The Vegetari

The Vegetarian Good Food Guide

Edited by Annabel Whittet

Published by Consumers' Association and Hodder & Stoughton

Which? Books are commissioned and researched by
The Association for Consumer Research
and published by
Consumers' Association,
2 Marylebone Road, London NW1 4DX and
Hodder & Stoughton,
47 Bedford Square, London WC1B 3DP

Typographic design by Paul Saunders;
maps by Eugene Fleury; cover photograph by Eric Carter; cover design by
Philip Mann (ACE Ltd)

British Library Cataloguing in Publication Data

The vegetarian good food guide.
1. Great Britain. Vegetarian restaurants. Directories
I. Whittet, Annabel *1947–* II. Consumers' Association
647.9541

ISBN 0-340-51442-6

Typeset by Rowland Phototypesetting Ltd,
Bury St Edmunds, Suffolk
Printed on part-recycled paper and bound in Great
Britain by
BPCC Hazell Books
Aylesbury, Bucks, England
Member of BPCC Ltd

Contents

The rise and rise of green cuisine

It seems almost incredible that Cranks, that pioneer among vegetarian restaurants and a model for many ventures, first opened its doors in London nearly thirty years ago, in 1961. What a beacon in the wilderness it must have been then and how things have changed for the vegetarian in search of a decent meal. Changed for the better, of course, though there is no reason for complacency. Meat-eating friends who heard about this book in preparation said, 'But surely nowadays all restaurants offer a vegetarian main course?' Would that this were the case. A glance through *The Good Food Guide* will show that even today, many of our most esteemed restaurants do not cater automatically on their standard menu for non-meat, non-fish eaters.

As little as fifteen years ago a vegetarian had to travel many miles to find a restaurant meal, and then it would probably have been a predictable nut cutlet or righteous brown rice, rather than a gourmet experience. Anyone wanting to dine with a meat-eater had to search hard to find a restaurant providing a suitable main dish. Now, as this book shows, many predominantly meat-oriented restaurants do an excellent job of catering for vegetarians and are a godsend to those with meat-loving partners or friends. Purely vegetarian restaurants have also come a long way: some have stuck to the simple formula of lasagne, stews, pizzas and vegetables in sauces, providing fresh food at low prices and offering perhaps a more adventurous menu in the evening. Others have set their aspirations at the highest level – a visit to Quince and Medlar at Cockermouth or Abbey Green in Chester proves what vegetarian cuisine can achieve and will be as delightful for a meat-eater as for a vegetarian.

Three per cent of the adult population now claims to be vegetarian, with a further 5.5 per cent claiming to avoid red meat. Gallup, who reported these results, point out that these figures have more than doubled since 1984. Women, interestingly, are leading the trend: 10.7 per cent of women say they eat no red meat, compared to 6.1 per cent of men. Often it is the younger generation who give up meat first and converts the family. When you appreciate the dramatic change in public awareness of cruelty to animals, it is not surprising that some choose to give up meat on moral grounds. Others are persuaded by arguments about healthy diets: evidence shows that vegetarians have lower blood cholesterol than the general population (vegans have even lower); most studies show that their blood pressure is lower; a South Bank Polytechnic study found vegetarians had a lower incidence of cancer of the colon and other problems associated with low-fibre diets; and according to work carried out at Oxford University and in America, female vegetarians seem less likely to get gallstones or suffer osteoporosis than female meat-eaters.

Many restaurants ask, 'What kind of vegetarian are you?' Since many of those who call themselves vegetarian eat fish and sometimes even white meat, the confusion is understandable, and often results in fish being included in the vegetarian section of the menu. Restaurateurs may equally be unsure of the definition of vegan. Then there are problem areas they may choose not to think of: the animal rennet in the cheese they use, for example; soups made with meat stocks; mousses and cold soufflés containing gelatine; a mincemeat recipe that demands suet. If in doubt about the constituents of a dish, ask. If a restaurateur has told us that the kitchen uses vegetarian cheese, this is mentioned in the text of the entry.

As this guide proves, the overall picture for vegetarians eating out is heartening, if erratic. Those who live in large cities have a great deal more choice of places than those in the country; those in London have the best range (though they have lacked an upmarket, reasonably priced, purely vegetarian restaurant, as opposed to café, since Christy's closed some years ago). Manchester, Bristol, Oxford and Cambridge are all well represented in the guide, probably a reflection of their large student populations. The South-East is well provided for, closely followed by the Lake District (perhaps because, as one restaurateur noticed, walkers have vegetarian leanings); the West Country and Wales have isolated pockets of vegetarian brilliance; East Anglia is pulling its socks up; vegetarians in Scotland and the North of England are sparsely catered for. Vegetarians finding themselves in one of those deserts without a listing in the vicinity will do best by searching out an Indian restaurant. Indians have always understood the needs of vegetarians and a collection of vegetable dishes will make a good meal; Italian restaurants usually have a suitable pasta dish. For vegans the picture is gloomier: though many vegetarian restaurants make an effort to provide a vegan dish of the day, centres of vegan cuisine, such as Veganomics and Country Life in London, and Ploughshares in Glastonbury, are rare.

Researching the guide has shown how exciting vegetarian food can be: those places that do make an effort and come up with imaginative dishes often find that meat-eaters choose them. Our criteria for inclusion were that a restaurant must have at least one interesting vegetarian main dish on its menu *at all times*, with no prior notice required, and that the dish must not be just an omelette, quiche or salad. It was difficult to be firm and exclude restaurants which can provide excellent meals for vegetarians given a little notice – places like the Old Vicarage, Witherslack, the Cemlyn, Harlech, or Gidleigh Park, Chagford. But our aim is to stop vegetarians being ghettoised as a special case, so we held firm.

Our researches have turned up various types of restaurant. There are plenty of ethnic entries, of course – among them Greek, Indian, Spanish, Malaysian, African, Chinese, Mexican, Thai – whose cuisines have traditionally used cheap vegetables and pulses. The burgeoning bars that serve fresh pasta with a range of freshly made sauces are a good choice for vegetarians, as are pizzerias, many of which provide vegetarian toppings and the best of which, for example Pizzeria Condotti in London, the Pizza Express chain, the Pizza Margherita chain in the north, La La Pizza in Kingston and the Pizza Piazza chain, are nearly as good as those in Italy. We found that Indian vegetarian restaurants have also proliferated; the staples of their menus, Southern Indian delicacies such as masala dosas, chaats and pooris are tasty and unusual, their prices offer very good value, and many of them are diversifying with other dishes – for instance Rani, Sabras and Spices in London, and Kalpna in Edinburgh.

It's sad to see some meat-oriented restaurants putting a token vegetarian main dish on the menu and leaving it unchanged for months, even years, while the meat dishes change around it. Imaginations that concoct the most enterprising combinations based on meat or fish seem to go blank when presented with the challenge of providing a vegetarian dish, even when some of their starters may be vegetarian and show flair. One has the impression that all over the country chefs are rolling up vegetables in filo pastry: in compiling the guide, filo pastry parcel is the dish I seem to have seen most often on menus, followed closely by lasagne. In other restaurants, vegetarians and meat-eaters are more equitably provided for, yet the vegetarian dishes show evidence of thought and care: the Moon in Kendal, Kites in York, the Milkhouse in Montacute and Moorings in Wells-next-the-Sea, for instance. Entries range from the front-parlour style of the Bubbling Kettle in Betws-y-Coed (which served one of the best lasagnes tasted in the course of research) to the splendours of Burts in London.

Wholly vegetarian restaurants cover the spectrum from unpretentious cafés to elegant places like Lupton Tower (Kirkby Lonsdale), Quince and Medlar (Cockermouth) and Abbey Green (Chester). Many at the cheaper end could, to some benefit, broaden their repertoires beyond those endlessly repeated pizzas, lasagnes and pastas, but as sources of cheap, fresh cooking, with a different menu each day at extremely reasonable prices, they are underrated. Outstanding examples are Food for Thought and Neal's Yard Bakery in London, Ryton Gardens at Ryton-in-Dunsmore and the Everyman Bistro in Liverpool, where you can have a feast for about a fiver. Often these places make all the food they serve on the premises, including the bread. Those with higher aspirations may provide such delights as leeks en croûte with béarnaise sauce (Town House, Southampton), Glamorgan sausages with laverbread sauce (Roots, Swansea), quenelles de fromage sauce saffron (Lupton Tower, Kirkby Lonsdale), Mediterranean pie with Feta and wholemeal yoghurt pastry (Lancrigg Country House Hotel, Grasmere), parsnip and cashew terrine (Quince and Medlar, Cockermouth) or choux buns with olive and nut cream (Abbey Green, Chester).

In the entries, outstanding vegetarian food is indicated by a star after the restaurant name; there is a list at the end of the book. The Editor's top ten on page 12 lists a personal selection of the best. Let us hope that this guide will be a spur to restaurants to buck up their ideas and realise that the delicate, subtle, light flavours of good vegetarian cuisine are where the future lies. Many thanks to all those who have contributed reports for this edition; your help is much appreciated. Please continue to let us have reports on restaurants in the guide, other places we should include or, for that matter, places where you've been disappointed. Either write a letter or, if you prefer, use one of the report forms at the back of the book (please give as much information as possible about what you ate, atmosphere and décor). The address is *The Vegetarian Good Food Guide*, FREEPOST, 2 Marylebone Road, London NW1 1YN. With your help the next edition will be even better.

Annabel Whittet
March 1990

About this guide

Although this is a guide to restaurants that serve vegetarian food, it's not *just* for vegetarians. Whether you are vegetarian or vegan (and whether you are strict or flexible), whether you eat out with, or want to entertain, someone who is, or might be vegetarian, or simply if you appreciate sitting down in a restaurant, looking at the menu and having the option to choose a meal without meat or fish, this book is for you.

The growing numbers of vegetarians (*see* The rise and rise of green cuisine) mean that most of us probably number a vegetarian among our friends and relatives; that parents are having to cater for offspring choosing to 'go veggie'; that anyone entertaining a stranger for a business lunch should consider that the guest may not wish to eat meat. This guide is a handbook to be used on all sorts of occasions, for meals at all price levels. It points the way to somewhere handy for a quick lunch, just as much as signalling the restaurants where the object is to enjoy a relaxed meal in style.

The main criterion for inclusion in the guide is that an eating place offers a vegetarian main course on the standard menu – that is, at all times, without any need for 'prior arrangement' or '24 hours' notice' or any of those other get-out clauses loved by restaurateurs. Equally, the food on offer should be more interesting and imaginative than an omelette or a salad. All the restaurants listed have been sent a questionnaire and have said that vegetarian food is available at all times. If you find otherwise, please tell us. Catering is a volatile business and a change of chef or owner may mean a change in kitchen policy. Short-term difficulties might also affect whether vegetarian food is being served.

The guide has been compiled in the same way as *The Good Food Guide* and is based on reports from consumers backed up by anonymous inspections. We have, however, tried to provide a geographical spread of entries. For example, vegetarians new to an area will, we trust, appreciate being able to find out about the only suitable eating places in the vicinity, even if the food may tend to the straightforward. For some areas, notably Scotland and some parts of Wales, finding entries has been difficult. One *Good Food Guide* inspector, on a touring holiday in Scotland in the summer of 1989, asked every restaurant visited whether they offered vegetarian food (mindful not only of us, but of a vegetarian relative). Almost universally, the answer was a dismal 'no'.

To campaign for better choice, we need your feedback. Please write and tell us about any vegetarian meals you eat: either use a report form or, if you prefer, write a letter to the FREEPOST address given on page 9.

Practicalities

Ⓥ after a restaurant name indicates that it serves only vegetarian food.

★ after a restaurant name indicates that the vegetarian cooking is especially good. The Editor's top ten restaurants are given on page 12.

Cost The cost of a three-course vegetarian meal without wine is indicated by **£** symbols to the right of the restaurant name.
£ = up to £7.50; **££** = £7.50 to £15; **£££** = £15 and over.

The details underneath the text of an entry are based on information given to us by the proprietor and availability of meat, fish and vegan dishes is signalled here. 'Wheelchair access' indicates that entrances are at least 33 inches wide, passages 4 feet wide, and that there are a maximum of two steps, unless otherwise stated.

The Editor's top ten restaurants

Throughout the guide, restaurants providing an exceptional service for vegetarians have been awarded stars; a list appears at the end of the book. Of those, it was difficult to pick out only ten as supreme. Like the guide, this list reflects a huge range of eating places, from inexpensive cafés to grand establishments; some are purely vegetarian, others serve meat and fish as well. They have been chosen for the success with which they achieve their aims; the list is alphabetical, not in order of merit.

Abbey Green, CHESTER A charming restaurant with a relaxed atmosphere, where lunch and dinner menus are imaginative as well as extensive and prices are extremely reasonable.
Burt's, LONDON This offers fine cooking in formal and stylish surroundings and beautiful presentation. Though fish and meat dishes are also offered, the vegetarian choice is stunning.
Clement's, PLAISTOW A purely vegetarian restaurant where the ambitions and execution are higher than average, ingredients are excellent and the cooking skilled.
Food for Friends, BRIGHTON Reasonable prices at this unpretentious café represent amazing value for wholesome, freshly cooked food.
Food for Thought, LONDON From breakfast to dinner, vegetarians can eat well in the relaxed, cosmopolitan atmosphere.
Lupton Tower, KIRKBY LONSDALE A purely vegetarian establishment with high aspirations, amply fulfilled in the delicate cuisine. Recommended for dining out and for overnight stays.
Moon, KENDAL A cheerful bistro serving vegetarian and meat dishes, where new ideas are constantly emerging from a resourceful kitchen.
Quince and Medlar, COCKERMOUTH Dinner in quiet, peaceful surroundings provides a vegetarian with a gourmet experience with a relatively small price tab.
Rani, LONDON One of the best Indian vegetarian restaurants; the cooking is exotic, flavours subtle and textures varied.
Stannary, TAVISTOCK Dining here is a special treat; in the attractive restaurant, food is as good as it looks and almost any dietary requirement can be met.

London

Ajimura

£££ MAP 14

51–53 Shelton Street, WC2 TEL 071-240 0178

All the hallmarks of Japanese cuisine are here in the beautifully presented food, which includes a welcome number of vegetarian dishes. A set dinner of vegetable tempura starts with hors d'oeuvre with avocado and gomasu, a sesame dressing, proceeds to seasoned vegetables with nori-sui clear soup, then vegetable tempura and finally fresh fruit. Individual hors d'oeuvre include oshitashi, spinach rolled in seaweed with roasted sesame seed, or age dofu, deep-fried bean curd with tempura sauce. By some oversight, the helpful 'v' symbol for vegetarian has not been applied to the assorted vegetable sushi or nimono, the simmered dish of the day.

Open Mon to Sat, exc Sat L, noon to 2.30, 6 to 11 **Closed** bank hols Booking advisable. Table service. Licensed. Meat dishes. Fish dishes. Vegan dishes. Takeaways. Access, Amex, Diners, Visa

Almeida Theatre Wine Bar

£ MAP 13

1A Almeida Street, N1 TEL 071-226 0931

The wine bar caters mainly for visitors to the highly esteemed theatre, and on nights when the theatre is open, the wine bar is at its crowded and cheery best; the menu is also more extensive. Even when less crowded, the place has an austere charm with its bare boards, rickety chairs and small tables. 'For a wine bar, the food is quite reasonable if limited on choice.' However limited, there will always be a vegetarian main dish. A typical non-performance night produced a rather thin leek and potato soup, Mozzarella fritters, hot and very rich with a well presented winter salad, and fruit for dessert. Other days might reveal stuffed celery au gratin, spanakopita with tomato sauce, stuffed courgettes or French onion tart. Theatre nights may offer desserts such as chestnut and prune mousse. What is essentially simple fare is done well and is occasionally inspired by new ideas.

Open Mon to Sat 12.30 to 2.30, 6 to 10 Table service L. Counter service D. Licensed. Meat dishes. Fish dishes. Snacks at other times. No-smoking area. Wheelchair access. Access

Al-Omaraa ££ MAP 12

27 Queensway, W2 TEL 071-229 9898

There is an authentic feel to this Lebanese restaurant, enhanced by the countrymen and women who patronise it. Lunches are particularly good value, as you can help yourself to the buffet as many times as you wish for £5.50, including a pudding. Of the hot dishes two might be vegetarian, on a typical day herby baked potatoes and a cauliflower dish; as well as tangy baba ganoush, hummus, crisp falafel, fried pitta bread salad (rather sharp and soggy), beans and a moussaka. The sweet is home made: a baklava look-alike was in fact stuffed with sweetened cheese, and was very good. Lebanese coffee is spicy and fragrant. In the evening there is a set vegetarian menu for two.

Open all week noon to 1am Booking advisable. Table service. Licensed. Vegan dishes. Take-aways. Wheelchair access

Andrew Edmunds ££ MAP 13

46 Lexington Street, W1 TEL 071-437 5708

A wine bar that sets modest aims and achieves them. The surroundings are pleasantly unkempt, the menu is concise. Salads are a strong point, for instance avocado and almond, and hot dishes might be couscous or spinach and ricotta tortellini. Pleasant service.

Open Mon to Fri 12.30 to 3, 5.30 to 10.45 (Sat and Sun 1 to 3.30, 5.30 to 10) **Closed** 23 Dec to 3 Jan Booking advisable. Table service. Tables outside. Licensed. Meat dishes. Wheelchair access. Access, Visa

The factual details under the text are based on information supplied by the restaurateur.

Auberge de Provence

£££ MAP 13

St James Court Hotel, 41 Buckingham Gate, SW1 TEL 071-821 1899

'Now I know what they eat in heaven' said one reporter at the end of a meal. St James Court is expensive and luxurious, inevitably catering mainly to business people and tourists; food and service are high class. Such an avowedly French restaurant deserves full marks for providing three vegetarian main dishes. Starters are fairly limited: provençale salad or wild mushrooms in puff pastry; main dishes include home-made pasta with tomato compote, ratatouille tartlet and vegetable-filled filo pastry. Accompanying vegetables are expensive. The restaurant requires that hot puddings must be ordered at the beginning of a meal: some find this pedantry trying.

Open Mon to Sat exc Sat L 12.30 to 2.30, 7.30 to 11 **Closed** 1 to 14 Jan, bank hols Booking advisable. Table service. Licensed. Meat dishes. Fish dishes. Other diets catered for on request. Wheelchair access. Access, Amex, Diners, Visa

Au Provencal

££–£££ MAP 12

293–295 Railton Road, SE24 TEL 071-274 9163

Reports have been somewhat mixed since new owners took over a year ago. None the less, there is a vegetarian main dish, such as broccoli in cheese and mushroom sauce with muesli crumble topping and accompanying vegetables are good; so is the summer pudding. This part of London is not overendowed with vegetarian eateries, so it might answer for a meal with fish- or meat-eaters.

Open Tue to Sun 12.30 to 2.30 (3 Sun), 5.30 to 10.30 (7.30 to 10 Sun) Booking advisable. Table service. Licensed. Meat dishes. Fish dishes. No-smoking area on request. Wheelchair access. Access, Visa

Baalbek

££ MAP 12

18 Hogarth Place, SW5 TEL 071-373 7199

A small Lebanese café a minute's walk from Earls Court tube station with authentic food and authentic Middle-Eastern atmosphere, its dark walls enlivened with posters of Beirut. Tables are rather cramped. Best to ask the advice of helpful staff when ordering because, for instance, a starter of ful medames proves to be plenty for two. Other starters include falafel, motabal (otherwise known as baba ganoush) and six vegetarian, in fact, vegan, main dishes take in bean and vegetable stews and a generous couscous, the vegetable sauce true and thick. Good Lebanese coffee rounds off a meal that is certainly value for money.

Open Mon to Sat, D 6 to 11 Booking advisable. Table service. Licensed, also bring your own: no corkage. Meat dishes. Vegan dishes. Snacks at other times. Take-aways. Wheelchair access. Access, Visa

Baba Bhel Poori House Ⓥ ★ £ MAP 12

29–31 Porchester Road, W2 TEL 071-221 7502

Diners are greeted at this Indian vegetarian restaurant by a delightful, smiling, saried lady who serves in an attentive and swift manner: food appears unbelievably fast. A take-away customer has been known to place an order and a minute later be presented with his paperbag of purchases. The menu contains the usual range of puris, channa chat, bhel puri, dosas and curries, with lassi and falooda to drink and rasogula, shrikhand, goolab gamun and ras malai as well as three kinds of kulfi for dessert. Samosas come fresh and hot, the pastry flaky, not too greasy, and the filling spiced medium hot; a splendid potato poori dish is served cold, with yoghurt, onion and sev. The kulfi is outstanding and unlike many Indian restaurants, they make the three different varieties on the premises; texture and flavour are perfect.

Open Tue to Sun noon to 3, 6 to 11 **Closed** 25 Dec Table service. Licensed. Vegan dishes. Take-aways. Access, Visa

Bahn Thai ££ MAP 14

21A Frith Street, W1 TEL 071-437 8504

Despite cramped tables, lighting so dim you can't see 'whether you are eating chillis or spring onions', the food has been highly praised – 'quite the best Thai restaurant in London'. Vegetarians can choose from various vegetables with oyster sauce, vegetarian rice noodles, Thai-style stuffed omelette and steamed vegetables with coconut cream, 'though this last has been reported as a 'boring julienne of vegetables and coconut flavour'.

Open all week noon to 2.45 (12.30 to 2.30 Sun), 6 to 11.15 (6.30 to 10.30 Sun) **Closed** 25 Dec, Easter, some bank hols Booking advisable. Table service. Licensed, also bring your own: corkage varies. Meat dishes. Fish dishes. Vegan dishes. Other diets catered for on request. Take-aways. No pipes or cigars. Wheelchair access. Access, Amex, Visa

Bambaya £££ MAP 12

1 Park Road, Crouch End, N8 TEL 081-348 5609

The owners describe the cuisine as West African and Caribbean; they shun meat and only cook fish and vegetables. The restaurant, on two levels, is decorated with pen-and-ink Caribbean sketches and one wall, elaborately tiled in pattern and white, appears to be a remnant of a former shop. Starters are mostly soups and the peanut variety is rather bland. It might be best to plunge straight into some of the vegetarian main courses, which include a good medium-hot vegetable curry, full of exotic items. Aubergines créole are chunky and tasty, served with dhal, and 'hoppin John', the best of all, is rice with black-eyed peas cooked in coconut milk. Caribbean specialities such as corn bread, plantains and Red Stripe beer are also on offer. A refreshing taste experience for those with jaded palates.

Open Tue to Sun 6.30 to 11 **Closed** bank hols Booking advisable. Table service. Licensed, also bring your own: corkage £2.50. Fish dishes. Vegan dishes. Wheelchair access. Access, Amex, Visa

Bedlington Café ££ MAP 12

24 Fauconberg Road, W4 TEL 081-994 1965

By day the Bedlington is simply a café serving fry-ups; by night a Thai restaurant of the highest order. The outside seems not to have changed in years; the phone number is still painted as Chiswick 1965. 'It's a gem of a place, 100 per cent unpretentious but serving really fresh, aromatic, authentic food.' Diners sit at Formica tables on functional chairs, under crude lighting, but select meals from a feast of 66 dishes, of which the soups are stunning, rich, creamy and scented. Vegetarian dishes are curry, mushroom and ginger and fried vegetables in batter. All ingredients are reliably fresh. The café's fame entices customers from far and wide, so booking is a necessity; every night there is queuing in the street.

Open Mon to Sat 9 to 2, 6.30 to 10 **Closed** July Booking advisable. Table service. Tables outside. Unlicensed, but bring your own: corkage 50p per person. Meat dishes. Fish dishes. Vegan dishes. Snacks. Take-aways

Beech ££ MAP 12

322 Kentish Town Road, NW5 TEL 071-284 0455

A cheerful, unpretentious and bright addition to the restaurant scene in Kentish Town. Start with tagliatelle with cream and herbs or soup of the day and go on to wild rice, raisins and nuts in filo pastry on a bed of spinach with cider sauce.

Open Mon to Sat 12.30 to 3, 6.30 to 11.45 Booking advisable. Table service. Tables outside. Licensed. Meat dishes. Fish dishes. Snacks at other times. No children under 6 for D. Wheelchair access. Access, Visa

Bellamy's Brasserie ££ MAP 12

181 Stoke Newington Church Street, N16 TEL 071-241 6305

A local gathering place with a pleasant atmosphere, the bar/brasserie regularly turns out filo pastry with vegetables, a couple of pasta dishes and vegetarian burgers along with a vegetarian daily special on the main menu. There is also 'lunch munch fare' available during morning and afternoon open hours, and the wine list includes organic wines.

Open all week noon to 2.45, 6.30 to 10.30 **Closed** weekday L Oct to Mar Table service. Tables outside. Licensed. Meat dishes. Fish dishes. Vegan dishes. Other diets catered for on request. Access, Amex, Diners, Visa

Bengal Lancer ££ MAP 12

253 Kentish Town Road, NW5 TEL 071-485 6688

Steadfastly popular, the Lancer offers a vegetarian thali and an aubergine Lancer, hot and crispy. There are also the usual vegetable biriani, paratha stuffed with vegetables, or mushroom pilau.

Open all week noon to 3, 6 to midnight (12.30am Fri and Sat) Booking advisable. Table service. Licensed. Meat dishes. Fish dishes. Take-aways. Wheelchair access. Access, Amex, Diners, Visa

Bennett & Luck ⓥ

£ MAP 12

Islington Park Street, N1 TEL 071-226 3422

Go through the healthfood store selling some unusual items and organic fruit and vegetables to this tiny café of six tables, spotlessly clean, lit from above by skylights. It is popular at lunchtime and getting a table can be difficult, though take-aways account for much of the trade. There are endless variations on a few basic dishes, so they do not pall. Salads are consistently good and a mixed plate of warm chilli beans, beets, brown rice and tofu in soy, greens and fruits makes a good, satisfying meal. Scotch eggs are crisp and nicely coarse in texture. Portions of puddings such as a cinnamon apple crumble with oat topping are huge, and cakes are home made (including Hilary's special 'not cheese cake', vegan style). The very reasonable prices point to another reason for the café's popularity.

Open Mon to Sat 10am to 5.30 **Closed** 1 week at Christmas Table service. Counter service. Vegan dishes. Other diets catered for on request. Snacks. Take-aways. Wheelchair access. Access, Visa

Bhel Poori House ⓥ ★

£ MAP 13

92–93 Chapel Market, N1 TEL 071-837 4607

'Very much one of the new generation of Indian vegetarian establishments, attractively decorated in light green and – far more importantly – serving lovely food,' comments one reporter. The pooris with chickpeas in tamarind sauce are fine in taste and texture and dosas (a range of five is listed) are fresh and lacy, arriving with potato mixture and coconut chutney. The house speciality, thali, would satisfy a giant, is flavoursome and includes a dessert: the other suitable thali does not. An excellent place for value.

Open all week noon to 2, 6 to 11 Table service. Licensed. Vegan dishes. Snacks. Take-aways. Wheelchair access. Access, Amex, Carte Blanche

Blue Elephant

££–£££ MAP 12

4–6 Fulham Broadway, SW6 TEL 071-385 6595

The exoticism of this Thai restaurant, with its tropical plants and staff in colourful dress, is brought down to earth by the substantial prices and lengthy waits between courses. Nevertheless, there is a vegetarian menu of spring roll, muak lek (cornmeal cake), a sweet-and-sour bean curd dish, devilled ladies' fingers and a massaman curry of potatoes, beans, cauliflower and cashew-nuts.

Open all week, exc Sat L, noon to 2.30, 7 to 12.30 (10.30 Sun) **Closed** 24 to 27 Dec Booking advisable. Table service. Licensed. Meat dishes. Fish dishes. Vegan dishes. Take-aways. Wheelchair access. Access, Amex, Diners, Visa

Bombay Brasserie

££ MAP 13

Courtfield Close, 140 Gloucester Road, SW7 TEL 071-370 4040

There are shades of imperial splendour in this large and spacious Indian restaurant with a reputation as one of the first to go upmarket. If you can, eat in the conservatory extension, filled with plants, a pleasant place to enjoy what can be a long drawn-out affair. The cuisine ranges over India – Goan, tandoori, Parsi and Moghlai dishes are offered, plus a section of extra-hot dishes. For those of faint palate, the ordinary dishes are quite hot enough. There are two vegetarian thalis and other vegetable dishes can be interesting: brinjal patiala, mustard leaves, and gucchi and khumbi – wild Indian and fresh mushrooms.

Open all week 12.30 to 2.45, 7.30 to midnight Booking advisable. Table service. Tables outside. Licensed. Meat dishes. Vegan dishes. Wheelchair access. Access, Amex, Diners, Visa

Brewer Street Buttery

£ MAP 14

56 Brewer Street, W1 TEL 071-437 7695

The clean, friendly and popular café serves some Jewish dishes, some Polish and some from other cuisines. Standard are Polish cheese piroshki or stuffed dumplings, but daily options always include one vegetarian choice – perhaps aubergines provençale. Various cakes and gateaux, stregatini liqueur ice-cream and cassata are some of the possible desserts. Fresh fruit juices are available. For the heart of London, prices are reasonable.

Open Mon to Fri noon to 3.30 **Closed** bank hols Table service. Unlicensed, also bring your own: corkage £2. Meat dishes. Fish dishes. Snacks at other times. Take-aways. No-smoking area. Wheelchair access

Burt's ★

£££ MAP 14

42 Dean Street, W1 TEL 071-734 3339

At last, a restaurant in the capital where the excellence of the vegetarian choice, the comfort of the surroundings and the relaxed helpfulness of the staff contribute to an occasion on a par with the best anywhere. The staff used to be at Inigo Jones, where vegetarianism began to infiltrate haute cuisine; here it is unashamedly in ascendancy. The owners began the restaurant with the idea of serving vegetarian and fish only – thus the arty photographs of fish and vegetables. However, stalwart meat-eaters from the Inigo Jones clientele campaigned for the occasional meat dish. The place is not nearly as awe-inspiring as Inigo Jones was: the long room is pink and grey with grey upholstered cane chairs and large mirrors faintly marked with 'Bs'. Choice is the main difficulty when presented with such a wealth – a rarity for vegetarians. From one meal, it would seem that the four-course vegetarian menu is the best option, though dessert is limited to sorbet. That meal began with marinated vegetable fritters with piquant sauce, lightly battered in a tempura style, all vegetables preserving their flavours, then went on to an aubergine mousse wrapped in a finely sliced courgette with fresh tomato sauce. Like all the dishes, this looked wonderful but was just a bit too subtle in taste. Then a woodland mushroom, artichoke and spinach lasagne, that old friend hardly recognisable in this version of individual round layers, the pasta frail and thin, the whole tasty and light. The only reservation was that accompanying vegetables were, apart from mange-tout, the same as in the fritters. The delights on the main menu include home-made gnocchi with Stilton, spinach and tomato, a special of toasted onion brioche with goats' cheese; blanquette of vegetables in brioche; celeriac spring rolls with oriental vegetables which were cunningly sliced celeriac strips rolled around an oriental assortment of beanshoots, with carrots sitting on a cabbage mound: excellent, if lacking in celeriac flavour. Aubergine sausages had a delicate, thyme flavour. A chocolate assembly of coconut cream, mousse, chocolate and mint sorbet and white chocolate mousses was an inspired collection of tiny, beautiful delicacies; the jalousie of winter fruits with caramel ice-cream got a similarly enthusiastic reception. The set menu as we went to press was £19.95, which for cooking and ambience at this level, is not unreasonable.

Open Mon to Sat exc Sat L 12.15 to 2.30, 5.30 to 11.30 Booking advisable. Table service. Licensed. Meat dishes. Fish dishes. Snacks 5.30 to 7. Wheelchair access. Access, Amex, Diners, Visa

Café Delancey — ££ MAP 13

3 Delancey Street, NW1 TEL 071-387 1985

A café that anyone would like to have at the end of their road: a comfortable, cosmopolitan version of the continental café, with wooden floor, marble tables, and newspapers. The day starts with breakfast, and there seems to be no objection to people just having coffee and a piece of bread, even at lunchtime. Don't panic when the printed menu has no vegetarian main dish: it will be on the blackboard. It varies daily and might be deep-fried aubergines stuffed with cream cheese or a cream cheese, tomato and mushroom filo bundle. Freshly squeezed orange juice is a bonus. The trio of chocolate mousses is a subtle arrangement in three layers with a fudgy chocolate topping.

Open all week 9.30am to 11.15 **Closed** 25 Dec, 1 Jan, bank hols Booking advisable. Table service. Licensed. Meat dishes. Fish dishes. Other diets catered for on request. No cigars. Access, Visa

Café Flo — ££ MAP 12

205 Haverstock Hill, NW3 TEL 071-435 6744

A useful brasserie offering French provincial cookery; one eats to the strains of jazz and blues in an atmosphere acceptably free and easy. The vegetarian main dish might be a tian of courgettes and tomatoes; the starters a salad of Gruyère, Roquefort, avocado and vegetables or fusilli au pistou. Locals flock to the café so it tends to be crowded. Flo's Bar and Grill opposite (071-794 4125) is open noon to 3, 6 to 11.30 Monday to Saturday and 11 to 4 and 7 to 11 on Sunday. There's also a branch in St Martin's Lane, WC2 (071-836 8289) which, suitably for its location, is open from 8.30am to midnight all week.

Open all week noon to 3, 6 to 11 Booking advisable. Table service. Tables outside. Licensed. Vegan dishes. No cigars or pipes. Access, Visa

Café Pelican

££ MAP 14

45 St Martin's Lane, WC2 TEL 071-379 0309 and 0259

The authentic French brasserie atmosphere, with waiters to match, can be marred by some lapses of service and cuisine, but you can eat or drink all day. A *menu vegetarien* includes such dishes as crème vichyssoise; vegetables marinated in vinegar, tarragon and shallots; tomato and courgette in puff pastry with rosemary cream, and spinach canneloni with cheese sauce. A £1 cover charge comes into effect at 6pm.

Open all week 11am to 12.30pm **Closed** 24 Dec to 2 Jan Table service. Counter service. Tables outside. Licensed. Meat dishes. Fish dishes. Vegan dishes. Snacks at other times. Wheelchair access. Access, Amex, Diners, Visa

Café Pelican du Sud

££ MAP 13

Hay's Galleria, London Bridge City, Tooley Street, SE1
TEL 071-378 0096/7

Yuppiedom is here! Hay's Galleria is a converted warehouse development full of places to spend money and look glamorous. The Café Pelican is no exception: it spills into the covered atrium, plants abound, and waiters and waitresses appear characteristically French. There is a full vegetarian menu, and, although not a lot of imagination has been applied, it is a plus. A sample menu took in cauliflower soup, wild mushroom tartlet, marrow and squash with cheese sauce, fresh noodles with pesto, and a fricassee of baby vegetables. Asparagus tartlet proved to be filled mainly with a rather unremarkable, bland scrambled egg mixture. The restaurant is on the pricey side, but at least it puts vegetarianism on the agenda.

Open Mon to Fri 10 to 9.30, L noon to 9.30 **Closed** 22 Dec to 3 Jan Booking advisable. Table service. Tables outside. Licensed. Meat dishes. Fish dishes. Snacks. No babies L. Wheelchair access. Access, Amex, Diners, Visa

Café Society

££ MAP 13

Procter Street, WC1 TEL 071-242 6691

A glass front with canopies marks this French restaurant where vegetarians can find grilled goats' cheese or roasted peppers as starters, tagliatelle with aubergine or spinach and cheese-stuffed filo pastry with mushroom sauce as main courses. Lunch is from noon to 3 and snacks take over from then to closing. It may not be cheap, but answers well for a vegetarian and meat-eater out together.

Open Mon to Fri noon to 8 **Closed** 22 Dec to 2 Jan Booking advisable. Table service. Tables outside. Licensed. Meat dishes. Fish dishes. Snacks. Take-aways. Wheelchair access. Access, Amex, Visa

Calabash ££ MAP 14

38 King Street, WC2 TEL 071-836 1976

Almost hidden in the basement of the Africa Centre, this offers authentic African food. Though not cosy or intimate in atmosphere, it is attractively decorated with bright tablecloths in ethnic prints and original pictures and artefacts by African artists. The cuisine is fascinating, tending towards the spicy, and vegetarians are well catered for: the Calabash speciality of black-eyed beans, vegetable stew, fried plaintain, sweet potatoes and mixed salad could overwhelm a timid appetite. The dish called 'peanut butter' is actually a combination of sweet corn, carrots, peas, green beans and pepper akin to a thick soup and served with fried plaintain or rice. Among the sweets, kanufa and basbusa are a kind of solid honey cake, very filling.

Open Mon to Sat, exc Sat L, 12.30 to 2.30, 6 to 10.30 **Closed** bank hols Booking advisable. Table service. Licensed. Meat dishes. Fish dishes. Take-aways. Access, Amex, Diners, Visa

Canal Brasserie ££ MAP 12

Canalot Studios, 222 Kensal Road, W10 TEL 081-960 2732

On the western reach of the Grand Union Canal here is yet another warehouse conversion especially popular with the local moneyed young. It may be hard to find through a maze of cul de sacs and one-way streets, but once there, the entrance is pretty with a fountain, open lift and a view of the canal, and the atmosphere is good. On the modern British menu are two vegetarian main dishes – perhaps a puff pastry parcel of artichoke hearts, spiced vegetable ragout or aubergine and pasta charlotte. Start with Japanese salad, chilled mould of watercress with lemon vinaigrette or chilled carrot soup. Feta-filled filo triangles have proved to be 'too large, too deep-fried and had no sauce to help them along.' Lighter dishes, such as soup, Boursin and spinach in pastry, or cheese puffs with pesto are available, too. Steamed puddings are a treat.

Open Mon to Fri noon to 3.30, 6 to 10.30 Booking advisable. Table service. Counter service. Tables outside. Licensed. Meat dishes. Fish dishes. Vegan dishes. Other diets catered for on request. Snacks at other times. Take-aways. Access, Visa

Chapter House ££ MAP 13

Montague Close, SE1 TEL 071-378 6446

Attached to Southwark Cathedral and run by Milburns, as are several entries in this guide. Vegetarians are offered such items as tomato and basil soup, grilled mushrooms with Stilton and cream, and ratatouille lasagne. Reserve some space for puddings.

Open Mon to Fri 10.30am to 4 **Closed** bank hols Booking advisable. Table service. Tables outside. Licensed. Meat dishes. Fish dishes. Vegan dishes on request. No-smoking area. Access, Amex, Diners, Visa

Cherry Orchard Ⓥ ★ £–££ MAP 12

241–245 Globe Road, E2 TEL 081-980 6678

It would be hard to stumble across the Cherry Orchard by chance, but once found, often visited. Witness the regular clientele. The décor is clean, modern and a cut above café; modern paintings for sale hang on the walls, and there is a blissful absence of music. The food is excellent with lots of choice for vegans. A typical menu will offer main dishes such as stuffed peppers or ratatouille with brown rice. A chunky corn chowder was deemed tasty and good; stuffed peppers contained fresh dill and came with a 'sensational' sesame cream sauce. Vegan chocolate cake might figure among the puddings.

Open Tue to Sat noon to 3, 6.30 to 10.30 **Closed** 1 week at Christmas, 4 days at Easter Booking advisable D. Table service D. Counter service L. Tables outside. Unlicensed, but bring your own: corkage £1. Vegan dishes. Other diets catered for on request. Take-aways. No-smoking. Children's portions. Wheelchair access (not wc). Access, Visa

Christian's

£££ MAP 12

1 Station Parade, Burlington Lane, W4 TEL 081-995 0382 and 0208

Station Parade, not in the London A–Z, links Burlington Lane and Sutton Court Road, and the restaurant looks more like a florist's – windows filled with weeping figs and wooden tubs outside stuffed with night-scented stocks. The open plan exposes the kitchen to the diner, with Christian in evidence. The atmosphere is 'slightly shabby, with lots of charm'. Eggy quiche nibbles are welcomed, and starters of goats' cheese and lentil salad or perhaps an English cheese soufflé are provided for vegetarians. There is one main dish, perhaps a vegetable stew. Desserts are recited: chocolate terrine with coffee sauce was a success, but apricot and almond tart failed to reveal its almond origins. There's an authentic Frenchness about the cooking and the portions are generous.

Open Tue to Sat D 7.30 to 10.15 **Closed** 25 Dec, bank hols Booking advisable. Table service. Tables outside. Licensed, also bring your own: corkage £7. Meat dishes. Fish dishes. Other diets catered for on request. No pipes or cigars. No children under 10. Wheelchair access

Chutneys Ⓥ ★

£ MAP 13

124 Drummond Street, NW1 TEL 071-388 0604

Perhaps the fact that branches have been successfully opened up in Bombay and Los Angeles makes this restaurant a target for the 'yuppie Indian vegetarian' label or perhaps it's the smart black and white décor. Lunch is the most popular time to eat here and the buffet provides a range of dishes, among them excellent black-eyed beans, potatoes and peas, ladies' fingers, nan, and puddings. The selection of twelve dishes for £3.50 is great value. Bhel pooris, samosas, thalis and dosas appear on the evening menu. One of the best of its kind.

Open all week noon to 2.45, 6 to 11.25 **Closed** 25 and 26 Dec, 1 Jan Booking advisable Fri, Sat. Table service. Counter service L. Licensed. Vegan dishes. Other diets catered for. Smoking discouraged. Access, Amex, Diners, Visa

The Vegetarian Good Food Guide *has been compiled in the same way as* The Good Food Guide *and is based on reports from consumers and anonymous inspections.*

Connolly's

£££ MAP 12

162 Lower Richmond Road, SW15 TEL 081-788 3844

This inconspicuous converted corner shop run by a brother and sister team – Eamonn and Kate Connolly – delights in some inventive modern British cuisine. What may sound peculiar combinations – puff pastry with noodles, spinach and saffron, for instance – can be surprisingly successful. Modern pastels hang on the walls, and although tables are close and usually filled, the high ceiling prevents claustrophobia. Vegetarians must look to the à la carte menu, which always has one dish on offer: maybe a four-cheese pizza with aubergines, peppers and sage; ricotta and spinach pancakes with peanut butter sauce or aubergine gratin with saffron custard. About a dozen puddings, rather on the sweet side, include sticky-toffee pudding ('a delicious, light, American muffin-sized sponge in a pool of equally light sauce'), home-made kumquat ice-cream and banoffi tartlets, burnt ice-cream and iced chocolate soufflé. There is a cover charge of 75p.

Open Tue to Sun, exc Sun D, noon to 2.30 (4 Sun), 7 to 10.30 Table service. Tables outside. Licensed, also bring your own: corkage £3 per bottle. Meat dishes. Fish dishes. Vegan dishes. Other diets catered for on request. No pipes. Wheelchair access. Access, Visa

Cordon Vert ⓥ

££ MAP 12

136 Merton Road, SW19 TEL 081-543 9174

This vegetarian and vegan restaurant tries to provide a more ambitious choice of dishes than many. The dining-room is small, the ceiling quaintly hung with string bags; all the cooking is done in the tiny kitchen at the back, from where the sound of Radio 4 emanates. The blackboard lists the day's dishes, of which a number are vegan. Portions are generous, prices on the high side. There's a tendency towards breadiness in the cooking – a mushroom and celery roast suffered from this, though it was flavoursome. There is also the lamentable habit of putting pink salad cream on the salad. Good cheesecake. Something of an oasis.

Open Tue to Sat noon to 10 (11 Fri and Sat), L noon to 3, D 7 to 10 **Closed** 23 Dec to 3 Jan **Booking advisable.** Table service. Counter service. Unlicensed, but bring your own: corkage 95p. Vegan dishes. Snacks. Take-aways. No smoking. Wheelchair access

Cork & Bottle

£ MAP 14

44–46 Cranbourn Street, WC2 TEL 071-734 7807

The flagship of Don Hewitson's chain of excellent wine bars (see Shampers and Methuselah's), this was probably the first in London to have a vegetarian special available every day; the dish now might be a spinach roulade or oriental salad. Follow with a pudding, perhaps first-class Pavlova with strawberries. Look for a narrow door and stairs down or you could miss this crowded, noisy rendezvous.

Open all week exc Sun L 11am to 3, 5 to 10.45 (7 to 10.15 Sun) Counter service. Licensed. Meat dishes. Fish dishes. No children under 14. Access, Amex, Diners, Visa

Cranks Ⓥ

£–££

8 Marshall Street, W1 TEL 071-437 9431 MAP 13
Open Mon to Sat, 8am to 10.30pm; Take-aways 8am to 6pm Mon to Fri, 9.30am to 5.30pm Sat Access, Amex, Diners, Visa
11 The Market, WC2 TEL 071-379 6508 MAP 14
Open Mon to Sat, 9.30am to 8pm, 10am to 6pm Sun
9–11 Tottenham Street, W1 TEL 071-631 3912 MAP 13
Open Mon to Fri, 8am to 8pm, 9am Sat
17–19 Great Newport Street, WC2 TEL 071-836 5226 MAP 14
Open Mon to Fri, 8.30am to 8.30pm, 10am Sat, 11am to 6pm Sun
10 Adelaide Street, WC2 TEL 071-379 5919 MAP 14
Open Mon to Sat, noon to 10.30pm, 6pm Sun Access, Visa
23 Barrett Street, W1 TEL 071-495 1340 MAP 13
Open Mon to Fri, 8am to 7pm, 9am Sat

It used to be possible to declare that Cranks was the best vegetarian restaurant in London. Partly because of other excellent rivals, this is no longer the case. Lunches still offer good salads, tasty pizzas, homity pies, quiches and soups; the bread is as good as ever – among the best – and the cakes are ace. Candlelit dinners, however, available at Marshall Street and Adelaide Street, have disappointed. One inspector who wanted mixed salad found the large bowls empty, to be told curtly that there was no more – and this at mid-evening. Poor crudités, watery garlic mushrooms and over-salty Greek salad can precede main dishes, all of which for some reason have been topped with orange and lemon wedges. Of the puddings, the trifle gets highest marks. Best to put up with the crowds and go at lunchtime for salads, hot dishes, and cakes. As we went to press, a new branch opened at 31 The Circle, EC2, and three new take-away branches were planned for the City.

Booking advisable D. Table service D. Counter service. Licensed. Vegan dishes. Other diets catered for on request. Snacks. No-smoking. Access, Amex, Diners, Visa

Crowthers

£££ MAP 12

481 Upper Richmond Road West, SW14 TEL 081-876 6372

Described by one reporter as a 'delightful restaurant with a European flavour', Crowthers has a good reputation for its cooking. There is no differentiation made between starters and main dishes on the vegetarian menu, so take your pick from spinach and mushroom roulade with hollandaise, filo pastry parcels, vegetable ravioli, Caerphilly cheese ramekin, Pithiviers of carrot with orange and cardamom, shii-take mushroom parcels and cream of artichoke soup. Opinion is divided: some find the place a touch self-satisfied, others are happily impressed.

Open Mon to Sat, exc Mon L and Sat L, noon to 2, 7 to 10 **Closed** 24 Dec to 2 Jan, 2 weeks in summer Booking advisable. Table service. Licensed, also bring your own: corkage £4. Meat dishes. Fish dishes. Vegan dishes and other diets catered for on request. Wheelchair access. Access, Amex, Visa

Country Life Ⓥ ★

£ MAP 13

123 Regent Street, W1 (entrance 1 Heddon Street) TEL 071-434 2922

The rural theme is reflected in the enormous photographs of the countryside on the walls; otherwise the décor of the basement room is unprepossessing. The vegan buffet offers a good range of freshly cooked dishes at very reasonable prices. Help yourself to the home-made bread, which includes oatmeal and raisin as well as wholewheat, and such exotic spreads as tahini and unusual nut butters. Salads can be assembled from numerous ingredients and topped with tofu cheese, cashew and pimento cream, Italian or French dressings. Huge trays of hot food for self-service include ratatouille, sunshine timbales or vegetable pastry rolls. This is lively vegan food: there's a purée of mixed fruits to top puddings and pumpkin or sunflower seeds, diced fruit, oatmeal crunch and other delights to top a fruit salad. The system for paying is unexpected: your plate is scrutinised as you leave the food queue and a bill is issued, to be paid on the way out.

Open Mon to Fri 11.30am to 2.30 (2 Fri)   Counter service. Vegan dishes. Snacks. Take-aways. No-smoking

Deals

££ MAP 12

Chelsea Harbour, SW10 TEL 071-376 3232

Comparison has been made between this and the Hard Rock Café – American style with lots of burgers and steaks and very popular. The one vegetarian dish on the menu seems unvarying – aubergine steaks charbroiled and topped with provençale sauce. For American puddings read very sweet: slightly bland pecan pie and rich but good chocolate mud – gooey fudge, chocolate, butterscotch cream on a thick biscuit base.

Open all week 11am (noon Sun) to 11 (10 Sun)   **Closed** 25 and 26 Dec   Booking advisable. Table service. Tables outside. Licensed. Meat dishes. Fish dishes. Snacks. Take-aways. Wheelchair access. Access, Amex, Visa

De Blank, Natural History Museum

£ MAP 13

Cromwell Road, SW7 TEL 071-938 9185

Exhausted families and other visitors can be refreshed by soups and vegetarian dishes of roulades, stuffed aubergine, leek and ricotta strudel or moussaka; sweets are a strong point. Run by Justin de Blank.

Open all week 10 (1 Sun) to 5   **Closed** 24 to 26 Dec   Counter service. Licensed. Meat dishes. Snacks. No smoking. Wheelchair access

Diana's Diner

£ MAP 14

39 Endell Street, WC2 TEL 071-240 0272

The small, steamy café, now something of an institution, serves vegetarian versions of Italian dishes such as spaghetti and cannelloni, and a risotto al funghi that gets a glowing mention. 'Chips are excellent, as are the salads.' Other recommendations include the special ice-creams and chocolate sponge cheesecake. Huge portions of eggs and chips are well cooked and quickly served.

Open Mon to Sat 7am to 7 (3 Sun) **Closed** 1 day every 2 weeks Table service. Counter service. Unlicensed. Meat dishes. Fish dishes. Snacks. Take-aways. Wheelchair access. Access, Amex, Diners, Visa

Dining Room Ⓥ £££ MAP 13

1 Cathedral Street, SE1 TEL 071-407 0337

Macrobiotic food is done well in this vegetarian basement. Cooking is taken seriously but flavours may be bland. Portions of the one main course are large: a goulash of lentils, haricot beans and chickpeas with fried barley would sink most hearty eaters. To start, a green pea and aubergine soup is good, but date and sesame pâté may be too sweet to get the digestive juices going. Ingredients are all carefully chosen and cheeses are excellent. The place is now anachronistic: surrounded by post-modernist architecture, it remains in an old building with imitation Roman mosaic on the floor and bare brick walls. Wines are organic.

Open Tue to Fri 12.30 to 2.30, 7 to 9.45 **Closed** 25 Dec, bank hols Booking advisable. Table service. Licensed

Diwana Bhel Poori Ⓥ ★ £ MAP 13

121 Drummond Street, NW1 TEL 071-387 5556

A busy, popular restaurant offering excellent value in what has become an Indian enclave, now extended to accommodate trade from the previous annexe over the road. The dedicated clientele queues up at lunch and dinner times to savour the South Indian cooking and can choose from six different dosas, pooris, bhel poori, idli sambar and thalis which include a house speciality. No stinting on the spices. Three kulfis are available as well as mango ice-cream or water ice and that very rich and sweet yoghurt-based shrikhand. Indian spiced tea has had favourable reports.

Open all week noon to 11.40 Table service. Unlicensed. Vegan dishes. Take-aways. Access, Diners, Visa

Dolphin Brasserie

££ MAP 13

Dolphin Square, Rodney House, Chichester Street, SW1
TEL 071-828 3207

An aquamarine geometric décor combined with a swimming-pool conspire to produce a feeling of being aboard a liner, descending from poop to promenade deck to look over the water. The large restaurant nods towards vegetarians: though there is nothing suitable on the set-lunch menu, the full menu offers a couple of starters – soup or poached egg on a muffin with avocado hollandaise – and a single main stir-fry of vegetables on puff pastry base served with saffron and coriander butter. A place for a special evening out, with dancing on Friday and Saturday nights.

Open all week, exc Sat L, 12.30 to 2.15, 7 to 10.45 Booking advisable. Table service. Licensed. Meat dishes. Fish dishes. Vegan dishes. Other diets catered for on request. Snacks at other times. Wheelchair access. Access, Amex, Diners, Visa

Dukes Hotel

£££ MAP 13

St James's Place, SW1 TEL 071-491 4840

Old-fashioned British discretion and Edwardian gentility reign in the heart of St James's and foreign visitors with large wallets come to appreciate the marble bathrooms and four-poster beds. If they are also vegetarian, they are catered for by a token vegetarian dish – perhaps stuffed baby marrows baked and served with chervil sauce. Ices and sorbets are home made and there is a renowned bread-and-butter pudding. Despite the high-class atmosphere, service doesn't always come up to expectations.

Open all week noon to 2, 6 to 10 Booking advisable. Table service. Licensed. Meat dishes. Fish dishes. Other diets catered for on request. Snacks at other times. No children under 7. Wheelchair access. Accommodation. Access, Amex, Carte Blanche, Diners, Visa

The main criterion for inclusion in the guide is that an eating place offers a vegetarian main course on its standard menu, at all times, that is more than just an omelette, quiche or salad. If you find that a listed restaurant no longers caters for vegetarians, please inform the guide; the address to write to is on page 9.

East West ⓥ

£ MAP 13

188 Old Street, EC1 TEL 071-608 0300

Purely vegan and if you're not used to this style of food, the cooking might strike you as heavy and bland. The ingredients are of good quality and everything appears to be freshly made. Mixed salads are a good bet – beetroot, pasta and millet among other. The daily set meal is enormous, with lots of unseasoned rice and bulgur with vegetables added in purée and other forms. Puddings sometimes look better than they taste: fools made from seaweed; couscous cake. One pear 'trifle' turned out to be basically fruit jelly. The surroundings are wholesome, worthy and informal, and it's a mecca of its kind in this part of London.

Open all week, exc Sat D and Sun D, noon **Closed** 25 Dec and bank hols Counter service. Licensed. Vegan dishes only. Other diets catered for on request. Snacks. Take-aways. Access, Visa

El Flamenco

££ MAP 13

114 Denby Street, SW1 TEL 071-828 0687

Pimlico does not have much to offer vegetarians, so this Spanish restaurant could be useful for either a snack of tapas or a more expensive full meal. Vegetarian choices are patatas bravas – potatoes in their skins in spicy hot sauce – juicy wedges of good tortilla, marinated olives or a plate of good quality Manchego cheese. On the restaurant menu is a main dish crêpe with aubergines and onions with white cream sauce.

Open all week restaurant 12.30 to 2.30, 6.30 (7 Sun) to 10.30; tapas bar Mon to Sat 11am to 11, Sun noon to 3, 7 to 11 Booking advisable. Table service. Tables outside. Licensed. Meat dishes. Fish dishes. Snacks. Wheelchair access. Access, Visa

English Garden

£££ MAP 13

10 Lincoln Street, SW3 TEL 071-584 7272

You might be seated under a domed roof in the pleasant and relaxed restaurant in a discreet house off the Kings Road. There is one vegetarian main dish on offer, perhaps a pie of artichokes and asparagus under puff pastry in good creamy sauce. Starters might produce a fresh basil and tomato salad or a huge summer salad, American style, with strawberries. Both a summer pudding with clotted cream and a wild strawberry fool were more-ish. Portions, despite the nouvelle appearance of the food, are generous and service is good. A fine place to come with meat- and fish-eaters.

Open all week 12.30 to 2.30, 7.30 to 11.30 **Closed** 25 and 26 Dec Booking advisable. Table service. Licensed. Meat dishes. Fish dishes. Other diets catered for on request. No children D. Access, Amex, Diners, Visa

L'Escargot £££ MAP 14

48 Greek Street, W1 TEL 071-437 2679

Smart and expensive, the Snail helpfully marks its vegetarian options: leek and watercress soup; chilled cucumber soup; filo pastry filled with ricotta, spinach and avocado; spinach and Gruyère tart; and leek and Cheddar tart give the cheese-dominated tone. The incidentals of bread, orange juice, coffee and accompanying snail-shaped chocolates are good. Service tries to be helpful, but is sometimes confused.

Open Mon to Sat, exc Sat L, noon to 3, 6 to 11.15 **Closed** Easter and Christmas Booking advisable. Table service. Licensed, also bring your own: corkage £3.50. Meat dishes. Vegan dishes on request. Take-aways by arrangement. No pipes or cigars. Access, Amex, Diners, Visa

Ethiopia 2002 £–££ MAP 12

341A Harrow Road, W9 TEL 071-286 5129

This stylish bright blue restaurant is adorned with various fly-whisks, straw plates and baskets and lit by stunning pyramidal blue lights covered in clouds. Brown paper is placed over the tablecloths, and pencils are put out for customers to doodle while waiting. The menu, on a vast wooden board, gives a potted history of Ethiopia and has a vegetarian section with useful notes on what is hot and what is not. All the starters are vegetarian and include baked sweet potato and cottage cheese chilli dip, both good. Follow this with the chef's suggested vegetarian dishes which, if mildness is stipulated, tend to be stodgy. A large, flat sourdough bread called injera is spread over a tray piled with aubergine, lentil, potato and bulgur. Ethiopian honey wine is sweet and fragrant, and coffee comes with frankincense and myrrh. A donation is made from each meal to the reforestation of Ethiopia.

Open all week noon to 4.30, 7 to 11 **Closed** 25 Dec to 1 Jan Booking advisable. Table service. Licensed, also bring your own: corkage £1.25. Meat dishes. Vegan dishes. Take-aways. Wheelchair access. Access, Visa

Fleet Tandoori £ MAP 12

104 Fleet Road, NW3 TEL 071-485 6402

At the back of the Royal Free Hospital, this small reliable restaurant offers a good-value vegetarian thali and a short list of vegetable dishes. Though the range is standard, the execution is careful and results consistently good: try excellent muttar paneer and channa masalada. Breads are fresh and soft. The branch at 346 Muswell Hill Broadway (081-883 8252) has the same menu and opening times.

Open all week noon to 2.30, 6 to 11.30 (11pm Sun) **Closed** 25 Dec Table service. Licensed. Meat dishes. Fish dishes. Vegan dishes. Take-aways. Wheelchair access. Access, Amex, Diners, Visa

Food for Thought Ⓥ ★ £ MAP 14

31 Neal Street, WC2 TEL 071-836 0239

One of the oldest established vegetarian restaurants in town, this cramped basement is as good as ever, extremely popular at lunchtime when queues are frequent and long. The food is excellent, freshly made from high-quality ingredients and served in hearty quantities. Home-made wholewheat cheese and onion bread and soup make a meal. Several hot main dishes include such choices as avial, gado-gado, stir-fried vegetables, and quiche. The butterbean rarebit, really a dish of glorified vegetables and beans in cheese sauce, is sensational. The menu changes twice a day. Everything is prepared on the premises, and cakes are unusually light and creamy for a vegetarian restaurant: the combinations of flavours in a chocolate raspberry flan worked well and the result was a real success. Freshly squeezed orange juice is another plus.

Open Mon to Sat noon to 3, 5.30 to 8 **Closed** 2 weeks at Christmas Counter service. Vegan dishes. Other diets catered for on request. Snacks at other times. Take-aways. No-smoking

Four Seasons

£ MAP 13

64 Union Street, SE1 TEL 071-378 1988

By day a take-away and buffet café where vegetarians and meat-eaters from the burgeoning local offices jostle and help themselves from an island bar loaded with salads, charged for by weight. Hot daily dishes such as good lasagne and curry are also doled out. What really sticks in the mind, however, are the cakes – in the afternoon, the smell of freshly baked cakes is hard to resist. From Wednesday to Saturday nights there is live jazz in the candle-lit dining-room. The menu may offer only one vegetarian dish, but that will be good: perhaps spiced lentil and cauliflower soup or delicately flavoured stuffed crêpes, freshly made. 'Ludicrously cheap for this part of town.'

Open Mon to Sat exc Sat L 11.30am to 3, 9 to 1am Table service D. Counter service L. Licensed. Meat dishes. Vegan dishes. Snacks. Take-aways

Frith's

£££ MAP 14

14 Frith Street, W1 TEL 071-439 3370

This idiosyncratic restaurant has more than a touch of the designer about its appearance, the simple dining-room hung with good pictures and a tiny garden with a couple of tables, but there is a very serious interest in food. Owner Carla Tomasi brings Italian influences to bear on what is otherwise modern British cooking with a difference. One of the differences is her dislike of salt, and diners may find its addition a help. Try starters such as broccoli and ginger soup, red onion and raisin tart or broccoli and walnut mousse and follow, perhaps, with a timbale of aubergine with smoked Mozzarella, parsnips and walnut cake with baked garlic, or baked field mushrooms with marinated tofu. Puddings include chocolate truffle cake with nectarine caramel and a subtly flavoured home-made purple berry ice-cream. The plaited bread is also home made. As we went to press, Frith's Vegetarian Café was opened in the basement, with a short menu and the same hours.

Open Mon to Sat, exc Sat L, 12.30 to 2.30, 7.30 to 11.15 **Closed** 25 Dec, Easter, bank hols Booking advisable. Table service. Tables outside. Licensed. Meat dishes. Fish dishes. Vegan dishes. No pipes or cigars. Wheelchair access. Access, Visa

Gate Ⓥ

£ MAP 12

Temple Lodge, 51 Queen Caroline Street, W6 TEL 081-748 6932

A welcome re-opening of a vegetarian café in a central location. Go through the wrought-iron gate at the side of the religious bookshop, into the courtyard and up the outside stairs: the new Gate, formerly the Angel Gate, is at the top. Plans for the future include suspending a large parachute from the ceiling. In one corner there is a piano for live music evenings. A trial meal on the second day of opening is a stringent test, but the food proved to be well-cooked and fresh, and one hopes that wrinkles such as lengthy delays will be ironed out. The menu is short: dhal, tabouleh and Greek salad as starters, followed by a choice of Windy City pie, lasagne or curry; and one dessert, apple pie. Interestingly enough (other restaurateurs note) most customers on that second day chose the Windy City pie; a wholesome layering of spinach, ricotta, Mozzarella and mushrooms under a light crust. Apple pie had a pleasant lemon tang, and good pastry.

Open Mon to Sat noon to 3, 6 to midnight Table service. Tables outside. Unlicensed, but bring your own: no corkage. Vegan dishes. Take-away. No-smoking area. Access, Visa

Gilbert's

££–£££ MAP 13

2 Exhibition Road, SW7 TEL 071-589 8947

The restaurant on two floors lies in museumland; it was set up by Ann Wregg and Julia Chalkley with the aim of offering very good home cooking. Despite grappling with the hand-operated lift to convey the food to diners, they manage to keep sufficiently cool to allow customers a view of the kitchen, and most seem delighted with the results. Examples of starters include leek and mushroom soup, Camembert crêpes, baked mushrooms with goats' cheese, hot Stilton tart; main dishes take in spinach timbales with sorrel sauce, herb tart, parsnip and walnut soufflé. Try to save some space for Atholl Brose, home-made ice-creams, Queen's pudding or chocolate tipsy cake. Bread is home made, as are the cakes and even the biscuits.

Open Mon to Sat, exc Mon L and Sat L, 12.30 to 2, 6.15 to 10.15 **Closed** 23 Dec to 2 Jan, 2 weeks Aug Booking advisable. Table service. Licensed. Meat dishes. Fish dishes. No pipes or cigars. Wheelchair access. Access, Amex, Visa

Golden Duck

££ MAP 12

6 Hollywood Road, SW10 TEL 071-352 3500/4998

Virtually opposite St Stephen's Hospital and one of the few Chinese restaurants operating a vegetarian set menu. Eight courses for two people run on the lines of vegetable-filled Peking dumplings; spring rolls with sweet and spicy cabbage salad; and Lohan Tsai, described as 'a Buddhist monk's vegetarian treat', which includes seasonal vegetables, lotus nuts, winter mushrooms, and seaweed. A Szechuan influence emerges in vegetarian options on the main menu – bean curd and Szechuan pickle salad, for instance. A hefty 12.5 per cent is levied for service.

Open all week 7.30 to 11.30, plus 1 to 3 Sat and Sun Booking advisable. Table service. Licensed. Meat dishes. Take-aways. Wheelchair access. Access, Amex, Diners, Visa

Govinda's ⓥ

£ MAP 13

9 Soho Street, W1 TEL 071-437 3662

The self-service counter offers an eat-as-much-as-you-can meal, various curries and thalis and a wide range of salads. Some of these are not completely successful, for example, rather sour yoghurt potatoes. Spices and herbs are used well and cakes of various kinds are lined up for dessert. Seasonal freshly squeezed juices and fruit nectars made with yoghurt are refreshing drinks. A useful venue for shoppers and office workers who take advantage of the very reasonable prices. Run by Krishna followers.

Open Mon to Sat, exc Sat D, 12.30 to 3, 5 to 7 Counter service. Licensed. Vegan dishes. Snacks. Take-aways. Access

Great Nepalese

£ MAP 13

48 Eversholt Street, NW1 TEL 071-388 6737

Tucked away on the east side of Euston Station, the newly redecorated Great Nepalese displays Nepalese traditions on the walls and on the menu. Vegetarian specialities include masco bara, a black lentil pancake with piquant curry sauce; aloo bodi tama, bamboo shoots, potato and beans; and aloo keranko achar, cold potatoes, peas, green chilli and powdered sesame seeds. The loyal following enables this friendly place to leave trendiness to others.

Open all week noon to 2.45, 6 to 11.45 **Closed** 25 and 26 Dec Booking advisable. Table service. Licensed, also bring your own: corkage £1 per bottle. Meat dishes. Fish dishes. Vegan dishes. Take-aways. Wheelchair access. Access, Amex, Diners, Visa

Greenhouse ⓥ ★ £ MAP 13

16 Chenies Street, W1 TEL 071-637 8038

In contrast to the daylight outside, the basement can appear dark and gloomy, but soon comes to feel cosier: closely packed tables are populated by people listening to old-fashioned rock music. The cooking is streets ahead of many vegetarian cafés and vegans will find at least one daily dish. Pizza and quiche are invariably supplemented by specials, for instance a tangy, cheesey, spinach and corn tian made with fresh spinach, at least four fresh salads, for which you may have to ask for dressing. Puddings are flavoursome and light: a home-made cheesecake has pretty layers of lemon and chocolate and a thin, crunchy wholewheat base. A typical day's range would also offer trifle, lemon meringue pie and fruit salad. Wheelchair customers can have food brought up to a ground-floor bar, preferably by prior arrangement. Lunchtimes can be a better bet than evenings, when dishes may begin to seem jaded.

Open Mon to Sat noon to 2.30, 5 to 9 exc Mon D **Closed** 1 week at Christmas, bank hols Counter service. Unlicensed. Vegan dishes. Other diets catered for on request. Snacks at other times. Take-aways. No smoking

Heal's £££ MAP 13

196 Tottenham Court Road, W1 TEL 071-636 1666

Catering to the well-hee ed (or Healed) shopper and occasional stray from Bloomsbury publishing, the roomy restaurant has stylish Japanese overtones in the black trellis screens dividing the tables. Afternoon tea has been praised: unlimited quantities can be taken from the trolley laden with sandwiches and cakes. Set-price lunch menus always feature one vegetarian main dish – perhaps a fresh pasta in pesto sauce – and it is well done. The food is carefully presented and ingredients are sometimes unusual. Summer pudding and strawberry charlotte have come in for special notice. Avid readers will find newspapers provided.

Open Mon to Sat, L noon to 2.30 Booking advisable. Table service. Licensed, also bring your own: corkage £3.75 to £4.50. Meat dishes. Fish dishes. No pipes or cigars in dining-room. Wheelchair access. Access, Amex, Diners, Visa

ICA

£ MAP 13

12 Carlton House Terrace, SW1 TEL 071-930 8535

This better-than-average café offers vegetarian dishes among others in the avant-garde surroundings of the Institute of Contemporary Arts. You must take out a day membership (£1 at the time of going to press) even to visit the café, but it is certainly worth it if you are going to see a film or exhibition, as there are few other places to eat nearby. The café is opposite the bar, through the gallery, and serves plenty for vegetarians – southern pasticcio, red dragon pie, moussaka, Hungarian pie and salads are just some examples.

Open all week noon to 9 Counter service. Tables outside. Licensed, also bring your own: corkage £2 per bottle. Snacks. No smoking. Wheelchair access

India Club

£ MAP 13

143 The Strand, WC2 TEL 071-836 0650

As in India, the menu here is divided into non-vegetarian and vegetarian dishes: honey to a vegetarian's eyes. The fairly standard curries include a well-flavoured vegetable version, as well as beans and coconut, a couple of dosais, tomato omelette, uppama, and raitha. Described as 'Good cooking with no frills,' and prices are reasonable.

Open all week noon to 2.30, 6 to 10 (Sun 6 to 8) Booking advisable. Table service. Unlicensed, but bring your own: no corkage. Take-aways

Jamdani

££ MAP 13

34 Charlotte Street, W1 TEL 071-636 1178

Jamdani muslin was famed for its delicacy and transparency, said to be so fine that a dress made of it could pass through a wedding ring. This restaurant sets itself the high task of replicating such fineness in its cuisine – not always successfully, as reports continue to vary considerably. The room is attractive; prices are relatively high. Vegetarians don't get much of a look in, except for a thali and a range of vegetable dishes that include navratan korma – nine vegetables in a cream spiced sauce – baheer e baingan – aubergine – and undhya, of green bananas, beans, aubergine, potato. There are also some interesting breads. For a change from kulfi, try the South Indian coconut ice-cream.

Open all week 12.30 to 2.45, 6.30 to 11.30 **Closed** 25 and 26 Dec Booking advisable. Table service. Licensed. Meat dishes. Fish dishes. No-smoking area. Wheelchair access. Access, Amex, Diners, Visa

Jazz Café

££ MAP 12

56 Newington Green, N16 TEL 071-359 4936

Not just of interest because of the music: the café functions as a vegetarian restaurant with an extensive menu offering such items as hummus, skordalia, spiced hazelnut and vegetable pâté, lasagne, tandoori burgers, couscous, tian and pasta bake as well as salads and quiche. Follow with fruit crumble, fudge cake or perhaps lemon and almond cake. The menu changes daily. There's an entrance fee if you also want to hear the music that starts after 9pm – go at lunchtime or between 6.30 and 7pm to avoid it (or arrive and leave between 7 and 9 and the charge is refunded). The first dining-area, doubling as the stage, quickly gets crowded, but further seating can be found through the bar in an attractive kind of conservatory. Popular and friendly, this is a must for any vegetarian jazz enthusiast.

Open all week noon to 3, 6.30 to 11 **Closed** 2 days at Christmas Table service. Counter service. Vegan dishes. Wheelchair access

Julie's

£££ MAP 12

135 Portland Road TEL 071-229 8331

Vegetarians might be inclined to bypass the Champagne bar and the bar for the more upmarket restaurant, which provides the most reliable main-course dish: often Swabian noodles on field mushrooms. Starters include watercress mousse with minted yoghurt, tomato parfait with quails' eggs and ragout of wild mushrooms in a puff pastry basket. The

Gothic bar next door, filled with dark carvings, large low sofas and little round tables at the back and cushioned benches at the front with daily newspapers, is less formal, more relaxing and intriguing, but might only offer soup for non-meat eaters.

Open all week exc Sat L 12.30 to 2.45, 7.30 to 11 (10.15 Sun) Booking advisable. Table service. Licensed. Meat dishes. Access, Amex, Diners, Visa

Justin de Blank

££ MAP 13

54 Duke Street, W1 TEL 071-629 3174

Although this is self-service, the ambience promises more: large cane sofas and metal tables are ranged down one side and an attractive lit array of dishes down the other. Justin de Blank has a good name for bread and cakes, but sadly the food may sometimes look better than it turns out to be – and prices are relatively high. A spinach roulade with cottage cheese was disappointing, though a stuffed pepper with pine nuts was better. Try the fruit brûlée or meringue brûlée, both of which have been much enjoyed. Handily placed for those who can brave Oxford Street, and the products of the bakery make this an attraction for afternoon tea.

Open Mon to Fri 8am to 5.30, Sat 9am to 3.30 Counter service. Licensed. Meat dishes. Fish dishes. Other diets catered for with 24 hours' notice. Snacks. Take-aways. No-smoking area. Wheelchair access. Access, Visa

Kanishka

££ MAP 13

15 Warren Street, W1 TEL 071-388 0860 and 0862

The great Emperor Kanishka was a vegetarian who allowed his courtiers to eat meat. He might turn in his grave at the sight of the few vegetarian dishes on the menu at his namesake restaurant. Of interest are cashew-nut rolls Kashmiri, two vegetarian thalis, sobji kebab cooked in the tandoor and a wild-and-cultivated mushroom curry. The bread is better than average and the buffet lunch is good value.

Open all week noon to 3, 6 to 11.30 (midnight Thur, Fri and Sat) **Closed** 25 and 26 Dec Booking advisable. Table service. Tables outside. Licensed. Meat dishes. Fish dishes. Vegan dishes. Take-aways. No-smoking area. Wheelchair access. Access, Amex, Diners, Visa

Kastoori ⓥ

£ MAP 12

188 Upper Tooting Road, SW17 TEL 081-767 7027

Starters of puris, dahi puris, patras, bhel puris, corn bhel and many others can be followed by main dishes of dosas, various curries, chats, utappam, paav bhai – described on the menu as an exotic collection of chosen vegetables made into curry served with fried buns – and three thalis, one of which is only available on Sundays. Lassi, falooda and masala tea are typical drinks; shrikhand, rasmalai, kulfi and gulab jamun the sweets.

Open all week, exc Mon L and Tue L, 12.30 and 3, 6 to 10.30 (11 Fri, Sat and Sun) **Closed** 25 Dec, 1st week Jan Booking advisable. Table service. Licensed. Vegan dishes. Other diets catered for on request. Snacks at other times. Take-aways. No-smoking area. Access, Visa

Kettners

££ MAP 14

29 Romilly Street, W1 TEL 071-734 6112

It's like a club without the bores: a huge building in the heart of Soho spawns tiled wine bar, Champagne bar, panelled dining-rooms, cosy and luxurious alcoves – and there's live music every night. Despite such luxury, the prices are not high and vegetarians can indulge in the excellent pizzas à la Pizza Express, of which chain this is a part. There are a few extra puddings in addition to the usual ones – apple pie or ice-cream bombe – and freshly squeezed orange juice is available. Private rooms can be hired. No bookings are taken but the complicated system of allotting tables works surprisingly well.

Open all week 11am to midnight **Closed** 25 Dec Table service. Licensed, also bring your own: corkage £5. Meat dishes. Fish dishes. Vegan dishes. Snacks. Take-aways. No-smoking area. Wheelchair access. Access, Amex, Diners, Visa

Lakorn Thai

££ MAP 13

197–199 Rosebery Avenue, EC1 TEL 071-837 5048

There's a whole page of vegetarian offerings in the huge menu of over 100 dishes and the restaurant has no equal for convenience to the Sadler's Wells Theatre. The service is attentive and efficient, making it possible to be out comfortably within an hour – though dessert might have to be skipped. Try special fried noodles Thai-style, mixed vegetables fried in tempura batter or hot-and-sour omelette. Mixed reports suggest that standards sometimes wobble, perhaps because of the larger size after expansion, but the reasonable prices still attract.

Open Mon to Sat noon to 3, 6 to 11.15 **Closed** bank hols Booking advisable. Table service. Licensed. Meat dishes. Take-aways. Wheelchair access. Access, Amex, Diners, Visa

Launceston Place ££ MAP 12

1A Launceston Place, W8 TEL 071-937 6912

From the elegant lettering on the delightful curved exterior to the subdued and restrained furnishings and crowded walls of the interior, this speaks of class. A higgledy-piggledy collection of rooms has been opened into two curiously shaped dining-areas, a long sofa running underneath the window; the impression is of being in someone's sitting-room. Service is friendly rather than obsequious and the food can be splendid. A vegetarian usually has several choices of starter, perhaps baked tomato salad with goats' cheese, a thick, straightforward celeriac soup, or cold grilled mixed vegetables, the burnt skins giving an exotic flavour, prettily arranged around a home-made pesto. Do not refrain from a pudding, since the chocolate truffle cake is one of the best – light and rich – and a prune and armagnac home-made ice-cream a great invention. Main courses get mixed reports: gratin of turnips, Jersey Royals and morels with a fine butter sauce was appreciated, having 'a delicate yet crunchy texture'. On another occasion tagliatelle with girolles was oily, bland and stodgy, depressing to face when adjacent meat-eaters were exclaiming over their delights.

Open all week exc Sat L and Sun D 12.30 to 2.30, 7 to 11.30 **Closed** bank hols Booking advisable. Table service. Licensed. Meat dishes. Fish dishes. Vegan dishes. No pipes. Wheelchair access. Access, Visa

Laurent ££ MAP 12

428 Finchley Road, NW2 TEL 071-794 3603

In the unfashionable part of Finchley Road, with tacky décor, this authentic couscous café does a good job within the limits it has set itself.

Couscous is the only main course; one variety is vegetarian. The token starter is brique à l'oeuf – deep-fried egg pancake – and puddings include crêpes Suzettes and crème caramel. The couscous is spiced with caraway and cumin seeds; the little pot of harissa could blow your head off, and the accompanying vegetables – a very generous pot full of courgettes, carrots, leeks, chickpeas, celery, green pepper and turnips – is hot enough without it. The good North African mint tea is black tea with mint added, but thankfully no sugar.

Open Mon to Sat noon to 2, 6 to 11 **Closed** first 3 weeks Aug Booking advisable. Table service. Licensed. Meat dishes. Take-aways. Access, Visa

Leith's ★ **£££** MAP 12

92 Kensington Park Road, W1 TEL 071-229 4481

It's still a rarity to find a first-rate restaurant offering a completely separate vegetarian menu. Leith's goes further and states, 'If you are a vegan, please tell the manager.' Whenever possible, organically grown produce is used from Leith's own farm, and vegetarian dishes are guaranteed not to contain meat stock or gelatine. A visit makes you feel pampered: dark rich furnishings, excellent tableware and the sight of temptingly laden trolleys all contribute, though service has been criticised as uninterested. The trolleys of starters and desserts often seem the best choice, but the vegetarian menu will add such dishes as chilled beetroot and Greek yoghurt soup; red pepper mousse with warm olive oil vinaigrette or summer leaf salad with goats' cheese and croûtons; home-made pasta with creamed seaweed, tomato and summer herbs; tartlet of spinach with quails' eggs; a 'sandwich' of kalaif pastry and celeriac; timbale of spiced bulgur wheat. The sweets trolley purveys some sweet moussey delights and a recommended hot bread-and-butter pudding, alternatively there is a poppy seed and almond parfait or a savoury of scrambled eggs and mushrooms on toast. Traditional and new British cheeses can be followed by petits fours and tea, coffee or herb teas, which are included in the fixed-price menus.

Open all week, D 7.30 to 11.30 **Closed** 4 days Christmas, 2 days Aug bank hol Booking advisable. Table service. Licensed. Meat dishes. Vegan dishes. No pipes or cigars. No children under 7. Access, Amex, Diners, Visa

See the back of the guide for a list of restaurants awarded stars for especially good vegetarian cooking.

Le Lion £££ MAP 12

103 Black Lion Lane, W6 TEL 081-748 9070

Discovered down a side street off King Street, this tiny ground-floor restaurant with antique Parisian posters does a couple of vegetarian main dishes on an interesting menu. Service is intelligent and informed and crudités are served courtesy of the house. For a vegetarian, starters might be a good leek and Gruyère strudel or an asparagus and quails' eggs tartlet with hollandaise. Main courses could be croustade of vegetables and herbs, crépinette of spinach with leeks or a good spinach and sorrel mousse. Sticky-toffee pudding, made with dates, is a must.

Open Mon to Sat, exc Mon L and Sat L noon to 3, 7 to 11 **Closed** 25 and 26 Dec Booking advisable. Table service. Tables outside. Licensed. Meat dishes. Fish dishes. Other diets catered for on request. Wheelchair access. Access, Amex, Diners, Visa

Mandalay ££ MAP 12

100 Greenwich South Street, SE10 TEL 081-691 0443

One of the very few Burmese restaurants in Britain, the Mandalay is very unusual, and certainly somewhere to refresh a bored palate. From the outside, set in the small parade of shops, it doesn't look overly smart but inside the rattan chairs, ceiling fan and wicker furniture create a Somerset Maugham-style effect. Instead of attempting to order for yourself, ask the proprietor for advice about the Burmese meals, as he is extremely helpful; the resulting food is interestingly flavoured, spicy, with good use of fresh herbs, and not too hot. Portions are large and doggy bags are offered. Vegetarians might choose an okra curry, a mixed vegetable curry, or a Burmese omelette curry. Burmese 'soups' are used more as a dip or gravy than as starters. Puddings include semolina cakes, a seaweed dish with coconut and a mango ice-cream that could have benefited from more stirring in the freezing.

Open Tue to Sun 7 to 10.30, Sun L 12.30 to 3 **Closed** Christmas week Booking advisable. Table service. Licensed. Meat dishes. Fish dishes. Vegan dishes. Other diets catered for on request. Access, Amex, Visa

Report forms are at the back of the book; write a letter if you prefer.

Mandeer ⓥ

£ MAP 13

21 Hanway Place, W1 TEL 071-323 0660

The low lighting cannot wholly disguise a tackiness in this basement Indian vegetarian restaurant, though the round tables are well spaced, which gives a spacious feel. In the café, choice is limited but the food is good value. The restaurant itself aims higher, with dearer dishes and an extensive dinner menu featuring some interesting vegetarian versions of Indian dishes: puffed lotus savoury, tofu special and paneer kurma, for instance. Lunches are set meals of South Indian snacks such as bhel, dosa, patra and pani puri. Kachoris are delicately though powerfully flavoured and freshly cooked, moist inside and crisp out. Take with a pinch of salt – or sugar – any advice about dishes 'not being hot'. Puris are fresh and warm. Organic wines are available. As we went to press, Hanway Place was under threat of development, which might mean Mandeer has to close; best to check by telephone.

Open Mon to Sat noon to 2.30, 6 to 9.45 **Closed** 25 Dec, 1 Jan, bank hols Booking advisable. Table service restaurant. Counter service café. Licensed, also bring your own: corkage £3. Vegan dishes. Other diets catered for on request. Snacks at other times. Take-aways. Access, Amex, Diners, Visa

Manna ⓥ

££ MAP 12

4 Erskine Road, NW3 TEL 071-722 8028

This could almost be a shrine to traditional vegetarianism. All the ingredients are there – long, shared pine tables, large portions of wholefood, lots of brown rice and seaweed, a committed clientele. There's nothing frivolous about the food, not even the puddings. Vegetables and brown rice will almost certainly be on the menu, with other dishes such as broccoli and nut loaf, leek, Feta and almond tart and starters of gazpacho, carrot and coriander soup or mixed bean pâté. Vegans are always catered for. The wholewheat bread is baked on the premises daily. It's certainly good value, and few could leave feeling hungry.

Open all week, D 6.30 to 11 **Closed** 25 and 26 Dec Table service. Licensed, also bring your own: corkage £1.75. Vegan dishes. Take-aways. No-smoking area. Wheelchair access

Mary Tandoori ★

££ MAP 12

17 New Road, E1 TEL 071-247 0855

Rated as one of the better Indian eating places in the East End, this compares favourably with upmarket West End restaurants. The family who own and run it put you at your ease in the dimly lit, flock-wallpapered dining-room. There is a separate vegetarian menu on request, which has half a dozen bhel pooris, assembled to your order, so spicing can be adjusted, a thali and three dosas. The cooking is subtle and there's no oiliness or taste of reheating. Aloo papri chat with a sweet-and-sour yoghurt, tamarind and spiced topping and ragada patties – a mound of chilli-hot chickpeas – make excellent starters that could even be a meal, and there are freshly cooked vegetable dishes with good chapatis. Prices are very reasonable.

Open all week noon to 2.30, 6 to midnight **Closed** bank hols Booking advisable. Table service. Licensed. Meat dishes. Snacks. Take-aways

Melati

££ MAP 14

21 Great Windmill Street, W1 TEL 071-437 2745

The central location and good-value food are the two great attractions here; expect to queue at main meal times if you haven't booked. Vegetarian options have been increased to include a vegetable satay, spring roll, potato cakes, sweetcorn fritters and noodles with mixed vegetables. Highly recommended is the bean curd omelette: it may not sound inviting but the combination of bean curd, egg and the spicy gravy called tahu telor is surprisingly successful. For pudding there are some exotic sweet dishes based on jack fruit, mango, papaya, young coconut and jelly. The recent redecoration is stripped pine on three floors.

Open all week, noon to 11.30pm (12.30am Fri and Sat) **Closed** 25 Dec Booking advisable. Table service. Licensed. Meat dishes. Fish dishes. Other diets catered for on request. Take-aways. Wheelchair access. Access, Amex, Carte Blanche, Diners, Visa

★ *after a restaurant name indicates that the vegetarian cooking is especially good. A list of starred restaurants appears at the end of the book.*

Ménage à Trois

££ MAP 13

15 Beauchamp Place, SW3 TEL 071-584 9350 and 589 4252

The cramped conditions do not deter the devotees from an unusual enterprise: it's been around for eight years, but there's still nothing like it. The idea is to avoid the usual categories of starters and main course. All portions are nouvelle-sized, and meals can be made up from vegetables, warm salads, eggs and pasta – one or more to be eaten together or separately. The approach works to the benefit of vegetarians. Though the vegetables section is a motley collection of crudités, lasagne, crispy potato skins, there are also the more interesting 'rendezvous' of baby stuffed vegetables and a trio of wild mushrooms – mushroom ravioli with truffle sauce, feuilleté of wild ceps with garlic and parsley and stuffed cap with mushroom soufflé). Chocoholics will revel in the 'chocolate dreams' section, which offers three mousses, a truffle, dark and white ice-cream, and a sorbet. The Ménage à Trois could compete, comprising three hot pastry parcels with pear and chocolate, banana and rum, and apple and raspberry fillings served with praline cream.

Open Mon to Fri L 11.30am to 3, all week, D 7 to 11.30 Booking advisable. Table service. Licensed, also bring your own: corkage varies. Meat dishes. Fish dishes. Vegan dishes. Other diets catered for. Take-aways. Access, Amex, Diners, Visa

Methuselah's

££ MAP 13

29 Victoria Street, SW1 TEL 071-222 3550

Part of Don Hewitson's chain, Methuselah's has a wine bar and brasserie, both of which offer a vegetarian choice. It's heartening to know that the vegetarian dish of the day in the Burgundy Room is one of the most popular dishes. The food is way above that in run of the mill wine bars and portions have even been described as too large. Vegetable gratin and the renowned mushroom pâté are available in the wine bar, and the Burgundy Room might have stuffed baked onion Côte d'Azur or stuffed peppers. Try the frozen lemon soufflé with raspberry and cassis sauce or mango and passion-fruit mousse.

Open Mon to Fri 11am to 3, 5 to 10.45 Table service restaurant. Counter service bar. Tables outside. Licensed. Meat dishes. Wheelchair access. Access, Amex, Diners, Visa

Mildred's ★

£ MAP 14

58 Greek Street, W1 TEL 071-494 1634

This looks like a coffee-bar, has no frills, crams in the Formica tables and decorates the walls with what appear to be kitsch sculptures akin to cuckoo clocks. But the food is excellent, and with such reasonable prices that at peak times it is predictably crowded with a mainly young student clientele. Start with a garlicky aubergine and olive pâté with Neal's Yard bread; follow perhaps with stir-fry vegetables with a satay sauce and brown rice and a fresh well-dressed mixed-leaf salad. Cakes, fruit salad and ice-cream are home-made: the orange ice-cream is rich and creamy, the trifle uninspired. Freshly squeezed orange juice or pink grapefruit juice make a welcome change from carton juices.

Open Mon to Sat noon to 10 Table service. Unlicensed, but bring your own: corkage £1. Fish dishes. Vegan dishes. Snacks at other times. Take-aways. No smoking

Millwards ⓥ

££ MAP 12

97 Stoke Newington Church Street, N16 TEL 071-254 1025

The large plate-glass windows are filled with plants and the casual furniture yet comfortable trimmings make this a pleasant, faintly 1960s place, not demandingly smart. The menu calls itself 'Continental' and has a good choice of starters – spiced lentil pâté, falafel, sweet-and-sour Chinese leeks, baby sweetcorn à la grècque – and main courses – leek and lentil terrine with a sour cream sauce, broccoli and almond strudel, chestnut filo with red wine sauce. Sadly, some dishes have fallen short of expectations. None the less, vegans are always well catered for, and a 'Taistie Maisie' offers a selection of first and main courses for £7.50. Traditional crumbles and trifles to follow, or a more adventurous lemon fudge cake.

Open weekdays 6pm to 11pm (11.30pm Fri); noon to 11.30pm Sat; noon to 11pm Sun **Closed** 1 week at Christmas Booking advisable. Table service. Licensed, also bring your own: corkage £2.50. Vegan dishes. Other diets catered for on request. Take-aways. Wheelchair access. Access, Visa

See the back of the guide for an index of restaurants listed.

Mijanou

££££ MAP 13

143 Ebury Street, SW1 TEL 071-730 4099

There's nothing trendy or designer about this discreet French restaurant à la bourgeoise, with its stained-glass ceiling in the basement and its butterfly tableware. It's a shame that the extensive and ambitious vegetarian menu, extremely high in price, should turn out to be something of a disappointment. Five starters have included tasty cream cheese lasagne, just a touch on the dry side, and a pleasant vichyssoise tartlet heaped with potatoes and leeks on a crisp pastry base. Main courses, of which there are four, could not be criticised on grounds of meanness: in fact it may be hard to finish them. A Pithiviers à la fondue de Gruyère aux epinards was a solid pastry-topped pie containing a delicious sauce, but providing no escape from that strong sauce and the pounds of pastry. The chartreuse of riz sauvage, full of wild rice and a 'truffle-flavoured mousse' was also a struggle. Some dishes give an impression of having been reheated. A strong-flavoured white cheese ice-cream with prunes soaked in armagnac and Earl Grey, the cheese and tea not detectable, is a good end to a meal.

Open Mon to Fri 12.30 to 2, 7.30 to 10 **Closed** 2 weeks at Christmas, 1 week at Easter, 3 weeks Aug Booking advisable. Table service. Tables outside. Licensed, also bring your own: corkage for 2 is cost of a bottle of house wine. Meat dishes. Fish dishes. Vegan dishes. Other diets catered for on request. No-smoking in dining-room. Wheelchair access. Access, Amex, Diners, Visa

Ming

££ MAP 14

35–36 Greek Street, W1 TEL 071-734 2721

A delicate blue restaurant which serves an interesting Peking menu and comes up with some unusual Chinese vegetarian dishes, for instance ratatouille Chinese style, hot and spicy tofu, and an onion pancake. The more usual fried noodles and stir-fried root vegetables with sweet-and-sour seasonings are reported to be good, too.

Open all week noon to 11.45 **Closed** 25 and 26 Dec Booking advisable. Table service. Counter service. Licensed. Vegan dishes. Take-aways. Access, Amex, Diners, Visa

If in doubt about the constituents of a dish, ask.

Mon Plaisir

££–£££ MAP 14

21 Monmouth Street, WC2 TEL 071-836 7243

Fondly remembered for consistently providing authentic, simple French food in Continental fashion, Mon Plaisir continues in the same vein, although it has now grown to four rooms. The crowded, busy atmosphere has not changed. Perhaps one of the few innovations is the inclusion of a couple of vegetarian main dishes on the menu – crêpe fourrée and a wild mushroom tart. If you chose the latter you would bypass the mushroom brioche that featured as a starter on the same menu, but other starters included a salad and a gratinée à l'oignon.

Open Mon to Sat, exc Sat L, noon to 2.15, 6 to 11.15 **Closed** bank hols Booking advisable. Table service. Licensed. Meat dishes. Fish dishes. Vegan and other diets catered for with prior notice. Wheelchair access. Access, Amex, Diners, Visa

National Gallery

£ MAP 14

Trafalgar Square, WC2 TEL 071-930 5210

Pleasantly large and airy; the food, provided by Justin de Blank, includes hot dishes such as soup, quiche, roulade or strudel. A useful bolt-hole.

Open all week 10 (2 Sun) to 5 **Closed** Christmas Counter service. Licensed. Meat dishes. Fish dishes. Snacks. No-smoking area. Wheelchair access

Neal Street Restaurant

£££ MAP 14

26 Neal Street, WC2 TEL 071-836 8368

The high reputation is borne out by the clean, simple décor, artistic menu and very good service. Mushrooms are the speciality here, so there are wild mushroom soup, brawdelli of pasta with morel sauce or egg tagliolini with wild mushrooms for starters and vegetables include cannellini beans with fungi. The token main dish is parmigiana of courgette. Go to town on puddings by indulging in the pot au chocolat, crème brûlée or tiramisu, Sicilian trifle with vanilla cream, cake and coffee – sensational.

Open Mon to Fri 12.30 to 2.30, 7.30 to 11 **Closed** bank hols, Christmas to New Year Booking advisable. Table service. Licensed. Meat dishes. Fish dishes.

Other diets catered for on request. No children under 5. Wheelchair access. Access, Amex, Visa

Neal's Yard Bakery & Tea Room Ⓥ ★ £ MAP 14

6 Neal's Yard, WC2 TEL 071-836 5199

In summer the yard, surrounded by a bakery, an apothecary and cheese shop, is filled with people perched on wooden benches under the tub-planted trees. They are probably eating take-aways from the bakery, which offers such choices as really good soups, pizzas, pies, rice balls and daily specials such as lasagne or ratatouille. Above the bakery and under the rafters is a café with big glass windows at each end. From the bakery counter, food is taken up here – the same choice as for take-away. Hippy-style low tables and cushions have been replaced by more prosaic pine tables, of which there were always a few, but the atmosphere is much the same: unhurried, un-yuppy. The bread is outstanding, perhaps the best in London: as well as the plain wholemeal, which is more like cake than bread, there are sunflower seed, three-seed and yet others. Cakes are also excellent, particularly the boozy fruit cake. If trifle is on, make a beeline: made with black treacle or molasses cake, it is quite one of the best in the city.

Open Mon to Fri 10.30am to 6.30 (4.30 Sat) **Closed** 25 and 26 Dec Counter service. Tables outside. Unlicensed, but bring your own: no corkage. Vegan dishes. Other diets catered for on request. Snacks. Take-aways

Neal's Yard Soup and Salad Bar £ MAP 14

2 Neal's Yard, WC2 TEL 071-836 3233

On the other side of the yard from the bakery is the mainly take-away soup and salad kitchen, where, in addition to freshly made soups and organic salads, there are also three hot dishes a day: stir-fried vegetables, vegetarian shepherd's pie, dhal, lasagne, baked potatoes or marinated tofu with vegetables. Every day there will be a cheese bake and a quiche of some kind. Juices are freshly squeezed; no sugar is used; soups are always vegan.

Open Mon to Sat 11 to 5.30 Counter service. Vegan dishes. Snacks. Take-aways. No smoking

New Restaurant, Victoria and Albert Museum

£ MAP 13

Henry Cole Wing, Cromwell Road, SW7 TEL 071-589 6371

The large, airy space is charming – a long gallery at basement level with bare brick walls, columns and arches, running alongside the road. Some of the old Victorian tiles are displayed; tables are pine, set with tiny vases of flowers; newspapers on poles are a welcome touch. A range of salads are served buffet style. There is always one vegetarian main dish, different each day, maybe spinach pasta with basil cream, mixed vegetable roly poly and tomato sauce, curry, or Yorkshire cheese-and-herb pudding. A pasta with cream cheese, eagerly forked up after lengthy queueing, was sadly tepid, dull in taste and cloggy in texture. But bread-and-butter pudding, piquant and not in the least stodgy, with good custard, was a triumph.

Open all week 10am (2.30 Sun) to 5 **Closed** bank hols Counter service. Licensed. Meat dishes. Fish dishes. Other diets catered for on request. Snacks. Take-aways. No-smoking area. Wheelchair access

New World

£ MAP 14

Gerrard Place, W1 TEL 071-734 0677/0396

Dim-sum are the draw – but why are there no vegetarian ones? Otherwise there's a list of vegetarian dishes includes fried seaweed, braised aubergine, monks style vegetables, spicy bean curd and a large range of other reasonably priced choices.

Open all week 11am to 11.45 **Closed** 25 Dec Booking advisable. Table service. Licensed, also bring your own: corkage £2 per bottle. Meat dishes. Fish dishes. Vegan dishes. Take-aways. Wheelchair access. Access, Amex, Diners, Visa

Nuthouse Ⓥ

£ MAP 13

26 Kingly Street, W1 TEL 071-437 9471

This long, narrow restaurant just behind Regent Street is handy for shoppers and office workers. There is nothing fussy about the plain décor: Formica tables and naive paintings. The cooking belongs to the old school of vegetarianism with huge vats of hot dishes such as mixed bean casserole, moussaka, and pasta or, the speciality, cheesy mixed vegetables, jostling alongside bevies of pies, rissoles, plenty of salads and rather heavy puddings. For an extremely reasonable price, you could satisfy a hefty appetite.

Open Mon to Sat 10.30 to 7 Counter service. Licensed. Vegan dishes. Other diets catered for on request. Snacks. Take-aways. No-smoking area

Odette's

£££ MAP 13

130 Regent's Park Road, NW1 TEL 071-586 5486

There's an assured feel about this established restaurant, though the front room is rather overwhelming and the conservatory behind light and chilly. It's a trendy place to come, and trendy vegetarians will be catered for with one main dish (there's also one available in the attached wine bar). The food, rather over-written on the menu, impresses some more than others. The menu might start with a hot vegetable soup, a chilled soup of cucumber, fennel and dill or an interesting wild mushroom ravioli made with beetroot pasta. Main dishes might include a potato and carrot gateau or a timbale of carrot and Gruyère cheese. The bread-and-butter pudding and the trio of chocolate mousses were a disappointment. The kitchen makes rather imaginative bread rolls, such as tomato, spinach and walnut flavours.

Open Mon to Sat 12.30 to 2.30 (exc Sat L), 7.30 to 11 **Closed** last 2 weeks Aug: Christmas to New Year Booking advisable. Table service. Tables outside. Licensed. Meat dishes. Fish dishes. Vegan and other diets catered for on request. Take-aways. Wheelchair access. Access, Amex, Diners, Visa

Olive Tree

£ MAP 14

11 Wardour Street, W1 TEL 071-734 0808

Opposite the Swiss Centre, this popular Lebanese restaurant has food displayed in the window and along the counter to the left of the entrance. Beyond are small tables packed closely together, usually full. Two menus, vegetarian and non-vegetarian, are offered to all diners. Substantial aubergine dip has a smoky, garlicky flavour, served with a generous basket of three or four hot brown and white pitta breads as a starter. Main courses are generous portions: couscous is packed with seasonal vegetables; moussaka would satisfy the most hungry. For pudding, large slices of baklava help offset the strength of the coffee. Good value in a very central area.

Open all week noon to 11pm **Closed** 25 Dec Table service. Licensed. Meat dishes. Vegan dishes. Snacks. Take-aways. No smoking. Access, Visa

One Two Three

£££ MAP 13

27 Davies Street, W1 TEL 071-409 0750

Fairly pricey upmarket Japanese restaurant where a vegetarian could start with a couple of bean curd dishes or baby mushrooms with white radish and go on to fried aubergine covered with miso and sesame seed and grilled, or vegetable tempura. Vegetable sushi is like a Swiss roll, the vegetables rolled with rice and sheets of seaweed – before being sliced in rings.

Open Mon to Fri noon to 2.30, 6.30 to 10.30 Booking advisable. Table service. Licensed. Meat dishes. Fish dishes. Take-aways. No babies. Access, Amex, Diners, Visa

Orso

£££ MAP 14

27 Wellington Street, WC2 TEL 071-240 5269

The entrance to this upmarket Italian restaurant is inconspicuous – just a simple wooden door with glass plate above bearing the name. Stairs lead down to a basement that is always crowded, where famous faces sit cheek by jowl with after-theatre goers and Covent Garden lovers. Tables are laid with white linen. Drinks are offered immediately, and orange juice is freshly squeezed. Service manages to be smooth and efficient without the frantic bustle that might be expected. This is not a place for addicts of basic pizza/pasta chains. Pizzas have crispy thin bases and generous toppings: try goats' cheese and garlic, with pungent cheese and whole toasted garlic cloves. Vegetables are cooked admirably: broccoli full of flavour and firm, presented with a wedge of lemon. Note that credit cards aren't accepted.

Open all week noon to midnight **Closed** 24 and 25 Dec Booking advisable. Table service. Licensed. Meat dishes. Fish dishes. Other diets catered for on request

Otters

££ MAP 12

271 New Kings Road, SW6 TEL 071-371 0434

This bright and tasteful restaurant is located at the elegant end of Kings Road. Decorated in plum, it has that now fashionable air of genteel quality as opposed to stark modernity. A reputation for trying out bizarre combinations of food doesn't seem to extend to the single vegetarian dish, which could be Caerphilly and walnuts wrapped in vine leaves, or cauliflower and wild mushroom timbale with sorrel cream. Starters are limited, especially if you don't eat fish – peach and cream cheese wrapped in filo on apricot coulis might be the only possibility, or a spinach and curly endive salad with red and yellow cherry tomatoes. The home-made ice-creams are worth tasting: the highly original rose-water ice-cream was delicately flavoured, honey another success. Chocolate parfait was rich and ice-crisp. Prices, though not cheap, are reasonable.

Open all week noon to 3, 7 to 11 exc Sun D **Closed** Christmas to New Year Booking advisable. Table service. Licensed. Meat dishes. Fish dishes. Vegan dishes. Other diets catered for on request. Wheelchair access. Access, Amex, Diners, Visa

Pacifico

££ MAP 14

5 Langley Street, WC2 TEL 071-379 7728

As Mexican restaurants go, this one is a good bet, offering vegetarian versions of typical dishes such as tacos, tortillas, nachos and quesadillas. These are mainly based on tomato and cheese. The American saloon décor and strong music seem rough and tumble, but the atmosphere is cosmopolitan.

Open all week noon to 11.45 Table service. Licensed. Meat dishes. Vegan dishes. Other diets catered for on request. Snacks. Take-aways. Access, Visa

Pearl of Siam

££ MAP 12

107 Roman Road, E2 TEL 081-980 1676

Offers Thai cuisine at fairly hefty prices; portions vary, the food is genuine and good. Inside, the walls are plain cream and seating consists of bamboo chairs. The vegetarian section of the menu includes quick-fried seasonal vegetables, pastry leaves filled with mixed vegetables and deep fried, fried bean curd and vegetable salad with peanut sauce, as well as a soup with bean curd. The fried bean curd, rather like Hovis mini loaves in appearance, earns an accolade: 'the best of its kind I've ever tasted'. However, the vegetables with peanut sauce has disappointed, being mainly hardboiled egg with slivers of cabbage and a few slices of tomato.

Open Mon to Sat noon to 3, 6 to 11 **Closed** Christmas and New Year Booking advisable. Table service. Licensed. Meat dishes. Fish dishes. Vegan dishes catered for with prior notice. Take-aways. No-smoking area. Access, Visa

---

Pizza Express £££

23 Bond Street, W5 TEL 081-567 7690 MAP 12
252 Chiswick High Road, W4 TEL 081-747 0193 MAP 12
30 Coptic Street, WC1 TEL 071-636 3232 MAP 13
10 Dean Street, W1 TEL 071-437 9595 MAP 14
35 Earls Court Road, W8 TEL 071-937 0761 MAP 12
227 Finchley Road, NW3 TEL 071-794 5100 MAP 12
363 Fulham Road, SW10 TEL 071-352 5300 MAP 12
895 Fulham Road, SW6 TEL 071-731 3117 MAP 12
15 Gloucester Road, SW7 TEL 071-584 9078 MAP 13
94 Golders Green Road, NW11 TEL 081-455 9556 MAP 12
14 High Parade, High Road, SW16 TEL 081-677 3646 MAP 12
820 High Road, N12 TEL 081-445 7714 MAP 12
84 High Street, SW19 TEL 081-946 6027 MAP 12
Kettner's, 29 Romilly Street, W1 TEL 071-437 6437 MAP 14
11 Knightsbridge, SW1 TEL 071-235 5273 MAP 13
230 Lavender Hill, SW11 TEL 071-223 5677 MAP 12
137 Notting Hill Gate, W11 TEL 071-229 6000 MAP 12
26 Porchester Road, The Colonnades, W2 TEL 071-229 7784 MAP 12
64 Tranquil Vale, SE3 TEL 081-318 2595 MAP 12
144 Upper Richmond Road, SW15 TEL 081-789 1948 MAP 12
305 Upper Richmond Road West, SW14 TEL 081-878 6833 MAP 12
335 Upper Street, N1 TEL 071-226 9542 MAP 13
154 Victoria Street, SW1 TEL 071-828 1477 MAP 13
29 Wardour Street, W1 TEL 071-734 0355 MAP 14

The pizzas are better than many found in Italy. They are freshly made, swiftly and efficiently, before your eyes in huge batteries of ovens; the dough is crisp and tasty, the fillings herby, garlicky, well seasoned, and the toppings take vegetarians into account – there are five pizzas without meat or fish and ingredients can be substituted. Though the range of dishes is limited, with only a few starters and desserts, everything is so good that that is almost a bonus. For a reasonably priced meal out, one can hardly do better, and every restaurant in the chain comes up to the same high standard. The décor is usually clean, bright and cosmopolitan – marble-topped tables, Bauhaus type chairs, tiled floor – the service is good and, because of the cultural interests of the owner, Peter Boizot, there will often be good paintings on the walls and live jazz at some branches. Individual restaurants will have their own variations in décor – Coptic Street is particularly attractive, as it has original shop tiles; Notting Hill Gate has a rather dated modern rainbow mural and Knightsbridge is up-market Italian chic – but the menu, for vegetarians, is identical apart from some restaurants serving cheese and biscuits or cheesecakes with fruit toppings.

Open all week 11am to midnight Table service. Tables outside. Licensed, also bring your own: corkage £5. Meat dishes. Fish dishes. Vegan dishes. Snacks at other times. Take-aways. No-smoking area. Wheelchair access. Access, Amex, Diners, Visa

Pizzeria Castello £££ MAP 13

20 Walworth Road, SE1 TEL 071-703 2556

Still serving good, hot and sizzling, freshly made pizzas, though the pressure of popularity can take its toll: comments on the service range from 'staff are great pros' to 'surly, largely uninterested.' Packed out on Saturdays and almost always crowded on other nights.

Open Mon to Sat noon (5 Sat) to 11 **Closed** 24 Dec to 2 Jan Booking advisable. Table service. Licensed. Meat dishes. Take-aways. No-smoking area. Wheelchair access

Pizzeria Condotti ££ MAP 13

4 Mill Street, W1 TEL 071-499 1308

One of the smartest pizzerias in London, serving some of the best pizzas too – light, crisp, oiled bread bases covered with juicy toppings. The atmosphere is pleasant and the service speedy. Salads, unfortunately, are dull.

Open Mon to Sat 11.30am to midnight **Closed** 24 Dec to 3 Jan, bank hols Table service. Licensed. Meat dishes. Snacks. Take-aways. Access, Amex, Diners, Visa

Pizzeria Franco

£ MAP 12

4 Market Row, SW9 TEL 071-738 3021

A tiny café in the covered area of Brixton market, just off Electric Lane; posters, Italian pictures and press clippings cover the walls and smells of fresh pizzas and cappuccino drift out to the street. It is extremely popular and on Saturdays it may take half an hour to get a table; the owners may turn out 400 pizzas in the day. Said to be 'some of the best in London' they take in a standard range of fillings – four cheeses, margherita, imperial, and a soufflé version that oozes tomato, Mozzarella, ricotta, mushrooms and herbs. When the owners are not busy they will make up a topping of your choice.

Open Mon to Sat 11.30am to 4.30 Table service. Tables outside. Unlicensed. Meat dishes. Fish dishes. Snacks. Take-aways

Plummers

££ MAP 14

King Street, WC2 TEL 071-240 2534

Plum pink décor and rich velvet curtains, grey painted chairs, good modern paintings and candlelit tables make this a comfortable place for a reasonably priced meal. There are at least two suitable main dishes always available, augmented by specials – perhaps a vegetable casserole. Starters of chilled cucumber soup, crudités, a good apple and Stilton soup or egg and tomato mousse are followed by, invariably, nut crumble with spinach and cream cheese, something that works well under its crispy oat and nut topping, with perhaps garlic bread and salad. The banana and toffee pie is for those with a very sweet tooth; cheesecake, summer pudding or Loseley ice-creams are alternatives.

Open Mon to Sat, exc Sat L, noon to 2.30, 5.30 to 11.30 Booking advisable. Table service. Licensed. Meat dishes. Fish dishes. Wheelchair access. Access, Amex, Diners, Visa

Pollyanna's

££ MAP 12

2 Battersea Rise, SW11 TEL 071-228 0316

Pollyanna's has a fairly static menu, but it is extensive and there are three main courses for vegetarians. Meals vary in quality, some reports are lavish with praise, others more critical about service and food. A vegetable terrine, a melon and apple salad with mint and sour cream, or soup might be on offer as starters. Main dishes could include stir-fried vegetables, vegetable and cheese cobbler and almond-fried spinach and mushroom pancakes with apple and mint relish. A good place for a reasonably priced dinner.

Open Mon to Sat D 7 to midnight, Sun L 1 to 3 **Closed** 4 days at Christmas and 1 Jan Booking advisable. Table service. Tables outside. Licensed, also bring your own: corkage £3. Meat dishes. Fish dishes. Access, Visa

Punters Pie

££ MAP 12

183 Lavender Hill, SW11 TEL 071-228 2660

High-quality fare at acceptable prices: vegetarians can eat a pie with a peanut pastry crust; spinach and ricotta cheese in a pancake; or pasta with pesto, cream or tomato sauce. Organically grown vegetables are used and everything, from bread rolls to sorbets, is made on the premises. The conservatory can be booked for parties. Quick lunches for busy people are jacket potatoes (£1 reduction if the order isn't delivered within 10 minutes) with a variety of fillings.

Open all week noon to 3, 6 to 11.30 (7 to 11 Sun) Booking for groups of 6 or more only. Table service. Tables outside. Licensed. Meat dishes. Fish dishes. Access, Amex, Diners, Visa

Quaffers

££ MAP 13

8 Norfolk Place, W2 TEL 071-724 6046

It would be easy to walk past the unobtrusive wine bar with its restful grey and peach colours but a sandwich sign on the street helps announce it. The interior is clean and uncluttered, tables fresh with flowers. It is crowded, busy and the music is loud. The blackboard carries the day's vegetarian special, and the standard menu also has a main dish. On a sample day, the crudités, with a good garlic mayonnaise, were crunchily fresh and given an unusual touch with orange and melon chunks. Both the special vegetarian main dish of stuffed aubergines with spicy tomato sauce and cheese and the regular leek and potato bake – vegetables layered and baked in cheesy sauce – were tasty and good. But why, at 1.45pm, had the apple tart run out?

Open Mon to Fri noon to 2.30, 6.15 to 10.30 **Closed** 25 Dec Table service. Licensed. Meat dishes. Fish dishes. No children under 8. Wheelchair access. Access, Amex, Diners, Visa

Ragam

£ MAP 13

57 Cleveland Street, W1 TEL 071-636 9098

Although unimpressive from the street, this small restaurant with an informal air and rather cramped accommodation specialises in Kerala cuisine and has a good range for vegetarians. The menu gives helpful suggestions for combining dishes – one of the problems with South Indian cuisine based on dosas and idlis. Some of the more unusual items include green banana bhaji, less exciting than it sounds, and kaallan–yoghurt, coconut spices and sweet mangoes. The avial is delicate, good and mild; well-cooked mixed vegetable curry and coconut rice. Choose the kulfi to follow. The masala tea with its restrained spicing is good. Generous portions and reasonable prices make this an attractive choice in the area.

Open all week noon to 3, 6 to 11.30 **Closed** 25 and 26 Dec Table service. Licensed, also bring your own: corkage £1.50 per bottle. Meat dishes. Vegan dishes. Other diets catered for on request. Take-aways. Wheelchair access. Access, Amex, Diners, Visa

Raj Bhel Poori House Ⓥ

£ MAP 13

19 Camden High Street, NW1 TEL 071-388 6663

There's nothing very Indian about the lacquered pine tables and dark leaf patterned wallpaper of this South Indian vegetarian restaurant. The menu holds few surprises for aficionados, but a meal of light, good bhel pooris, dahi vadi (with strong sweet-and-sour sauce), paper and deluxe dosas (both interesting and delicious), iddly sambar, brinjal bhajia and raita, followed by mango kulfi and a rich cardamom-flavoured shrikhand, was much enjoyed.

Open all week noon to 11.30 **Closed** 25 Dec Booking advisable. Table service. Tables outside. Unlicensed, but bring your own. Vegan dishes. Snacks. Take-aways. Wheelchair access. Access, Amex, Diners, Visa

Rani ⓥ ★

££ MAP 12

7 Long Lane, N3 TEL 081-349 4386/2636

It may have expanded and gone posh, but the food is as good as ever and only slightly more expensive than it was. The menu gives helpful hints for choosing dishes, always a problem to avoid stodginess, and suggested combinations are made for two- and three-course meals. Hearty eaters will cheer the 'no additional charge for refills of any items from main course.' There are various thalis and some unusual dishes, such as stuffed aubergine and potato curry, banana methi and interesting breads: methi bhatoora is soft, puffed and deep-fried, made of yoghurt and fenugreek; methi roti is thick and flat, stuffed with sweetened lentils flavoured with cardamom and saffron. Each day of the week has its own special – if it's Wednesday it must be Rani Tiffin. Good samosas, bhel puris and an aubergine and lime bean curry well endowed with fresh coriander. For dessert try the Rani Nutty Delight of pistachio, almonds and cashew-nuts cooked in milk and sugar, or a hot gulab jamun with ice-cream.

Open Tue to Sun 12.30 to 2, 6 to 10.30 exc Sat L Booking advisable. Table service. Licensed. Vegan dishes. Take-aways. No children after 7pm. Access, Visa

Rasa Sayang

££ MAP 12

Kingswell Shopping Centre, Heath Street, NW3 TEL 071-435 6508

Related to its namesake in Frith Street in Soho, this Indonesian restaurant in the modern shopping plaza just up from Hampstead Underground is modern and slick. Defying most Indonesian décor, the colour scheme is black, white and pink; chairs are chrome and black leatherette, and tables are black marble. The vegetarian section of the menu has gado-gado, mixed vegetables in coconut gravy, fried beansprouts, fried bean curd and Lo han chai, a Chinese dish. A vegetarian satay made from soya-bean protein is chewy and juicy, but might work better using vegetables.

Open Tue to Sun 1 to 2.45, 6 to 11.30 (1 to 11 Sat and Sun) **Closed** bank hols Booking advisable. Table service. Licensed. Meat dishes. Vegan dishes. Take-aways. Wheelchair access. Access, Amex, Diners, Visa

Ravenscourt Park Teahouse £ MAP 12

off Paddenswick Road, W6 TEL 081-748 9513

Now run by the local council, the Teahouse has been spruced up, thereby losing some of its previous funky charm; it is spick and span but still welcoming. Situated in all that remains of Ravenscourt House – the stables – the pretty building sits in the middle of the park; in summer you can eat outside in its dog-free garden. Radio One plays, newspapers of the day are provided and chess and backgammon sets are available. A typical day offered a tomato soup (not home made, but with a dollop of cream), jacket potatoes, pizza, salads and a vegetarian hot dish of pasta with cream, mushrooms and broccoli. The Italian chef regularly chooses to offer pasta dishes, though alternatives might be curry or vegetables with rice. The setting, relaxed atmosphere and very low prices are the attractions.

Open all week, 10 to 4.30 **Closed** Christmas Counter service. Tables outside. Take-aways

Ravi Shankar Ⓥ ★ £ MAP 13

133 Drummond Street, NW1 TEL 071-388 6458

Drummond Street, like Hanway Street, is a mecca for fans of vegetarian Indian food. This double-fronted restaurant, brown in décor and with pine tables, serves the familiar South Indian dishes, well cooked and with some variations; there are six types of dosas, of which the paper dosa is served like a huge sail standing vertically on the plate. There are kebabs, uthapam, iddlis and a pan bhaji that is rather sour, served incongruously with an English toasted white roll. Potato poori – crisp pooris, onions, tamarind and yoghurt – is good: not too spicy, cool and tasty. Others have enjoyed dahi vala, hot potato cakes and a daily special of chick pea curry. There are sweet drinks and puddings such as falooda, lassi, three good kulfis (almond, pistachio, mango) and a strong, spicy masala tea tasting of aniseed and cardamom, as well as Mysore coffee. Orange, apple and carrot juices are freshly squeezed.

Open all week noon to 11 Table service. Licensed. Take-aways. Wheelchair access. Access, Amex, Diners, Visa

Raw Deal ⓥ

£ MAP 13

65 York Street, W1 TEL 071-262 4841

The name doesn't do justice to this café in a smart area, patronised by all kinds of people who enjoy the daily hot dishes and wide variety of salads, about ten every day. There's a delicacy of touch evident in the lemon zing to a red cabbage salad and the spicy sweetness to the pasta salad. Main dishes might be nutty aubergine, nut roast or butter bean savoury. Generous portions of home-made cakes and desserts include a good apple and almond tart. Deservedly popular.

Open Mon to Sat noon to 9.30 **Closed** 25 Dec to 1 Jan, bank hols Counter service. Tables outside. Unlicensed, but bring your own: corkage 10p. Vegan dishes. Other diets catered for on request. Take-aways. No-smoking area. Wheelchair access

Red Fort

££ MAP 14

77 Dean Street, W1 TEL 071-437 2525 and 2410

In the heart of Soho is one of the new-wave Indian restaurants, which means that prices are not low. It's a great bustling place, 'vibrant with life'. There are contradictory reports about the service, but the food is good: chutneys are memorable and a starter of masha – crisp vegetables and black-eyed beans wrapped in thin layers of onion, gently baked – was reckoned a success. Other vegetarian possibilities include aloo patishapta, a pancake with potato and carrot filling, niramish and more predictable dhals and curries; there is also a thali. Sunday lunch is a buffet, and good value.

Open all week noon to 3, 6 to 11.30 **Closed** 25 Dec and 26 Booking advisable. Table service. Licensed. Meat dishes. Fish dishes. Take-aways. Wheelchair access. Access, Amex, Visa

The availability of meat and fish dishes is indicated in the details underneath the text of an entry.

Sabras Ⓥ ★ £££ MAP 12

263 Willesden High Road, NW10 TEL 081-459 0340

A facelift has created a spotless, brightly lit café from the faded plastic of the old days, though this has resulted in a faintly clinical air. Tables are still close together too. Ladies perform miracles in the kitchen and the menu is extensive, with all food made on the premises, including arrays of traditional very sweet sweets such as burfi and galub jamun, sold at the counter. The range of breads includes stuffed paratha, four-layer paratha and a disappointingly leathery rotala. South Indian specialities include crisp, freshly made dosas, the masala accompaniment containing cashews, potatoes, onions and coconut; Kashmiri koftas; pilau; dhal tarka and mixed vegetables, all of which are tasty but fiery. Even the masala tea was made with such a generous hand in the spice jar that it had to be drunk in tiny sips.

Open Tue to Sun 1 to 2.45, 6 to 9.45 Booking advisable. Table service. Licensed. Vegan dishes. Other diets catered for. Snacks at other times. Take-aways. No-smoking area. Wheelchair access. Access, Visa

Safari-Afro Gallery ££ MAP 12

354 Cricklewood Lane, NW2 TEL 081-209 0116 and 455 5154

Specialising in African and Cajun cuisine and described as serving 'absolutely excellent food'. The menu is pretty intriguing and one cannot but wonder what 'manish water' is – of academic interest, since it is meaty. A 'vegetarian surprise' set meal starts with bean loaf, corn on the cob, young coconut meat or corn soup and goes on to tropical vegetables in groundnut sauce, noodles with vegetables or coconut jollof rice. Non-alcoholic fruit drinks include fresh virgin coconut water in the shell; alcoholic ones include Caribbean cocktails with a big kick.

Open all week 11 to 11, L 1 to 3, D 6 to 11 Tables outside. Licensed. Meat dishes. Fish dishes. Vegan dishes. Take-aways. Access, Amex, Diners, Visa

'Wheelchair access' indicates that, according to the proprietor, entrances are at least 33 inches wide, passages 4 feet wide, and that there are a maximum of two steps, unless otherwise stated.

Seasons Ⓥ

£ MAP 13

22 Harcourt Street, W1 TEL 071-402 5925

A pretty bow-fronted exterior and clean cool interior invite customers to this purely vegetarian enterprise that steers away from community-noticeboard style and gives plenty of room. Daily menus provide a couple of main dishes, one of which is invariably vegan – examples are courgette provençale, cheesy puff balls and spinach sauce, walnut cottage cheese layer and an excellent spinach potato. There is also a good range of fresh salads. The extensive choice of puddings ranges from some heavy cheesecake to a good, light trifle with walnuts and raisins, and an exceptional carrot cake.

Open all week noon to 10 (12.30 to 9 Sun) Table service D. Counter service L. Tables outside. Licensed, also bring your own: corkage £2.50. Vegan dishes. Other diets catered for on request. Snacks at other times. Take-aways. No smoking. Wheelchair access. Amex, Diners, Visa

Shahee Bhelpoori Ⓥ

£ MAP 12

1547 London Road, SW16 TEL 081-679 6275

Opposite Norbury BR station and offering good service, cleanliness and value for money. The menu, which is supplemented by daily specials, promises a familiar range of bhelpooris, pani pooris, dosas and a couple of thalis. Ravi onion dosa, muttar paneer and sag paneer are specialities. Falooda, several kinds of lassis and masala tea to drink.

Open all week, noon to 2.30, 6 to 11.30 Table service. Licensed. Vegan dishes. Other diets catered for on request. Take-aways. No-smoking area. Wheelchair access. Access, Amex, Diners, Visa

Shampers

££ MAP 13

4 Kingly Street, W1 TEL 071-437 1692

One of Don Hewitson's chain (see also Cork and Bottle), all of which have vegetarian dishes of the day. Starters of the house mushroom pâté or summer salad lead into main dishes such as oyster mushrooms with quails' eggs and hollandaise, stuffed tomatoes provençale or a pasta dish. The brasserie has more choice, with dishes such as aubergine caviare or cucumber mousse with red pepper sauce. Everyone lends their name to a dish here, so you might finish with Ruth's chocolate fudge ice-cream pie.

Open Mon to Sat, exc Sat D, 11am to 3, 5 to 10.45 Table service brasserie. Counter service bar. Licensed. Meat dishes. No children under 14. Wheelchair access. Amex, Access, Diners, Visa

Soho Soho £££ MAP 14

11–13 Frith Street, W1 TEL 071-494 3491

Vegetarians don't get much more than a look-in at the brasserie, but the menu changes quarterly. The chef is from Provence and starters might be a tomato salad with onion rings and French dressing or a cold artichoke casserole with fresh basil and herbs. The two main course might be a warm potato and Roquefort salad on a bed of watercress, or parcels of cabbage stuffed with carrots, ginger, turnips and raisins, served with potato purée. The dessert list of about 10 items includes an unusual fresh lemon sorbet with iced Stolichnaya vodka. Dine to live music in the evenings. The adjacent wine bar operates a simpler menu.

Open Mon to Sat noon to 3, 6 to 11.30 **Closed** 25 and 26 Dec Booking advisable. Table service. Licensed. Meat dishes. Access, Amex, Diners, Visa

Le Soleil ⓥ ££ MAP 12

110–112 Palmerston Road, E17 TEL 081-520 5898

A brave venture in the depths of Walthamstow: by day a take-away snack bar attached to a healthfood store, by night an austerely lit and stark white restaurant. It's rather bleak to sit in, but run by a very friendly couple. Customers should have plenty to talk about because the arrival of food is slow. What arrives might be a good thick watercress soup or creamy cheese with grapes and toasted almonds for starters; a solid asparagus and almond bake or a baked egg ratatouille for the main course. Mixed salads are disappointing. The menu is short: two each of starters and main courses. Puddings and cakes are home made. It may not be Cordon Bleu, but the owners try hard and where else could a vegetarian eat for miles around?

Open Mon to Sat 9am to 5.30 (7 Thur), D Thur Fri and Sat 7 to 10 **Closed** 25 and 26 Dec Booking advisable D. Table service D. Counter service L. Tables outside. Unlicensed, but bring your own: no corkage. Vegan dishes. Other diets catered for on request. Snacks at other times. Take-aways. Wheelchair access

Something Else Ⓥ

£ MAP 13

49 Cross Street, N1 TEL 071-226 6579

The atmosphere contributes to the success of this vegetarian venture where at weekends you may well have to wait for a table. The front parlour extends into a back room with servery, and a bustle of friends and relations coming and going into the kitchen area lends a warm, family atmosphere. The plain décor is enlivened by crowds of posters, plants, prints and bric à brac. Although the blackboard menu seems to display plenty of variety in its six or so dishes for each course, on closer inspection many of these rely on the same cooking method (on a random day, many starters were pâtés, and many dishes rely on pastry), making a well-designed meal difficult. A deep-coloured and deep-flavoured mushroom and spinach soup was a high spot among starters; a spicy Spanish dip could have done with more zing; mushroom Wellington resembled a mushroom purée in pastry, and spinach in filo didn't conform to the usual idea of filo. Salads are good, a winter salad being exceptionally well presented and dressed. The same difficulty in composing a meal without repetition arises with the puddings; again there are lots of pies on offer.

Open all week 6.30 to 11.30 Table service. Counter service. Licensed, also bring your own: corkage £1.50. Vegan dishes. Other diets catered for on request. Take-aways. Wheelchair access

Sonny's

££ MAP 12

94 Church Road, SW13 TEL 081-748 0393

The cool grey and white dining-room has a surreal touch in two imitation stuffed cheetahs by the bar; through the French windows is a pretty patio garden. Barnesians find loud voices an aid to summon waiters or waitresses but the food is consistently good. Vegetarian starters might be roasted red pepper, aubergine, green bean and Parmesan salad, goats' cheese and sun-dried tomato pizza or deep-fried polenta with butter and Parmesan; the single main dish varies from a warm spinach roulade with garlic mushrooms and Mornay sauce to asparagus and ricotta strudel or black-bean chilli with guacamole and corn muffins. Puddings are a strong point, so keep a space for a 'correctly grainy' espresso ice-cream with hot chocolate sauce that has the pungent aroma and strong taste of coffee.

Open all week exc Sat L and Sun D Booking advisable. Table service. Licensed. Meat dishes. Fish dishes. Other diets catered for on request. Wheelchair access. Access, Visa

South of the Border £££ MAP 13

8–10 Joan Street, SE1 TEL 071-928 6374

Off the Cut, at the Blackfriars Road end, this is a useful pre- or post-theatre venue. The restaurant is on one and a half floors, with a wooden balcony and stairs and a welcoming bar in the entrance. Indonesian food features strongly, so there is a good rijstaffel containing a reasonable number of vegetable dishes. There's peanut sauce in most of them, so steer clear if you don't like peanuts. A dish on its own from the Indonesian menu will probably not be enough to satisfy, so better to choose a separate vegetarian main dish of something like spinach and cheese roulade. There is plenty of room and service is excellent but prices are high for what you get, particularly for vegetarians.

Open Mon to Sat exc Sat L noon to 2.30, 6 to 11.30 Booking advisable. Table service. Tables outside. Licensed. Meat dishes. Fish dishes. Other diets catered for on request. Wheelchair access. Access, Amex, Diners, Visa

Spices ⓥ ★ £ MAP 12

30 Stoke Newington Church Street, N16 TEL 071-254 0528

How pleasant it would be to have this sophisticated, calm Indian vegetarian restaurant at the end of one's road. The Venetian blinds and bright, simple décor are inviting, service is discreet and the food excellent. As well as the usual dosas, crisp and faultless, are such dishes as ragara pattice – stuffed potato cakes rather like vegetable balls – and somtum – glorified grated carrot. Vegan dishes are clearly marked. Each day of the week has its own fixed speciality, for example, corn korma with lemon rice and raita on Thursday, and a slightly disappointing biriani with sambhar and salad on Friday. For those with feeble palates, the hotness level is acceptable. Vegan ice-cream is available as well as three kinds of kulfi.

Open Mon to Fri noon to 3, 6 to midnight (noon to midnight Fri and Sat) **Closed** 24 Dec D and 25 Dec Booking advisable. Table service. Licensed, also bring your own: corkage varies. Vegan dishes. Other diets catered for. Snacks at other times. Take-aways. No-smoking area. Wheelchair access. Access, Amex, Diners, Visa

Spread Eagle

£££ MAP 12

2 Stockwell Street, SE10 TEL 081-853 2333

Making an effort to please vegetarians, the restaurant regularly offers three suitable starters and two main courses; finely shredded vegetables in wine sauce served in puff pastry, and a main course of wild mushroom crêpe give the tone. Chocolate marquise with coffee-bean sauce has been praised but brown-bread ice-cream has been heavy and the sauce too sharp. Free-range eggs are used.

Open all week, exc Sat L and Sun D, noon to 2.30 (3 Sun), 6.30 to 10.30 **Closed** last 2 weeks Aug, 24 Dec to 31 Dec Booking advisable. Table service. Licensed. Meat dishes. Access, Amex, Diners, Visa

Sree Krishna ★

£ MAP 12

194 Tooting High Street, SW17 TEL 081-672 4250

The surroundings are fairly unassuming but the food is terrific, particularly for vegetarians: alongside the usual varieties of curry, including vegetable ones, is a good range of South Indian sambars, dahi vadai, and a couple of dosas. Reports enthuse about masala dosas, dahi vahdas, assorted bahjias – onion, spinach, cauliflower, mushroom – crisp bhindi, uppuma and well spiced mushroom biriani. The service is charming and children may be awarded Smarties on the way out. 'If it were done up it would vie with the best Indian restaurants in London.'

Open all week noon to 2.45, 6 to 10.45 (11.45 Fri and Sat) **Closed** 25 Dec Booking advisable. Table service. Licensed, also bring your own: corkage £1. Meat dishes. Seafood dishes. Other diets catered for on request. Snacks at other times. Take-aways. Wheelchair access. Access, Amex, Diners, Visa

See the back of the guide for a list of restaurants serving only vegetarian food.

Sri Siam ★

££ MAP 14

14 Old Compton Street, W1 TEL 071-434 3544

A long, narrow and noisy restaurant which has gained a reputation for serving some of the best vegetarian Thai food in London. At the end of the menu comes a long vegetarian section all à la carte, listing dishes such as spring rolls, vegetarian satay, deep-fried 'golden bags' made from delicate bean curd skin filled with vegetables, tempura pak, and Thai crêpes among other delicacies.

Open all week, exc Sun L, noon to 3, 6 to 11.15 Booking advisable. Table service. Licensed. Meat dishes. Fish dishes. Other diets catered for on request. Take-aways. Wheelchair access. Access, Amex, Diners, Visa

Suruchi ⓥ

£ MAP 13

18 Theberton Street, N1 TEL 071-359 8033

The food is the South Indian variety of dosas, bhel puris and pani puris: 'good quality, subtly spiced, well balanced'. Countering this is one report that the food seemed to have been sitting around in the kitchen for a while before being served. Décor is invitingly fresh and modern.

Open all week noon to 2.30, 6 to 10.30 Booking advisable for large parties. Table service. Unlicensed, but bring your own: no corkage. Vegan dishes. Take-aways. Wheelchair access. Amex, Visa

Surya

££ MAP 12

59–61 Fortune Green Road, NW6 TEL 071-435 7486

'Excellent, well-flavoured, well-differentiated cooking,' enthused one reporter about the food at this green and white restaurant with its profusion of plants. Muttar paneer is made with fresh curd cheese and plenty of coriander; potato and tomato curry is a subtle version. Bhel puri, sambar and kaddin have also all been praised, and ras malai is lemony and topped with pistachio nuts. If unsure what to order, ask advice. Each day of the week has its own special dish – spicy pumpkin on Tuesday, lotus stem on Saturday, for example. Drinks include a mango milk shake, falooda, lassi and a good masala tea. Sitar music.

Open all week, exc Sun D, noon to 2.30, 6 to 10.30 Booking advisable. Table service. Licensed. Vegan dishes. Other diets catered for on request. Snacks at other times. Take-aways. No-smoking area. No children under 6 at D. Wheelchair access. Access, Amex, Diners, Visa

Sutherlands £££ MAP 13

45 Lexington Street TEL 071-434 3401

Sutherlands is an intriguing mixture of originality, lack of snobbery and expensive, highly elaborate food. Pick your way past the dustbins, up the alley and arrive at the exterior which looks to some like a boarded-up shop. Inside, minimalist décor is matched by the hairdos of the staff; they are cheerful, friendly and down-to-earth and all obviously care about the food. Chef Garry Hollihead has high ambitions; six types of bread, for instance, include sesame, dill, and excellent hazelnut and walnut. There have been paeans of praise from reporters, particularly for some inspired puddings, such as lavender ice-cream, chocolate truffle torte with marmalade mousse and orange sorbet and chocolate rum roulade. Tucked away at the bottom of the menu is a vegetarian dish such as filo parcel filled with shards of winter vegetables with tomato coulis, or a mille-feuille of asparagus and crispy pastry in a basil and tomato sauce with poached quails' eggs. Organic wines are available. An experience, and one for which you need a deep pocket.

Open Mon to Fri 12.15 to 2.30, inc Sat 6.30 to 11.15 Booking advisable. Table service. Licensed. Meat dishes. Fish dishes. Vegan and other diets catered for on request. Wheelchair access. Access, Visa

Tarantula ⓥ ★ £ MAP 13

Diorama Arts Centre, 14 Peto Place, NW1 TEL 071-487 2891

The café is a delight in this slightly down-at-heel arts centre: the serving counter stands shyly at one side of an octagonal room, once used for projecting the 'diorama', an early form of moving picture. Tables are arrayed in the octagon and in the narrow room radiating from it. The 'best veggie burger in London', made to a secret formula, appears every day, as do freshly made soups and a fruit crumble of varying kinds. Because of what the staff describe as a 'chronic shortage of space' in the kitchen, soups are the only starters, and the day's main dishes are two or three in number: a good stir-fry of vegetables with brown rice; a strudel variously stuffed; tortilla stuffed with avocado, mushroom and cheese with brown rice, salsa, refried beans and sour cream. Beloved by its clientele for excellent value.

Open Mon to Fri, L 12.30 to 3 Counter service. Vegan dishes. Other diets catered for on request. Snacks. Take-aways. Wheelchair access

Tea Rooms des Artistes **££** MAP 12

697 Wandsworth Road, SW8 TEL 071-720 4028

Carpets thrown over sofas and low tables remind people of a certain age of halcyon hippie days. Although the food is no longer purely vegetarian, fish being on offer too, there are several vegetarian choices. The daily dish might be a good fennel and Mozzarella bake, served with excellent buttered and parsleyed potatoes and a fresh and interesting salad. Strawberry and apple flan has disappointed. The building, with its faded grandeur, has a fascinating history and diners in the small garden to the side can see remains of what were farm buildings – in the centre of Wandsworth, they seem almost incredible.

Open Mon to Fri 6 to 11, Sat and Sun 11.30am to 11 (10.30 Sun) **Closed** Christmas week, bank hols Counter service. Tables outside. Licensed. Fish dishes. Vegan dishes. Snacks at other times. Wheelchair access

Theatre Museum Café **££** MAP 14

Russell Street, WC2 TEL 071-836 7891

Part of the Milburns chain, providing above-average vegetarian choices of mixed vegetable casserole, ratatouille or risotto, as well as snacks during the day.

Open Tue to Sun 11 to 7.15 (hot food from 2.30) **Closed** 24 to 26 Dec Table service. Licensed, also bring your own: corkage £1.50. Meat dishes. Fish dishes. Snacks. No-smoking area. Wheelchair access

The Place Below Ⓥ ★ **£–££** MAP 13

St Mary le Bow, Cheapside, EC2 TEL 071-329 0789

This vegetarian restaurant has a unique crypt atmosphere, with bare bricks and arches. It gets enthusiastic recommendations for excellent tomato and miso soups, delicate Gruyère and almond, or cheese and apple, quiches and wholesome wholegrain rolls. Every day there is a good selection of hot dishes such as chilli bean guacamole, Caribbean bean stew with coconut, or courgette and Feta filo pie, accompanied by a variety of salads; puddings are in the vein of crumble, fruit cheesecake, fruit fool or chocolate cake. The only gripe is that portions could be larger.

Open Mon to Fri 7.30 to 3, L 11.45 to 2.30 **Closed** 22 Dec to 2 Jan Counter service. Vegan dishes (Tue and Thur). Other diets catered for on request. Snacks. Take-aways.

Topkapi

££ MAP 13

25 Marylebone High Street, W1 TEL 071-486 1872

A popular, good-value Turkish restaurant: food and service get praise, and the menu draws attention to dishes for vegetarians. Starters include aubergine salad and tabouleh and the main dish could be courgettes and aubergine in a tomato sauce. Sweets are the familiar sticky array.

Open all week noon to 11.30 **Closed** 25 and 26 Dec Booking advisable. Table service. Licensed. Meat dishes. Take-aways. Wheelchair access. Access, Amex, Diners, Visa

Tuk Tuk

££ MAP 13

330 Upper Street, N1 TEL 071-226 0837

Tuk Tuk is best described as a smart 'mid-tech' café with black and red décor, serving Thai food at reasonable prices without the usual over-emphasis on lemon-grass and large hot-pots. Dishes include spring rolls, which, though fresh and crisp, may tend towards the greasy, and Thai noodles. The food is reliable, and this draws an enthusiastic crowd so booking is recommended.

Open Mon to Sat 12 to 3, 6 to 11.30 **Closed** 22 Dec 1 week Booking advisable. Table service. Licensed. Meat dishes. Fish dishes. Take-aways. Access, Amex, Diners, Visa

All letters to the guide are acknowledged.

Twenty Trinity Gardens £££ MAP 12

20 Trinity Gardens, SW9 TEL 071-733 8838

The unknowing are unlikely to come across this spacious restaurant that advertises its presence only with an array of greenery down a residential street in Brixton. Those who know it are faithful customers. Classical music plays, the walls are hung with oriental carpets and tables are laid with white linen and pink napkins. Both lunch and dinner fixed-price menus include vegetarian starters and a main course; of these, the starters – for example a delicious terrine that is more like a timbale – may be more tempting than the main dishes: rather stodgy Mozzarella, tomato and olive lasagne and bland risotto, for instance. Peaches poached in brandy with fresh almond paste and raspberry coulis are delicious.

Open Mon to Sat exc Sat D 12.30 to 2.30, 7 to 10.30 **Closed** Christmas to New Year Booking advisable. Table service. Tables outside. Licensed. Meat dishes. Fish dishes. No-smoking area. Wheelchair access. Access, Visa

Veganomics ⓥ ★ ££ MAP 12

314 Lewisham Road, SE13 TEL 081-852 7978

Full marks for enterprise to this purely vegan restaurant that goes to extraordinary lengths to make vegan food interesting. Mr Bailey (the joint owner) even combs the surrounding parks and countryside for guelder berries, wild service berries and elderberries for sauces. The restaurant was a hardware store in the 1880s, and wooden shelves and tiny drawers remain, as do the original gas fittings, still operational, and giving a dim glow to the room. The lack of music is much appreciated, and yet, since a healthy number of customers come to eat here, there is no deadly hush. On Thursdays, Melody Lovelace (yes, it is her real name), the joint owner, sings with a guitarist. Given the limitations of vegan food, what they achieve is remarkable: a typical menu has starters of soya bean pâté, root soup, Veganomics special salad, cauliflower pakoras lightly fried in thin crispy batter with sweet-and-sour sauce, and rosemary potato balls which were overwhelmingly rosemary flavoured. This problem was repeated in a main course (of a choice of six) of millet cakes, which had little intrinsic flavour other than that of the herbs, and a pumpkin with hazelnut and chestnut stuffing which didn't quite succeed. But the accompanying vegetables – different with each dish – show a lot of thought: fresh peas (in November!), steamed leeks with roasted sesame and sunflower seeds and potatoes with tofu and garlic. Puddings are a speciality, and they even make their own ice-cream. The vegan cream in a trifle was delicious, but a ras malai, overwhelmingly saffron in taste, turned out disappointingly rubbery. But careful choice from the menu and a bottle of organic wine should combine for an enjoyable evening.

Open Thur to Sat 7 to 10.30 (11 Sat) Booking advisable. Table service. Licensed. Vegan dishes only. Other diets catered for on request. Take-aways. No smoking. Wheelchair access

Véritable Crêperie

£ MAP 13

329 King's Road, SW3 TEL 071-352 3891

This used to be Astérix, one of the pioneer theme restaurants; Véritable Crêperie has kept the bare brick walls, deep-blue wall lights, blue gloss-painted highlights and round tables. The theme is pancakes, either galettes made with buckwheat flour for savoury fillings or crêpes for sweet. Suggested fillings are listed or you can make up your own from a long list of ingredients and it's easy to choose meatless versions. The pancakes are made in front of you and served, crisp and good, in tidy packet form. Good French cider and citron pressé.

Open all week noon to midnight **Closed** 2 days Christmas Table service. Tables outside. Licensed, also bring your own: corkage £1.50. Meat dishes. Fish dishes. Snacks. Take-aways. Wheelchair access. Access, Visa

Veronica's

££ MAP 12

3 Hereford Road, W2 TEL 071-229 5079

Veronica herself is a gentle hostess and her restaurant is cosy with its subdued lighting and flower-strewn suspended ceiling. The menu changes every five or six weeks, adhering to a formula of regional or historical themes, always British: the products of the research can be fascinating. Even the art exhibition that hangs in the restaurant will, whenever possible, follow the theme. An East Anglian season came up with a seventeenth-century recipe of mushrooms in red wine with horseradish and orange, Essex sweet spinach tart with goats' cheese topping, and a sweet-sour autumn salad of dried apricots, dill cucumbers, walnuts, olives, raisins and capers, as well as a flavoursome leek and apple soup. Sadly, the four vegetarian main dishes fall a little below the meat ones, although efforts are clearly made: vegetable hot-pot had a very delicate almond flavour, baked eggs on a bed of creamy leeks were saved from stodginess by the surprise of horseradish. Good home-made ice-creams. There are nice touches like the thick peanut dip with crudités; in short, you feel pleasantly pampered, and the food is varied and well done.

Open Mon to Sat, exc Sat L, noon to 3, 7 to midnight **Closed** bank hols, 2 days at Christmas Booking advisable. Table service. Tables outside. Licensed. Meat dishes. Fish dishes. Vegan dishes. Other diets catered for on request. Take-aways. Wheelchair access. Access, Amex, Diners, Visa

Village Restaurant ££ MAP 12

61 Blythe Road, W14 TEL 071-328 1087

The delicatessen above sells some of the things you can enjoy downstairs in this cosy basement with bare brick walls, pine tables and large modern posters. Excellent French bread and butter is automatically provided, and locals gather to eat perhaps a vichyssoise soup followed by farci vegetarien – courgettes, green peppers and tomato filled with two kinds of bready stuffing, one dominated by tomato and one by mushroom. Salads are good. The tarte Tatin takes some beating, though the chocolate mousse concealing an Amaretti biscuit base comes close.

Open all week, exc Sun, L 11.30am to 3.30, 7 to 10.30 Table service. Licensed, also bring your own: corkage £3. Meat dishes. Fish dishes. Vegan dishes. Snacks at other times. Take-aways. Visa

Wholemeal Café £ MAP 12

1 Shrubbery Road, SW16 TEL 081-769 2423

Opposite the Police Station is this spruce, pine-furnished vegetarian café beloved by locals, offering meals of more than quiche and jacket potatoes: a pepper nut roast with stir-fry vegetables and new potatoes was tasty, vegetables fresh. You might find interesting soup of onion and sunflower seed, and an Indian chickpea casserole. Puddings include banana cream, fruit crumble and an apricot slice that's agreeably gluey and filling, but made with dried apricots even in the apricot season.

English elderflower and gooseberry wines are available. The system of delivering food after it has been ordered at the counter – and, presumably, after heating – means there's a wait.

Open all week noon to 10 **Closed** 25 Dec Table service. Counter service. Licensed. Snacks. Take-aways. Wheelchair access

Wilkins ⓥ

£ MAP 13

53 Marsham Street, SW1 TEL 071-222 4038

Wilkins is an oasis of wholefood cooking in a desert of sandwich and pizza bars and expensive restaurants of little acclaim. Some dishes change daily – perhaps ratatouille and rice or mixed vegetables and cheese sauce – and some standards remain, such as curried meat loaf or cheese flan. The proprietors say that 90 per cent of dishes are home made every day. Plenty of sweets and cakes, such as crumbles, date slice and fruit pudding, with the carrot cake a speciality. Excellent value, though the stools and wooden chairs at communal pine tables don't promise or deliver much comfort. A shop a couple of doors away is under the same management.

Open Mon to Fri, L 11.30 to 2 Counter service. Tables outside. Unlicensed. Vegan dishes. Other diets catered for on request. Snacks at other times. Take-aways. No smoking

Wilsons

££–£££ MAP 12

236 Blythe Road, W14 TEL 071-603 7267

A spruce French-style bistro serving rather pricey modern British food. The menu is distinctly expensive in the evening, but the set-price lunch can be better value. For too long the vegetarian main dish has been an asparagus, Roquefort and walnut filo pastry parcel and tomato coulis, occasionally supplemented by a Stilton and pear tart with watercress sauce: tasty, indeed, but a change might be welcome. Starters do not offer a great choice either, sometimes merely a tomato soup with basil. Good puddings include summer pudding, chocolate marquise, sorbets, fruit salad with muscat and elderflower syrup, and bread-and-butter pudding 'out of this world'. Service is amiable. Lunches tend to be busy.

Open all week, exc Sat L, Sun D, 12.30 to 2.30, 7.30 to 10 **Closed** 2 weeks Aug,

2 weeks at Christmas, bank hols. Booking advisable. Table service. Licensed. Meat dishes. Fish dishes. Other diets catered for on request. Wheelchair access (toilets downstairs). Access, Amex, Visa

Windmill ⓥ

£ MAP 12

486 Fulham Road, SW6 TEL 081-788 3844

A homely atmosphere in this long thin café that offers wholefood, vegetarian, vegan and sugar-free dishes and uses organically grown vegetables. Lunch menus are shorter than for dinner: a couple of starters, which might be soup and chestnut pâté; main dishes of, for example, shepherd's pie, stuffed peppers, an 'organic' Florentine (vegetables in a good if saltless sauce, served with brown rice). Puddings suffer from the bland vegan syndrome but the vanilla in the wheat cream redeems a fruit slice. Other puddings include sherry trifle, cheesecake and fig custard. Organic beer and wine is available by the glass. Don't expect great comfort.

Open all week noon to 10.30 Table service D. Counter service L. Licensed. Vegan dishes. Snacks at other times. Take-aways. No smoking. Wheelchair access

Woodlands ⓥ

£–££ MAP 13

77 Marylebone Lane, W1 TEL 071-486 3862

One of a chain of Indian vegetarian restaurants, presumably modelled on the famous ones in the home country. Although the owners are aiming at a higher level than many others, with prices pitched accordingly, the plush surroundings and courteous service are not always matched by the food. The South Indian menu offers many different versions of dosas, uthappam, vegetable cutlets, samosas, good cashewnut pakoras, three thalis and some fiery curries. Drinks include khir – milk with saffron and crushed almonds – as well as lassi. The other branches are at 37 Panton Street, SW1 (tel. 071-839 7258) and 402A Wembley High Road, Wembley (tel. 081-902 9869).

Open all week noon to 2.30, 6 to 10.30 Booking advisable weekends. Table service. Licensed, also bring your own: corkage £9 to £10. Vegan dishes. Take-aways. Access, Amex, Diners, Visa

Yours Naturally Ⓥ

£ MAP 14

London Ecology Centre, 45 Shelton Street, WC2 TEL 071-497 2723

A collection of six small tables and green plastic chairs form the sitting area of the café; at lunchtime it's a matter of queuing and sharing. In addition to regular menu items such as quiche, rice balls, tortillas and pizzas, there are hot daily dishes: mushroom risotto, homity pie with a cheesy flavour, red cabbage. Salads come undressed. The cakes are many: flapjacks, date slices, carob, moist carrot, and a banana that is restrained and intriguing with a cream cheese icing. A vegan dish is only on offer some of the time.

Open Mon to Sat 10am to 9 Counter service. Licensed. Take-aways. No smoking. Wheelchair access

Zamoyski's

££ MAP 12

85 Fleet Road, NW3 TEL 071-794 4792

It's not chic, but it's pleasant: in the wine bar below, the bar stretches along one wall, the other bare brick wall is lined with tables, and a spiral stair leads to the peaceful wood-furnished restaurant above. For starters try the hearty beet soup with chunks of beetroot; crisp, tasty potato and walnut latkes; tagliatelle or pierogi dumplings stuffed with cheese and potatoes and coated in dill sauce. The last are also served as a main course, the only other one being ruski pierog of vegetables baked in puff pastry. Puddings include a solid cheesecake, faworki of shallow-fried sweet pastry dusted in icing sugar, and a very good semifreddo of savoiardi biscuits, mascarponi cheese, whipped cream and egg whites soaked in marsala.

Open Mon to Sat, exc Sat L, noon to 2, 5.30 to 11 **Closed** 24 Dec to 2 Jan, Easter Booking advisable. Table service. Licensed. Meat dishes. Fish dishes. Take-aways. Visa

Zzzzzz's Café Ⓥ

£ MAP 13

238 Gray's Inn Road, WC1 TEL 071-278 5391

The bed shop out front inspires the name and the trade is mainly take-away, but there are a few seats on which to perch and eat generous portions of quiche, pizza, lasagne or nut roast. Although the culinary style may lack finesse, there is satisfaction in choice, including for vegans and other diets. Fresh orange juice is a plus and wholefood cakes and biscuits are baked daily. Be prepared to queue at lunchtime. Breakfast is served from 8am.

Open Mon to Fri, L 11.30 to 3.30 Counter service. Tables outside. Vegan dishes. Other diets catered for on request. Snacks. Take-aways

England

ABBEY DORE Hereford & Worcester MAP 6

Stables £

Abbey Dore Court Gardens, Abbey Dore Court
TEL Golden Valley (0981) 240279

Although Mrs Sage only cooks quiches, what quiches! And where else is there for a hungry vegetarian to eat in the middle of Herefordshire? Here at the Abbey Dore Gardens, home of the National Euphorbia Collection and close to the ruined abbey, you can eat either in the courtyard of the Victorian house or in the new conservatory. The quiches are outstanding, and the salads, all freshly made, are interesting and varied. Cakes and home-made ice-creams complete the picture. Many items are also available for sale; they have their own herd of Jersey cows (whose younger members peer out of barns and stables), and dollops of Jersey cream adorn everything possible. The cream can also be bought to take away.

Open all week 11 to 6, L noon to 2.30 **Closed** end Oct to Mar Table service. Counter service. Tables outside. Meat dishes. Snacks. Take-aways. Wheelchair access

ABINGDON Oxfordshire MAP 4

Frageos £

9 East Street TEL Abingdon (0235) 23260

Behind a boutique. Many come to drink tea out of the splendid collection of china cups and teapots; vegetarians will find, alongside meat and fish, dishes such as spicy vegetable casserole in baked potatoes, nut loaf and salad and soups.

Open Tue to Sat 9.30 (1 Sun) to 10, Mon 9.30 to 5.30 Table service. Licensed. Meat dishes. Fish dishes. Vegan dishes. Other diets catered for on request. Snacks. Take-aways. Access, Visa.

ALDEBURGH Suffolk MAP 5

Regatta ££

171–173 High Street TEL Aldeburgh (0728) 452011

The cooking is declared to be 'modern eclectic'. For vegetarians this means starters such as goats' cheese, mushroom and spinach terrine, or broccoli tartlet and toasted almonds, and main dishes such as potato and peanut chop with fresh tomato coulis. Bread and ice-cream are home made.

Open Mon to Sat noon to 2.30 (12.30 to 2 Sun), 7 to 10.15 **Closed** Aldeburgh Carnival Day Booking advisable. Table service. Tables outside. Licensed. Meat dishes. Vegan and other diets catered for on request. Snacks at other times. Wheelchair access. Access, Visa

ALNWICK Northumberland MAP 10

John Blackmore's ££

1 Dorothy Foster Court, Narrowgate TEL Alnwick (0665) 604465

The eighteenth-century house in a narrow street near the castle has a Jacobite history, explained on a plaque by the door. The dining-room, complete with old range, is the front room of a typical town house, brightly decorated and hung with paintings from a local gallery. Dinners are the focus of effort and much praised for service and cooking. A vegetarian will find a meal to suit, starting perhaps with a light broccoli mousse filled with Mozzarella and mushrooms with carrot and tarragon sauce, or baked eggs on braised celery with creamy Stilton sauce ('a very fine dish'), and continuing with a savoy cabbage parcel filled with vegetables, fresh basil and garlic with a cream fennel sauce, or choux buns filled with a purée of vegetables and pulses on an onion sauce with fresh herbs, baked with Emmental. Chocolate mousse, roulade and cheesecake have been well received. Lunches are simpler with jacket potatoes, quiche, open sandwiches and daily specials.

Open Tue to Sat exc Tue D 11.30am to 2.30, 7 to 9.30 **Closed** Jan Booking advisable at D. Table service. Licensed. Meat dishes. Fish dishes. Other diets catered for on request. Snacks. Wheelchair access. Access, Amex, Diners, Visa

ALTRINCHAM Greater Manchester MAP 7

Hilal ££

351 Stockport Road, Timperley TEL 061-980 4090

In a rare gesture to vegetarians the Hilal serves vegetable versions of all the styles of dish on the menu – biriani, rogan josh, Madras, sambar and vindaloo. The three-course lunch represents good value: onion bhajee followed by vegetable curry and a dessert, but no kulfi.

Open all week noon to 1.45, 6.30 to 11 **Closed** 25 and 26 Dec Booking advisable. Table service. Counter service. Licensed. Meat dishes. Vegan dishes. Other diets catered for on request. Take-aways. Wheelchair access. Access, Visa

Nutcracker Ⓥ £

43 Oxford Road TEL 061-928 4399

It is fitting to find this archetypal pine-furnished restaurant so close to the UK Vegetarian Society. Lunches display innovative touches: carrot, apple and cashew-nut soup, zyldyke casserole (a Dutch mixed vegetable dish), spinach pancake layer, pasanda with brown rice (a curry) and chestnut fricassee are some of the dishes on offer. Salads are a particular feature and there is a standard selection of home-made soups, quiche, jacket potatoes and a feast of cakes and puddings. Vegetarian cheese and free-range eggs are used. A choice of organic wines is available.

Open Mon to Sat noon to 2.30 Counter service. Licensed. Vegan dishes. Take-aways. No-smoking area

The cost of a three-course vegetarian meal without wine is indicated by £ symbols to the right of the restaurant name:
£ = up to £7.50
££ = £7.50 to £15
£££ = £15 and over

AMBLESIDE Cumbria **MAP** 10

Chesters £

Kirkstone Gallery, Skelwith Bridge TEL Ambleside (053 94) 332553

Situated in the Kirkstone Green Slate Quarries, Chesters is surrounded by show areas selling everything imaginable made from slate. The name of the coffee-shop comes from the leaseholder's dog, and the walls are hung with black-and-white sketches of dogs as well as dried flowers. Naturally the floor and many of the tabletops are made from slate. The sight of the home-made cakes, rich fruit cakes and sponges is mouth-watering and lunches, listed on the blackboard, are largely vegetarian: soups are nearly always suitable; cheese and bread is accompanied by a good salad; main dishes include a tasty, though runny, lasagne or a cheesy bean bake or lentil moussaka. For those who like Christmas pudding, the rich fruit pudding is a must – it is a lighter version, full of fruit and chopped nuts.

Open all week, L noon to 2 Counter service. Tables outside. Licensed, but bring your own: no corkage. Meat dishes. Fish dishes. Wheelchair access

Drunken Duck Inn £

Barngates TEL Hawkshead (096 66) 346

A black and white country pub at the crossroads on the Tarn Hows road; the garden has views over the fells and to Windermere. Inside, the small rooms, low-ceilinged and beamed, are warmed by one real log fire and one gas version. Vegetarians should turn a blind eye, if they can, to the hunting trophies, for the blackboard listing daily dishes will provide starters of egg and asparagus or mushroom and nut pâté and main dishes such as bean moussaka, red onion and Gruyère tart, and fennel, orange and butterbean bake. Prices are not cheap, but vegetarian real ale drinkers will find a visit worthwhile.

Open all week, noon to 2, 6.30 (7 Sun) to 9 Table service. Tables outside. Licensed. Meat dishes. Fish dishes. Wheelchair access. Accommodation. Access, Visa

Harvest Vegetarian Ⓥ ★ £££

Compston Road TEL Ambleside (053 94) 33151

Brightened up with a lick of cream paint, beige carpets, pine furniture, rather fine photos on the walls, and alcoves formed by trelliswork, this vegetarian restaurant gives plenty of elbow room – though there is a feeling that 'time was not for languishing'. Soup of the day might be a rich, dark, lentil and vegetable, served with wholewheat rolls; the Stilton and hazelnut pâté is pleasant, with the true texture of hazelnuts and the taste of Stilton. Three special dishes are cooked daily, in addition to the fixture – Harold's vegetable pie, made with outstanding wholemeal pastry and a moist and tasty vegetable filling. The daily dish might be a cauliflower, spaghetti and courgette bake in cheese sauce, described by one reporter as a very satisfying dish that doesn't rely on heavy herbing for flavour. The dark chocolate raisin pudding and blackcurrant and banana syllabub with home-made ice-cream are both highly recommended.

Open all week, D 5 to 9.30, Sat and Sun L noon to 2.30 **Closed** weekdays Nov to Mar Table service. Licensed. Vegan dishes. Other diets catered for on request. Take-aways. No smoking. Wheelchair access

Kirkstone Foot Country House Hotel £££

Kirkstone Pass Road TEL Ambleside (053 94) 32232

The country-house hotel offers self-catering accommodation in the delightful grounds, watered by streams. One hopes that even self-caterers allow themselves a restaurant meal since the family produces much-admired food along traditional English lines – until recently heavily into roasts, but now diversified and always including one vegetarian dish, maybe spinach-filled profiteroles with sweet-and-sour sauce. Starters could be orange, starfruit and pineapple salad or cream of bean and fennel soup. The sweets trolley brings forth much delight.

Open all week, D 8 **Closed** Jan to early Feb Booking advisable. Table service. Licensed. Meat dishes. Fish dishes. Other diets catered for on request. No smoking. No children under 7. Wheelchair access. Accommodation. Access, Visa

See the back of the guide for an index of restaurants listed.

Rothay Manor £££

Rothay Bridge TEL Ambleside (053 94) 33605

'As good as Miller Howe and a lot more friendly' claims one reporter – and, to its credit, it has a full vegetarian menu. The atmosphere is informal, food excellent. Not all the extensive vegetarian menu may be available to non-residents, but there will be something, perhaps liptauer (a spicy Czechoslovakian pimento and cream cheese salad), apple with date and walnut stuffing, or Stilton, port and herb pâté with home-made oat biscuits for course one; then fresh vegetable soup or sorbet; then goulash, crumble, herb and nut rissoles, risotto, lasagne, curry or savoury pasties.

Open all week 12.30 to 2, 8 to 9 **Closed** Jan to mid-Feb Booking advisable D and Sun L. Table service. Counter service L. Tables outside L. Licensed. Meat dishes. Fish dishes. Other diets catered for on request. Snacks at other times. No smoking in dining-room. No children at L. Wheelchair access. Accommodation. Access, Amex, Diners, Visa

Wilf's Café £

3–4 Cheapside TEL Ambleside (053 94) 33660

Go through the Rock and Run Shop, selling climbing and running gear, and Wilf's is upstairs. Café stalwarts of baked potatoes, sandwiches and cheese on toast are augmented with vegetable pasta bake, brown lentil chilli and vegetable and chickpea curry, the last two served with brown rice. Carrot cake or fruit crumble with custard, yoghurt or cream to finish. Wilf (Iain Williamson) also provides meals such as mushroom stroganoff and Mexican lasagne on Friday, Saturday and Sunday evenings (7 to 9pm) at the Golden Rule pub, Smithy Bow, Ambleside.

Open Thur to Tue 9 to 4.30 Counter service. Meat dishes. Other diets catered for on request. Snacks. No-smoking. Access. Visa

Zeffirelli's Ⓥ £

Compston Road TEL Ambleside (053 94) 33845

The complex includes a cinema, a shopping arcade, a conservatory café, lounge bar and this Japanese-looking pizzeria. Unusually and hearteningly, the successful venue serves purely vegetarian wholefood. As well as home-baked wheatmeal and sesame-seed pizzas cooked to order, there are lasagne, cream and Stilton pasta, Mexican red bean and vegetable chilli. Finish off with home-made cakes, cheesecake and a 'horribly sweet sticky-toffee pudding if you like it'. An unexpected bonus is the real, fresh apple juice. Three-course candlelit dinners offer a vegan option.

Open all week, D 5 to 9.45, Sat and Sun L noon to 2 **Closed** Tue and Wed Nov to Mar Table service. Licensed, but bring your own: corkage varies. Vegan dishes. Take-aways. No smoking in dining-room. Access, Visa

AMERSHAM Buckinghamshire MAP 4

Paupers ££

11 Market Square TEL Amersham (0494) 727221

Paupers belongs to an old world school of décor; there are church pews as seats, with privacy lent by brass rails and red curtains. Thursday offers 'beggar's feast' of a three-course dinner. There is a full vegetarian menu, but it may not be proffered, so ask. It may list lasagne, gratin, sweet-and-sour quorn (quorn being the latest soya product), tandoori quorn, moussaka and curry. A sample meal started with good, authentic-tasting gazpacho with ice-cubes and olives; ravioli resembled the commercial variety, but sweet-and-sour quorn was acceptable. Good home-made chocolate and orange gateau; cheese is in good condition and well presented.

Open Tue to Sun noon to 2, 7 to 11.30 Booking advisable. Table service. Licensed. Meat dishes. Wheelchair access. Access, Visa

ASHFORD Kent MAP 3

Cornerstone £

25A High Street TEL Ashford (0233) 642874

Run by a Christian charity but not intrusively proselytising, the café serves good snacks, teas and coffees and mainly vegetarian lunches of such dishes as cashew-nut and mushroom flan, lentil bake, pizza or nut roast. There is always a vegetarian soup available and home-made wholegrain bread.

Open Tue to Sat 10 to 5.30 Counter service. Tables outside. Meat dishes. Fish dishes. Other diets catered for on request. Snacks. Take-aways. No-smoking. Wheelchair access

ASHFORD-IN-THE-WATER Derbyshire MAP 7

Riverside Hotel £££

Fennel Street TEL Bakewell (062 981) 4275

There's a five-course set dinner at this country-house hotel on the banks of the River Wye, in one of Derbyshire's prettiest villages. Examples of the vegetarian offerings include deep-fried button mushrooms and ratatouille, hot or cold, for starters. To follow, the single vegetarian option might be a stroganoff of avocado and pistachio in a sauce enriched with brandy. Chocolate terrine and raspberry and blackcurrant mousse give the style of the puddings, and the cheeseboard, if somewhat lacking in enterprise, none the less arrives with grapes, celery and home-made walnut bread.

Open Mon to Sat 7.30 to 9.30, Sun L noon to 2 Booking advisable. Table service. Tables outside. Licensed. Meat dishes. Vegan and other diets catered for on request. No babies. No smoking in dining-room. Wheelchair access. Access, Amex, Visa

ASTON CLINTON Buckinghamshire MAP 4

Bell £££

Aston Clinton TEL Aylesbury (0296) 630252

Noisy main road aside, all else is as near perfection as can be managed in both hotel and garden. The cuisine is nouvelle and expensive, but with larger than usual portions. A tendency to elaboration can be detected even in descriptions – 'cold avocado soup perfumed with a hot curry glaze' – but the dishes are innovative: a gateau of ratatouille and ravioli of mushrooms in a piquant Champagne sauce are examples from the exclusive vegetarian menu that offers four starters and four mains. Allow plenty of time for a meal, as service can be slow. Extras, such as cream cheese with walnuts as a titbit before the starter and a sorbet before dessert, are excellent and the grapefruit soufflé and blackcurrant sorbet have met with approval. Non-alcoholic wine and even a non-alcoholic cocktail are available.

Open all week noon to 1.45, 7 to 9.45 Booking advisable. Table service. Licensed. Meat dishes. Fish dishes. Other diets catered for on request. No smoking in dining-room. Wheelchair access. Accommodation. Access, Visa

AVEBURY Wiltshire MAP 2

Stones ⓥ ★ £

High Street TEL Avebury (067 23) 514

Converted from a stable block, the long, low restaurant has a rustic air with pine tables and stone floor. The food is appealing and reports praise. To some it is reminiscent of Cranks – everything is served on hand-thrown pottery – but more colourful. Typical dishes are spinach polpettini (spinach balls combined with wheatgerm, pine nuts, raisins, eggs and seasonings, tasty though sweetish) and beefsteak tomato with provençal stuffing of mushrooms, cheese and olives, which is highly recommended by one reader. Other options include starters such as French bean and pecan pâté, mung bean and pepper croquettes with coriander, and potato soup with Red Leicester and Cognac, and for pudding, Cornish licky pie with clotted cream and cider or lumpia with fresh mango sauce. Salads are also good. There is good, still, locally produced cider, various country wines such as raspberry, gooseberry, elderflower and silver birch. Vegans are always catered for.

Open all week 10 to 6 **Closed** Jan and Feb, weekdays Nov to Christmas and Mar to Easter Booking advisable for large groups. Counter service. Tables outside. Licensed. Vegan dishes. Other diets catered for on request. Take-aways. Snacks. No-smoking area. Wheelchair access

AYLESBURY Buckinghamshire MAP 4

Bottle and Glass ££

Gibraltar, Nr Aylesbury TEL Aylesbury (0296) 748488

This pub has set aside a couple of large rooms as a restaurant and provides really good food: extensive snacks at lunchtime always include one vegetarian hot dish and full meals in the evening. Then a three-course menu might include vegetarian dishes such as pan-fried asparagus and wild mushrooms garnished with pine kernals served with lentil and apricot sauce; wild mushroom and chestnuts in filo pastry with lentil and ginger sauce (from the Christmas menu); or mixed vegetables in filo pastry with yoghurt, banana and coriander sauce. Follow this with a chocolate mousse or caramel oranges.

Open all week noon to 2.30, 7 to 10 Booking advisable. Table service. Tables outside. Licensed. Meat dishes. Fish dishes. Other diets catered for on request. Snacks at other times. Wheelchair access. Access, Amex, Carte Blanche, Diners, Visa

BAKEWELL Derbyshire MAP 7

Green Apple £–££

Diamond Court, Water Street TEL Bakewell (0629) 814404

Roger Green runs a mixed meat and vegetarian establishment where lunches tend to be casual affairs of rolls, salads and a couple of hot dishes, of which one will be vegetarian – perhaps courgette and cheese bake, rather disappointingly bland and overpoweringly cabbagey according to one report. In the evening menus become more elaborate, meat tends to dominate and prices rise. The vegetarian main dish then might be marrow stuffed with brown rice, mushrooms and tomatoes. Home-made banoffi pie, Bakewell pudding or fruit brûlée to finish.

Open Mon to Sat exc Mon and Tue L noon to 2, 7 to 10, Sun L summer **Closed** 2 weeks Jan Booking advisable for Sat D. Table service D. Counter service L. Tables outside. Licensed, but bring your own: corkage £2. Meat dishes. Fish dishes. Other diets catered for on request. Take-aways. No smoking. Wheelchair access

BARNARD CASTLE Co Durham MAP 10

Market Place Teashop £

29 Market Place TEL Teesdale (0833) 690110

It may look like any other teashop but the inside is remarkable, with a cherished collection of silver-plated teapots and antique furniture. The cooking is straightforward, honest and unpretentious, with prices to suit. Dishes vary with quiches, pancakes and bakes among the vegetarian choices; home-made samosas, and baked spinach with cheese and brown rice have pleased. Praise of the puddings, pies and cakes is unqualified. The Bertorelli ice-cream on sale is one of the best commercial brands available.

Open all week 10am (3pm Sun) to 5.30pm **Closed** Sun Jan to Mar, Christmas Eve to 4 Jan Table service. Licensed. Meat dishes. Fish dishes. Snacks at other times. Wheelchair access

Priors ⓥ

£

7 The Bank TEL Teesdale (0833) 38141

Pleasant if modest surroundings for lunches and snacks along the lines of salads, baked potatoes, quiches and pizzas, supplemented by daily specials of perhaps savoury pancake gateau, croustade or cashew and mushroom loaf. Good honest cakes and Yorkshire curd tart. 'A good cheap place to eat.' Organic wines are served.

Open all week 10am (noon Sun) to 5 (6 Fri and Sat), last Fri of month, D 7.30 to midnight **Closed** Sun Christmas to Easter Counter service. Tables outside. Licensed. Vegan dishes. Other diets catered for on request. Snacks at other times. Take-aways. No-smoking area. Wheelchair access. Access, Amex, Diners, Visa

BARNET Hertfordshire MAP 12

Clock House

££

251 East Barnet Road, East Barnet TEL 081-449 6010

Fondues for two are a speciality and a West Country cheese version would suit vegetarians, otherwise there are casseroles, including chickpea for vegans. Spinach castles with spicy tomato sauce is another standard dish, and daily blackboard specials always include a vegetarian option. Steaks and grills for meat-eaters, plus a good-value roast lunch on Sunday.

Open Tue to Sun 7 to 10.30, Sun L 1 to 3.30 **Closed** 2 weeks Feb Booking advisable. Table service. Licensed. Meat dishes. Fish dishes. Vegan dishes. Other diets catered for on request. Take-aways. No children under 7. Wheelchair access exc WC. Access, Visa

BARNSTAPLE Devon **MAP 1**

Heavens Above ⓥ ★ £

4 Bear Street TEL Barnstaple (0271) 77960

This is one of the better vegetarian wholefood cafés, with stripped pine furniture, pictures that are for sale and a noticeboard bearing information about Greenpeace and yoga classes. The fixed menu has pizza, quiche, jacket potatoes with vegetarian cheese, salads, rissoles and Brazil nut and rice loaf. There is a different hot dish every day, perhaps lentil and spinach lasagne, mushroom and spinach roll or bobotie. Freshly made desserts include a very good bread-and-butter pudding. Free-range eggs are used. Prices are reasonable and certainly represent good value. Organic wines.

Open Mon to Sat, L noon to 2 **Closed** 25 Dec to 2 Jan, bank hols Counter service. Licensed. Vegan dishes. Other diets catered for on request. Snacks, 10am to noon. Take-aways. No-smoking area

Lynwood House ££

Bishop's Tawton Road TEL Barnstaple (0271) 43695

To find this pleasant small hotel with five bedrooms, use the North Devon link and take the Newport turn-off. A warm welcome awaits the visitor, backed up by attentive service. Although the menu is almost exclusively dedicated to fish, a vegetarian section contains starters such as melon and orange, Greek salad or garlic mushrooms, and main dishes of samosas with sorrel sauce, or noodles with cheese and vegetables. For those staying overnight, the cooked breakfast is excellent.

Open Mon to Sat noon to 2, 7 to 10 Booking advisable. Table service. Tables outside. Licensed. Meat dishes. Fish dishes. Vegan dishes. Other diets catered for on request. Take-aways. No smoking. Wheelchair access. Accommodation. Access, Visa

A restaurant doesn't have to be able to serve all items on the menu, although it should have most. If you think the restaurant is deliberately trying to mislead people, tell the local Trading Standards Officer.

BARRINGTON Cambridgeshire MAP 5

Royal Oak £

31 West Green TEL Cambridge (0223) 870791

'Worth a trip out from Cambridge for a vegetarian in search of a good pub meal in pleasant surroundings and at a very reasonable price.' The pub is a large, timber-framed East Anglian building with authentic interior – 'not plastic and Dralon' – with studwork partitioned bars and a large central fireplace. The menu is predominantly vegetarian: the odd vegetarian dish was introduced a few years ago and these proved so popular that now the menu has three vegetarian starters and six main dishes that change every two to three months. The vegetarian pâté is rather like dry ratatouille purée, but none the worse for that; nut cutlets have a pleasant smooth texture with cashews and walnuts in evidence and comes with a good mushroom sauce; the cashew capri, obviously cooked to order, comes with al dente tagliatelle and a good tomato sauce topped with pistachios. Puddings are not so exciting.

Open all week noon to 2, 6.30 to 10.30 Table service. Counter service. Tables outside. Licensed. Meat dishes. Fish dishes. Vegan dishes. Wheelchair access. Access, Visa

BATH Avon MAP 2

Broad Street Café Ⓥ £

14 Broad Street TEL Bath (0225) 462631

This vegetarian café caters for an appreciative clientele who visit regularly for snacks and quick lunches of pizza, soups, flans and hot dishes such as chestnut, aubergine and chickpea casserole (an excellent combination of ingredients in a succulent sauce), spinach roulade, mushroom croustade, cabbage and nut parcels or braised leeks and mushrooms in red wine. Good wholemeal quiches. Some salads are more successful than others – hazelnut and banana in mayonnaise was one that didn't quite work. 'Super selection of home-made breads.' Bath is well endowed with vegetarian eateries but this certainly merits a visit.

Open Mon to Sat 11.30 to 3 Counter service. Unlicensed. Vegan dishes. Other diets catered for on request. Snacks. Take-aways. No smoking

Canary £

3 Queen Street TEL Bath (0225) 424846

Though this has been a tea-shop since 1928, the name Canary was bestowed in the 1950s by a canary-keeping owner. Now run by Simon Davis, it upholds the tradition of serving a wide selection of teas – five different Darjeelings, for example – and coffees; these are also for sale. Breakfasts start the day and snacks and lunches include such vegetarian options as Somerset rabbit, tyropitta, coulibiac and cauliflower and broccoli cheese. There are also cakes, biscuits and other sweet pies. All food is prepared in the kitchens, and there are organic wines.

Open Tue to Sun 9 to 7; Mon 9 to 5.30 Booking advisable. Table service. Licensed. Meat dishes. Vegan dishes. Snacks. No-smoking area. Wheelchair access. Access, Visa

Demuth's Ⓥ £

2 North Parade Passage TEL Bath (0225) 462631

A little coffee-shop in the town centre, purely vegetarian and vegan. Daily specials are posted on the blackboard – mushrooms with fresh coriander, sweet-and-sour chestnuts, mushroom and spinach moussaka, organic parsnip soup or aubergine pâté, for example. Good cakes and baked items can be taken away, as can the speciality of smoked tofu-filled pitta bread. Smokers are directed 'outside in the yard'!

Open all week L 11.30 to 3 Table service. Tables outside. Licensed. Vegan dishes. Other diets catered for on request. Snacks at other times. Take-aways. No smoking

Edouards ££

31 Belvedere, Lansdown Road TEL Bath (0225) 333042

The basement bar and informal ground-floor wine bar are topped by a smart first-floor restaurant; the food in the top two is the same. Vegetarians, though provided with a main course along the lines of stir-fry vegetables, vegetable gratin or carrot and walnut loaf in wine sauce, are invited specifically to request a suitable starter. Puddings are rather a dull collection, such as chocolate and brandy mousse or fresh fruit cheesecakes.

Open all week noon to 2.15 (exc Sun L), 6.30 to 10.15 (7 to 10.45 Fri and Sat) **Closed** bank hols, 25 to 28 Dec Booking advisable. Table service. Tables outside. Licensed. Meat dishes. Fish dishes. Vegan dishes and other diets catered for on request. Wheelchair access. Access, Visa

Garlands £££

7 Edgar Buildings, George Street TEL Bath (0225) 442283

In a row of shops this ambitious, rather expensive restaurant makes the effort to provide vegetarians with a main course of some sort, though the repertoire is limited: puff pastry tartlet, filo pastry parcel or puff pastry horn filled with vegetables and cheese sauce or tomato coulis give an idea of the scope. Although Bath offers a wealth of vegetarian choices this could be suitable for a special meal out with non-vegetarians. Worthy of particular attention is a crème brûlée, the usual recipe varied by a layer of sliced apple under the glaze.

Open Tue to Sun 12.15 to 2.15 (exc Sun L), 7 to 10.30 **Closed** 3 weeks Jan Booking advisable. Table service. Licensed. Meat dishes. Fish dishes. Wheelchair access. Access, Amex, Visa

Hat and Feather ⓥ £

14 London Street TEL Bath (0225) 425672

An unusual venture: a totally vegetarian pub. The 'international' cooking includes broccoli soup, sweetcorn soup, lasagne, moussaka and vegetable curry.

Open all week 11.30 to 11 (Sun 12 to 3, 7 to 10.30) Counter service. Licensed. Snacks. No children in the evening. Wheelchair access

Huckleberry's ⓥ £

34 Broad Street TEL Bath (0225) 464876

The friendly, studenty atmosphere, together with good food, earn this purely vegetarian restaurant a loyal following. The cooking is inspired by Mediterranean and Middle Eastern cuisines, with the menu changing daily – no microwave cookery here! Lunches might comprise falafels with tahini dip, butterbean bourguignonne, leek and potato Mornay, quiche, Huck's salad plate and starters such as carrot, tomato and orange soup, hummus or guacamole. Breakfast is served from 9.30am.

Open all week L 11.45 to 3.30 Table service Sun only. Counter service. Licensed. Vegan dishes. Other diets catered for on request. Snacks. Take-aways. No-smoking area. Access

Number Five £££

5 Argyle Street TEL Bath (0225) 69282

Near Pulteney Bridge on the main road is this attractive bistro-style restaurant where, from breakfast onwards, you can find a large choice of vegetarian dishes on a mixed menu. Such things as a good, crispy pancake with ratatouille, twice-baked cheese soufflé with cheese straws or Mozzarella and peperonata tart can be ordered either as a starter or main course.

Open all week 10am to 10 (noon to 5 Sun) Booking advisable. Table service. Tables outside. Licensed. Meat dishes. Fish dishes. Other diets on request. Snacks. No-smoking area. Wheelchair access. Access, Amex, Diners, Visa

Popjoy's £££

Beau Nash's House, Sawclose TEL Bath (0225) 460494

Once the home of Juliana Popjoy, Beau Nash's mistress, the house is splendid in fine Regency tradition. The red dining-room is filled with portraits of dandies and the drawing-room upstairs puts the portrait of Beau Nash in pride of place over the fireplace. The restaurant commands a high place in Bath's culinary hierarchy. One vegetarian dish is always available – perhaps a spring roll with spinach, nuts and tomato. The bread is excellent; nibbles are good; accompanying vegetables are varied and well cooked, and ingredients, for example, nettles in soup/or seaweed, can be intriguing. Rhubarb and ginger pudding is one stalwart and comes with toffee sauce and clotted cream. Service can sometimes be slow.

Open Tue to Sat noon to 2, 6 to 10.30 **Closed** 2 weeks Jan Booking advisable. Table service. Licensed. Meat dishes. Fish dishes. Other diets catered for on request. No pipes or cigars. Wheelchair access. Access, Amex, Visa

Priory Hotel £££

Weston Road TEL Bath (0225) 331922

The elegant house, built in 1835 of Bath stone and surrounded by a pretty garden, has excellent facilities, good service and a token vegetarian dish such as cannelloni or a filo pastry with leek and watercress sauce. The starter might be mushrooms stuffed with apple, cheese and celery, breadcrumbed and deep-fried. Creamy desserts – choux swans, mille-feuille and apricot strudel with vanilla sauce and ginger ice-cream – or a savoury such as Stilton, egg and brandy on toast, can complete the meal.

Open all week 12.30 to 2, 7.30 to 9 Booking advisable. Table service. Licensed, but bring your own: corkage £5. Meat dishes. Other diets catered for on request. No smoking in dining-room. Wheelchair access. Accommodation. Access, Amex, Diners, Visa

Pump Room ££

Stall Street TEL Bath (0225) 444474 and 444488

The Regency pump room is worth visiting in its own right, and the restaurant has a certain glamour, enhanced by a pianist at the grand piano. This is the second Milburns restaurant in Bath (see Number Five) and the food is similar, with a ratatouille pancake and possibly a soup for vegetarians. Snacks and cakes are served during the day, and tea-time starts at 2.30.

Open all week 10 to 5.30 (4.30 Nov to Mar, 6.30 July and Aug) **Closed** 25 and 26 Dec Table service. Tables outside. Licensed. Meat dishes. Fish dishes. Snacks. No-smoking area. Wheelchair access

Scoffs (V) £

20 Kingsmead Square TEL Bath (0225) 462483

This wholefood bakery used to sell only its own produce, but has now extended into a café. Everything is made on site – bread is hand-rolled in lots of varieties, including pumpernickel, three-seed and fruit-and-muesli Balkan. Cakes include two that are sugar-free and two made with honey, while cheese is vegetarian and eggs are free-range. The menu, with main dishes such as homity pies, flans, spinach turnovers and spring rolls, as well as breads and sweets, contains a high proportion of vegan items, clearly marked with a green diamond. Salads are good; orange and grapefruit juices are freshly squeezed. With its reasonable prices and excellent quality, it's a popular place.

Open Mon to Sat 11am to 5.30pm Counter service. Vegan dishes. Other diets catered for on request. Snacks. Take-aways. Wheelchair access

Tarts £££

8 Pierrepont Place TEL Bath (0225) 330280 and 330201

A cellar restaurant off Pierrepont Street, entered through the pillars by the Fernley Hotel. Tables are laid with damask cloths and the presentation of food is nouvelle and attractive; prices are reasonable for the quality and ambience. The à la carte menu, available both at lunch and dinner, yields a vegetarian main dish such as a brioche case filled with fresh seasonal vegetables, or deep-fried aubergine with pesto and parmesan. All daily specials are meat or fish. Starters could be choux pastry fritters or baby artichoke salad with coriander and fresh herbs. Ice-creams are home made. 'Music varies from Mozart to modern.'

Open Mon to Sat noon to 2.30, 6.45 to 11 **Closed** 3 days Christmas and New Year Booking advisable. Table service. Licensed. Meat dishes. Fish dishes. Other diets catered for on request. No pipes or cigars except in private rooms. Access, Visa

Walrus and the Carpenter ££

28 Barton Street TEL Bath (0225) 445081

This pub caters better than most for vegetarians. You might find avocado and blue cheese pâté, vegetable soup, crêpes, leek bake or nut roast with watercress, whether at lunchtime or in the evening. Organic wines.

Open all week noon to 2.30 exc Sun L, 6 to 10 **Closed** Dec 25 and 26, Jan 1 Table service. Licensed. Meat dishes. Vegan dishes. No pipes or cigars. Wheelchair access. Access, Visa

Wife of Bath

££

Pierrepont Street TEL Bath (0225) 461745

The eclectic menu will yield a meal that might begin with garlic mushrooms and go on to a provençal vegetable casserole with chestnuts and mushrooms. Fish is the speciality.

Open all week noon to 2.30 (exc Sun L), 5.30 to 11 **Closed** Closed 1 Jan Booking advisable. Table service. Tables outside. Licensed, but bring your own: corkage £2.50. Meat dishes. Fish dishes. No-smoking area during the week. Access, Visa

BATTLE East Sussex MAP 3

La Vieille Auberge

££

27 High Street TEL Battle (042 46) 5171

Built in 1688 of stones from Battle Abbey, the hotel curiously combines some of the less tasteful elements of British décor in the bar, and the more tasteful ones of French country cosiness in the dining-room. There is a separate vegetarian set menu of four courses which opens with beignets of seasonal vegetables, goes on to a sorbet and then a vegetarian dish of the day, perhaps ratatouille ravioli with a chive beurre blanc, or potato, mushroom and leek wrapped in cabbage and served with lentils, onion and a cep sauce. Puddings are particularly highly rated – an iced honey timbale was a 'dessert worth returning for': separate portions of lemon and honey ice-creams on top of what appeared to be strips of frozen honey, all on vanilla sauce. Coffee comes with home-made petits fours. A good place to eat out with non-vegetarians.

Open all week noon to 2, 7 to 10 Booking advisable. Table service. Licensed. Meat dishes. Fish dishes. Other diets catered for on request. Wheelchair access. Accommodation. Access, Amex, Diners, Visa

A restaurant manager can't insist on people not smoking, unless it's specifically a non-smoking restaurant or a non-smoking area. If it is, smokers could be asked to leave if they don't stop. If it's important to you, check beforehand what the smoking arrangements are.

BEACONSFIELD Buckinghamshire MAP 4

Old Hare £

Aylesbury End TEL Beaconsfield (0494) 673380

Some imagination goes into the vegetarian daily specials at this pub: goulash, cheese and red lentil loaf and spaghetti are typical. A red-dragon pie and a curry are on the standard menu. On Sundays only a limited selection of snacks is provided for vegetarians. No puddings.

Open all week exc Sun D, noon to 2, 7.30 to 10 Table service. Counter service. Tables outside. Licensed. Meat dishes. Fish dishes. Vegan dishes. Other diets catered for on request. No children. Wheelchair access. Access, Visa

BEAULIEU Hampshire MAP 2

Montagu Arms £££

Palace Lane TEL Lymington (0590) 612324

Remarkably, the hotel has not been smothered by the heritage blanket that has fallen over many British hotels and restaurants: in such a renowned beauty spot, it is almost a curiosity not to discover ye olde trappings. A vegetarian dish is always available – filo pastry with spinach and goats' cheese or wild mushrooms in brioche. The food has been reported as excellent. The prices assure a high standard of comfort.

Open all week 12.30 to 2, 7.30 to 9.30 Booking advisable. Table service. Licensed, also bring your own: corkage £5. Meat dishes. Fish dishes. Vegan dishes. Other diets catered for on request. No children under 5. Wheelchair access. Accommodation. Access, Amex, Diners, Visa

BECKENHAM Kent MAP 3

Pizza Express £

189 High Street TEL 081-650 0593

A satellite of the excellent London-based chain that was founded twenty-five years ago. See London entry.

Open Mon to Sat 11.30 to midnight, Sun noon to 11.30. Table service. Licensed, also bring your own: corkage £2.50. Meat dishes. Fish dishes. Take-aways. No-smoking area. Wheelchair access. Access, Amex, Diners, Visa

BEDFORD Bedfordshire MAP 5

Pizza Express £

22 St Peters Street TEL Bedford (0234) 53486

A satellite of the excellent London-based chain that was founded twenty-five years ago. See London entry.

Open Mon to Sat 11.30 to midnight, Sun noon to 11.30. Table service. Licensed, also bring your own: corkage £2.50. Meat dishes. Fish dishes. Take-aways. No-smoking area. Wheelchair access. Access, Amex, Diners, Visa

Ye Three Fyshes Inn £

Bridge Street TEL Turvey (023 064) 264

A cosy old-fashioned pub with beams, flag-stoned floors and an inglenook fireplace. The food is good, as is the beer, and on the fixed menu are aubergine and mushroom lasagne and mung bean and mushroom biriani; occasionally you might find a chilli. In summer, the setting by the river makes this a good place to visit for a snack lunch or supper.

Open all week noon to 2.30, 7 to 9.30 Table service. Tables outside. Licensed. Meat dishes. Vegan dishes. Wheelchair access. Access, Visa

BERKHAMSTED Hertfordshire MAP 5

Cook's Delight Ⓥ £–£££

360–362 High Street TEL Berkhamsted (0442) 863584

It's hard to believe from the outside that there's a restaurant here. The entrance is through an Aladdin's cave of a shop, worth a detour for rare oils, flavourings, seaweed, organic vegetables, seed and grain breads. Downstairs is a little dining-room, upstairs a more expansive one. Vegan and macrobiotic cooking are special interests here, and it may be best to check in advance what is planned. Gourmet dinners on Saturdays – at a considerably higher price – derive from Malaysian cuisine. Clay-pot dishes are a speciality, and a vegetable casserole cooked this way acquires a smoky taste, subtle and good. What looks like thin mixed vegetable soup is deceptive: it's full of flavour with a hint of sweetness from chunks of an orange squash (not the bottled kind), said to be so tasty because it's organic. Bread has to be requested, and comes without butter, but it is a moist, wonderful, heavy three-seed variety. Puddings, which are macrobiotic, can be solid. Another plus for some diners are the 92 organic wines, 40 monastic and natural ales and dry organic cider.

Open Thur to Sat D 7.30 (8 Sat) to 9.30, Sat and Sun L 10 to 3 **Closed** 2 weeks Aug/Sept Booking advisable. Table service. Tables outside. Licensed. Vegan dishes. Other diets catered for on request. Snacks. Take-aways. No smoking. Wheelchair access. Access, Visa

BEXHILL-ON-SEA East Sussex MAP 3

Corianders ⓥ £

66 Devonshire Road TEL Bexhill-on-Sea (0424) 220329

In a food desert, Corianders offers decent lunches with good salads and a basic range of dishes dominated by mushroom sauce and cheese sauce. Soup of the day, cakes, good coffee and herb tea can be enjoyed.

Open Mon to Sat 9.30 to 5, L noon to 2 Counter service. Tables outside. Licensed. Vegan dishes. Snacks. Take-aways. Wheelchair access

BIDEFORD Devon MAP 1

Banks Coffee Shop £

16 High Street TEL Bideford (0237) 476813

This used to be a branch of the Midland Bank, hence the name; now it is bright, clean and homely with pine tables, cream walls and brown cord on the floor. The food is predominantly, but not purely, vegetarian, and prices are low. Baked pies and quiche are good and there is a blackboard dish that changes every day – lentil and mushroom curry, mushroom stroganoff or vegetable risotto, for example. There are lots of cakes, sponges and scones, all baked on the premises and also sold from the associated shop. This is a pleasant spot to visit for lunch or a snack during the day.

Open Mon to Sat 9 to 5 (2.30 Wed in winter) Counter service. Meat dishes. Fish dishes. Vegan dishes. Snacks. Take-aways. No smoking. Wheelchairs exc wc

Sloops £–££

Bridge Street TEL Bideford (023 74) 71796

There is a bar area and a small, pleasantly decorated cream dining-room here. More vegetarian dishes are available at lunch than dinner, plus standard snacks of quiches, jacket potatoes, good vegetable soups and a dish of the day. An excellent sweetcorn chowder packed with corn and potato, followed by crempog las, a thick pancake made with parsley batter and filled with onions and mushrooms, provided a very satisfactory lunch. Spicy vegetable and nut tart, cashew and mushroom roast might be sampled at dinner. Good pies and clotted cream.

Open Tue to Sat 10.30 to 2, 6.30 to 9.30 **Closed** 2 weeks in Nov Booking advisable. Table service. Licensed. Meat dishes. Fish dishes. Vegan dishes and other diets catered for on request. Snacks. No smoking. No children under 14 Fri and Sat D. Access, Visa

Thymes ⓥ £–££

The Bakehouse, Queen Street TEL Bideford (023 72) 73399

This wholefood vegetarian café is part of the Bakehouse Craft Studios. The food is variable, ranging from a 'lovely spaghetti in spicy cheese sauce' to, on one occasion, disappointing nut rissoles. During the day there are quiches, pizzas, chickpea burgers and salads that seem to have been through a mechanical chopper, with ingredients all of a size. Cakes include a wide selection: carrot, chocolate, spicy apple, date slice and coconut cream. The evening menu is more formal and more pricey, but takes in soup, pâté or melon boats, goes on to lasagne, mushroom and leek croustade, stuffed peppers or quiche, and finishes with desserts such as Pavlova, chocolate chestnut gateau or apricot mousse.

Open Mon to Sat, L 10am to 3pm, Thur to Sat, D 7 to 9.30 Table service D. Counter service L. Licensed. Vegan dishes. Other diets catered for on request. Snacks. Take-aways. No-smoking area. Wheelchair access

BIRCHOVER Derbyshire MAP 7

Druid Inn ★

Main Street TEL Winster (062 988) 302

An astonishing range of vegetarian dishes is on offer here – ten main courses and seven starters. With gargantuan portions and excellent quality ingredients, it is not surprising that tables are fully booked week after week. Just some of the dishes you might find are spinach roulade with cream cheese and garlic, Californian walnut pâté, steamed Chinese vegetables in sweet-and-sour sauce and almond risotto with peanut and garlic sauce. Certainly worth a journey.

Open all week noon to 2, 7 to 9 (9.30 summer) **Closed** 25 Dec Booking advisable. Counter service. Tables outside. Licensed. Meat dishes. Fish dishes. Vegan dishes. Other diets catered for on request. No-smoking area. No children after 8.30. Wheelchair access. Access, Visa

BIRDLIP Gloucestershire MAP 4

Kingshead House ££–£££

TEL Gloucester (0452) 862299

The eighteenth-century building houses a restaurant and some well-furnished and comfortable bedrooms. The Knocks, who own it, are interested in cooking and pay attention to the small details, offering for example home-made jams for breakfast. Bread is baked on the premises and organically grown local vegetables are used where possible. Judy Knock is an avid reader of old English recipe books, and produces some unusual puddings. The four-course dinner menu has a vegetarian main dish that varies: aubergine and tomato charlotte with red pepper sauce; timbale of courgettes with spinach and red pepper sauce; three filo parcels filled with broccoli, mushrooms and cheese, served with fresh tomato sauce. For dessert, try the chocolate mousse, gooseberry and elderflower mousse, home-made ice-creams or interesting sorbets.

Open Tue to Sun exc Sat L and Sun D, 12.15 to 2, 7.30 to 10 **Closed** 25 and 26 Dec Booking advisable. Table service. Tables outside. Licensed. Meat dishes. Fish dishes. Other diets catered for on request. Wheelchair access. Accommodation. Access, Amex, Diners, Visa

BIRMINGHAM West Midlands MAP 4

Adil £

148–150 Stoney Lane, Sparkbrook TEL 021-449 0335

The first established balti house in the area, the restaurant has a solid local following and a good reputation for its cooking. There are 13 vegetarian baltis (dishes cooked in an iron skillet) among the 50-plus on the menu, including the unusual Kashmiri beans and mustard leaf, along with spinach, aubergine, potato and okra. Six vegetable birianis ring the changes with dhal and chickpea versions. Breads are satisfyingly fresh.

Open all week noon to midnight Booking advisable. Table service. Unlicensed, but bring your own: no corkage. Meat dishes. Fish dishes. Vegan dishes. Take-aways. Access, Amex, Carte Blanche, Diners, Visa

Chung Ying ££

16–18 Wrottesley Street TEL 021-622 5669/1793

That this large restaurant is nearly always full is testimony to the good cooking and generous portions. Vegetarians can choose from the 'vegetable and side dishes' menu for such choices as mixed vegetables in casserole, grilled vegetables with walnuts, stewed bean curd with green vegetables and fried noodles with bean sprouts. Sadly, of the thirty or so dim-sum, only three are vegetarian.

Open all week noon to midnight (11 Sun) **Closed** 25 Dec Booking advisable. Table service. Licensed. Meat dishes. Fish dishes. Take-aways. No children under 7. Access, Amex, Diners, Visa

If you think you have been ill as a result of a restaurant meal, tell your doctor and the local Environmental Health Officer. The EHO can investigate the incident and may decide to prosecute; under the Food Act, it's an offence for a restaurant to serve food unfit for human consumption. If it can be proved that the restaurant caused your illness – which can be difficult – it could be fined and made to compensate you. In serious cases, it may be worth getting legal advice about suing the restaurant yourself.

Chung Ying Garden £–££

17 Thorp Street TEL 021-666 6622

It's a treat to find a separate vegetarian section on a Chinese restaurant menu. Even better is the choice of 15 dishes of substance and interest, such as deep-fried dumplings or wun-tun, bean curd braised in black-bean or sweet-and-sour sauce, and fried mixed vegetables with cashew-nuts in bird's nest. The large room is pleasantly decorated; service draws mixed reports.

Open all week noon to 11.45 (10.45 Sun) **Closed** Closed 25 Dec Booking advisable. Table service. Licensed. Meat dishes. Fish dishes. Vegan dishes on request. Take-aways. Wheelchair access. Access, Amex, Diners, Visa

Cornerstone Coffee House £

25 Woodbridge Road, Moseley TEL 021-449 3324

There's a gentle Christian influence at this café run by a charity. Dark wood tables and spindleback chairs are pleasant, classical music plays and the atmosphere is tranquil and tolerant. 'It's the sort of place one could take grandparents to, along with bohemian friends.' Posters and books are for sale. Lunches are mainly vegetarian, there are snacks all day, and a choice of two vegetarian dishes is available on four nights of the week. Typical of what might be found are lasagne, crispy mushroom layer or bulgur Mexicana. The vegetable and coriander soup of a sample meal was as one would make it at home. Bulgur pilaf with mushroom sauce was flavoursome but the treacle tart proved almost too sweet.

Open Mon to Sat, exc Mon D and Tue D, 10.30am to 3, 7 to 10 Table service. Meat dishes D. Snacks. Take-aways. No smoking. Wheelchair access

Days of the Raj ££

51 Dale End TEL 021-236 0445

The small but smart entrance of this Indian restaurant leads into an upmarket Raj setting, where some excellent dishes – all subtly spiced – are available. Vegetarian main dishes include stuffed tomatoes, punjabi sabjee, aloo gobi and shani paneer. Service can disappoint.

Open Mon to Sun exc Sat Sun L noon to 2.30, 7 to 11.30 Booking advisable weekends. Table service. Counter service. Licensed, also bring your own: corkage £3 wine, £10 spirits. Meat dishes. Vegan dishes. Take-aways. Wheelchair access. Access, Amex, Diners, Visa

Gingers ⓥ £££

7A High Street, Kings Heath TEL 021-444 0906

On the A435, four miles south of Birmingham, opposite MFI, Gingers has been a vegetarian restaurant for about ten years. Inside, it is cosily decorated, with pictures of famous vegetarians, ornaments, tables covered with green tablecloths and laid with interesting pottery cruets and candle-holders. It's a good place to go for a relaxed evening. The menu has two or three starters and three main dishes; 'spiced' tomato and onion soup, when tasted, was thin and rather lacking in spice; garlic mushrooms also seemed underseasoned. Main dishes of spinach and mushroom tabbouleh and Turkish pilaff were good, but could have been punchier in flavour; five accompanying salads offered a good range of textures. A whisky and ginger cake had plenty of whisky and tasted genuinely of orange and ginger. Presentation and service have been praised, and the place is obviously extremely popular.

Open Mon to Sat 6.30 to 9 **Closed** bank hols, 1 week at Christmas Booking advisable. Table service. Unlicensed, but bring your own: no corkage. Vegan dishes. Other diets catered for on request. Take-away. No-smoking area. Wheelchair access

Jewel in the Crown ££

125 Alcester Road, Moseley TEL 021-449 4335

The bold frontage advertises this Indian restaurant in the middle of a suburb of Birmingham. Though not particularly vegetarian, it does have a vegetarian section on the menu; somewhat annoyingly, three out of eight of these items are fish dishes, but there is a suitable balti and a thali. Spicing, for those of tender palate, is agreeably subtle. Pistachio kulfi is good. In short, 'a very competent Kashmiri budget restaurant where vegetarians and vegans could feel comfortably catered for.'

Open all week , exc Tue L and Sat L, noon to 2.30, 6 to midnight Booking advisable. Table service. Licensed. Meat dishes. Fish dishes. Take-aways. Wheelchair access. Access, Amex, Visa

Lombard Room £££

The Patrick Collection, 180 Lifford Lane, King's Norton
TEL 021-459 9111

How vegetarianism spreads – even into the realms of a motor museum-cum-conference centre. This converted paper mill off the A34 is set in recently landscaped grounds. As well as a motor collection, exhibited in period context, there is an art collection and the Lombard Room restaurant. Not only is there a vegetarian menu, but it shows some flair. A typical day offered a fan of melon with fresh fruits and strawberry coulis, and avocado and wild mushroom salad as starters, and aubergines on red cabbage with mustard sauce or spinach roulade filled with crisp vegetable and melted cheese as main dishes.

Open all week noon to 2.30, 7 to 9.45 Booking advisable. Table service. Licensed, also bring your own: corkage £5–£7.50. Meat dishes. Fish dishes. Vegan dishes and other diets catered for on request. No smoking. Wheelchair access. Access, Amex, Diners, Visa

Maharaja ££

23–25 Hurst Street TEL 021-622 2641

The vegetarian dishes, though they hold no surprises, are praised for flavour and texture. The question is, why is there no set vegetarian menu when fish- and meat-eaters get them? The central location is an asset; the smoke-filled atmosphere a debit.

Open Mon to Sat noon to 2.30, 6 to 11.30 **Closed** bank hols, last week of July and 1st week Aug Booking advisable. Table service. Licensed. Meat dishes. Fish dishes. Take-aways. Access, Amex, Diners, Visa

Nutters ★ £–££

422 Bearwood Road TEL 021-420 2528

This mainly vegetarian restaurant reverses the usual procedure and offers a token meat dish. Décor is a bit spartan, but spotlessly clean. The food is excellent for such low prices: guacamole, leek and potato soup, stuffed courgettes and baked spaghetti in tomato and cream sauce cooked in an earthenware pot have all been enjoyed. Lunches offer less choice than dinner, when the range might include cashew, onion and sweetcorn vol-au-vent, pasticcio, curry or risotto in filo pastry. Vegans have several options. Puddings will provide vegans with, perhaps, apple strudel alongside bread pudding, pineapple shortcake or orange and chestnut roulade.

Open all week, exc Sun D and Mon D, noon to 2.30 (3 Sun), 7 to 11 (11.30 Fri and Sat) Booking advisable Fri and Sat. Table service. Licensed, also bring your own: corkage £1. Meat dish. Fish dish. Vegan dishes. Other diets catered for on request. Snacks at other times. Take-aways. No-smoking area. Wheelchair access. Access, Amex, Diners, Visa

La Santé/Michelle £££

182–184 High Street, Harborne TEL 021-426 4133

Two restaurants run by the same owners, with the same chef. Whether you sit upstairs, in La Santé, or downstairs in Michelle, may depend on how many customers there are. Both serve the same vegetarian menu and certainly it is a relief to find not a single quiche or ratatouille; the selection of six starters and five main courses is inventive. Sad, then, that the execution is not better. A vegetable terrine was served with a rather tired mayonnaise and the cheese for the 'raclette' dish was vegetarian Cheddar, served with potatoes. Also, in a French restaurant one might reasonably expect better pastry than formed the base of a tarte de saison. None the less, couscous and leeks in cream and puff pastry have been well liked.

Open Mon to Sat noon to 2, 7 to 10 (10.30 Fri and Sat) Booking advisable. Table service. Tables outside. Licensed, also bring your own: corkage £1. Meat dishes. Vegan dishes. Other diets catered for on request. Take-aways. Access, Visa

Wild Oats ⓥ ★ £

5 Raddlebarn Road, Selly Oak TEL 021-471 2459

There are only about five tables in this purely vegetarian restaurant that is popular with students and locals for its consistently good cooking and relaxed atmosphere. The printed menu has five or six salads and starters such as hummus and baked potatoes. For dessert there are banana and apple crunch, a home-made ice-cream, cheesecake, and fruit fool and crumble whose fruit depends on the season. On the blackboard are the day's hot dishes and the soups. The soups are always imaginative and good. Hot dishes include stuffed peppers, sweet-and-sour vegetables or French mushroom tart. All are freshly cooked and served in extremely generous portions. Everything is home made, down to the bread. Excellent value.

Open Tue to Sat noon to 2, 6 to 9 Table service. Unlicensed, but bring your own: corkage 50p. Vegan dishes. Other diets catered for on request. Take-aways. No smoking. Wheelchair access

BIRTLE Greater Manchester MAP 7

Normandie £££

Elbut Lane, Nr Bury TEL 061-764 3869/1170

It's hard to know whether the view or the food is the main attraction: both are splendid. To reach the stone building, take the old Rochdale Road going east and, after Fairfield Hospital on the right, continue to the Methodist Church, after which turn left. The accommodation draws enthusiastic praise for elegance. The menu carries a single vegetarian starter and main course; the former being scrambled eggs with duxelles, tiny pistou tartlets or celery and Stilton soup, for example, and the main dish a light vegetable and herb clafoutis or millefeuille of vegetables with a herb cream sauce. If you like chocolate, don't miss the 'exquisite chocolate soufflé in a pastry case'; the gratin of oranges has also been recommended. Well worth a trip either for a meal or to stay – there are home-made croissants, brioches and jam for breakfast.

Open Mon to Sat exc Mon and Sat L, noon to 2, 7 to 9.30 **Closed** 26 Dec to 8 Jan Booking advisable. Table service. Licensed. Meat dishes. Fish dishes. No pipes or cigars in dining-room. Wheelchair access. Accommodation. Access, Amex, Diners, Visa

The Editor's top ten restaurants providing an exceptional service for vegetarians, chosen for the success with which they achieve their aims, are listed on page 12.

BISHOP'S CLEEVE Gloucestershire MAP 4

Cleeveway House

££

Evesham Road TEL Bishop's Cleeve (024 267) 2585

Sadly, there is only a token vegetarian main dish at this ambitious restaurant that changes its extensive menu frequently. Vegetarians might cast longing looks at meat-eaters' plates while making do with curried nut roast or lasagne, perhaps. Starters begin with well-flavoured celery soup or delicate cheese soufflé. Ice-creams are home-made, and some say they're on the heavy side, if that's possible. Sorbets and the hazelnut meringue deserve special mention.

Open Tue to Sat 12.15 to 1.45, 7.15 to 9.45 **Closed** 25 Dec, 2 weeks Feb Booking advisable. Table service. Tables outside. Licensed. Meat dishes. Fish dishes. Take-aways. No pipes or cigars in dining-room. Wheelchair access. Accommodation. Access

BLACKBURN Lancashire MAP 7

Pizza Margherita

£

New Park House, Preston New Road TEL Blackburn (0254) 665333

One of a chain of good, simple, stylish pizzerias, where pizzas are cooked freshly to order and come on wholemeal bases with generous toppings. There are four varieties for vegetarians, plus a lasagne and an Idaho bake of mushroom, cheese and tomato on a potato base, and four or five suitable starters.

Open Tue to Sun 10.30am to 10.30 Table service. Tables outside. Licensed. Meat dishes. Snacks. Take-aways. No-smoking area. Wheelchair access. Access, Visa

BODMIN Cornwall MAP 1

Pots

£

Fore Street TEL Bodmin (0208) 74601

The 'pots' are huge steaming bowls of 'more-than-a-soup stews', one of which is a very tasty vegetable selection. You can also compose fillings for a sandwich or jacket potato if preferred. In the evening a vegetarian main course might be lasagne or stuffed aubergine with provençale sauce; with notice, and for a vegetarian group, this menu could be extended. Starters are egg mayonnaise, crispy mushrooms with garlic dip, or melon with ginger or grape cocktail. It's a place reckoned to be 'well worth supporting'.

Open Mon to Sat 9 to 5.30, 7.30 to 9 Fri and Sat only Booking advisable evenings. Table service. Licensed. Meat dishes. Vegan dishes. Other diets catered for on request. Snacks. Wheelchair access. Access, Visa

Waffles £

Market Arcade, Fore Street TEL Bodmin (0208) 75500

Highly recommended for lunch, when you will always find two hot dishes for vegetarians along the lines of bean and lentil casserole with herb dumplings, curry, or vegetable lasagne, in addition to soups, jacket potatoes and quiche. The curry, filled with a wide selection of vegetables (carrots, courgettes, celery, tomato and cauliflower florets) arrived in a pleasantly spiced sauce with properly cooked rice. There's a good choice of salads and a tempting selection of home-made pies and cakes.

Open Mon to Sat L 11.30 to 2 Counter service. Licensed. Meat dishes. Vegan dishes. Other diets catered for on request. Snacks at other times. Take-aways. No-smoking area. Wheelchair access

BOURNEMOUTH Dorset MAP 2

Coriander ££

14 Richmond Hill TEL Bournemouth (0202) 552202

This Mexican restaurant just off the square is worth a visit if you are in the area as it provides a sizeable range of dishes for vegetarians: chilli-and-cheese-filled potato skins, enchiladas, nachos, lasagne and vegetarian Vesuvius (vegetable and bean casserole topped with deep-fried potatoes, cheese and sour cream, then grilled). There is also a set vegetarian dinner for two. Specify the amount of heat you require and the kitchen will temper the seasoning accordingly.

Open all week noon to 2.15 exc Sun L, 6 to 10.30 Booking advisable. Table service. Licensed. Meat dishes. Vegan dishes. Other diets catered for on request. No-smoking area. Access, Visa

Henry's Wholefood Ⓥ

£

6 Lansdowne Road TEL Bournemouth (0202) 297887

The restaurant is in a terraced house and informality reigns. Lunches are wholefood dishes such as vegetable pakoras or lentil and walnut pâté. Three-bean pie, or crisp ratatouille layer with satay sauce might be on offer in the evening. Side dishes of vegetables are included in the price. Vegetarian cheese is used and bread and sorbets are home made. There's a wide range of organic wines and non-alcoholic drinks.

Open Mon to Sat 11.30 to 2 (exc Mon L), 6 to 10 Booking advisable weekends. Table service. Licensed, also bring your own: corkage £2. Vegan dishes. Other diets catered for on request. Take-aways. No smoking area. Wheelchair access

Pizza Piazza

£

1 Yelverton Road TEL Bournemouth (0202) 22412

A branch of a growing chain that offers an enterprising choice of reliably good pizzas. See entry under New Malden for more detail.

Open all week noon to 11 Table service. Licensed. No-smoking area. Wheelchair access. Access, Visa

Salad Centre

£

Post Office Road TEL Bournemouth (0202) 21720

Not just a salad place, for there are hot dishes of curry, cottage pie, vegetable hot-pot, nut roast or cheese, onion and potato pie. There are nine or ten salads daily, reflecting the café's name.

Open Mon to Sat 10am to 3 Counter service. Vegan dishes. Take-aways. No smoking

When you book a restaurant table, you're making a contract with the restaurant and they must give you a table, in reasonable time. If they don't, they're in breach of contract and you can claim a reasonable sum to cover any expenses you had as a result, eg travelling costs.

BOVEY TRACEY Devon MAP 1

Granary Café, Devon Craftsmen's Guild £

Riverside Mill TEL Bovey Tracey (0626) 832223

It seems that nowadays where there's a craft centre, there's a café – a most admirable trend. Located in a large converted mill, the café has polished floors, white painted walls and the sound of the river rushing past. 'It's immaculately clean, and though it's humble, the quality is good.' Unpretentious vegetarian specials of the day might include tagliatelle, bean and lentil casserole or vegetable bake, all served in craft pottery. Clotted cream accompanies desserts of a cake-like nature, and there are two local ice-creams with 10 flavours to choose from.

Open Mon to Sun noon to 1.30 Counter service. Tables outside. Licensed. Meat dishes. No smoking. Wheelchair access. Access, Visa

BOVINGDON Hertfordshire MAP 5

Bobsleigh Inn £££

Hempstead Road TEL Bovingdon (0442) 833276

In the heart of the Home Counties, the Bobsleigh provides a high degree of comfort; tables are well spaced and laid with pink linen, velvet curtains line the windows of the conservatory extension, wicker chairs and unobtrusive efficient service are in evidence. Despite the irony of the owner being a butcher, there are two vegetarian main dishes available. A sample meal opened with an avocado that had been scooped out of its skin, mixed with carrot, celery, peppers and basil and yoghurt, and put back; then continued with peppers stuffed with mushrooms, broccoli and courgettes provençale that also turned up as the accompanying vegetables. Other vegetables were well judged – carrots, minty potatoes and leeks in cream. Excellently crisp profiteroles with a good bitter chocolate sauce were the dessert. A good dining-out venue when with non-vegetarians.

Open Mon to Sat noon to 2 (exc Mon, Sat), 7 to 9.30 **Closed** 26 Dec to 6 Jan Booking advisable. Table service. Licensed. Meat dishes. Vegan dishes. Other diets catered for on request. Snacks. Wheelchair access. Accommodation. Access, Amex, Diners, Visa

BOWNESS-ON-WINDERMERE Cumbria MAP 9

Hedgerow £

Lake Road TEL Windermere (096 62) 5002

Sadly this is no longer solely vegetarian, but a typical snack bar with some concessions to vegetarians. You reach the pleasant room up a narrow staircase and are greeted by the aroma of fresh coffee. Small posies of flowers brighten up the bare wood tables. The printed menu has only a few vegetarian offerings, but there is a daily special. This might be home-made nut cutlets, which proved to be two triangle-shaped cutlets that 'smelled greasy and were greasy'. A salad is served with all dishes, whether starter or main, and seems redundant when the main dish itself is a salad. The redeeming feature of a disappointing visit was a blackberry and apple pie made with excellent short pastry, filled with luscious blackberries and served with Jersey ice-cream.

Open all week 10.30 to 5.30 Table service. Licensed. Meat dishes. Fish dishes. Snacks. Access, Visa

BRADFORD West Yorkshire MAP 7

Bharat ££

502 Great Horton Road TEL Bradford (0274) 521200

Though all the expected meat and king prawn standards are here, the vegetarian thali is one of the chef's specialities. Choice is extended with vegetable biriani, navratan, kofta and bhuna and korma curries, as well as some 10 solo vegetables. A report on the kofta declared it to be one of the best-textured ever encountered: crisp on the outside and firm on the inside with the vegetables still identifiable. Pilau that is fragrant and not oily, and home-made kulfi thick with pistachios represent 'excellent value'.

Open Tue to Sun, noon to 2, 6 to 12 Booking advisable. Table service. Licensed. Meat dishes. Fish dishes. Vegan dishes. No-smoking area. Access, Amex, Diners, Visa

The availability of vegan dishes is indicated in the details underneath the text of an entry.

Pizza Margherita £

Argus Chambers, Hall Ings TEL Bradford (0274) 724333

A branch of a good north-country chain of simple, clean and stylish pizzerias that serve freshly cooked pizzas with wholemeal bases, and four vegetarian possibilities. In addition to the pizzas, there are lasagne and a potato bake.

Open all week 11am to 10.30 Table service. Licensed. Meat dishes. Snacks. Take-aways. No-smoking area. Wheelchair access. Access, Visa

Quiet Greek ££

1099 Thornton Road TEL Bradford (0274) 815760

Once inside the new stone building you could be in a modern taverna in Greece: walls are whitewashed and deliberately uneven to give a stone effect, quiet Greek music plays and many of the customers are families. Further, on Wednesday and Saturday evenings after 11pm, Greek dancing and plate smashing are on the agenda. Vegetarians will find starters like a good, thick, tomato-ish minestrone, slightly oily but crisp tiropitta, tsatsiki and melintzanasalata. A comprehensive meze includes dips, olives, stuffed vegetables, moussaka made from aubergine, courgette and other vegetables with a creamy yoghurt topping, and beans. Sweets are unexceptional.

Open all week exc Sat and Sun L noon to 2, 7 to 11 Table service. Licensed, also bring your own: corkage £2 per bottle. Meat dishes. Seafood dishes. Other diets catered for on request. Wheelchair access. Access, Visa

Shiraz £

113 Oak Lane TEL Bradford (0274) 490176

The savoury dishes served in the rather plain café are authentic and extremely good value and the sweets in the window are attractive. Various vegetarian curries, as well as vegetable masala and biriani are on the menu – all dishes served with three chapatis or two tandoori chapatis. In addition to the traditional sweets, there are three kinds of kulfi and barfi, gulab jamun and ras malai.

Open Sun to Thur 11am to 2, Fri and Sat 11am to 3.30am Table service. Counter service. Unlicensed. Meat dishes. Vegan dishes. Snacks. Take-aways. Wheelchair access

BRADWELL Derbyshire MAP 7

Lyndale Café £

Nr Sheffield TEL Hope Valley (0433) 20567

An honourable mention for value: soup, vegetarian pâté, salads and a range of hot meals are all cooked to order and reasonably priced. Vegans won't go hungry. There are at least three hot dishes available every day, hot dishes along the lines of fidgetty pie, lasagne, moussaka, stir-fry vegetables and nut roast.

Open all week 9am to 7 (6 in winter), D by appointment **Closed** 25 and 26 Dec Table service. Licensed. Meat dishes. Vegan dishes. Other diets catered for on request. Snacks. Take-aways. Accommodation

BRENT KNOLL Somerset MAP 1

Goat House £

Bristol Road TEL Brent Knoll (0278) 760650

On the A38, near M5 exit 22. As you might imagine, the enterprise has a lot to do with goats. What you would not imagine is the range of items made from the herd kept here – from milk through to three goats' cheeses, butter, fudge and ice-cream, even cosmetics and shampoo. Alongside meat and fish are served some good vegetarian dishes such as courgette au gratin, pizza, aubergine and pepper stew, pasta bake and shepherd's pie without meat. Puddings take in an outstanding bread-and-butter and a good chocolate and mocha fudge cake. Homely and welcoming.

Open Wed to Sat, Mon 9 to 5, Tue 12 to 5, Sun 10 to 5 Counter service. Tables outside. Unlicensed, but bring your own: no corkage. Meat dishes. Fish dishes. Snacks. Take-aways. No-smoking area. Wheelchair access

See the back of the guide for a list of restaurants serving only vegetarian food.

BRENTWOOD Essex **MAP 5**

Pizza Express £

5 High Street TEL Brentwood (0277) 233569

A satellite of the excellent London-based chain that was founded twenty-five years ago. See London entry.

Open Mon to Sat 11.30 to midnight, Sun noon to 11.30. Table service. Licensed, also bring your own: corkage £2.50. Meat dishes. Fish dishes. Take-aways. No-smoking area. Wheelchair access. Access, Amex, Diners, Visa

BRIDLINGTON Humberside **MAP 8**

Vittles £

64 Quay Road TEL Bridlington (0262) 604826

Gleaning dishes from all over the world, Vittles none the less has a Middle Eastern bias. This is evident in the generously endowed special platter offered at dinner only – it takes in stuffed cabbage, Feta pasties, hummus, tsatsiki, tabouleh and deep-fried aubergines and courgettes – as well as falafel and couscous. American dishes include gumbo, burritos and succotash; from India there's pasanda; from the Far East, stir-fried tofu. Vegetables get unusual treatment too: aubergines are filled with apricots; stuffed courgettes are poached in red wine. Lunch is a simpler affair, but still international: moussaka, curry, chilli, fruit and vegetable casserole are among the varying choices.

Open Tue to Sat 11.45 to 2.30, Fri and Sat 7.30 to 9.30 Booking advisable evenings. Table service evenings. Counter service lunch. Licensed, but bring your own: corkage 75p. Vegan dishes. Snacks. Take-aways. No smoking. Wheelchair access

BRIGHOUSE West Yorkshire **MAP 7**

Brook's ££

6–8 Bradford Road TEL Brighouse (0484) 715284

This relatively new restaurant could be a haven for a vegetarian eating out with meat-eaters, as the regularly changing menu always has a vegetarian main course: after a starter such as broccoli and almond parcels or warm leek and onion quiche with beurre blanc sauce, you might be tempted by a choux pastry ring filled with wild mushrooms and spinach or a savoury roulade of artichokes and asparagus. Modern British leanings are represented by bread-and-butter pudding, treacle tart with vanilla cream or citrus fruit and mint terrine.

Open Mon to Sat 7 to 11 Booking advisable. Table service. Licensed. Meat dishes. Fish dishes. Vegan and other diets catered for on request. No smoking

BRIGHTON East Sussex MAP 3

Annie's £–££

Middle Street TEL Brighton (0273) 202051

Tucked down a tiny alley in the Lanes, opposite Dukes Lane, this cramped up-and-down restaurant serves reasonably priced food without any flourishes – every day and all day. Home-made pies are the house speciality and a vegetable and bean version with potato and cheese topping may be supplemented with macaroni cheese or spaghetti. Banoffi pie, trifle, chocolate mousse or treacle sponge pudding round things off.

Open all week noon to 11 Booking advisable. Table service. Tables outside. Licensed, also bring your own: corkage 50p per bottle. Meat dishes. Vegan dishes. Other diets catered for on request. Snacks at other times. Children's menu up to 7.30pm, though not always vegetarian. Access, Amex, Diners, Visa

La Caperon ££

113 St George's Road, Kemp Town TEL Brighton (0273) 680317

La Caperon has taken over the premises previously occupied by Oat Cuisine, which was a purely vegetarian restaurant. Having inherited a vegetarian clientele, the owners sensibly offer vegetarian dishes as well as French meaty dishes. The food is good and unpretentious; a typical day's vegetarian menu has steamed cockles and mussels (a mistake, surely); potato mille-feuille with mushrooms, tomatoes and caper sauce; stir-fried egg noodles with vegetables, peanuts and sweet-and-sour sauce; large tomatoes stuffed with vegetables, pasta and tomato sauce and a tofu and cashew-nut stroganoff. Start with gnocchi romaine or avocado and nut pâté perhaps. Dishes tend to rely heavily on pasta; otherwise they are well prepared.

Open Tue to Sun noon to 2, 7 to 10.30, exc Sun D Table service. Licensed. Meat dishes. Fish dishes. Vegan dishes. Other diets catered for on request. No-smoking area. Access, Visa

Food for Friends ⓥ ★ £

17A–18 Prince Albert Street, The Lanes TEL Brighton (0273) 202310

A fixture of the Brighton scene, popular not only for its high-quality food but also for the relaxed atmosphere where strangers seem to chat readily, classical music plays and newspapers can be borrowed. Breakfast begins the day, with croissants, pastries and cakes from the bakery behind the restaurant. Lunch is good value: choose from a daily changing menu offering salads, quiche, and the likes of black-eyed bean and mushroom stroganoff with rice; tortellini alla Firenza; kebabs and a light, tasty spinach pancake. Stir-fried vegetables are the only constant. If main dishes sometimes have a chunky tendency, puddings and cakes are light and creamy: chocolate roulade and a fresh raspberry cake, for example. Portions are generous.

Open all week, 9am to 10pm (L noon to 3, D 5.30 to 10) Counter service. Licensed. Vegan dishes. Other diets catered for on request. Snacks. Take-aways. No-smoking area. Wheelchair access. Visa

Latin in the Lane ££

10 Kings Road TEL Brighton (0273) 28672 and 21600

One of the best up-market Italian restaurants in the area. Spacious and light, it has black-and-white floor tiles, white tables with marble-type tops and plenty of flowers. Home-made pasta is the thing to try – there is not a pizza in sight – and plenty of the sauces and fillings are vegetarian. Ravioli arrives light and soft, a far cry from many slimy, sticky parcels; alla fritta is a spinach version. Well reported are fettucine al pesto (made with cream as well as the usual basil, pine nuts and garlic), fettucine medici (with cream, mushrooms and peas), and rigatoni Siciliana. For dessert, ice-cream and zabaglione have been enjoyed. On Saturday nights there is live music. Somewhere to come for a reasonably priced evening out with well cooked food professionally presented.

Open all week noon to 2.15, 6.15 to 11 (11.15 Fri and Sat) **Closed** 25 and 26 Dec Booking advisable. Table service. Licensed. Meat dishes. Fish dishes. Other diets catered for on request. Access, Amex, Diners, Visa

Pizza Express £

22 Prince Albert Street, The Lanes TEL Brighton (0273) 23205
90 Western Road TEL Brighton (0273) 26333

A satellite of the excellent London-based chain that was founded twenty-five years ago. See London entry.

Open Mon to Sat 11.30 to midnight. Sun noon to 11.30. Table service. Licensed, also bring your own: corkage £2.50. Meat dishes. Fish dishes. Take-aways. No-smoking area. Wheelchair access. Access, Amex, Diners, Visa

Slims Ⓥ £

92 Churchill Square TEL Brighton (0273) 24582

Slims caters largely for those in need of refreshment during their travails in the shops and is in the heart of the modern shopping centre. Purely vegetarian, it serves reasonably priced snacks of flans, salads, jacket potatoes, hot dishes such as curry, ratatouille, mushroom stroganoff and courgette and hazelnut bake. A good choice of flapjacks, cakes, shortbreads and specialities – fresh fruit roulades and cheesecakes.

Open Mon to Sat 11.30 to 2.30 Counter service. Tables outside. Licensed. Vegan dishes. Other diets catered for on request. Snacks. Take-aways. No-smoking area. Wheelchair access exc wc

BRISTOL Avon MAP 2

Bakers ££

3 Ninetree Hill, Stokes Croft TEL Bristol (0272) 47242

The small menu in this attractive restaurant changes regularly but always keeps a high proportion of vegetarian dishes. There is a lively interest in meatless cooking – a parsnip timbale with green herb mayonnaise, walnut and spring onion tart, and curried egg loaf have featured as starters; aubergine cheesecake, vine leaves with spiced pine kernel and rice stuffing, and cauliflower and pear pie with walnut pastry set the tone for the main courses. If you can't manage dark chocolate cake or autumn pudding, try a home-made ice-cream; the range varies, but might include rhubarb and orange, apricot, banana, or brown bread.

Open Tue to Thur 7 to 10.30 (11 Fri, Sat) **Closed** Christmas Eve to 2 Jan, first 2 weeks Sept Booking advisable. Table service. Licensed. Meat dishes. No-smoking area on request. Wheelchair access

Bell's Diner £££

1 York Road, Montpelier TEL Bristol (0272) 240357

This converted corner shop has a menu that changes regularly and always has a couple of dishes for vegetarians, coming up with some adventurous ideas. A typical menu revealed starters of celeriac soup, avocado, quails' eggs and walnut salad with walnut oil vinaigrette, and main dishes of baked stuffed pattipan (small butternut squash with pinenuts, garlic and parsley with cider sauce) and garlic and basil pasta with sun-dried tomatoes, olives and yoghurt cream topping. Well worth a visit.

Open Tue to Sat 7 to 11, Sun L noon to 4 Booking advisable. Table service. Licensed, also bring your own: corkage £3. Meat dishes. Fish dishes. No smoking. Wheelchair access. Access, Visa

Café de Daphne £

12 York Road, Montpelier TEL Bristol (0272) 426799

A popular café providing a modest all-day service of meat and vegetarian food. No lavish sums have been spent on décor – linoleum floor, no curtains – but there is a pleasant lack of trendiness and some nice touches, such as fresh carnations on the tables. Breakfasts offer variety (Jamaican brunch consists of fried banana, egg, beans and Jamaican bread) and lunch dishes are internationally inspired and rather unusual: bagels with home-made curd cheese; polenta and verzata; frittata, peppers, herb and filo pie; three-grain and aubergine risotto; Italian ratatouille. Regional Italian and Algerian dishes are specialities.

Open all week 10 to 6 **Closed** 1 week at Christmas Table service. Tables outside. Licensed. Meat dishes. Vegan dishes. Other diets catered for on request. Snacks. Take-aways. No-smoking area.

Cherries Vegetarian Bistro ⓥ £££

122 St Michael's Hill TEL Bristol (0272) 293675

At the top of the hill, conveniently close to the University, is this pleasant vegetarian bistro loved by students and locals alike. Enjoy good food and organic wines at reasonable prices: as well as stalwarts such as hummus, there might be an orange and walnut pâté; smoked tofu mélange; a fritatta of spinach, mushrooms, courgettes and cream cheese; farmhouse onions stuffed with fruit, vegetables, nuts and herbs with a rich red wine gravy, or puff pastry baskets. Vegans will always be offered a suitable gateau; other puddings include fruit salad trifle, chocolate mousse, and spiced apple and raisin crumble.

Open Mon to Sat, D 7 to 10.30 **Closed** 2 weeks summer, 25 Dec Booking advisable. Table service. Licensed, but bring your own: corkage £2 per bottle. Vegan dishes. Other diets catered for on request. No-smoking area. No children after 8.30pm or at weekends. Wheelchair access. Access, Visa

Edwards ££

24 Alma Vale Road, Clifton TEL Bristol (0272) 731254

There have been many positive reports for this restaurant tucked away in a quiet back street behind Clifton Down shopping centre. The ominous note at the bottom of the menu, 'omelettes and vegetarian dishes always available', might translate into vegetables and cheese en croûte, or pasta provençale. Starters are the likes of broccoli mousse and broad beans with almonds and cheese sauce. Some think that cheese features too strongly on the menu.

Open all week exc Sat L, Sun D, noon to 2.30, 7 to 11 **Closed** first 2 weeks Aug Booking advisable. Table service. Licensed. Meat dishes. Fish dishes. Vegan dishes. Other diets catered for on request. No-smoking area. Wheelchair access. Access, Visa

If in doubt about the constituents of a dish, ask.

Ganges £££

368 Gloucester Road TEL Bristol (0272) 245234 and 428505

Don't be deterred by the Technicolor décor. There's a range of consistently good vegetarian dishes, some composed into a thali and a reasonably priced set menu. The latter calls for a full appetite with its samosas, chana bhaji, sobji curry with fresh vegetables of the day, bagun bhaji (aubergine), sag bhaji (spinach), pilau rice, dessert and coffee.

Open all week noon to 2, 6 to 11.30 **Closed** 25 and 26 Dec Booking advisable. Table service. Licensed. Meat dishes. Vegan dishes. Take-aways. Wheelchair access. Access, Amex, Diners, Visa

Glasnost ££

1 William Street, Totterdown TEL Bristol (0272) 723217

Well, the name will certainly date it! 'An excellent atmosphere for a party with mixed dietary requirements' says a devotee. The bistro is decorated simply, with cubicles, high-back benches and oilcloth-covered tables; the day's menu is listed on a blackboard. The food is excellent value and gives vegetarians an interesting choice with starters such as hot devilled mushrooms, avocado, tomato and Brie salad, carrot and coriander soup. Main courses could include lentil and spinach loaf with fresh tomato and herb sauce, winter vegetable and bean casserole, slightly bland buckwheat pancakes or spinach tikon. Round things off with profiteroles or sticky toffee pudding.

Open all week D 6.30 to 10, Sun L 10 to 5 **Closed** bank hols Booking advisable. Table service. Licensed, also bring your own: corkage £2. Meat dishes. Fish dishes. Vegan dishes and other diets catered for on request. Access, Visa

Jameson's ££

30 Upper Maudlin Street TEL Bristol (0272) 276565

A bistro opposite Bristol Royal Infirmary, displaying dishes of the day on the blackboard in addition to the printed menu. The vegetarian main courses, pretty unchanging, are broccoli and blue cheese pancakes or two croûtes, one with avocado and celery, the other with leeks, mushrooms and nuts with a sharp tomato sauce. Accompanying vegetables are pleasantly crunchy, cooked in separate ironware. Of the starters, meatless ones include mushroom and hazelnut pâté, endive salad and hot avocado with Stilton filling. The orange ice-cream filled with chocolate and Grand Marnier has been recommended, as have the profiteroles. Be prepared for some lengthy pauses between courses.

Open Mon to Thur, D 7 to 11 (11.30 Fri and Sat) **Closed** 3 weeks Aug Booking advisable. Table service. Licensed. Meat dishes. Fish dishes. Wheelchair access. Access, Visa

McCreadies Ⓥ £

26 Broad Street TEL Bristol (0272) 265580

A vegetarian and vegan restaurant conveniently situated in the heart of the city; it serves tasty, fresh and reasonably priced food. A high proportion of the vegetables are organic and all the dishes are home made. During a week, the range might include a variety of soups, hummus, deep-fried tempeh with salad, garlic mushrooms, and main dishes of chickpea cobbler, ratatouille bake, curries, various pastas, and tempeh and mushroom pie. Salad is served with all main dishes.

Open Mon to Fri 8.30 to 7 (11 Thur, 4 Fri), Sat 11 to 11 Counter service. Licensed, but bring your own: corkage £1. Vegan dishes. Other diets catered for on request. Snacks. Take-aways. No-smoking area. Wheelchair access

Michael's £££

129 Hotwell Road TEL Bristol (0272) 276190

It may be in a scruffy part of Bristol, but this restaurant, furnished with antique furniture and with an attractive décor, treats its vegetarian customers well. Starters on the fixed-price menu marked as suitable for vegetarians include feuilleté of Stilton with mixed vegetables; mushroom, fennel and watercress timbale; and twice-baked soufflé with celery sauce. The main dish might be a pastry box with mushrooms and nuts in a herb sauce. Good selection of home-made desserts and ices.

Open Mon to Sat 7 to 11.30 Booking advisable. Table service. Licensed, also bring your own: corkage £2.50. Meat dishes. Fish dishes. Other diets catered for on request. No smoking. Wheelchair access (also wc). Access, Visa

Millwards ⓥ £££

40 Alfred Place, Kingsdown TEL Bristol (0272) 245026

Sister to the Millwards in London (see entry), this branch also aspires to be an above-average vegetarian café; tables are laid with cloths, the atmosphere is tranquil and diners can see the preparation of food, which is always a heartening sign. Vegans will find plenty to suit – sesame and tofu dip with crudités, orange hummus, tofu terrine and vegetable korma, for instance. Other starters might be cashew-nut and cream cheese pâté, and spinach and pistachio nut roulade with Dijon mustard sauce. Main course dishes of coulibiac with watercress sauce, layered almond and cashew roast with fresh tomato sauce or mushroom filo with walnut yoghurt might be followed by apple and Mozzarella tart, Millwards' own sorbets, hunza apricots with nut cream (vegan), chocolate peppermint parfait or cheesecake on a chocolate base. Organic wines and herbal teas are also available.

Open Tue to Sat 7 to 10.30 Booking advisable. Table service. Licensed, but bring your own: corkage £2.50. Vegan dishes. Other diets catered for on request. No smoking. Wheelchair access. Access, Visa

Muset ££

12 Clifton Road, Clifton TEL Bristol (0272) 732920

A noisy bistro on three floors placing emphasis on fresh ingredients. Though shellfish is the speciality, vegetarians will find dishes on the lines of button mushrooms in cheese sauce, cottage cheese flavoured with herbs and peaches, stir-fried vegetables on a bed of pasta, or nut, herb and vegetable cutlets. Home-made brandy-snap baskets, fresh tropical fruit salad, or home-made peach ice-cream in a crêpe served with peach and brandy sauce to follow.

Open Tue to Sat 7 to 10.30 **Closed** 1 week at Christmas, 2 weeks in summerEngl-andBooking advisable. Table service. Licensed. Meat dishes. Vegan dishes and other diets catered for on request. Wheelchair access. Access, Visa

A change of owner or chef may mean a change of menu policy. If a restaurant is no longer serving vegetarian food, please inform the guide; the address to write to is on page 9.

Pizza Express £

31 Berkeley Square TEL Bristol (0272) 260300

A satellite of the excellent London-based chain that was founded twenty-five years ago. See London entry.

Open Mon to Sat 11.30 to midnight, Sun noon to 11.30. Table service. Licensed, also bring your own: corkage £2.50. Meat dishes. Fish dishes. Take-aways. No-smoking area. Wheelchair access. Access, Amex, Diners, Visa

Pizza Piazza £

8–10 Baldwin Street TEL Bristol (0272) 293278

A branch of a growing chain that offers an enterprising choice of reliably good pizzas. See entry under New Malden for more detail.

Open all week noon to 11 Table service. Licensed. No-smoking area. Wheelchair access. Access, Visa

Plum Duff £££

6 Chandos Road TEL Bristol (0272) 238450

In a narrow back street behind Whiteladies Road, the plum-coloured restaurant is attractive and quirky, with modish rag-rolled walls and an assortment of newly upholstered antique chairs. There are home-made rolls and crudités already on the tables as you arrive. Roquefort cheese with nuts and pears in pastry, baked green pepper with chilli beans, tomato and cheese, or mushrooms and chestnuts with mustard and tarragon have been successful; two vegetarian main dishes are always available. The style is smarter than that of the average bistro, prices are not outrageous.

Open Tue to Sat, D 7 to 10.30 **Closed** 24 Dec to 10 Jan Booking advisable. Table service. Licensed. Meat dishes. Fish dishes. No pipes or cigars. No children under 8. Wheelchair access. Access, Visa

The Vegetarian Good Food Guide *is totally independent, accepts no free hospitality and makes no charge for inclusion.*

Pushpanjli £

217A Gloucester Road, Horfield TEL Bristol (0272) 40493

Bristol's Gujerati vegetarian restaurant, spruce but hardly luxurious, serves snacks such as bhel puri, dosas, patras and onion bhajias, along with some more unusual items such as mogo chips, khanvi (an Indian pasta made with chickpea flour, yoghurt, chillies, and other seasonings). There are various vegetable curries as well as Indian-style spaghetti, three dhals and a thali.

Open all week noon to 10, Sun 4 to 7.45 **Closed** 1 week at Christmas Table service. Tables outside. Licensed. Vegan dishes. Snacks. Take-aways. No-smoking area

Rajdoot ££

83 Park Street TEL Bristol (0272) 268033 and 291242

A long, narrow restaurant at the top of the main shopping street. The mildly spiced and reasonably priced Indian food includes a set vegetarian menu of vegetable cutlet, onion kulcha, aloo jeera, dhal, vegetable pilau, raita and a choice of sweets from the trolley or more prosaic tinned fruits or ice-cream.

Open all week noon to 2.30, 6.30 to 11.30 **Closed** 25 and 26 Dec, bank hols Booking advisable. Table service. Licensed. Meat dishes. Fish dishes. Take-aways. Wheelchair access. Access, Amex, Diners, Visa

Rocinante's ££

85 Whiteladies Road TEL Bristol (0272) 734482

A tapas bar serving Mexican food to meat-eaters and vegetarians; there have been appreciative reports of the friendly service, good food and organic vegetables. Soup, chickpeas in spinach and tomato sauce, and vegetable casserole give a flavour of the menu.

Open all week 9 to 11, L 12.30 to 3, D 6 to 11 (exc Sun D) **Closed** 25 and 26 Dec, 3 days at Easter Table service. Counter service. Tables outside. Licensed, but bring your own: corkage £3. Meat dishes. Vegan dishes. Other diets catered for on request. Snacks. Wheelchair access. Access, Visa

BROADSTAIRS Kent MAP 3

Mad Chef's Bistro £

The Harbour TEL Thanet (0843) 69304

The Chef may be mad but provides a perfectly sane vegetarian menu. Some 10 dishes are helpfully marked with double asterisks to indicate that no animal products have been used. The place specialises in fish and is menu-mad, with *cartes* for the bistro, for specials, for vegetarians, and for lunch, snack and supper. The supper menu lists some eight vegetarian choices, including spinach nut rissoles, cauliflower cheese and vegetable pie, risotto and curry. These are also on the main menu along with lentil and mushroom bolognese, aubergines stuffed with mushrooms and cashew-nuts, and aubergines sauté with yoghurt and Feta. With desserts such as no-name cake, Mississippi mud pie, home-made apple pie and home-made chocolate fudge pudding comes the offer of cream, ice-cream or both. Where can such madness lead?

Open all week noon to 2.30, 6 to 10 Booking advisable Sat and Sun. Table service. Licensed. Meat dishes. Fish dishes. Vegan dishes. Take-aways. Access, Amex, Diners, Visa

Marchesi Bros ££

18 Albion Street TEL Thanet (0843) 62481

Described as 'Anglo-French', the restaurant is over 100 years old, but up-to-date when it comes to catering for vegetarians. A separate menu of some six dishes offers dishes on the lines of spinach pancake with cream mushroom sauce, stroganoff in brandy sauce with wine, and Brie and goats' cheese fritters with Cumberland sauce.

Open all week noon to 2, 6.30 to 9.30 **Closed** 25, 26 and 27 Dec Booking advisable. Table service. Tables outside. Licensed, also bring your own: corkage £2.50. Meat dishes. Fish dishes. Other diets catered for on request. No-smoking area by prior arrangement. Wheelchair access. Accommodation. Access, Diners, Amex, Visa

The Vegetarian Good Food Guide *has been compiled in the same way as* The Good Food Guide *and is based on reports from consumers and anonymous inspections.*

BROADWAY Hereford & Worcester MAP 4

Collin House ££

Collin Lane TEL Broadway (0386) 858354

It's a pleasure to find an old-fashioned traditional English hotel serving refreshingly authentic and unpretentious food with attention to details such as home-made bread and crudités with home-made mayonnaise. The old stone house with flagstones and massive beams is cosy, with an inglenook fireplace. Starters include hazelnut and cheese soufflé with watercress sauce, and tomato and tarragon jelly with lime-flavoured yoghurt sauce. Double Gloucester cheese, hazelnut and parsley croquettes served on a bed of green noodles with sweet red pepper and tomato sauce is a speciality; other dishes include walnut and Stilton choux pastry served with a ragout of mushrooms flavoured with marjoram; sweet pepper and walnut pasta with lemon, thyme and sherry vinegar dressing. Home-made meringues with fruity home-made ice-cream, bread-and-butter pudding and date and butterscotch pudding satisfy the sweet tooth.

Open all week noon to 1.30, 7 to 9 Booking advisable. Table service. Tables outside. Licensed. Meat dishes. Fish dishes. Vegan dishes. Other diets catered for on request. No children under 8 at D. Wheelchair access. Accommodation. Access, Visa

Lygon Arms £££

TEL Broadway (0386) 852255

Lovers of old oak beams will enjoy this high-class establishment, with its long tradition of luxury and service. There is a four-course vegetarian menu; it might consist of a pastry case of asparagus with ginger, mint and lime butter sauce, an iced cucumber and yoghurt soup and a summer vegetable ravioli in basil sauce. Sorbets follow. Of the puddings, the orange mousse with Cointreau has been recommended.

Open all week 12.30 to 2, 7.30 to 9.15 Booking advisable. Table service. Licensed. Meat dishes. Fish dishes. Other diets catered for on request. Snacks at other times. Wheelchair access. Access, Amex, Diners, Visa

BROMLEY Kent MAP 3

Carioca £

239 High Street TEL 081-460 7130

An extremely popular Indian restaurant, well above the usual high street standard. The menu is mostly meat, but there's a good-value vegetarian thali and an unusual selection of vegetable side dishes. Courgettes with tomatoes and garlic, dhal makhani, with a special mix of spices, muttar paneer and also damn – potatoes fried in butter with tomatoes, rosemary and fresh cream – would make up a good meal.

Open Mon to Sat noon to 2, 7 to 11. Booking advisable. Table service. Licensed. Meat dishes. Take-aways. No-smoking area. Wheelchair access. Access, Amex, Diners, Visa

Pizza Express £

15 Widmore Road TEL 081-464 2708

A satellite of the excellent London-based chain that was founded twenty-five years ago. See London entry.

Open Mon to Sat 11.30 to midnight, Sun noon to 11.30. Table service. Licensed, also bring your own: corkage £2.50. Meat dishes. Fish dishes. Take-aways. No-smoking area. Wheelchair access. Access, Amex, Diners, Visa

BROMSGROVE Hereford & Worcester MAP 4

Grafton Manor ££–£££

Grafton Lane TEL Bromsgrove (0527) 579007

The building of the manor was commissioned in 1567 by Sir Gilbert Talbot, then Earl of Shrewsbury, and though it was rebuilt in the early eighteenth century after a fire, much of its sixteenth-century charm persists. The present owners, the Morris family, have restored it to make an elegant and comfortable country-house hotel with six acres of grounds leading to a lake. Dinner is a grand affair, with food generally of a high standard: bread, canapés and chocolates are all home made. A separate four-course vegetarian menu might offer a broad bean and hazelnut soup, followed by Ogen melon with fruit sorbet or salad with sauté cheese and onions, then either wild mushrooms sauté with garlic and pink peppercorns or wholemeal spiced vegetable pie. Afterwards good sweets or, at a supplementary charge, English cheese with home-made biscuits. Coffee and petits fours are extra.

Open all week exc Sat L 12.30 to 1.30, 7.30 to 9 Booking advisable. Table service. Licensed, also bring your own: corkage £5.75. Meat dishes. Fish dishes. Other diets catered for on request. No children under 8. Wheelchair access. Accommodation. Access, Amex, Diners, Visa

BUNGAY Suffolk MAP 5

Rebecca's £–££

42 St Mary's Street TEL Bungay (0986) 4691

The double-fronted café in the main street was once a bakery; it now sports a menu outside that promises a selection of vegetarian delights such as poached pear with cream and tarragon dressing; melon, grape and port appetizer; ratatouille with creamy mushroom-filled ring; cheese, nut and vegetable loaf with piquant sauce, or puff pastry cases with cream cheese, mushrooms and coriander. It is disappointing that this range is only available on the one night of the week that they open, Saturday. Lunches offer only a couple of dishes, perhaps mushroom stroganoff, broccoli, cream cheese and cauliflower pie, lasagne, curry, or pasta with fresh herb and cheese sauce.

Open Tue to Sat 11.30 to 5, plus 7.45 to 9.30 Sat **Closed** Christmas to New Year Booking advisable. Table service. Unlicensed. Meat dishes. Fish dishes. Other diets catered for on request. Snacks. Take-aways. Smoking. Wheelchair access. Access, Visa

BURGH LE MARSH Lincolnshire MAP 8

Windmill £–££

TEL Skegness (0754) 810281

The Windmill is an important element in the enterprise, since it grinds all the flour used to bake the bread for the restaurant. The bread is Granary-style, with a good crust and moist inside. Originally a tea-shop, the dining-room is spacious, free from Muzak, with floral Austrian blinds and papered arches. Ingredients are of a high quality and a typical meal might be vegetarian pancakes with chilli sauce, kebabs with peanut sauce, followed by a choice of meringues, home-made walnut and maple syrup ice-cream, crème brûlée and other sweets. Ice-cream is excellent, coffee arrives with home-made fudge. One of the best places to eat for miles around.

Open Tue to Sat 7 to 9.30, Sun noon to 1.45 **Closed** 25 and 26 Dec Booking advisable. Table service. Licensed. Meat dishes. Fish dishes. Vegan dishes. Other diets catered for on request. Wheelchair access

BURNLEY Lancashire MAP 7

Top Table £

11 Brown Street TEL Burnley (0282) 416732

This café in the centre of town serves wholesome vegetarian lunches: soups, mushroom pâté, hummus, courgette provençale with garlic bread, ratatouille-stuffed pittas or hazelnut-stuffed mushrooms are just some of the savoury items. Almond flan with seasonal fruits or fruit brûlée for pudding.

Open Mon to Sat 9 to 5 Table service. Counter service. Unlicensed. Meat dishes. Snacks. Take-aways. Wheelchair access

BURY ST EDMUNDS Suffolk MAP 5

Angel Hotel ££

Angel Hill TEL Bury St Edmunds (0284) 753926

The Georgian elegance of the Angel Hotel makes it a landmark in the square opposite the ruined Abbey in Bury St Edmunds. An enlightened policy on vegetarianism, plus a financial controller who as resident vegetarian samples the dishes, results in a vegetarian menu of three starters and four main courses. Eat in either the main dining-room or the medieval undercroft (the Vaults restaurant). Take your pick of avocado fan, a 'first-class' pot of white mushrooms in garlic butter or a salad of melon, orange and grapefruit segments; avocado with walnuts and tomato soup have been praised. Main dishes might be puff pastry parcels, pancakes, Stilton fritters or a mild vegetable curry. It's also a good haunt for afternoon teas.

Open all week noon to 2, 7 to 9.30 Booking advisable. Table service. Licensed. Meat dishes. Vegan dishes. Other diets catered for on request. Snacks. No-smoking in dining-room. Accommodation. Access, Amex, Diners, Visa

Beaumont's Health Stores Ⓥ £

6 Brent Grovel Street TEL Bury St Edmunds (0284) 706677

Behind the healthfood store, the vegetarian restaurant falls into the varnished pine school of décor; in the courtyard are a few more tables. A short menu has such dishes as aduki bean shepherd's pie, savoury slice of kasha baked with vegetables, and some conservative salads. There is more for the sweet-toothed to get excited about: an orange gateau made with bitter orange marmalade is described as 'stately' and a brandy chocolate slice has been liked. 'Clean, unpretentious and excellent value for money. Certainly worthy of recommendation.'

Open Mon to Sat 9.30am to 5 Table service upstairs. Counter service downstairs. Tables outside. Vegan dishes. Other diets catered for on request. Snacks. Take-aways. Wheelchair access. Access, Visa

CALVERTON Nottinghamshire MAP 7

Patchings Farm Art Centre £

Oxton Road TEL Nottingham (0602) 653479

Follow the signposts from the A614 to find the restaurant in the farm art centre, where vegetarians will sometimes find fancifully named home-made dishes such as Pearl's pastie (cheese and onion stuffing in pastry), groom's slice (a nut dish) and country casserole. The rural English theme continues with Auntie Betty's supper (home-made fruitcake with Stilton cheese and a glass of cider or apple juice), cream teas, bread-and-butter pudding, and tipsy trifle. English fruit wines are available; all wines stocked are produced without the use of chemical weedkillers, fertilisers or pesticides.

Open all week 9 to 10 **Closed** 25 and 26 Dec Booking advisable. Table service. Tables outside. Licensed. Meat dishes. Vegan dishes. Other diets catered for on request. Take-aways. No smoking. Wheelchair access. Access

CAMBERLEY Surrey MAP 2

Pizza Express £

52 Park Street TEL Camberley (0276) 21846

A satellite of the excellent London-based chain that was founded twenty-five years ago. See London entry.

Open Mon to Sat 11.30 to midnight, Sun noon to 11.30. Table service. Licensed, also bring your own: corkage £2.50. Meat dishes. Fish dishes. Take-aways. No-smoking area. Wheelchair access. Access, Amex, Diners, Visa

CAMBRIDGE Cambridgeshire MAP 5

Browns ££

23 Trumpington Street TEL Cambridge (0223) 461655

Busy, bright and lively, the Cambridge branch of Browns is popular and seems to please. Vegetarians don't have a wide choice, but this is compensated for by sound food and capable cooking in the kitchen. Lasagne noodles layered with cheese and ratatouille have been reported as bubbling and well seasoned, the pasta al dente, the cheese mellow, and the ratatouille unoily. Mrs Brown's vegetarian salad proves to be a riotous combination of fresh fruit and vegetables, marinated pulses, nuts, raisins and olives with a choice of dressings. There is also a vegetarian dish chalked up on the board of daily specials. Service is young, cheerful and prompt enough in view of the bustle. A student haunt where animated conversations are accompanied by recorded jazz.

Open all week 11am to 11.30pm **Closed** 24–26 Dec Table service. Tables outside. Licensed. Corkage £1. Meat dishes. Vegan dishes. Snacks. No-smoking areas. Wheelchair access. Access, Amex, Visa

Hobbs Pavilion £

Park Terrace TEL Cambridge (0223) 67480

No relation to the adjacent Hobson's, this former cricket pavilion on the edge of Parker's Piece is essentially a crêperie. Ingredients are good and there's an enterprising selection of vegetarian fillings. Soup is usually vegetarian as are some main-course salads, for example, mixed salad leaves topped with wholemeal pasta spirals with sliced button mushrooms cooked in curry, ginger and turmeric. Of the puddings, try the home-made and tangy lemon cheesecake. Orange, grapefruit and lemon juice are freshly squeezed. This is somewhere to come and relax over a meal: the day's papers are provided and service is friendly and efficient. Water and glasses are brought to the table on arrival – a nice touch.

Open Tue to Sat noon to 2.30, 7 (8.30 Thur) to 10 **Closed** mid-Aug to mid-Sept Table service. Tables outside. Licensed. Meat dishes. Fish dishes. Other diets catered for on request. No-smoking area.

King's Pantry Ⓥ £–££

9 King's Parade TEL Cambridge (0223) 321551

The Pantry's situation – in the centre, opposite King's College – could hardly be better, even though it's in a basement. This strictly vegetarian restaurant is very popular. Lunches offer casseroles, salads and wholesome cakes. Cream teas, complete with cucumber sandwiches, are available. Evenings, with tablecloths and candlelight, deliver a set-price menu with two main dishes (oh dear! pasta and moussaka) or an à la carte menu which has more tempting suggestions, such as a terrine, asparagus mousse, croquette noissette or pipérade. Vegans are well catered for generally and the sorbet is specifically vegan. All cheese is vegetarian. Hungry early in the morning? The café opens at 8am.

Open all week L noon to 5.30, Wed to Sat D 7 to 9.30 **Closed** 25 Dec Booking advisable D. Table service. Licensed, but bring your own: corkage £2. Vegan dishes. Other diets catered for. Snacks at other times. Take-aways. Access, Visa

Myttons £–£££

Jesus Lane TEL Cambridge (0223) 324033

What was a Turkish bath is now a posh brass and velvet restaurant with sporting prints on the walls, and a less formal brasserie. The restaurant menu cannot be relied upon always to list a vegetarian main dish, but the brasserie has several options – ratatouille, pasta, cheesy potatoes and carrot timbale, for instance, on a menu that makes no distinctions between main dishes and starters. This means that the bill can be very modest. Daily specials listed on the blackboard will usually include one vegetarian dish, well executed: home-made green tagliatelle with half a roasted aubergine was 'cooked to perfection'. Finish with highly rated toffee pudding or strawberry mousse with wild strawberries, for example.

Open all week 11am to 3, 6 to 11, exc Sun D **Closed** 3 days after Christmas Booking advisable in restaurant. Table service. Tables outside. Licensed. Meat dishes. Fish dishes. Vegan dishes. Other diets catered for on request. Snacks at other times. Wheelchair access. Access, Amex, Diners, Visa

Nettles Ⓥ £

6 St Edwards Passage TEL Cambridge (0223) 872419

Tiny and primarily a take-away. The food, though, is good value and much appreciated by the clientele: both a vegetable curry and an apple crumble have been relished. A valuable place to know about.

Open Mon to Sat 9 to 8, L from 11.30 **Closed** 23–27 Dec; bank hols Counter service. Vegan dishes. Other diets catered for on request. Snacks. Take-aways

Pizza Express £

28 St Andrews Street TEL Cambridge (0223) 61320

A satellite of the excellent London-based chain that was founded twenty-five years ago. See London entry.

Open Mon to Sat 11.30 to midnight, Sun noon to 11.30. Table service. Licensed, also bring your own: corkage £2.50. Meat dishes. Fish dishes. Take-aways. No-smoking area. Wheelchair access. Access, Amex, Diners, Visa

Twenty Two £££

22 Chesterton Road TEL Cambridge (0223) 351880

'The food was the best we tried in Cambridge: good ingredients, everything home made with attention to taste, quality and presentation. We will go back.' Given the dearth of upmarket places providing a vegetarian main dish, this is a useful recommendation. The restaurant is an end-of-terrace house near the river; light classical music plays and tables are laid with pink cloths, candles and flowers. A short menu on a typical day offers mushroom and hazelnut soup or deep-fried Camembert, followed by vegetable goulash with potatoes. A complimentary salad makes a welcome refresher between courses. Sorbets are good. Service is pleasant and efficient.

Open Tue to Sat, D 7.30 to 9.30 **Closed** 1 week Christmas Booking advisable. Table service. Licensed, but bring your own: corkage £3. Meat dishes. Fish dishes. Other diets on request. Take-aways. No children under 12. Access, Visa

Upstairs £££

71 Castle Street TEL Cambridge (0223) 312569

One reporter describes the menu as a 'complex brew' of authentic Middle Eastern dishes. Above Waffles, this tiny enterprise is unique in its dedication to ethnic cuisine. As well as predictable hummus and tabouleh are starters such as leeks dressed in lime juice, olive oil and tarragon, followed by main dishes that might be a tajine of peppers and courgettes oven-baked in an egg and parmesan cheese base, or a badeny mahshi min tamar of aubergine filled with nuts and dates, or a combination of kizi inzi – stuffed vegetables – leeks and walnuts oven-baked in a spicy egg base, then sprinkled with pine kernels. Spicing is discreet.

Open all week, D 6.30 to 10.15 Booking advisable. Table service. Licensed. Meat dishes. Fish dishes. Vegan dishes. No-smoking area. No children

Waffles £

71 Castle Street TEL Cambridge (0223) 312569

A waffle-lover's paradise! There is nothing but waffles on the menu, but they come with either sweet or savoury toppings, which vary daily. The place is small, and suitable for a quick meal.

Open Tue to Sun 6.30 to 11, Sun L 9.30 to 2 **Closed** 2 weeks Sept Table service. Licensed. Meat dishes. No smoking

'Wheelchair access' indicates that, according to the proprietor, entrances are at least 33 inches wide, passages 4 feet wide, and that there are a maximum of two steps, unless otherwise stated.

CANTERBURY Kent MAP 3

George's Brasserie £–£££

71–72 Castle Street TEL Canterbury (0227) 765658

Open at the start of the day for coffee and croissants, the brasserie comes up with such dishes for vegetarians as goats' cheese tarts, wild mushroom tart and home-made pasta with pesto. Warm Stilton tartlet gets a favourable mention. Portions are enormous. Be prepared for some lengthy delays – even in ordering.

Open all week 11.30am to 10 (10.30 Fri and Sat) Table service. Licensed, also bring your own: corkage £2.50. Meat dishes. Fish dishes. Vegan dishes. Other diets catered for on request. Snacks. Take-aways. No-smoking area. Wheelchair access. Access, Amex, Visa

Mother Earth £–££

34 St Peter's Street TEL Canterbury (0227) 463175

A tea-room-type café that prides itself on the 200 varieties of tea it provides. Although not exclusively vegetarian, suitable lunch dishes could be soup, curry, or mushroom bake.

Open all week 10 to 5.30 **Closed** 24 to 26 Dec Table service. Tables outside. Licensed. Vegan dishes. Snacks. Wheelchair access

CARLISLE Cumbria MAP 10

Grapevine £

22 Fisher Street TEL Carlisle (0228) 46617

When in Carlisle, vegetarians do not have a lot of choice! The Grapevine, however, run with Christian commitment, has a menu on the lines of pizza, lasagne, pasta verde with cheese in cream hazelnut sauce, sweet-and-sour vegetables, pasties, nut roast and various salads. The menu marks with an asterisk items suitable for vegetarians; by a slip of the system, smoky bacon quiche has been included. Sticky toffee pudding is a speciality. There's a good selection of scones, cakes and biscuits.

Open Mon to Sat 11 to 4.30 Counter service. Unlicensed. Meat dishes. Snacks. Take-aways. No-smoking area

CASTLE ACRE Norfolk **MAP** 8

Ostrich Inn £

TEL Castle Acre (076 05) 398

A visit to what one reporter claims is 'the most romantic village in England' could be made memorable with a meal at this unpretentious pub. Chairs and tables are an eclectic mix and the old beams and fireplaces have not been glamorised. Vegetarians will always find a home-made pizza plus home-cooked specials. Crumble turned out to be a well-seasoned mix of leeks, carrots and celery with a crunchy peanut topping; spinach and almond lasagne was equally good, the tomato base to the sauce tasting fresh. Salads are generous, fresh and imaginative, for example, a minty kasha and light and creamy coleslaw. Tempting sweets include a nutty filo. Very good value.

Open all week noon to 2, 7 to 10.30 **Closed** 25 Dec Table service. Tables outside. Licensed. Meat dishes. Fish dishes. Other diets catered for on request. Take-aways. Accommodation

CASTLE CARY Somerset **MAP** 2

Old Bakehouse ⓥ £

High Street **TEL** Castle Cary (0963) 50067

Found at the top of the narrow High Street, this wholefood shop and café has a pleasant, homely atmosphere and turns out what is described as 'early Cranks-style' wholefood. Mushroom croustade, curry, pizza, lentil rissoles with tomato sauce, lentil cakes, salads and soups all are obviously home made, if sometimes on the bland side. Allow room for a sweet since the cook obviously enjoys making the popular toffee date pudding, coffee fudge flan and others, all served with a very thick dollop of Somerset cream. Delicious selection of ice-creams.

Open Tue to Sat 11 to 5 Booking advisable. Table service. Tables outside. Licensed. Other diets catered for on request. Snacks. Take-aways. No smoking

CASTLETON North Yorkshire MAP 10

Lion Inn £

Blakey Ridge TEL Lastingham (075 15) 320

Hikers and others can find a welcome break in the North York Moors National Park and indulge in a meal in either the restaurant or the bar of this remote and dramatically situated pub on the top of the moors, on Blakey Ridge between Hutton le Hole and Castleton. A full vegetarian all-day menu offers seven main dishes that come in generous portions, for example lasagne, pine kernel and cashew-nut loaf, or a vegetarian hot-pot.

Open all week noon to 10 Table service. Licensed. Meat dishes. Vegan dishes. Other diets catered for on request. Take-aways. Wheelchair access. Accommodation

CAULDON LOWE Staffordshire MAP 7

Old School Restaurant £

Staffordshire Peak Arts Centre
TEL Waterhouses (0538) 308431

The good home cooking attracts regulars for home-made soup, egg mayonnaise and cheese and pepper starter, and three vegetarian main dishes – perhaps mushroom burgers, homity pie and cashew-nut and celery loaf. There's also a local speciality: Staffordshire oatcakes with fillings ranging from plain cheese to mushroom and garlic, or tomatoes, onions and chilli. Drinks include Disos wine, with no added sugar, as well as English fruit wines such as damson, plum, gooseberry, and raspberry. Afternoon teas with scones and cream or high teas are available. The Peak Arts Centre is worth a visit for its contemporary craft and fine art displayed in the Old School.

Open all week noon to 2.30, Thur to Sat 6 to 9 Booking advisable Sun and D. Table service. Tables outside. Licensed. Meat dishes. Vegan dishes. Other diets catered for on request. Snacks. No smoking. Wheelchair access. Accommodation. Access, Visa

All letters to the guide are acknowledged.

CHAGFORD Devon **MAP** 1

Teignworthy Hotel £££

Frenchbeer TEL Chagford (0647) 33355

When approaching from Chagford, take the Fernworthy road and go one mile, then turn right to Thornworthy to discover this charming, Lutyens-style country house. The vegetarian main course is a fixture on the menu: it might be stir-fried vegetables in a sweet-and-sour sauce with brown rice; asparagus and wild mushroom tartlet with morel butter sauce or a vegetable feuilleté with saffron cream sauce. The choice of starters might include a cream of pumpkin and tarragon soup or a hot spinach gateau with beurre blanc and girolles. Sweets may perhaps be 'over-rich' – which could be construed as praise by some – for example poached pear and almond cream tart with vanilla sauce, or iced nougatine parfait with raspberry coulis. Good local cheeses.

Open all week 12.15 to 1.45, 7.15 to 9 Booking advisable. Table service. Tables outside. Licensed. Meat dishes. Fish dishes. Other diets catered for on request. No smoking in dining-room. No children under 10. Wheelchair access. Accommodation. Access, Visa

CHATHAM Kent **MAP** 3

Food for Living Eats ⓥ £

116 High Street TEL Medway (0634) 409291

At the back of a wholefood shop, the little green-and-white vegetarian café is a haven of real food – somewhere you can feel positively cared for amid the anonymous chainstore-land of the High Street. Shoppers take advantage of the array of cakes and muffins. At lunchtime, as well as such fare as burgers, lasagne, falafel and pizzas, are dishes of the day: a vegetable chilli with salad and pitta has honest chunks of carrot, courgette and aubergine in a commercial-tasting sauce, and an astonishing selection of salads – tabouleh, curried rice and peas, pasta whirls, coleslaw, rice, carrot and sunflower seeds. Excellent value. Only free-range eggs and vegetarian Cheddar are used. Vegans get much consideration.

Open Mon to Sat 9am to 4.30 Counter service. Unlicensed. Vegan dishes. Snacks. Take-aways. No smoking. Wheelchair access. Access, Visa

CHAWTON Hampshire MAP 2

Cassandra's Cup £

TEL Alton (0420) 83144

Dream yourself back to the eighteenth century in the busy tea-room over the road from Jane Austen's house. In summer the kitchen staff work flat out, but the food does not suffer, and for a light lunch or tea this is an ideal place. The cakes are home made, and the puddings outstanding – try pecan pie or blackcurrant and apple crumble. There are three vegetarian meals on the menu – typical examples are macaroni cheese, spring vegetables in cream sauce or spinach and mushroom lasagne. Cards, crafts and gifts are for sale adjoining the tea-rooms.

Open all week L to 2.30 (Wed to Sun in winter; Sat, Sun only in Jan) **Closed** 1 week at Christmas Booking advisable in summer. Table service. Tables outside. Licensed. Meat dishes. Fish dishes. Other diets catered for on request. Smoking discouraged. Wheelchair access exc wc

CHELMSFORD Essex MAP 5

Pizza Express £

219 Moulsham Street TEL Chelmsford (0245) 491466

A satellite of the excellent London-based chain that was founded twenty-five years ago. See London entry.

Open Mon to Sat 11.30 to midnight, Sun noon to 11.30. Table service. Licensed, also bring your own: corkage £2.50. Meat dishes. Fish dishes. Take-aways. No-smoking area. Wheelchair access. Access, Amex, Diners, Visa

CHELTENHAM Gloucestershire MAP 4

Moran's Eating House ££

127–129 Bath Road TEL Cheltenham (0242) 581411

An informal restaurant where a vegetarian could have a lunch or dinner along the lines of pickled pear and Brie salad, Stilton puffs with home-made apple chutney, or avocado with celery, apple and walnuts in a curry mayonnaise; followed by broccoli pancakes with Stilton and walnut sauce, Italian courgette and tomato casserole with fresh Parmesan or stuffed aubergines with garlic crumble topping.

Open Mon to Sat 11.30 to 2, 6.30 to 10.30, exc Mon L Table service. Licensed. Meat dishes. Vegan dishes and other diets catered for with prior notice. Wheelchair access

Pizza Piazza £

6–7 Montpellier Street TEL Cheltenham (0242) 221845

A branch of a growing chain that offers an enterprising choice of reliably good pizzas. See entry under New Malden for more detail.

Open all week noon to 11 Table service. Licensed. No-smoking area. Wheelchair access. Access, Visa

CHESTER Cheshire MAP 7

Abbey Green Ⓥ ★ £–££

2 Abbey Green, Northgate Street TEL Chester (0244) 313251

One would never stumble across Abbey Green, tucked away as it is down a slightly sleazy alley off Northgate Street facing an untidy patch of greenery. Inside the period double-fronted house all is peace, comfort and efficiency. Word of mouth has spread its reputation for excellent vegetarian cuisine and so plenty of customers find their way here. The impression is Victorian: sprigged wallpaper and dark sideboard with floral tablecloths in the dining-room and low chairs, an old fireplace and piano in the lounge. The food is outstanding: an extensive menu for lunch gives way to an even more extensive dinner menu, and prices are remarkably reasonable, particularly for lunch. 'Where's the complaints book – I want to complain that it's too cheap!' exclaimed one satisfied customer. At lunchtime starters might consist of tart black-olive pâté served with wholegrain bread, rightly without butter, or spiced garlic mushrooms with cider. The selection of main dishes might be carrot, apple and cashew-nut loaf with a tangy plum sauce; chilli and tofu burgers; Feta cheese and spinach strudel or a good, creamy mushroom and aubergine stroganoff with white wine served on spicy, gingery brown rice. Four kinds of salad or a baked potato are available as side dishes. In the evening, perhaps there will be warm Camembert and fruit salad or baby vegetables with an apricot sweet-and-sour sauce to start. If choice is difficult for the main course, a good decision might be the Abbey Green platter, which is a selection of what's on the menu – for example, sweet chestnut roll, avocado en croûte, stuffed tomatoes. On the sideboard are the desserts: sherry trifle, a fruit 'crackle' crumble with a cornflake base, and an apricot and lemon cheesecake which, despite its wizened appearance, tastes excellent. This is undoubtedly one of the best vegetarian restaurants in the country, not surprisingly a winner of the Vegetarian Society's Restaurant of the Year award. Worth making a long journey to visit.

Open Mon to Sat exc Mon D, noon to 2.30, 6.30 to 10 Booking advisable. Table service. Tables outside. Licensed. Vegan dishes. Other diets catered for on request. No smoking in dining-room. Wheelchair access. Access

Blue Bell ££

65 Northgate Street TEL Chester (0244) 317758

The Blue Bell's claim to fame is as Chester's oldest surviving domestic structure and only medieval inn. The building is lopsided, half-timbered and full of antique furniture, inglenooks and polished brass. The ambience, with discreet lighting and candle-lit tables is delightful. Service is courteous, and there is always one vegetarian dish on both the lunch and dinner menus. One reporter found the fennel and tomato ravioli 'tasted like school suet pudding'. However, other dishes, such as melon balls and mango sorbet, Stilton and pear quiche and mushrooms in madeira sauce with mille-feuille worked well.

Open Mon to Sat noon to 2.30, 7 to 10 Booking advisable. Table service. Tables outside. Licensed. Meat dishes. Fish dishes. Vegan dishes and other diets catered for with prior notice. Snacks. No-smoking area. Access, Visa

Francs ££

14 Cupin Street TEL Chester (0244) 317952

The modest frontage belies the pleasantly spacious interior of a self-consciously French café. The menu takes itself a mite seriously with its 'amuse-gueule du chef' and 'marmites de notre grandmère'. Vegetarians might choose to start with a salad of Roquefort, walnuts and melon, and go on to organic vegetable gratin or noissetine, a combination of vegetables, hazelnut pâté and fromage frais in pastry. Young fogeys and professionals congregate.

Open all week noon to 2.30, 6 to 11 Booking advisable. Table service. Licensed. Meat dishes. Fish dishes. Other diets catered for on request. Snacks at other times. Take-aways. Access, Amex, Visa

Marlborough Arms £

St John Street TEL Chester (0244) 23543

Chester's vegetarian scene is dominated by Abbey Green (see above), but if you want a reasonably priced pub meal, this could fit the bill. Vegetarian dishes are available at lunchtime only. Seating is on stools in the bar, rather closely packed around copper-topped tables. The walls are decorated with familiar jokey texts. There is a separate vegetarian menu of three dishes, such as chilli, bean and tomato casserole, nut roast, or vegetable chilli with rice.

Open Mon, Tue and Sat 11.30 to 4, 5.30 to 11 (6 Sat), Thur and Fri all day, Sun noon to 2, 7 to 10.30 Table service. Counter service. Licensed. Meat dishes. Vegan dishes. No children under 14. Wheelchair access

CHICHESTER West Sussex MAP 2

Clinchs Coffee Shop £

Guildhall Street TEL Chichester (0243) 789915

Choose your dish at the counter, then move to a larger room, furnished with round tables covered with floor-length tablecloths, with a large chintz-curtained window running the length of the room looking on to a conservatory. All food is cooked daily; savoury dishes are flans, crêpes, pasta, pizzas and salads. Cakes will suit all tastes – try the cheesecake, a Duke of Cambridge (with nuts, angelica, fruit, brown sugar and egg topping), Danish pastries or a chocolate cake with fudge icing and walnut bread.

Open Mon to Sat 8.30am to 5.30pm Counter service. Tables outside. Licensed. Meat dishes. Other diets on request. Snacks. Take-aways. No-smoking area. Wheelchair access. Access, Visa

Pizza Express £

27 South Street TEL Chichester (0243) 786648

A satellite of the excellent London-based chain that was founded twenty-five years ago. See London entry.

Open Mon to Sat 11.30 to midnight, Sun noon to 11.30. Table service. Licensed, also bring your own: corkage £2.50. Meat dishes. Fish dishes. Take-aways. No-smoking area. Wheelchair access. Access, Amex, Diners, Visa

St Martin's Tea-Rooms £

3 St Martins Street TEL Chichester (0243) 786715

To reach the tea-rooms, which are set in a typical period terraced house with a pretty garden, turn first left in East Street going from the Cross. Meals of a mainly vegetarian nature (with the addition of smoked salmon and gammon) are served all day. It is claimed that all food and drink is, as far as can be ascertained, free from artificial flavours, colours and preservatives. Savoury dishes, soups and cakes are made on the premises using organic produce and are wholefood as far as possible. Lunches consist of choices such as red dragon pie, vegetable goulash, mushroom courgette and bean bake.

Open Tue to Sat 10am to 6pm Table service. Order at counter. Tables outside. Licensed. Meat dishes. Fish dishes. Other diets catered for on request. Snacks. Take-aways. Smoking in garden only. Wheelchair access

Salad House/No. 13 ££

13 Southgate Street TEL Chichester (0243) 788822/776634

Sister establishments, of which Salad House opens in the day time and No. 13 in the evening. Both offer meat and vegetarian dishes cooked to wholefood principles. As well as the anticipated salads, the Salad House could come up with a lunch of cheese, apple and onion bake, lasagne, or moussaka. At No. 13, a meal might start with soup or walnut and Cheddar cheese balls, and go on to a bean gratiné or lasagne.

Open Salad House L Mon to Sat 11.45 to 2.30; No. 13 Tue to Sat D 5.30 to 8.30 (9.30 Sat) **Closed** bank hols Booking advisable. Table service. Licensed. Meat dish. Vegan dishes. Other diets catered for on request. Take-aways. No-smoking area. Access, Visa

CHILGROVE West Sussex MAP 2

White Horse Inn ££–£££

Chilgrove TEL East Marden (024 359) 219

Set between Chichester and Petersfield on the B2141, this inn with restaurant has drawn good reports for set-price lunches and higher-priced dinners. Lunch might offer fennel and tomato salad, ricotta and spinach pancakes with gnocchi as main courses and dinners often manage to escape the standard filo pastry purse. Instead there might be a spinach roulade or walnut pâté in pastry. Chilled sweet-corn soup or cream of French bean soup and home-made spinach ravioli with sage butter are among the initial courses at dinner. Ice-creams are home made and the meringue cake concoction has been described as 'yummy and unsophisticated'. Finish with coffee with Jersey cream and complimentary mint crisps.

Open Tue to Sat D 7 to 9.30, Sun L 12.15 to 1.45 **Closed** Feb Booking advisable. Table service. Tables outside. Licensed. Meat dishes. Other diets catered for on request. No pipes or cigars during meals. No children under 14. Wheelchair access. Access, Carte Blanche, Diners, Visa

CHIPPING CAMPDEN Gloucestershire MAP 4

Bakers Arms £

Broad Campden TEL Evesham (0386) 840515

Stone walls, beams and log fires, and an assortment of tables and chairs give plenty of rustic attraction to this country pub with, in pride of place, a rugwork picture of the building. The menu is gratifyingly marked with vegetarian 'v's: two kinds of lasagne, fettuccine, omelettes and chilli as well as a ploughman's.

Open all week noon to 2, 6 to 9.45 (7 to 8.45 Sun) Tables outside. Licensed. Meat dishes. Vegan dishes. No children after 9pm. Wheelchair access

CHIPPING NORTON Oxfordshire MAP 4

Nutters £

10 New Street TEL Chipping Norton (0608) 41995

The emphasis is on healthy eating for all, so the food is low in fat, sugar and salt, but high in fibre and with a careful eye on the vitamin and mineral content. The menu changes daily, everything being freshly made, and offers a variety of salads for self-selection, hot jacket potatoes or brown rice with various meat and vegetarian fillings, quiches and other main dishes such as broccoli with ginger or lentil casserole. Special slimmer's fruit cake, without fat or sugar, is undermined by a wickedly fattening chocolate fudge cake.

Open Tue to Sat 10 to 6 (5.30 Nov to Mar) Counter service. Tables outside. Licensed. Meat dishes. Other diets catered for on request. Snacks. Take-aways. No smoking. Wheelchair access

CHISWORTH Derbyshire MAP 7

Woodheys Farm ★ ££

Glossop Road TEL Glossop (045 74) 2704

From Marple Bridge take the A626 to Glossop; Chisworth is about a mile before Charlesworth and the restaurant is just after a dangerous bend in the road. The Farm perched high above the heavily wooded Etherow Valley must surely have one of the loveliest and most spectacular restaurant sites in the region: sitting inside and looking out is like viewing from the air. The old farm buildings have been tastefully developed and smartly modernised in light brown with stained brown panelling. Though meat is much in evidence, vegetarians have a choice of three dishes which could be mushroom croustade, leek and walnut croûtes or aubergine chasseur. One diner found his vegetable soup perfectly balanced with carrot, turnip and celery, accompanied by a still warm wholewheat bap; his aubergine chasseur was rendered successful by the rich, tomato-thickened, red wine sauce, served with excellent vegetables. Try goodies such as syllabub, sherry trifle or fruit salad.

Open Tue to Sat noon to 2 (exc Sun L), 7 to 10 **Closed** 4 days Jan Booking advisable. Table service. Tables outside. Licensed, also bring your own: corkage £2. Meat dishes. Vegan dishes. Other diets catered for on request. No-smoking area. Wheelchair access. Access, Visa

CHULMLEIGH Devon MAP 1

Eggesford Garden Centre £

Eggesford TEL Chulmleigh (0769) 80250

Offers humble fare, but very fresh. There's a cold salad buffet and always two or three specials for vegetarians – quiche, homity pie or pasties. Prices are low. Home-baked teas are a delight.

Open all week, L noon to 2 Table service on request. Counter service. Tables outside. Licensed. Meat dishes. Snacks. Take-aways. Wheelchair access. Access, Visa

CHURCH STRETTON Shropshire MAP 6

Acorn £

26 Sandford Avenue TEL Church Stretton (0694) 722495

By day a small and homely café, by night a restaurant where you can dine at leisure, this is a place to find good-value wholefood. Lunches might produce bulgur wheat and lentil pilau, minted field-bean casserole or oven-baked spaghetti; dinners might yield bean pâté or grape, melon and tomato vinaigrette followed by chilli-bean casserole or provençale bean stew. Good home-made blackberry and apple pie shares billing with specialities of baklava, apple strudel and wholemeal scones.

Open all week, exc Tue, mid-Oct to Easter, 9.30am to 5.30 (10 to 6 Sun); all week exc Sat D (by arrangement) Easter to mid-Oct 10am to 6 **Closed** 2 weeks Nov Booking advisable D. Table service. Counter service. Tables outside. Unlicensed, but bring your own: corkage 99p. Meat dishes. Vegan dishes. Other diets catered for on request. Take-aways. No-smoking area

A restaurant must display a menu and a wine list outside, or immediately inside the door. Prices shown must be inclusive of VAT. If they aren't, tell the local Trading Standards Officer.

CIRENCESTER Gloucestershire MAP 4

Coffee House £

Brewery Court, Cricklade Street TEL Cirencester (0285) 654791

Up the wooden stairs in the Arts Workshops, the Coffee House provides a predominantly vegetarian daily menu. Starters of pâté – avocado, aubergine or Stilton and walnut – or perhaps a soup (hot in winter and cold in summer), might be followed by quiche; jacket potato; risotto; mushroom stroganoff; broccoli and ginger gratin; florentine cheesecake or chestnut pie. Desserts include a rich chocolate and almond crunch cake, plum and banana brûlée, rich chocolate mousse, plus the various home-made cakes and scones that are available throughout the day.

Open Mon to Sat 10 to 5.15, L 12 to 2 Counter service. Licensed. Meat dishes. Other diets catered for on request. Snacks. Take-aways. No smoking

CLEVELEYS Lancashire MAP 7

Cleveleys Wholefood & Vegetarian Restaurant ⓥ ★ £

44 Victoria Road West TEL Cleveleys (0253) 865604

Above the Health from Herbs shop, which also sells take-away dishes, is a long, narrow restaurant papered in Laura Ashley style, with a coal fire and aspirations beyond those of many vegetarian cafés. Lunches during the week offer straightforward dishes such as tomato and hazelnut cannelloni; vegetable crumble, hazelnut loaf, chestnut and orange pâté and Armenian soup. Friday evening, however, is when the restaurant is at its best, with a different menu every week: two starters, three main dishes and sweets from the trolley (three courses represent very good value). A sample dinner began with a watercress, mushroom and walnut roulade, acceptable if slightly overpowered by mushroom flavour; and continued with a 'formidable' and authentically exotic vegetable korma on saffron rice, and a layered terrine, of cheese, celery, onions and tomato. The dessert trolley offers puddings on the lines of gooseberry cheesecake, strawberry and nut meringue, lemon mousse, a gingery choux ring and a banana roll with tangy lemon cream centre.

Open Tue to Sun 11.30 to 4.45, Fri D 6.30 to 8.45 Table service. Licensed. Vegan dishes. Snacks. Take-aways. No smoking

CLUN Shropshire MAP 4

Old Post Office £££

9 The Square TEL Clun (058 84) 687

The original post office is one dining area and additional space in a new conservatory at the back has splendid views. A short menu yields a vegetarian starter – perhaps terrine of baby leeks served with hazelnut vinaigrette – followed by a main dish of baked Mediterranean tomato filled with nuts and wrapped in filo on a bed of vegetables with teriyaki sauce. The cooking is first-rate and accompanying vegetables can't be bettered. To follow try a sharp lemon tart, a chocolate terrine with refreshing mango coulis or one of the excellent range of English and Welsh cheeses. The home-made bread should not be missed.

Open Wed to Sat D 7.15 to 9.30 (8.30 Sun), L by arrangement **Closed** mid-Jan to mid-Mar Booking advisable. Table service. Tables outside. Licensed. Meat dishes. Fish dishes. Other diets catered for on 24-hours' request. Wheelchair access. Snacks at lunchtime. Accommodation. Access, Visa

COCKERMOUTH Cumbria MAP 9

Quince & Medlar Ⓥ ★ ££

13 Castlegate TEL Cockermouth (0900) 823579

In a tall period house beside the castle is one of the best vegetarian restaurants in the UK, its merits borne out by full tables and heavy bookings. Walking in, you would not think it vegetarian: there's not a stripped pine table in sight; instead the atmosphere is Victorian, with Laura Ashley-style wallpaper, pretty patterned carpet, linen tablecloths, candles and fresh flowers on each table. There are even flowers and bowls of pot-pourri in the charming loos, down a winding stone stair in what was presumably the old kitchen – a black range stands in the passageway. Almost everything, say the proprietors, is made on the premises, from wholegrain rolls to ice-cream; the only exceptions are wine and butter. It is difficult indeed to choose from such a superb menu: hazelnut and mushroom pâté in puff pastry; chilled carrot, apricot and orange soup; grapefruit, melon and orange medley; tomato pesto soup; an egg gnocchi parisienne and a warm asparagus salad, which arrives beautifully arranged with baby corn, baby tomatoes and mixed leaves, the asparagus and mange-tout just warm. Six main dishes continue the inventiveness: parsnip and cashew terrine; cheese and leek roulade; aubergine and courgette timbale and a seed and nut ring more like a small tart, tasty, crisp and filled with vegetables. Accompanying vegetables are a triumph: cauliflower in white sauce, baby potatoes, French beans in a courgette slice ring and swede with sesame seeds (the last not quite sufficient a delicacy to overcome some prejudices against swedes). Save space for the delights to follow: apricot syllabub, pear frangipane or a chewy brown bread ice-cream in a crisp brandysnap basket with a small pool of custard sauce. Tea ('Which variety would you prefer?') and coffee are served with a home-made biscuity chocolate. For great food, delightful surroundings and excellent service it is almost unbeatable.

Open Tue to Sun D only, 7pm to 9.30pm **Closed** 3 weeks Jan Booking advisable. Table service. Licensed, but bring your own: corkage £2.50. Vegan dishes. Other diets catered for on request. No smoking. No children under 5. Access, Visa

COLCHESTER Essex MAP 5

Warehouse Brasserie ££

Chapel Street TEL Colchester (0206) 765656

Directions and parking suggestions are essential: park in the multi-storey at the top of Balkerne Hill, cross the dual carriageway at the lights and walk down past the T-junction. The restaurant draws praise for both vegetarian and meat cooking and is reckoned to be excellent value for money. It's heartening to find a kitchen that really thinks about its vegetarian food: typical are bitkis in tomato sauce with fresh pasta, bitkis being little savoury patties made with nuts and fresh herbs. Main courses come either in 'light' or 'main' portions and the three or four daily specials always include vegetarian ones. Falafel or twice-baked cheese soufflés might be the light dishes and curried nut roast, stuffed field mushrooms or aubergine au gratin the main ones. Bread is home made. If you can resist mud pie – rich chocolate mousse on a chocolate-biscuit base with cream and grated chocolate – then perhaps you might try the highly rated steamed date pudding with vanilla custard.

Open Mon to Sat noon to 2, 7 to 10.30 **Closed** 23 Dec to 2 Jan Booking advisable. Licensed. Meat dishes. Other diets catered for on request. Snacks at other times. Wheelchair access. Access, Visa

COLNBROOK Buckinghamshire MAP 4

Ostrich Inn ££

High Street TEL Slough (0753) 682628

Just over a mile from M4 junction 5. Colnbrook being on the old road west from London, it has long been serving up food to travellers; there has been an inn on the site of the Ostrich since Norman times. The present building conforms to the image of the traditional English pub in almost picturebook fashion with its Elizabethan façade, the coaching entry into the courtyard, heavy beams, log fireplaces and antique furniture. Vegetarians can find starters of cheese and port pâté, or celery soup. Main dishes of stuffed peppers or mushroom stroganoff, followed by bread and butter pudding, might be a sample meal on offer.

Open all week noon to 2.25, 6 to 10.30 Booking advisable. Table service. Licensed. Meat dishes. Fish dishes. Vegan dishes and other diets catered for on request. Snacks. Access, Amex, Diners, Visa

CONGRESBURY Avon MAP 1

Paddingtons £

Broad Street TEL Yatton (0934) 838908

Useful for a light lunch: the choice might include salads, jacket potatoes, nut roast, millet and cheese fissole, leek and egg gratin, cassoulet, and many of the more traditional choices such as mushroom pancakes, quiche and ratatouille. Everything is freshly cooked each day. The menu changes daily and is chalked on a blackboard on the wall. Home-made cakes and crumbles to finish.

Open Mon to Sat L noon to 2.30 Table service. Counter service. Licensed. Meat dishes. Vegan dishes. Other diets catered for on request. Snacks at other times. Take-aways. Wheelchair access

The main criterion for inclusion in the guide is that an eating place offers a vegetarian main course on its standard menu, at all times, that is more than just an omelette, quiche or salad. If you find that a listed restaurant no longers caters for vegetarians, please inform the guide; the address to write to is on page 9.

CORBRIDGE Northumberland **MAP** 10

Ramblers ££

Farnley **TEL** Hexham (0434) 632424

A far-flung outpost of German cuisine may seem an unlikely spot for vegetarians, judging by what the home country offers the visitor, but four main dishes of some originality include a broccoli soufflé topped with hollandaise sauce, almonds and asparagus surrounded by rice, and onion mousse rolled in a pancake and baked in tomato sauce. Starters are also unusual: small cheese fritters with almonds, cream of courgette soup with mint, or a vegetarian pâté of lentils and pistachios. The menu is in German with full English descriptions.

Open Tue to Sat 7 to 10, L by prior arrangement Booking advisable. Table service. Licensed. Meat dishes. Fish dishes. Other diets catered for on request. Wheelchair access. Access, Amex, Diners, Visa

CORSE LAWN Gloucestershire **MAP** 4

Corse Lawn House Hotel ★ ££–£££

Corse Lawn **TEL** Tirley (045 278) 479

On a summer's day, tables are laid outside by the duck pond that faces the Queen Anne house. The atmosphere is welcoming, not at all intimidating, and an unusually extensive vegetarian menu lists five starters and six main dishes. All have been well thought out: terrine of wild mushrooms with soy and madeira or hot mousseline of vegetables with beurre blanc, for example, as starters; croustade of baby sweetcorn or brochette of mixed vegetables with saffron rice to follow. Generous portions of vegetables accompany main dishes. Salads are modern-style mixed leaves, well dressed with walnut oil. Of the old-fashioned puddings, butterscotch sponge and toffee ice-cream, hot passion-fruit soufflé and brochette of tropical fruit in brandy sauce have been praised. Presentation and service all contribute to making this a place for a special meal or an overnight stay – sample mangoes in lime juice for breakfast.

Open all week noon to 2, 7 to 10 Booking advisable. Table service. Tables outside. Licensed, also bring your own: corkage £2. Meat dishes. Fish dishes. Vegan dishes. Other diets catered for on request. No smoking in the dining-room. Wheelchair access. Accommodation. Access, Amex, Diners, Visa

COVENTRY West Midlands **MAP 4**

Cocked Hat ££

Rugby Road, Binley Woods TEL Coventry (0203) 440777/458004

The Cocked Hat continues to provide a selection of meals for vegans and vegetarians in the comfy old house that is also a hotel. The menu system is rather confusing: the so-called vegetarian menu is in fact a vegan one. It is extensive – there are usually five starters and six main dishes – sweet-and-sour stuffed peppers, curry, Cocked Hat special macaroni with sambal, nut cutlets, vegetable casserole and medallions of lentil, walnut and dill. Puddings include crêpes Suzette, Caribbean gateau or mandarine impériale.

Open all week noon to 2, 7 to 10 Booking advisable. Table service. Licensed. Meat dishes. Fish dishes. Vegan dishes. Other diets catered for on request. Snacks. Wheelchair access. Accommodation. Access, Amex, Diners, Visa

Ostlers £

166 Spon Street TEL Coventry (0203) 226603

The attractive building is in one of the last remaining old streets in Coventry. Crock-pots are a speciality, examples of which are vegetable goulash and a cheese and onion pie. The handwritten menu may supplement these with courgette crumble, broccoli bake, bean medley or pasta provençale. This is really somewhere for a convenient meal rather than a lengthy dinner.

Open Mon to Sat 11 to 10.30pm (11.30 Fri and Sat), Sun 7pm to 10.30 Booking advisable. Table service. Licensed. Meat dishes. Vegan dishes. Snacks. Wheelchair access. Access, Amex, Visa

The cost of a three-course vegetarian meal without wine is indicated by £ symbols to the right of the restaurant name:
£ = up to £7.50
££ = £7.50 to £15
£££ = £15 and over

CRANBROOK Kent MAP 3

Cranes ££

2 Waterloo Road TEL Cranbrook (0580) 712396

A cottagey, intimate and friendly restaurant in the attractive village of Cranbrook. One vegetarian dish, the same at lunch and dinner, is on the monthly menu – stuffed aubergine, avocado and chestnut bake or ratatouille in filo pastry basket.

Open Tue to Sat noon to 1.45, 7 to 10 **Closed** 1 week spring bank hol, 25 and 26 Dec Booking advisable. Table service. Licensed. Meat dishes. Fish dishes. Other diets catered for on request. Access, Visa

CRICKLADE Wiltshire MAP 2

Whites

93 High Street

As the Guide went to press, Whites closed and Colin White moved north to cook at Sharrow Bay, Ullswater, Cumbria.

CROYDON Surrey MAP 3

Hockneys Ⓥ ★ £–££

98 High Street TEL 081-688 2899

Apart from the fact that no alcohol is served, you might not guess that this is run as a Buddhist co-operative – the Buddhist centre is at the rear of the restaurant. Upstairs the large spacious room is stylish and modern with green rag-rolled walls, Patrick Proctor prints and stained wooden tables: at night the effect can be stark because of unsubtle overhead

A change of owner or chef may mean a change of menu policy. If a restaurant is no longer serving vegetarian food, please inform the guide; the address to write to is *on page 9.*

lighting. The menu changes daily, though some things are unvarying: falafels, quiches, samosas and veggieburgers, and also variations on the home-made rich ice-cream parfaits. Much the same is available at lunch and dinner, but the prices are higher and there is more choice at night. Starters might include melon, hummus, baked goats' cheese and a good thick potato and watercress soup or a garlicky pâté de campagne, mostly mushroom. There are at least three main courses, a typical selection being lasagne made of Brie, a good, spicy, fruit curry that comes with dhal and vegetable rice, and a mushroom brioche served as a slice from a large roll – a touch too much sage in it and, served with only cranberries and a crude heap of cucumber, something that could do with more outside interest. Alcohol may be proscribed as a drink – though you can bring your own – but it is a favourite flavouring in puddings – sherry trifle, and rum-and-raisin, brandy or crème de menthe parfaits.

Open Tue to Sat noon to 5.30, 5.30 to 10 Booking advisable Fri and Sat D. Table service D. Counter service L. Unlicensed, but bring your own: corkage £1 L, £1.50 D. Vegan dishes. Other diets catered for on request. Snacks. Take-aways. No smoking. Access, Amex, Diners, Visa

Karat £££

164 Cherry Orchard Road TEL 081-681 3402

This Thai family enterprise caters well for vegetarians, in deference to customers of the totally vegetarian restaurant that was previously on the site. Though there are several dishes with oyster sauce – and therefore not truly vegetarian – others are found to be excellent, beautifully prepared and 'gutsily spiced yet delicate at the same time.' The tiny restaurant is decorated dramatically with a pair of peacock feathers and other Thai hangings. A tom yum hed, hot-and-sour mushroom soup, tastes as good as it smells, a fine combination of lemon-grass, Thai basil and a kind of ginger; kang ped pak is a lightly cooked collection of vegetables in spicy curry sauce, and kao phad kai, egg-fried rice, has the

Under the Trade Descriptions Act, a restaurant must provide food and drink as described on the menu or by the waiter. If you think what you're served doesn't match the description, don't start eating. Complain immediately and ask for something else. You could also tell the local Trading Standards Officer that the restaurant is misleading customers.

same honest flavouring. The steamed banana pudding with sesame seeds is sugar-free.

Open Tue to Sun D 6.30 to 11 Booking advisable. Table service. Tables outside. Licensed. Meat dishes. Vegan dishes. Other diets catered for on request. Take-aways. No children under 5 Fri and Sat. Access, Visa

Kelong ££

1B Selsdon Road TEL 081-688 0726

The two rooms of the Malaysian/Singaporean restaurant have a pleasant ambience, and feature characteristic ceiling fans. The separate vegetarian menu – which reports say would easily do for two – represents 'staggeringly good value'. Start with a choice of soup or spring rolls served with three sauces. Then choose four main dishes from a list of ten, each portion gigantic. Finish with ice-cream or sorbet. At a sample meal an okra curry made with fresh okra was full flavoured; soy-flour omelette, rather like a large tortilla with bean sprouts and shredded cabbage, was good; sugar peas were crisp and green; noodles 'pleasant enough' but gado-gado disappointing.

Open Mon to Sat noon to 2.45, 6 to 10.45 **Closed** 2 weeks Aug Booking advisable. Table service. Licensed. Meat dishes. Fish dishes. Snacks at other times. Take-aways. Wheelchair access. Access, Amex, Diners, Visa

Pizza Express £

3 South End TEL 081-680 0123

A satellite of the excellent London-based chain that was founded twenty-five years ago. See London entry.

Open Mon to Sat 11.30 to midnight, Sun noon to 11.30. Table service. Licensed, also bring your own: corkage £2.50. Meat dishes. Fish dishes. Take-aways. No-smoking area. Wheelchair access. Access, Amex, Diners, Visa

The Vegetarian Good Food Guide *has been compiled in the same way as* The Good Food Guide *and is based on reports from consumers and anonymous inspections.*

Tiffin £–££

466 London Road TEL 081-683 4411

Don't be put off by a drab exterior to this Indian restaurant that is light and bright inside, with Indian paintings and ethnic music. In typical sub-continental fashion, the menu is split into vegetarian and non-vegetarian. Vegetarian tiffin for two is a set menu of starter, main course, side dishes, bread, sweet and coffee. Among these might be potato croquettes stuffed with peas, fried onion and sweetcorn served with a sweetish piquant sauce, channa masala. The à la carte dishes include good, crunchy, non-greasy samosas with that sweet-sour sauce. Both the makhani nan and onion kulchi – an onion-stuffed nan – are tasty. Palak paneer comes in a very spicy sauce, and the hot vegetable curry has a good consistency. One report says 'a hungry vegetarian could be satisfied here with only three dishes.'

Open all week noon to 3, 6.30 to midnight Booking advisable. Table service. Licensed, also bring your own: corkage £2. Meat dishes. Fish dishes. Take-aways. Wheelchair access. Access, Diners, Visa

DARLINGTON Co Durham MAP 10

Darlington Arts Centre Bistro £

Vane Terrace TEL Darlington (0325) 483271

Handy if you're visiting events at the arts centre, the bistro provides vegetarians with crêpes, curries, burgers and vegetable Mornay, though most of the menu is meat. A Christmas menu for vegetarians is a welcome touch.

Open Mon to Sat, exc Sat D, 11.30 to 2, 5.30 to 9 Counter service. Licensed. Meat dishes. Vegan dishes. Other diets catered for on request. Take-aways. No smoking. Wheelchair access. Accommodation. Access, Visa

Some restaurants have started to take customers' credit card numbers when they book and say that if they don't turn up, a charge will be made. As long as they tell you beforehand, restaurants are within their rights to do this. But the charge should only be reasonable compensation for their loss, not a penalty.

Victor's £

84 Victoria Road TEL Darlington (0325) 480818

Vegetarians are catered for only at lunchtime, so please note. The fare might be spiced mushroom tartlet with yoghurt and spring onion sauce or white nut rissoles.

Open Tue to Sat noon to 2.30, 7 to 10.30 Booking advisable. Table service. Licensed. Meat dishes. Other diets catered for on request. Wheelchair access. Access, Amex, Diners, Visa

DARTINGTON Devon MAP 1

Cranks ⓥ £

Cider Press Centre, Shinners Bridge TEL Totnes (0803) 862388

Opened by the Cranks team in the 1970s (see also London entry) and still providing the traditional, if rather solid, Cranks bill of fare: hearty soups, substantial salads, quiches, pizzas, baps, cakes and puddings. The rectangular room with its pine tables and chairs has a light, welcoming feel, and can get packed out at lunchtime. Part of the growing Cider Press Centre, where local craftspeople work as well as exhibit, and set by the River Dart; there are good riverside walks nearby.

Open Mon to Sat 10am to 5 Counter service. Tables outside. Licensed. Vegan dishes. Other diets catered for on request. Snacks. Take-aways. No smoking. Wheelchair access

DEBENHAM Suffolk MAP 5

Cretingham Bell £

Cretingham TEL Debenham (072 882) 419

The large attractive pub near Debenham has good jazz nights, for which booking might be advisable. There are a couple of vegetarian dishes available – a vegetable and pasta crumble that is more or less a fixture, and another dish that might be curry; starters might be home-made mushroom pâté and deep-fried jacket potato skins filled with cheese and onion sauce. Other dishes that have been enjoyed include garlic mushrooms, a very good vegetable and bean pie with peanut-butter pastry and home-made quiche. The proprietors are willing to make up vegan dishes when asked. Good-looking home-made apple and blackcurrant pie to follow.

Open all week noon to 2.30 (2 Sun), 7 to 9.30 (9 Sun) Booking advisable. Table service. Tables outside. Licensed. Meat dishes. Fish dishes. Vegan dishes and other diets catered for on request. Snacks. No-smoking area. Accommodation. Access, Visa.

DEDHAM Essex MAP 5

Marlborough Head Hotel £

Mill Lane TEL Colchester (0206) 323124 and 323250

Under the influence of a young woman vegetarian who works in the kitchen, two daily vegetarian dishes appear on the extensive menu at this pub/hotel: a typical day provides chestnut and mushroom bake and fried lentil croquettes with spicy tomato sauce. Both were found to be well cooked, well presented and made with fresh vegetables. 'A very good meal at a reasonable price.'

Open all week noon to 2, 7 to 10 **Closed** 25 and 26 Dec Counter service. Tables outside. Licensed. Meat dishes. Fish dishes. Wheelchair access. Accommodation

DENT Cumbria MAP 10

Dent Crafts Centre ★ ££

Helmside TEL Dent (058 75) 400

The old stone building in the picturesque Dentdale setting is run as a crafts shop selling local knitwear, pottery, jewellery and toys, as well as a coffee-shop and restaurant. During the day light snacks are served in this tasteful room with stone floor, natural stone and whitewashed walls, and oak tables. On Friday, Saturday and Sunday evenings there is an excellent four-course menu that always provides one vegetarian main dish out of the three, 'prepared with obvious consideration for flavour, texture and colour.' Everything is home made, except for brown and white baguettes that come from Limesdale Bakery. A typical menu starts with chef's salad or fruit cocktail, proceeds to a thick home-made vegetable soup or blackcurrant sorbet, then to a September pie of thin wholewheat pastry filled with tomatoes, courgettes, aubergine, beans and parsnips. Puddings usually feature one hot and two cold – often crumble in the first instance and an interesting fruit salad, cherry meringue or greengage cream in the second.

Open Tue to Sun D 7.30 to 8.30 June to Aug; Wed and Fri Sun D mid-Feb to June **Closed** Jan to mid-Feb Booking advisable. Table service. Licensed, but bring your own: corkage £1.50. Meat dishes. Other diets catered for on request. Snacks at other times. No-smoking in dining-room. Access, Visa

Stone Close £–££

Main Street TEL Dent (058 75) 231

This café also offers bed-and-breakfast accommodation and evening meals can be arranged. Otherwise, lunches give excellent value for money: start with tea-leaf eggs – a dish of marbled eggs subtly flavoured with tea, herbs and spices – potted cheese; follow with crispy mushroom layer, quiche or baked potato with filling. Apple pie is served in local manner with Wensleydale cheese: 'superb pastry, with slightly under-cooked pieces of apple that genuinely taste of apple'. If you do arrange dinner, you might have aubergine Parmesan, stuffed aubergine, leek and mushroom pie or vegetable and bean bake.

Open all week 10.30 to 5.30, D by arrangement **Closed** Jan, first 2 weeks Feb, Mon to Thur L Nov to Feb Booking advisable D. Table service. Licensed. Meat dishes. Other diets catered for on request. Snacks at other times. Wheelchair access. Accommodation

DERBY Derbyshire MAP 7

Calke Abbey £

Ticknall TEL Derby (0332) 864803

Converted by the National Trust from a byre and cattle shed, the restaurant is unexpectedly elegant and modern, lit by minimalist lighting. Local traditions and ingredients inform the cooking, particularly in the cake line – Derbyshire cold tea cake, short cake and Derby scones. Vegetarians can enjoy such dishes as Derbyshire carrot soup, mushroom and cream cheese pâté, tomato and parsnip bake. Sugar-free scones and banana cakes take their place alongside lots of sugar-rich ones. The

National Trust has a policy that cafés serving light lunches must offer a hot and a cold vegetarian dish. Lunch hours are designated as noon to 2 and tea as 2 to 5. One drawback is that you have to pay for admission to the abbey to get in.

Open all week exc Thur and Fri, 11am to 5 **Closed** Nov to Easter exc weekends Counter service. Tables outside. Licensed. Meat dishes. Snacks. Wheelchair access. Access, Visa

Footlights Bistro, Derby Playhouse £

Eagle Centre TEL Derby (0332) 363677

Theatre-goers and others may be pleased to know that, in addition to baked potatoes, there is always one vegetarian main dish on the menu here – it could be vegetable bake topped with Red Leicester, pasta or a good-value vegan burger; suitable starters could be Stilton and walnut loaf, crudités with a dip or garlic mushrooms.

Open Mon to Sat noon to 2, plus 6 to 11 when there's a performance Booking advisable. Table service. Counter service. Licensed. Meat dishes. Fish dishes. Vegan dishes. Other diets catered for on request. Snacks. Take-aways. No-smoking area. Wheelchair access. Access, Amex, Visa

Sarang ⓥ ££

14 Pear Tree Road TEL Derby (0332) 44815

'Refreshingly different' is part of the praise for this Indian wholefood vegetarian restaurant. It serves an extensive range, from chaats, pakoras, sobjis, bhajis, wholemeal chapatis, paratas and puris to the more rarely found marrow curry and a green turnip curry in special spiced sauce (tinda masala). Mixed bean bhaji, bhindi bhaji, vegetable samosas and also tikki have all been enjoyed. Don't ignore the puddings, as the halva of the day and the khir – a vermicelli-based pudding with raisins and almonds – have been regarded as 'highlights of the meal'.

Open Mon to Sat, D 6 to 10.30 (midnight Fri and Sat), L by arrangement Booking advisable. Table service. Licensed. Vegan dishes. Take-aways. Wheelchair access. Access, Visa

DEVIZES Wiltshire **MAP** 2

Wharfside £

13 Coach Lane TEL Devizes (0380) 6051

By the newly restored Kennet and Avon canal is a modern, brick-built development with numerous craft shops selling straw hats, wood-turned bowls and pot pourri. The café is part of the complex and also sells knick-knacks and watercolours. The food is home made, tasty and fresh, if not startlingly original. There's a salad buffet of beets, red cabbage, coleslaw, corn and bean sprouts, apple and celery, and greens, undressed. Hot dishes include cauliflower cheese, a tasty lasagne made with fresh tomatoes, mushrooms and celery with strong cheese, and a good spinach quiche. Desserts offer various cakes and a creamy strawberry roulade. Reasonably priced, and a good place for snacks or lunch, especially family outings.

Open Mon to Sat 9 to 4.30 (5 in summer), L noon to 2 **Closed** 24 Dec to 2 Jan Booking advisable. Counter service. Licensed, also bring your own: no corkage. Meat dishes. Fish dishes. Other diets catered for on request. Snacks. Take-aways. Wheelchair access

Wiltshire Kitchen £

11 St John's Street TEL Devizes (0380) 4840

The light, airy café has some six tables on the ground floor and more in the cellar downstairs. All food is prepared by the staff. A day's menu could yield potato and coriander or carrot and tomato soup; lasagne, moussaka, quiche and an innovative range of salads including brown rice in tomato sauce with mint and green peppers; celery, apple, grape, pumpkin seed, peanut and carrot; lettuce, nasturtium flowers, mint and other fresh herbs. Lasagne is hot, flavoursome and not overcooked. Roulades are the house speciality – try perhaps chocolate and rum, lemon and honey or a savoury watercress and orange. Other puddings might be blackberry and apple tart or fruit meringue nests. Good cakes and scones. Freshly squeezed orange juice and home-made lemonade to drink. Reliable and friendly.

Open Mon to Sat 9 to 5.30 **Closed** 1 week at Christmas Table service. Counter service. Tables outside. Licensed, also bring your own, corkage varies. Meat dishes. Fish dishes. Other diets catered for on request. Snacks. Take-aways. Wheelchair access

DORCHESTER Dorset MAP 2

Bridge Between ££

8 High East Street TEL Dorchester (0305) 68438

The proprietors call the cuisine 'traditional British with a hint of wholefood'. Examples of the vegetarian dishes are nut croquettes or spinach timbale to start, Tibetan roast or mushroom and cashew-nut roast to follow. The atmosphere is curiously formal.

Open Mon to Sat (all week Aug) 6 to 9.30 **Closed** 1 week at Christmas Table service. Tables outside. Licensed, also bring your own: corkage £2. Meat dishes. Fish dishes. Vegan dishes. Other diets catered for on request. Take-aways. Wheelchair access

Potter In £

19 Durngate Street TEL Dorchester (0305) 68649

Though not purely vegetarian, this wholefood café provides plenty of choice for non-meat eaters: soups, vegetable pâtés, vegetable hotpot or walnut and Brie roulade with spinach. With up to 28 different salads on offer, no one should go hungry.

Open Mon to Sat noon to 2.30 **Closed** bank hols Counter service. Tables outside. Licensed. Meat dishes. Fish dishes. Other diets catered for on request. Snacks at other times. Take-aways. No smoking. Wheelchair access. Access, Visa

DORKING Surrey MAP 3

Pizza Express £

235 High Street TEL Dorking (0306) 888236

A satellite of the excellent London-based chain that was founded twenty-five years ago. See London entry.

Open Mon to Sat 11.30 to midnight, Sun noon to 11.30. Table service. Licensed, also bring your own: corkage £2.50. Meat dishes. Fish dishes. Take-aways. No-smoking area. Wheelchair access. Access, Amex, Diners, Visa

Pizza Piazza £

77 South Street TEL Dorking (0306) 889790

A branch of a growing chain that offers an enterprising choice of reliably good pizzas. See entry under New Malden for more detail.

Open all week noon to 11 Table service. Licensed. No-smoking area. Wheelchair access. Access, Visa

DOULTING Somerset MAP 2

Brottens Lodge £££

Doulting TEL Cranmore (074 988) 352

Directions are important: turn south off the Frome to Shepton Mallet road in the village of Doulting; 500 yards past the railway bridge and side road to Shepton, take the lane to the left; the Victorian country house is found up a hill on the right – a haven of rural peace, with splendid views. The set-price menu features one vegetarian main dish – mushroom and celery stroganoff with brown rice. The food is good value and a serious effort is made for non-meat eaters. Bread is home made.

Open Mon to Sat exc Mon and Sat L, noon to 1.30, 7 to 9 **Closed** first 2 weeks Jan Booking advisable. Table service. Licensed, also bring your own: corkage varies. Meat dishes. Vegan dishes. Other diets catered for on request. No pipes or cigars in dining-room. Wheelchair access. Accommodation

DULVERTON Somerset MAP 1

Crispin's ££

23 High Street TEL Dulverton (0398) 23397

Both lunch and dinner are good value in this bistro that always lists three choices for vegetarians. Begin with mushroom aïoli or deep-fried Camembert, perhaps, and carry on with peppers stuffed with pine nuts, hazelnut loaf with fresh tomato and basil sauce or walnut slice with apricot sauce. Puddings are traditional favourites such as summer pudding, treacle tart or chocolate and chestnut mousse, all served with vanilla ice-cream or cream.

Open all week, exc Sun D, noon to 2, 7 to 9.30 **Closed** Feb, Mon in winter Booking advisable. Table service. Tables outside. Licensed. Meat dishes. Fish dishes. Vegan dishes. Wheelchair access. Accommodation

DUNSTER Somerset MAP 1

Tea Shoppe £

3 High Street TEL Dunster (0643) 821304

A charming tea-shop in the only brick-faced building in Dunster High Street – built 1495 – pride of place is given to a very interesting cupboard with carvings by North American Indians. The décor is blue and white, the kitchen spotless and there's an admirable display of vegetables. The home baking is excellent: try Bramley apple cake, clotted chocolate with ginger and various others. Puddings include banoffi pie, hot bread pudding and West Country treacle tart. Lunches of salads, mushroom and peanut pâté, cheese and walnut pâté, quiche and a vegetable bake are available. Highly recommended.

Open all week 9.30 to 6.30 (weekends Mar, to 5pm) **Closed** Nov to Feb Booking advisable. Table service. Licensed. Meat dishes. Snacks. No-smoking area. Wheelchair access exc wc. Access, Visa

DURHAM Co Durham MAP 10

Almshouses £

Palace Green TEL Durham (091) 3861054

The Almshouses are seventeenth-century in origin and sit virtually next to the Cathedral. There's a strong and imaginative vegetarian bias: pâtés, such as tofu, olive and walnut, or butterbean, garlic, herb and olive oil kick off the short menu (there's also always a soup), then main courses might embrace cheese and lentil loaf with a tomato and basil sauce, or vegetable strudel, served with a choice of salad or vegetables. Organic wines; Italian coffee.

Open all week June to Sept 9 to 8, L noon to 2.30, winter 9 to 5 Table service. Counter service. Licensed. Meat dishes. Vegan dishes. Other diets catered for on request. Snacks. Take-aways. No smoking during meal times. Wheelchair access

EASINGWOLD North Yorkshire MAP 7

Truffles £

Snowdon House, Spring Street TEL Easingwold (0347) 22342

In a desert for vegetarians this could be a useful spot for a lunch of soup, deep-fried mushrooms, pancakes with crunchy vegetables and cheese sauce, mushroom stroganoff or pasta dish. All dishes are home cooked. Home-made cheesecake, cream teas and cakes are served.

Open Mon to Sat L 11.45 to 2.15 Booking advisable. Table service. Licensed. Meat dishes. Other diets on request. Snacks. Take-aways. No-smoking area. Wheelchair access

EASTBOURNE East Sussex MAP 3

Pizza Piazza £

4 Pevensey Road TEL Eastbourne (0323) 410312

A branch of a growing chain that offers an enterprising choice of reliably good pizzas. See entry under New Malden for more detail.

Open all week noon to 11 Table service. Licensed. No-smoking area. Wheelchair access. Access, Visa

EAST MOLESEY Surrey MAP 3

Tiltyard £–££

Hampton Court Palace TEL 081-943 3666

The jouster's lunch of cheese, apple, chutney and celery seems appropriate for the setting, as the self-service restaurant lies within the curtilage of Hampton Court Palace. It is one of the Milburn chain, which successfully caters at the upper end of the mass market. There is a vegetarian daily hot dish, which might be quiche, cauliflower cheese or vegetable terrine. Puddings are usually good. There is no entrance fee to the grounds and therefore no charge to get into the restaurant.

Open all week 10am to 6.30 **Closed** 25 Dec Counter service. Tables outside. Licensed. Meat dishes. Fish dishes. Snacks. Take-aways. No-smoking area. Wheelchair access

EDGWARE Greater London MAP 12

Wing Ki ££

29 Burnt Oak Broadway TEL 081-205 0904

Very popular with the locals and offering a separate vegetarian menu, though not a set vegetarian meal, there is a Szechuan and Peking bias, and a number of the choices are gratifyingly out of the ordinary: spring rolls served with hot sweet cabbage, vegetables with pancakes, cucumbers and spring onion, fried lady fingers with chilli or garlic sauce, and baby corn with mange-tout.

Open all week noon to 2.30, 6 to 11.30 **Closed** 24–26 Dec Booking advisable. Table service. Licensed. Meat dishes. Fish dishes. Vegan dishes. Other diets catered for on request. Take-aways. Wheelchair access. Access, Visa

ELLAND West Yorkshire MAP 7

Berties Bistro ££

7–10 Town Hall Buildings TEL Elland (0422) 371724

Named after Bertie, Prince of Wales, the atmosphere of this popular restaurant is outstandingly Victorian. Reasonably priced food comes in generous portions, and there is always one vegetarian dish on the menu, if not two. The verdict is that a little more of the imagination shown in other dishes could be applied to the vegetarian food; there is a sense of eating vegetables with vegetables. Starters may be limited to one dish of perhaps over-rich creamed button mushrooms with rum, garlic and parsley; main courses might be good ratatouille layered with pasta shells, moistened with tomato sauce and topped with cheese, or rather bland vegetable, cabbage and mushroom roll. Follow with a good plum and almond sponge, though the custard is reminiscent of the commercial variety, or a gin and lime mousse, the two flavourings working surprisingly well together.

Open Tue to Sun D; Tue to Thur 7 to 10.30, Fri 7 to 11, Sat 6.30 to 11, Sun 5 to 9 Table service. Licensed. Meat dishes. Fish dishes. Vegan dishes. Other diets catered for on request. Wheelchair access

EPSOM Surrey MAP 3

Pizza Piazza £

34 South Street TEL Epsom (037 27) 24049

A branch of a growing chain that offers an enterprising choice of reliably good pizzas. See entry under New Malden for more detail.

Open all week noon to 11 Table service. Licensed. No-smoking area. Wheelchair access. Access, Visa

ERPINGHAM Norfolk MAP 8

Ark ★ ££

The Street TEL Cromer (0263) 761535

A pretty red-brick cottage deep in the countryside with its own kitchen garden providing vegetables. Much thought goes into the dishes, vegetarian as well as meat, and portions are good. Warmly recommended are cream cheese pâté and a simple but highly effective two-mushroom terrine with fresh frisée and radicchio salad to start. Main dishes such as walnut pâté en croûte, an 'absolutely superb' asparagus with hot lemon cream, or spinach layer with nuts may follow. Puddings, which are on the lines of apple and cinnamon crunch have been known to raise a cheer in the dining-room. Coffee is accompanied by home-made chocolates. Excellent value.

Open Tue to Sat D 7 to 9.30, Sun L 12.30 to 2 **Closed** 3 weeks Oct, Tue Mar to Oct Booking advisable. Table service. Licensed. Meat dishes. Fish dishes. Other diets catered for on request. Wheelchair access

★ *after a restaurant name indicates that the vegetarian cooking is especially good. A list of starred restaurants appears at the end of the book.*

ESKDALE GREEN Cumbria MAP 9

Brook House £

Boot TEL Eskdale (094 03) 288

Though the restaurant specialises in regional Cumbrian cuisine, the vegetarian might not notice this with the limited choice and style of food: a savoury nut loaf, for example. The price is right, though.

Open all week 8am to 8.30 (D from 7) in summer, 9.30 to dusk in winter **Closed** 24 to 26 Dec Booking advisable. Table service. Tables outside. Licensed, but bring your own: corkage £3.50. Meat dishes. Fish dishes. Other diets catered for. Snacks. Take-aways. Wheelchair access. Accommodation. Access, Visa

ETON Berkshire MAP 2

Eton Wine Bar ££

82–83 High Street TEL Windsor (0753) 854921/855182

In north Windsor, near Eton bridge, the Wine Bar has a reputation for good food, with some adventurous dishes alongside more predictable ones. A real gas fire (rather than an electric log fire) contributes to the pleasant atmosphere. Satisfied vegetarians have eaten avocado with nuts, chives and mayonnaise, and a bean and asparagus risotto. Other examples of the daily main vegetarian dish might be cashew-nut, bean shoot, and baby corn stir-fry or a wholemeal hazelnut pancake with broccoli, soured cream and chive filling. Victorian brown-bread ice-cream served with a red fruit kissel is hard to resist.

Open all week noon to 2.30, 6 (7 on Sun) to 10.30 (11 on Fri and Sat) **Closed** 24 to 27 Dec Booking advisable. Table service. Licensed. Meat dishes. Fish dishes. Wheelchair access. Access, Visa

EVESHAM Hereford & Worcester MAP 4

Cedar Restaurant, Evesham Hotel ££

Cooper's Lane TEL Evesham (0386) 765566

A family-run black and white hotel, previously known as the Mansion House, set back from the main road that follows the Avon. The eponymous cedar was planted in 1809. Inside, everything is plain and homely, though there is an ambitious menu. At least five out of the ten starters and one main dish are vegetarian; as well as predictable pancakes and filo parcels of vegetables are some more unusual items, such as a nut and watercress cake. Ice-creams are home made – the brown bread one called Mother's Pride. A children's menu can be ordered.

Open all week 12.30 to 2, 7 to 9.30 **Closed** 25 and 26 Dec Booking advisable. Table service. Licensed. Meat dishes. Fish dishes. Other diets catered for on request. No pipes or cigars in dining-room. Wheelchair access. Accommodation. Access, Amex, Diners, Visa

Vine Wine Bar £

16 Vine Street TEL Evesham (0386) 446799

A friendly wine bar, good for a quick meal. The selection of vegetarian dishes includes breaded courgettes with blue cheese dip; mushrooms stuffed with cheese and nuts; peppers stuffed with rice, nuts, raisins, wine and mushrooms, and rösti served with quiche and salad.

Open Tue to Sun noon to 2, 7 to 10 (exc Sun D) Booking advisable (Thurs, Fri, Sat). Table service. Tables outside. Licensed. Meat dishes. Wheelchair access. Access, Visa

EXETER Devon MAP 1

Café at the Meeting House £–££

38 South Street TEL Exeter (0392) 410885

In an old converted chapel with a retail shop in front, this light and airy café is on two floors, its trellis-trimmed gallery overlooking the main part. The fact that booking is recommended even at lunchtime attests to its popularity. Purely vegetarian at lunch, the menu promises and fulfils with a good selection of hot and cold dishes; fish is added at dinner. Starting off, there might be asparagus and walnut tart, chestnut pâté, and cream of cauliflower soup with melon and thyme. Main course offerings could be an aubergine, red cabbage and red bean casserole that has been enjoyed; a lentil and carrot shepherd's pie that was well-seasoned; spinach in filo pastry; fresh tagliatelle with broccoli, Brie and almonds, or red wine ratatouille. There are always make-a-meal salad selections for lunch, for which the dressings are fresh and tasty – there's a tang in the yoghurt one. 'We will return,' was one verdict.

Open Mon to Sat 11 to 5, 7.30 to 9.30, exc Mon D **Closed** bank hols Booking advisable. Table service. Counter service. Tables outside. Licensed. Fish dishes. Vegan dishes. Other diets catered for on request. Snacks. Take-aways. No-smoking area. Access

Cooling's £

Gandy Street TEL Exeter (0392) 34183/4

Useful for its long opening hours and hot and cold selection of food that shows care in vegetarian cookery. Oeufs à la russe and quiche are among the cold offerings; hot options might include macaroni Brazoni, spinach and cheese pancakes, haricots provençale and leek and butterbean bake. Round off with a home-made pudding.

Open all week noon to 9.30 **Closed** bank hols only, 25 and 26 Dec Counter service. Tables outside. Licensed. Snacks. Meat dishes. Fish dishes. Wheelchair access. Visa

Gallery Café £

Exeter and Devon Arts Centre, Bradninch Place, Gandy Street
TEL Exeter (0392) 219741

A lunch-time only café whose vegetarian items show some flair: pumpkin and peanut soup, fennel goulash, tomato and basil cheese-cake, and Sicilian stuffed aubergine. These rub along with more traditional homity pies, ratatouille pancakes and stuffed mushrooms with garlic. Ten daily salads have an individual touch, for example, courgette and Chinese leaf with honey dressing, bean sprouts and ginger.

Open Mon to Sat noon to 2.30 **Closed** bank hols, 2 weeks at Christmas Booking advisable. Table service. Counter service. Licensed. Meat dishes. Take-aways. No-smoking area. Wheelchair access

The factual details under the text are based on information supplied by the restaurateur.

Gueridon £

Dolphin Inn, Thorverton, Nr Exeter TEL Exeter (0392) 860205

In a large rambling Georgian pub, the lurid pink restaurant with tureen lids decorating the wall may look a little shabby but is comfortable. On offer normally are four vegetarian main courses, perhaps fettuccine in cream sauce, lentil bake, nut rissoles or cashew-nut balls in sauce. Both the fettuccine, with mushrooms and cashew-nuts in the sauce, and the moist lentil bake, topped with breadcrumbs and walnuts, have been enjoyed. Accompanying vegetables are particularly good, for example tasty carrots, mange-tout, white cabbage and broccoli, all crunchy and full of flavour. Also recommended are a blackberry and apple and a treacle tart. Service is good.

Open all week noon to 1.45, 7 to 10 Table service. Tables outside. Licensed. Meat dishes. Fish dishes. Vegan dishes. Take-aways. Wheelchair access. Accommodation. Access, Visa

Herbies Wholefood Ⓥ £–££

North Street TEL Exeter (0392) 58473

This vegetarian café conforms to the pine table tradition of décor. The vegan proprietor ensures that vegans are well catered for, even making lassi with soya milk. Daily specials supplement staples of Mexican bean pie, cheese and vegetable pie, pizza, samosas, and baked potatoes, and there are exquisite green salads. Follow with sweets such as crumble, cheesecake and Quicke's very good ice-cream. There are organic wines and non-alcoholic beer.

Open Mon to Sat, noon to 2.30, 7 to 9.30 exc Mon D Booking advisable. Table service. Licensed, also bring your own: corkage £1.50. Vegan dishes. Other diets catered for. Take-aways. No-smoking area. Wheelchair access. Access, Visa

Pizza Piazza £

44–45 Queen Street TEL Exeter (0392) 77269

A branch of a growing chain that offers an enterprising choice of reliably good pizzas. See entry under New Malden for more detail.

Open all week noon to 11 Table service. Licensed. No-smoking area. Wheelchair access. Access, Visa

Tudor House £££

Tudor Street TEL Exeter (0392) 73764

Dating from at least 1450 – the date on the flagstone at the portal – Tudor House was inhabited by a maltster of the city, Isaac Burche in 1628 and remained a family house after that. The Leat Room has a hand-carved oak ceiling; outside the old mill leat runs by the windows. All the rooms are delightful, with mullioned windows and lots of beams. The restoration of the building received a European Heritage Award. One vegetarian main dish is always available to follow starters such as field mushrooms baked en cocotte with spinach and tarragon, cheese soufflé or a soup – carrot and coriander, cucumber and shallots, watercress with chervil, for example. The main dish could be fennel casserole with onions, tomatoes and herbs. This rates as a special-occasion place when there are non-vegetarians in the party: good food, beautiful surroundings, modest cost.

Open Tue to Sat, exc Sat L, 12.15 to 1.45, 7.15 to 9.5 **Closed** 24 to 30 Dec Booking advisable. Table service. Licensed. Meat dishes. Fish dishes. Other diets catered for on request. No-smoking area. Wheelchair access. Accommodation. Access, Amex, Diners, Visa

EXMOUTH Devon MAP 1

Round the Bend ⓥ £

53 The Strand TEL Exmouth (0395) 264398

This exclusively vegetarian restaurant on two floors, with assorted tables covered in floral plastic cloths, has basic, fairly unimaginative, though fresh fare, during the day. Hummus is home made and pleasantly crunchy. Salads are good but the ingredients were repeated in a main course making the range of ingredients appear limited. Other lunchtime possibilities are soup, baked potato, quiche or nut cutlet. Dinners improve in variety, with croustades, stir-fried vegetables, lasagne, or fried cheese. It may not be Cordon Bleu but local vegetarians find the catering consistent.

Open Tue to Sat noon to 2, Fri and Sat D 7 to 9.30 Table service. Licensed. Take-aways. No smoking at L

FARNHAM Surrey MAP 3

Pizza Piazza £

68A Castle Street TEL Farnham (0252) 721383

A branch of a growing chain that offers an enterprising choice of reliably good pizzas. See entry under New Malden for more detail.

Open all week noon to 11 Table service. Licensed. No-smoking area. Wheelchair access. Access, Visa

FELSTED Essex MAP 5

Rumbles Cottage ££

Braintree Road TEL Great Dunmow (0371) 820996

Joy Hadley seems to be achieving that delicate balance of cooking with style but not pretension – good, simple but imaginative food is the result, says one reporter. The one vegetarian choice might be mild cashew-nut curry with a fruit pilaff, or vegetable and bean couscous. Service in this authentic cottage setting has drawn almost unanimous praise.

Open Tue to Sat 7 to 9, Sun noon to 2 **Closed** 3 weeks Feb, 1 week Aug Booking advisable. Table service. Licensed. Meat dishes. Fish dishes. Vegan and other diets catered for on request. No-smoking area. Wheelchair access. Access, Visa

FEOCK Cornwall MAP 1

Trelissick Garden ££

TEL Truro (0872) 863486

Benefiting from the National Trust's policy that its cafés provide a vegetarian hot and cold dish at all times, this café for visitors to the splendid gardens caters well – indeed, better than most. Tam White, the cook, creates innovative salads such as carrot and cashew-nut with yoghurt dressing; courgette and red pepper; green pea and red kidney bean; and red cabbage, apple and sultana. The main hot dish might be a vegetable loaf. During the summer there is a parking fee.

Open all week, 11am (12.30 Sun) to 6; 11am to 4 Sun Nov and Dec **Closed** Jan and Feb Booking advisable Sun. Counter service exc Sun. Licensed. Meat dishes. Snacks. Wheelchair access. Access, Amex, Visa

FEWSTON North Yorkshire MAP 7

Swinsty Tea Garden ⓥ ★ £

Fewston House, Fewston TEL Blubberhouses (094 388) 637

A discovery in the middle of nowhere – a tea-room that offers only wholefood vegetarian meals. For lunch, choose from soup and a couple of main dishes (one of which is vegan), such as cashew-nut and vegetable croustade, spinach roulade or a tender kidney bean and aubergine casserole, served with a wholemeal roll. There is a wide choice of cakes, among them lemon cheesecake of a good Continental type, and apple cake with a pastry bottom and crumbly top, well flavoured with cinnamon and other spices.

Open Sat and Sun 11 to 5, also Thur and Fri May to Oct, 2 to 5 Counter service. Tables outside. Unlicensed, but bring your own. Vegan dishes. Other diets catered for. Snacks. No smoking

FLITWICK Bedfordshire MAP 5

Flitwick Manor £££

Church Road TEL Flitwick (0525) 712242

A country-house hotel with some old world touches, for example four-poster beds, and some more modern touches, as in an interesting collection of rare cartoons. Prices are high and the company can be daunting; it's definitely somewhere to dress smartly. The extensive menu has a couple of vegetarian dishes daily – wild mushroom crumble and ratatouille pasties with dill-flavoured cream, for example – or a three-course vegetarian menu, with the same crumble as main course. The home-made plum or strawberry yoghurt ice-creams could be good choices but be sure to leave room for hand-made truffles that come with coffee, all included in the set price.

Open all week 12.30 to 2, 7.30 to 9.30 **Closed** 24 D, 25, 26 Dec Booking advisable. Table service. Tables outside. Licensed. Meat dishes. Fish dishes. Other diets catered for on request. No pipes or cigars in dining-room. Wheelchair access. Accommodation. Access, Diners, Visa

FLIXTON Suffolk MAP 5

Buck Inn £–££

TEL Bungay (0986) 2382

Found by following signs towards Flixton Aviation Museum, if coming from Bungay, the Buck Inn has an astonishing array of vegetarian options. Among the 10 main dishes you might find chilli-bean casserole, vegetable crumble, haricot hot-pot, three-bean curry and nut bake.

Open all week 11 to 2, 7.30 to 10.30 Booking advisable. Table service. Counter service. Licensed. Meat dishes. Fish dishes. Vegan dishes. Wheelchair access.

FOLKESTONE Kent MAP 3

Alfresco £

45 Bouverie Road West TEL Folkestone (0303) 43831

Set behind Sainsbury's. The main à la carte menu has no vegetarian dishes but monthly menus offer a vegetarian speciality: this could be vegetable and pasta gratin, vegetable and rice stuffed marrow on tomato coulis, or sorrel, tomato and Mozzarella pillows with oriental sauce. Starters might be home-made soup, crumbed aubergine with tomato and Parmesan or Mozzarella, tomato and avocado salad with basil sour cream. That rare and delicious Sicilian pudding, tiramisu, is on offer as well as little pots of chocolate, apple and blackberry strudel pie and full dairy ice-creams.

Open Mon to Sat L 11 to 3, Fri and Sat D 7 to 9 Booking advisable. Table service. Licensed. Meat dishes. Fish dishes. Vegan dishes. Take-aways. Wheelchair access. Access, Visa

Holland & Barrett ⓥ £

80 Sandgate Road TEL Folkestone (0303) 43615

Hearty snacks can be found in this centrally located branch of the Holland & Barrett chain. Savoury daily dishes might be ratatouille, Mexican corn bake and mushroom and butterbean stroganoff supplemented by those old regulars, jacket potatoes and quiches. Walnut tart, Florentine pie, coffee fudge pie, plum and orange sponge and cheesecake can satisfy the sweet tooth.

Open Mon to Sat 9.30 to 5 **Closed** bank hols Counter service. Unlicensed. Other diets catered for on request. Snacks. Take-aways. No smoking

FOWEY Cornwall MAP 1

Stanton's ££

11 Esplanade TEL Fowey (072 683) 2631

'A well-run family business where you can be sure of excellent food and a friendly relaxed atmosphere.' Alongside the meat menu is an extensive vegetarian one of seven starters and eleven main dishes (some of which are larger versions of the starters). The chef experiments with new dishes, and as well as old favourites like corn-on-the-cob, egg mayonnaise and platter of vegetables with cheese sauce, you can have such home-made creations as vegetable and soya-bean curry, chestnut ragout, hazelnut loaf with ratatouille or Stilton and spinach croquettes. Vegans also have a good range to choose from. Puddings on offer might be pecan pie, cheesecake, meringues with clotted cream and chocolate fudge cake among others. Good value and well recommended for mixed eating.

Open Tue to Sun 7 to 10 **Closed** 3 to 5 weeks Feb to Mar Booking advisable. Table service. Licensed. Meat dishes. Vegan dishes. Other diets catered for on request. Wheelchair access. Access, Amex, Diners, Visa

A restaurant manager can't insist on people not smoking, unless it's specifically a non-smoking restaurant or a non-smoking area. If it is, smokers could be asked to leave if they don't stop. If it's important to you, check beforehand what the smoking arrangements are.

FROGHALL Staffordshire **MAP 7**

Wharf £££

Foxt Road TEL Ipstones (0538) 266486

A 200-year-old warehouse on the banks of the Caldon Canal provides a scenic setting for diners. The inside has been restored to preserve the original character: a new blue quarry-tiled floor harmonises with bare brick walls and exposed beams. The cooking is described as 'modern British' and experimentation with sauces extends to the two vegetarian main dishes – lentil and banana cakes with ginger and pineapple sauce, or Mozzarella, tomato and basil pastries in a purée sweetcorn sauce, for example. Start perhaps with Stilton and celery soup, chilled raspberry and almond soup or hot cucumber boats with pistachio nut and tomato filling in a pool of red wine sauce. Puddings may be more traditional; lemon soufflé and a chocolate mousse cake have been praised. Bread, sorbet and after-dinner chocolates are usually home made.

Open Tue to Sat D 7.30 to 9.15, Sun L noon to 1.30 **Closed** 2 weeks in autumn Table service. Licensed. Meat dishes. Fish dishes. Other diets catered for on request. Wheelchair access. Access, Visa

GATESHEAD Tyne & Wear **MAP 10**

Ship £

Eighton Banks TEL 091-416 0273

Said to be a current Tyneside champ for bar meals, though vegetarians don't have much choice of hot dishes – garlic mushrooms or the special of the day. However, there is a superb salad bar with up to 20 freshly made varieties every day. If you have the daily special, perhaps deep-fried pancakes with wine and mushroom stuffing, you can have salad as a side dish.

Open Mon to Sat noon to 2.30, 7 to 10 (exc Fri D, Sat D) **Closed** 25 Dec L Booking advisable. Table service. Tables outside. Licensed. Meat dishes. Fish dishes. Vegan dishes. Take-aways. No-smoking area. No children under 14. Wheelchair access

GATWICK West Sussex **MAP 3**

Garden Restaurant, Gatwick Hilton £££

Gatwick Airport TEL Crawley (0293) 518080 ext 2

The food is reasonable in terms of quality, if high in price. The choice of three clearly indicated vegetarian main dishes was, in the summer, curry with wild rice, fresh fettuccine with field mushrooms and celery and mushroom stroganoff. Amy's coffee-shop, which is in the same building and handily open 24 hours a day, offers tortellini and mushroom stroganoff.

Open all week, exc Sat L, noon to 2.30, 7 to 10.30 Booking advisable. Table service. Counter service. Licensed. Meat dishes. Fish dishes. No smoking area. Wheelchair access. Access, Amex, Carte Blanche, Diners, Visa

GLASTONBURY Somerset **MAP 2**

Ploughshares Café ⓥ ★ £

4A High Street TEL Glastonbury (0458) 35233

Early Pink Floyd and deep-fried tandoori tofu combine at this entirely vegan café – after all, Glastonbury is a focus for New Age culture. The cooking is splendidly enterprising, taking in soufflés, flans, bakes, tempeh pizzas, quiche, bolognese and basic dishes of tofu and tempeh. As far as possible ingredients are organic, from vegetables and wholewheat flour to coffee. Meals typically consist of a selection of salads with tofu dressing, a large assortment of pastries such as samosas, vegi-rolls, mushroom swirls or English country-style pasties, a home-made soup and a main dish, perhaps tofu and almond loaf with roast parsnips and rich brown sauce. Puddings and cakes are served with Ploughshares' sweet tofu cream; sugar-free, wheat-free, gluten-free varieties are available. The wholesale delivery service even reaches to London (try the Carob frig cake – sensational).

Open all week 10.30 to 7 (9 Fri and Sat) Counter service. Tables outside. Licensed. Vegan dishes only. Other diets catered for on request. Snacks. Takeaways. No smoking. Wheelchair access

See the back of the guide for an index of restaurants listed.

Rainbow's End Café ⓥ £

17A High Street TEL Glastonbury (0458) 33896

Half-way up the High Street on the left, this stripped-pine café serves lunches of soups, curries, lasagne, Greek cheese pie and cauliflower croustade.

Open Mon to Sat L noon to 2.30 Counter service. Tables outside. Licensed. Vegan dishes. Snacks at other times. Take-aways. No-smoking area

GLOUCESTER Gloucestershire MAP 4

Down to Earth ⓥ £

11 The Forum, Eastgate Shopping Centre
TEL Gloucester (0452) 305832

'A local centre for the health conscious, with a shop area selling green goods,' this self-service café is popular at lunchtime for dishes such as vegetarian shepherd's pie, Brazil nut roast, lasagne and various quiches. Prices are reasonable and it's best to arrive in good time to guarantee choice. Puddings might be Bakewell tart, apple and blackcurrant pie, apple and apricot flan or carrot cake. Good for vegans.

Open Mon to Sat 8.30 to 4 **Closed** bank hols Counter service. Licensed. Vegan dishes. Other diets catered for on request. Snacks. Take-aways. No smoking

Undercroft £

Church House, College Green TEL Gloucester (0452) 307164

One of the Milburns chain of restaurants, catering on a level above the usual, with a vegetarian option. It might be, for instance, a ratatouille casserole or vegetable flan. Puddings are generally a strong point.

Open all week 10am (noon Sun) to 4.30 (5 in summer) Booking advisable. Counter service. Tables outside. Licensed. Meat dishes. Fish dishes. Snacks. No-smoking area. Wheelchair access

If in doubt about the constituents of a dish, ask.

GODALMING Surrey MAP 3

Pizza Piazza £

78 High Street TEL Godalming (048 68) 29191

A branch of a growing chain that offers an enterprising choice of reliably good pizzas. See entry under New Malden for more detail.

Open all week noon to 11 Table service. Licensed. No-smoking area. Wheelchair access. Access, Visa

GRASMERE Cumbria MAP 9

Baldry's Wholefood £

Red Lion Square TEL Grasmere (096 65) 301

Baldry's cooks both meat and vegetarian dishes, with an emphasis on organic ingredients; staples such as hummus, grilled goats' cheese with walnut oil and pear salad, Wensley rarebit, mushrooms on toast, potato bake, quiche and cheese platter are supplemented by specials which appear regularly according to the day of the week. Apart from Friday (which is a fish day) there is always one vegetarian special: shepherd's pie, casserole with wholemeal parsley dumplings, pasta and cauliflower gratin, baked onions with nut stuffing, broccoli and cashew-nut bake or chestnut and mushroom roast. Hot puddings are the likes of hot sticky gingerbread and Cumberland rum nicky, and there are locally made cakes. A speciality is home-made double chocolate ice-cream.

Open Fri to Wed L noon to 3 **Closed** weekdays Dec to Feb Counter service. Tables outside. Licensed. Meat dishes. Snacks at other times. Take-aways. No smoking. Wheelchair access

Lancrigg Vegetarian Country House Hotel ⓥ ★ ££

Easedale Road TEL Grasmere (096 65) 317

Robert and Janet Whittington started the Rowan Tree in Grasmere and then embarked on running this first-rate vegetarian hotel. 'The house and location alone are worth a visit on a summer evening.' Décor and furniture are tasteful and comfortable; classical music plays; organic home-grown vegetables are used whenever possible and organic wines are served. Let us hope that other restaurants and hotels will be induced to follow suit when they hear that about half the visitors are not vegetarian, but come to enjoy the natural good food and peace and quiet. Daily menus are short, with no choice of main dish: it might be cheese gougère with mushrooms and red wine sauce; vine leaves stuffed with pine kernels, apricots and organic Basmati rice or Mediterranean vegetable pie with Feta cheese and wholemeal yoghurt pastry. Middle Eastern inspired falafel, crudités with tahini, Stilton, port and walnut pâté or apple and cashew-nut soup with sunflower seed rolls have appeared as starters. An extensive range of puddings includes lemon and cardamom meringue pie, blackcurrant and tofu fool or traditional lemon pudding. Warmly recommended.

Open all week exc Mon L noon to 2, 7 to 7.30 Booking advisable. Table service. Tables outside. Licensed. Vegan dishes. Other diets catered for on request. Snacks at other times. No smoking in dining-room. Wheelchair access. Accommodation. Access, Visa

GRANTHAM Lincolnshire MAP 8

Ferns ⓥ £

15A Bridge Street TEL Grantham (0476) 76981

This purely vegetarian café gets its inspiration from around the world – dishes from Mexico, France, Italy, India and the Middle East are likely to appear, as well as some invented to take advantage of what fresh ingredients are available. Lunches offer a predictable range of quiche, jacket potatoes and soup with daily specials such as leek and pasta bake or cassoulet. More imagination goes into dinners of such dishes as pasta alla genovese, vodka pasta with vodka and tomato cream sauce with a hint of chilli, or enchiladas.

Open Mon to Sat L noon to 2, Fri and Sat D 7.45 to 8.45 **Closed** first 2 weeks Aug, bank hols Booking advisable D. Table service. Tables outside. Licensed. Vegan dishes. Other diets catered for on request. Snacks at other times. No-smoking area. Wheelchair access

The availability of meat and fish dishes is indicated in the details underneath the text of an entry.

Knightingales £

Guildhall Court, Guildhall Street TEL Grantham (0476) 79243

Don't be put off by the pun: the vegetarian food is straightforward and listed on a separate menu. After a starter such as cream cheese and cashew-nut pâté or a choice of soups – perhaps courgette, tomato and walnut, parsnip and apple or tomato and garlic – there are such main dishes as mushroom and cashew-nut lasagne, spinach roulade or mushroom and celery stroganoff. Desserts include strawberry and kiwi Pavlova, date, walnut and caramel flan and brown sugar meringues.

Open Mon to Sat 9 to 4.30pm Counter service. Tables outside. Licensed. Meat dishes. Vegan dishes. Other diets catered for on request. Snacks. Take-aways. Wheelchair access

GREAT MALVERN Hereford & Worcester MAP 4

Only Natural Ⓥ £

99B Church Street TEL Malvern (0684) 561772

In the courtyard opposite Oxfam is this purely vegetarian café where almost all the ingredients of lunches and snacks are organic and eggs are free-range. There is almost always a soup, followed by hot dishes of curry, nut roast, quiche, pizza, various savoury pies, and a good range of salads. Cakes are home made from organic flour; there are sugar-free and vegan varieties. Vegan ice creams are also available.

Open Mon to Sat 9 to 5, L noon to 2 Counter service. Tables outside. Vegan dishes. Snacks. Take-aways. No-smoking

St Ann's Well Ⓥ £

Victoria Walk, St Ann's Road TEL Malvern (0684) 560285

Splendidly situated at the top of the Malvern hills above the town; follow St Ann's Road until it turns into a path winding up the hill. Housed in the original octagonal spa house it has the Malvern spring still running into a marble basin at the entrance. The food in the café is basic home-made fare of pizza, veggie burger, quiche and filled rolls. Lots of cakes and shortbreads. You can sit outside the café on benches cut into the side of the hill.

Open all week 10 to 5.45, D 7 to 10 with prior booking **Closed** weekdays Nov to Mar Booking advisable. Counter service. Tables outside. Licensed. Vegan dishes. Other diets catered for on request. Snacks. Take-aways. No-smoking area. Wheelchair access

GREAT MISSENDEN Buckinghamshire MAP 4

The George ££

94 High Street TEL Great Missenden (024 06) 2084

This fifteenth-century pub on the main road between Aylesbury and Amersham would be a pleasant venue for a vegetarian accompanied by a meat-eater, as there is always a good selection of dishes of reliable quality – vegetable stroganoff, wheat and walnut casserole, crêpes and pasta dishes in one or more combinations. Specials on offer as we went to press included chestnut patties in red wine sauce and cashew-nut balls in mushroom sauce. What are known as 'worker's wodge' lunches (served Monday to Friday except bank holidays) also list a fritto misto vegetaire (potato-flake-coated vegetables served with a dip), home-made vegetable soup and onion bhajias.

Open all week noon to 2, 6.45 to 9.45 exc Sun Booking advisable. Table service. Tables outside. Licensed. Meat dishes. Fish dishes. Vegan dishes. Other diets catered for on request. Wheelchair access. Access, Visa

GRIMSBY Humberside MAP 10

Brit's ££

29 Abbey Road TEL Grimsby (0472) 354442

Filling a gap in something of a culinary desert is this relatively new restaurant featuring English food, though it is pricey. Organically grown vegetables are used and sauces are reckoned to be a speciality. No vegetarian dish is described on the menu, but a note says 'vegetarian meals are available on request'. Sample possibilities are reassuring – nut stroganoff on wild rice pilaff, giant mushroom mille-feuille and a strudel of vegetables (what would we do without filo?). Home-made ice-creams, sorbets, chocolates and petits fours.

Open Tue to Sat exc Sat L noon to 2.30, 7.30 to 10 **Closed** first 2 weeks Jan Booking advisable. Table service. Licensed. Meat dishes. Fish dishes. Vegan dishes. Other diets catered for on request. Wheelchair access. Access, Visa

GUILDFORD Surrey MAP 3

Tithe Barn Restaurant £

Loseley Park TEL Guildford (0483) 571881

This is the headquarters of the Loseley company, which makes the famous yoghurts, ice-creams and other high-quality dairy foods from the milk of the herd that grazes in the fields around. Vegetarian dishes are limited in the restaurant – housed in an old tithe barn – but vegetarian cheese and organic produce are used if possible. Dishes could be lasagne, leek and potato bake or ratatouille. Quiches are a popular item on the menu too. A range of organic breads and cakes are also on sale at the farm shop.

Open Wed to Sat noon to 2.30 **Closed** Oct to May Table service (booked parties only). Counter service. Tables outside. Licensed; also bring your own. Snacks. No smoking. Wheelchair access

HADLEIGH Suffolk MAP 5

Spinning Wheel ££

High Street TEL Hadleigh (0473) 822175

Vegetarians get a look in at this mainly meat restaurant. Starters of stuffed pear, fruit cup, cottage cheese and tomato salad or mushrooms Spinning Wheel might be followed by ratatouille, lasagne, filo pastry roll or vegetable and bean casserole.

Open all week noon to 2, 7 to 11 Table service. Licensed. Meat dishes. Other diets catered for on request. No-smoking area. Wheelchair access. Access, Amex, Diners, Visa

See the back of the guide for a list of restaurants serving only vegetarian food.

HANLEY Staffordshire MAP 7

Dylans ⓥ £

99 Broad Street TEL Stoke-on-Trent (0782) 286009

Run by women, this vegetarian restaurant has an informal atmosphere with only a few tables set close together. The prices are reasonable and the food is good; vegans particularly are able to find interesting choices as about half the day's menu is vegan. Huge blackboards cover the walls and display a menu that might include pumpkin and white radish soup, a good herby lentil pâté or garlic dip with crudités; unstinting portions of main dishes such as sweet-and-sour peppers and beans, Brazil and peanut loaf with red wine and mushroom or mustard sauce, and cheese and lentil loaf with barbecue sauce. The extensive range of sweets might include carrot and cinnamon cake or sticky chocolate orange mousse; vegan ice-cream is a staple. Organic wines.

Open Mon to Sat 11am to 2.30, 6 to 10.30 Booking advisable. Table service. Licensed. Vegan dishes. Other diets catered for on request. Wheelchair access. Access, Visa

HARROGATE North Yorkshire MAP 7

Bettys £–££

1 Parliament Street TEL Harrogate (0423) 502746

The old-fashioned tea-rooms that specialise in a good range of teas and coffees also serve high-quality snacks all day and an evening menu from 6pm. Welsh rarebit is a speciality and home-baked cakes are good. For supper or a light dinner, try soured cream and herb potatoes, deep-fried mushrooms with tartare sauce or salads. Everything is reasonably priced – and live piano music is thrown in for good measure.

Open all week 9am to 9 **Closed** some bank hols Table service. Licensed. Meat dishes. Fish dishes. Snacks at other times. Take-aways. Access, Visa

A restaurant doesn't have to be able to serve all items on the menu, although it should have most. If you think the restaurant is deliberately trying to mislead people, tell the local Trading Standards Officer.

Dr B's Kitchen £

13–15 Knaresborough Road TEL Harrogate (0423) 884819

Dr B's Kitchen, run by Barnardo's, gives vocational training work to young people with special needs and provides some interesting vegetarian dishes; organic vegetables and free-range eggs are used whenever possible. The lunch menu changes every day; starters might be Stilton-stuffed mushrooms, courgette and orange soup, Stilton and port pâté or aubergine fritters, and main dishes red dragon pie, spinach roulade, mung bean dahl, potato and lentil bake, nut cutlets with spicy tomato sauce or hot asparagus tart.

Open Mon to Fri noon to 2 Table service. Tables outside. Meat dishes. Other diets catered for on request. Snacks. Take-aways. No-smoking area. Wheelchair access

Tiffins on the Stray ⓥ ★ £–££

11A Regent Parade TEL Harrogate (0423) 504041

There's a genuine commitment to ingredients and choice at this wholly vegetarian restaurant that gives special consideration to vegans. Treacle loaf is home baked, to accompany soup; prune and brandy ice-cream is also home produced. Prices reflect the effort applied. Lunch and dinner menus each provide five starters and an equal number of mains: nut croquettes with apple sauce or tagliatelle verdi with tomato and basil sauce to begin, followed by chilli bean and bulgur wheat casserole; cauliflower, pear and pepper pie with walnut pastry; vegetable kebabs with smoked tofu and a sweet-and-sour sauce. Sweets arrive with a welcome choice of yoghurt, cream or fromage frais and might include sticky toffee pudding, raw sugar brûlée, muesli crumble and Tayberry sponge pie. To complete the operation, from 10am to noon there are brunches of fruit compote, filled pancakes, toasted muffins and eggs, then afternoon teas with home-made cake. Five leaf teas feature, plus a range of herbal choices; three degrees of roast coffee served in cafetières indicate the level of customer care.

Open Tue to Sat 10 to 2, 7 to 10 **Closed** 25, 26 Dec and 1 Jan Booking advisable. Table service. Unlicensed, but bring your own: no corkage. Vegan dishes. Other diets catered for on request. Snacks. Take-aways. No cigars or pipes. Wheelchair access. Access, Visa

HARROW Greater London **MAP** 12

Pizza Express £

2 College Road **TEL** 081-427 9195

A satellite of the excellent London-based chain that was founded twenty-five years ago. See London entry.

Open Mon to Sat 11.30 to midnight, Sun noon to 11.30. Table service. Licensed, also bring your own: corkage £2.50. Meat dishes. Fish dishes. Take-aways. No-smoking area. Wheelchair access. Access, Amex, Diners, Visa

HASLEMERE Surrey **MAP** 2

Crowns £

Weyhill **TEL** Haslemere (0428) 3112

This busy pub constantly varies its blackboard menu and always provides something for vegetarians: deep-fried Camembert with gooseberry conserve, and mushrooms with Stilton and garlic dip are sample starters. Follow with cheese, leek and potato pie; aubergine and mushroom lasagne; pizza; cauliflower cheese, or pasta.

Open Mon to Sun 11.30 to 2.15, 6.30 to 10.30 **Closed** 25 and 26 Dec Booking advisable weekends. Table service. Tables outside. Licensed. Meat dishes. No children under 14 at D. Access, Visa

Morels £££

25–27 Lower Street **TEL** Haslemere (0428) 51462

Run by Jean-Yves and Mary Anne Morel, this is an outstanding restaurant with a formidable reputation. Jean-Yves is French and cooks; Mary Anne is English and serves. The ambience is delightful and the food excellent. Vegetarians can rejoice that such a bastion of French cooking has come up with a main dish for them, but may find it predictably a strudel, here filled with wild mushrooms and fresh herbs. Starters are limited to perhaps scrambled egg with aubergine and peppers, served cold. The desserts stun with their appearance and flavours don't disappoint.

Open Tue to Sat exc Sat L 12.30 to 2, 7 to 10 **Closed** last 2 weeks Sept, first week Oct Booking advisable. Table service. Licensed. Meat dishes. Fish dishes. Vegan dishes. Other diets catered for on request. No-smoking area. No pipes or cigars. Wheelchair access. Access, Amex, Diners, Visa

HASTINGS East Sussex MAP 3

Millies £

45 High Street TEL Hastings (0424) 431896

The daily menu has one vegetarian and one meat or fish dish. A typical week might take in walnut and rice bake, spinach lasagne, broccoli cheese bake, pasta shells with tomato and mushroom bake, shepherdess pie and aubergine and Parmesan cheese bake. A daily selection of half a dozen salads, three or four quiches, and jacket potatoes is also available. Formerly called Brants.

Open Mon to Sat noon to 3 Counter service. Tables outside. Licensed. Meat dishes. Fish dishes. Snacks. Take-aways. No smoking. Wheelchair access

Pure Treats Ⓥ £

50 George Street TEL Hastings (0424) 717801

Near the town centre and on a pedestrian-only street the co-operatively-run wholefood restaurant serves daily dishes such as mushroom timbale, shepherdess pie with onion sauce, Brazil nut roast, lasagne, vegetables in cheese sauce and a good lentil and courgette bake. There are various salads. Drop in for tea or coffee and choose from an array of wholesome cakes: banana, carrot, chocolate brownies, date slices, cashew and carob slices and scones. Sunday lunch is a nut or bean roast with all the trimmings of Yorkshire pudding, gravy and vegetables.

Open Mon to Sat 10 to 4; all week in summer 10 to 10 Counter service. Tables outside. Unlicensed, but bring your own: corkage 50p. Vegan dishes. Other diets catered for. Snacks. Take-aways. No smoking. Wheelchair access exc wc

The Vegetarian Good Food Guide *is totally independent, accepts no free hospitality and makes no charge for inclusion.*

HATHERSAGE Derbyshire **MAP 7**

Longland's Eating House £

Main Road TEL Hope Valley (0433) 51978

Above the Outside outdoor equipment shop, next to the petrol station, this is a café by day but turns into a slightly more upmarket restaurant in the evening. Daytime offerings might take in kidney bean and mushroom lasagne and courgette and lentil gratin; in the evening, main courses are along the lines of cheese and spinach enchilada and red dragon pie, made with aduki beans, wheat grain and vegetables, topped with mashed potato. Home-made cakes naturally include Bakewell tart, as this is Derbyshire, but also embrace banana and walnut and chocolate fudge. Two dozen wines. Hungry walkers and others might like to know that on Saturdays and Sundays breakfast is served from 9 to 11.30am.

Open Tue to Sun L 11.30 to 5, Wed to Sat D 6.30 to 9.30 Booking advisable Sat D. Table service D. Counter service. Licensed, also bring your own: corkage £1. Meat dishes. Fish dishes. Snacks. Access, Visa

HAVANT Hampshire **MAP 2**

Nutmeg Ⓥ £

Old Town Hall, East Street TEL Havant (0705) 472700

This daytime café attached to the Havant Arts Centre also opens when there's an evening performance. It has an informal collection of pine tables and chairs, pleasantly brightened with fresh flowers and pot plants. Food is wholesome: potato, lentil and apricot soup and a moist, crumbly apricot cake were found to be good and came in generous portions. Shepherd's pie, vegetable curry, broccoli and walnut bake and chilli bean casserole have featured as hot daily dishes. Vegans have a good choice.

Open Tue to Sat 9.30 to 4.30 **Closed** Christmas, Easter Counter service. Tables outside. Licensed, also bring your own: corkage 50p. Vegan dishes. Snacks. Takeaways. No smoking. Wheelchair access

Report forms are at the back of the book; write a letter if you prefer.

HAWORTH West Yorkshire MAP 7

Weavers ££

15 West Lane TEL Haworth (0535) 43822

Once a group of weavers' cottages, now a relaxed restaurant where northern dishes feature on a menu that changes regularly. Even vegetarian dishes show the regional influence – vegetable casserole with herb dumplings, or spinach and Wensleydale pie. Other dishes might include samosas, stuffed cabbage with onion sauce or mushroom terrine with sherry sauce. Everything is home produced including ice-creams and sorbets. There's a nursery note to the puddings: old school pud, sticky-toffee, and nannies meringue surprise.

Open Tue to Sat D 7 to 9.15, Sun L 12.15 to 1.30 **Closed** 1 week at Christmas, 2 weeks June Booking advisable. Table service. Licensed. Meat dishes. Fish dishes. Other diets catered for on request. No-smoking area. Access, Amex, Diners, Visa

HAYLE Cornwall MAP 1

Lelant Garden Centre Restaurant £

Nut Lane TEL Hayle (0736) 753732

Even if not buying plants, one might be tempted in by hot dishes featuring a reasonable vegetarian choice: leek croustade, nut roast, spaghetti and home-made soups. There is a good selection of serve-yourself salads and home-made wholemeal cakes.

Open all week, L 10am to 5.30 Counter service. Tables outside. Unlicensed, but bring your own: corkage £4.50. Meat dishes. Vegan dishes. Snacks at other times. Take-aways. No-smoking area. Wheelchair access

HELSTON Cornwall MAP 1

Nansloe Manor ££

Meneage Road TEL Helston (0326) 574691

The hotel is off the A394 on the south side of Helston. Although vegetarians are restricted to one dish, that much can be a godsend in this part of the world. The manor, set in its own grounds, is homely and friendly. Light dishes have a place as well as three-course meals; well cooked bar meals have drawn praise. 'An interesting vegetarian dish' is what the menu offers – it could be cheese and garlic purée roulade, lentil and spinach timbale, or yellow lentil and leek loaf. There might be only one starter, Brie soufflé, deep-fried mushrooms or gnocchi, perhaps. Save room for a light, fluffy lemon cheesecake or one of the other puddings that come with copious quantities of clotted cream.

Open all week noon to 2, 7 to 9.30 **Closed** 6 days at Christmas Booking advisable. Table service. Tables outside. Licensed, but bring your own: corkage £3.50. Meat dishes. Fish dishes. Vegan dishes. Other diets catered for on request. No children under 10. Accommodation. Access, Visa

HENLEY-ON-THAMES Oxfordshire MAP 4

As You Like It £££

60 Bell Street TEL Henley-on-Thames (0491) 410071

The vegetarian set menu serves a minimum of two, but the components are well thought-out: crispy seaweed to start, sweet-and-sour vegetables with steamed rice or Singapore rice noodles to follow. The regular menu takes in a couple of bean curd dishes, one in Szechuan style and one braised in brown sauce. Soups include a welcome hot-and-sour vegetarian version and the toffee treatment in desserts extends beyond apple and banana to pineapple. Enjoy the ambience, too – a rich gold and blue interior and carefully chosen accessories.

Open all week 12.30 to 2.15, 6.30 to 11 (midnight Fri and Sat) **Closed** 25 and 26 Dec Booking advisable. Table service. Licensed. Meat dishes. Fish dishes. Takeaways. Wheelchair access. Access, Amex, Visa

HEREFORD Hereford & Worcester MAP 4

Gaffers Ⓥ ★ £

89 East Street

A popular and relaxed vegetarian café where a jeweller may be working in one corner. All kinds of people gather here to share tables and enjoy good food at extraordinarily reasonable prices. A typical day's menu might include several quiches, various imaginative salads – curried cauliflower, roasted seedy cauliflower, mushroom, greens and potato – pizza, cider and lentil loaf with mushroom sauce, cashew paella or vegetable bake. To follow, country pie consists of purée fruit on a crunchy flapjack base with a cream topping, or choose a moist home-made cake.

Open Mon to Sat 10 to 4.30 Counter service. Tables outside. Unlicensed. Vegan dishes. Other diets catered for on request. Snacks. Take-aways. No smoking after 12.30pm

Nutters ⓥ £

Capuchin Yard, off Church Street TEL Hereford (0432) 277447

A tiny shoppers' café serving vegetarian snacks and a few hot nut roasts. Though the curried pie, cheese puffs and other items are made off the premises, they are made to the owner's specifications and are good.

Open Mon to Sat noon to 4.45 Counter service. Tables outside. Licensed. Vegan dishes. Other diets catered for on request. Snacks. Take-aways. No-smoking. Wheelchair access

Restaurant Ninety Six ££

96 East Street TEL Hereford (0432) 59754

Formerly known as Effy's, this pretty and cosy restaurant tries some ambitious ideas without forgetting vegetarians: chilled pea and fennel soup works very well, a mixed leaf salad is excellent and a main dish of vine leaves stuffed with wild rice served with tomato coulis is good. Service is not overwhelming, and the water-melon and cucumber titbits and slim, crisp biscuits with puddings are nice touches. Imagination tends to run riot with the puddings – brown-bread ice-cream stands on its own without the addition of a chocolate sauce, and pears in the summer pudding are obliterated by gooseberries and blackcurrants. In all, good and reliable.

Open Tue to Sat D 7 to 9.30 **Closed** 1 week at Christmas, 2 weeks summer Booking advisable. Table service. Licensed. Meat dishes. Fish dishes. Other diets catered for. No pipes. No children under 4. Wheelchair access. Access, Visa

HERSTMONCEUX East Sussex **MAP 3**

Sundial £££

Gardner Street TEL Herstmonceux (0323) 832217

The Sundial goes from strength to strength, one of them being its vegetarian menu. The upmarket dining-room is cottagey, with black beams, and in summer there are tables on a delightful terrace. As well as predictable dishes, vegetarian fare is enlivened with choices such as leek terrine with a green sauce three-cheese soufflé, and pasta with tomato and basil. Rich gateaux follow. Sharpen up your French to understand the menu.

Open Tue to Sun exc Sun D 12.30 to 2 (2.30 Sun), 7.30 to 9.30 (10 Sat) **Closed** 25 Dec to 20 Jan, 7 Aug to first week Sept Booking advisable. Table service. Tables outside. Licensed. Meat dishes. Fish dishes. Other diets catered for on request. Take-aways. No-smoking until after dessert. Wheelchair access. Access, Amex, Diners, Visa

HINTLESHAM Suffolk **MAP 5**

Hintlesham Hall £££

Nr Ipswich TEL Hintlesham (047 387) 334

Once famed as Robert Carrier's flagship, now owned by the Watsons, Hintlesham offers very ambitious and rich food at high prices in splendid surroundings. The attribution of fish dishes as vegetarian is worrying, but there is a valid if unexciting vegetarian main dish – a strudel or noodles, perhaps. Starters of 'poached egg in creamy leek-lined tartlet with red Burgundy and mushroom sauce' or 'friture of deep-fried vegetables served with garlic and almond mayonnaise' are more adventurous. There is a good selection of French and British cheeses and desserts include a hazelnut, walnut and pistachio hot soufflé with maple sauce, orange, lemon and lime crème brûlée and 'a little caramelised rice pudding served with poached fruits' which earns high praise.

Open all week, exc Sat L, noon to 1.30, 7 to 9.30 Booking advisable. Table service. Licensed, also bring your own: corkage from £7.50. Meat dishes. Fish dishes. Vegan dishes. Other diets catered for on request. Snacks at other times. No smoking in the dining-room. No children under 10 in dining-room. Wheelchair access. Accommodation. Access, Amex, Visa

HITCHIN Hertfordshire MAP 5

Pizza Piazza £

87 Bancroft TEL Hitchin (0462) 421101

A branch of a growing chain that offers an enterprising choice of reliably good pizzas. See entry under New Malden for more detail.

Open all week noon to 11 Table service. Licensed. No-smoking area. Wheelchair access. Access, Visa

HOCKLEY HEATH West Midlands MAP 4

Nuthurst Grange £££

Nuthurst Grange Lane TEL Lapworth (056 43) 3972

Just off the A34 half a mile south of Hockley Heath is this small hotel decorated in Liberty style, where the cooking is of a high standard. A vegetarian main course is on the cheaper of the set-price dinner menus – Feta cheese and spinach pie, roulade of spinach, nuts and pulses, or nut and mushroom ragout with sesame seed sauce, for example. Mousseline of broccoli and celeriac, lovage and sweetpea soup, and avocado, melon and mango with minted yoghurt dressing are starters. The crême brûlée has been praised and there is a wide variety of properly ripe cheeses.

Open all week exc Sat L, noon to 2, 7 to 9.30 Booking advisable. Table service. Licensed, also bring your own: corkage by arrangement. Meat dishes. Fish dishes. Vegan dishes. Other diets catered for on request. Wheelchair access. Accommodation. Access, Amex, Diners, Visa

HOLT Norfolk MAP 8

Yetman's ★ ££

37 Norwich Road TEL Holt (0263) 713320

This part of the world is sometimes described as a desert for good food, but Yetman's comes to the rescue. The vegetarian dishes, though limited, demonstrate that the chef gives them full and exacting attention; starters might be fennel and apple soup or walnut brioche filled with cream cheese and herbs with tomato salad; main dishes have included gougère filled with ratatouille, mushroom pâté layered with leeks, parsnip and Gruyère layer or herb pancakes with spinach and mushroom pâté. Courgettes stuffed with green peppers and chives served on a mushroom pâté with Parmesan sauce, was found to be 'a novel combination that worked well and tasted delicious.' Polish off with home-made ice-creams, spotted Dick or a highly rated peach Melba. Home-made truffles arrive with the coffee. The primrose interior with elm chairs and tables, crisp white napery and fresh flowers go further to making the restaurant an oasis.

Open Wed to Sun 12.30 to 2, 7.30 to 9 **Closed** 2 weeks Nov Booking advisable. Table service. Licensed. Meat dishes. Fish dishes. Other diets catered for on request. No smoking. Wheelchair access

HONITON Devon MAP 2

Honeybees £

110 High Street TEL Honiton (0404) 43392

Although the range of dishes on the menu of this chaotic and cluttered wholefood café is restricted, the place has eccentric charm and it is a good place to pop in for a quick bite. Tables and chairs are randomly placed and objects such as gnomes lie around – either part of the décor or unclaimed belongings. It's open from breakfast to tea-time for exotic teas, coffees, fabulous cakes, cream teas and mainly vegetarian lunches offer soup, hummus, pâté, quiche, salads, baked potatoes and home-made ice creams. Toasted banana sandwich and the passion cake are recommended. Unusual fruit juices.

Open Mon to Sat L noon to 5 Table service. Counter service. Unlicensed, but bring your own: no corkage. Meat dishes. Vegan dishes. Other diets on request. Snacks at other times. Take-aways. No-smoking area. Wheelchair access

HOPE Derbyshire MAP 7

Poachers Arms ★ ££

Castleton Road TEL Hope Valley (0433) 20380

A village pub in a very busy area of the Peak District: the restaurant is cosy and service is good, though quite formal. Reporters praise the vegetarian section of the menu, one describing it as 'more adventurous than usual in a pub of this type', and fruit and nut vegetable risotto has been specially noted. There are eight dishes on the menu, a high proportion of which are pasta – panzerotti, cannelloni, lasagne, spaghetti and noodle and ratatouille bake – as well as pancakes and curry.

Open all week noon to 2, 6.30 to 10 Booking advisable. Table service. Counter service. Tables outside. Licensed, also bring your own: corkage £2.50 to £10.50. Meat and fish dishes. Vegan dishes. Accommodation. Access, Amex, Diners, Visa

HORSHAM West Sussex MAP 2

Pizza Piazza £

3 Denne Road TEL Horsham (0403) 62029

A branch of a growing chain that offers an enterprising choice of reliably good pizzas. See entry under New Malden for more detail.

Open all week noon to 11 Table service. Licensed. No-smoking area. Wheelchair access. Access, Visa

HOWDEN Humberside MAP 7

Bridgegate House £

15 Bridgegate TEL Howden (0430) 431010

This daytime-only eatery, where home cooking and baking prevail, is reached through the healthfood shop in front. One of the owners is an ex-cookery teacher. There are daily blackboard specials, but even the standard fare has an unusual touch: moussaka is made with green lentils layered with onions, garlic, aubergines, potatoes and tomatoes topped with a Cheddar cheese sauce, and chilli bean casserole has bulgur wheat and red wine for added interest. Daily wholefood cakes are also marked-up on the blackboard; otherwise, desserts are soya or natural ice-creams and yoghurts. Fish eaters get a look in with one main course normally on offer.

Open Mon to Sat 9 to 4.30pm **Closed** 2 weeks Aug Table service. Unlicensed. Fish dishes. Vegan dishes. Other diets catered for on request. Snacks. Take-aways. No smoking. Wheelchair access exc wc. Accommodation

HUDDERSFIELD West Yorkshire MAP 7

Byrams ££

3 Byram Street TEL Huddersfield (0484) 530243

The Greenwoods, who have owned the bistro for the last eight years, began to offer vegetarian dishes four years ago, and now take this side of the venture seriously enough to provide half a dozen options. Flamiche aux poireaux – white leek tartlet with puff pastry; petits fondues – deep-fried cheese and nutmeg balls; chickpea and fennel casserole and a gougère all show that thought goes into the cooking. The gougère is delightfully crisp on top, soft and cheesey inside, filled with a herbed mixture of courgettes and peppers. The dim and cosy ambience encourages a leisurely meal.

Open Mon to Sat noon (11.30am Sat) to 2.30, 6 to 10.30 (11 Fri and Sat) **Closed** 25 Dec Booking advisable Fri and Sat. Table service. Licensed. Meat dishes. Fish dishes. Vegan dishes. Other diets catered for on request. Wheelchair access. Access, Amex, Visa

HULL Humberside MAP 8

Chaplin's El Gringo £

73 Princess Avenue TEL Hull (0482) 494195

The Mexican menu here will offer a couple of vegetarian versions for an enthusiast of Tex Mex cuisine – huevos rancheros and chimichanga.

Open all week noon to 2, 6 to 11.30, exc Sun L Booking advisable. Table service. Licensed. Meat dishes. Fish dishes. Vegan dishes. Other diets catered for on request. Take-aways. No-smoking area. Wheelchair access. Access, Visa

4626 Restaurant, Crest Hotel ££

Ferriby High Road, North Ferriby TEL Hull (0482) 645212

It is enlightened of the Crest Hotel to provide vegetarians with alternatives: pear with tarragon cream; celery, apple and pine kernel salad; asparagus and mushroom pastry case can be starters and main dishes might be pipérade, saffron rice pilau or pasta with mushrooms, peppers, cream and cheese. Diners enjoy a view of the Humber Bridge.

Open all week 12.30 to 2, 7 to 10 Booking advisable. Table service. Licensed. Meat dishes. Vegan dishes. Other diets catered for on request. No-smoking area. Wheelchair access. Accommodation. Access, Amex, Diners, Visa

HUNGERFORD Berkshire MAP 2

Galloping Crayfish ££

The Courtyard, 24 High Street TEL Hungerford (0488) 84008

Recent refurbishments have coincided with the arrival of a new chef. Vegetarians will continue to be catered for with a minimum of one starter and one main dish (even though the proprietor admits to hearing that Berkshire has the highest proportion of vegetarians in Britain). Dishes might be tomato and basil salad with walnut oil, warm goats' cheese salad, tagliatelle, chanterelle mushrooms with a julienne of vegetables, or stir-fried vegetables.

Open Tue to Sun exc Sun D noon to 2, 7 to 10 Booking advisable. Table service. Tables outside. Licensed, also bring your own: corkage £3. Meat dishes. Fish dishes. Other diets catered for on request. Wheelchair access. Access, Amex, Visa

ILFORD Essex MAP 3

Mandarin Palace ££

559 Cranbrook Road, Gants Hill TEL 081-550 7661

Though it's right on Gants Hill roundabout, once inside you wouldn't know, since the tables in the spacious room are cunningly placed away from the windows. The décor is in red and gold and there are fat, bald, male statues. A complete vegetarian menu shows some conviction: before you order you may be warned that the spicy aubergine with garlic sauce is hot, so an alternative (cashew-nuts with mixed vegetables) is suggested. Crispy roll, sweetcorn soup and mooshoo vegetables with pancakes are all good, if a little bland; braised bean curd and the cashew-nut vegetable dish have been more successful. The finishing touch is a toffee banana: great if you like them. This would certainly be somewhere a vegetarian would feel happy to come with a meat eater.

Open Mon to Sun noon to 3, 6 to midnight Booking advisable. Table service. Counter service. Licensed, also bring your own: corkage £1.50. Meat dishes. Vegan dishes. Take-aways. Wheelchair access. Access, Amex, Diners, Visa

ILFRACOMBE Devon MAP 1

Angel ★ ££

23 Church Street TEL Ilfracombe (0271) 66833

How strange that what was formerly a butcher's shop – and one that rejoices in its ancestry with Victorian tiles and ox's head – should now cater well for vegetarians and vegans as well as fish eaters. Known locally as 'the bovine revenge', the menu is about 50 per cent vegetarian (about nine starters and three main dishes). Dishes are sophisticated, for example a good spinach roulade with imaginative salad; pasta in wine and cheese sauce; hazelnut roast; bean goulash, or mushrooms on rice stuffed with Brazil nuts, apples and onions with lemon herb butter and creamy mushroom sauce. A sampled avocado and lemon water-ice worked extremely well as a starter, tortellini stuffed with mushrooms and pine nuts in cheese and white wine sauce came piping hot, was 'first rate' and was accompanied by an excellent salad – lettuce, tomatoes and onions, Waldorf packed with walnuts and red cabbage and kidney beans in tomato mayonnaise. There are home-made ice-creams and sorbets, and fresh fruit juices and organic wines. One dessert a day is hot, served as the others, with yoghurt for the light touch or cream for the heavy. You can order half portions 'for your cherub'.

Open Tue to Sat noon to 2.30, 6.30 to midnight Booking advisable. Counter service. Tables outside. Fish dishes. Vegan dishes. Other diets catered for. Snacks at other times. Take-aways. No smoking. Access, Amex, Diners, Visa

ILKLEY West Yorkshire MAP 7

Bettys £–££

32–34 The Grove TEL Ilkley (0943) 608029

What began as tea and coffee importers many years ago has grown into a chain of tea and coffee specialists and old-fashioned tea-shops all serving the same kind of high-quality snacks. Vegetarian dishes include deep-fried mushrooms, Yorkshire cheese lunch, cheese and herb pâté or Welsh rarebit. Specials might be smoked Wensleydale croquettes or mushroom croustade. A children's menu is available and savouries, bread and cakes can be bought from the adjoining shop.

Open all week 9am to 7 (9 Fri to Sun) **Closed** some bank hols Table service. Licensed. Meat dishes. Fish dishes. Snacks at all times. Take-aways. Wheelchair access, exc wc. Access, Visa

Sous le Nez ££

19–21 Church Street TEL Ilkley (0943) 600566

Two places to eat: a muted and tasteful restaurant on the first floor and downstairs a busy bistro. The same menu – and prices – operate in both; vegetarian dishes are clearly marked with a 'V'. Pepper-stuffed nut roast, a strudel of stir-fried vegetables, nuts and smoked cheese, and baby goats' cheese and nut roast rolled in breadcrumbs and deep-fried are examples of main dishes.

Open all week, exc Sun L, noon to 2.15, 6 to 10.30 (11 Fri and Sat) Booking advisable. Table service. Licensed. Meat dishes. Fish dishes. No children under 5 after 8. Wheelchair access. Access, Amex, Visa

IPSWICH Suffolk MAP 5

Café Marno £

14 St Nicholas Street TEL Ipswich (0473) 53106

A relaxed place for a lunch chosen from a daily changing blackboard selection: good apple and parsnip soup might be followed by tagliatelle with mushrooms and cream, nut roast or vegetable moussaka. Reports recommend the home-made Pavlova, or try kishmish, dried fruits stewed in brandy, pecan pie, or Guinness and chocolate cake.

Open Mon to Sat 10.30 to 4, Sat D 7.30 to 10 **Closed** Christmas to 2 Jan Table service in evening. Licensed. Vegan dishes. Snacks. Take-aways. No-smoking area. Wheelchair access. Access, Visa

See the back of the guide for a list of restaurants awarded stars for especially good vegetarian cooking.

Marlborough Hotel £££

Henley Road TEL Ipswich (0473) 257677

Though reports of the food vary, the Marlborough Hotel does at least rally to provide vegetarians with alternatives to the main meat menu. Some rather interesting dishes are available as a first or main course: layers of courgettes, aubergines and peppers; special vegetarian salad in a light watercress dressing, or a roulade of rice, peppers and nuts baked in filo pastry with a marmalade sauce. Other examples include pasta flavoured with Stilton under a walnut and breadcrumb crust, and mixed vegetable and Lymeswold pancakes.

Open all week 12.30 to 2, 7.30 to 9.30 Booking advisable. Table service. Licensed, also bring your own: corkage £4.25. Meat dishes. Fish dishes. Snacks. Wheelchair access. Accommodation. Access, Amex, Diners, Visa

Singing Chef ££

200 St Helen's Street TEL Ipswich (0473) 255236

There's no doubt that Kenneth Toyé – who, given half a chance, will break into song to live up to the name of the restaurant – really likes cooking, and it's cheering to find a vegetarian main course now a fixture on his menus. The double-fronted restaurant, in a residential part of Ipswich, parades its Frenchness; inside, a rather bleak room is softened by candlelit, café-style tables. Cheese croustade, a salad with croûtons or a slightly disappointing pissaladière might lead on to a pipérade, mixed pasta and bean ragout or onion tart. Puddings may be on the weighty side, but never contain gelatine: Grand Marnier pancakes or coupe Jeanine, for example.

Open all week D 7 to 11 **Closed** 1 week after Easter week, last week Aug Booking advisable Fri and Sat. Table service. Tables outside. Licensed. Meat dishes. Fish dishes. Other diets catered for on request. No-smoking tables. Take-aways on advance order only. Access, Visa

When you book a restaurant table, you're making a contract with the restaurant and they must give you a table, in reasonable time. If they don't, they're in breach of contract and you can claim a reasonable sum to cover any expenses you had as a result, eg travelling costs.

IRONBRIDGE Shropshire MAP 4

Meadow Inn £

Buildwas Road TEL Ironbridge (095 245) 3193

'Very good pub grub in huge portions and very cheap,' is one verdict on the food. The fixed menu has a spicy bean bake and a vegetable Mornay, while blackboard special may also include something without meat or fish, such as mushroom stroganoff or pasta in cream sauce with cheese and tomato.

Open all week noon to 2 (2.15 Sun), 6 to 10 (9.30 Sun) Table service. Tables outside. Licensed. Meat dishes. Fish dishes. Vegan dishes. Other diets catered for with prior notice. Wheelchair access. Access, Visa

Olivers ⓥ £

Upstairs, 33A High Street TEL Ironbridge (095 245) 3086

Olivers is near the famous iron bridge. A small, pretty bistro rather than a café, set above the Au Pont de Fer restaurant, it serves exclusively vegetarian food. Lunches and dinners aim to follow wholefood principles as far as possible. Examples of starters are herb pâté, warm salad of cashew and orange, or home-made soup; main dishes include zucchini lasagne, leek, Stilton and apple flan, chilli or vegetables in cheese sauce.

Open Tue to Sun 11.30 to 2.30, 7 to 9.30 exc Sun D Booking advisable. Table service. Licensed, also bring your own: corkage 50p. Vegan dishes. Other diets catered for on request. Snacks. No smoking

IXWORTH Suffolk MAP 5

Pickerel £

High Street TEL Pakenham (0359) 30398

As well as being such a pretty pub, the Pickerel is worth a visit for its food. Curry and apple soup, ratatouille and a good pineapple cassis to follow were all enjoyed. Other vegetarian items are featured on the blackboard – spicy spinach filos, mushroom and bean pancakes, stroganoff, vegetable and hazelnut cutlet or cheesy leek and potato bake. Service is excellent.

Open all week noon to 2, 7 to 9.30 Booking advisable. Table service. Tables outside. Licensed. Meat dishes. Fish dishes. Other diets on request. Access, Visa

JEVINGTON East Sussex MAP 3

Hungry Monk £££

Jevington TEL Polegate (032 12) 2178

A cosy, intimate restaurant made up of a labyrinth of small rooms filled with an array of objects. The food is high quality with prices to match. Starters, such as a croustade of quails' eggs or gazpacho, are more interesting than main dishes of goats' cheese in filo pastry with sweet pepper sauce or feuilleté of wild mushrooms with chestnuts. Accompanying vegetables have been overcooked, but there's praise for puddings, ginger ice-cream and crème brûlée in particular.

Open all week, D 7 to 10, Sun L noon to 2 **Closed** 24 Dec, 25 Dec, bank hols Booking advisable. Table service. Licensed. Meat dishes. Fish dishes. Vegan dishes. Other diets catered for on request. No smoking in dining-room. No children under 4

KENDAL Cumbria MAP 9

Moon ★ ££

129 Highgate TEL Kendal (0539) 729254

An excellent place for a night out – and the meat-eater will find a wide choice as well. The décor is modern bistro, with red wooden folding chairs and red check tablecloths. The heavy rock music may not be to everyone's liking. Walls are hung with objects and pictures on the moon theme; upstairs the attractive black and white tablecloths and upholstered chairs create a relaxing venue for coffee or drinks. The food is terrific. Try, as starters, a Feta cheese strudel, not hot out of the oven but very tasty, containing fresh spinach; an inventive asparagus and Brie cream with a tangy texture and full Brie flavour. From a good choice of main dishes, try a creamy fennel, mushroom, sweetcorn and lemon cream tagliatelle; brioche filled with sweet-and-sour vegetables; a delicious, mildly spiced vegetable korma with baby sweetcorn, carrots, aubergines and okra with brown rice; or a very good red wine pilaff –

rice, spinach and tomatoes covered with Gruyère custard. Why, though, must every dish be adorned with mixed salad? Puddings include summer fruit kissel, strawberry and mango cream and meringue, an outstanding steamed sticky-toffee pudding, light and caramelly. Alternatively, there's garlic Lancashire cheese. What it lacks in terms of quality of bread and some of the trimmings, it makes up for in value-for-money food.

Open all week, D 6 to 10 (10.30 Fri and Sat) Table service. Licensed. Meat dishes. Fish dishes. Other diets catered for on request. No pipes or cigars. Wheelchair access. Access, Visa

Nutters Coffee House £

Yard 11, Stramongate TEL Kendal (0539) 725135

Tucked down a cobbled passageway off Finkle Street, Simon Nutter's idiosyncratic establishment has a quaint old-fashioned air and serves good vegetarian dishes alongside meat. The menu changes every day. Downstairs a fire is lit on chilly days. 'Neat and tidy it is not': postcards and foreign bank notes are pinned up and poems are chalked on blackboards in the passageway. Upstairs the blackboard bears the day's menu: good soups, particularly mushroom and watercress, hearty baked potatoes, perhaps a vegetable pie or a quiche. A good range of puddings and cakes includes a specially commended sticky-toffee pudding and a good lemon meringue pie. Toasted teacakes, scones, sponges, shortbreads and rich fruit cakes are on offer outside mealtimes.

Open Mon to Sat 8.30am to 6.30 Table service. Counter service. Tables outside. Licensed. Meat dishes. Snacks. Take-aways. No-smoking area. Wheelchair access

Pizza Margherita £

181 Highgate TEL Kendal (0539) 731303

One of a good small chain, set in a converted Victorian shop and clean and stylish in décor. Wholemeal pizzas, cooked to order, come in four vegetarian versions, alternatively try vegetable lasagne or a jacket potato with mushroom sauce. The coffee can be recommended.

Open all week 11am to 10.30 Table service. Licensed. Meat dishes. Fish dishes. Vegan dishes. No-smoking area. Wheelchair access. Access, Visa

Plough Inn £–££

Selside TEL Kendal (0539) 83687

Sometimes a pub meal is just the ticket, and there is at least one home-style vegetarian main dish at this pub. Vegetable stroganoff it might well be, with vegetable soup if a starter is a must.

Open all week noon to 2, 7 to 9 Counter service. Tables outside. Licensed. Meat dishes. Fish dishes. Other diets catered for on request. Snacks at other times. Wheelchair access. Accommodation

Waterside Wholefoods Ⓥ £

Kent View TEL Kendal (0539) 729743

Near the River Kent, overlooking an old stone bridge yet near the main shopping centre, is this popular vegetarian café, simply decorated with white walls and furnished in pine and oatmeal tweed. The food is prepared freshly each day in a kitchen that can be glimpsed from the café – customers can see the hot rolls, cheese and fruit scones and quiche brought out of the oven. Cakes are tempting, in particular fruit and almond tart and carrot cake. For lunch, there are salads, hot dishes such as quiche, Turkish pilau with yoghurt or a crisp wholemeal pastry leek and potato pie. Soups are recommended.

Open Mon to Sat, L 11.45 to 2 Counter service. Tables outside. Unlicensed. Other diets on request. Snacks. Take-aways. No smoking. Wheelchair access

KENILWORTH Warwickshire MAP 4

Ana's Bistro ££

121–123 Warwick Road TEL Kenilworth (0926) 53763

This cluttered, low-beamed bistro has a daily menu providing straightforward fare with one vegetarian main-course option – stroganoff, pancake or deep-fried mushrooms, perhaps. Starters might include mushrooms in garlic and herb butter, pasta provençale, melon and pineapple cocktail, or avocado vinaigrette.

Open Tue to Sat, D 7 to 10.30 **Closed** 3 weeks Aug, 1 week Easter Booking advisable. Table service. Licensed. Meat dishes. Fish dishes. Other diets catered for on request. Access, Visa

KESWICK Cumbria **MAP 9**

Brundholme Country House Hotel **£–£££**

Brundholme Road TEL Keswick (076 87) 74495

A small country-house hotel in what Coleridge described as a 'delicious situation'; things haven't changed much and there are splendid views. Dishes adhere to traditional lines, and vegetarians get a small look-in on a five-course set-dinner menu: soup or Lanarkshire blue cheese as starters, then sorbet followed by one dish that might be crumble, stroganoff or lentil and spinach roulade. Sweets can prove a disappointment. In general the cooking is careful, but beware of meaty stocks used in soups.

Open all week 12.30 to 1.45, 7.30 to 8.30; L by arrangement **Closed** 25 Dec to Feb Booking advisable. Table service. Tables outside. Licensed. Meat dishes. Fish dishes. Vegan dishes. Other diets catered for on request. No smoking in dining-room. Wheelchair access. Accommodation. Access, Visa

Maysons **£**

33 Lake Road TEL Keswick (076 87) 74104

All the food here is made on the premises and portions are generous. Suitable main courses might include Indonesian vegetable curry on brown rice, lasagne, stuffed vegetables and mushroom rissoles, while starters are on more predictable lines of hummus and onion soup. Carrot cake is delectable and moist.

Open all week 11.30am to 8.45 **Closed** D Nov to June Counter service. Licensed. Meat dishes. Vegan dishes. Other diets catered for on request. Snacks. Take-aways. No-smoking area

A restaurant must display a menu and a wine list outside, or immediately inside the door. Prices shown must be inclusive of VAT. If they aren't, tell the local Trading Standards Officer.

KIDDERMINSTER Hereford & Worcester **MAP 4**

Natural Break £

6–7 Blackwell Street TEL Kidderminster (0562) 743275

Part of a small chain of vegetarian and meat-serving cafés, open all day for snacks, teas and cakes. See entries under Worcester.

Open Mon to Fri 9.30 to 4 (5 Sat) Counter service. Meat dishes. Vegan dishes. Low-fat dishes on request. Snacks. Take-aways. No-smoking area. Wheelchair access

KING'S LYNN Norfolk **MAP 8**

Garbo's ★ ££

7 Saturday Market Place TEL King's Lynn (0553) 773136

A sparkling restaurant in Saturday Market Place in this most attractive East Anglian town; the atmosphere is warm and staff are informal and cheerful. 'The vegetarian element of the menu is exceptional,' comments one reporter, while another praises the presentation. An extensive menu changes every couple of days: starters might include artichoke stuffed with broad bean and pistachio purée topped with puff pastry, an excellent leaf salad with croûtons topped with poached egg, or cheese and herbs in filo pastry. Main dishes include grilled avocado with wild mushrooms and cashew-nut crumble, stir-fried vegetables in puff pastry with cider and parsley sauce and various pastas. Home-made ice-creams include a good blackberry version.

Open Tue to Sat 7 to 10 Booking advisable. Table service. Licensed, also bring your own: corkage £2 per bottle. Meat dishes. Fish dishes. Other diets catered for on request. No-smoking area. Access, Amex, Visa

Riverside £–££

King's Lynn Arts Centre, 27 King Street
TEL King's Lynn (0553) 773134

Delightfully situated overlooking the river, the terrace would be a good choice for a summer day. Lunch dishes are limited and vegetarians are offered quick, inexpensive meals of spinach and mushroom pancakes, red kidney bean casserole or lasagne. Evening meals are more upmarket and vegetarian dishes are always available. Most vegetables are organically grown in the restaurant's own garden. Fresh lime cheesecake, sweet roulade or hazelnut meringues are home made. A new wine list includes organic wines.

Open Mon to Sat noon to 2, 7 to 10 Booking advisable. Table service. Tables outside. Licensed. Meat dishes. Fish dishes. Other diets catered for on request. No-smoking area. Access, Visa

KINGSTON-UPON-THAMES Surrey MAP 3

La La Pizza ££

138 London Road TEL 081-546 4888

Owned by an Italian and exuding a busy, boisterous air that precludes a quiet tête à tête, but the dedicated clientele obviously enjoy it. Excellent pizzas come with an almost overwhelming variety of toppings, of which a good many are vegetarian. The pizza-dough garlic bread is soft and moist inside, crisp outside, as it should be. Prices are reasonable. With so much going for it, it is a serious competitor to Pizza Express.

Open all week, D 5.30 to 11.30 Booking advisable weekends. Table service. Licensed. Meat dishes. Fish dishes. Take-aways. Wheelchair access

Pizza Express £

41 High Street TEL 081-546 1447

A satellite of the excellent London-based chain that was founded twenty-five years ago. See London entry.

Open Mon to Sat 11.30 to midnight, Sun noon to 11.30. Table service. Licensed, also bring your own: corkage £2.50. Meat dishes. Fish dishes. Take-aways. No-smoking area. Wheelchair access. Access, Amex, Diners, Visa

The main criterion for inclusion in the guide is that an eating place offers a vegetarian main course on its standard menu, at all times, that is more than just an omelette, quiche or salad. If you find that a listed restaurant no longers caters for vegetarians, please inform the guide; the address to write to is on page 9.

KIRKBY LONSDALE Cumbria MAP 10

Lupton Tower ⓥ ★ ££

Lupton TEL Crooklands (044 87) 400

The tower of this eighteenth-century country house contains some of the best bedrooms, with views on two sides. Family run, the hotel is luxurious without being overly opulent: log fires burn, the small dining-room is decorated with fresh flowers and linen cloths and napkins grace the tables. A warning that all the food is vegetarian is given on booking, but surely even the most hide-bound flesh eater could not criticise a four-course menu that shows imagination and 'inspired confidence that an entire meal could be interesting without meat' – this from a meat-eater. Many visitors are not vegetarian. Modern British presentation makes the most of a vegetarian terrine, surrounded with puff pastry and a tomato salad; cauliflower and almond soup is good and tasty and the sole main course might be an intriguing quenelles de fromage sauce saffron – cheese dumplings made of three different cheeses, one very strong, one mild and one waxy. Pear tarte Tatin is made with flaky pastry and the apple and blackcurrant mousse is excellent. There are special culinary events, for instance a Caribbean dinner and Midsummer madness.

Open all week, D 7.30 Booking advisable. Table service. Licensed, but bring your own: corkage £2. Vegan dishes by prior arrangement. No-smoking. Wheelchair access. Accommodation

KIRKBY STEPHEN Cumbria MAP 10

Old Forge Bistro £

39 North Road TEL Kirkby Stephen (076 83) 71832

The seventeenth-century smithy now converted to a bistro provides bar snacks and home-made blackboard specials; all vegetarian dishes appear on the blackboard. A typical day's menu might be sweet-and-sour aduki bean braise, butterbean and mushroom stroganoff with wholemeal rice, lentil and walnut loaf with tomato and tarragon sauce, as well as a curried apple soup. Soup is always vegan. There's sticky toffee pudding and Cumberland rum nicky to finish.

Open Tue to Sun noon to 2, 6 to 10 Booking advisable. Table service. Licensed.

Meat dishes. Other diets catered for on request. Take-aways. No smoking. Wheelchair access

KIRKHAM Lancashire MAP 7

Cromwellian ££

16 Poulton Street TEL Kirkham (0772) 685680

Somewhat inconspicuous in the main street of Kirkham is this small white-painted town house said to be 300 years old. Smartly set tables are scattered informally round two small ground-floor rooms and upstairs. The colour scheme is burgundy and grey. A husband and wife team shares the running of the restaurant – she does most of the cooking, though he makes the soups, of which parsnip and ginger has been well regarded. Starters on the set-price menu are limited – maybe a spiced banana and seasonal salad or savoury profiteroles. All the menu promises is a 'vegetarian dish of the day': this might turn out to be Brazil nut terrine, Alsace-style onion tart or bean and vegetable casserole. For puddings there might be sticky-toffee pudding or walnut tart, both tried and recommended, or good almond sponge with coffee cream sauce. Hand-made chocolate petits fours come with coffee but both at additional cost.

Open Tue to Sat D 7 to 10, Sun L 12.30 to 2.30 Booking advisable. Table service. Licensed. Meat dishes. Fish dishes. Other diets catered for on request. Wheelchair access. Access, Visa

KIRKOSWALD Cumbria MAP 9

Prospect Hill Hotel ££

Eden Valley TEL Lazonby (076 883) 500

Prospect Hill indeed, with commanding views over the Eden Valley. Eighteenth-century farm buildings have been converted into this cosy hotel decorated with antique farm implements, old sewing machines, flat irons and measuring scales. The dining-room is semi-circular, the original gin casing platform forming extra floor space. A full vegetarian menu has about five starters and five main dishes: start perhaps with a thick and flavoursome vegetable-stock soup, wine and nut pâté or hot avocado stuffed with cheese and nuts; go on to a good, nutty, herby mixed vegetable crumble or a light courgette roulade with cream cheese and courgette filling and rich hollandaise-type sauce. Cherry chocolate cake makes a rich and alcoholic dessert; fruit salad would be a lighter pudding. Cheeses are local. Coffee comes with excellent home-made fudge.

Open all week, D 7 to 8.45 **Closed** Feb Booking advisable. Table service. Licensed, but bring your own: corkage £1.50 per bottle, extra for Champagne. Meat dishes. Fish dishes. Other diets catered for on request. Wheelchair access (also wc). Accommodation. Access, Diners, Visa

KNARESBOROUGH North Yorkshire MAP 7

Bengal Dynasty £

6–8 Bond End TEL Harrogate (0423) 863899

'I'm glad to have discovered the Dynasty,' was one reader's verdict on a place where the food is not too salty and the kulfi, which is of a particularly creamy texture, hits just the right note for sweetness. Onion bhajias to start and vegetable korma for the main dish, plus that kulfi, would satisfy a vegetarian visitor.

Open all week 6 to midnight Table service. Licensed. Meat dishes. Take-aways. Wheelchair access. Access, Amex, Diners, Visa

KNUTSFORD Cheshire MAP 7

Longview Hotel ££

Manchester Road TEL Knutsford (0565) 2119

Pauline and Stephen West have worked hard on this corner Victorian building. Inside is somewhat old-fashioned and eccentric – not the ideal romantic venue perhaps, but certainly somewhere to find robust vegetarian food in very generous portions. The chefs don't rely on old favourites and have come up with some new and successful ideas: egg, tomato and cucumber mousse, a tasty mushroom and cheese 'puff' served as a wedge of pie, tofu à la printanière. The last is a treat for those who like tofu – it is marinated with ginger, spring onions, sherry and soy sauce and then pan fried. Accompanying vegetables are a feast in themselves, a typical array being moussaka, rice with almonds and orange chips, fried potatoes, asparagus, leeks, cauliflower and carrots. Lush creamy puddings include good lime cheesecake and strawberry mallow.

Open Mon to Sat, D 7 to 8.30, L by arrangement Fri and Sat **Closed** 25 Dec to 1 Jan Booking advisable. Table service. Licensed. Meat dishes. Fish dishes. Other diets catered for on request. Snacks. Wheelchair access (also WC). Accommodation

LACOCK Wiltshire MAP 2

Red Lion £

High Street TEL Lacock (024 973) 456

The building dates from the seventeenth century and is decorated in rustic fashion inside: corn dollies hang from the ceiling beams, there are stuffed birds and animals, furniture is upholstered in tapestry and antique agricultural implements abound. Huge logs burn in the large old fireplace and at the other end of the pub a more utilitarian wood-burning stove gives off a glow. In addition to standard pub fare of jacket potatoes and ploughman's, vegetarians are offered a blackboard dish that might be a bake of some kind, depending on what vegetables are in season. A courgette and mushroom version, served with spinach in a thick cheesy sauce, was much enjoyed. Soups are usually made with meat stock.

Open all week 12.15 to 2.30, 6.30 to 10 **Closed** 25 Dec Table service. Tables outside. Licensed. Meat dishes. Snacks. Wheelchair access. Accommodation

LANCASTER Lancashire MAP 7

Duke's £

Duke's Playhouse, Moor Lane TEL Lancaster (0524) 843215

The Playhouse aims to be a community centre and the restaurant, for it is now more than a café, provides high-quality meals. There are special menus for those of limited time going to the theatre or, in contrast, those who want a more relaxed evening. Main vegetarian dishes include nut roast, gratin dauphinois or curried mushrooms. Lunch offerings might be tagliatelle, cauliflower bake or snacks such as jacket potatoes.

Open Tue to Sat noon to 2, 5.30 to 9 Booking advisable pre-performance. Table service. Licensed. Meat dishes. Fish dishes. Vegan dishes. Other diets catered for on request. Wheelchair access

Libra ⓥ £

19 Brock Street TEL Lancaster (0524) 61551

Libra is a long-established vegetarian restaurant and conforms to the pattern of café-with-counter serving lunches of jacket potatoes, quiches and salads. There are tables in the back garden for fine-weather eating. Daily dishes might be broccoli and sweetcorn filo parcels, a bake, or perhaps a quiche so freshly cooked that you have to wait for it to emerge from the oven: it comes in a light wholemeal pastry with a generous filling. The sugar-free fruit cake is good and well endowed with fruit.

Open Mon to Sat 11am to 3 Counter service. Tables outside. Licensed. Vegan dishes. Other diets catered for on request. Snacks. Take-aways. No smoking. Wheelchair access

Pizza Margherita £

2 Moor Lane TEL Lancaster (0524) 68820

Part of a small chain. The building used to be derelict, now it's neat and clean, inside and out. The floor is tiled, tables are marble-topped and there are plenty of plants, large mirrors and modern prints on the walls. The menu warns that there might be a wait for pizzas cooked to order. In the meantime, try one of the many vegetarian starters – minestrone, red and white bean salad, baked mushrooms, salads. The pitta bread arrives piping hot. Of the pizzas, vegetarians can have four versions, which arrive with a thin wholemeal base and lavish topping. Other dishes available are a lasagne and a bake consisting of mushroom, cheese and tomato on a potato base. Apple pie is made with good, sweet shortcrust pastry.

Open all week 11am to 10.30 Table service. Licensed. Meat dishes. Snacks. Take-aways. No-smoking area. Access, Visa

All letters to the guide are acknowledged.

Warehouse Café ⓥ £

78A Penny Street TEL Lancaster (0524) 63021

This workers' co-operative is open all day and serves lunches such as salads, shepherd's pie, gougères filled with peppers and avocado, mushroom and nut roast in red pepper sauce, and stuffed vine leaves. The veggie burgers, made to the kitchen's own recipe, are a speciality. Unlimited coffee for 65p is a plus.

Open Mon to Sat 10.30 to 4.30 Table service. Tables outside. Licensed. Vegan dishes. Other diets catered for on request. Snacks. Take-aways

LAUNCESTON Cornwall MAP 1

Greenhouse ⓥ £

Madford Lane TEL Launceston (0566) 3670

'An airy, green-painted, conservatory-type of place, a sort of daytime healthfood bistro/coffee-bar,' is one description of this wholefood restaurant. Every day there are quiches, pizzas and some five different salads with hot dishes of tomato and lentil bake, green bean layer, mushroom bake, or aduki pie. The mixed bean curry made with haricot, flageolet and broad beans was spicy and came with brown rice. Home-made cakes are good, and the sticky gingerbread is particularly recommended.

Open Mon to Sat L only, 10 to 4 **Closed** 1 week after Christmas Counter service. Licensed. Vegan dishes. Other diets catered for on request. Snacks. Take-aways. No smoking. Wheelchair access exc wc

LEAMINGTON SPA Warwickshire MAP 4

Wishing Well ⓥ ★ £–££

29 Bath Street TEL Leamington Spa (0926) 315001

Converted from an Indian take-away, this vegetarian restaurant resembles a clearing in a wood, complete with trees and wishing well. The food – a large proportion of which is suitable for vegans – is freshly prepared, well presented and tastes extremely good. At lunchtime there are snacks as well as more complete meals. A sample meal, much appreciated, consisted of a nut roast with tasty red wine and herb sauce, surrounded by an array of vegetables, nuts, seeds and fruits, and buckwheat pancakes filled with ratatouille and covered with a delicate lemon sauce, then a traditional Bakewell tart with soya custard to finish, the portion almost too generous. Had starters been ordered, the choice would have been between nut pâté, garlic mushrooms or parsnip and apple soup. One criticism is that main dishes too often resort to tofu, an ingredient not to everyone's liking.

Open Tue to Sat 10am to 5, 7 to 10   Booking advisable. Table service D. Counter service L. Licensed. Vegan dishes. Other diets catered for on request. Snacks. Take-aways. No-smoking area. Wheelchair access. Access, Amex, Diners, Visa

LEDBURY   Hereford & Worcester   MAP 4

Apple Charlotte   £–££

44 The Homend   TEL Ledbury (0531) 4181

Both bar and bistro menus have at least one vegetarian dish. The bistro, tiny and cosy in this ancient half-timbered building, always makes a soup to cater for vegetarians. The daily dish might be artichoke strudel or savoury profiteroles. The bar, as well as offering pizzas, might list a curry or hazelnut and brown rice roast served on herb rösti. 'Alternatives can usually be provided for vegans,' say the owners.

Open Mon to Sat noon to 2.30, 7.30 to 9.30   Booking advisable. Table service. Licensed. Meat dishes. Vegan dishes. Other diets catered for on request. Take-aways. No children after 9 in upstairs bistro. Wheelchair access. Access, Visa

Market Place   £–££

1 The Homend   TEL Ledbury (0531) 4250

A pretty, old building facing the ancient market, which still functions as such. Inside, the resturant is all green – dark green walls, green-stained wood furniture and even a carpet to match. Lunches are self-service and have much more to offer vegetarians than the evening menu: typically there will be quiche, nut roast, a few salads and a hot dish. Black-eyed bean casserole is good, with a hint of caraway. A good variety of cakes, shortbreads, flapjacks and scones includes an unusual treacle tart made with cornflakes rather than breadcrumbs; the pastry is good, the filling overly sweet. Evening choices are rather limited, the menu being mainly pasta and burgers.

Open all week noon to 2, 7.30 to 10 (exc Mon D) Booking advisable D. Table service D. Counter service L. Licensed, also bring your own. Meat dishes. Snacks. No-smoking area. Wheelchair access. Access, Visa

LEEDS West Yorkshire MAP 7

Cocina £

84–86 Vicar Lane TEL Leeds (0532) 465754

Apart from the odd Mexican artefact, there is little atmosphere to this Mexican restaurant which, if anything, is more trans-Atlantic than ethnic. The menu has eight vegetarian main dishes: enfrijolada – steamed corn tortillas rolled and filled with bean stew and topped with guacamole – rates highly: baja tomotillo is more like filo pastry than a pancake (which is how it is described on the menu), the filling tasty and subtly flavoured with cinnamon, is perhaps too rich; enchiladas are also recommended – two different fillings, one much hotter than the other. The enfrijolada is vegan. Of the desserts, only capirotada (cooked apple and raisins on top of sliced bread) is vegan, and only it and the toffee pudding are made on the premises. Failure to obtain certain ingredients (avocados for instance) can lead to some items being unavailable. Service is helpful and pleasant.

Open all week noon to 3, 5 to 10.30 exc Sun L Table service. Licensed. Meat dishes. Snacks. Take-aways. No-smoking area. Wheelchair access. Access, Visa

Hansa ⓥ £

North Street TEL Leeds (0532) 444408

What used to be a row of Victorian shops is now a splendid Gujerati restaurant, five minutes' drive from the city. Excellent channa bateta (chickpeas and potatoes cooked in coconut and garnished with crisps, onions and roasted peanuts) is a feature, as well as masala dosa, patra and a 'rather oily' aubergine bhaji. Home-made ice-creams flavoured with almond and saffron, mango or cardamom vie with classic kulfi on the sweets list. Unusual puddings include ghari, crusted sweet pie served hot with cream, and lapsi, a vegan concoction of bulgur cooked in vegetable ghee with sultanas and spiced with cardamom, fennel and cinnamon.

Open Tue to Sun, exc Sat L and Sun L, noon to 2, 7 to 10.30 Booking advisable. Table service. Licensed. Vegan dishes. Other diets catered for on request. Take-aways. No-smoking area. Wheelchair access. Access, Diners, Visa

Mandalay £

8 Harrison Street TEL Leeds (0532) 446340 and 4454563

Though it's now fashionable for Indian restaurants to avoid flock wall-paper, the resulting décor can be lacking in character, something that has been mentioned about the Mandalay. The food, however, has plenty of identity: slightly sweet aloo tikki and vegetable samosas have been praised, pakoras are recommended, and good vegetable biriani has fragrant saffron spiced rice and a welcome addition of cashews and raisins. Creamy dhal and Peshwari nan make good accompaniments. A vegetarian set menu is surprisingly more expensive than the others, and offers onion bhaji, aloo tikki, vegetable samosas, malai kofta, bhindi bhaji, muttar paneer, dhal, nan, rice, raita and a dessert of kulfi.

Open Mon to Sat, exc Sat L, noon to 2.30, 6 to 11.30 Table service. Licensed. Meat dishes. Fish dishes. Take-aways. Wheelchair access. Access, Amex, Diners, Visa

Olive Tree ££

Oaklands, Rodley Lane TEL Leeds (0532) 569283

A jetty leads from the car park up to the large stone Victorian house, far from the stereotype of a Greek restaurant. Inside looks like an old-fashioned English dining-room: a spacious ground floor room boasting high ceilings and large windows. Staff may have the Yorkshire way of speech, but the food is authentically Greek. A good selection of the starters is vegetarian – tandiki, hummus, melintzanosalata, dolmades – then there might be a vegetarian moussaka. The cooking is above average and salads get good reports. Ingredients indicate wise buying.

Open all week, exc Sat L, noon to 2.30, 6.30 to 11 **Closed** 25 and 26 Dec, 1 Jan Table service. Licensed. Meat dishes. Vegan dishes. Other diets catered for on request. No-smoking area. Wheelchair access. Access, Visa

Strawberryfields Bistro £

159 Woodhouse Lane TEL Leeds (0532) 431515

As well as serving pizza and burgers, Strawberryfields claims to borrow from less well-known cuisines, though this is more obvious in meat and fish items than the vegetarian ones. On the standard menu are moussaka, croustade, lasagne, mushroom and nut pancake, and nutmeat pâté in brioche. The speciality board changes every week and also has some vegetarian ideas – walnut and bulgur balls in mushroom and wine sauce or three-bean stroganoff, for instance. For the sweet-toothed, death by chocolate, Mississippi mud pie or a fudge brownie.

Open Mon to Sat, exc Sat L, 11.45 to 2.15, 6 to 11 **Closed** 24, 25 and 26 Dec Booking advisable Fri and Sat. Table service. Licensed. Meat dishes. Vegan dishes. Other diets catered for on request. No-smoking area. Wheelchair access, exc WC. Access, Visa

LEICESTER Leicestershire MAP 4

Blossoms £

176 Cank Street TEL Leicester (0533) 539535

The snack bar is in a pedestrianised, newly refurbished part of Leicester. The atmosphere is homely, the main clientele shoppers. For lunch there are home-made soups, jacket potatoes, various quiches and hot dishes such as bean hot-pot, goulash, curry, lentil bolognese, mushroom bake. Good home-made sweets run the gamut of fruit and lemon meringue pies, crumble, flapjacks, cheesecake, banana and walnut cake, and date and apricot slice.

Open Mon to Sat 11.30am to 2.30 Counter service. Licensed. Vegan dishes. Snacks. Take-aways. No-smoking area

Bobby's £

154–156 Belgrave Road TEL Leicester (0533) 660106 and 662448

In the heart of Leicester's Indian community, Belgrave Road supports several cafés, of which Bobby's is among the best. The food is excellent, even if the style of furnishing is fairly spartan and the ambience a little severe. Thalis are especially good. Like many Indian vegetarian restaurants it has a counter selling home-made sweets and other items, as well as the dining areas. In all, authentic and good value.

Open Tue to Sun 11am to 10.30 (11 Sat and Sun) Table service. Unlicensed, but bring your own: no corkage. Vegan dishes. Snacks. Take-aways. No-smoking area. Wheelchair access. Access, Amex, Visa

Bread and Roses ⓥ £

70 High Street TEL Leicester (0533) 532448

A Middle-Eastern bias dominates the menu: falafel rissoles, vegetarian kibbeh and bulgur pie with cashew-nuts all appear as main courses, and desserts include baklava and date slices. There are various quiches, among them spinach, mushroom or sweetcorn.

Open Tue to Sat noon to 4 **Closed** 25 Dec, 1 Jan Booking advisable. Table service. Tables outside. Licensed, also bring your own. Vegan dishes. Other diets catered for on request. Take-aways. No-smoking area. Access, Visa

Chaat House ⓥ ££

108 Belgrave Road TEL Leicester (0533) 667599

South Indian cuisine is vegetarianism in its element, and the choice here. There are two set thalis, one more substantial than the other, but both come with either puri or chapati. Some 10 vegetable curries are on offer, as well as choley bhature, chaats, dosas, four different kulfis and five other traditional sweets. Is the masala milk a first among drinks?

Open all week exc Tue, noon to 8.30 Table service. Unlicensed. Vegan dishes. Snacks. Take-aways. No smoking. Wheelchair access. Access, Amex, Diners, Visa

Good Earth ⓥ £

19 Free Lane TEL Leicester (0533) 626260

Above a healthfood store specialising in organic produce, the restaurant in the centre of town provides counter lunches and dinner on Fridays; about six nights a year it holds a gourmet evening. All the day's dishes are home made: vegetable bake, a selection of salads buffet style, pies, rissoles and quiches. Home-made puddings include apple and black-currant crumble and lemon syllabub.

Open Mon to Sat, L noon to 3, Fri, D 6 to 11 Counter service. Licensed. Vegan dishes. No-smoking area

Hayloft, Holiday Inn ££

129 St Nicholas Circle TEL Leicester (0533) 531161

Buffet meals are taken from a central area (Mon to Fri 10.30–2, 7–10). An enterprising à la carte offers four main-course vegetarian options (in addition to a veggie-burger available on the all-day menu): Tibetan roast, with spinach, walnuts, buckwheat and tahini; cold corn and cashew-nut roast; raised vegetable pie and chilli bean casserole. Puddings are from the trolley. Service has been praised.

Open all week 12.30 to 2.15, 7 to 10.15 Booking advisable. Table service. Counter service. Licensed, also bring your own: corkage £5. Meat dishes. Vegan dishes and other diets catered for on request. Snacks. No-smoking area. Wheelchair access. Accommodation. Access, Amex, Carte Blanche, Diners, Visa

LEIGHTON BUZZARD Bedfordshire MAP 4

Swan Hotel ££

High Street TEL Leighton Buzzard (0525) 372148

The Swan attracts kind comments about the food and friendly service: details such as automatically serving iced water are appreciated. A complete vegetarian dinner menu offers three starters and three main dishes. Choose from melon with pink champagne sorbet, a fan of avocado pear with yoghurt and grapefruit salad; hot pastry case with field mushrooms and spinach in madeira sauce; bean and nut stroganoff with salad leaves; aubergine and tomato casserole. Sticky-toffee pudding for those who fancy nursery puddings, home-made sorbets for those who don't.

Open all week noon to 2, 7 to 9.30 Booking advisable. Table service. Tables outside. Licensed, also bring your own: corkage £5. Meat dishes. Fish dishes. Other diets catered for on request. No-smoking area. Wheelchair access. Accommodation. Access, Amex, Diners, Visa

LEWES East Sussex **MAP 3**

Kenwards £££

Pipe Passage, 151A High Street TEL Lewes (0273) 472343

Down narrow Pipe Passage off Lewes High Street, Kenwards pleasantly defies the traditions of 'liveried flunkeys', being determinedly individualistic. The food relies on good simple ingredients and doesn't overwhelm with super-rich sauces. Vegetarians also eat well – but take careful note, not so well at lunchtime. Menus change often, with main dishes of Bonchester cheese with mushrooms and cider, or courgette and mushroom with Stilton and tarragon. Starters include beetroot terrine with leeks and orange or artichokes and leeks with ginger and parsley. British cheeses are served just at maturity and the attached shop sells them too. Home-made sorbets are intriguing – rose petal and mint served with wild strawberries, for instance. Wintry puddings which are variations on British favourites might be hot ginger sponge with lemon sauce or walnut and apricot tart. It's comparatively expensive, but certainly somewhere to have a special dinner with relish.

Open Mon to Fri noon to 2.15, Tue to Sat 7.30 to 9 **Closed** 1 week spring, 1 week summer Booking advisable. Table service. Tables outside. Licensed. Meat dishes. Fish dishes. Other diets catered for on request. Access, Visa

Old Needlemakers Café £

Market Lane TEL Lewes (0273) 476822

The former candle factory houses various craft shops as well as this Café, which, though not purely vegetarian, serves rudimentary fare such as quiches, jacket potatoes, pizzas, and tasty soups. There are various salads too.

Open Mon to Sat 9.30 to 5 Counter service. Tables outside. Unlicensed, but bring your own. Meat dishes. Fish dishes. Snacks. Take-aways. Wheelchair access

'Wheelchair access' indicates that, according to the proprietor, entrances are at least 33 inches wide, passages 4 feet wide, and that there are a maximum of two steps, unless otherwise stated.

LINCOLN Lincolnshire **MAP 8**

Harvey's Cathedral Restaurant/Troffs £–£££

1 Exchequer Gate, Castle Square TEL Lincoln (0522) 510333

A vegetarian dish may not always be available at lunchtime, though one will be produced if requested. At dinner in both Troffs bistro and the more upmarket Harveys, the story has a happier ending: always main courses, often with a fruity bias, as in mild fruit curry, pasta bake, nut cutlet or cashew and tofu stir-fry. Try the home-made steamed sponge pudding or the petit pot au chocolat for dessert.

Open all week, exc Sat L and Sun D noon to 1.55, 7 to 9.55 Booking advisable. Table service. Licensed, also bring your own: corkage £6.50. Meat dishes. Fish dishes. Other diets catered for on request. Access, Visa

Love & Barley ⓥ £

Newland TEL Lincoln (0522) 510128

To be described as 'a vegan restaurant with a very informal "ageing hippy" feel to it, presenting the sort of food Cranks used to, in the early days,' is quite a recommendation. Prices are extremely reasonable for lunches and dinners of soup, tagliatelle and carrot ragout in white wine sauce.

Open Tue to Sat noon to 3, 7 to 9.30, (exc Tue D and Wed D) Booking advisable. Table service. Unlicensed, but bring your own. Vegan dishes only. Other diets catered for on request. No-smoking area. Wheelchair access

LITTLE WALSINGHAM Norfolk **MAP 8**

Old Bakehouse ££

33 High Street TEL Walsingham (0328) 820454

An overnight stay can follow dinner in this beamed old building with its winding stairs; guests are given a key to come and go as they please. Vegetarians will find a starter of, perhaps soup, savoury peach with cheese and herbs, smoked spinach roulade or cheese and herb filo pastries, and main dishes along the lines of five-bean casserole, curried nut roast, or tomato and courgette bake. All puddings are home made apart from locally made sorbets. Cointreau and marmalade ice-cream is reported to be 'very, very good indeed' and the Danish whisky cake is 'rich and soggy'. Lavish portions of cream are added.

Open Tue to Sat D 7 to 9.15, Sun L 12.30 to 2 **Closed** Sun L and Tue Nov to Easter Booking advisable. Table service. Licensed, also bring your own: corkage £2.75. Meat dishes. No children under 4. Wheelchair access. Accommodation. Access, Visa

LIVERPOOL Merseyside MAP 7

Armadillo ££

20–22 Matthew Street TEL 051-236 4123

A clean, stylish and bright restaurant serving inventive, moderately priced food with a couple of vegetarian main dishes. There are modern prints on the walls and fresh flowers on the tables. Starters at lunchtime might include stuffed vine leaves and main dishes may be spicy lentil fritters served on a bed of spinach. For dinner the offer is, perhaps, potato and herb cake with melted goats' cheese followed by asparagus mousse baked en croûte. The cooking is not always consistent, and one reporter felt let down by a 'tired' lasagne. A pear and ginger crumble has been described as 'most impressive', a strawberry tart 'acceptable'. It's one of the trendy Liverpudlian eating places, so take it at that.

Open Tue to Sat 11.45 to 3, 7 to 10.30 **Closed** 24 to 27 Dec, bank hols Booking advisable. Table service. Licensed. Meat dishes. Fish dishes. Vegan dishes. Other diets catered for on request. Take-aways. Access, Visa

Bluecoat Chambers Bistro £

Bluecoat Chambers, School Lane TEL 051-709 5297

A bistro in an art centre, where prices will not make too large a dent in the pocket. The atmosphere is slightly arty and it can be a quiet place for a lunch of soup, hummus, cheese and potato bake, quiche, salad or a good stir-fry. Leave some room for puddings, which have been described as 'extravagant and wonderful'.

Open Mon to Sat 10 to 5 Counter service. Licensed. Meat dishes. Vegan dishes and other diets catered for on request. Snacks. Take-aways. No-smoking area. Wheelchair access

Eureka £

7 Myrtle Parade, Off Myrtle Street TEL 051-709 7225

A characteristically friendly, authentic Greek restaurant with a vegetarian section to the menu offering moussaka, spinach pie, and fasulya. All are well cooked and recommended.

Open Mon to Wed 10 to 8, Thur 10 to 9, Fri 10 to 10, Sat 11 to 10 **Closed** 2 weeks in summer Booking advisable. Table service. Counter service. Licensed, also bring your own: corkage 50p per person. Meat dishes. Fish dishes. Snacks. Take-aways. Wheelchair access

Everyman Bistro ★ £

9–11 Hope Street TEL 051-708 9545

'It's noisy, ebullient, casual and somewhat scruffy. But it does achieve an extraordinary high standard of food.' In three subterranean rooms below the Everyman Theatre, the restaurant with its bare brick walls, well-worn tables and stone floor is something of a legend. Food is selected and then microwaved. This should not deter as the quality and cooking are first-class. The enormous choice offers five different salads and such main dishes as aubergines in red wine sauce, stuffed red peppers, dhal and yoghurt, cheese and spinach roulade, leek and almond filo pastry. This last contains pencils of leek bound with a subtle savoury almond sauce. Among the many sweets are pears in hot fudge sauce, which is all that it should be, apple pie, mango cheesecake, Greek fritters, Caribbean bananas, eclairs, fruit in yoghurt, walnut and coffee gateau. It would take a great many visits to get bored with this cheap and cheerful place that also delivers freshness, quality and choice.

Open Mon to Sat noon to midnight Counter service. Licensed. Meat dishes. Vegan dishes. Snacks. Take-aways. No-smoking area. Wheelchair access

Far East £

27–35 Berry Street, (top of Bold Street) TEL 051-709 3141

Above a Chinese supermarket, a welcome effort is made for vegetarians, with over a dozen items on offer. Soups, such as sweetcorn and egg drop, and a vegetable hot-and-sour version, are followed by sweet-and-sour mixed vegetables, braised rainbow bean curds or Chinese mixed vegetables with rice vermicelli, served in a hot-pot. Useful for its long hours and virtually year-round opening.

Open all week noon to 11.25 **Closed** 25 and 26 Dec Booking advisable. Table service. Licensed. Vegan dishes. Other diets catered for on request. Take-aways. No young children. Wheelchair access. Access, Amex, Diners, Visa

Grande Bouffe ££

48A Castle Street TEL 051-236 3375

In the heart of the business part of Liverpool is this busy French restaurant which has received mixed comments – those who admire the inventions of the dishes don't mind the rather scruffy interior and uninviting exterior. Vegetarians are catered for with a starter of, perhaps, lentil and spinach roulade, and main courses of baked goats' cheese with basil and pine nuts in filo pastry, or pancakes with carrots and sultanas.

Open Mon to Sat exc Sat L, noon to 2.30, 6 to 10.30 **Closed** bank hols Booking advisable. Table service. Counter service. Licensed, also bring your own: corkage £2 per bottle. Meat dishes. Fish dishes. Vegan dishes and other diets catered for on request. Snacks. Take-aways. Access, Amex, Visa

Greenbank Ⓥ £

332–338 Smithdown Road TEL 051-734 2378

The Greenbank Project is a scheme for physically handicapped and able-bodied young. The food is all wholefood vegetarian and varies from snacks of veggie-burgers and pizzas to a choice of 10 starters and 13 main dishes: kidney bean and mushroom bordelaise, Caribbean casserole, okra cutlets, aduki bean rissoles and spicy nut and bean loaf with sweetcorn sauce are some of the more inventive ones. A three-piece band plays on Sundays and in the evenings.

Open Tue to Sun 11 to 3, 5 to midnight exc Sun D Booking advisable. Table service. Counter service. Licensed, also bring your own: corkage £2.50. Vegan dishes. Other diets catered for on request. Snacks. Take-aways. No-smoking area. Wheelchair access. Access

Keith's Wine Bar £

105 Lark Lane TEL 051-728 7688

Students find the prices here attractive and vegetarians especially like the food. Though meat and fish are also served, there are non-meat soups, home-made bread, salads, and a hot dish – perhaps lentil bake, spinach lasagne, or carrot and thyme pie, served with a baked potato. This is a good place to come for a relaxed evening. Portions are generous and cakes get particularly favourable mentions.

Open all week noon to 3, 5 to 11 **Closed** 24 to 30 Dec Counter service. Licensed. Meat dishes. Fish dishes. Snacks. Wheelchair access

Tate Gallery Coffee-Shop £

The Albert Dock TEL 051-709 3223

The Albert Dock complex is now one of the city's attractions and the Tate's appeal is not just for the art but also for this exceptionally good café, perched on a balcony on the mezzanine floor. Seating is either on high stools, or at small grey metal tables looking out over the waters of the nineteenth-century dock. The café may be modest, but attention to detail means that, within its limits, it excels. Soup, sandwiches, quiche, cakes, biscuits and salads are supplemented with a few hot daily dishes such as spinach and cream-cheese filo parcels, or vegetable bake. Cakes and puddings include warm spiced apple crumble, clementine cheesecake, fresh lemon cake, Borrowdale tea-bread, scones and shortbread. Some supplies come from the excellent Melmerby village bakery and ice-creams come from Loseley Farm. Salads are all freshly made. Justly popular, and there may be queues at weekends.

Open Tue to Sun 10 to 5 (11 to 6.45) in summer) Counter service. Licensesd. Meat dishes. Fish dishes. Vegan dishes. Other diets catered for on request. Snacks. Take-aways. No-smoking. Wheelchair access.

LOUGHBOROUGH Leicestershire **MAP 4**

Dizzi Heights ⓥ **£–££**

27 Biggin Street TEL Loughborough (0509) 262018

The dizzy heights are the first floor above a healthfood shop. The bright, spotless dining-room is filled with an array of souvenirs from the owners' travels. The cooking is always to a high standard and deserves more recognition and support. Home-made bread is available with dhal soup, ratatouille croustade or corn-and-potato bake at lunch. For dinner there might be soup, garlic mushrooms, rainbow terrine and yoghurt sauce. Nut roast and a pancake are always on offer and the special might be broccoli and mushrooms in gratin or a Middle-Eastern platter. All the wine is organic.

Open Tue to Sat 10am to 5, Sat, D 7 to 10.30 Booking advisable D. Table service D. Counter service L. Licensed, also bring your own: corkage £1. Vegan dishes. Other diets catered for on request. Snacks. Take-aways. No smoking

LOUTH Lincolnshire **MAP 8**

Ferns **££**

40 Northgate TEL Louth (0507) 603209

Formerly a wet-fish shop, now up-market, and run by a couple 'keen that everything should be just as you would like it. So many places don't seem to care if you eat or drop dead.' Don't panic when no vegetarian dish is listed on the main courses on the menu; a note at the bottom says 'A vegetarian dish is always available, and we are pleased to prepare any dish of your choice given prior notification.' This might turn out to be kebabs, tagliatelle or a trio of stuffed capsicums. You may however have trouble starting with the starters; apart from a daily soup, which just might be vegetarian, all other starters on a typical menu are meat or fish – even the mushrooms are sizzled in 'best pork dripping'.

Open Tue to Sat D 7 to 10 Booking advisable. Table service. Licensed, also bring your own: corkage £3. Meat dishes. Fish dishes. Other diets catered for on request. No children under 8 after 7.30. Access, Amex, Diners, Visa

See the back of the guide for an index of restaurants listed.

LUDLOW Shropshire **MAP 4**

Dinham Hall £££–£££

TEL Ludlow (0584) 6464/3669

Restaurants at the upper end of the market have come a long way to accommodate vegetarians – as they should – but there is still some way to go: wider choice and set dinners to match those of meat-eaters would be welcome. Here is a case in point: only one vegetarian starter and main course on the à la carte in a dining-room applauded for the value of its five-course set menu. On one occasion, the choice was a 'remarkable combination that looked as wonderful as it tasted' – a puff base filled with wild mushrooms and onions served on a sauce of hazelnut and cream. Another time the offering was herb blinis topped with marinated vegetables bound in honey and Greek yoghurt scented with coriander. The 20-minute wait for an apricot soufflé at the end was declared 'worth it for an exquisite dish'. Add the distinctive surroundings of this former schoolhouse opposite the castle and this becomes a contender for a special night out.

Open all week 12.30 to 2.15, 7.30 to 9.15 (exc Sun D) **Closed** 25 and 26 Dec Booking advisable. Table service. Tables outside. Licensed. Meat dishes. Fish dishes. Vegan dishes. Other diets catered for on request. No children under 4. Wheelchair access. Accommodation. Access, Amex, Diners, Visa

Dinham Weir ££

Dinham Bridge TEL Ludlow (0584) 874431

Picturesquely situated with a view from the garden over the weir, the restaurant lists one vegetarian dish, along the lines of asparagus pancakes, stuffed aubergines, bulgur wheat casserole or vegetable lasagne. For a peaceful traditional English meal with non-vegetarians, it could be a good choice.

Open all week 12.30 to 1.30, 7 to 9 exc Sun D Booking advisable. Table service. Tables outside. Licensed. Meat dishes. No children under 5. Accommodation. Access, Amex, Diners, Visa

See the back of the guide for a list of restaurants serving only vegetarian food.

Hardwicks £

2 Quality Square TEL Ludlow (0584) 6470

Enter Quality Square opposite Woolworths, off Castle Square. It's refreshing to find somewhere where family cooking concentrates on vegetarian dishes, of which three or four will appear daily, alongside a token meat or fish dish. Every day produces something different, though a soup always features; leek and mushroom bake, spinach soufflé, creamy vegetable crumble, cauliflower and potato pie or courgette and tomato bake are typical. Lemon delight, apple and ginger, blackcurrant surprise and apricot and orange are just some of the home-made cakes which should not be missed.

Open Mon to Sat noon to 4.45 **Closed** 2 weeks at Christmas Table service. Tables outside. Licensed. Meat dishes. Fish dishes. Snacks. Take-aways. No-smoking area

Olive Branch £

2–4 Old Street TEL Ludlow (0584) 4314

This wholefood café serves meat and vegetarian lunches of the soup, moussaka and vegetable bake variety. Macaroni cheese, mushroom and walnut bake and vegetable lasagne – all with a choice of three salads – are well reported. Oven-fresh scones and cakes are also available. Sharing a table may be necessary, but, given the friendly atmosphere, that's no hardship.

Open Mon to Fri 10 to 3 (5 Sat, noon to 5 Sun) Counter service. Licensed, also bring your own: corkage £2.50. Meat dishes. Snacks. Take-aways. No-smoking area. Wheelchair access

LUTTERWORTH Leicestershire MAP 4

Denbigh Arms ££

High Street TEL Lutterworth (0455 55) 3537

With décor described as 'DIY designer country house', the Arms offers a friendly welcome and a full vegetarian menu of cannelloni, pasta, lasagne, vegetable pie and stuffed peppers or tomatoes. Other dishes might include lentil and pulse casserole with madeira or bean curd and nut curry with wild rice and spinach.

Open all week noon to 2, 7 to 9.30 Booking advisable. Table service. Licensed. Meat dishes. Fish dishes. Other diets catered for on request. Wheelchair access. Accommodation. Access, Amex, Diners, Visa

LYNDHURST Hampshire MAP 2

Mad Hatter Tearooms £

10 High Street TEL Lyndhurst (042 128) 2341

Be warned that the Mad Hatter operates flexible opening times; such is the nature of a small enterprise. There is a limited vegetarian repertoire for lunch; come for soup and a pasta dish such as mushroom and nut fettucine, perhaps.

Open Tue to Sun 10 to 5 Table service. Tables outside. Meat dishes. Vegan dishes. Snacks. Take-aways. No-smoking area. Wheelchair access

LYNTON Devon MAP 1

Chough's Nest Hotel ££

North Walk TEL Lynton (0598) 53315

Priority is given to residents at this hotel with a spectacular view across to Countisbury headland, but it is possible for non-residents to book for dinner. A good-value set meal might start with a choice of home-made soup or fruit cocktail, followed by wholewheat vegetable lasagne or hazelnut and sweetcorn roast plus potatoes, vegetables and sometimes salad too. Crumbles or pies to finish, or ask for a fresh fruit salad. Guests staying over can benefit from free-range eggs and hot wholegrain bread at breakfast. This is Lorna Doone country, and once a week there's a celebratory dinner.

Open all week, D 7 **Closed** mid-Oct to Easter Booking advisable. Licensed. Meat dishes. Fish dishes. Other diets catered for on request. No smoking in public rooms. No children under 2. Accommodation

Hewitt's

££

North Walk TEL Lynton (0598) 52293

The Victorian house, with turrets, balustrades, manorial staircases and chimney breasts, clings to the hill in its 27 acres overlooking the Bristol Channel. It is 'the epitome of the country-house hotel environment' according to one reporter. The excellent food has earned much praise. Breakfasts include home-made yoghurts and croissants; ingredients are fresh and the cuisine is of a high quality. An endearing criticism is that portions are too large. Set menus do not cater for vegetarians, but the main menu has a selection of three dishes that can be ordered either as starters or main courses: 'seaweed' with toasted almonds; deep-fried Somerset Brie with cranberry jelly, and carrot and chervil timbale with tomato sauce. In addition to almond tuile with vanilla ice-cream and fresh strawberries there has been home-made lemon tart with clotted cream, hot pear soufflé with poire William sauce, chocolate and vanilla Bavarois, an imaginative wild cherry tea-flavoured sorbet. There's also a selection of local cheeses served with home-made walnut bread.

Open all week noon to 2, 7 to 9 Booking advisable. Table service. Tables outside. Licensed. Meat dishes. Vegan and other diets catered for on request. Snacks. No smoking. Wheelchair access. Accommodation. Access, Amex, Diners, Visa

Neubia House Hotel

£

Lydiate Lane TEL Lynton (0598) 52309

Not a posh establishment, but its claims to provide good vegetarian food have been borne out by visitors' reports. One of the owners is vegetarian, and there is always a choice of four vegetarian starters and a main course on the set menu, on the lines of gougère, stuffed vine leaves, stuffed courgettes or aubergine au ménage. Pistachio nut and cream cheese pâté, hazel and walnut terrine or carrot and courgette soup are among the more enterprising starters. A short selection of puddings includes raspberry trifle, blackcurrant pie and rum and raisin cheesecake. Children under five can eat at 5.30pm and there's a babysitting service for residents during dinner.

Open all week D 6.45 to 7.30 **Closed** 26 Nov to 10 Feb Booking advisable. Table service. Licensed. Meat dishes. Fish dishes. Other diets catered for on request. No smoking in dining-room. No children under 4. Accommodation. Access, Visa

MAIDSTONE Kent **MAP 3**

Pizza Express £

32 Earl Street TEL Maidstone (0622) 683549

A satellite of the excellent London-based chain that was founded twenty-five years ago. See London entry.

Open Mon to Sat 11.30 to midnight, Sun noon to 11.30. Table service. Licensed, also bring your own: corkage £2.50. Meat dishes. Fish dishes. Take-aways. No-smoking area. Wheelchair access. Access, Amex, Diners, Visa

Russett £

34 King Street TEL Maidstone (0622) 53921

Despite the very English image conjured up by the name, the short menu is dominated by pasta, with three options for vegetarians on the lines of fettucine topped with ratatouille. Salads to start; sweets such as walnut splendour, with ice-cream and cream, to finish. Five wines, plus house wine by the glass.

Open Mon to Wed 10 to 5.30, Thur to Sat 10 to 10 Table service. Licensed. Meat dishes. Wheelchair access

MALTON North Yorkshire **MAP 7**

Camphill Book and Coffee Shop £

9A Saville Street TEL Malton (0653) 695265

Good for a lunch of soup (made from local organic vegetables and using a different grain each day of the week), quiche, flan or vegetable pie. There are vegan cakes and biscuits, though vegan hot dishes are usually not on the menu. Yoghurt comes from organic farms in Botton Village. Home-made apple, pear, strawberry, blackcurrant or lemon juices are served hot or cold. Excellent value.

Open Mon to Sat (exc Thur) 9 to 5 **Closed** 24 Dec to 6 Jan Counter service. Meat dishes. Fish dishes. Snacks. No-smoking area

MALVERN WELLS Hereford & Worcester **MAP 4**

Cottage in the Wood

Holywell Road TEL Malvern (0684) 573487

Under a new regime, the cottage is favourably inclined towards vegetarianism. The menu changes every month with a variety of starters including avocado eclair, spinach pâté or melon with blackberries, and a couple of main dishes: spinach and cream cheese in a crêpe; aubergine stuffed with olives, onion, capers and tomatoes. Chocolate mint ice-cream is home made, or try pashka, a Russian dessert of cream cheese, candied fruit and raisins.

Open all week 12.30 to 2, 7 to 8.30 (9 Fri and Sat) Booking advisable. Table service. Tables outside. Licensed, also bring your own: corkage £5. Meat dishes. Other diets on request. Wheelchair access. Accommodation. Access, Visa

MANCHESTER Greater Manchester **MAP 7**

Cornerhouse £

70 Oxford Street TEL 061-228 7621

On the first floor of an arts and cinema complex, this convenient café may be functional and a trifle spartan but a local reporter says, 'I do not know of anywhere in the city centre where palatable food can be obtained more cheaply.' Vegetarian food predominates, and the cooking ranges through international cuisines to come up with pastas, chillis, curries, lentil bakes, three-bean casserole, blinis, falafels and hummus. A sample meal included a good lentil bake, passable carrot and oatmeal bake, vegetable strudel made with flaky pastry, mild aloo tikka and good couscous. A useful place to know about, open for drinks and cold food from 10am to 10pm.

Open all week noon to 2.30, 5 to 8 **Closed** 25 Dec Counter service. Licensed. Meat dishes. Snacks at other times. Take-aways. No-smoking area. Wheelchair access

The meal price guide that appears to the right of each restaurant name is based on prices given to us by the restaurateur.

Greenhouse ⓥ £

331 Great Western Street, Rusholme TEL 061-224 0730

Open from breakfast until late, the Greenhouse has an extensive regular menu that also gives vegans plenty of choice. Stuffed dates (with cream cheese and herb filling), baked aubergine pâté, hazelnut pâté, spring roll, or boursinette (herb and cream cheese dip) are just some of the starters; the Greenhouse strudel is considered the speciality dish (filo rolled around mushrooms, spinach, cream, wine, cheese and herbs) but there are some other exciting ideas, such as smoked tofu and banana pie, sweet potato goulash or satay mushroom pie with Indonesian-style peanut sauce, as well as more run-of-the-mill curries, lasagnes and roasts. Specials each day might include asparagus spanakopita, or mushrooms in coriander cream, and a sweet mango and mocha mille-feuille. There is a good range of organic and country wines – gooseberry, elderflower, damson, blackberry, and raspberry. Though perhaps a little scruffy, food and service are reliable and prices reasonable.

Open Mon to Fri 10 to 11, Sat and Sun 1 to 11 **Closed** 1 week at Christmas Booking advisable. Table service. Licensed, also bring your own: corkage £1. Vegan dishes. Other diets catered for on request. Snacks. Take-aways. No-smoking area. Wheelchair access

Greens ⓥ £

43 Lapwing Lane, West Didsbury TEL 061-434 4259

A café offering adventurous dishes at reasonable prices: starters include vegetable and wakame soup, sweetcorn blinis, blue cheese and walnut croquettes and spinach and cheese profiteroles. Interestingly different main dishes might be mushroom, broccoli and tomato galette with red pepper sauce, watercress and cottage cheese lasagne or Persian millet pilaff with almonds and satay sauce.

Open Tue to Sat 10 to 9.30 Booking advisable. Table service. Tables outside. Unlicensed, but bring your own: no corkage. Vegan dishes. Other diets catered for on request. Snacks. Take-aways

The factual details under the text are based on information supplied by the restaurateur.

Hong Kong £

47 Faulkner Street TEL 061-236 0565

The newly redecorated Hong Kong preserves good standards of Cantonese food. Dim-sum is praised but, sadly, there are no vegetarian fillings. There is a vegetarian section on the menu offering such basic choices as fried mixed vegetables with satay sauce and fried baby sweetcorn with cashew-nuts.

Open all week noon to midnight **Closed** 25 and 26 Dec Booking advisable. Table service. Licensed. Meat dishes. Fish dishes. Other diets catered for on request. Snacks. Take-aways. Access, Amex, Diners, Visa

Kathmandu Tandoori £

42–44 Sackville Street TEL 061-236 4684 and 2436

A long-established Nepalese restaurant in a basement on the fringe of Manchester's Chinatown, entered through a door set in the side of a large warehouse. The décor is pleasantly uncluttered and the food is consistent, praise being given to the 'excellent-value' vegetarian set menu that includes onion pakora, mixed vegetables, dhal, muttar paneer, nan and pilau rice. One regular reports, 'We have eaten here many times and have never been disappointed!'

Open all week noon to 2.30, 6 to 11.30 Booking advisable. Table service. Licensed, also bring your own: corkage £1 wine, £3 spirits. Meat dishes. Fish dishes. Vegan dishes. Other diets catered for on request. Snacks at other times. Take-aways. Wheelchair access. Access, Amex, Diners, Visa

Koreana ££–£££

Kings House, 40 King Street West TEL 061-832 4330

In the heart of the city, this family-owned restaurant serves authentic Korean food inviting to vegetarians since there are two set dinners and various main dishes to suit. First courses of cold vegetables may not look exciting but taste delicious; try also the noodle and vegetable dish japchae – it may sound boring but is superb, garlicky and full of flavour. Other good items include bindae tok, pancakes made from bean flour and topped with vegetables, and potato pancake. For dessert, Korean rice cake is oddly reminiscent of Christmas cake.

Open Mon to Sat exc Sat L, noon to 2.30, 6.30 to 10.30 (11 Fri and Sat) Booking advisable. Table service. Licensed. Meat dishes. Vegan dishes. Access, Visa

Kosmos Taverna £

248 Wilmslow Road TEL 061-225 9106

Jostled by chip shops and take-aways is this consistently good Greek restaurant. Service is of the warm Mediterranean style that makes you feel loved – so loved that the clientele can get carried away. Start with good hummus, falafel or melintzanosalata and go on to moussaka, roovithi – chickpeas with chopped spinach in a spiced tomato sauce – or fasulya – haricot beans with olive and lemon dressing. Sunday lunch is served until 5pm and there are usually daily specials, including some vegetarian options, at the weekend.

Open all week D 6.30 to 11.30 (12.30 Fri and Sat), Sun 1pm to 11.30 **Closed** 25 and 26 Dec, 1 Jan Booking advisable. Table service. Licensed. Meat dishes. Fish dishes. Vegan dishes. Take-aways. Wheelchair access. Access, Visa

Lime Tree ££

8 Lapwing Lane, West Didsbury TEL 061-445 1217

Apart from the best Indian and Chinese restaurants, there are few other places in the area that take their cooking as seriously and come up with a successful formula. Here the spare décor, wooden floors and sewing-machine tables suggest a bistro atmosphere; it is so popular that the premises have been extended with a conservatory. The menu lists a vegetarian dish of the day, which might be aubergine baked with spices, for example. Accompanying vegetables are seasonal, steamed and various (good dauphinois potatoes, mange-tout, carrots and cauliflower on a typical day). Try the splendid steamed hot chocolate pudding with butterscotch sauce, described by one reporter as 'just right, light, more chocolate than sponge'. There's a branch at 9–11 Wilmslow Road, Rusholme (telephone 061-227 7108).

Open Tue to Sat 6.30 to 10.30, Sun noon to 2 **Closed** 25 and 26 Dec Booking advisable. Table service. Tables outside. Licensed. Meat dishes. Wheelchair access. Access, Visa

Market Restaurant £££

104 High Street TEL 061-834 3743

There is great originality in the cooking, claims one reporter and the menu, which changes monthly, has two or three vegetarian starters and main courses. These may be on the lines of aubergine sesame cream with home-made water biscuits, dill, cream cheese and pink peppercorn filo tart, or apple, chive and calvados soup to start. Main dishes might include Genoese Easter pie of spinach, artichoke hearts and Dolcelatte, parsnips 'Molly Parkin' baked with Gruyère, cream and tomatoes, and cabbage coulibiac with sour cream sauce. Choosing a pudding from the five or so on offer could be a dilemma: consider chocolate pecan pie, tangerine and almond tart, rhubarb baked in honey and saffron custard or plum and gin sorbet. Those who crave more can join the monthly Pudding Club and sample five at one sitting.

Open Tue to Sat 5.30pm (7 Sat) to 9.30 **Closed** 1 week at Christmas, 1 week spring, Aug Booking advisable. Table service. Licensed. Meat dishes. Fish dishes. Wheelchair access. Access, Amex, Visa

On the Eighth Day ⓥ £

109 Oxford Road, All Saints TEL 061-273 1850

In terms of choice of food, this purely vegetarian and vegan workers' co-operative does not, unfortunately, achieve as much as similar ventures in Edinburgh, Glasgow and Aberdeen. Inside it is spacious but rather akin to a transport café. A typical lunch menu might include baked potatoes, chilli pâté, pea and mint soup, one mixed salad, a chick pea and aubergine curry and nut roast.

Open Mon to Sat 10 to 7 (4.30 Sat) Counter service. Unlicensed. Vegan dishes. Other diets catered for. Snacks. Take-aways. No smoking. Wheelchair access

Pizza Express £

Old Colony House, South King Street TEL 061-834 0145

A satellite of the excellent London-based chain that was founded twenty-five years ago. See London entry.

Open Mon to Sat 11.30 to midnight, Sun noon to 11.30. Table service. Licensed, also bring your own: corkage £2.50. Meat dishes. Fish dishes. Take-aways. No-smoking area. Wheelchair access. Access, Amex, Diners, Visa

That Café ★ £££

1031–1033 Stockport Road, Levenshulme TEL 061-432 4672

The owner used to run an antique shop which metamorphosed into this successful restaurant in an area of small terraced houses. It's attractively green with plants filling the windows, and the 1930s décor includes an authentic lack of central heating, hard wooden chairs and lots of teapots. 'The best vegetarian food in Manchester' is one verdict on the varied and imaginative dishes (all are freshly cooked). Six-bean casserole, broccoli and Brie crêpes, mushroom strudel and starters such as mint pâté of black-eyed beans, onions and mint or wholemeal tartlet filled with mushrooms and brandy custard give an idea of the range. A reasonably priced set menu might include vegetarian starters of soup, Stilton and walnut pâté or guacamole, followed by nut roast with spinach sauce and puddings like hot fudge sundae, banana pudding, a variation on bread-and-butter pudding, or fresh fruit salad.

Open Tue to Sat D 7 to 10.30, Sun L 12.30 to 2.30 Booking advisable. Table service. Licensed. Meat dishes. Fish dishes. Vegan dishes. Other diets catered for on request. Access, Amex, Visa

MANSFIELD Nottinghamshire MAP 7

Pepperwood £

Longdale Rural Craft Centre, Longdale Lane, Ravenshead
TEL Mansfield (0623) 796952

Yet another of the burgeoning breed of craft centres to support a restaurant with vegetarian undertones. This enterprising version provides home-made hot dishes (available all day) of spicy tomato and chickpea casserole, savoury nut roast, country pie or macaroni cheese, followed by sherry trifle, apple crumble, golden syrup pudding with fresh cream and other truly traditional cakes and puddings. The evening menu has a single dish of cashew and mushroom roast. English fruit wines and mead to drink.

Open all week 9am to 10pm **Closed** 25 and 26 Dec Booking advisable. Table service. Tables outside. Licensed. Meat dishes. Vegan dishes. Other diets catered for on request. Take-aways. No smoking. Wheelchair access. Access, Amex

MARLBOROUGH Wiltshire MAP 2

Polly Tea Rooms ££

High Street TEL Marlborough (0672) 52146

A slightly tatty exterior gives way to a charming old world interior with beams, flowery tablecloths and crockery, and prints on the walls. Cakes and confectionery made on the premises are the speciality and scones include a muesli version. Parsnip and apple soup is a successful combination of flavours, served with excellent fresh bread, while the vegetarian special of the day might be a cauliflower bake or carrot and courgette roulade. Quick, efficient service and freshly squeezed orange juice are pluses.

Open all week 9.30am to 6, L noon to 3 Table service. Licensed, also bring your own: no corkage. Meat dishes. No-smoking area. Wheelchair access. Access, Amex, Diners, Visa

MARTLESHAM Suffolk MAP 5

Black Tiles £

Main Road TEL Ipswich (0473) 624038

A pub near Woodbridge, in the same group as the Cretingham Bell (see Debenham) and the Pickerel at Ixworth (see Ixworth). A vegetarian will find something suitable on the blackboard – perhaps a starter of spicy spinach filos, waldorf appetiser with citrus dressing or mushroom and bean pancake; and for a main dish perhaps stroganoff, vegetable and hazelnut cutlet or cheesy leek and potato bake.

Open all week noon to 2.15, 7 to 9.30 Booking advisable. Table service. Tables outside. Licensed. Meat dishes. Fish dishes. Other diets catered for on request. Access, Amex, Visa

If in doubt about the constituents of a dish, ask.

MARKET HARBOROUGH Leicestershire MAP 4

Wine Bar & Bistro ££

22 High Street TEL Market Harborough (0858) 63975

The owners are the cooks at this informal wine bar. Kerry Shaw prepares the extensive vegetarian offerings and her husband Colin takes care of the carnivores. Dishes are mostly tested favourites such as chilli, lasagne, stroganoff, crumble and crêpes, but there are some new ideas like risotto al Gorgonzola, savoury leek and nut layer and cabbage layer. Fruit crumbles are a speciality.

Open all week exc Mon D and Sun L, 11.30 to 2.30, 7.30 to 10 Booking advisable at weekends. Table service. Licensed. Meat dishes. No children under 4. Wheelchair access. Access, Amex, Visa

MATLOCK Derbyshire MAP 7

Riber Hall £££

TEL Matlock (0629) 582795

There's an air of old world luxury at this Elizabethan stone manor house, now a pricey country-house hotel: there are plenty of magnificent beams, oak fireplaces and four-posters. Furniture veers towards the chintzy. Gardens, including a walled garden, orchard and conservatory, are delightful. A vegetarian menu of four main courses lists quiche, nut roast, soufflé omelette and a trio of vegetable mousses with tomato coulis. Try the rich Bakewell tart: 'a world away from the ordinary Bakewell'.

Open all week noon to 1.30, 7 to 9.30 Booking advisable. Table service. Licensed. Meat dishes. Fish dishes. No children under 10. Accommodation. Access, Amex, Carte Blanche, Diners, Visa

MAYFIELD East Sussex MAP 3

Rose and Crown £

TEL Mayfield (0435) 872200

This pretty pub with a garden in which you can eat in summer does a good line in home-cooked food. Inside, you can eat either in the dining-room or bar. The menu changes daily and there are always a couple of vegetarian dishes: broth for instance, served with French bread, avocado aïoli, or melon tsatsiki. Main dishes include ratatouille pancakes, crumble, curry, tortelloni and mushroom bake, spaghetti, vegetable pie, macaroni cheese and quiches. There's a choice of sweet, solid puddings such as crumbles or fresh fruit desserts.

Open Mon to Sun noon to 2, 7 to 9.30 Table service. Tables outside. Licensed. Meat dishes. Vegan dishes. Other diets catered for on request. Accommodation. Access, Visa

MELBOURN Cambridgeshire MAP 5

Pink Geranium £££

TEL Royston (0763) 260215 and 262503

The pretty pink thatched cottage markets itself vigorously and bills can be hefty, though there are such benefits as a Rolls-Royce chauffeur service and a free crèche for under twos. The seasonal menu reflects English cooking; emphasis is placed on the use of fresh ingredients. The 'fish and vegetarian' section lists a couple of possibilities: mushrooms in cream sauce with noodles and a trio of pancake parcels with various fillings served with herb sauce. There is always a soufflé, one of the kitchen's specialities, as a starter, but it may not be cheese: otherwise, vegetarians might choose, coulibiac, or quails' eggs with pine kernels and watercress sauce. Crème brûlee gets a favourable mention.

Open Tue to Sun exc Sat L and Sun D, noon to 2.15, 7 to 10 Booking advisable. Table service. Tables outside. Licensed. Meat dishes. Fish dishes. Vegan dishes. Other diets catered for on request. No children at D but crèche facilities. Wheelchair access. Access, Carte Blanche, Visa

MELMERBY Cumbria MAP 10

Village Bakery £

Melmerby TEL Langwathby (076 881) 515

Not just a bakery, also a very good restaurant and craft gallery connected to a smallholding run on organic principles. The bakery uses flour from the local watermill for pies, cakes and breads; the smallholding grows the organic vegetables and soft fruit that is served in the restuarant; 120 free-ranging hens supply eggs. Cakes and snacks can be enjoyed all day and there are at least three vegetarian dishes for lunch – noodles baked with mushrooms and cream cheese, fennel à la grecque, or buckwheat pancake with courgettes in tarragon cream, for example. The creamy vegetable pie is a speciality and the baker's lunch is a selection of home-made breads and local cheeses. Home-made ice-creams and sorbets, including brown bread and honey and ginger, are available all day. Try the simnel cake, Westmorland parkin or Grasmere gingerbread, for old-fashioned goodness. Despite seasonal closing for lunch, snacks are served from 8.30am to 12.30pm Monday to Saturday.

Open Tue to Sun, L noon to 2 **Closed** L Christmas to Easter Table service. Licensed. Meat dishes. Vegan dishes. Other diets catered for on request. Snacks. Take-aways (snacks only). No smoking. Wheelchair access. Access, Visa

MESSING Essex MAP 5

Old Stores Bistro ££

The Street TEL Tiptree (0621) 815868

A red-painted restaurant with an old-fashioned feel, in the centre of an out-of-the-way village. As well as meat dishes, it offers a full vegetarian menu and, if you phone in advance, an extra dish of the day will be prepared. Vegetarians are thus not treated as second-class citizens, though some comments have slipped through to suggest that they are none the less regarded as oddities. Inside, presided over by Mrs Kimber, a tea-shop atmosphere is smartened up by pink linen tablecloths and maroon overcloths. Mr Kimber cooks. Of the five starters on the vegetarian menu, Old Stores mushrooms have been well reported, with good white sauce and correctly cooked mushrooms. Hazelnut loaf with mushroom and pepper sauce has equally been praised; courgette and lentil gratin was disappointing. Puddings are well worth a try: sample good strawberry meringues or a rich and filling walnut and butterscotch sponge gateau.

Open Tue to Sun 7.30 to 10.30, Sun L 12.30 to 2.30 Booking advisable. Table service. Licensed, also bring your own: corkage £2 per bottle. Meat dishes. Other diets catered for on request. Wheelchair access. Accommodation. Access, Visa

MEVAGISSEY Cornwall MAP 1

Mr Bistro ££

East Quay TEL Mevagissey (0726) 842432

Though specialising in fresh fish cookery, Mr Bistro caters for vegetarians with such main courses as a nut roast, vegetable lasagne, or huevas rancheros.

Open all week noon to 2.30, 7 to 10 **Closed** Nov to Mar Booking advisable. Counter service. Tables outside. Licensed. Fish dishes. Meat dishes. Wheelchair access. Access, Diners, Visa

Palm Restaurant ££

2 Polkirt Hill TEL Mevagissey (0726) 842055

What was originally a town house is now a modest, friendly restaurant furnished in cheap and cheerful style, with lots of pictures, photographs and fancy curtains. The owners are aiming to feed the holiday trade, and they usually provide about three vegetarian dishes on the menu. A sample meal proved enjoyable, if rather average – salty leek soup and a lasagne overprovided with tomato purée. However, goulash with cream and wine was tasty, the portions hearty, and ingredients good.

Open Wed to Sat 7 to 9 **Closed** 3 weeks Nov Booking advisable. Table service. Licensed, also bring your own: corkage £2. Meat dishes. Vegan dishes. Other diets catered for on request. Wheelchair access. Access, Visa

MINCHINHAMPTON Gloucestershire MAP 4

Burleigh Court £££

Nr Stroud TEL Brimscombe (0453) 883804

Health awareness is high at this elegant E-shaped manor set on a hillside overlooking the River Frome. A daily changing à la carte menu highlights low-cholesterol and low-calorie dishes and includes two or three vegetarian options at each stage: tomato and thyme soup, spinach and ricotta crêpes, or beetroot roulade might be followed by vegetable coulibiac, aubergine parmigiana or cheese and lentil loaf. Even the sweets include a low-calorie version. The owner states that 'vegan dishes are available always, even if not on the menu.' One reporter described the cream and forget-me-not-blue dining-room as 'very lovely, very English; the best of the public rooms.'

Open all week exc Sun D noon to 2, 7 to 8.45 **Closed** 2 weeks Christmas Booking advisable. Table service. Tables outside. Licensed. Meat dishes. Fish dishes. Vegan dishes. Other diets catered for on request. Snacks at other times. Take-aways. No smoking in dining-room. Wheelchair access. Accommodation. Access, Amex, Diners, Visa

MONTACUTE Somerset MAP 2

Milk House ★ ££

17 The Borough TEL Martock (0935) 823823

The Duftons took up catering late in life but have made this old stone building opposite Montacute House an idiosyncratic and homely attraction. Log fires blaze in the fifteenth-century house which is furnished with antiques. The dining-room was a later addition, which explains why the original well is now in the middle of it. Cooking is described as 'French wholefood, if that's not a contradiction' and includes organic produce and wholemeal pastry in classic French dishes, as well as some inspired by India, the Middle East and Russia. Good-value set menus, two- and three-course, offer a couple of vegetarian starters and main dishes, for example, green spinach crêpes filled with spiced mushrooms; artichoke bottoms with a cheese sauce; or cashew-nut and sunflower seed fricadelle, served with fresh tomato coulis. Try the banoffi crumble – brandied and spiced bananas with crunchy oat topping, with cream – home-made sorbets, a 'light and lovely' chestnut and chocolate flummery or chocolate mousse. Everything is made on the premises except for the rolls, sometimes.

Open Wed to Sat D 7 to 9, Sun L noon to 2 Booking advisable. Table service. Tables outside. Licensed. Meat dishes. Fish dishes. Vegan dishes. Other diets catered for on request. No smoking in dining-room. No children under 12. Wheelchair access. Accommodation. Access, Visa

The availability of vegan dishes is indicated in the details underneath the text of an entry.

MORPETH Northumberland **MAP 10**

La Brasserie ££

59 Bridge Street TEL Morpeth (0670) 516200 and 516205

Navigate the tricky stairs and arrive in a pretty pink and green restaurant that cossets its customers and has a full vegetarian menu as well as a vegetarian choice on the good value set-lunch menu. The range of six starters and six main dishes rarely deviates, the starters being pizza, spaghetti or salads, followd by less predictable vegetable and Stilton crumble, filled pancakes, and fruit and vegetable curry.

Open Tue to Sun exc Sun D noon to 2, 6.30 to 10.30 Booking advisable. Table service. Licensed. Meat dishes. Fish dishes. Other diets catered for on request. Take-aways. Access, Amex, Diners, Visa

Dobson Restaurant, Linden Hall ££

Longhorsley TEL Morpeth (0670) 516611

Dobson's is one of the magnificent reception rooms of the Linden Hall country-house hotel, a Georgian beauty set in 300 acres of wooded grounds. The upmarket menu lists starters such as melon and mango or vegetable delice – layers of cauliflower, carrot and broccoli wrapped in spinach on a watercress sauce. Main courses for vegetarians – stuffed aubergine or stuffed pancake, for example – can be eaten as an 'intermediate course' by others at almost half the cost, presumably in smaller portions. Prices are irritatingly written out in words rather than in numbers.

Open all week 12.30 to 2, 7 to 10 Booking advisable. Table service. Meat dishes. Fish dishes. Vegan dishes. Other diets catered for on request. Snacks. No pipes or cigars in dining-room. Wheelchair access. Accommodation. Access, Amex, Carte Blanche, Diners, Visa

Some restaurants have started to take customers' credit card numbers when they book and say that if they don't turn up, a charge will be made. As long as they tell you beforehand, restaurants are within their rights to do this. But the charge should only be reasonable compensation for their loss, not a penalty.

MUCH WENLOCK Shropshire MAP 4

Scott's £

5 High Street TEL Much Wenlock (0952) 727596

A useful lunchtime venue for a vegetarian who could eat fairly predictable dishes such as quiche, lasagne, soup, or bean cottage pie. The owners sell frozen vegetarian meals and stock Hadley Park Farm additive-free ice-creams.

Open all week 10 to 5 **Closed** 2 weeks at Christmas; Wed Nov to Easter Table service. Licensed, also bring your own: corkage 50p. Meat dishes. Other diets catered for on request. Snacks. Take-aways. No-smoking area. Wheelchair access

NAILSWORTH Gloucestershire MAP 4

Flynns £££

3 Fountain Street TEL Nailsworth (045 383) 5567

This stylish restaurant celebrates its food with paintings, done by a local artist, of the dishes that Garry Flynn and his brigade produce. A typical evening menu might provide avocado with tomato and chive cream mousse, fresh fig and an olive oil dressing, to start, and broccoli and cauliflower in filo pastry with Stilton cream on a tomato coulis for a main dish. Other evenings have offered carrot and almond gateau with coriander and beetroot vinaigrette, and baked potato terrine with mild curry cream sauce. Round things off with poached peach on home-made peach ice-cream with crème anglaise or pink and white grapefruit terrine with passion-fruit coulis.

Open Mon to Sat exc Mon L, 12.30 to 2.30, 7 to 9.30 Booking advisable. Table service. Licensed. Meat dishes. Fish dishes. Other diets catered for on request. No-smoking area. Access, Visa

Markey's Stone Cottage £££

Old Market TEL Nailsworth (045 383) 2808

The old stone building recognises the twentieth century with smooth white brick and plate-glass windows. Inside, the two dining-rooms are flowery and cottagey, verging on the twee. Various daily dishes supplement the fixed menu and may give an alternative to the one vegetarian main course, perhaps savoury pancake in Stilton sauce, half an aubergine filled with vegetables with Stilton sauce, or avocado and mushrooms in brioche. Terrine of chestnuts, chocolate and armagnac is recommended. Although the cooking is on nouvelle lines, portions are generous. Good brown rolls and petits fours are made on the premises.

Open Tue to Sat 7.30 to 10 Booking advisable at weekends. Table service. Licensed. Meat dishes. Fish dishes. No children under 12. Wheelchair access. Access, Diners, Visa

NANTWICH Cheshire MAP 7

Oddfellows Arms £

97 Welsh Row TEL Nantwich (0270) 624758

This pub offers an outstanding number of vegetarian dishes – of the seven main courses, four are vegan. Start with sweetcorn and watercress chowder, Creole pâté or breaded mushrooms and go on to burgers, nutty Stilton and mushroom pie, chilli bean casserole, cashew paella, lasagne, stroganoff or curry. Round this off with hot chocolate fudge cake, butterscotch and walnut cake or daloon rolls (apple and blackberry pancake rolls).

Open all week noon to 2.30, 7 to 9 Table service. Tables outside. Licensed. Meat dishes. Vegan dishes

NETHERFIELD East Sussex MAP 3

Netherfield Place £££

TEL Battle (042 46) 4455

The spacious country house was built in 1924 of typical soft-red brick and set in grounds that contain a walled kitchen garden and tennis-courts. As well as the restaurant, there are 13 bedrooms. A separate fixed-price vegetarian menu should be offered; if not, ask for it. Not all the dishes listed may be available but the choice could be three cheesy filo pastry parcels, artichoke soup, ogen melon with strawberries, deep fried goats' cheese, or wild mushroom and hazelnut soup, as starters; followed by stir-fried vegetables, asparagus pancake (fresh asparagus), vegetable risotto, puff pastry case filled with vegetables and wild mushrooms or kebabs. Produce from the garden is used in the restaurant, including fresh cultivated and wild mushrooms, herbs, vegetables, fruit and flowers. Ice-creams and bread are home made.

Open all week noon to 2, 7 to 9.30 (9 Sun) **Closed** 21 Dec to 14 Jan Booking advisable. Table service. Licensed. Meat dishes. Fish dishes. Vegan dishes and other diets catered for on request. Snacks. Wheelchair access. Accommodation. Access, Amex, Diners, Visa

NEWARK Nottinghamshire MAP 7

Gannets £

35 Castlegate TEL Newark (0636) 702066

Although not purely vegetarian, this snack-oriented café serves vegetarian main dishes such as quiche, jacket potatoes, rissoles, hazelnut roulade and peanut and lentil roast. Everything is home made except breads and bread-related products. Regular salads include a good one of greens, a beetroot version and a brown rice version. There are many kinds of cakes including carrot, banana bread and scones. Freshly squeezed orange juice is a plus. Lunch starts at noon and continues 'until the food runs out'.

Open all week 10am to 5 **Closed** 25 and 26 Dec Counter service. Tables outside. Licensed. Meat dishes. Snacks. Take-aways. No smoking noon to 2

NEWCASTLE UPON TYNE Tyne & Wear MAP 10

Café Procope £–££

35 The Side, Quayside TEL 091-232 3848

Not as spruce as it once was, but the Café Procope still rings interesting changes on its wide-ranging menu, with a fair choice for vegetarians. It's possible to eat at any time of day here on snacks such as Mexican pitta burritas, toasted bagel sandwiches and hot filled croissants. Lunches and dinners start with herbed hummus with pistachios, falafel and salads, leading to more substantial main dishes such as vegetables with groundnut sauce served over fried plantains or Jambalaya, a Louisiana Creole dish traditionally made with chicken or seafood but for vegetarians with okra, peppers and Cajun spices.

Open Tue to Sun exc Sun D, 9.30am to 10.30pm (10 to 5 Sun) **Closed** 2 weeks in summer, 2 weeks at Christmas Booking advisable. Table service. Licensed. Meat dishes. Fish dishes. Vegan dishes. Other diets catered for on request. Snacks at other times. Take-aways. No-smoking area. Wheelchair access

Dragon House ★ £££

30–32 Stowell Street TEL 091-232 0868

Imaginative food at sensible prices can be enjoyed in a luxurious atmosphere. The young owners are rarely absent and are keen to maintain standards. Rather than the usual Chinese habit of producing stir-fry dishes with oyster sauce for vegetarians, the Dragon House has a separate health and vegetarian menu. There are various soups, including one made from seaweed, and a 'hot-and-sour' soup which proved to be a large bowl of very hot strong stock with fresh bean curd, shredded bamboo shoot, carrot and egg. Other starters are crispy seaweed, pancake roll, deep-fried bean curd with chilli and salt and impressive spring rolls – obviously home-made and splendidly crisp – the filling 'so tasty it makes you wonder why anyone would want to eat pork again.' Main dishes are again a far cry from the unoriginal with aubergine hotpot, bean curd dumpling, vegetarian bird's nest, and satay, as well as rice and noodles of which a vermicelli dish proved huge, interestingly flavoured and with no greasiness. 'Not only is the cooking good and value for money, but even more importantly the menu is as interesting as that offered to meat eaters.'

Open all week noon to 2, 5 to 11 (Sun noon to midnight) **Closed** 25 Dec and 1 Jan Booking advisable. Table service. Licensed. Meat dishes. Fish dishes. Snacks. No-smoking area. Access, Amex, Diners, Visa

Eastern Taste £

277 Stanhope Street TEL 091-273 9406

The two brothers who run this café have no pretensions about style – there are strip lights, Lino on the floor, Formica tables and folded kitchen-roll napkins. It is an Halal tandoori, because so many customers are Muslim, but about 25 per cent are vegetarian, and this accounts for the strong vegetarian emphasis on the menu. Value is extraordinarily good: most starters cost 95p and main dishes (and these are big Pakistani dishes, not typical Indian side-dish size) are £1.60. Starters vary, one reporter found the samosas insipid and onion bhajees too large, but the pakoras were good and vegetable tikki (mashed potato into which other vegetables and spices are mixed, coated with gram flour batter and deep fried) is outstanding, if extremely spicy. Curries and breads are all well reported and at such low prices the place has a large following. To avoid the queues go early for dinner, or at lunchtime.

Open all week noon to 12.30 **Closed** 25, 26 Dec and 1 Jan Booking advisable. Table service. Unlicensed, but bring your own. Meat dishes. Vegan dishes. Snacks. Take-aways. Wheelchair access

Edoardo's £££

6–7 Drury Lane, Cloth Market TEL 091-261 7608

This city-centre Italian restaurant is unusually vegetarian in leaning: apart from starters which run through the usual prawn cocktail and Parma ham routine, the pizza and pasta sections of the menu are both divided into vegetarian and non-vegetarian, with seven pizzas and four pasta dishes listed. For those with hearty appetites it's good to find somewhere doing a vegetarian calzone (a folded pizza); this one has a broccoli, onion and garlic filling. The pizza toppings are also imaginative – courgettes, potatoes and aubergines; or asparagus, spinach, sweetcorn and peas are a couple of examples. Of the puddings, crêpes suzettes and zabaglione might be good choices.

Open all week, exc Sun L, noon to 2.30, 5.30 to midnight Booking only for big parties. Table service. Licensed. Meat dishes. Vegan dishes and other diets catered for on request. Take-aways. Wheelchair access. Access, Visa

Great Wall ££

35–39 Bath Lane TEL 091-232 0517/7616

Newcastle has many suitable vegetarian venues but this is one to head to for Chinese cuisine. The unprepossessing appearance and basic décor belie good food and the welcome surprise of two vegetarian set dinners, one for two people and one for four. Don't panic at the sight of 'vegetarian chicken' or 'vegetarian sweet-and-sour pork': the ancient tradition of Chinese vegetarian cooking describes dishes in this way and they are usually made up of vegetables, tofu and nuts. Excellent jasmine tea is served.

Open Mon to Sat noon to 1.45, 6 to 11 **Closed** 25, 26 Dec and 1 Jan Booking advisable. Licensed. Meat dishes. Vegan dishes. Wheelchair access. Access, Amex, Diners, Visa

Red Herring £

3–4 Studley Terrace, Fenham TEL 091-272 3484

The café is in a Victorian suburb and faces the Little Moor part of Newcastle's Town Moor; what was once a corner shop is now a whole-food shop, café and bakery run by a co-operative whose members cook to a rota. It resembles a workers' café, with simple furnishings and basic décor and lots of agit. prop. notices, but has a warm friendly air. Bread, pizza, quiche and curried vegetable pasties are produced daily in the bakery and organic ingredients are used whenever possible. Latin American dishes are a speciality. Reports of stuffed aubergines and ratatouille are encouraging, though a curry with brown rice tended to be dry. A nut purée en croûte, diminutive in size and pricey, was soggy and covered in a disappointing sauce. Home-made croissants, cherry-and-almond slices and various buns are all good.

Open Tue to Sat 10 to 10, Sun 11 to 8 Table service. Counter service. Vegan dishes. Other diets catered for on request. Snacks. Take-aways. No-smoking area. Wheelchair access

Rupali ££

6 Bigg Market TEL 091-232 8629

The eclectic Indian menu lists dishes from all over the sub-continent and extensive provision is made for vegetarians; prices are reasonable. All tastes can be catered for, from hot Madras sambar of vegetables and lentils to Gujerati thali and a very mild korma. Good dhals include coconut-flavoured lundal and a lemon-flavoured version. Follow with mangoes, lychees or guavas; sadly there's no kulfi.

Open all week noon to 2.30, 6 to 11.30 (7 Sun) Table service. Licensed. Meat dishes. Seafood dishes. Vegan dishes. No smoking area. Access, Amex, Diners, Visa

Sachins £££

Forth Banks TEL 091-261 9035

Good Punjabi food is provided on a short menu. The vegetable and bean section includes some interesting items, such as bhein aloo of lotus roots and sauté potatoes, and dhal makhani of split black and yellow beans cooked in butter and fresh cream. Breads are particularly good.

Open Mon to Sat noon to 2, 6 to 11.15 Booking advisable. Table service. Licensed. Meat dishes. Other diets catered for. Access, Diners, Amex, Visa

Tandoori Nights £

17 Grey Street TEL 091-221 0312

This Indian restaurant closely follows the style of the elegant stone street it inhabits and is exceptionally tasteful inside; despite its expensive looks, prices are not unreasonable. Choices for vegetarians are starters of bhajias, pakoras, samosas or channa chat. Main dishes are vegetarian versions of korma, Madras, vindaloo, dhansak and dopiaza. A sampled samosa was 'lovingly folded and pinned together with three cloves' and tasted sweet and unusually of cinnamon. The vegetable dhansak was excellent and other vegetable side dishes, such as sag panneer, were good. Service is impeccable. 'This will be my regular place for a treat when I'm skint,' commented one convert.

Open all week noon to 2.30, 6 to midnight **Closed** 25 and 26 Dec Booking advisable. Table service. Licensed. Meat dishes. Take-aways. Wheelchair access. Access, Amex, Diners, Visa

NEW MALDEN Surrey MAP 3

Pizza Piazza £

69 High Street TEL 081-942 2865

Comparisons are odious but inevitable between Pizza Piazza and Pizza Express. Both chains at the top of the pizza range, serving excellent products with many clearly marked choices for vegetarians, and sharing a continental atmosphere of marble-topped wrought-iron tables with tiny vases of flowers. Although Pizza Piazza lists fewer pizzas, the combinations are more inventive: Alba, for instance, has mushrooms, gorgonzola and garlic; Principe has leeks, Feta and basil; and there are plenty of extras that can be added. The menu is the same in every branch, with occasional 'specials'. Avocado Helena – avocado with tomato slices and Feta topped with yoghurt, cucumber and olives – or hot buttery garlic bread make light starts to a meal, and puddings include a dark chocolate ice-cream bombe, lemon sorbet, hazelnut ice-cream and cassata. There are some pasta dishes, but they're all meaty.

Open all week, noon to 11.30pm Table service. Licensed. No-smoking area. Wheelchair access. Access, Visa

NEW MILTON Hampshire MAP 2

Marryat Room, Chewton Glen Hotel £££

Christchurch Road TEL Highcliffe (0425) 275341

Captain Marryat wrote *The Children of the New Forest* while living here and many of his books are displayed in the bar. The hotel has some grand amenities, including helipad and croquet lawn, and prices reflect this. Nice details come with the price tag – a slice of vegetable terrine as a tempter on each table, and good petits fours with coffee. The separate vegetarian menu starts well with some unusual variations on old themes – asparagus in puff pastry with lime butter sauce – but for main dishes resorts to some tired ideas such as omelette with morel mushrooms, risotto, and mille-feuille with pink pepper. The home-made ice-creams and sorbets are praised; other puddings include iced lime soufflé, sabayon-glazed fresh apricots with wild strawberries, and coconut ice-cream.

Open all week 12.30 to 2, 7.30 to 9.30 Booking advisable. Table service. Tables outside. Licensed. Meat dishes. Fish dishes. Other diets catered for on request. Snacks at other times. No pipes or cigars in dining-room. No children under 7. Wheelchair access. Accommodation. Access, Amex, Carte Blanche, Diners, Visa

A restaurant manager can't insist on people not smoking, unless it's specifically a non-smoking restaurant or a non-smoking area. If it is, smokers could be asked to leave if they don't stop. If it's important to you, check beforehand what the smoking arrangements are.

NEWPORT PAGNELL Buckinghamshire MAP 4

Glovers Wine Bar £

18–20 St John Street TEL Newport Pagnell (0908) 616398

In a converted seventeenth-century building. The menu provides vegetarians with such dishes as cashew and mushroom roast with asparagus sauce, or vegetable biriani. Quiches and pizzas are home made. Happy hour between 7 and 8.

Open Tue to Sat 12.15 to 2 exc Sat L, 7.30 to 10 **Closed** Christmas to New Year Counter service. Tables outside. Licensed, also bring your own: corkage £3. Meat dishes. Other diets catered for. Wheelchair access. Access, Visa

NEWTON POPPLEFORD Devon MAP 1

Jolly's Ⓥ ★ ££

The Bank TEL Colaton Raleigh (0395) 68100

Purely vegetarian, with a classy air: order your meal sitting in a comfortable lounge and proceed to a modest but carpeted dining-room hung with embroideries and boasting linen tablecloths. Starters include pasta with lentil and tomato sauce, hummus, guacamole, a sweetcorn chowder full of corn and potato and exemplary mushrooms in garlic and cream. Quantities can defeat when it comes to main courses, appealing as they are: a Caribbean casserole of sweet potatoes, courgettes and pineapple, and a hot chilli casserole have both been praised. Puddings tend towards the traditional; try the pecan pie.

Open Mon to Sat exc Mon L, noon to 2, 7 to 9 Booking advisable. Table service. Licensed. Vegan dishes. Other diets catered for on request. No smoking. Wheelchair access. Accommodation. Access, Visa

NORTHALLERTON North Yorkshire MAP 7

Bettys £–££

188 High Street TEL Northallerton (0609) 775154

The chain of old-fashioned tea-rooms offers excellent teas and coffees and serves splendid regional snacks and light meals all day. A Yorkshire cheese lunch, Welsh rarebits – one with local cheese – and salads as well as home-made cakes, pastries and breads are delicious. Fresh orange juice is available and there is a children's menu.

Open all week 9am to 5.30 (10am Sun) **Closed** some bank hols Table service. Licensed. Meat dishes. Fish dishes. Snacks at other times. Take-aways. No-smoking area. Wheelchair access, exc wc. Access, Visa

NORWICH Norfolk MAP 8

Lloyd's ££

66 London Street TEL Norwich (0603) 624978

The vegetarian choice here can be limited, but at lunchtime a few of the starters may be taken as a main course with a salad; for instance fresh pasta with a cream, basil and walnut sauce. Otherwise, the vegetarian offering might be cashew and Brazil nut roast with tomato sauce, aubergine pie or a crêpe stuffed with spinach and cottage cheese. Thirty wines, including house wine by the glass.

Open all week noon to 2, 6.30 to 9.30 Booking advisable Sat D. Table service. Tables outside. Licensed, also bring your own: corkage £3. Meat dishes. Fish dishes. Vegan dishes. Other diets catered for on request. No-smoking area. Access, Amex, Diners, Visa

Pizza Express £

15 St Benedict Street TEL Norwich (0603) 622157

A satellite of the excellent London-based chain that was founded twenty-five years ago. See London entry.

Open Mon to Sat 11.30 to midnight, Sun noon to 11.30. Table service. Licensed, also bring your own: corkage £2.50. Meat dishes. Fish dishes. Take-aways. No-smoking area. Wheelchair access. Access, Amex, Diners, Visa

The Vegetarian Good Food Guide *has been compiled in the same way as* The Good Food Guide *and is based on reports from consumers and anonymous inspections.*

Pizza Piazza £

1 All Saints Street TEL Norwich (0603) 667809

A branch of a growing chain that offers an enterprising choice of reliably good pizzas. See entry under New Malden for more detail.

Open all week noon to 11 Table service. Licensed. No-smoking area. Wheelchair access. Access, Visa

Treehouse ⓥ £

16 Dove Street TEL Norwich (0603) 625560

A bright yellow, pine-furnished restaurant in the centre, above a wholefood shop. Popular for lunch with shoppers and office workers, it is described by one regular as 'a dedicated vegetarian establishment offering an interesting and thoughtful choice and excellent value for money.' Every day a different menu is chalked up on the board. Choice is limited, with dishes such as curry; tofu, tomato and basil flan; cheesy sweet potato; mushroom croustade, or Brazil and millet burger with mushroom sauce – the last enjoyable, if short on seasoning. All cakes are freshly baked and a plum and lemon version with butterscotch sauce gets special praise.

Open Mon to Sat 11.30am to 3 Table service. Unlicensed. Vegan dishes. Other diets catered for on request. Take-aways. No smoking

Waffle House £

39 St Giles TEL Norwich (0603) 612790

There's a hint of wholefood about this café where almost half the toppings are vegetarian and free-range eggs are used. Smart with its two shades of pink and bamboo furniture, it is a pleasant place for coffee, a snack or a meal. Even a 'small' waffle is a hearty portion. Toppings are savoury or sweet and waffles are plain or wholemeal. Ingredients are well chosen for their freshness and combinations work well.

Open all week 11am (noon Sun) to 10 (9 Sun, 11 Fri and Sat) Table service. Licensed, also bring your own: corkage £1.25. Meat dishes. Fish dishes. Snacks. No-smoking area. Wheelchair access

NOTTINGHAM Nottinghamshire MAP 7

Artistes Gourmands/Café des Artistes ££–£££

61 Wollaton Road, Beeston TEL Nottingham (0602) 228288/430341

A dual operation, very popular locally. The upmarket restaurant, Artistes Gourmands, comes up with specials such as avocado with wild mushrooms baked with cream, wine, basil and tomato; lettuce leaves rolled and stuffed with mixed vegetables and fresh herbs; or ceps filled with asparagus mousse and served with asparagus spinach soufflé. Dishes are simpler and cheaper in the Café: crudités with saffron mayonnaise; chilled ratatouille; free-range eggs poached in vegetable stock with avocado and Roquefort sauce flavoured with walnuts, or baked aubergine in a lemon cream sauce. Home-made desserts include a light biscuit layered with chocolate and apricot mousse with Cointreau sauce; tarte tatin; vacherin and other layered and filled extravaganzas.

Open Mon to Sat 7 to 9.30, Tue to Fri noon to 1.30 **Closed** 2 weeks Jan Booking advisable. Table service. Licensed. Meat dishes. Fish dishes. Wheelchair access. Access, Amex, Diners, Visa

Jack Sprats ★ £–££

23–25 Heathcote Street TEL Nottingham (0602) 410710

Vegetarians are spoiled for choice at this former Victorian corner shop, now black and white outside and inside, and decorated with posters for various causes. The dinner menu normally offers some seven starters and main courses and four sweets, most of them suitable for vegans. There is also a generous fish menu. Two vegetarians and a fish-eater dining together reported eating a beautifully presented cheesy aubergine Parmesan, an elegant cashew and mushroom roast with an excellent sherry sauce, and tender green tagliatelle interwoven with strips of smoked salmon. Other starters included chestnut and orange pâté, masala mushrooms or mixed bean salad, and main courses a raised almond and fennel pie with celery sauce, Brazil nuts and chickpeas en croûte or sweet-and-sour vegetables on mushroom rice. Round off with home-made chocolate cake or brandy oranges in caramel. Lunch menus feature lighter and cheaper dishes which sometimes turn up as starters on the dinner menu. Atmosphere and service are cheerful.

Open Tue to Sat noon to 3, 7 to 10.30 Booking advisable weekends. Table service. Licensed. Fish dishes. Other diets catered for on request. Snacks. Take-aways. No-smoking area. Wheelchair access

Maxine's Salad Table ⓥ £

56 Upper Parliament Street TEL Nottingham (0602) 473622

Maxine's title doesn't do her justice, for the restaurant offers much more than salads, every day: soup, quiche and a dish of the day that might be a crumble, spaghetti bake or tomato hot-pot. Naturally, there is a good choice of salads. Everything is home made including such sweets as chocolate mousse and fresh cream trifle.

Open Mon to Sat 10am to 3 **Closed** bank hols Counter service. Licensed. Vegan dishes. Snacks. Take-aways. No-smoking area. Wheelchair access

Ocean City £

100–104 Derby Road TEL Nottingham (0602) 475095

The vegetarian set menus are a big plus. A set dinner for two has six dishes, starting with sweetcorn soup and followed by deep-fried silver rolls, sweet-and-sour bean curd, and fried bamboo shoots and water-chestnuts with cashew-nuts. For four people there are eight dishes, which include the same soup, fried vegetable cubes with cashew-nuts in a bird's nest, fried bean curd with chilli and black-bean sauce, and sweet-and-sour mixed vegetables. Aside from the set menus there are a meagre four choices.

Open Mon to Fri noon to 3, 6 to 11.30; noon to midnight Sat, noon to 10.30 Sun **Closed** 25 Dec Booking advisable. Table service. Licensed. Meat dishes. Fish dishes. Take-aways. Wheelchair access. Access, Amex, Diners, Visa

'Q' in the Corner £

3 Victoria Street TEL Nottingham (0602) 506956

Discovered within Ziggi's Boutique, the queue in the corner will be for home-cooked lunches; the balance of dishes at the café is more in favour of vegetarians than meat and fish eaters. Shoppers during the day can eat various cakes, pies such as lemon meringue, and, for lunch, find home-cooked moussaka, hot-pots, nut roast and pasta meals among a range of about a dozen dishes.

Open Mon to Sat 9.30 to 5 Counter service. Meat dishes. Fish dishes. Snacks. No-smoking area. Access, Visa

Rita's Café ⓥ £

15 Goosegate TEL Nottingham (0602) 481115

This vegan café is upstairs, above Hiziki Wholefoods, and is run as a co-operative. Lunches are reasonably priced, drawing on a wide range of international cuisine to come up with cauliflower thermidor; tempeh cutlets in orange sauce with stir-fried courgettes; moussaka; pea and cider soup; falafels, and sea vegetable soup. Specialities are tempeh dishes, peanut stew and a ploughperson's lunch of creamy vegan cheese, pâtés and chutneys. Vegan gateaux and cheesecakes are available.

Open Mon to Sat 10 to 5 **Closed** Christmas Counter service. Unlicensed, but bring your own: no corkage. Vegan dishes. Other diets catered for on request. Snacks. No-smoking area

Sagar ££

473 Mansfield Road, Sherwood TEL Nottingham (0602) 622014

A traditional but wide-ranging menu and competent cooking of good, fresh ingredients are the attractions here. The vegetarian curries in the Madras, methi, Bangalore and bhuna styles are typical but a vegetable kebab starter is more unusual. There is Indian cake for dessert, alongside the standard kulfi, carrot halva and gulab jamun.

Open all week noon to 2.30, 5.30 to 12.30 **Closed** 25 Dec Booking advisable. Table service. Licensed. Meat dishes. Fish dishes. Take-aways. No pipes. No children under 8. Wheelchair access. Access, Amex, Visa

★ *after a restaurant name indicates that the vegetarian cooking is especially good. A list of starred restaurants appears at the end of the book.*

Shama Tandoori £

33 The Square, Beeston TEL Nottingham (0602) 250364

Useful in an otherwise poor area for vegetarians is this Indian restaurant with a separate vegetarian menu. Highly recommended is the sabzi special of mushrooms, cauliflower, bindi and potatoes cooked together with onions, garlic, green peppers and tomatoes. Other dishes include vegetarian biriani, methi, bhuna, rogan josh and pathia as well as a mild Kashmiri curry, and various typical Indian side dishes and desserts.

Open Tue to Sat noon to 2.30, 6 to 12.30 (1 Fri and Sat) Table service. Licensed. Meat dishes. Take-aways. Wheelchair access. Access, Diners, Visa

Ten Ⓥ ££

10 Commerce Square, Lace Market TEL Nottingham (0602) 585211

The purely vegetarian restaurant off High Pavement is in the basement of a converted warehouse; its high aspirations are not always totally borne out by the food, but it is worth supporting and is one of the few vegetarian ventures in the area. The night's menu could have seven starters and nine main dishes with mixed nut roast with red wine sauce, spinach Mount Ararat (a base of lightly seasoned carrots and mushrooms, then broccoli, topped with chick peas, onions and mixed herbs, served with vermouth sauce), nut cutlet Diane (brandy, cream and tomato and mushroom sauce) or noisettes grand duc (two noisettes of cashew-nuts and avocado, wrapped in vine leaves, one with artichoke bottom and supreme sauce, one with asparagus tips and provençale sauce). Saturday lunches feature snacks, with savoury herb waffles, jacket potatoes and falafels, as well as a hot dish or two. Silver birch wine, made from birch sap, features on the wine list.

Open Tue to Fri 5.30 to 11, Sat noon to 11. Booking advisable. Table service. Licensed. Vegan dishes. Other diets catered for on request. Take-aways. No-smoking area. Access

A change of owner or chef may mean a change of menu policy. If a restaurant is no longer serving vegetarian food, please inform the guide; the address to write to is on page 9.

NUNEATON Warwickshire MAP 4

Millers Hotel ££

Main Road, Sibson TEL Tamworth (0827) 880223

There may not be any startling vegetarian dishes at this hotel, but it does have the virtue of a choice of four main courses – stroganoff, pancakes, stuffed peppers and mushroom pie on a typical menu. Greek Disos wine, with no added sugar, is also served.

Open Mon to Sun noon to 2.15, 7 to 9.45 Table service. Licensed. Meat dishes. Fish dishes. Vegan dishes. Diabetic dishes. Wheelchair access. Access, Amex, Diners, Visa

OKEHAMPTON Devon MAP 1

Partners ££

38 Red Lion Yard, Fore Street TEL Okehampton (0837) 54662

The round red dining-room looks like a tea-room and indeed you can indulge in teas, coffees, cakes and cream teas during the daytime. Though the Bealeys say they prefer to be told of vegetarian preference in advance, there is always something suitable on the lunch and dinner menu, perhaps a pancake or a croustade. Occasionally there is a vegetarian evening with a good demonstration of what we all should know by now: that 'the staple diet of the vegetarian is not nut roast and raw vegetables, but an endless array of tastes and textures'.

Open Tue to Sun exc Sun D, noon to 2.30, 7 to 9.30 Booking advisable. Table service. Tables outside. Licensed. Meat dishes. Fish dishes. Other diets catered for on request. Snacks at other times. No pipes or cigars. Wheelchair access

OLDBURY West Midlands MAP 4

Jonathans ££

16–20 Wolverhampton Road TEL 021-429 3757

The Victorian theme runs through the décor, the waitresses are in mob caps and the menu is quaintly divided into 'first removes' and 'main removes'. The idea of using old shillings and pence to indicate pounds and pence may amuse, but is also confusing – 3/8d represents £3.80, some inflation! As well as a mushroom Yorkshire, an intriguing Yorkshire pudding with onion gravy and whole mushrooms, there is a separate vegetarian menu buried in the à la carte menu with first and main removes – four dishes on each – showing some lively vegetarian cooking: filbert gateau, Cheddar and onion surprise and cucumber and almond ragout. The treacle and coconut tart is recommended. Vegetarians are also catered for at Sunday lunch.

Open all week noon to 2, 7 to 10.30 Booking advisable. Table service. Licensed, also bring your own: corkage £3. Meat dishes. Fish dishes. Other diets catered for on request. Snacks at other times. Access, Amex, Diners, Visa

OLDHAM Greater Manchester MAP 7

Woody's ⓥ £££

5 King Street, Delph, Saddleworth TEL Saddleworth (0457) 871197

Behind a small shop-front, Woody's aspires to full restaurant status. A lot of effort has been put into making the interior attractive, and, more importantly, into the creation of the menu. Five starters and five main courses include French onion soup, pakoras, pear fan with cream and walnut dressing, and sweetcorn tartlets; main courses might be hazelnut escalopes, potato pinwheels, autumn slice with a cheese sponge base, courgette and cumin bake and Caribbean medley. At a sample meal pakoras proved to be mushrooms in spicy batter, light and crisp with the mushroom flavour satisfactorily sealed in. Nut pâté and courgette and cumin bake tended to be on the bland side; hazelnut escalope with apricot and cream sauce succeeded. Puddings – of which chocolate and coffee mousse cake and wholemeal profiteroles were tried – are less exciting. Vegans will find two or three dishes and organic wines are available.

Open Tue to Sun D 7.30 to 10 Booking advisable. Table service. Licensed. Vegan dishes. No smoking. Wheelchair access. Access, Visa

The Vegetarian Good Food Guide *has been compiled in the same way as* The Good Food Guide *and is based on reports from consumers and anonymous inspections.*

OMBERSLEY Hereford & Worcester MAP 4

Crown and Sandys Arms £

TEL Worcester (0905) 620252

Look on the blackboard, not the printed bar meals menu, for vegetarian options such as chestnut and mushroom pie, bean and vegetable biriani, spicy aubergine parcels or spinach and cream cheese roulade. An à la carte menu operates in the evening from Tuesday to Saturday. Good puddings.

Open all week noon to 2.30, 5.30 (7 Sun) to 10 **Closed** 25 Dec Booking advisable. Table service. Counter service. Tables outside. Licensed, also bring your own: corkage £1 per bottle. Meat dishes. Fish dishes. Vegan dishes on request. Accommodation. Access, Visa

OSWESTRY Shropshire MAP 4

Granary 2 £

16 Leg Street TEL Oswestry (0691) 670210

Meat and vegetarian dishes deserve equal praise in this sister of the restaurant in Welshpool (see entry). Snacks are available all day; lunch dishes might include broccoli cheese flan, pizza, vegetable bake, leek and mushroom bake, lasagne, or cheese and potato bake.

Open Mon to Sat 9.30 to 4.45 Counter service. Licensed. Meat dishes. Snacks. Take-aways. No-smoking area. Wheelchair access

OTLEY West Yorkshire MAP 7

Curlew Café Ⓥ £–££

11–13 Crossgate TEL Otley (0943) 464351

The Curlew occupies two eighteenth-century cottages whose rooms are rustically furnished with country-style tables and chairs. Many of the original features remain. Despite interesting international dinner menus on Friday and Saturday nights, a sample lunchtime meal proved disappointing. Beetroot and red cabbage soup might be a better choice than a thin pasta, sweetcorn and mushroom soup that had almost no mushrooms. Spinach and Feta cheese pie, though acceptable in flavour, suffered from a soggy base, and a farmhouse casserole had rendered its constituents almost indistinguishable. There are several main dishes to suit vegans.

Open all week L noon to 4.30 (5 Sun), Thur to Sat D 7.30 to 10   Booking advisable D. Table service. Vegan dishes. Other diets catered for on request. Snacks. Take-aways. Wheelchair access

OTTERBURN   Northumberland   MAP 10

Redesdale Arms Hotel ★   ££

TEL Otterburn (0830) 20668

The attractive square, stone building, though somewhat remote, should attract vegetarians from miles around, as the separate vegetarian menu is unusually good. Despite being a hotel, the atmosphere is that of a country pub, and the décor is one of the main drawbacks for vegetarians: quantities of hunting prints and a fox head on the wall. If you can find a seat where you don't have to view that, you can enjoy some original, freshly cooked vegetarian food. Yes, lasagne is on the menu but so too are vegetable pie with walnut; or puff pastry, leek and lentil cobbler; bean and cider casserole; cheese and rice puffs; and nut, corn and cheese casserole. The leek and lentil cobbler, a stew of leeks and other vegetables, thickened with lentils, was topped with dumplings more like thick, crispy, wholemeal biscuits and served with fresh green salad and good vegetables. Cheese and rice puff resembles a fat pasty, filled with cottage cheese, rice and vegetables. Portions are generous. 'Although it's a good hour's drive from home, I'll be going a lot,' said one enthusiastic reporter.

Open all week 11.30 to 3, 7 to 9   Table service. Tables outside. Licensed. Meat dishes. Fish dishes. Vegan dishes. Other diets catered for on request. Snacks. Wheelchair access. Accommodation. Access, Diners, Visa

If you book a table at a restaurant, you must turn up in reasonable time. If you don't keep your booking, or are very late, you're in breach of contract and the restaurant could sue you for compensation. Let the restaurant know as soon as possible if you can't make it, so the restaurant can reduce its loss by rebooking the table.

OVINGTON Hampshire MAP 2

Bush ££

TEL Winchester (0962) 732764

Near the A31 by the River Itchen, this popular pub gives a few vegetarian alternatives on a mainly fish and meat menu: stir-fry of vegetables, nuts, herbs and rice; lentil and bean curry with fruit garnish; tagliatelle topped with fried courgettes and aubergines. Starters are basic and puddings rich – from oranges in Grand Marnier to meringue Jamaica with coffee ice-cream, chocolate sauce, pineapple and Tia Maria. The terrace is an attraction in summer.

Open Mon to Sat exc Sat L, noon to 1.30, 7.30 to 9.30 Booking advisable. Table service. Tables outside. Licensed, also bring your own: corkage £2.50. Meat dishes. Fish dishes. Vegan dishes. Other diets catered for on request. No children under 8. Wheelchair access. Access, Amex, Visa

OXFORD Oxfordshire MAP 4

Baedekers ££

43A Cornmarket TEL Oxford (0865) 242063

'More fun, we thought, than Brown's.' And offering more choice for vegetarians! As the name might indicate, the menu flies around the world with Mexican, Cajun, Chinese, Indian and many other cuisine inspirations. Vegetarians might look to Mexico for starters of nachos or guacamole and India for a main course thali – curries arrive, 1950s-fashion, with sliced bananas and coconut – then come back to England for bread-and-butter pudding. Afternoon teas are also served and organic wines are listed.

Open all week noon to 2.45, 6 to 11.30 Table service. Licensed. Meat dishes. Fish dishes. Snacks at other times. Access, Visa

Bandung £

124 Walton Street TEL Oxford (0865) 511668

Near the city centre, this Indonesian/Malaysian restaurant practises authentic cooking without concessions to western tastes. Batik fans, a colourful fish tank and background strains of Javanese flutes give it a genuine ambience. There are 'excellent' gado gado, rojak and tahu goreng, the latter so dominated by the peanut sauce that it is recommended only for those who like peanuts, a fiery nasi lemak, and a properly crisp and crunchy tangeh goreng. Pisang goreng – tiny bananas cooked in crisp batter and coated with honey – make a simple finish.

Open Tue to Sun, exc Sun L, noon to 2.30, 6 (7 Sun) to 11 **Closed** 25, 26 and 27 Dec Booking advisable Fri and Sat. Table service. Licensed. Meat dishes. Fish dishes. Wheelchair access. Access, Amex, Diners, Visa

Fifteen North Parade ££

15 North Parade TEL Oxford (0865) 513773

Both the set dinner and à la carte menu have a vegetarian dish of the day, obviously the result of some thought – corn crêpe filled with vegetables and cheese served with spicy tomato relish perhaps, or an aubergine mould with three cheeses; this last was declared good but somewhat spoiled by a coarse-flavoured fresh hyssop sauce. Starters veer into filo pastryland or stick to the soup and melon formula. The cuisine is rich. Home-made ice-creams are recommended, and three-chocolate marquise well reported. In all, 'somewhere for well-heeled vegetarians whose arteries are in good nick.'

Open all week noon to 2, 7 to 10 (10.30 Sat) Booking advisable. Table service. Tables outside. Licensed, also bring your own: corkage £6.75. Meat dishes. Fish dishes. Other diets catered for on request. Access, Visa

Gee's ££

61A Banbury Road TEL Oxford (0865) 511472

Gee's is refreshingly unpretentious and produces good modern British cooking at reasonable prices. The conservatory restaurant is tasteful: the décor is plain and stylish, with long slender banquettes, peach cushions and plenty of hanging plant baskets. Deservedly popular with meat-eaters and vegetarians; the vegetarian main course among the short list of lunchtime specials or on the evening menu might be vegetable bake, pancakes, oyster mushrooms in pastry tarts with fennel and Richard sauce, or grilled goats' cheese salad. Round off with an excellent crème brûlée, or the visual delight of a fruit vacherin.

Open all week noon to 2.30, 7 to 11 Booking advisable at weekends. Table service. Tables outside. Licensed, also bring your own: corkage £4. Meat dishes. Vegan dishes. Other diets catered for on request. No-smoking area. Wheelchair access. Access, Amex, Visa

Museum of Modern Art £

30 Pembroke Street TEL Oxford (0865) 722733

Below the Museum of Modern Art is this white-painted, uncluttered modern café with plastic tables and chairs and a long, low bench with low tables to one side. Maybe because this is in Oxford, it reminds one of a common room, and is popular at lunchtime. Salads are good and fresh with lavish use of fresh herbs. Vegetarian dishes dominate – for instance, a mushroom and courgette loaf, quiche, or a curiously sweet cottage cheese and walnut loaf. Snacks include spinach and cheese filo pastry triangles and lentil and walnut burgers with tomato sauce. Of the very few desserts trifle or a walnut cheesecake are acceptable.

Open Tue to Sun L noon to 4 Counter service. Licensed, also bring your own: corkage 50p per head. Meat dishes. Fish dishes. Snacks. No smoking. Wheelchair access

Pizza Express £

The Golden Cross TEL Oxford (0865) 790442

A satellite of the excellent London-based chain that was founded twenty-five years ago. See London entry.

Open Mon to Sat 11.30 to midnight, Sun noon to 11.30. Table service. Licensed, also bring your own: corkage £2.50. Meat dishes. Fish dishes. Take-aways. No-smoking area. Wheelchair access. Access, Amex, Diners, Visa

St Aldate's Church Coffee House £

94 St Aldate's TEL Oxford (0865) 245952

The Gothic dark wood of the ground-floor room opposite Christ Church College reinforces the impression of being in a church hall. The cakes, flapjacks and buns in this snack-type café are all home baked and simple lunches might be soup, jacket potatoes and quiches, plus a hot vegetarian dish such as lentil and mushroom bolognaise. A useful spot in the city centre and very reasonably priced.

Open Mon to Sat noon to 2 Counter service. Tables outside. Meat dishes. Snacks. Take-aways. No smoking. Limited wheelchair access

PAIGNTON Devon MAP 1

Natural Break £–££

75 Torquay Road TEL Paignton (0803) 524771

This wholefood café on the main road to Torquay could be a useful stopover for a meal of vegetable crumble, homity pie, nut roast, vegan bake, lentil bolognaise, risotto or various pastas.

Open Mon to Sat noon to 3, plus Fri and Sat 7 to 10 Table service D. Counter service L. Licensed. Meat dishes. Snacks. Take-aways. No-smoking area

PANGBOURNE Berkshire MAP 2

Copper Inn £££

Church Road TEL Pangbourne (0734) 842244

A half-timbered hotel with a modern dining extension which has an 'old pine' feel to it. The menu lists three vegetarian main courses, of which the twice-baked spinach and cheese soufflé is a speciality that meat-eaters are offered as a starter; others are cheese and almond sausages on a tomato coulis and filo pastry with wild mushrooms. Try the rhubarb crème brûlée or marquise of bitter chocolate to finish.

Open all week 12.30 to 2, 7.30 to 9.30 (10 Fri and Sat, 9 Sun) Booking advisable. Table service. Tables outside. Licensed, also bring your own: corkage £4 per bottle, £7.50 for champagne. Meat dishes. Fish dishes. Other diets catered for on request. Snacks at other times. Wheelchair access. Accommodation. Access, Amex, Carte Blanche, Diners, Visa

The Editor's top ten restaurants providing an exceptional service for vegetarians, chosen for the success with which they achieve their aims, are listed on page 12.

PARKHAM Devon **MAP 1**

Penhaven Country House ££

TEL Horns Cross (023 75) 388

Although it also serves meat, this hotel advertises the fact that it caters for vegetarians, and the resulting food is varied, excellently presented and draws largely on local produce. The cooking is described as traditional English; a vegetarian meal might start with mushroom and nut pâté and continue with lentil rissoles with a herb sauce.

Open all week D 7.15 to 9 Booking advisable. Table service. Licensed. Meat dishes. Fish dishes. Wheelchair access. Accommodation. Access, Amex, Diners, Visa

PENRITH Cumbria **MAP 9**

In Clover £

Poets' Walk TEL Penrith (0768) 67474

Situated in a small modern shopping centre is this rather functional restaurant, meagrely decorated and furnished with pine. Items are written on the blackboard, and the rapidity of erasings and rewritings suggests fresh cooking. The food is 95 per cent vegetarian and includes dishes such as asparagus roulade, stuffed mushrooms and vegetable strudel. A sample meal started with spicy apple, celery and tomato soup, and went on to a Wensleydale cheese, onion and tomato pie and a pasta and broccoli bake. Sadly the cheese in the first dish and the broccoli in the second were not much in evidence. Good home-made puddings and cakes to finish.

Open Mon to Sat 9 to 6 Counter service. Tables outside. Licensed. Vegan dishes. Other diets catered for on request. Snacks. Take-aways. No smoking. Wheelchair access

The main criterion for inclusion in the guide is that an eating place offers a vegetarian main course on its standard menu, at all times, that is more than just an omelette, quiche or salad. If you find that a listed restaurant no longers caters for vegetarians, please inform the guide; the address to write to is on page 9.

PENZANCE Cornwall **MAP 1**

Olive Branch ⓥ £

3A The Terrace, Market Jew Street TEL Penzance (0736) 62438

On the first floor and if you have a window seat (best to book for a meal) you can enjoy a view of St Michael's Mount. Daily specials of cottage pie, mushroom roast and other dishes supplement a menu of home-made soup, bean burgers, nut cutlets, parsnip and cashew-nut patties, cheese patties, peanut mince balls with sweet-and-sour sauce, cauliflower cheese bake, sweetcorn, egg and cheese bake, veggie-burgers and curries. Soggy rice and overcooked vegetables have been a disappointment. Home-made cakes, and cream teas for non-vegans. 'Full of teenagers drinking the cheapest coffee in town!'

Open Mon to Sat 10.30 to 2.30, 6 to 9 **Closed** D New Year to Easter Booking advisable. Table service. Unlicensed, but bring your own: no corkage. Vegan dishes. Snacks. Take-aways. No-smoking area

PERRANUTHNOE Cornwall **MAP 1**

Ednovean House Hotel ££

TEL Penzance (0736) 711071

A separate vegetarian menu awaits residents and non-residents to the hotel, set just off the A394 between Penzance and Helston. Six starters and nine main dishes include asparagus in cream and cheese sauce, mushroom pâté, curry, lasagne, nut roast, mushroom stroganoff and chilli. All vegetables are either home grown or local farm produce. There are a couple of organic French wines listed and a non-alcoholic wine.

Open all week D 7 to 9 Booking advisable. Table service. Licensed. Meat dishes. Other diets catered for on request. No smoking. Wheelchair access. Accommodation. Access, Amex, Visa

When you book a restaurant table, you're making a contract with the restaurant and they must give you a table, in reasonable time. If they don't, they're in breach of contract and you can claim a reasonable sum to cover any expenses you had as a result, eg travelling costs.

PINNER Greater London **MAP 3**

La Giralda **££**

66 Pinner Green TEL 081-868 3429

British and Spanish cuisines are combined in this noisy, busy restaurant, certainly not advisable for a romantic, intimate evening. The habit of not putting prices on the menu can be annoying. After gazpacho or melon, do not despair at the thought of the 'vegetarian specialities platter': it is not the appalling collection of accompanying vegetables one often receives, but changes daily and might be rice-stuffed peppers, aubergines and nuts in filo pastry or vegetable lasagne. The crème brûlée to finish has been applauded as authentic. Dinner is cheaper before 8pm.

Open Tue to Sat noon to 2.30, 6.30 to 10 Booking advisable. Table service. Licensed. Meat dishes. Fish dishes. Vegan dishes. Wheelchair access. Access, Amex, Diners, Visa

PLAISTOW West Sussex **MAP 2**

Clements ⓥ ★ **£–£££**

Rickmans Lane TEL Plaistow (040 388) 246

Converted from a pub, this has a spacious, tranquil atmosphere. At either end of the large dining-room there is a fireplace, plants abound, the lighting is low and gentle folk music plays. Tables are well spaced and attractively set with fresh flowers, candles and fine glasses. With aperitifs come home-made crudités, perhaps hummus with a good, strong flavour, served with peppers and cauliflower florets. The menu choice is somewhat limited, with just three starters, three main courses and four puddings, and while the dishes break no new ground, execution is good. Starters might be fennel au gratin or spinach, courgette and lentil soup. At a sample meal cashew and carrot roulade with a dill yoghurt dressing was excellent – full of flavour, light and moist. To follow, the Special Indian dish is made with aubergines and served with a carrot and toasted sesame seed salad. Puddings are on the lines of lemon cheesecake, mocha cream mousse or compote of pears. Good coffee and home-made petit fours.

Open Tue to Sat noon to 2, Thur to Sat 7 to 9.30 **Closed** 25 Dec Booking advisable. Table service. Tables outside. Licensed. Vegan dishes. Other diets catered for on request. No smoking. Wheelchair access. Visa

PLYMOUTH Devon MAP 1

Clouds £–££

102 Tavistock Place TEL Plymouth (0752) 262567

A basement restaurant where smart people come for an inexpensive lunch, and vegetarians are catered for with three choices of main course. Deep-fried potato skins, accompanied by olive and cream dip, vine leaves filled with rice, tomatoes and herbs in a tomato sauce and a nut roast full of cashew and pecan nuts have all been praised. Home-made puddings take in excellent banoffi pie, lemon meringue pie, rich chocolate mousse and exotic fresh fruit salad. With an open fire in winter the atmosphere is cosy, tables are decently spaced.

Open Mon to Fri noon to 2, Wed to Sat 7.30 to 10 Booking advisable. Table service. Licensed. Meat dishes. Vegan and other diets catered for on request. Access, Amex, Diners, Visa

Kurbani £–££

1 Tavistock Place, Sherwell Arcade TEL Plymouth (0752) 266778

Near the City Museum and Library, opposite the Polytechnic. As well as providing vegetarians with starters such as aloo bonda, pakora, onion bhajia and chana chat, the menu offers a couple of vegetarian birianis and a vegetarian thali.

Open noon to 2.30, 5.30 to 11.30 Booking advisable. Table service. Licensed. Meat dishes. Vegan dishes. Take-aways. Wheelchair access. Access, Amex, Diners, Visa

Plymouth College of Further Education ⓥ £

King's Road, Devonport TEL Plymouth (0752) 264739

The Department of Hotel and Catering restaurant offers a vegetarian menu only twice a week, but the outstanding value and sound cooking attract regulars, and it is well worth knowing about. The set menus provide two or three choices at each course, and sometimes take a national theme. For instance, the African menu offers Kenyan beans with coconut, or yam curry with groundnut and cassava pudding; the Russian menu choice might include Kiev-style beetroot soup and mushrooms with vegetables. At other times, there may be nut croquettes with a red wine sauce, broccoli and cheese roulade or stuffed pepper rolls.

Open Tue, L noon; Thur, D **Closed** July and Aug Booking advisable. Table service. Licensed. Vegan dishes. Other diets catered for on request. Wheelchair access. Access, Visa

Theatre Royal £

Broadway Restaurant, Royal Parade TEL Plymouth (0752) 665432

If you want a quick meal before the show the foyer bar could be useful. Pizzas are cooked to order; though there are fancy names for the toppings (Evita, South Pacific), you can devise your own from ingredients such as peppers, mushrooms, tomatoes, sweetcorn and cheese. In the main restaurant vegetarians will find dishes of the day: vegetable terrine; vol-au-vent with mushrooms, cream and wine; courgette provençale; mushroom stroganoff; moussaka; nut cutlets or curry.

Open Mon to Sat 10 to 2.30, 6 to 11 Booking advisable in restaurant. Table service. Counter service in foyer bar. Tables outside. Licensed, also bring your own: corkage £5.50. Meat dishes. Other diets catered for on request. Snacks. No-smoking area. Wheelchair access. Access, Amex, Diners, Visa

POLPERRO Cornwall MAP 1

Kitchen ££

The Coombes TEL Polperro (0503) 72780

The tiny restaurant, with matching pink walls and tablecloths, has some inventive set-price menus, one of which is vegetarian. Starters and desserts are the same on all five menu choices. Home-made white rolls come with a light, spicy lentil and red pepper soup, tasty with the addition of salt. Little ramekins of garlicky cashew-nut, and cheese and cardamom mushrooms on a large croûton work well. Main courses of aduki bean burgers or curried nut roast with mango and mint sauce are possible. As well as the ubiquitous banoffi pie, said to be good here, there's a variation – strawberry toffee pie. Excellent value, and all meals are a little cheaper at lunchtime.

Open all week, exc Tue Easter to Nov, D 6.30 to 10 **Closed** Nov to Easter, Sun to Thur Booking advisable. Table service. Licensed. Meat dishes. Fish dishes. No children under 5; children at 6.30 only. Wheelchair access. Access, Visa

POOLE Dorset **MAP** 2

Clipper £

100 Dolphin Centre **TEL** Poole (0202) 683334

The Clipper restaurant, a large self-service operation in the new Dolphin Centre, has a vegetarian counter called Inn a Nutshell. Everything is made on the premises daily. A typical day's menu includes broccoli roulade, mushroom burger, courgette and tomato Mornay, cauliflower and potato gratin, kontiki pie and vegetable casserole. Wholemeal cakes and cookies are freshly baked.

Open Mon to Sat 9.30 to 5.30 Counter service. Licensed. Meat dishes. Fish dishes. Snacks. Take-aways. No-smoking area

Warehouse £££

Poole Quay **TEL** Poole (0202) 677238

The style of the restaurant is pleasantly straightforward, the décor plain, tables with white linen tablecloths ranged down the wall so that each has a window overlooking the quay. The position, right on the harbour, offers perpetual entertainment in the endless pageant of boats. The cooking is reportedly professional, without gimmicks, and very English. Vegetarians have lean pickings on starters: on one occasion only an 'intoxicating array of fruits' was possible and on another the pineapple, mushroom, nut, celery and pepper dish was obviously the same in content as one of the two main courses. These are low on originality: quiche or risotto. Crème brûlée turned out to be all that it should be; other desserts are bread-and-butter pudding, lemon or orange pancakes, spotted Dick and ice-creams.

Open all week noon to 2, 7 to 10 Booking advisable. Table service. Licensed. Meat dishes. Fish dishes. Vegan dishes. Other diets catered for on request. Access, Amex, Diners, Visa

POOL IN WHARFEDALE West Yorkshire MAP 7

Pool Court £££

Pool Bank TEL Leeds (0532) 842288

A pioneer among high-class restaurants in its provision for vegetarians. The price of the four-course dinner is determined by the price of the main dish and the vegetarian option is the cheapest. First courses might include asparagus and leek ramekin; the middle course a salad of avocado with pine kernels and croûtons, and the main course a combination of a stuffed sweet pepper, asparagus quiche and a garden herb risotto or globe artichokes with the three fillings of leek and spinach in butter sauce, oyster mushrooms, and sweet peppers with ginger. Homemade sorbets follow for those with no room left for delights such as velvet truffle torte flavoured with Framboise, or the chef's choice of the day's sweets in combination.

Open Tue to Sat 7.30 to 9.30, L for parties of 10 or over by appointment **Closed** 10 days at Christmas, 2 weeks July to Aug Booking advisable. Table service. Licensed, also bring your own: corkage varies. Meat dishes. Fish dishes. Other diets catered for on request. No pipes or cigars in dining-room. Wheelchair access except wc. Accommodation. Access, Amex, Diners, Visa

PORTSMOUTH Hampshire MAP 2

Memories of India £

21 High Street, Old Portsmouth TEL Portsmouth (0705) 751209

As an antithesis to red flock, this Indian restaurant is almost overdesigned in the other direction – pastel colours and swags of chintz, pink tablecloths and linen. Vegetarian set meals of three courses are good value. Try vegetable dhansak in rich spicy sauce, excellent with nan bread and raita. There are also a couple of suitable birianis and a mixed vegetable curry on the menu.

Open all week noon to 2.30, 6 to 11 (noon to 11 Sat) **Closed** 25 and 26 Dec Table service. Licensed. Meat dishes. Snacks. Take-aways. No-smoking area. Wheelchair access. Access, Amex, Diners, Visa

POWERSTOCK Dorset MAP 2

Three Horseshoes ££

Powerstock TEL Powerstock (030 885) 328 and 329

The inn faces the church in the tiny village of Powerstock. There is the bar, the old dining-room and the smarter new dining-room to choose from, with the same food available in all. Vegetarians will find one dish on a menu specialising in fish – perhaps mushroom and cashew roulade, pine kernel roast or spinach and cheese pie with filo pastry crust. Reports of the food vary, with a spinach pancake getting a high rating and hors d'oeuvre a low one.

Open all week noon to 2, 7 to 9.30, exc Mon, Thur, Sun D **Closed** 2 weeks Nov, 2 weeks Feb Table service. Tables outside. Licensed, also bring your own: corkage £3. Meat dishes. Fish dishes. Other diets catered for on request. Snacks at other times. No smoking in dining-room. Wheelchair access. Accommodation. Access, Amex, Visa

PRESTON Lancashire MAP 7

Eat Fit £

20 Friargate TEL Preston (0772) 555855

Close to St George's Shopping Centre and the market, Eat Fit dedicates itself to 'a healthier style of eating' with good home cooking that includes scones and cakes. There are hearty soups and hot dishes of the likes of mushroom stroganoff, broccoli casserole, butterbean and mushroom crunch and spinach roulade.

Open Mon to Sat 11 to 3.30 Counter service. Unlicensed. Meat dishes. Fish dishes. Other diets catered for on request. Snacks. Take-aways. No-smoking area. Wheelchair access

Report forms are at the back of the book; write a letter if you prefer.

Roobarb (V) £

24 Adelphi Street TEL Preston (0772) 59179

Fresh ingredients and low prices are the attractions at this predominantly vegan café run by a co-operative near the library and the Students' Union. Lunchtime sandwiches and snacks are bolstered with such good basic fare as nut roast with pecan casserole and chilli con vege with rice. On Thursday and Saturday evenings there are daily specials on the lines of spinach and tofu bhuna, hazelnut and courgette bake, and mushroom and Guinness pie. Fruit crumble, vegan ice-cream or cinnamon and carrot cake to finish. There's flavoured soya milk to drink, as well as the more usual herbal teas and fruit juices.

Open Mon to Sat 10 to 3, Thur and Sat D 7 to 10 Table service. Unlicensed, also bring your own: no corkage. Vegan dishes. Other diets catered for on request. Snacks. Take-aways. Wheelchair access

PUCKERIDGE Hertfordshire MAP 5

White Hart ££

High Street TEL Ware (0920) 821309

Vegetarians are promised at least six starters and twelve main courses at this family-run pub with a dining-room. The separate vegetarian menu does not fall short of the promise. Two interesting starters are hot grapefruit with sherry, and home-made ratatouille with garlic bread. There is a vegan wholemeal pasta and bean hot-pot among the main courses, which also include tomato pancakes with a rich cream thermidor sauce, cracked wheat and walnut casserole, mushroom and nut fettuccine, and lentil crumble. All dishes are served with a seasonal salad or fresh vegetables and offer a substantial meal at a reasonable price. Bar meals are more informal and snack-like.

Open all week noon to 1.55, 6.30 to 9.45 Table service. Tables outside. Licensed, also bring your own: corkage £2. Meat dishes. Vegan dishes. Other diets catered for on request. Take-aways. Children under 14 only if eating. Access, Diners, Visa

PUDSEY West Yorkshire **MAP 7**

Aagrah

£

483 Bradford Road TEL Bradford (0274) 668818

This family-run restaurant has a vegetarian section on the menu and lists Kashmiri vegetables, mushroom biriani, vegetable biriani, as well as vegetarian versions of curries such as Madras, vindaloo and korma. There is a thali and a vegetable karahi with fresh ginger, garlic, onions and fresh coriander. Follow with traditional kulfi or burfi.

Open all week D 6 (noon Sun) to 11.30 Booking advisable. Table service. Licensed. Meat dishes. Seafood dishes. Vegan dishes. Other diets catered for on request. No-smoking area. Wheelchair access. Access, Amex, Diners, Visa

PULBOROUGH West Sussex **MAP 2**

Barn Owls

££

London Road, Coldwaltham TEL Pulborough (079 82) 2498

Vegetarian meals have been served for ten years here, and one of the cooks is vegan. To promote vegetarianism there are also sometimes wholly vegetarian evenings to tempt the unconverted with such dishes as deep-fried cabbage and hazelnut rolls served with a light creamy tomato sauce, or pasta parcel filled with devilled vegetables topped with mushroom and sherry sauce. All pâtés, mousses, sauces, soups, and sweets are home made. There is a three-course Victorian menu and also, 'for those with a discerning healthy appetite', an eight-course dinner, featuring lentil croquettes, spinach cheese puffs, strudel, or vegetable pudding or crumble.

Open all week 7 to 9.30pm, Sun L noon to 1.30 Booking advisable. Table service. Licensed. Meat dishes. Fish dishes. Vegan dishes. Other diets catered for on request. No children under 12. Accommodation. Access, Visa

A restaurant doesn't have to be able to serve all items on the menu, although it should have most. If you think the restaurant is deliberately trying to mislead people, tell the local Trading Standards Officer.

Stane Street Hollow £££

Codmore Hill TEL Pulborough (079 82) 2819

Anne Kaiser gives a charming welcome at this Swiss restaurant where high-quality food comes at a price – and it's good to see free-range chickens and ducks running about outside to provide eggs (that's all, we hope). To begin a vegetarian meal, there might be a melon, tomato and mint mayonnaise cocktail, mushroom pâté or cheese soufflé. To follow, the choice could be a wholewheat pancake with aubergine, leek, ginger and cayenne; puff pastry with assorted mushrooms and almonds, and a vegetarian platter of a home-grown pepper filled with pumpkin, onion, ginger, mushrooms and garlic, topped with yoghurt and sour cream sauce and served on brown rice. Banana fritters get good reports, though home-made ice-cream might be the lighter alternative. The set lunch menu is good value; the main menu changes every four weeks.

Open Wed to Sat, exc Sat L, 12.30 to 1.15, 7.15 to 9.15 **Closed** 2 weeks May and Oct, 24 Dec D, 25 and 26 Dec, 31 Dec to 4 Jan Booking advisable. Table service. Licensed. Meat dishes. Fish dishes. Other diets catered for on request. No-smoking in dining-room

QUORN Leicestershire MAP 4

Quorn Grange £££

Wood Lane TEL Quorn (0509) 412167

A double-gabled house, red pantiled and solid, with delightful gardens viewed from the pink, plush and comfortable dining-room. The vegetarian element in the menu could be a starter of vegetable terrine or avocado soufflé and a main course of ravioli, vegetable tartlet or pancakes with tomato and coriander sauce.

Open Mon to Sat 7 to 9.30, Sun noon to 2 Booking advisable. Table service. Tables outside. Licensed. Meat dishes. Vegan and other diets catered for on request. Wheelchair access. Accommodation. Access, Amex, Diners, Visa

The availability of meat and fish dishes is indicated in the details underneath the text of an entry.

READING Berkshire MAP 2

Pizza Express £

56 St Mary's Butts TEL Reading (0734) 391920

A satellite of the excellent London-based chain that was founded twenty-five years ago. See London entry.

Open Mon to Sat 11.30 to midnight, Sun noon to 11.30. Table service. Licensed, also bring your own: corkage £2.50. Meat dishes. Fish dishes. Take-aways. No-smoking area. Wheelchair access. Access, Amex, Diners, Visa

REDHILL Surrey MAP 3

Pizza Piazza £

3 Linkfield Street TEL Redhill (0737) 66154

A branch of a growing chain that offers an enterprising choice of reliably good pizzas. See entry under New Malden for more detail.

Open all week noon to 11 Table service. Licensed. No-smoking area. Wheelchair access. Access, Visa

REDLYNCH Wiltshire MAP 2

Langley Wood ££

Hamptworth Road TEL Romsey (0794) 390348

The delightful garden leads directly into acres of woodland, where deer roam; inside, the lounge is a cross between old world hunting lodge and 1930s semi. The cooking is said to be good, with home-made bread and, if you are staying overnight, croissants for breakfast. A meal might include baked spinach and Gruyère served in turmeric sauce with toasted cashew-nuts, an interesting savoury bread pudding with onion marmalade or nut pâté en croûte. Vegetarian dishes can tend towards the heavy; cheer things up with a 'gorgeous, light' lemon soufflé.

Open Sun 12.30 to 2, Wed to Sat 7.30 to 11 **Closed** 3 weeks Jan/Feb Booking advisable. Table service. Licensed. Meat dishes. No cigars or pipes in the dining-room. Wheelchair access. Accommodation. Access, Amex, Diners, Visa

RICHMOND Surrey MAP 12

Mrs Beeton's £

58 Hill Rise TEL 081-940 9561

This light, airy old shop, with boarded walls and floor, is run by a co-operative whose cooks take turns each day. Opening times could be noon to 5 and 6 to 10, but it's best to check beforehand. The style is simple and food can vary as much as the hours, depending on who is cooking. Vegetarians will always find one main course but Friday is their best day, when fresh spinach soup, carrot and lentil soup, spiced vegetable crumble or buckwheat pancakes might be on the menu. Other days might produce only a quiche. Puddings, all home made, are limited: death by chocolate seems to appear almost invariably, but sometimes there are cheesecake, walnut tart or apple pie.

Open all week, times vary daily Booking advisable D. Table service. Tables outside. Unlicensed, but bring your own: no corkage. Meat dishes. Fish dishes. Snacks. Take-aways. Wheelchair access

Pizza Express £

20 Hill Street TEL 081-940 8951

A satellite of the excellent London-based chain that was founded twenty-five years ago. See London entry.

Open Mon to Sat 11.30 to midnight, Sun noon to 11.30. Table service. Licensed, also bring your own: corkage £2.50. Meat dishes. Fish dishes. Take-aways. No-smoking area. Wheelchair access. Access, Amex, Diners, Visa

Refectory ££

6 Church Walk TEL 081-940 6264

Ecclesiastical in name only – deriving from proximity to the churchyard and its previous function as vestry office – this is much praised. Martin and Harriet Steel provide home cooking which they describe as wholesome, with a daily vegetarian choice such as soup, guaranteed to be without meat stock; cheese and vegetable flan; spiced bean casserole; lentil, rice and celery bake. Leave room for traditional British puddings, in particular the butterscotch tart. Open for morning coffee and afternoon tea, and for dinner for private parties of 15 or more.

Open Tue to Sun L noon to 2 **Closed** 25 Dec, 1 Jan and Easter Booking advisable at weekends. Table service. Tables outside. Licensed, also bring your own: corkage £5 per bottle. Meat dishes. Other diets catered for. Snacks at other times. No smoking. Wheelchair access. Accommodation. Access, Visa

Richmond Brasserie **£££**

Bridge Street TEL 081-332 2524

This might be right for those occasions when you are the only vegetarian among meat-eaters who are dining out without counting the pennies. The vegetarian choice is very limited – perhaps artichokes with hollandaise to start and mushrooms in puff pastry to follow. However, the restaurant had been open only six months at the time of going to press, so things may look up. The view and service are praised.

Open all week noon to 3, 7 to 11 Booking advisable. Table service. Licensed. Meat dishes. Vegan and other diets catered for on request. Access, Amex, Visa

Richmond Harvest Ⓥ ★ **£–££**

5 Dome Buildings, The Quadrant TEL 081-940 1138 and 8584

Well known on the Richmond scene, this spruce basement with bare brick walls is inviting for vegans and vegetarians. Wholefood, includes home-made starters such as a soup of the day served with home-baked bread; aubergine and tomato pâté; guacamole, or tamari mushrooms. Follow these with aubergine and bulgur wheat crumble, courgette and tomato lasagne or vegetable and butterbean Kashmir on brown rice. All puddings are home made too. Excellent freshly cooked dishes and plenty of choice make this well worth a visit.

Open all week 11.30 to 11 (1 to 10 Sun) Booking advisable. Table service. Licensed. Vegan. Other diets catered for on request. Take-aways

The availability of vegan dishes is indicated in the details underneath the text of an entry.

ROCHFORD Essex MAP 3

Chatters ££

64–66 West Street TEL Southend-on-Sea (0702) 540083

The 250-year-old weatherboarded restaurant used to be a workmen's café; now it has 'more than a touch of Laura Ashley' in the décor. The colour scheme is green – paint, carpet, upholstery – and tables are laid with small vases of flowers and candles. Both the ordinary and the vegetarian menus are extensive: nine starters and eight main dishes for a vegetarian to choose from. As well as mundane items on the lines of avocado vinaigrette and melon are good mushrooms beelzebub in a cream curry sauce, avocado stuffed with walnuts and tangy sauce, and aubergine stuffed with mushrooms, nuts and onions. Vegans will find two main dishes. Side vegetables let the meal down.

Open Tue to Sat D 7 to 11, Sun L noon to 2 Booking advisable. Table service. Tables outside. Licensed. Meat dishes. Fish dishes. Vegan dishes. Other diets catered for on request. Take-aways. Access, Visa

Renoufs £££

1 South Street TEL Southend-on-Sea (0702) 544393

The cuisine at both Renoufs and the restaurant in the Hotel Renouf 100 yards away has a continental influence. The vegetarian menu sticks fairly closely to the stalwarts: onion soup au gratin, avocado and fruit cocktail, vegetable risotto, nut cutlets, vegetable strudel with ginger sauce – and less usual oyster mushroom with Provence, tomatoes and artichokes. There's a sweets trolley to finish. 'A relaxing, friendly and warm place,' comments one reporter.

Open Tue to Sat 12.30 to 1.45 (exc Sat L), 7.30 to 9.45 **Closed** 3 weeks Jan, 2 weeks in summer Booking advisable. Table service. Licensed. Meat dishes. Fish dishes. Access, Amex, Diners, Visa

A restaurant manager can't insist on people not smoking, unless it's specifically a non-smoking restaurant or a non-smoking area. If it is, smokers could be asked to leave if they don't stop. If it's important to you, check beforehand what the smoking arrangements are.

ROSS-ON-WYE Hereford & Worcester **MAP 4**

Meader's ££

1 Copse Cross Street TEL Ross-on-Wye (0989) 62803

There are no pretensions in décor or culinary trimmings at this Hungarian café in the town centre. It used to be purely vegetarian, but now provides meat dishes as well. Hungarian and other continental cuisines predominate, with lunches along the lines of snacks or lasagne, nut roast, curry or mushrooms in cream sauce. Special Hungarian menus are available in the evening at a fixed price for two, with one vegetarian dish of mushroom goulash. Everything is freshly made. Eat to Muzak except on Saturday nights when live music and candlelight set the scene. All things considered, a good value place to eat.

Open Mon to Sat exc Mon D 11.45 to 2.15, 7 to 9.30 **Closed** Tue and Wed D Jan to Easter Booking advisable for Sat D. Table service D. Counter service L. Licensed. Meat dishes. Fish dishes. Snacks at other times. Take-aways. No-smoking area at lunchtime

ROWSLEY Derbyshire **MAP 7**

Caudwell's Country Parlour Ⓥ £

Caudwell's Mill Craft Centre TEL Matlock (0629) 733185

By the time of publication, the wholefood tea-room should be in its new building in a craft centre with five workshops; the aim is to provide more and better seating. The successful food formula will remain the same: morning coffees, lunches and teas offering natural ingredients, and home baking made with flour milled on site and free-range eggs. Main meals provide dishes such as cream of watercress and potato soup, vegan nut roast, mushroom pâté, or Country Parlour savoury crumble. Scones and cakes feature strongly on the list of dessert and teatime treats.

Open Mon to Sun 11.30 to 5.30 **Closed** Mon to Fri Jan and Feb Counter service. Tables outside. Meat dishes (Jul and Aug only). Vegan dishes. Other diets catered for on request. Snacks. Take-aways. Wheelchair access

ROXWELL Essex MAP 5

Farmhouse Feast £££

The Street TEL Roxwell (024 548) 583

The half-timbered house, next to the Chequers, has a suburban air, but its idiosyncratic style of producing large tureens of soup from which you help yourself may suit vegetarians rather well. The tureens may contain lentil, onion and carrot, curried parsnip, or carrot and split pea soup, and main dishes might be Essex roulade with lentil and spinach, buckwheat and red pepper loaf, stuffed aubergines or mushroom, garlic and chick-pea pancakes. Puddings are also help-yourself. As we go to press the restaurant is up for sale and so sadly may not continue in its present form. Best to check before visiting.

Open Wed to Fri noon to 1.30, Tue to Sat D 7.30 to 9.30, Sun L by arrangement only (parties over 6) **Closed** 2 weeks June, first week Jan Booking advisable. Table service. Licensed. Meat dishes. Fish dishes. Vegan dishes. Other diets catered for on request. No-smoking area. Wheelchair access exc wc

RUGBY Warwickshire MAP 4

Grosvenor Hotel ££

Clifton Road TEL Rugby (0788) 535686

There are not many places in the area suitable for vegetarians and a meal here would provide a choice of main dishes; it's a pleasant venue for a special occasion at moderate cost. Roquefort and pistachio pâté with shredded apple and Cumberland sauce might be the starter, followed by dishes such as asparagus and bean ragout 'cascading from a puff pastry pillow' or a like puff pastry pillow but with a ragout of wild mushrooms and Brie served on leaf spinach with port glaze. Follow with hot raspberry soufflé, chilled dark chocolate fondant with orange and Cointreau syrup. Home-made chocolates are served with coffee.

Open all week, exc Sat L, noon to 2, 7 to 10 Booking advisable. Table service. Licensed. Other diets catered for on request. No pipes in the dining-room. Accommodation. Access, Amex, Diners, Visa

Peppers Coffee Shop £

25 Sheep Street TEL Rugby (0788) 61819

The coffee-house confines itself to serving vegetarian and fish dishes; lunches are predictable wholefood choices such as quiches, pizzas, jacket potatoes and lasagne; there are also some specialities of savoury stuffed potatoes, stuffed aubergines, courgette and tomato pie and vegetable risotto.

Open all week 9.30 to 5 Counter service. Tables outside. Fish dishes. Vegan dishes. Other diets catered for on request. Snacks. Take-aways. No smoking. Wheelchair access

RYE East Sussex MAP 3

Chilka House £

The Black Boy, 4 High Street TEL Rye (0797) 226402

Look for the Black Boy Tea-Rooms sign; that unlikely oak-panelled setting houses this restaurant named after the large inland lake in India. Although the vegetarian choice is pretty much of the side-dish variety, the house speciality is a vegetarian dish called dhokar dalna: large vegetable cubes specially fried and served in a sauce. All vegetable dishes are prepared with pure corn oil. The vegetable kofte starter is an interesting carrot and beetroot combination in breadcrumbs. Nan have been praised and it is said that the proprietor grinds flour for the bread.

Open Wed to Sat 6.30 to 10.30 **Closed** 21 Dec to 4 Jan, Feb Table service. Licensed. Meat dishes. Fish dishes. Vegan dishes. Take-aways. Wheelchair access. Access, Amex, Diners, Visa

RYTON-ON-DUNSMORE West Midlands MAP 4

Ryton Gardens Café Ⓥ ★ £

National Centre for Organic Gardening TEL Coventry (0203) 303517

A café connected to the National Centre for Organic Gardening ought to serve good vegetarian food – and this does so consistently. As would be expected, great emphasis is placed on organic ingredients. A typical day's menu offers freshly cooked hot dishes of a good parsnip and apple soup, fennel and lemon soup, mushroom layer and an oriental special, which is a selection of vegetables in spicy batter. Some interesting innovations include broad bean cutlet and onion sauce. Salads include such rarities as mizuna, rocket, miners lettuce and land cress. The sweet-toothed will relish the fresh fruit fools, Bakewell tarts, ginger and honey cheesecake and upside-down pineapple pudding. There is a comprehensive range of organic wines. Cream teas are also served.

Open all week 9am to 4, L noon to 2.30 **Closed** 24 to 30 Dec Counter service. Licensed. Other diets catered for on request. Snacks. Take-aways. Wheelchair access. Access, Visa

ST AGNES Cornwall **MAP 1**

Frins, Porthvean Hotel ★ £££

Churchtown TEL St Agnes (087 255) 2581

Frin is the pet name of the co-owner and chef and although not a vegetarian, she brings flair and imagination to a menu that labels clearly vegetarian and vegan dishes in addition to meat and fish. As well as the more predictable garlic mushrooms, pasta and corn on the cob, there might be vegetarian pâté to start. For mains, meatless moussaka is packed with chunks of aubergine and tomato, while nut roast takes in almonds, walnuts, pecans, peanuts and herbs and arrives with a sherry and cream gravy described by one diner as 'truly memorable'. Vegetables are plain and unadorned; green salad is a good mixture of leaves. Crème caramel and well-reported chocolate pot give a flavour of the puddings. Cut-price rates for B&B in January and February.

Open Mon to Sat 7 to 9 **Closed** Christmas and New Year Booking advisable. Table service. Licensed. Meat dishes. Fish dishes. Vegan dishes. Other diets catered for on request. No smoking. Accommodation. Access, Visa

The cost of a three-course vegetarian meal without wine is indicated by £ symbols to the right of the restaurant name:
£ = up to £7.50
££ = £7.50 to £15
£££ = £15 and over

ST ALBANS Hertfordshire MAP 5

Pizza Express £

11–13 Verulam Road TEL St Albans (0727) 53020

A satellite of the excellent London-based chain that was founded twenty-five years ago. See London entry.

Open Mon to Sat 11.30 to midnight, Sun noon to 11.30. Table service. Licensed, also bring your own: corkage £2.50. Meat dishes. Fish dishes. Take-aways. No-smoking area. Wheelchair access. Access, Amex, Diners, Visa

Upstairs Downstairs ££

1–2 Waxhouse Gate, High Street TEL St Albans (0727) 54843

The cosy atmosphere can be enjoyed for lunches or dinners, when three or more vegetarian dishes will be on offer: aduki pie, carrot and nut loaf, moussaka, chickpea curry, lemon pea croquettes and spinach roulade are examples. A home-made tomato soup with basil has been much enjoyed; other starters might be pan-fried mushrooms with sesame seed, vegetable pâté, avocado with raspberry sauce.

Open all week 10 to 3, 6.30 to 12 Booking advisable. Table service. Tables outside. Licensed. Meat dishes. Vegan dishes. Other diets catered for on request. Snacks. Wheelchair access. Access, Visa

ST AUSTELL Cornwall MAP 1

Thin End £

41A Fore Street TEL St Austell (0726) 75805

A coffee-house that serves home-made German-style cakes, meringues with clotted cream, light meals, salads and jacket potatoes all day; there is one vegetarian dish, a nut roast with salad. In the winter it's full of students sitting over endless cups of coffee and sticky cakes; in the summer it's the haunt of holiday-makers. The patisserie downstairs sells the same cakes and baked items.

Open Mon to Sat 9 to 5 Table service. Licensed. Meat dishes. Snacks. Take-aways. No-smoking area

ST IVES Cornwall MAP 1

Woodcote Hotel Ⓥ £

The Saltings, Lelant TEL Hayle (0736) 753147

This purely vegetarian and vegan hotel serves a fixed-price dinner menu (£7.50 as we went to press). Combinations might be walnut and aubergine pâté followed by stuffed aubergine with cashew-nut and butter bean casserole; home-made soup followed by apricot and lentil-stuffed vine leaves served with mixed salad and pasta; or spinach lasagne followed by savoury pancakes with red cabbage and jacket potatoes. Puddings are on the lines of cheesecake, lemon meringue pie or blackberry and apple pie.

Open all week D 6.30 to 8 **Closed** Nov to Feb Booking advisable. Table service. Unlicensed, also bring your own: no corkage. Vegan dishes. Other diets catered for on request. Snacks. No smoking. No babies. Accommodation

SALISBURY Wiltshire MAP 2

Bishop's Mill £

The Maltings TEL Salisbury (0722) 412127

Flexibility is the key here: starters and main courses are interchangeable, and portions are for one or two people. The mix-and-match selection includes courgettes or cauliflower in breadcrumbs with cranberry or garlic sauce, and such main courses as wholemeal flan with layers of courgettes, carrots and tomato with custardy cheese topping, or different kinds of pasta with a selection of four sauces: tagliatelle with a generous pile of mushrooms in a strongly flavoured garlic sauce has been good. Well-spiced apple pie might be a pleasant finish. The building looks like a restored warehouse and has a wine bar at the front, heavily populated by young customers enjoying the loud music, but there is a more sedate dining area at the back where the music isn't too intrusive.

Open all week 10 to 11 (8.30 to 11 Sat) **Closed** 25 Dec Table service. Tables outside. Licensed. Meat dishes. Snacks. Take-aways. Wheelchair access. Access, Amex, Diners, Visa

Harper's £££

7 Ox Row, The Market Square TEL Salisbury (0722) 333188

Conveniently situated in the middle of Market Square, Harper's is really a glorified café – none the worse for that, as the food is very good and the upstairs gives a good view over the market. Various menus are available, with vegetarian dishes marked 'v': a minor criticism is that sometimes a starter will also appear as a main course. Vegetable nest-cream and tarragon vol-au-vent, a very good gazpacho with traditional garnish are examples of starters, vegetable bake with cheese and crumb topping is a main course. Bread-and-butter pudding made with cream and served in an individual dish is not to be missed.

Open Mon to Sat noon to 2, 6.30 to 10 (10.30 Sat) **Closed** 25 and 26 Dec, 1 Jan Booking advisable. Table service. Licensed, bring your own: corkage £3. Meat dishes. Vegan dishes. Other diets catered for on request. Access, Diners, Visa

Hob Nob Coffee Shop £

The Kings House, 65 The Close TEL Salisbury (0722) 332151

Attached to the South Wiltshire Museum, the Hob Nob serves vegetarian soup and a range of hot dishes, perhaps ratatouille crumble; basil and tomato crumble; mushroom bake or mushroom and coriander vol-au-vent; as well as a pizza or quiche. Cakes are home made.

Open Mon to Sat 10.30 to 4 plus 2 to 5 Sun July and Aug **Closed** Nov to Easter Booking advisable. Table service. Counter service. Unlicensed, but bring your own, corkage: charge by arrangement. Vegan and other diets catered for on request. Snacks. Cold take-aways. No smoking. Wheelchair access

Michael Snell Tea Rooms £

8 St Thomas's Square TEL Salisbury (0722) 336037

Locals rate the tea-rooms highly and the shop on the same premises sells quality products such as home-made chocolates and biscuits, honeys, jams, coffees and teas. Ice-creams and sorbets are also home made without artificial colourings or flavourings. Outside the lunchtime hours Swiss-style cakes and cream teas can be enjoyed. Lunches are limited but good, typical dishes being mushroom flan, baked jacket potato, moonraker vegetable pie and a really good, light, cheese flan with a satisfactorily crisp base. Three salads are served with each main course.

Open Mon to Sat 9 (8.30 Sat) to 5.30 Table service. Tables outside. Unlicensed. Meat dishes. Fish dishes. Take-aways. No-smoking area. Wheelchair access

Mo's ££

62 Milford Street TEL Salisbury (0722) 331377

The brightly lit transatlantic-style restaurant is centrally placed and popular in the evenings. The menu rarely changes and a vegetarian main course section includes six dishes – lasagne, burger, 'lentil creation', bulgur wheat chilli, pine kernel roast and croustade. These may be supplemented by a daily special. Try the speciality of chocolate crumb pudding from a wide selection of sweets available.

Open all week, exc Sun L, noon to 2.30, 5.30 to 11.30 Bookings advisable. Table service. Licensed. Meat dishes. Take-aways. Access, Diners, Visa

Wheatsheaf £

TEL Middle Woodford (0722) 73203

This eighteenth-century inn has a welcome vegetarian section on its menu; the food is well thought of, most cooked on the premises. The surroundings are attractive. The building was originally a farmhouse and the dining area has been formed from the barns; ceilings are low, beams abound and there are low wooden tables and a spacious garden with further tables. One day's offerings included: lentil soup, avocado vinaigrette, vegetable chilli and rice, macaroni cheese, vegetable curry, broccoli bake, mushroom and nut fettucine, two kinds of lasagne, one an Italian version with spinach and mushrooms. Macaroni cheese was found to be well cooked, with flavoursome cheese sauce, a hot and healthy portion; the broccoli bake equally good, topped with crunchy oatmeal. Also a good range of real ales.

Open all week noon to 2, 7 to 10 Table service. Tables outside. Licensed, also bring your own, corkage varies. Meat dishes. Other diets catered for on request. Take-aways. Access, Amex, Visa

SALTASH Cornwall **MAP 1**

Cotehele Barn ££

Cotehele House, St Dominick TEL Liskeard (0579) 50652

Inside the beautiful National Trust medieval manor but accessible without paying the admission fee. Carrying out the National Trust policy that caterers should always feature one hot and one cold vegetarian dish, the Barn does well. There are imaginative soups, such as celery and almond or Stilton and onion, lentil and nut pâté and a vegetable bake or lasagne. Salads are also recommended.

Open all week, exc Fri, 11am to 6 (4 Nov and Dec) **Closed** Jan to Mar Booking advisable Sun. Table service. Licensed. Meat dishes. Other diets catered for on request. Snacks. Wheelchair access. Access, Amex, Visa

SANDBACH Cheshire **MAP 7**

Rumours £

148 Congleton Road TEL Crewe (0270) 763664

Brown walls and elaborately framed prints strive for an Edwardian effect in this wine bar that makes a genuine attempt to provide a good range of vegetarian food. Waitresses are friendly and enthusiastic about the meals. Daily choices are written on the blackboard and about six are vegetarian; even Christmas menus remember non-meat-eaters. Gourmet evenings extend the repertoire and may produce Alsatian dumplings in corn sauce, or aubergine and mushroom fritters. The gourmet evenings do not invariably contain vegetarian dishes, however, so it is best to check. Cheese filo parcels are the equal of many a smarter restaurant, and the celery and cashew-nut risotto, which arrives in vast quantities, is tasty with the rice separated and the cashew-nuts crunchy. Raleigh cheese and egg, complicated though it is, works very well. Puddings have been a let-down, brandy cake rating a comment of 'mundane'.

Open all week noon to 2.15, 5 to 10.15 Booking advisable at weekends. Table service. Licensed. Meat dishes. Fish dishes. Vegan dishes. Other diets catered for on request. Snacks at other times. Children's menu up to 7.30. Wheelchair access. Access, Diners, Visa

SCARBOROUGH North Yorkshire **MAP** 10

Gemini ⓥ £

13 Victoria Road **TEL** Scarborough (0723) 360054

Starters of baked stuffed peppers, hummus and fruit cup, tofu and cheese bake, lead on to main dishes of aduki bean bake, savoury nut roast and hazelnut and chickpea croustade. Leek and Stilton flan, carrot cake and home-made ice-creams are particularly recommended. Organic wines. 'Generous portions, as you'd expect in Scarborough. Prices are reasonable and I can't imagine that you'd ever leave dissatisfied,' writes one visitor.

Open Mon to Sat exc Mon D 11.30am to 3, 7 to 9.30 Table service D. Counter service L. Tables outside. Licensed. Vegan dishes. Take-aways. No-smoking area. Wheelchair access. Access, Visa

Square Cat £

Stephen Joseph Theatre, Valley Bridge Parade
TEL Scarborough (0723) 368463

Taking its name from Alan Ayckbourn's first play (he's the theatre's artistic director), the Square Cat welcomes shoppers as much as theatre-goers, offering a standard lunchtime bill of baked potatoes, sandwiches, salads and quiches, amplified in the evening by a couple of vegetarian choices such as mushroom and nut fettucine, lentil bake, cashew-nut risotto. Wholemeal quiche is made with crisp, crumbly pastry and soup is always vegetarian. Tables are well spaced and the atmosphere crackles when there's a performance. Good coffee.

Open Tue to Sat noon to 2, 6 to 11 **Closed** when theatre is shut Counter service. Licensed. Meat dishes. Wheelchair access. Access, Visa

SCARISBRICK Lancashire **MAP** 7

Cathay Garden ££

63 Southport Road **TEL** Southport (0704) 30071

This lively Chinese restaurant, relatively unadorned, can build up a fug on a crowded night, but is a good choice for vegetarians and meat-eaters alike. The vegetarian set dinner offers seven dishes and the vegetarian banquet nine, in addition to a good range of separate vegetarian starters and main dishes. At a sample meal both a large plateful of assorted hors d'oeuvre – with among other things, seaweed, pickled cabbage, corn, carrots – and spring onion pancakes (two crispy folded pancakes with onion filling) were good starters, followed by equally well received family-style bean curd and vegetables in a spicy hot sauce and mixed vegetables in black-bean sauce. The only quibble was over an incorrect bill. See also Southport.

Open Tue to Sat 5.30 to 11 **Closed** 25, 26 and 27 Dec Booking advisable. Table service. Licensed. Meat dishes. Vegan dishes. Take-aways. Wheelchair access. Access, Amex, Diners, Visa

SCUNTHORPE Humberside MAP 8

Giovanni's ££

44 Oswald Road TEL Scunthorpe (0724) 281169

Italian cooking is by nature adaptable for vegetarians and this pizzeria-cum-restaurant offers excellent sauces and a high consistency of cooking. Macaroni Villalbese with tomatoes, peas, onions and fresh mushrooms in a cream and red wine sauce; spaghetti vegetariani with artichokes, mushrooms, spinach, onions and peppers; and risotto al funghi are all good examples; the sauces are repeated in pizza versions. Disappointingly, the half dozen or so vegetarian starters hold few surprises.

Open Mon to Sat noon to 2, 6 to 11 (11.30 Fri and Sat) Table service. Tables outside. Licensed. Meat dishes. Fish dishes. Vegan dishes and other diets catered for on request. Wheelchair access. Access, Visa

SEAFORD East Sussex MAP 3

Quincy's ££

42 High Street TEL Seaford (0323) 895490

An ex-cobbler's shop is the scene for a tiny, rather cottagey restaurant with clapboard walls and, inside, tongue-and-groove walls hung with motley pictures. Low music seems to induce whispered conversations.

Adventurous combinations may not always be successful, but some dishes, such as croustade of mushrooms and quails' eggs with chive and lemon sauce, has been praised. Other vegetarian dishes might be asparagus and wild mushroom tart or stuffed mushroom pastry. Other puddings are freely confessed to be 'a bit over the top', for example chocolate gluttony, composed of three kinds of chocolate pudding.

Open Tues to Sat, D 7.15 to 10 **Closed** 2 weeks Sept Booking advisable. Table service. Licensed, also bring your own: corkage £2.50. Meat dishes. Fish dishes. Vegan dishes and other diets catered for on request. No children under 8. Access, Visa

SEAVIEW Isle of Wight MAP 2

Seaview Hotel £

The High Street TEL Seaview (0983) 612711

A family-run Victorian hotel which has a good reputation for its food; the restaurant menu has a vegetarian section offering dishes such as vegetable puff and noodles. Starters might be home-made soup, melon or vegetable terrine with tomato coulis. Vegetarians can also eat in the bar – a typical dish is pasta with vegetables, cream and cheese. Finish with crème brûlée, chocolate mousse or peach sorbet in a brandy-snap basket.

Open all week noon to 1.30, 7.30 to 9.15 exc Sun D Booking advisable. Table service. Tables outside. Licensed, also bring your own: corkage by arrangement. Meat dishes. Fish dishes. No children under 5 at D. Accommodation. Access, Amex, Visa

SEEND Wiltshire MAP 2

Seend Bridge Farm ££

Nr Melsham TEL Seend (038 082) 8534

Mr Podger runs the farm and Mrs Podger runs the restaurant – a restaurant with a difference. Two rooms of the farmhouse have been turned into dining-rooms: service is unpretentious but charming; the food is all fresh, home-cooked traditional English fare, the vegetables grown on the farm in many cases. It's so popular that booking must be done well in advance. And here's the difference: the menu is sent to you and your choice must be phoned through well before the night you've booked. There are seasonal menus: the winter vegetarian main dish was parsnip nut cream. How it was made is a mystery, but the result was a stunningly light, creamy dish sprinkled with nuts, remembered with relish. Starters included cream of spinach canelloni, soup, garlic and herb-baked mushrooms, and tomato salad with garlic bread. The baked Alaska meets with universal acclaim: it is huge. Other puddings are chocolate Amaretti mousse, farmhouse trifle, apple pie.

Open Wed to Sat D 7 to 9 **Closed** 24 to 26 Dec, 1 Jan Bookings only. Table service. Unlicensed, but bring your own. Meat dishes. Fish dishes. Other diets catered for on request. Wheelchair access. Accommodation

SEVENOAKS Kent MAP 3

Pizza Piazza £

3C Dorset Street TEL Sevenoaks (0732) 454664

A branch of a growing chain that offers an enterprising choice of reliably good pizzas. See entry under New Malden for more detail.

Open all week noon to 11 Table service. Licensed. No-smoking area. Wheelchair access. Access, Visa

SHEFFIELD South Yorkshire MAP 7

Bay Tree £

119 Devonshire Street TEL Sheffield (0742) 759254

This mainly vegetarian restaurant offers some fish dishes, so it is a good place to eat with companions who like the food of rivers and seas. There is nothing unusual among the starters, which are of the soup-pâté-hummus variety, but the pressed apple juice and freshly squeezed orange juice are welcome. Main courses might be celery, Gruyère and almond bake, green peppercorn roulade, and potato and mushroom gratin. The modest prices are gratifying.

Open Mon to Sat noon to 3, Thur and Fri 6.30 to 9 Counter service. Unlicensed, but bring your own: corkage 50p. Fish dishes. Vegan dishes. Other diets catered for on request. Snacks. Take-aways. Wheelchair access

Fat Cat £

23 Alma Street TEL Sheffield (0742) 28195

The main attraction are the real ales, of which there are plenty, and additional 'guest' ones that change regularly. None the less, the tall building set in the drab streets of the old industrial area will do a vegetarian proud. Good-value lunches can be eaten in front of the coal fire without the intrusion of canned music. A vegetable lentil soup came piping hot and well seasoned; vegetable chilli and cauliflower in light mustard sauce have been enjoyed, and salads are fresh and crisp. Perhaps to weigh down the beer, puddings tend to be on the heavy side – an orange passion-cake could be lighter but jam sponge is popular.

Open all week noon to 2.30 Table service. Tables outside. Licensed. Meat dishes. Vegan dishes. Take-aways. Wheelchair access. No-smoking area

Just Cooking ★ £

16–18 Carver Street TEL Sheffield (0742) 27869

Partly due to its central location, but mainly due of course to the excellent food, Just Cooking can get busy at lunchtimes, and on Saturdays expect queues, snappy ordering, a rushed feel, and perhaps food not as hot as it might be. Having said that, it is well worth a trip, for, in addition to meaty dishes, vegetarians will find a good main course at lunch and dinner. Although the restaurant is large and airy, seating tends to be a bit cramped. The menu gains inspiration from around the world, Greece being a favourite, hence lots of filo pastry, Feta and ketalotiri cheeses. Starters might be savoury apple with cheese and herb pâté with tarragon cream, or courgette and leek soup with yoghurt; main dishes include gourmet vegetable pie with artichoke hearts and Gruyère or spinach roulade with mushrooms in marsala. When sampled, an aubergine bake was a delicately flavoured combination of courgettes, tomatoes and aubergines; a rice salad to accompany was interestingly full of bean-shoots, red beans, white cabbage, nuts and apple. Good kiwi-fruit Pavlova, crisp on the outside and marshmallowy inside; trifle was almost too creamy. Special occasions include jazz and gala evenings with menus that always feature a vegetarian dish.

Open Tue to Sat 11.45 to 3.30, D Wed 5.30 to 7.30, Fri 7 to 9.45 **Closed** Christmas to New Year, 3 weeks Aug to Sept Counter service (Table Fri D). Licensed. Meat dishes. Other diets catered for (1 week's notice). Take-aways. No-smoking area. Wheelchair access by arrangement

Nirmal's £

189–193 Glossop Road TEL Sheffield (0742) 724054

This family-run Indian restaurant has achieved a long-standing reputation for sound and consistent cooking. As well as the usual dhals, pakoras and bhajias, there are vegetarian dishes such as koftas, mushroom and bamboo shoot bhaji and a set vegetarian menu for two which includes sag paneer, channa, aubergine with green peppers, mixed vegetable pilau, puri, sweet yoghurt and kulfi. Each day of the week brings forth a different dhal.

Open all week, exc Sun L, noon to 2.30, 6 to midnight (1am Fri and Sat) Booking advisable. Table service. Licensed. Meat dishes. Fish dishes. Vegan dishes. Snacks at other times. Take-aways. Wheelchair access. Access, Amex, Visa

SHEPTON MALLET Somerset MAP 2

Bowlish House ★ £££

Wells Road TEL Shepton Mallet (0749) 2022

This elegant Georgian hotel with stone-flagged hall and comfortable furniture, filled with fresh flowers from the garden, is run by Bob and Linda Morley, formerly of the Sun Inn, where vegetarian cuisine was a speciality. Linda Morley is a vegetarian and prepares all the food herself. Only one suitable main course appears on the set-price menu, but a light puff pastry with mushrooms and avocado, and a cervelas of spinach and almonds with pine kernels and sweet pepper coulis have both been enjoyed. Other dishes might be choux pastry on spinach cream sauce, filled with herbed sauté mushrooms or a tartlet of mushrooms and leeks on a lemon cream sauce. Puddings are said to be exceedingly generous, and the chocolate mousse has been recommended.

Open all week D 7 to 9.30 Booking advisable. Table service. Licensed. Meat dishes. Fish dishes. Other diets catered for on request. Accommodation. Access, Visa

SHIFNAL Shropshire MAP 4

Park House Hotel ££

Park Street TEL Telford (0952) 460128

Meat- and fish-eaters will be catered for by French cuisine but vegetarians have a separate menu weaving strands of cooking from all over the world – lasagne, vegetables à la Créole, French crêpes and curry are some examples. Unusual ideas include a strawberry yoghurt soup flavoured with fresh limes.

Open all week noon to 2.30, 6 to 10 Booking advisable. Table service. Licensed. Meat dishes. Fish dishes. Vegan dishes. Other diets catered for on request. Snacks. Wheelchair access. Access, Amex, Carte Blanche, Diners, Visa

Raphael's ££

4 Church Street TEL Telford (0952) 461136

The seventeenth-century cottage off the main Telford to Wolverhampton road in the centre of Shifnal, houses a simply furnished restaurant. The area is not well served with places serving good vegetarian meals, so this is a welcome eating place. There's a choice of starters and main courses: spicy chickpeas with rice; grapefruit and grapes in wine; and baked goats' cheese in puff pastry to begin; mushroom croustade, red bean and aubergine delight or gado-gado to follow. The lentil crumble is well presented and herby, if a little dry; chestnuts and rice has been enjoyed as have excellent vegetables.

Open Tue to Sat 7.30 (7 Sat) to 10 Booking advisable. Table service. Licensed. Meat dishes. Fish dishes. Vegan dishes. Other diets catered for on request. No-smoking area. Wheelchair access. Access, Visa

SHIPLEY West Yorkshire MAP 7

Aagrah ££

27 Westgate TEL Bradford (0274) 594660

A small Indian restaurant offering a vegetarian thali in addition to a biriani, mushroom pilau and other vegetable dishes.

Open all week, D 6 to 12.45 Booking advisable. Table service. Licensed. Meat dishes. Vegan dishes. Other diets catered for on request. Take-aways. No-smoking area. Wheelchair access. Access, Amex, Diners, Visa

SHIPTON GORGE Dorset **MAP** 2

Innsacre Farmhouse Hotel £££

Shipton Gorge TEL Bridport (0308) 56137

A happy atmosphere prevails at this pleasant and welcoming hotel offering good food with a propensity for sauces. Starters may provide lean pickings but the main courses are adventurous – deep-fried vine leaf parcels filled with aduki beans, mung beans and fresh dates coated in coconut batter; beansprout nutlets with sweet-and-sour aubergines. Good fresh fruit flan and alcoholic gateau. Picnic lunches can be packed for guests.

Open all week noon to 2, 7 to 9.30 Table service. Tables outside. Licensed. Meat dishes. Vegan dishes. Other diets catered for on request. No pipes in dining-room. Wheelchair access. Accommodation. Access, Amex, Diners, Visa

SHOTLEY BRIDGE Co Durham **MAP** 10

Manor House Inn ★ ££

Carterway Heads, Nr Consett TEL Edmundbyers (0207) 55268

'I feel sure this is a rising star', writes one satisfied customer. The inn, a long, low period building on the A68, overlooks Derwent Reservoir and very pleasant countryside; the interior has recently been renovated to a high standard. For vegetarians there are starters of hot cheese beignets, leek gratin with rosemary rolls, crespolini with spinach, and pine nut and garlic tartlet. Main dishes show commendable flair – broccoli croustade, mushroom stroganoff, mushroom choux ring and an excellent piperade, creamy and fluffy, with onions, peppers and tomatoes. Ice-cream is home made.

Open Tue to Sat noon to 2.30, 7.30 to 10 Table service. Tables outside. Licensed. Meat dishes. Fish dishes. Other diets catered for on request. No children under 12. Wheelchair access

SHREWSBURY Shropshire **MAP** 7

Good Life Ⓥ

Barracks Passage, Wyle Cop **TEL** Shrewsbury (0743) 50455

Just below the Lion Hotel on Wyle Cop is this tiny, two-roomed restaurant in a restored fourteenth-century building. Vegetarian whole-food of a high order is served, the daily range usually including between eight and ten kinds of salad, four different quiches and two nut loaves. Hot dishes of the day might be five-bean cheese pot, bean goulash, mushrooms and peppers in wine, African pilaff or spinach moussaka. Tarts, sweet flans and home-made cakes to finish.

Open Mon to Sat 9.30 to 3.30 (4.30 Sat) **Closed** 25, 26 Dec, bank hols Counter service. Licensed. Vegan dishes. Other diets catered for on request. Snacks. Take-aways. No-smoking area. Wheelchair access

SKIPTON North Yorkshire **MAP** 10

Herbs Ⓥ £

10 High Street **TEL** Skipton (0756) 60619

At the Town Hall end of the High Street and attached to the Healthy Life Natural Food Centre, Herbs celebrates its decade this year. There is a basic range of salads, flans and sandwiches plus a couple of daily dishes: mushrooms cooked in a mustard cream sauce, served with herb bread; ratatouille pancakes; apple and onion bake. Puddings and cakes take up virtually half the menu and range from lemon Pavlova to hot plum pie and treacle tart. A dozen herbal teas and an equal number of fruit juices.

Open Mon and Wed to Sat 9.30 to 4.45 **Closed** 25 and 26 Dec Table service. Vegan dishes. Other diets catered for on request. Snacks. Take-aways. No smoking after 11.30am

The main criterion for inclusion in the guide is that an eating place offers a vegetarian main course on its standard menu, at all times, that is more than just an omelette, quiche or salad. If you find that a listed restaurant no longers caters for vegetarians, please inform the guide; the address to write to is on page 9.

STRATFORD-ON-AVON Warwickshire **MAP 4**

Café Natural ⓥ £

Unit 1, Greenhill Street TEL Stratford-on-Avon (0789) 415741

Next to Safeways and at the back of a healthfood shop, this wholefood vegetarian restaurant is busy, clean and offers the best selection of vegetarian food in Stratford. Pine tables are covered with Laura Ashley tablecloths, chairs are pine and rather hard. The ceiling is of bamboo lattice work with hanging baskets of dried flowers. Self-service meals are varied, with about eight salads, six or eight main dishes and biscuits, cakes and tarts. The day's hot dishes might include a very light and good savoury strudel, curried plait, lentil and tomato flan or a 'fairly substantial' nut roast. The selected dish may be microwaved. Service is by young and friendly staff.

Open Mon to Sat 11.45am to 4.45, Fri D 5 to 7 Counter service. Unlicensed, but bring your own: corkage 50p. Vegan dishes. Other diets catered for on request. Snacks. Take-aways. No smoking. Wheelchair access

Sir Toby's ££

8 Church Street TEL Stratford-on-Avon (0789) 68822

The menu changes only twice a year, so vegetarians who find the restaurant congenial as well as convenient for the theatre will have to make do with their one choice for six months: perhaps fresh vegetable tagliatelle with coconut cream sauce. Starters might yield a soup such as home-made tomato and basil with cream and croûtons or fresh summer fruits with savoury mint yoghurt. The pudding list is more extensive and includes home-made sorbets and ice-creams in eight varieties.

Open Mon to Sat 5.30 to 9.30 **Closed** 2 weeks in Feb Booking advisable. Table service. Tables outside. Licensed, also bring your own: corkage £1.75. Meat dishes. Fish dishes. Vegan dishes. Other diets catered for on request. No cigars. Wheelchair access. Access, Amex, Visa

The factual details under the text are based on information supplied by the restaurateur.

Vintner Bistro and Café £

5 Sheep Street TEL Stratford-on-Avon (0789) 297259

This old-world, all-day wine bar with beams and oak tables occupies a central position five minutes' walk from the theatre and serves whole-food meat and vegetarian dishes. Downstairs tends to be crowded. Food ordered at the bar is brought to the table. At least one vegetarian dish is always available, perhaps courgette provençale or curried vegetable lasagne. Tagliatelle, generously loaded with cheese, is well reported.

Open all week 10.30am to 10 Counter service. Licensed. Meat dishes. Snacks. Wheelchair access. Access, Amex, Visa

SOUTHALL Greater London MAP 3

Brilliant £

72–74 Western Road TEL 081-574 1928

Not always so brilliant, sadly. None the less vegetarians have a choice of the standard Indian vegetable dishes and egg curry, plus the unusual and unexplained 'Mexican mix'. All main dishes come with chapatis, rice or kulchis.

Open all week exc Sat and Sun L noon to 3, 6 to 11.30 **Closed** Aug Booking advisable. Table service. Licensed. Meat dishes. Fish dishes. Vegan dishes. Take-aways. Wheelchair access. Access, Amex, Diners, Visa

Shahanshah ⓥ £

60 North Road TEL 081-574 1493

The range of curries, samosas, aloo tikki, mutton paneer, dhal and channa may be standard but the food is consistent and prices low. Indian sweets are a speciality.

Open Wed to Mon 10 to 8 Table service. Counter service. Vegan dishes. Snacks. Wheelchair access

SOUTHAMPTON Hampshire MAP 2

Flying Teapot ⓥ £

25 Onslow Road, St Mary's TEL Southampton (0703) 335931

Eight people run this co-operative venture and all cook. Reasonable prices draw a steady student clientele; community and campaigning notices abound. Vegans can find plenty of choice among the pizzas, pasties, soups, pâtés and hot dishes such as chilli, Barcelona bake, nut roast and lasagne. There can be as many as eight salads. Wholemeal rolls are baked every day and cakes and puddings include sugar-free varieties among the flapjacks, carrot cake, bread pudding and trifles. Appropriately, there's a good range of teas.

Open Mon to Sat noon to 8.30 Counter service. Vegan dishes. Other diets catered for on request. Snacks. Take-aways. No-smoking area. Wheelchair access

Town House ⓥ ★ £–££

59 Oxford Street TEL Southampton (0703) 220498

In the fashionable area of Southampton is this small – almost too small – vegetarian restaurant, painted in pastel shades with looped blinds and potted plants. Lunches are usually jacket potatoes, samosas, curries, lasagne and home-made soups. Dinners call the culinary skills into action, with a set-price menu of six starters and six main courses, of which at least one is vegan in each course. The deep-fried Brie with apple sauce is crisp and ungreasy, with the cheese just melting. Samosas, good and crisp, are filled with spiced vegetables. A beautifully presented leeks en croûte with béarnaise sauce uses a slightly sweet pastry lattice topping, and vegan nut cutlets are moist and look good, surrounded by two sauces (of yoghurt and tomato) pooled on the plate. Other dishes might be Peking bake, beansprouts and other vegetables wrapped in a pancake and pastry and served with a cream mint sauce, or Town House crêpes, layers of pancakes filled with spinach, mushroom and tomato. All puddings are home made; as well as crème caramel and fruit salad there is banoffi pie, sweet and gooey. Organic wines are included on the wine list.

Open Mon to Sat exc Sat D, noon to 2, 6.30 to 9.30 (10.30 Fri) Booking advisable. Table service. Tables outside. Licensed. Vegan dishes. Wheelchair access. Access, Visa

SOUTHPORT Merseyside **MAP 7**

Cathay Garden £

Sandown Court, Leicester Street TEL Southport (0704) 30380

A Chinese restaurant with an associated branch in Scarisbrick (see entry). There are two vegetarian set dinners – one with seven dishes and one with nine. Many similar vegetarian dishes are on the main menu. Mixed hors d'oeuvre includes such things as seaweed, pickled cabbage, corn and carrots, spring onion pancakes, bean curd and vegetables in spicy hot sauce. Try toffee apples and bananas to follow.

Open all week 6 to 11 **Closed** 25 and 26 Dec Table service. Licensed, also bring your own: corkage £1. Meat dishes. Vegan dishes. Take-aways. Wheelchair access. Access, Amex, Diners, Visa

SOUTHSEA Hampshire **MAP 2**

Barnaby's Bistro £–££

56 Osborne Road TEL Portsmouth (0705) 821089

The dark red interior enhances the intimate ambience, created, perhaps, because the tables are close packed. One diner relished a tangy, creamy courgette and blue cheese soup with a selection of breads, followed by an aubergine bake stuffed with nuts and covered with tomato sauce and good accompanying salad of leaves with croûtons. Other possible dishes include Swiss fondue (for two), vegetables and mushrooms with cream in puff pastry with hollandaise sauce, or field mushrooms, spinach and poached egg au gratin. Prices are reasonable.

Open all week 12.30 to 2.30, 6 to 11 Booking advisable weekends. Table service. Licensed. Meat dishes. Wheelchair access. Access, Visa

Country Kitchen £

59 Marmion Road TEL Portsmouth (0705) 811425

Shoppers cram into the cosy, cluttered café at lunchtime. What may look like a familiar run of vegetarian dishes are not always so usual in execution: lentil soup tastes of cheese, rissoles are made from lentils and seaweed, a pâté is composed of wine and nuts. The macaroni with vegetables and cheese, says one reporter, is 'tangy, with a good crust'. There is a good selection of quiches, with combinations such as carrot, walnut and onion, or Stilton, sour cream and white wine. Free-range eggs and vegetarian cheese are used. The menu is on a blackboard with specials on a separate board, and customers order at the counter. A place that achieves its modest aims – as its popularity shows.

Open Mon to Sat 9.30 to 5 Counter service. Tables outside. Vegan dishes. Other diets catered for on request. Snacks. Take-aways. No smoking

Pizza Express £

41 Osborne Road TEL Portsmouth (0705) 293938

A satellite of the excellent London-based chain that was founded twenty-five years ago. See London entry.

Open Mon to Sat 11.30 to midnight, Sun noon to 11.30. Table service. Licensed, also bring your own: corkage £2.50. Meat dishes. Fish dishes. Take-aways. No-smoking area. Wheelchair access. Access, Amex, Diners, Visa

Rosie's Vineyard £

87 Elm Grove TEL Portsmouth (0705) 755944

The blackboard menu changes twice a month at the wine bar-cum-bistro. Vegetarians are offered the likes of spinach and Mozzarella cannelloni or wholemeal pancakes stuffed with ratatouille, served with salads. Otherwise, fish is the dominating theme. There are waffles and meringues for puddings, and over 50 wines.

Open all week D 7 to 10.45, Sun L noon to 3 Table service. Counter service. Tables outside. Licensed. Meat dishes. Fish dishes. Vegan dishes. Other diets catered for on request. Wheelchair access. Access, Visa

Under the Trade Descriptions Act, a restaurant must provide food and drink as described on the menu or by the waiter. If you think what you're served doesn't match the description, don't start eating. Complain immediately and ask for something else. You could also tell the local Trading Standards Officer that the restaurant is misleading customers.

SOUTHWOLD Suffolk MAP 5

Crown ££

90 High Street TEL Southwold (0502) 722275

The imposing exterior of this eighteenth-century coaching-inn in Southwold's main street might lead to high expectations; sadly, recent reports have been mixed. Some have found the vegetarian option disappointing while others say the vegetarian food is imaginative and good. Typical offerings are avocado with marinated mushrooms and cucumber or cream of carrot, celery and tomato soup to start, followed by vegetable ragout with rice or tagliatelle with peppers, mushroom, aubergine and cream.

Open all week 12.30 to 2, 7.30 to 9.45 Booking advisable. Table service. Tables outside. Licensed, also bring your own: corkage £4. Meat dishes. Fish dishes. No-smoking in dining-room. Accommodation. Access, Amex, Visa

STAFFORD Staffordshire MAP 7

Curry Kuteer £

31 Greengate Street TEL Stafford (0785) 53279

The oldest Indian restaurant in town has been rejuvenated with an ornate and elaborate décor, but the established good cooking continues. It is extremely popular. Vegetarians do not have a vast choice, however – vegetable samosa or onion bhajia for starters, and four main dishes, of which two are birianis, one a curry and one the chef's special vegetable thali.

Open all week noon to 2, 6 to midnight Booking advisable. Table service. Licensed. Meat dishes. Take-aways. No children under 4. Wheelchair access. Access, Amex, Diners, Visa

Some restaurants have started to take customers' credit card numbers when they book and say that if they don't turn up, a charge will be made. As long as they tell you beforehand, restaurants are within their rights to do this. But the charge should only be reasonable compensation for their loss, not a penalty.

STAMFORD Lincolnshire MAP 8

George ££

71 St Martin's TEL Stamford (0780) 55171

The coaching-inn was built by Lord Burghley, treasurer to Elizabeth I, in 1597. Now a comfortable hotel, its oak-panelled dining-room is adorned with heraldic banners. The menu has several vegetarian dishes with big appeal to mushroom lovers: wild mushrooms and vegetables baked in pastry with a butter sauce and forest mushrooms on a puff pastry case both feature on a summer menu, alongside vegetable and herb ravioli in a basil and tomato sauce. Stir-fried vegetables on a butter and black-bean sauce in filo pastry were found to be a good combination of tastes and textures at a sample meal. Pecan pie or a good fruity sorbet could follow. That a place renowned for its steaks should now offer vegetarian cuisine is a welcome sign of the times.

Open all week 12.30 to 2.30, 7.15 to 10.30 Table service. Counter service. Tables outside. Licensed, also bring your own: corkage £3. Meat dishes. Fish dishes. Vegan dishes. Other diets on request. Snacks at other times. Take-aways. No-smoking area. Wheelchair access. Accommodation. Access, Amex, Visa

STOCKPORT Greater Manchester MAP 7

Coconut Willy's Ⓥ £–££

37 St Petersgate TEL 061-480 7013

This wholefood vegetarian restaurant inhabits an old shop in one of the few remaining shopping streets in Stockport. The narrow room is cheerful with lots of hanging plants, some of them artificial, art deco mirrors and oilcloths on the tables. The menu ranges round the world for inspiration, with some interesting dishes, though all served with a redundant salad garnish. Starters show more invention than mains: stuffed vine leaves, hummus – 'properly prepared with good rough texture and lemony tang' – good crisp samosas, lightly spiced and filled with well-flavoured vegetables. Main dishes tend to be more mundane: quiche, pizza and daily specials such as a chestnut and green and red pepper casserole in dark vegetable stock which is well seasoned and accompanied by an appropriate brown rice mould. Organic wines and naturally fermented beers are available.

Open Tue to Sat 11.30am to 10.30 (D from 6) Table service. Counter service. Licensed, also bring your own: corkage 50p per person. Vegan dishes. Other diets catered for on request. Snacks. Take-aways. No-smoking area. Wheelchair access. Access, Visa

STOKE-BY-NAYLAND Suffolk MAP 5

Angel Inn ££

TEL Colchester (0206) 263245

A pretty group of old cottages with pleasant bars, logs blazing in fireplaces, attractive lamps and above-average furnishings, which give an air more of a hotel than a pub. Bar food is good and reasonable, the menu at lunch and supper chalked up daily on blackboards. There is a restaurant as well, where prices on an à la carte menu are higher. A vegetarian dish is always available. Typical dishes are cheese and almond croquettes with cucumber coulis, gratin of Mediterranean baked vegetables, and three-bean curry. Salads are good and all food is freshly prepared. Don't be put off by some odd descriptions of puddings: the 'iced coffee and chocolate chip terrine' is actually home-made coffee water and cream ice, and is well reported.

Open all week noon to 2, 6.30 to 9 Booking advisable. Table service. Tables outside. Licensed. Meat dishes. Fish dishes. No babies. Accommodation. Access, Amex, Diners, Visa

STON EASTON Somerset MAP 2

Ston Easton Park £££

TEL Chewton Mendip (076 121) 631

The Palladian elegance of this beautifully restored mansion, set in Repton-designed grounds, puts a high price on its meals and accommodation. The dining-room is light and airy, service is efficient and pampering includes tasty filled pastry nibbles and crudités with a walnut dip. The fixed-priced four-course menu begins with hors d'oeuvre, continues with such choices as chilled cucumber and chive soup or terrine of garden vegetables with tomato and thyme coulis. There is always one vegetarian main dish – globe artichoke soufflé flavoured with morels is the speciality – and the filo pastry tartlet filled with garden vegetables, wild mushrooms and pine kernels is well reported. The *pièce de résistance* for dessert is the tulip Ston Easton Park, but crumbles, home-made ice-creams and summer pudding impart a modern British flavour. 'No service charge included or gratuities expected.'

Open all week 12.30 to 2, 7.30 to 9.30 (10 Fri and Sat) Booking advisable. Table service. Tables outside. Licensed. Meat dishes. Fish dishes. Vegan dishes. Other diets catered for on request. Snacks. No pipes or cigars allowed in dining-room. No children under 12. Wheelchair access. Accommodation. Access, Amex, Diners, Visa

STONY STRATFORD Buckinghamshire MAP 4

Peking ££

117 High Street TEL Milton Keynes (0908) 563120

Unusually for a Peking restaurant, this one spares more than a passing thought for vegetarians. There is a meatless appetiser section of the menu with mixed hors d'oeuvre, tofu, spring rolls, wun tun, fried 'prawns' made with cauliflower, and deep-fried water-chestnuts and mushrooms on skewers among other items. Main dishes include such ersatz meat dishes as vegetarian 'duck' pieces with fresh vegetables, barbecued 'pork' with sauce as well as monk's vegetables and other typical vegetable dishes.

Open all week noon to 2.15, 6 to 11.15 Booking advisable. Table service. Licensed, also bring your own: corkage £4. Meat dishes. Fish dishes. Take-aways. No-smoking area. Wheelchair access. Access, Amex, Visa

STOW-ON-THE-WOLD Gloucestershire MAP 4

Grapevine Hotel £££

Sheep Street TEL Cotswold (0451) 30344

In a comfortable Cotswold stone building fully equipped with beams and conservatory. A vegetarian menu consists of such dishes as vegetable casserole, deep-fried vegetables, garlic mushrooms in puff pastry, stir-fried vegetables, tagliatelle in cream cheese and mushroom stroganoff.

Open all week noon to 2, 7 to 9 **Closed** 24 Dec to 10 Jan Booking advisable.

Table service. Tables outside. Licensed, also bring your own: corkage £5. Meat dishes. Vegan dishes. Other diets catered for on request. No-smoking. Wheelchair access. Accommodation. Access, Amex, Diners, Visa

STRETTON Leicestershire MAP 4

Ram Jam ££

Great North Road TEL Castle Bytham (078 081) 410776

An A1 roadside stop with a difference, serving good, authentic English food in an informal atmosphere. Real fresh orange juice arrives for breakfast; Stilton is outstanding. Vegetarians will only find one main dish – perhaps pasta with cream, grated Parmesan, garlic and breadcrumbs – and starters of aubergine and mushroom fritters, minted green pea soup, asparagus and broccoli salad. Try the Ram Jam ices with fruit, chocolate or fudge topping or the fruit tartlet of the day to finish off.

Open all week 11 to 3, 6 to 11 (10.30 Sun) **Closed** 25 Dec Booking advisable. Table service. Tables outside. Licensed. Meat dishes. Fish dishes. Other diets catered for on request. Snacks. No-smoking area. Wheelchair access. Accommodation. Access, Amex, Visa

STROUD Gloucestershire MAP 4

Mother Nature Ⓥ £

This wholefood café serves lunches of purely vegetarian dishes, all given local names – Painswick Pottage, Lypiatt lasagne, Severn Valley bean bake, Stroud surprise and Gatcombe goulash. Portions of various salads are also available. There are no starters.

Open Mon to Sat noon to 4.30 Counter service. Unlicensed. Snacks. Takeaways. No smoking 12 to 2

The cost of a three-course vegetarian meal without wine is indicated by £ symbols to the right of the restaurant name:
£ = up to £7.50
££ = £7.50 to £15
£££ = £15 and over

STURMINSTER NEWTON Dorset **MAP 2**

Plumber Manor £££

Hazelbury Bryan Road TEL Sturminster Newton (0258) 72507

This small Jacobean country-house hotel, owned by the Prideaux-Brune family since the early seventeenth century, is two miles south-west of Sturminster Newton on the Hazelbury Bryan road. Described as a 'restaurant with bedrooms'; there are some in the main house, and a recently converted barn has further rooms, overlooking the stream and garden. Free stabling for those who wish to ride is provided on a do-it-yourself basis (straw and water are provided). The main attraction here is the stylish restaurant – decorated in pale blues and greens and pleasantly free from Muzak. The food, though old-fashioned, is of a high order. Start perhaps with asparagus and artichoke casserole, vegetable terrine or hot mushrooms with brandy, basil and cream, and go on to a single vegetarian option which might be lentil Wellington, nut loaf, stuffed courgettes or stuffed mushrooms.

Open all week 7.30 to 9.30 **Closed** 2 weeks Feb Booking advisable. Table service. Licensed. Meat dishes. Other diets catered for on request. Wheelchair access. Accommodation. Access, Visa

SUDBURY Suffolk **MAP 5**

Mabey's Brasserie ££

47 Gainsborough Street TEL Sudbury (0787) 74298

A husband-and-wife team runs this small brasserie where diners eat in pleasant private booths. Of the six starters and three main courses at least one each will be vegetarian – perhaps gazpacho followed by provençale lasagne, better and more exciting than most lasagnes with its oozing, ratatouille-type filling. Jacket potato chips, one of the specialities of the house, are reportedly delicious and crunchy one day and soggy the next. Rich sauces and croûtons with everything seem to be hall-marks. Home-made ice-creams.

Open Mon to Sat noon to 2, 7 to 10 **Closed** 2 weeks Feb, 2 weeks Aug Booking advisable. Table service. Licensed, also bring your own: corkage £3 per bottle. Meat dishes. Fish dishes. Other diets catered for on request. Wheelchair access. Access, Visa

SUNDERLAND Tyne & Wear **MAP 10**

Raffles Coffee Lounge £

24 Frederick Street TEL 091-514 0623

You may be starved of choice when eating out in Sunderland, so Raffles might come as a welcome surprise: choose from macaroni cheese, quiche, pizza and a vegetable roast with salad. Banoffi pie is a speciality.

Open Mon to Sat 9 to 5 Counter service. Tables outside. Unlicensed. Snacks. Take-aways. No-smoking area

SURBITON Surrey **MAP 3**

Pavement ⓥ ££

A good venue for a relaxed evening out, as the collection of eating areas, all cosily lit, give a feeling of well-being. Food and service is much praised. Start a meal, perhaps, with spinach roulade or samosas, and proceed to sweet potato cutlets or cashew and mushroom roast. Organic wines are available.

Open Tue to Sat 7 to 11 **Closed** 2 weeks at Easter, summer and Christmas Booking advisable. Table service. Licensed. Vegan dishes. Other diets catered for with prior notice. No-smoking area. Wheelchair access. Access, Visa

SUTTON Surrey **MAP 3**

Pizza Express £

4 High Street TEL Sutton 081-643 4725

A satellite of the excellent London-based chain that was founded twenty-five years ago. See London entry.

Open Mon to Sat 11.30 to midnight, Sun noon to 11.30. Table service. Licensed, also bring your own: corkage £2.50. Meat dishes. Fish dishes. Take-aways. No-smoking area. Wheelchair access. Access, Amex, Diners, Visa

SUTTON COLDFIELD West Midlands **MAP 4**

New Hall £££

Walmley Road TEL 021-378 2442

Claims to be one of England's oldest inhabited moated houses; a medley of building styles date from the sixteenth century to 1988, when a very harmonious wing was added. Americans like it here, particularly the dark panelled Great Hall. Partly because the prices encourage it, guests tend to be business people. Aspirations in the kitchen are high. Vegetarian dishes are marked with an asterisk on the menu and might offer carrot and coriander soup or a timbale of leeks and chives on a tomato coulis with sliced avocado as starters, and fresh noodles in a cream and white wine sauce with fried aubergines and basil, or a tartlet of wild mushrooms with a tomato butter sauce and spätzli as main courses.

Open all week, exc Sat L, 12.30 to 2, 7 to 10 Booking advisable. Table service. Meat dishes. Fish dishes. Vegan dishes. Other diets catered for on request. No smoking area. Children only at early D. Wheelchair access. Accommodation. Access, Amex, Diners, Visa

SUTTON COURTENAY Oxfordshire **MAP 4**

Fish Inn ££

TEL Abingdon (0235) 848242

The recently installed landlord of this pub has been greeted with enthusiasm by locals, desperate for good things to eat. Mr Buchan has achieved a reputation for freshly cooked, interesting, high-quality dishes at affordable prices. A vegetarian might enjoy a tian of courgette with tomatoes and fresh basil, a butter puff of young leeks and wild mushrooms and, if he or she still had space, a lemon tart with clotted cream. Bread is freshly baked.

Open Sun to Thur, exc Tue D, noon to 2.15, 7 to 9.30 (10 Fri and Sat) Booking advisable. Table service. Licensed. Meat dishes. Fish dishes. Vegan. Other diets catered for with prior notice. No-smoking area. Wheelchair access. Access, Visa

SWINDON Wiltshire MAP 2

Pizza Express £

Havelock Square TEL Swindon (0793) 616671

A satellite of the excellent London-based chain that was founded twenty-five years ago. See London entry.

Open Mon to Sat 11.30 to midnight, Sun noon to 11.30. Table service. Licensed, also bring your own: corkage £2.50. Meat dishes. Fish dishes. Take-aways. No-smoking area. Wheelchair access. Access, Amex, Diners, Visa

TAPLOW Buckinghamshire MAP 4

Orangery £

Cliveden Estate TEL Burnham (0628) 661406

A visit to the café makes a good end to a stroll round the impressive estate gardens, owned by the National Trust. Do not confuse the Orangery with the extremely expensive restaurant in the main house; also, there is an admission charge. Maureen Smith, the chef, always provides a vegetarian dish: not content with churning out the standards, she tries new recipes according to what is available. Stilton, walnut and celery quiche, for instance, was invented to use up Christmas Stilton; a spiced vegetables and rice creation was to tempt wilting palates in the heat of the summer of 1989. Other dishes include red wine and lentil loaf and a mid-eastern style lemony butter bean pâté. Lunch hours are designated as noon to 2 and tea as 2.30 to 5. The National Trust's policy is that a hot and a cold vegetarian dish must be available in cafés that do light lunches.

Open Wed to Sun 11am to 5 (noon to 2 Sat and Sun Nov and Dec), bank hol Mons **Closed** Jan & Feb Counter service. Tables outside. Unlicensed. Meat dishes. Other diets catered for on request. No-smoking area. Wheelchair access

The Vegetarian Good Food Guide *has been compiled in the same way as* The Good Food Guide *and is based on reports from consumers and anonymous inspections.*

TAVISTOCK Devon **MAP 1**

Peter Tavy Inn £

Peter Tavy, near Tavistock TEL Mary Tavy (082 281) 348

The crowds at this pub on the edge of Dartmoor testify to the quality of the food: for vegetarians a range of excellent salads (coleslaw dressing especially praised), and main courses such as leek croustade with lots of nuts, and colourful spinach and cheese pancakes, with good, fresh-tasting spinach. To start, try vegetable soup or the speciality of cashew-nut finger, described by one reporter as 'tasty, moist and succulent, while keeping its shape'. Good real ales and room to eat outside in the summer.

Open all week noon to 2.15, 7 to 9.30 **Closed** Christmas Day Counter service. Tables outside. Licensed, also bring your own: corkage £5. Meat dishes. Vegan dishes. Wheelchair access

Stannary Ⓥ ★ ££

Mary Tavy, near Tavistock TEL Mary Tavy (082 281) 897/8

'If you do not see what you want on the menu, please ask. We cannot promise, but we will try our best to cater for all special diets.' Who could ask for more? The menu at this 'tea-room, vegetarian restaurant and guest-house' is annotated to show vegan dishes, gluten-free dishes, and dishes that can be provided in a vegan or gluten-free version. 'We feasted!' exclaimed one reporter. 'Presentation is always a work of art – nut pâté came garnished with radicchio, kiwi-fruit, tomato, cucumber, green-skinned apple and a whole lychee.' If the elaboration can sometimes seem excessive, there are none the less recommendations for main courses such as asparagus in pancake with lemon sauce, and tandoori-style nut rissoles with brown rice, plus the home-baked bread with fresh, unsalted butter. Puddings have been a disappointment, mitigated by excellent coffee and a large plate of chocolates. The place is 'beautifully decorated, with some of Michael Cook's own woodturnings on the banister rail. There is a roaring log fire in a stove, big, comfy chairs and a chesterfield; the ambience is warm and welcoming.' Cakes and snacks are served from 10am to 6.30pm.

Open all week noon to 3, 7 to 9.30 **Closed** some lunchtimes in winter Booking advisable. Table service. Tables outside. Licensed. Vegan dishes. Other diets catered for on request. Snacks. Take-aways. No-smoking area. Accommodation. Access, Visa

TETBURY Gloucestershire MAP 4

Harry's ££

7 New Church Street TEL Tetbury (0666) 503306

On the road leading west out of Tetbury towards Dursley, the restaurant occupies what was a small shop. Inside it has been given the designer touch. Curious details include Muzak and plastic flowers. Vegetarian main dishes, two in the evening and one at lunchtime, are fairly traditional – Creole eggs poached in a sauce of onion, peppers and tomatoes or pancake stuffed with avocado and pasta.

Open all week noon to 2, 7 to 10 exc Mon L, Sun D Booking advisable at weekend. Table service. Licensed. Meat dishes. Fish dishes. Other diets catered for on request. Wheelchair access. Access, Visa

THORNBURY Avon MAP 2

Thornbury Castle £££

Castle Street TEL Thornbury (0454) 418511

Take the last M4 exit before the Severn Bridge, on to the B-road to Gloucester; alternatively turn south to exit 16 of the M5. The castle, dating from the sixteenth century, was never completed but inside all is peace and tranquillity, 'sumptuous in the baronial style'. Prices match, and the one vegetarian main dish on the menu might seem poor value – a braise of vegetables in a herb pancake, fettuccine with wild mushrooms, or freshly made Cannelloni. For dessert, there is a magnificent chocolate and rum mousse in Cointreau. When one visitor disliked the pudding, another was offered; when declined, the original was not charged for. This rare gesture of civility is indicative of the very high level of service, for which, the menu says, 'gratuities are not expected'.

Open all week noon to 2, 7 to 9.30 **Closed** 2 to 13 Jan Booking advisable. Table service. Licensed. Meat dishes. Fish dishes. Vegan dishes. Other diets catered for on request. No-smoking in dining-room. No children under 12 years. Accommodation. Access, Amex, Diners, Visa

THORNTON-CLEVELEYS Lancashire MAP 7

Victorian House £££

Trunnah Road TEL Cleveleys (0253) 860619

When Louise Guerin greets you at the door in her turn-of-the-century dress, you may feel you are in a time-warp. Inside the villa is like a Victorian stage set, full of bric-à-brac – some repro, some authentic – with some really stunning pieces. Bedrooms have four-poster beds and footstools. Waitresses also don Victorian garb, but there the Victorian touch ends, giving way to piped music and a modern menu. An extensive array of dishes includes a gratin of eggs, leek and cream quiche or watercress soup as starters, leading on to a brown rice and hazelnut roast with an exquisite nutty cream sauce, perhaps. An unusual variation on modern British cooking produces pineapple and pistachio steamed pudding with rum custard. Ice-creams, sorbets and bread rolls are home made.

Open all week D 7 to 9.30, L by arrangement Booking advisable. Table service. Tables outside. Licensed. Meat dishes. Fish dishes. Vegan dishes. Other diets catered for on request. No children under 6. Wheelchair access. Accommodation. Access, Visa

TIDESWELL Derbyshire MAP 7

Sara's Kitchen £

Commercial Road TEL Tideswell (0298) 871625

Sara Marcus and her husband escaped from London to run this café, which has been described as a 'beans on toast-plus sort of place'. One of the pluses is a good range of vegetarian options – about three dishes a day. Sara calls herself a practising hypocrite; she is not vegetarian herself but cooks plenty of vegetarian items. When you find a delicious cream onion soup (at only 90p), sweet chestnut and celery loaf with white wine sauce, green pepper and Parmesan bake, spinach and curd cheese lasagne, courgette and double Gloucester bake, all very reasonably priced, who is complaining? There is nothing fancy about the place, which is functional and simple and has a reputation locally for very good value combined with imaginative cooking.

Open Summer: Mon to Tue 8.30 to 2; Wed to Fri 8.30 to 4.30; Sat and Sun 10 to 5. Winter: Mon to Fri 10 to 2; Sat and Sun 10 to 5 **Closed** 25 and 26 Dec, 31 Dec to

2 Jan Table service. Unlicensed, but bring your own. Meat dishes. Fish dishes. Vegan dishes. Other diets catered for on request. Snacks. Take-aways. Wheelchair access

TIVERTON Devon MAP 1

Angel Food £

Angel Terrace TEL Tiverton (0884) 254778

Go through the shop to the wood-floored, wood-furnished vegetarian café, where the kitchen is strict about the freshness of the produce and prices are reasonable. Locals enjoy the food and the place is busy. Choice at lunchtime will be soups, small tarts, cheese and mushroom pie or some other hot dish, and various pasties. Sizzilian is a special type of vegetarian hot-dog.

Open Mon to Sat 8.30am to 5.30 (2.30 Thur, 4.30 Sat) **Closed** 24 Dec to 2 Jan Table service. Vegan dishes. Other diets catered for on request. Snacks. Take-aways. No smoking

Reapers ⓥ £

23 Gold Street TEL Tiverton (0884) 255310

Attached to a healthfood shop that sells organic fruits and vegetables as well as the more usual food and medicinal items. A basic, sensibly priced menu takes in a seasonal soup, four different salads and a hot main course on the lines of mushroom layer, vegetable croustade and spaghetti bean bake. Cakes and scones are available either side of lunch, which is from noon to 2.30.

Open Mon to Sat 10 to 3 Counter service. Vegan dishes. Other diets catered for on request. Take-aways. No smoking

If you book a table at a restaurant, you must turn up in reasonable time. If you don't keep your booking, or are very late, you're in breach of contract and the restaurant could sue you for compensation. Let the restaurant know as soon as possible if you can't make it, so the restaurant can reduce its loss by rebooking the table.

TOCKINGTON Avon MAP 2

Kitchen Garden £

Old Down House TEL Thornbury (0454) 413605

An authentic kitchen garden that grows fruit and vegetables, much of it sold as pick-your-own; there is an arable and dairy farm attached and the farm shop sells fresh vegetables, free-range eggs and farmhouse cheeses; a craft gallery sells local products. The restaurant serves wholefood lunches and teas throughout the day and home-made ice-cream and live yoghurts are a special attraction. Vegetarian dishes might include leek au gratin, nut roast or stuffed pepper.

Open Tue to Sun 9 to 5, L noon to 2.30 Booking advisable. Table service. Tables outside. Licensed. Meat dishes. Snacks. Take-aways. Wheelchair access. Access

TODMORDEN West Yorkshire MAP 7

Dumb Waiter ★ £–££

23 Water Street TEL Todmorden (070 681) 5387

Find Water Street and the maroon-painted bistro is about halfway along in a row of shops, with its name on the window. Inside the décor is cheery, with clouds painted round the walls and upturned umbrellas hung from the ceiling as lampshades. Tables are lit by candles. There is plenty of choice for vegetarians: six starters and four main dishes, with separate lunch and dinner menus. From the starters, the moist spicy lentil and potato filling could be more generous in its filo parcel; crisp, deep-fried mushrooms come with a sweetish Stilton dressing. Good main dishes are leek and cheese crumble, enchiladas, pancakes, broccoli fritters and a herby brazil nut and tomato loaf. Brown rolls with caraway seeds are home made. Puddings might include key lime pie with gingery biscuits and tangy apple and raspberry meringue pie. Coffee comes with good home-made caramel shortbread topped with chocolate.

Open Wed to Sun, exc Sun L, noon to 1.45, 7 to 9.30 Booking advisable. Table service. Licensed. Meat dishes. Fish dishes. Other diets catered for on request. Wheelchair access. Access, Visa

Hazel's

££

26 Burnley Road TEL Todmorden (0706) 815058

A relatively new bistro already popular with locals. Cooking is imaginative and along French lines with at least one – sometimes more – vegetarian main dishes, all using fresh ingredients and with an eye to health-conscious diners. Starters for vegetarians could include marinated pears with Stilton and walnuts, watercress and asparagus mousse or home-made carrot and orange soup, while main courses could be mushroom and cashew-nut stroganoff, spicy vegetarian tacos with onion, chutney, cheese and sour cream or tricolour pasta with baby sweetcorn, mange-tout and blue cheese. Banoffi pie is a stalwart on the pudding list; others might be pot au chocolat or mango and Malibu fool.

Open Wed to Mon 7 to 10 **Closed** last 2 weeks Feb Booking advisable. Table service. Licensed. Meat dishes. Fish dishes. Vegan dishes and other diets catered for on request. Access, Visa

TONBRIDGE Kent MAP 3

Office Wine Bar

££

163 High Street TEL Tonbridge (0732) 353660

A reasonably priced wine bar offering up to four vegetarian main dishes on the lines of curried mushrooms, lucky pie or leeks and mushrooms with cream in herb pastry, oat pancakes stuffed with vegetables and curried vegetables. Puddings are good: banoffi, toffee nut fudge cake, sorbets are indicative of the style.

Open Mon to Sat noon to 2, 7 to 9.30 Booking advisable. Table service. Licensed, also bring your own: corkage £1. Meat dishes. Fish dishes. Other diets catered for on request. Wheelchair access. Access, Amex, Diners, Visa

Platform Five

££

20 Barden Road TEL Tonbridge (0732) 358457

Near the station (back entrance), as the name indicates. The vegetarian section of the menu offers Stilton mushrooms or deep-fried Camembert, then five main dishes – mushroom crêpes, quiche, vegetarian loaf (a speciality), curry or aubergine galette. Puddings are profiteroles, Pavlova, crème caramel.

Open Mon to Sat 7 to 10, Sun noon to 3 Bookings advisable. Table service. Licensed. Meat dishes. Wheelchair access. Access, Visa

TOPSHAM Devon **MAP 1**

Toppers ££

41 Fore Street TEL Exeter (0392) 874707

Good-value wholemeal vegetarian and fish dishes top the bill here, with one meat dish only. Hummus and garlic mushrooms or tempura might precede cashew-nut and mushroom bake with watercress sauce, stuffed vine leaves or spinach roulade.

Open Tue to Sun D 6.30 to 10, Sat and Sun L 12.30 to 2, Tue to Fri L by arrangement Booking advisable weekends. Table service. Licensed, also bring your own: corkage £2. Meat dishes. Fish dishes. Vegan dishes. Other diets catered for on request. No pipes or cigars in dining-room. Wheelchair access. Accommodation. Access

TORQUAY Devon **MAP 1**

Mulberry Room ££

1 Scarborough Road TEL Torquay (0803) 213639

There have been many recommendations for this restaurant which at lunchtime provides good-value daily dishes from the blackboard and on Saturday evening expands to a six-course menu which can either be treated as a *carte* or taken in entirety. Starters might be lettuce and mint soup, mushroom soup with port, cream cheese and herb pâté, and rissole of nuts, mushrooms, onions and herbs; while main dishes have included lemon and lentil patties with cashew-nut and honey sauce, aubergines and courgettes in dhal and, a speciality, Guatemalan pasties. Confusingly arranged, the menu makes up the six courses with sorbet, cheese and coffee. 'Everything seemed just right, from the delightful furnishings to the aroma of good cooking and a display of home-made meringues.' Gluten-free, low-cholesterol and additive-free meals can be arranged. Traditional cream teas, teas, coffees, and fresh milk shakes are on offer during the day.

Open Wed to Sun L, 12.15 to 2.30, plus Sat D, 7.30 to 9 Table service. Tables outside. Licensed. Meat dishes. Other diets catered for on request. Snacks at other times. Wheelchair access. Accommodation

TOTNES Devon MAP 1

Willow ⓥ £

87 High Street TEL Totnes (0803) 862605

A stripped-pine café in a converted shop at the top of the High Street, near the castle. Breakfasts feature croissants baked with organic flour and set the wholefood style: at lunchtime organic herb and tofu dip might be followed by tagliatelle parmigiana, mushroom roast, or almond and organic mushroom stroganoff. There is always at least one vegan dish. Every Wednesday evening brings forth an Indian menu, and international dishes also feature at other times. Organic wines and natural beers lead the drinks list.

Open Tue to Sat, L noon to 2.30, Wed, Fri and Sat, D 6.30 to 10, Tue and Thur, D July to Sept Booking advisable D. Table service D. Counter service L. Licensed. Vegan dishes. Other diets catered for on request. Snacks at other times. Take-aways. No-smoking. Wheelchair access

TREBARWITH Cornwall MAP 1

House on the Strand ££

Trebarwith Strand TEL Camelford (0840) 770326

The old slate house is right on the beach and proves extremely handy for holiday-making families. The food is tasty and not too expensive. Cooking is eclectic, with bean and mushroom pâté, lentil and sesame fritters or mushroom soubise for vegetarians.

Open all week 10.30 to 9.30 **Closed** Nov to 2 weeks before Easter Table service. Tables outside. Licensed. Meat dishes. Fish dishes. Other diets catered for on request. Snacks. Wheelchair access. Accommodation. Access, Visa

See the back of the guide for an index of restaurants listed.

TRURO Cornwall MAP 1

Brasserie ££

Kenwyn Street TEL Truro (0872) 222279

Though attached to the Mounts Bay Trading Company, a real Aladdin's Cave of a shop, the Brasserie is separately run. The new building has a conservatory style with a chinoiserie influence, a 'real' coal fire burning with great effect at one end; the atmosphere is that of a bistro. The pasta trolley always has three vegetarian sauces to accompany a choice of shapes and fillings: ratatouille; cheese and mushroom; vegetables and cheese or cream and walnut are some examples. The ratatouille sauce is said to be good, the cream and walnut excellent. Quiches vary from day to day and there are a couple of other vegetarian dishes such as veggie burgers, nut loaf or pizza, freshly made each day according to the chef's fancy. The pudding trolley is worth sampling. Good value for money and popular.

Open Mon to Sat, exc Mon D, 9.30 to 5.30, 6.30 to 10 **Closed** 25 and 26 Dec Booking advisable. Table service. Counter service. Tables outside. Licensed. Meat dishes. Other diets catered for on request. Snacks. Wheelchair access. Access, Visa

Bustopher Jones £–££

62 Lemon Street TEL Truro (0872) 79029

'Bustopher Jones is not skin and bones – In fact, he's remarkably fat.' (T. S. Eliot) The wine bar, usefully situated in a central position, is pristine with its dark wood tables and chairs and dark green walls covered with paintings and prints for sale (American prints a speciality). It's a jolly place with a pleasant atmosphere and good vegetarian choices. As well as the ubiquitous jacket potato, there will be something on the lines of spinach and lentil roulade with mushroom sauce. Light asparagus mousse has been very good; walnut pie (an anglicised version of pecan pie) with wholemeal crust, flavoursome and not too sweet. Puddings are a strong point.

Open all week noon to 2.30 (exc Sun), 6 to 11 (7 to 10.30 Sun) Counter service. Licensed. Meat dishes. No-smoking area. Access, Visa

Pottles £–££

Pannier Market, Back Quay TEL Truro (0872) 71384

Just behind the Pannier Market, up wooden outside stairs, is an extremely popular and efficient café, where customers are assured that their orders will be fulfilled within ten minutes. Casseroles in individual dishes are the speciality, with a vegetarian one that is spicy and tasty. Puddings can be crude concoctions of fruit – and dressing them up with Cornish cream does not redeem them. Sadly, the home-made cakes are rather boring. Plans were afoot to open for dinner on Friday and Saturday as we went to press.

Open Mon to Sat 11.30am to 3 Table service. Tables outside. Licensed. Meat dishes. Vegan dishes. Other diets catered for on request. Snacks at other times. Take-aways

TUNBRIDGE WELLS Kent MAP 3

Continental Flavour £

15 Ritz Buildings, Church Road TEL Tunbridge Wells (0892) 512215

A convenient place for lunch when shopping or sightseeing: there will always be something simple in the vegetarian line, such as a lasagne, moussaka, pancake or creamy leek croustade. All food is home made. Four salads, pasties, pizzas and cakes are served all day. Soup is good. Wholewheat rolls and bread are baked on the premises.

Open all week 8 to 6 **Closed** Sun Oct to Apr Counter service. Unlicensed. Vegan dishes. Snacks. Take-aways. No smoking

Eglantine ££–£££

65 High Street TEL Tunbridge Wells (0892) 24957

The young owner of Eglantine has high ambitions for her restaurant. The short lunch and dinner menus both offer vegetarian options: for starter, perhaps an asparagus and leek mousse, watercress soup with cream and croûtons, or tartlet with wild mushrooms, while the main dish might be hot avocado tart with lemon and sour cream, or a light pastry case with hazelnuts, mushrooms and a sour cream sauce. Puddings aren't quite so successful: Pithiviers filled with almond kept the almonds a closely guarded secret and a brown sugar meringue with butterscotch ice-cream on caramel sauce was just too sweet. Service tends to be formal and incongruously over-attentive.

Open Tue to Sat 12.15 to 1.45, 7.15 to 9.30 (10 Sat) **Closed** 2 weeks late Aug to early Sept Booking advisable. Table service. Licensed. Meat dishes. Vegan dishes and other diets catered for on request. No-smoking area. Access, Amex, Visa

Pizza Piazza £

76 Mount Pleasant Road TEL Tunbridge Wells (0892) 547124

A branch of a growing chain that offers an enterprising choice of reliably good pizzas. See entry under New Malden for more detail.

Open all week noon to 11 Table service. Licensed. No-smoking area. Wheelchair access. Access, Visa

TWICKENHAM Greater London MAP 12

Cézanne ££

68 Richmond Road TEL 081-892 3526

A plain, relatively small restaurant serving food that's worth waiting for, and catering for vegetarians only with slender choices – perhaps one starter, seasonal salad with Gruyère, baby corn and garlic croûtons, and one main course, cheese pastry tartlet filled with vegetables, asparagus and Mozzarella, or aubergine stuffed with goats' cheese, lemon and walnuts. Warmly recommended desserts are banana and sesame pudding in filo pastry, and butterscotch and date pudding.

Open Mon to Sat exc Sat L 12.30 to 2, 7 to 10.30 (11 Fri and Sat) **Closed** 1 week at Christmas Booking advisable. Table service. Licensed, also bring your own: corkage £2.50. Meat dishes. Fish dishes. No pipes or cigars during meals. Wheelchair access. Access, Amex, Visa

UPPER SHERINGHAM Norfolk MAP 8

Red Lion £–££

TEL Sheringham (0263) 825408

Upper Sheringham is a pretty village, and the pub, just outside Sheringham itself, is a low, white building. Inside is cosy with a log fire, pine tables and chairs, an old settle and a chalked-up menu, all overseen by a genial Scots landlord. Bar meals might feature a vegetarian croûte, pasta or bake, as well as excellent deep-fried sticks of aubergine in crisp batter with home-made dip. A Grand Marnier mousse, though highly calorific, was relished. 'Full of people there for the food.'

Open all week noon to 2, 7 to 9 Booking advisable. Table service. Tables outside. Licensed. Meat dishes. Fish dishes. Vegan dishes and other diets catered for with prior notice. Wheelchair access. Accommodation. Access, Visa

WALBERSWICK Suffolk MAP 5

Mary's £

Manor House TEL Southwold (0502) 723243

The nautically inclined restaurant with its bar-cum-gift shop is popular and serves good food. A large warning for vegetarians: suitable meals are only on the menu at lunchtime. But the chef will 'always cook one specially if we are asked on booking'. Cashew and Brazil nut roast with onion gravy, layered aubergine with spinach or courgette and potato fritters with tomato and garlic relish might be on the daily lunch specials list. Perhaps apple and blackberry crumble or a 'fabulous' pecan pie will please for dessert. Morning coffees and afternoon teas are available.

Open Tue to Sun noon to 2, Fri and Sat 7.15 to 9 **Closed** Tue to Thur Oct to Mar Booking advisable. Table service. Tables outside. Licensed. Meat dishes. Fish dishes. Other diets catered for on request. Snacks at other times. No smoking in dining-room. Take-aways (limited). Wheelchair access

★ *after a restaurant name indicates that the vegetarian cooking is especially good. A list of starred restaurants appears at the end of the book.*

WALKINGTON Humberside MAP 8

Manor House £££

Northlands TEL Hull (0482) 881645

Just north of the village of Walkington is this mock-Tudor mansion set in pleasant lawns with views over quiet countryside. Rooms are opulent ('gilt knobs with everything') and every mod. con. is provided. The kitchen calls itself modern British, but the menu starts in French, then turns itself back into English with some odd results: 'deep-fried knapsack filled with prawns', for example. Vegetarians will be limited to one starter, perhaps melon with a syrup of elderflower and apple, and one main course, but this shows some flair – for example 'a pudding wrapped in leaves of cabbage, rice, cashew-nuts, spinach, ricotta cheese and truffle on a yoghurt and chive sauce' or 'deep-fried nest filled with egg-shaped croquettes of vegetables, nuts and vegetarian cheese on fresh tomato sauce with herbs'. Soup or sorbet makes up the refresher between courses.

Open Mon to Sat D 7.30 to 9.15 Booking advisable. Table service. Tables outside. Licensed. Meat dishes. Fish dishes. Vegan dishes. Other diets catered for on request. No children under 12. Accommodation. Access, Visa

WALTON-ON-THAMES Surrey MAP 3

Pizza Piazza £

14 Bridge Street TEL Walton-on-Thames (0932) 220153

A branch of a growing chain that offers an enterprising choice of reliably good pizzas. See entry under New Malden for more detail.

Open all week noon to 11 Table service. Licensed. No-smoking area. Wheelchair access. Access, Visa

When you book a restaurant table, you're making a contract with the restaurant and they must give you a table, in reasonable time. If they don't, they're in breach of contract and you can claim a reasonable sum to cover any expenses you had as a result, eg travelling costs.

WAREHAM Dorset **MAP 2**

Worgret Manor ££

Worgret Road TEL Wareham (092 95) 52957

One mile out of Wareham on the A352. It's an attractive place for vegetarians since there is a full vegetarian menu, with five starters and four main dishes. The food could not be described as outstanding in its originality but has some unusual touches; mushrooms with orange and Pernod cream sauce; asparagus and cheese oatcake; and cucumber and almond soup. Flambé dishes are popular, and sweet varieties include crêpe Suzettes, bananes flambées and pêches flambées Benedictine.

Open all week noon to 1.45, 7 to 9 **Closed** 2 days at Christmas Booking advisable. Table service. Licensed. Meat dishes. Fish dishes. Other diets catered for on request. Wheelchair access. Accommodation. Access, Amex, Diners, Visa

WARKWORTH Northumberland **MAP 10**

Halberd, Hermitage Inn £

Castle Street TEL Alnwick (0665) 711258

The restaurant in the inn serves a range of fairly predictable items such as vegetable ratatouille, mushroom and nut fettuccine, curry and a country lentil crumble. Desserts are unremarkable but include peach Melba, banana split and a variety of ice-creams.

Open all week noon to 2, 7 to 9.30, exc Mon D Booking advisable. Table service. Tables outside. Licensed, also bring your own: corkage £3. Meat dishes. Fish dishes. Vegan dishes. Wheelchair access. Accommodation

WARWICK Warwickshire **MAP 4**

Pizza Piazza £

33–35 Jury Street TEL Warwick (0926) 491641

A branch of a growing chain that offers an enterprising choice of reliably good pizzas. See entry under New Malden for more detail.

Open all week noon to 11 Table service. Licensed. No-smoking area. Wheelchair access. Access, Visa

WATLINGTON Oxfordshire MAP 4

Well House ★ ££

34–40 High Street TEL Watlington (049 161) 3333

In this pretty fifteenth-century building, which at the back becomes a jumble of additions, ruined walls and a half-finished patio, there is a welcome vegetarian menu, though you may have to ask for it. Alan Crawford takes a keen interest in dietary requirements and worries about vegans who pop pills containing essential vitamins. Orders are taken in the bar that sports the well from which the name comes, curiously lit from below. The dining-room is warm, beamed, full of flowers and has a large fireplace. There is also a memorable Burmese cat. The vegetarian menu can be eaten as two or three courses, starting with grilled goats' cheese, curried fruits, leek soup or avocado with sour cream. Or pick and choose from one of the other menus – Stilton and apple filo pastry is tart and crisp, cooked to order. Main courses include vegetable pie, cheese and lentil loaf, pancakes with spicy vegetables in Mornay sauce and courgettes filled with a sensational smoked aubergine mixture, prepared by a company that normally smokes fish. Accompanying vegetables – baby corn, leeks, sweet purée of carrots and duchesse potatoes are given due care. Bread rolls – warm, tiny, soft and light brown – are home made. To finish are puddings such as coffee meringue, crème brûlée, fresh fruit salad in brandysnap and a version of banoffi pie with a thin pastry crust, a caramel and banana melange topped with strong coffee cream: excellent.

Open Tue to Sun, exc Sat L and Sun D, 12.30 to 2.15, 7.30 to 9.30 Booking advisable. Table service. Licensed, also bring your own: corkage £1. Meat dishes. Fish dishes. Other diets on request. Wheelchair access. Accommodation. Access, Amex, Diners, Visa

The main criterion for inclusion in the guide is that an eating place offers a vegetarian main course on its standard menu, at all times, that is more than just an omelette, quiche or salad. If you find that a listed restaurant no longers caters for vegetarians, please inform the guide; the address to write to is on page 9.

WELLS Somerset **MAP 2**

Good Earth Ⓥ £

4 Priory Road TEL Wells (0749) 78600

It is sad that, having had a reputation for enterprising wholefood vegetarian cuisine, the Good Earth seems to have lost some of its exuberance. None the less, go for simple lunches of soup and a jacket potato or a hot dish on the lines of chestnut roast with mushroom sauce.

Open Mon to Sat 9.30am to 5.30 Counter service. Tables outside. Licensed. Vegan dishes. Other diets catered for on request. Snacks. Take-aways. No smoking. Wheelchair access. Access, Amex

WELLS-NEXT-THE-SEA Norfolk **MAP 8**

Moorings ★ ££

6 Freeman Street TEL Fakenham (0328) 710949

Residents of Wells are lucky to have such a restaurant in their midst; although in an unprepossessing part of the port, inside is spacious and tasteful, with pottery oil lamps and fresh flowers. Carla Phillips, chef and co-owner, chats in an easy way with customers; her food is imaginative and prices are reasonable. Menus change almost daily. Typical of the two or three starters might be chilled tomato soup with dill and soured cream, olive and almond cream served with tomatoes and free-range eggs and aubergine purée made from locally grown aubergines, followed by a choice of mushrooms with Stilton sauce or stuffed pepper with bulgur, pine kernels and currants. An aubergine casserole was 'discreetly pungent with cumin and fresh tomatoes' and accompanying vegetables may also be cooked with various spices. 'Just too good to be true,' was one verdict on butterscotch pudding with crisp walnut topping; alternatively indulge in Norfolk temptation, composed of 'snow' cake, lemon curd cream and fruit, open fig tart or home-made ice-cream. Mrs Phillips uses agar, not gelatine, in puddings. Coffee, tea or herb tea comes with home-made chocolates.

Open Fri to Tue L, 12.30 to 1.50; Thur to Mon D, 7.30 to 9 **Closed** 3 weeks Nov to Dec, 2 weeks June Booking advisable. Table service. Licensed, also bring your own: corkage £2.75. Meat dishes. Fish dishes. Other diets catered for on request. Wheelchair access (also wc)

WEMBLEY Greater London MAP 12

Pizza Express £

456 High Road TEL 081-902 4918

A satellite of the excellent London-based chain that was founded twenty-five years ago. See London entry.

Open Mon to Sat 11.30 to midnight, Sun noon to 11.30. Table service. Licensed, also bring your own: corkage £2.50. Meat dishes. Fish dishes. Take-aways. No-smoking area. Wheelchair access. Access, Amex, Diners, Visa

WEST BEXINGTON Dorset MAP 2

Manor £–££

Beach Road TEL Burton Bradstock (0308) 897616

At the top end of an unremarkable village is this quiet and simple country house with large gardens and children's playground. It's an ideal family holiday hotel where evening set menus and Sunday lunch provide for vegetarians. Starters might be fruity cocktails or mushrooms in garlic cream; main dishes might be filled pancakes (tomatoes, onions, asparagus and creamed mushrooms) with a cheese sauce, pizza or lasagne. The fashionable conservatory houses the bar, where these dishes can also be ordered à la carte. The children's menu, which is less than half the price of dinner, includes the pancakes.

Open all week 12.15 to 1.30, 7 to 9.30 Booking advisable. Table service. Tables outside. Licensed. Meat dishes. Fish dishes. Other diets catered for on request. No-smoking area. Wheelchair access. Accommodation. Access, Visa

WEST HUNTSPILL Somerset MAP 1

Gi Gi ££

Old Pawlett Road TEL Burnham-on-Sea (0278) 783698

Although the owner describes the cooking as British, there is a strong French influence on the menu (the frogs' legs won't endear them to vegetarians, nor will the shark). None the less, a vegetarian monthly menu does come up with eight dishes – nut roasts, lasagne, baked stuffed peppers and a Hawaiian salad among them. Though there's nothing strikingly original, it could be a useful place to dine out with meat-eaters.

Open all week, exc Sun D, noon to 2.30, 7 to 10.30 Booking advisable. Table service. Licensed. Corkage £1.50–£2. Meat dishes. Vegan dishes. Other diets catered for on request. No-smoking area. Wheelchair access. Access, Amex, Diners, Visa

WEST MERSEA Essex **MAP** 5

Willow Lodge £££

108 Coast Road **TEL** Colchester (0206) 383568

Coast Road is the continuation of the High Street, and the restaurant is well marked with a large car park beside it. The modest restaurant, timbered on the outside in mock Tudor-style, can get so busy with regulars that you may have to sit at one of the bar areas to eat. This is comfortable enough though. There is plenty to choose from, not only for meat-eaters, but vegetarians also: three main dishes and several starters. At a sample meal lasagne and mushroom stroganoff were pronounced satisfactory. Portions are generous and accompanied by a selection of vegetables, on this occasion cauliflower, sauté and boiled potatoes, runner beans and broccoli.

Open Tue to Sun noon to 2, 7 to 10, exc Sun D Table service. Tables outside. Licensed. Meat dishes. Fish dishes. Vegan dishes and other diets catered for on request. Snacks. Wheelchair access. Access, Amex, Visa

WETHERAL Cumbria **MAP** 9

Fantails ££

The Green **TEL** Carlisle (0228) 60239

Built in the nineteenth century as a blacksmith's and stables, now converted tastefully into a roomy restaurant on the first floor, reached via a curving stone staircase. The home-made cream of cauliflower soup gets a positive mention as does the freshness of the produce. Main dishes of garlic bread box, aubergine and tomato layers or piperade are on offer for vegetarians.

Open Mon to Sat noon to 1.30, 6 to 9.30 Booking advisable. Table service. Licensed, also bring your own: corkage £1.50. Meat dishes. Access, Visa

WEYMOUTH Dorset MAP 2

Milton Arms £££

21 St Albans Street TEL Weymouth (0305) 782767

The proprietor has been a vegetarian for 35 years and is therefore sympathetic to problems encountered when eating out. The chef cooks all food to order, from a menu that changes periodically. He may present you with avocado Florentine – baked avocado with apricot and chestnut filling on bed of spinach flavoured with nutmeg – Montaroux mystery (his speciality), or crêpes with ratatouille, fennel and garlic served with hazelnut sauce.

Open Mon to Sat noon to 2, 6.30 to 10 **Closed** Mon Jan to Mar, 2 weeks Oct, 2 weeks Feb Booking advisable. Table service. Licensed. Meat dishes. Fish dishes. Other diets catered for on request. Snacks. No-smoking area. Access, Visa

Perry's ££

The Harbourside, 4 Trinity Road TEL Weymouth (0305) 785799

Vegetarians get a wee look in at this restaurant specialising in fresh fish, normally by way of lasagne but sometimes with an additional choice on the blackboard. Puddings can be good – bread-and-butter and Bakewell tart have rated mentions.

Open all week D 7.15 to 10 (10.30 Sat); Fri and Sat L noon to 2 Booking advisable in season. Table service. Tables outside. Licensed. Meat dishes. Fish dishes. Vegan dishes. Other diets catered for on request. Wheelchair access. Access, Visa

Westers Bistro Bar £

6 Westerhall Road TEL Weymouth (0305) 784904

A solitary vegetarian dish may be offered on the menu, but the supplementary blackboard specials always feature a suitable dish, such as carrot and tahini pancakes; Mexican crêpes filled with refried beans, cheese and spices; spaghetti with lentil sauce; or sweet-and-sour beans with wholegrain rice. Starters might include avocado with Stilton, mayonnaise and walnuts or savoury pears topped with cream cheese, toasted almonds and a piquant dressing.

Open all week noon to 2, 7 to 11.30 Table service. Counter service. Licensed. Meat dishes. Other diets catered for on request. Take-aways. Access, Visa

WHITBY North Yorkshire MAP 10

Magpie Café ★ £

14 Pier Road TEL Whitby (0947) 602058

This outstanding café serves excellent food at very reasonable prices and caters for many different diets – gluten-free, fat-free, dairy-free – among which vegetarian seems positively tame. Sit and look over the quay, while children are happily entertained by the toy box in the corner, an excellent idea. Naturally fish is good and so are the chips. A vegetarian crumble is available, and a novelty is a vegetarian salad with chips. Home-made cakes include simnel cake, maids of honour and a sugar-free fruit loaf; puddings are also home made and include Yorkshire curd cheesecake, sticky-toffee pudding, hazelnut and rum praline slice. An excellent venue for families.

Open all week 11.30am to 6.30 **Closed** 1 Nov to week before Easter Table service. Licensed. Meat dishes. Fish dishes. Vegan dishes. Other diets catered for on request. Snacks. No-smoking areas

Shepherd's Purse Ⓥ ££

Sanders Yard, 95 Church Street TEL Whitby (0947) 820228

In an old building in the old town, entered either through a cobbled courtyard or through an excellent shop selling pulses, dried fruit, good teas and coffees, cheeses and yoghurt. Festooned with dried flowers, corn dollies and puppets, the place has a happy feel. Be sure to arrive in good time for a meal since popular items like soup or cheesecake run out quickly. Main dishes might be lentil and fennel bake, Mediterranean casserole, cannelloni or curry. The meal is microwaved for serving. Salads are outstanding. Cloyingly sweet but good puddings include pecan pie. In all, good value and generous portions, with a choice of organic wines too.

Open all week 10am to 5 (L from noon), 6 to 9.30 **Closed** Wed Nov to Feb Table service D. Counter service L. Tables outside. Licensed. Vegan dishes. Other diets catered for on request. Snacks. Take-aways. No smoking. Wheelchair access. Accommodation. Access, Visa

WHITNEY ON WYE Hereford & Worcester MAP 6

Rhydspence Inn ££

TEL Clifford (049 73) 262

This pretty half-timbered inn with a beamed porch and ancient cider press at the front displays a bar blackboard with the day's specials; sadly none of these is vegetarian. However, the main menu contains a section of five main dishes: curry, vegetable platter, lasagne, spaghetti and mushroom gratiné. Starters are soup, garlic mushrooms and deep-fried Pencarreg (crisply coated at a sample meal, though the cheese was not quite mature). Curry comes as an anglicised version with a tray of chutneys containing banana, diced tomato, diced green pepper and desiccated coconut (often also cream), but it is certainly hot. A lavish pudding trolley includes sherry trifle and brandy and chocolate cake.

Open all week noon to 1.45, 7 to 9.30 Booking advisable. Table service. Counter service. Tables outside. Licensed. Meat dishes. Other diets catered for on request. Wheelchair access. Accommodation. Access, Amex, Visa

WILLINGTON Co. Durham MAP 10

Stile ££

97 High Street TEL Bishop Auckland (0388) 746615

The old stone cottages have been converted to a restaurant with the addition of two conservatories. A large trailing plant hangs over the entrance to the dining-room, and dried flowers adorn the walls. The garden is a delight in summer. The menu is in general conventional, with such starters as mushrooms in garlic butter and avocado vinaigrette, but vegetarian main courses are more adventurous: Brazil and cashew-nut loaf with chestnut stuffing and fresh tomato sauce, mushroom and leek pudding or, their speciality, cheese gougère with spinach and onion filling. Accompanying vegetables are particularly noted – salsify in red wine, deep-fried, herbed cauliflower and shallots in red wine. To follow, try the apple and almond pudding, light yet satisfying; bananas Barbados or orange liquor pancakes could be alternatives. Gaelic, Jamaican and various other speciality coffees can be indulged after dinner.

Open Tues to Sun 7 to 9.45 **Closed** 2 weeks Sept Booking advisable Sat. Table service. Licensed. Meat dishes. Fish dishes. Other diets catered for on request. No smoking in dining-room. Wheelchair access. Access, Visa

WILMSLOW Cheshire MAP 7

Stanneylands Hotel £££

Stanneylands Road TEL Wilmslow (0625) 525225

It is good to find that this bastion of ambitious cuisine comes up with options for vegetarians. The atmosphere is country house-cum-gentlemen's club, and – apart from Sunday lunch – the food is relatively expensive. Praise has been lavish for a 'velvet cream of watercress and spinach soup crowned with toasted almonds'; a typical meal might offer aubergine and mushroom fritter with pears, cheese and coriander dressing as a starter, followed by a gratin of wheatmeal pancakes with layers of artichoke hearts and Feta cheese, accompanied by a coulis of sweet peppers.

Open all week 12.30 to 2, 7 to 10.30 (exc Sun D) **Closed** 25 Dec, New Year's Day and Good Friday Booking advisable. Table service. Licensed. Meat dishes. Fish dishes. Snacks. Wheelchair access. Access, Amex, Diners, Visa

WINCHESTER Hampshire MAP 2

Brann's ££

9 Great Minster Street TEL Winchester (0962) 64004

Attractive décor, a delightful view of the cathedral and close from an upstairs seat and friendly service may help to compensate for the lack of vegetarian choice on the menu – only one daily main course. Poached pear with Roquefort mousse to start might be followed by a ragoût of girolles, cèpes and garlic. The choice of desserts widens admirably: chocolate truffle cake on a pool of crème anglaise; white chocolate marquise with mint cream or fresh fruit pastry.

Open Mon to Sat noon to 2.30, 7 to 10.30 Booking advisable. Table service. Licensed, also bring your own: corkage £5–£8. Meat dishes. Fish dishes. Snacks. No-smoking area. Access, Amex, Visa

Minstrels £

18 Little Minster Street TEL Winchester (0962) 67212

The menu is predominantly vegetarian at this café near the shopping centre. Its popularity – perhaps due to lack of competition – does not seem to have ironed out some of the wrinkles, for instance food insufficiently re-heated. Salads show imagination, for example curry-spiced cauliflower, cole-slaw, carrot, nut, spice and bean; main dishes include courgette and potato bake, lasagne, pancakes, strudel or chilli. Stuffed aubergines and baked courgette with walnut sauce are house specialities.

Open all week 9.30 to 5 Counter service. Licensed. Meat dishes. Fish dishes. Vegan dishes. Other diets catered for on request. Snacks. No-smoking area. Amex, Diners

WINDERMERE Cumbria MAP 9

Holbeck Ghyll ££

Holbeck Lane TEL Ambleside (053 94) 32375

The nineteenth-century country house stands in its own acre of grounds high above Lake Windermere; the welcome is friendly and the burning log fires and newspapers add to the comfort. The food is well reported. The five-course dinner menu might start with a choice of kiwi-fruit grapefruit and nectarines in a light juniper sauce or warm spinach and Feta cheese filo pastry on a purée of tomato and basil; then offer cream of fennel soup with Pernod before a refresher course of celery and apple soup or leaf salad. There is no choice of main dish for vegetarians; it might be a filo pastry money-bag filled with stir-fried vegetables on hot potato salad or savoury vegetable crumble.

Open all week, D 7 to 8.45 **Closed** Jan Booking advisable. Table service. Licensed. Meat dishes. Fish dishes. Other diets catered for on request. No children under 7. Wheelchair access. Access, Visa

WINDSOR Berkshire MAP 2

Chaos Café ⓥ £

Windsor Arts Centre, St Leonard's Road TEL Windsor (0753) 859421

A purely vegan café with a rotating menu offering the likes of nut roast, stuffed marrow with mushroom sauce, goulash, ratatouille, chalked up each day on a board. Otherwise there are baked potatoes, chunky salad sandwiches, home-made cakes and a good range of herbal teas with a helpful list of their beneficial qualities.

Open Tue to Sat 11 to 2 **Closed** 2 weeks mid-Aug Counter service. Tables outside. Unlicensed (bar open Sat). Vegan dishes. Take-aways. No-smoking area. Wheelchair access

Country Kitchen £

3 King Edward Court, Peascod Street TEL Windsor (0753) 868681

There's not much of either the country or a rustic kitchen about this place, the pine stools, tables and tiled floor looking much the same as elsewhere. It caters on a large scale mainly to shoppers, the food arrayed on long counters and new dishes arriving constantly. There are 14 types of salad, jacket potatoes, puffy white rolls, soups and a daily vegetarian dish – on one occasion an average vegetable bake with cheese topping. Things look up for the sweet-toothed as there is a vast choice of home-made sweets and cakes – good hazelnut shortcake, moist chocolate rolls with brandy flavour, plus brownies, Danish pastries and flapjacks. Good for a snack in the heart of Windsor.

Open all week 11.30am to 3pm **Closed** 25 Dec Counter service. Licensed. Meat dishes. Vegan dishes. Snacks. No-smoking area

WINSCOMBE Avon • MAP 1

Penscot Farmhouse Hotel ££

Shipham TEL Winscombe (093 484) 2659

Once the Shipham Inn, the hotel, in the centre of Shipham, a couple of miles east of Winscombe, serves dinners where the price of the main course includes the starter, dessert, coffee and mints. In addition to those old favourites of breaded mushrooms, melon, and corn on the cob there is a vegetarian pâté; then home-made nut loaf, farmhouse pie, tomato and mushroom lasagne, cashew and mushroom bake and Mexican bean pie as possible main course choices.

Open all week D 7 to 9 (residents only Mon and Tue) Booking advisable. Table service. Tables outside. Licensed, also bring your own: corkage £1.50. Meat dishes. Vegan dishes. Other diets catered for on request. Snacks. Wheelchair access. Accommodation. Access, Amex, Carte Blanche, Diners, Visa

WITHAM Essex MAP 5

Crofters ££

25 Maldon Road TEL Witham (0376) 511068

An eighteenth-century house, all oak beams, exposed brick and open fireplaces, has been transformed into a wine bar/restaurant. The day's meat dishes are chalked on a blackboard but the four or so vegetarian choices will be recited. These might include winter vegetable crumble, courgettes and tomatoes layered in cheese sauce, vegetable risotto and leeks in cheese sauce, the first two described by a reporter as 'well cooked and presented. Each came with a side salad, among the best we have had for a long time, anywhere.' Recommended for a simple meal of ample portions at reasonable prices.

Open all week 11.45am to 2.15, 8.45 to 9.15 Booking advisable. Table service. Licensed. Meat dishes. No children at D. Wheelchair access. Access, Visa

WITHYPOOL Somerset MAP 1

Royal Oak £££

TEL Exford (064 383) 506/7

Don't be deterred by the fact that the bar menu has no vegetarian dishes – the restaurant has a full vegetarian menu. This pretty pub, a tourist's delight with its inglenook, low beams, hunting prints and bits of brass, set in a tiny village on the edge of Exmoor, is a haven for a vegetarian. The food is interesting and well cooked, and the cheeses deserve particular mention. The only drawback is the presence of fish on the so-called vegetarian menu. However, there are dishes such as mushrooms in cream and garlic on croûton, baked avocado cheese with tomatoes, or egg mayonnaise as starters, and main dishes of tagliatelle, vegetable casserole with butterbeans or Spanish omelette. Prices are not cheap, though, despite this being a pub.

Open all week noon to 2, 7 to 9 **Closed** 25 Dec Booking advisable. Table service. Tables outside. Licensed. Meat dishes. Fish dishes. Vegan dishes. Other diets catered for on request. No children under 10. Accommodation. Access, Amex, Diners, Visa

WOKINGHAM Berkshire MAP 2

Maryline's, Cantley House Hotel ££

Milton Road TEL Wokingham (0734) 789912

A three- or a four-course menu is available at this hotel where vegetarians are not relegated to a single dish at each course: there is a choice of three. The first course could be melon with raspberry sauce, or a mousse of red peppers; the second Roquefort cheese cream, light vegetable soup, vegetable terrine or asparagus with palm hearts and lychees. For mains there might be asparagus duxelle, aubergine and Gruyère cheese gateau or baked peaches with Stilton and walnuts. Full marks for effort.

Open Mon to Sat 12.30 to 2 (exc Sat L), 7.30 to 9.30 (10 Fri, Sat) Booking advisable. Table service. Tables outside. Licensed. Meat dishes. Fish dishes. Other diets catered for on request. Accommodation. Access, Amex, Diners, Visa

WOODBRIDGE Suffolk MAP 5

Wine Bar ££

17 Thoro'fare TEL Woodbridge (039 43) 2557

The weekly menu at this idiosyncratic wine bar sports one vegetarian main dish, perhaps three cheesy pastry galettes served with mange-tout, peppered leeks and braised lettuce with lovage; vegetable and crêpe timbale served with pesto sauce; or ratatouille filo strudel with onion and raisin compote. Care is shown in the vegetarian starters too: sauté fennel with gorgonzola, for example.

Open Tue to Sat noon to 2, 7 to 10 **Closed** 25 Dec, bank hol Mons Booking advisable. Table service. Licensed. Meat dishes. Fish dishes. Other diets catered for on request. No children under 16

WOODSTOCK Oxfordshire MAP 4

Brothertons Brasserie ££

1 High Street TEL Woodstock (0993) 811114

Tables are large, round, and simply laid in this collection of small gas-lit rooms. The place is popular and doesn't take bookings; there's a hustle and bustle and plenty of children around, who are well tolerated. The food is traditional and there's only one vegetarian main course, usually a basic lasagne or mushroom stroganoff. Full marks though for a home-made vegetable soup and good desserts: one slice of rum truffle cake would adequately feed two. Staff seem relaxed about people ordering only a bowl of soup for a meal at lunchtime, always a good sign.

Open all week 10.30 to 10.30 **Closed** 25 Dec Table service. Tables outside. Meat dishes. Fish dishes. Snacks. Access, Amex, Diners, Visa

WOOLHOPE Hereford & Worcester MAP 4

Butchers Arms ££

TEL Fownhope (043 277) 281

This typical half-timbered Herefordshire pub, with accommodation, gets its name from the fact that it used to be a butcher's shop as well as a pub. The food is wholesome and not expensive. Both bar and restaurant menus offer vegetarian choices – in the bar a lasagne, in the restaurant a mushroom biriani served with dhal, perhaps. Five possible starters are deep-fried mushrooms with blue cheese sauce, courgette mousse or spinach and goats' cheese strudel. Ice-creams are locally made: brown-bread, chocolate and fudge or chestnut, for example; other desserts include frozen ginger and coffee meringue cake and profiteroles.

Open bar, all week noon to 2, 7 to 9; restaurant, Wed to Sat D 7 to 9 Booking advisable. Table service. Licensed. Meat dishes. Fish dishes. Other diets catered for on request. Snacks at other times. Take-aways. No cigars or pipes in dining-room. Wheelchair access. Accommodation

WORCESTER Hereford & Worcester **MAP 4**

Natural Break £

4 The Hopmarket TEL Worcester (0905) 29979

Good for a snack or lunch. The counter provides flans that are made with vegetarian cheese and 20 varieties of salad – beetroot, egg and cress, cauliflower in spicy mayonnaise, carrot and nut, pasta and fruit are just some of the combinations. Hot dishes might be courgette and leek bake or jacket potatoes.

Open Mon to Fri 9.30 to 4 (5 Sat) Counter service. Tables outside. Meat dishes. Seafood dishes. Vegan dishes. Other diets catered for on request. Snacks. Take-aways. No-smoking area. Wheelchair access

Natural Break £

17 Mealcheapen Street TEL Worcester (0905) 26417

Related to the entry above, this café does a good line in snack lunches and teas; there is a good range of salads as well as jacket potatoes, flans made with vegetarian cheese and vegetarian specials. Baked items range from scones to florentines.

Open Mon to Fri 9.30 to 4 (5 Sat) Counter service. Meat dishes. Vegan dishes. Other diets catered for on request. Snacks. Take-aways. No-smoking area. Wheelchair access

Pizza Express £

1 St Nicholas Street TEL Worcester (0905) 726126

A satellite of the excellent London-based chain that was founded twenty-five years ago. See London entry.

Open Mon to Sat 11.30 to midnight, Sun noon to 11.30. Table service. Licensed, also bring your own: corkage £2.50. Meat dishes. Fish dishes. Take-aways. No-smoking area. Wheelchair access. Access, Amex, Diners, Visa

Sally Ann Café Ⓥ £

Vesta Tilley Centre, Lowesmoor TEL Worcester (0905) 726506

Home-cooked vegetarian lunches and dinner one evening a week are available at this café. Open for breakfasts and lunches, it serves dishes such as soup and wholegrain bread, pâté, moussaka, lasagne, vegetable cobbler, lentil bake and 'sausage' surprise. There is also a good range of cakes and biscuits. All eggs are free-range, and salt is not used. The evening menu consists of three courses: typical starters are crudités, soup, pâté and hummus; followed by pasta or pancakes with a choice of three sauces; then puddings of knickerbocker glory, chocolate tipsy cake, pancakes (again) or cheese. Good value. The only time that meat gets a look in is at monthly gourmet dinners, when a token meat main course will make an appearance. These dinners present a national cuisine, for instance Mexican.

Open Tue to Sun 11 to 4, Fri 11am to 10; otherwise D by arrangement Booking advisable D. Table service D. Counter service L. Tables outside. Unlicensed also bring your own. Vegan dishes. Other diets catered for on request. Snacks. Take-aways. Wheelchair access

WORTHING West Sussex MAP 3

Pizza Express £

Stanford Cottage, Stanford Square, Warwick Street
TEL Worthing (0903) 821133

A satellite of the excellent London-based chain that was founded twenty-five years ago. See London entry.

Open Mon to Sat 11.30 to midnight, Sun noon to 11.30. Table service. Licensed, also bring your own: corkage £2.50. Meat dishes. Fish dishes. Take-aways. No-smoking area. Wheelchair access. Access, Amex, Diners, Visa

Poppies Ⓥ £

165 Montague Street TEL Worthing (0903) 31132

This friendly vegetarian restaurant, open all day for teas, coffees, home-made cakes and scones, prides itself on its cooking and lack of artificial flavourings. Not only are ingredients fresh, but many of the fruits and vegetables are organic. Lunches start with Scotch broth, lentil soup or a salad bowl mix and go on to hot dishes of lentil and buckwheat slice, tortilla, quiche, curry or soya chilli con carne. Cakes are devil's food, carrot, ginger fruit and Victoria plum.

Open Mon to Sat (all week in summer) 10am to 5pm **Closed** 2 weeks Feb Table service. Tables outside. Unlicensed. Vegan dishes. Snacks. Take-aways. No-smoking area. Wheelchair access exc wc

YELVERTON Devon MAP 1

Buckland Abbey £

Buckland TEL Yelverton (0822) 855024

A particularly good National Trust café run by Teresa Owen. The restaurant, set in the Old Monk's guest-house, is a delight. The chef is a vegetarian herself, so meatless dishes get more than usual attention: spinach pâté served in a ramekin with home-made soda bread is a mix of spinach, eggs, cream cheese and soy sauce to give it piquancy. Substantial main dishes include mushroom and vegetable stroganoff, mixed bean casserole or croustade with a cheese, almond, sesame seed and walnut base. The National Trust has a policy that cafés serving light lunches must offer a hot and a cold vegetarian dish. There is an admission charge to the abbey, and consequently to the café.

Open all week exc Thur, L noon to 2 **Closed** Nov to 31 Mar Booking advisable Sun. Table service. Licensed. Meat dishes. Other diets catered for on request. Snacks. No smoking. Wheelchair access. Access, Amex, Visa

YORK North Yorkshire MAP 7

Bettys £–££

St Helen's Square TEL York (0904) 659142

As at other branches of this renowned chain of northern tea-rooms (see Ilkley, Harrogate and Pickering), the old-fashioned atmosphere is combined with home cooking and an excellent provision of teas and coffees, supplemented by fresh home-made lemonade and freshly squeezed orange juice. Daytime snacks include home-made breads, cakes and cream teas and a special rarebit. In the evening, to the accompaniment of a pianist, choices might be deep-fried mushrooms with tartare sauce or smoked Wensleydale croquettes.

Open all week 9am to 9 **Closed** some bank hols Table service. Licensed. Meat dishes. Fish dishes. Snacks. Take-aways. Wheelchair access, exc WC. Access, Visa

Blake Head Ⓥ ★ £

104 Micklegate TEL York (0904) 623767

A vegetarian café attached to a bookshop, where the food is of consistently high quality. The light, airy eating area is in an extension of the handsome 300-year-old building and has furniture made specially by a Welsh designer. Piped music is classical. Two of the chefs are vegan and so vegan food has a higher profile than usual: tofu and spinach lasagne or Mediterranean three-bean casserole might feature. Cakes are baked on the premises and include apricot and almond, tassajara – a sugar-free vegan cake of fresh and dried fruit, oats, coconut and sunflower seeds – fruit flan and carob cake. Freshly squeezed apple, carrot or orange juice, organic wines and beers are also available. Lunches are a cut above the average – unusual soups might be spinach and coconut or lentil and lemon, and hot dishes include vegetable casserole with swede and orange topping, and hazelnut stuffed peppers with orange sauce. Staff are unusually helpful.

Open all week 11.45 to 2.30 Counter service. Tables outside. Licensed. Vegan dishes. Snacks. No smoking. Wheelchair access. Access, Amex, Visa

Kites ★ ££

13 Grape Lane TEL York (0904) 641750

Some poky stairs lead to this characterful, informal, and unpretentious restaurant on the second and third floors. Simple furniture, well-spaced tables and red-painted floorboards create an inviting atmosphere. The cooking is excellent and vegetarianism is to the fore; as in a starter of aubergine caviare flavoured with garlic, fennel, cumin, ginger and tarmarind. Main dishes might be tacos with a hot chilli vegetable filling, couscous, South Indian curry with almonds and spinach, or chestnut-stuffed cabbage. There are also three kinds of cheese fondue, all of which are for two. Follow with highly rated banoffi pie, home-made ice-creams or a very rich chocolate and sour cream cheesecake. Good value.

Open Mon to Sat D 7 to 10.30, Sat L noon to 2 Booking advisable. Table service. Licensed, also bring your own: corkage £3. Meat dishes. Fish dishes. Other diets catered for. No-smoking area. Access, Amex, Carte Blanche, Diners, Visa

Miller's Yard Café ⓥ £

Miller's Yard, Gillygate TEL York (0904) 610676

Close to the Minster but a restful place to eat, whether in the old stone building itself or, in summer, outside in the small courtyard. The food is all vegetarian and good-value lunch dishes might include excellent cheese and vegetable roast; stir-fried vegetables with tofu and rice; broccoli and sweetcorn quiche; Italian layer bake with tagliatelle and spinach; a fresh tomato, lentil and pinto bean soup. Vegans are catered for and other diets can be, with notice. Eggs are free-range; cheeses are animal rennet-free. The same co-operative runs the Gillygate Bakery, which provides the excellent bread and cakes for the café.

Open Mon to Sat L noon to 2pm Counter service. Tables outside. Unlicensed. Vegan dishes. Other diets catered for on request. Snacks at other times. Take-aways. No smoking inside. Wheelchair access

Plunkets ££

9 High Petergate TEL York (0904) 637722

Petergate runs to one side of York Minster. Plunkets is an old building and inside the décor is simple, with candles on tables. As there is no booking, and it is popular, you might have to wait for a table. One drawback is the lack of a non-smoking area, and some find the pop music rather too loud. The menu – steaks, pies, spaghetti and hamburgers – has a corner devoted to vegetarians: chickpea stew, curry and a spaghetti dish, the last two found to be slightly bland, anglicised versions of what you would find in authentic Indian or Italian restaurants. There was nothing but praise however for lemon torte, served as a large portion with plenty of cream. Other desserts are cheesecake, chocolate fudge cake, apple pie, treacle tart and various ice-cream concoctions.

Open all week noon to 11 Table service. Tables outside. Licensed. Meat dishes. Wheelchair access. Accommodation

St William's £

3 College Street TEL York (0904) 634830

Make your way towards the Minster; St William's College is signposted. The large fifteenth-century building was a college for priests until the Dissolution. The restaurant is not purely vegetarian but has a hot dish of the day, perhaps cheese, pepper and carrot slice, tomato, basil and onion flan or aubergine and tomato moussaka. A home-made carrot and coriander soup was pronounced tasty and a leek and tomato croustade, though lacking much croustade, was otherwise good. Desserts, such as Queen of Puddings, chocolate and orange mousse, crème caramel, sticky toffee pudding and tangerine flan with dates, should be bought with your main course to save re-queueing.

Open all week noon to 2.30 Counter service. Tables outside. Licensed, also bring your own: corkage £1.75. Meat dishes. Fish dishes. Other diets catered for on request. Snacks. Take-aways. No-smoking area

Taylors £–££

46 Stonegate TEL York (0904) 622865

A fixture on the York café scene, Taylors was originally a purveyor of teas and coffees and these continue to be a central feature. Try the excellent range here, and eat good hot dishes upstairs in the old-style tea-room: mushroom croustade, mushroom vol-au-vent, smoked Wensleydale croquettes, a renowned Welsh rarebit and soups.

Open all week 9am to 5.30 Table service. Meat dishes. Fish dishes. Snacks. No-smoking area. Access, Visa

Scotland

ABERDEEN Grampian **MAP 11**

Jaws Café ⓥ ★

St Katherine's Centre, 5 West North Street
TEL Aberdeen (0224) 6456767

Based in a community centre and run by a workers' co-operative. The food is outstanding, with a range of hot dishes, including vegan options, bolstered by pizzas, pies and salads. Vegetarian goulash, colourfully decorated, is excellent, and salads, for instance kale, seaweed and potatoes, flavoursome and unusual. Bread is home baked and puddings take in crumbles, fruit salad and a rich date slice. Very reasonable prices make it justifiably popular. As we went to press, a move to larger premises nearby was mooted for summer 1990.

Open Mon to Sat noon to 3 (9pm Thur and Fri) Counter service. Vegan dishes. Snacks. Take-aways. No-smoking area. Wheelchair access

Shehbaaz £

19 Rose Street TEL Aberdeen (0224) 641786

Ask the waiter to recommend the best vegetarian dish on the menu (there isn't a separate section). One customer who did so ordered vegetable karai, which proved to be much better than one she had eaten elsewhere two nights earlier. Onion bhajias come in a flat pancake form rather than the familiar round puff, and are well flavoured. Though the cooking is not remarkable, it is of a reliably good standard. Service is good, and the pink flock wallpaper and grey upholstery of the décor tasteful.

Open all week noon to midnight, L noon to 2, D 5 to midnight **Closed**

25 Dec Booking advisable. Table service. Licensed. Meat dishes. Snacks. Take-aways. Wheelchair access. Access, Amex, Diners, Visa

Wild Boar £

19 Belmont Street TEL Aberdeen (0224) 624216

Definitely a yuppie-style establishment; a long room with stairs leading down in the centre, it is furnished with dark green painted tables and chairs. It's a good place to come for helpful service and a vegetarian choice that starts with pâté, four main dishes on the menu, and an extra blackboard choice, perhaps quiche. The vegetable kebab of aubergines, courgettes, mushrooms and onions with barbecue sauce is recommended. Fresh fruit salad to finish.

Open all week 10.30 to midnight, Sun 6.30 to 11 **Closed** 25 and 26 Dec, 1 Jan Table service. Licensed. Meat dishes. Snacks. No unaccompanied under 18s at D. No-smoking area. Wheelchair access

ARISAIG Highland MAP 11

Old Library Lodge ££

TEL Arisaig (068 75) 651

Formerly an eighteenth-century stable, now a restaurant with guest-house, plain exterior and Habitat-style interior. Simple meals offer vegetarian starters of smoked aubergine pâté, beetroot and apple soup or carrot and coriander. Follow with a creamy mushroom ragout with rice, hot avocado with wine and cheese stuffing, vegetable tartlet or wholemeal pancakes. Try rhubarb fudge crumble for dessert. Cigarette smoke can be a problem.

Open all week 11.30 to 2.30, 6.30 to 9.30 **Closed** Nov to Easter Booking advisable. Table service. Tables outside. Licensed. Meat dishes. Fish dishes. Other diets catered for on request. Accommodation.

'Wheelchair access' indicates that, according to the proprietor, entrances are at least 33 inches wide, passages 4 feet wide, and that there are a maximum of two steps, unless otherwise stated.

AUCHMITHIE Tayside MAP 11

But'n'Ben £

near Arbroath TEL Arbroath (0241) 77223

No frills, just good plain regional cooking 'as it must have been done from time immemorial.' There's no need to dress up, children and their mothers spill out of the kitchen all the time, the staff pop in and out to see that everyone is happy. The cottage, cosy with its coal fire, acts as a local meeting place. High tea is the big event here, and sadly there isn't much for vegetarians. Dinner, however, will have a dish suitable for non-meat eaters – cheese, sweetcorn and onion flan or spicy rice pilaff, for instance. Bread and cakes are home made, vegetables are home grown in the garden and Scots fare is a speciality. Freshly squeezed orange juice is available.

Open all week exc Tue, Sun D, noon to 2.30, 7.30 to 9.30 Booking advisable. Table service. Tables outside. Licensed. Meat dishes. Vegan dishes. Other diets catered for on request. Snacks at other times. Wheelchair access. Visa

AYR Strathclyde MAP 9

Fouters Bistro ££

2A Academy Street TEL Ayr (0292) 261391

Within a stone's throw of the River Ayr, down a narrow street, is this mainly meat and fish restaurant where you may have to ask for the vegetarian dish of the day. The restaurant is in the cellar and the dim lighting and dark maroon paint can make it difficult to read the menu. For vegetarians starters might be soup, mushrooms in cream sauce, tarte aux champignons or curate's garden salad; the main dish could be black-bean hot-pot, lasagne, stuffed peppers with wild rice or aubergine bake. Puddings are all made on the premises and white chocolate cheesecake is highly praised.

Open Tue to Sun noon to 2 (exc Sun L), 6.30 to 10.30 **Closed** 25 to 27 Dec, Jan Booking advisable. Table service. Licensed. Meat dishes. Fish dishes. Vegan dishes. Other diets catered for on request. No-smoking area. Access, Amex, Carte Blanche, Diners, Visa

BLAIR DRUMMOND Central **MAP** 11

Broughton's £–£££

TEL Doune (0786) 841897

Customers feel well looked after in this converted nineteenth-century farm building just under a mile west of Blair Drummond on the A873. Many of the herbs and vegetables are grown in the seven and a half acres that surround the restaurant, and wholegrain bread is home made. Vegetarians will find a mushroom and nutmeg cream tart for lunch and a rice, mushroom and tomato pancake or perhaps lentil stuffed aubergine for dinner.

Open Tue to Sun exc Sun D 12.30 to 2, 7 to 10 **Closed** 1 month during Jan and Feb Booking advisable. Table service. Licensed, also bring your own: corkage £3. Meat dishes. Other diets catered for on request. No-smoking in dining-room. No children at D. Wheelchair access. Access, Visa

CARNOUSTIE Tayside **MAP** 11

Crumbs £

Queen Street **TEL** Carnoustie (0241) 54044

A vegetarian in Carnoustie will not have much choice when it comes to eating out so this good-value and basic, if rather unexciting, coffee-shop would be worth visiting. Vegetarian dishes have almost the same weight as meat and fish dishes. Fairly standard fare such as deep-fried mushrooms in garlic butter, nut roast, leek croustade, lentil and tomato soup with good home-baked bread, lasagne and pizzas make up the list. Prices are very low.

Open Mon to Sat 9.30 to 4.30 (4 on Fri and Sat), 7 to 9.30 Fri and Sat Booking advisable. Table service. Licensed. Meat dishes. Fish dishes. Vegan dishes and other diets catered for on request. Snacks. Take-aways. Wheelchair access. Access, Visa

See the back of the guide for a list of restaurants awarded stars for especially good vegetarian cooking.

DERVAIG (Isle of Mull) Strathclyde MAP 11

Druimard Country House ££

TEL Dervaig (068 84) 345/291

Beside the Mull Little Theatre is this small hotel which inspires praise for accommodation and, particularly, food. 'This is the best value we have ever obtained in some 35 years of holidaying,' was one bold claim. The atmosphere is that of a country house and the vegetarian options are as good as the meat and fish. Daily menus will offer starters on the lines of home-made asparagus mousse, avocado with cream cheese, herbs and walnuts or spinach roulade with spicy tomato sauce, and main dishes of creamy mushrooms with crunchy almond and garlic topping, spicy strudel with herb mayonnaise or tart provençale.

Open all week 6 to 9 **Closed** Jan to Easter Booking advisable. Table service. Tables outside. Licensed. Meat dishes. Fish dishes. Vegan dishes and other diets catered for on request. No pipes or cigars. Wheelchair access. Accommodation. Access, Visa

DUMFRIES Dumfries & Galloway MAP 11

Opus £

95 Queenberry Street TEL Dumfries (0387) 55752

A longstanding and good-value meat-and-vegetarian café upstairs next to a gift shop; if anything, it's better now than ever though it may be crowded. Salads are good and plentiful, and hot dishes include the likes of vegetable pie, mushroom loaf, pancake or savoury crumble. There are cakes and simple puddings such as apple pie, banana pie and cheese-cake.

Open Mon to Sat 9 to 4.30 (2.15 Thur) Counter service. Licensed. Take-aways. Access

A change of owner or chef may mean a change of menu policy. If a restaurant is no longer serving vegetarian food, please inform the guide; the address to write to is on page 9.

DUNDEE Tayside **MAP 11**

Parrot Café £

91 Perth Road TEL Dundee (0382) 24813

Parrot is the name and parrots are the visual theme of the café; there are pictures of them everywhere. The furniture is good, old-fashioned stuff, and the range of snacks and meals for vegetarians shows some invention. A sample day has vegetable stroganoff, and cottage cheese, apple, walnut and raisin rye bread open sandwich. A regular customer praises the quality of scones and home-made wholemeal rolls, and mentions in particular the lentil and cumin soup and rhubarb fool.

Open Tue to Sat noon to 6 (5 Sat) **Closed** 2 weeks at Christmas and 2 weeks in summer Table service. Unlicensed, but bring your own. Meat dishes. Fish dishes. Snacks. Wheelchair access

DUNVEGAN (Isle of Skye) Highland **MAP 11**

Three Chimneys £–££

Colbost TEL Glendale (047 081) 258

An old crofter's cottage on the shores of Loch Dunvegan is the setting for a sophisticated, yet cosy restaurant. Shirley Spear cooks everything freshly – even the 100 per cent stoneground wholewheat bread – and menus vary at lunch and dinner. Lunches might be home-made soup and fresh cream crowdie (traditional Highland soft cheese) with oatcakes, pizza or bread and cheese. Evenings might produce leek and hazelnut crowdie, cream roulade with blackcurrant sauce, red bean Brazil nut crumble or aubergine, apricot and sweet almond pancakes. All puddings are home made – try a 'delicious' hazelnut and raspberry meringue. Vegetarian cheeses are local.

Open Mon to Sat 12.30 to 2, 7 to 9 **Closed** mid-Oct to Easter Booking advisable. Table service. Tables outside. Licensed. Meat dishes. Fish dishes. Vegan dishes. Other diets catered for on request. Access, Visa

EDINBURGH Lothian MAP 11

Bamboo Garden £–££

57A Frederick Street TEL 031-225 2382

The restaurant is large and spacious with Chinese artefacts in little alcoves. The menu is kind to vegetarians with two starters: dainty vegetable spring rolls and the less-usual fried seaweed with nuts, then main courses (a bit heavy on the bean curd, but high in protein) of sizzling vegetables with bean curd, bean curd in curry, bean curd with baby corn and mushrooms. There are also sizzling wheat gluten with vegetables – again not so usual – and vegetable chop suey. For dessert, toffee pineapple or light and crunchy banana fritters.

Open all week noon to midnight, L noon to 2 **Closed** 4 days Jan Booking advisable. Table service. Licensed. Meat dishes. Vegan dishes. Snacks. Take-aways. Access, Amex, Diners, Visa

Caprice £

327 Leith Walk TEL 031-554 1279

Not a name that conjures up pizzas, but that's what is served. An Italian family owns this pizzeria of high esteem. To aficionados, it is the traditional wood-burning oven – this one among the few in Britain – that produces an authentic pizza. Enjoy the artistry of the chefs as they knead and twirl the dough in full view of the customers.

Open all week, exc Sun L, noon to 2, 5.30 to 11 (11.30 Fri and Sat) **Closed** 1 and 2 Jan Booking advisable. Table service. Tables outside. Unlicensed. Meat dishes. Other diets catered for on request. Snacks at other times. Take-aways. No-smoking area. Access, Amex, Diners, Visa

Chans £

1 Forth Street TEL 031-556 7118

Two light, airy drawing-rooms are decorated in typical ethnic style at this Chinese restaurant, one of the few to have a chef specialising in vegetarian food. The result is an extensive menu of four starters, four soups and twenty main courses. Crispy vegetable wun-tun – small pastries filled with sweetcorn, deep fried and served with sweet-and-sour sauce – and spring rolls were both found to be light and good. Fried seaweed is crisp and sprinkled with spices. The trouble with the main dishes is that, despite their number, they tend to lack variety: mushrooms feature heavily and sauces are similar. Banana fritters are good, or try toffee apples and bananas.

Open all week noon to 1.45, 5.30 to 11.45 Booking advisable Fri and Sat. Table service. Licensed, also bring your own: corkage £1 per bottle. Meat dishes. Fish dishes. Vegan dishes. Access, Amex, Diners, Visa

Coconut Grove £££

3 Lochrin Terrace TEL 031-229 1569

The Mexican/South American restaurant clearly caters for students; prices are reasonable and there are no pretensions. The dimly lit interior is gaudy but spacious; food comes fairly crudely spiced, in large portions. Vegetarian dishes take in black-bean soup, creamy guacamole, mushrooms marinated in vinegar with a touch of chilli served with tacos. The menu is divided into burritos, enchiladas, tostadas and nacos, all of which have vegetarian versions. The burritos may be filled with rather flavourless vegetables; enchiladas are better.

Open Mon to Sat D 6 to 11 **Closed** 25 and 26 Dec Booking advisable. Table service. Licensed. Meat dishes. Other diets catered for on request. Take-aways. Wheelchair access. Access, Amex, Diners, Visa

Doric Wine Bar ££

15 Market Street TEL 031-225 1084

The Doric Wine Bar (not to be confused with the Doric Tavern downstairs, which is a pub) started life as Edinburgh's first French restaurant; and the waft of garlic still greets you. Although the room is basic, with bare painted floors and PVC tablecloths, the food remains varied and reasonably priced. Avocado and orange salad with raspberry mayonnaise, gazpacho, mushrooms cooked in cream with coriander, or hummus could be starters; aubergines with tomatoes and garlic, stuffed peppers, chillied root vegetables, tagliatelle with avocado, stuffed artichoke hearts, asparagus, and skewered vegetables with peanut sauce are the main course dishes. A mushroom and spinach lasagne with salad proved tasty and came in a sizeable portion.

Open Mon to Wed noon to 2.30 (2 Thur to Sat), 6 to 10.30 **Closed** 25 Dec and 1 Jan Booking advisable. Table service. Licensed. Meat dishes. Vegan and other diets catered for on request. Snacks. No children after 8pm. Access, Amex, Visa

Dragon Pearl ££

20 Union Place TEL 031-556 4547

The first Chinese restaurant in Edinburgh to feature a separate vegetarian menu. The kitchen prepares the dishes to be truly vegetarian: no oyster sauce sneaks in. There are five soups and eleven main dishes, most variations on vegetables, only one with bean curd and one a much-relished spicy rice vermicelli. The oyster mushrooms with cashew-nuts are well cooked with the nuts roasted, the monk's vegetables with deep-fried tofu has pleasant contrasts, and fried shredded vegetables, though less spicy than they might be, are also enjoyable. A useful tip for dessert: choose lotus cream and red bean paste dumplings from the dim-sum menu. Definitely a good place for vegetarians, the only snag being that the menu appears to be fixed in stone: it has not changed since it was introduced.

Open all week noon to 11 Booking advisable. Table service. Licensed. Meat dishes. Fish dishes. Take-aways. Wheelchair access. Access, Amex, Visa

Helios Fountain Ⓥ ★ £

7 Grassmarket TEL 031-229 7884

Although the café is in a Rudolf Steiner book and craft shop, dogma is not rammed down the throat with the red dragon pie. Rather, good dishes such as spinach and courgette tian, cheesy wheat berry bake or plantation casserole slide down enjoyably. Soups include Hungarian vegetable, potato and sweetcorn chowder. Daily choices are not many, but they will not disappoint. Particularly mentioned have been perfect, crisp-tender vegetables with peanut chilli sauce, a Boston bean pie topped with light wholemeal pastry and salads. Follow this with perhaps a 'moist and flavourful' pear tart or fruit crumble. It may be crowded, but with such good food and good value, that's no surprise.

Open Mon to Sat noon to 6 Counter service. Vegan dishes. Other diets catered for on request. Snacks. Take-aways. Wheelchair access. Access, Amex, Visa

Hendersons Ⓥ ★ £

94 Hanover Street TEL 031-225 2131

The crush and queues attest to the popularity of this vegetarian/vegan restaurant – and the weird decoration doesn't seem to daunt anyone. It's also a wine bar, which serves interesting Highland wines: elderflower, silver birch, gooseberry and blaeberry. The whole enterprise is a great success. The food is good, among which might be found a spinach tian, broccoli and Brie crumble, stuffed marrow and snacks such as spring rolls, nut rissoles and cakes. Vegetarian cheeses are a speciality and everything is made freshly on the premises.

Open Mon to Sat 11.30am to 2.30, 4.30 to 9; also Sun during Festival **Closed** 25 Dec, 1 Jan Counter service. Licensed. Vegan dishes. Other diets catered for on request. Snacks. Take-aways. No-smoking area. Access, Amex, Visa

Kalpna Ⓥ ★ £

2–3 St Patrick Square TEL 031-667 9890

A plain, down-to-earth café with a long-standing reputation for excellent Indian vegetarian food: tikkas of vegetables, kachoris and navratan korma are praised; other recommended dishes include makhani sobji – stir-fried vegetables in a sweet-and-sour sauce – mushroom bhaji and a good baingan bharta – crushed roast aubergines in yoghurt with cashew-nuts, onions and spices. The delicately spiced dishes are well reported and service described as excellent. Various thalis are offered, including a Gujerati version on Wednesdays. Unusual breads include dungree paratha with cheese and onion, paneer paratha with home-made cheese, onions and a touch of pepper. There are several kinds of kulfi and seero, a traditional sweet made from wholewheat, brown sugar, fresh ginger, raisins and cashews, to follow. Excellent value.

Open all week noon to 2, 5.30 to 10.30 Table service. Licensed. Vegan dishes. Take-aways. Wheelchair access. Access, Visa

Kelly's

££

46 West Richmond Street TEL 031-668 3847

Once a bakery, the small family-run restaurant offers modern British-style cooking, with generous portions. Set lunch and dinner menus will include vegetarian starters – warm Gruyère roulade with sweet red peppers and garlic cream cheese or broccoli and Stilton terrine with fresh pear dressing – and main courses such as leek and asparagus mille-feuille with creme fraîche and mint sauce or gougère with vegetables and squash in a sauce of Lanark Blue cream cheese. Puddings, made to order, are the forte: reports have praised a light lemon roulade and a shortbread with grapes covered with wine and grape juice glaze.

Open Tue to Sat D 6.45 to 9.30 Booking advisable. Table service. Licensed. Meat dishes. Fish dishes. Vegan dishes. Other diets catered for. No smoking until 9. Wheelchair access. Access, Amex, Visa

Lachana Ⓥ

£

3 Bristo Place TEL 031-225 4617

The most truly self-service of restaurants – a buffet where you help yourself to anything from one plate of food to two or three courses. It is run by Seventh Day Adventists. The two hot main dishes of the day might include lasagne, cashew roast or vegetarian haggis, and there are good salads – try the popular tofu cottage cheese. The price includes a slice of wholemeal bread. 'Some of the food has more salt than flavour but it certainly offers value for money', and it's particularly good for vegans since the only non-vegan food is yoghurt. Desserts will delight those with a sweet tooth.

Open Mon to Fri exc Fri D noon to 2.30, 5 to 7 Booking advisable. Table service. Counter service. Tables outside. Licensed. Vegan. Take-aways. No smoking. Wheelchair access

Lancers

££

5 Hamilton Place, Stockbridge TEL 031-332 3444 and 9559

There is a welcome vegetarian section as well as a thali on the menu of this Bengali restaurant aspiring to the posher end of the Indian scene.

Pakoras are good and the vegetable tikki 'well flavoured with a good texture'. Vegetable side dishes are successful, for example creamy dhal and aubergine bhaji and fresh chillis.

Open all week noon to 2.30, 5.30 to 11.30 Booking advisable. Table service. Licensed. Meat dishes. Seafood dishes. Vegan dishes. Take-aways. Wheelchair access. Access, Amex, Visa

Lilligs £

30 Victoria Street TEL 031-225 7635

The upstairs café with its jolly atmosphere is a series of small rooms intersected by stone arches. There are four or five daily dishes, for example, mushrooms in white wine with rosemary; cream-cheese-stuffed pancakes; vegetables baked in garlic sauce; potted cream of cauliflower bake; chestnut and mushroom pâté. On the negative side, service has been slapdash (when a hair was found in food, the waitress's response was a shrug), and one customer requesting vegetarian food was served meat croissants.

Open all week 11am to 11pm Table service D. Counter service L. Licensed. Meat dishes. Snacks. No-smoking area. Access, Amex, Diners, Visa

Maxies Bistro ££

32 West Nicholson Street TEL 031-667 0845

A fixture on the Edinburgh eating scene, Maxies could not be described as providing haute cuisine but it's good. Several vegetarian dishes are available at the bar; cheese and herb pâté, curried vegetables and deep-fried stuffed avocado with minted yoghurt dressing. The restaurant menu has much the same dishes with addition of vegetable cutlets and deep-fried stuffed mushrooms.

Open all week exc Sun L noon to 2.30, 5.30 to 11.30 **Closed** 25 Dec and 1 Jan Booking advisable. Table service. Counter service. Licensed, also bring your own: corkage £2 per bottle. Meat dishes. Fish dishes. Vegan dishes. Other diets catered for on request. Access, Visa

All letters to the guide are acknowledged.

Monsoon £

13 Dalry Road TEL 031-346 0204

The service is attentive in this Indian restaurant and the food – though not especially vegetarian-inclined – reliable. Vegetarian starters are kabak tava (fried courgettes in yoghurt sauce) or patlican tava (aubergine in the same sauce). There is a vegetarian meal for two consisting of vegetable masala, Madras sambar, onion kulcha, tarka dhal, sag bhajee, pulao rice and chutneys. Desserts are unremarkable but include kulfi, lychees and gulab jamun.

Open all week noon to 2.30, 5.30 to 11.45 Booking advisable. Table service. Licensed. Meat dishes. Vegan dishes. Take-aways. Wheelchair access. Access, Amex, Diners, Visa

Queen's Hall £

Clerk Street TEL 031-668 3456

Popular not only because of its convenience on concert days, but for its consistently good food. A typical day's menu could offer spinach and cheese loaf, nut croquettes and wholefood pizza; main dishes of tofu and vegetable flan, carrot and courgette roulade, vegetable spring rolls and lentil loaf have also featured. Seven desserts include pear crumble, apple and granola layer, banana and ginger flan.

Open Mon to Sat L, noon to 2, D before concerts 6 to 9 Counter service. Licensed, also bring your own: corkage £1.90. Meat dishes. Fish dishes. Snacks at other times. No-smoking area. Wheelchair access

St Jacques ££

King James Hotel, Leith Street TEL 031-556 0111

Don't be daunted by what must be one of the ugliest modern buildings in Edinburgh, for the restaurant in this fairly expensive hotel has a range of well-cooked vegetarian dishes. It is not clear whether they are meant to be starters or main dishes, as their pricing is way below meaty main dishes (vegetarian ones are about £3.75, meat and fish around £9.50). Aubergine and courgette mousse with a julienne of red peppers and saffron sauce, warm asparagus salad with sunflower seeds, salad with mange-touts, pineapple and strawberries, tomato and tarragon soup or stir-fry vegetables with flaked almonds give the flavour.

Open all week 12.30 to 2, 6.30 to 10.20 **Closed** 25 Dec Booking advisable. Table service. Licensed. Meat dishes. Fish dishes. Vegan and other diets catered for on request. Snacks. Wheelchair access. Accommodation. Access, Amex, Diners, Visa

Seeds Ⓥ £

53 West Nicholson Street TEL 031-667 8673

This vegetarian café is light and pleasant, relaxed and friendly; the food is fresh, varied, and filling without being too heavy. The range of salads, made from an imaginative array of ingredients, changes fairly frequently. There are several hot dishes, of which half portions can be ordered, never the same two days running, as well as filled rolls. The vegan baking is of a high order – try carob brownies and tofu cheesecake. The co-operative is so successful that space is at a premium: do not expect to be able to have a tête à tête.

Open Mon to Sat 10am to 8 **Closed** 1 week at Christmas, 2 days Easter Counter service. Unlicensed, but bring your own: no corkage. Vegan dishes. Other diets catered for on request. Snacks. Take-aways. No-smoking

Sunflower Country Kitchen £

4 South Charlotte Street TEL 031-220 1700

'An unusually successful attempt to present healthy food to a wide range of customers from ordinary Princes-Street-shopping meat-eaters to lactoveggies and vegans.' Meat and vegetarian dishes co-exist in roughly equal quantities on a more or less permanent menu. What a helpful idea to offer half portions at a lower price. Bread, cakes and desserts are home made. Specialities include a good mixed-grains salad, nuttie potatoes mashed with onion, rolled in flaked peanuts and deep-fried, nut roast, quiche made with free-range eggs and jumbo croissants.

Open all week 11.30am to 7 Counter service. Licensed. Meat dishes. Fish dishes. Vegan dishes. Other diets catered for on request. Snacks. Take-aways. No-smoking area

Szechuan House £

95 Gilmore Place TEL 031-229 4655

Don't be put off by the outside appearance; this Szechuan restaurant is very much better inside. Chinese poems adorn the walls – for instance, 'We thank all our customers who arrived in cars or on dragoned steeds, Flowing as gracefully as water.' A special vegetarian dish comprises vegetables, wheat gluten and cellophane noodles in a sweetish sauce, and a well-flavoured green bean dish and good stir-fried vegetables has been recommended. Spring rolls can be vegetarian. The Szechuan-style set meal is for four, several dishes of which – bean curd family-style and fried beans Szechuan-style – are declared to be hot and spicy. Toffee apples, sweet dumplings or banana fritters to finish.

Open Tue to Sun D 5.30 to 2am (3am Fri and Sat) **Closed** Chinese New Year Table service. Licensed, also bring your own: corkage 50p per bottle. Meat dishes. Fish dishes. Vegan dishes. Other diets catered for on request. Snacks at other times. Take-aways. Wheelchair access. Access, Visa

Verandah Tandoori ££

17 Dalry Road TEL 031-337 5828

A well-established Indian restaurant that continues to serve a good range of suitable dishes. In the vegetarian section are the expected sambar, karai, sag paneer malai and aloo gobi massallam, as well as a thali described by one reporter as 'lightly and fragrantly spiced'. The vegetarian special for two consists of a starter, main dishes with rice or nan, dessert and coffee.

Open all week noon to 2.30, 5.30 to 11.30 Booking advisable. Table service. Licensed. Meat dishes. Seafood dishes. Vegan dishes. Take-aways. Wheelchair access. Access, Amex, Diners, Visa

Viva Mexico £

10 Anchor Close, Cockburn Street TEL 031-226 5145

Authentic Mexican atmosphere and food with a concession to British tastes being a light hand with the spices. The typical dishes of tacos, enchiladas, quesada grandes and chimichangas are all listed on the menu with vegetarian versions. To complete the North American continent flavour, try Mississippi mud pie, pecan pie, Kahlua or mango mousse.

Open all week, exc Sun L, noon to 2.30, 6.30 to 10.30 **Closed** 25 Dec Booking advisable. Table service. Licensed. Meat dishes. Fish dishes. Vegan dishes. No children after 8.30pm. Access, Amex, Visa

FALKIRK Central MAP 11

Vegetarian Plus £

4 Melville Street TEL Falkirk (0324) 32615

Snacks are available all day but meals only from 11am. Hummus is served with oatcakes and main courses include creamed mushroom nut crunch or leek croustade. There's fish for non-vegetarian companions in eating.

Open Mon to Sat 9am to 5 (5.30 Fri and Sat) **Closed** first 2 weeks July Table service. Counter service. Licensed. Fish dishes. Vegan dishes. Other diets catered for on request. Snacks. Take-aways. No-smoking area

FORRES Grampian MAP 11

Bistro ££

High Street TEL Forres (0309) 75541

Formerly called Busters. There is reasonable variety on the menu and the bonus of three vegetarian main dishes – gado-gado, provençale-stuffed vegetables and tagliatelle in cream of tomato and mushroom sauce. The day begins at 9.30am with breakfast and lunch starts at noon – crêpes, pizzas and other such. The à la carte menu takes over at 6pm. Mint ice-cream is home made. Certainly worth a visit in an area of sparse catering for vegetarians.

Open Mon to Sat noon to 9.30 Table service. Licensed. Vegan dishes. Other diets catered for on request. Snacks at other times. Wheelchair access. Access, Amex, Visa

GLASGOW Strathclyde **MAP 11**

Babbity Bowster £–££

16–18 Blackfriars Street TEL 041-552 5055

Blackfriars Street was built as part of the eighteenth-century merchant city boom in Glasgow. Later, the villa that is the restaurant became derelict but it has been restored to former glory. The splendid décor of the café on the ground floor might make it worth visiting for this alone. Reports on the food are inconsistent. A vegetarian haggis is available in the café and lasagne might be offered in the first-floor restaurant.

Open restaurant: all week noon to 2.30, 5 to 11; café: 8am to 9pm Table service. Licensed. Meat dishes. Fish dishes. Accommodation. Access, Amex, Visa

Balbir's Vegetarian Ashoka Ⓥ £

141 Elderslie Street TEL 041-248 4407

Already having a name for good Indian food, Balbir's now ventures into vegetarian cuisine. With a décor that verges on the yuppy, the clientele are suitably young and the atmosphere lively. Main dishes of channa, stuffed parathas and vegetable masala have been enjoyed. Try the creamy ras malai for dessert.

Open all week exc Sun L noon to 2, 5 to 11.30 **Closed** 25 Dec and 1 Jan Booking advisable. Table service. Licensed. Vegan dishes. Snacks. Take-aways. No-smoking area. Access, Amex, Diners, Visa

Basil's Ⓥ ££

184 Dumbarton Road TEL 041-337 1416

The combination of a high-principled workers' co-operative (no South African or Chilean produce) with an attractive licensed table service restaurant has been described as unusual and appealing. Main dishes rely on old favourites such as mushroom moussaka, red pepper and cashew-nut roast and ratatouille, but the Spud de Lux – a baked potato filled with green peppers and mushrooms in a wine and mustard sauce – is recommended. Starters are more adventurous: smoked tofu and leek cocktail, mushrooms and sour cream or black olive and red wine pâté.

Organic vegetables are used and organic wines stocked. Occasionally there are organic cheeses.

Open Mon to Thur noon to 2, 6 to 10.30 (Fri to Sun to 11pm) Booking advisable weekends and evenings. Table service. Licensed. Vegan dishes. Other diets catered for with 24 hours notice. Snacks. Take-aways. No-smoking area. Wheelchair access. Access, Visa

Buttery ★ £££

652 Argyle Street TEL 041-221 8188

It's not easy to get to the restaurant, a solitary house in an island created by motorway flyovers and underpasses. Once inside, though, it's quiet, with a relaxed Victorian atmosphere created by a dark bar with old-style plush chairs and a dark wood-panelled dining-room. Vegetarian dishes are listed separately and draw praise: start with timbale of rice with cream, spinach and vegetables, a selection of deep-fried cheese with warm hazelnut dressing or a poached egg on toasted muffin with spinach coated in sweetcorn cream. Main dishes are somewhat less adventurous but have been enjoyed: mushrooms in filo pastry, curried vegetable raviolis, ratatouille filo or omelette.

Open Mon to Sat exc Sat L noon to 2.30, 7 to 10 **Closed** bank hols Booking advisable. Table service. Licensed. Meat dishes. Fish dishes. Other diets catered for on request. Access, Amex, Diners, Visa

Café Gandolfi ££

64 Albion Street TEL 041-552 6813

The modern furniture gives the café distinction; it feels like a continental brasserie, the menu going from croissants to profiteroles. The food looks smart and modern too. Aubergine purée, crudités, eggs en cocotte, vegetarian combo (rice, spiced beans, seasonal vegetables and aubergine purée), choux au fromage and vegetable filo parcels are the vegetarian offerings. Ice-cream is home made; chocolate pot has been enjoyed, being not too sweet, with a pleasant airy texture. There are organic wines, freshly squeezed orange juice and home-made lemonade.

Open Mon to Sat 9.30 to 11.30pm **Closed** bank hols Booking advisable. Table service. Licensed. Meat dishes. Fish dishes. Vegan dishes. Other diets catered for on request. Snacks. No children after 8 in the evening. Wheelchair access

Rab Ha's

££

83 Hutchson Street TEL 041-553 1545

Hearty eaters drift to Rab Ha's, named after a famous Glasgow glutton, Robert Hall, who reputedly could devour a calf at one sitting. Portions are large, but choice for vegetarians sadly is small – perhaps a starter of grilled mushrooms in garlic and sherry sauce and a main course of vegetable stroganoff. Desserts seem basic, along the lines of apple pie and strudel, chocolate mousse and sorbet. The restaurant with live music is downstairs, the bar with cheap lunches is on the ground floor.

Open Mon to Sat noon to 2.45, 7 to 10.30 exc Sat L Booking advisable. Table service. Licensed. Meat dishes. Vegan and other diets catered for on request. Snacks. Accommodation. Access, Amex, Diners, Visa

Rogano

££

11 Exchange Place TEL 041-248 4055

What is described as Queen-Mary-art-deco-style works well in this restaurant with downstairs café; service is excellent and food, particularly in the café, is good value. An otherwise inventive menu could perhaps be more so with vegetarian dishes – a stir-fry of vegetables, and hazelnut and wild mushroom pasta with herb cream are typical. Light syrup sponge with Amaretti cream and a strawberry shortcake have been praised.

Open Mon to Sat noon to 2.30, 7 to 10.30 **Closed** bank hols Booking advisable. Table service. Licensed. Meat dishes. Fish dishes. Vegan dishes. Other diets catered for on request. Snacks at other times. Access, Amex, Diners, Visa

Rajdoot

£

11–13 Hyndland Street TEL 041-334 0084

An upmarket Indian restaurant facing an 'only mildly vandalised' playground. Although people are safe in the area, property may not be if left in cars. Inside, waiters are courteous and efficient, and vegetarians do well. There's a thali of pakora, peas pilau, aloo gobi, dhal, fresh vegetables of the day and raita, as well as three vegetarian dishes.

Open all week noon to 2, 5 to midnight Table service. Licensed. Meat dishes. Fish dishes. Vegan dishes. Other dishes catered for on request. No-smoking area. Wheelchair access. Access, Amex, Diners, Visa

Third Eye Centre Ⓥ ★ £

350 Sauchiehall Street TEL 041-332 7521

The Third Eye Centre café, behind a new-age bookshop, is a long-term survivor on Glasgow's vegetarian scene. 'It's better than ever' is one verdict. Apart from soup, there's always a hot dish, often vegan – stuffed vegetables, lasagne, vegetarian haggis or calabrese cheese curry, perhaps – and an interesting selection of salads plus snacks of home-made oatcakes, cheesecakes and sweet cakes. The Centre, a lively and go-ahead arts forum that has hosted events such as Hungarian Arts, Polish Realities and Glasgow Style, is near the Glasgow School of Art. So, before going to the theatre, partake of the pre-theatre supper which is extraordinarily good value. Available all day are home-made soup, various stuffed vegetables and a hot dish of the day, and the counter stays open during shows.

Open Tue to Sun, exc Sun D, 11.30 to 8.30 (later when there's a performance) **Closed** 25 Dec, 1 Jan Table service D. Counter service early, L and during shows. Tables outside. Licensed. Vegan dishes. Other diets catered for on request. Snacks at other times. Take-aways. No smoking mornings and L. Wheelchair access. Access, Amex, Diners, Visa

Ubiquitous Chip ££

12 Ashton Lane TEL 041-334 5007

A lively restaurant, uninhibited by undue formality, where you can eat well either in the courtyard or in a kind of conservatory. Both bar and restaurant meals include vegetarian alternatives: in the bar a vegetarian haggis and neeps, and in the restaurant perhaps contrasting vegetable and nut baskets with pear and watercress sauce or spiced, almond-stuffed aubergine. Starters might be soup or a basket of mixed field mushrooms. Scots dishes are often featured, such as 'clapshot' – mashed potatoes and swedes – a very good oatmeal ice-cream and excellent strawberries with orange cream and Ayrshire shortbread. The kitchen tries to avoid using too much cream and butter.

Open all week exc Sun L noon to 2.30, 5.30 to 11 Booking advisable. Table service. Licensed. Meat dishes. Fish dishes. Snacks at other times. Wheelchair access. Access, Amex, Visa

Wholefoods £

Unit 7, Princes Square, 48 Buchanan Street TEL 041-226 4251

All soups are made with vegetable stock, which eases the choice of starter, but there's also a broccoli and Swiss cheese filo pastry with yoghurt and mint dressing or hummus. Daily vegetarian specials for the main course might be aubergine pie, mushroom stroganoff, vegetable bake or mushroom crumble. There is also a good range of salads.

Open Mon to Sat 10am to 7 (11 to 5 Sun) Counter service. Licensed. Meat dishes. Snacks. Take-aways. No-smoking area. Wheelchair access

Winter Green Café £

Winter Gardens, People's Palace, Glasgow Green TEL 041-554 0223

The setting is extraordinary, like a large conservatory with flowers, foliage and birds; so it's worth a visit for the experience alone. The wholefood café does serve meat, but the emphasis is on vegetarianism. The collective that runs the café is prohibited from cooking on the premises, so the food is brought in and re-heated; however, it is delivered fresh, with no additives, preservatives or artificial flavourings. The range is not large – soup, pizza, quiche, wholemeal pasties, filled rolls and croissants, oatcakes and cheese and salads for lunch. There are various cakes and puddings such as caramel shortcake, apple or rhubarb pie or cheesecakes.

Open all week 10 to 4, L 11.30 to 3 **Closed** 24 Dec to 3 Jan Counter service. Unlicensed, but bring your own: no corkage charge. Fish dishes. Snacks. Wheelchair access

The cost of a three-course vegetarian meal without wine is indicated by £ symbols to the right of the restaurant name:
£ = up to £7.50
££ = £7.50 to £15
£££ = £15 and over

HAWICK Borders MAP 10

Old Forge ££

Newmill, near Hawick TEL Hawick (0450) 85298

The former blacksmith's has recently been converted and one reporter's daughter used to have her pony shod here. Anvil and bellows are still on display, walls are rough cast and there are few tables. Food is imaginative, and there is a 'guinea-pig menu' for those willing to try new dishes. Sadly this cannot be relied upon to yield a vegetarian meal, but the set menu will. Four courses of first, say, avocado mousse; then a soup, perhaps chestnut, mushroom and orange; then perhaps mixed mushrooms cooked in red wine with garlic served with bulgur, or sweet-and-sour summer vegetables with brown rice. The bread is home made and an individual wholegrain loaf is placed on each table. Sticky-toffee pudding and coffee and brandy ice-cream to finish.

Open Tue to Sat D 7 to 9.30 **Closed** 2 weeks Nov and May Booking advisable. Table service. Licensed. Meat dishes. Fish dishes. Other diets catered for on request. Wheelchair access. Access, Amex, Visa

INVERGARRY Highland MAP 11

Glendale Guest House Ⓥ £

Mandally Road TEL Invergarry (080 93) 282

This good-value and unassuming guest-house off the A82, south of Invergarry, asks non-residents to book 24 hours' in advance for dinner and there's no choice on the set three-course menu (though customers are asked when they book whether they have any particular dislikes). None the less, value is outstanding – the set meal cost £6.50 as we went to press – and the food is well reported. Typical main dishes are spinach and flageolet pie; tofu and vegetable kebabs with gado-gado; and carrot and coriander curry, while starters are on the lines of chestnut soup, hummus or marinated mushrooms. Simple lunches are served to residents.

Open all week 6.30 to 7 Booking advisable. Table service. Vegan dishes. Other diets catered for on request. No-smoking area. Wheelchair access. Accommodation

INVERNESS Highland **MAP 11**

Culloden Pottery £

The Old Smiddy, Gollanfield TEL Ardersier (0667) 62749

Ten miles north-east of Inverness on the A96, the pine-furnished self-service café is above the pottery, with wonderful views over the Moray Firth. The owners are vegetarian but feel they have to offer fish as well. They use only vegetarian cheese, vegan margarine and local free-range eggs; there is always at least one vegan main dish. Likely dishes include soups, butterbean pâté, nut roast, lasagne, Brazil nut and broccoli pie and home-made pizzas, as well as salads and cakes. Most dishes are available in children's portions.

Open all week, L 9.30am to 5.30, Fri and Sat D 8.30 **Closed** 24 Dec to 2 Jan Counter service. Licensed. Fish dishes. Vegan dishes. Snacks at other times. No-smoking area. Chair lift for wheelchair access

Culloden House £££

TEL Inverness (0463) 790461

Three miles north-east of Inverness off the A96, Culloden House is an elegant Georgian mansion; the interior has an impressive Adam-style dining-room, four-poster beds and Jacuzzis in the bathrooms. The five-course menu has a vegetarian dish – perhaps wild mushrooms and walnuts in a parcel or a mousse of carrot and broccoli on creamed vegetable sauce – but that still leaves a vegetarian to twiddle his or her fork while others have a fish course. Still, three courses are better than none. The dessert buffet means that one can indulge oneself fully on such delights as chocolate roulade, passion-fruit soufflé, lemon tart, fresh fruit salad, French strawberries and a superb strawberry shortcake, with pitchers of cream, strawberry and raspberry purée that can be poured on top. It is not cheap, and vegetarians may not get as good a deal as meat-eaters, but they will have a splendid evening all the same.

Open all week 12.30 to 2, 7 to 9 Booking advisable. Table service. Licensed. Meat dishes. Fish dishes. Vegan dishes and other diets catered for on request. Accommodation. Access, Amex, Diners, Visa

IONA (Isle of Iona) Strathclyde **MAP 11**

Argyll Hotel ££

TEL Iona (068 17) 334

The hotel (handily 200 yards from the jetty) serves snack lunches such as salads, quiche and perhaps a vegetable lasagne; dinner is four courses, including coffee, and menus rotate on a four-week basis. Starters for vegetarians might be soup, cheese and sweetcorn vol-au-vent, lentil pâté, hummus or curried eggs. The one main dish could be ratatouille, nut roast, curry, red dragon pie, cashew-nut fritters, pasta or spicy chickpea casserole. Follow on with cranachan, apple and apricot mousse or blackcurrant fool.

Open all week 12.30 to 1.30, D at 7 **Closed** 21 Oct to Easter Booking advisable. Table service. Licensed. Meat dishes. Vegan dishes on request. Other diets catered for on request. No smoking in dining-room and 1 lounge. Wheelchair access exc bedrooms. Accommodation. Access, Visa

KILDONAN (Isle of Skye) Highland **MAP 11**

Three Rowans £

near Edinbane TEL Edinbane (047 082) 286

Facing west to the Outer Hebrides – the view claimed to be 'one of the finest from any restaurant' – the Three Rowans is a workshop as well as old croft house converted into a restaurant and tea-shop. Inside, bare timbers and bric à brac give an impression of old crofting life. Vegetarians will find several dishes to tempt – home-made pâté, soup, a lasagne and stuffed peppers. Specialities include home-made wholemeal bread baked daily and cloutie dumpling, a traditional Scottish dumpling with treacle and spices served hot with whipped cream.

Open Mon to Sat 10 to 4, 7 to 8.30 **Closed** mid-Oct to mid-Mar Table service. Tables outside. Licensed. Meat dishes. Snacks

The Editor's top ten restaurants providing an exceptional service for vegetarians, chosen for the success with which they achieve their aims, are listed on page 12.

KILMELFORD Strathclyde MAP 11

Cuilfail Hotel £

TEL Kilmelford (085 22) 274

Now refurbished, the public rooms are of a high standard. The bar and bistro serve vegetarian soup, mushroom vol-au-vent or date, banana and walnut salad as starters and almond risotto with peanut sauce, wine and nut pâté, vegetables en croûte or butterbean and cider risotto as main courses. Brown bread is home made. A very tart lemon tart is one of the home-made puddings, which include a vegan sorbet.

Open all week noon to 2, 6.30 to 9 **Closed** Jan and Feb Table service. Tables outside. Licensed. Meat dishes. Vegan dishes. Other diets catered for on request. No-smoking area. Wheelchair access. Accommodation. Access, Visa

KYLE OF LOCHALSH Highland MAP 11

Wholefood Café £–££

Highland Designworks, Plockton Road TEL Kyle (0599) 4388

A café affording at least three vegetarian main courses and a similar number of starters: spicy peanut dip with crudités, cashew and cheese pâté with sesame crackers or a variety of soups including tomato and basil, or carrot and oatmeal. Main dishes on the menu include buckwheat pancakes filled with fresh spinach and cream cheese, and aubergine, brown lentil and red wine moussaka. The raspberry fool is made from locally grown fruit, cheeses are served with oatcakes and there is usually one ice-cream and several other choices are available on the dessert list.

Open June to Oct, all week 12.30 to 9; April and May, Wed to Sun 12.30 to 9 **Closed** mid-Nov to mid-Mar Table service. Counter service. Tables outside. Licensed. Fish dishes. Vegan dishes. Other diets catered for on request. Snacks. Take-aways. No smoking. Wheelchair access. Access, Visa

The availability of meat and fish dishes is indicated in the details underneath the text of an entry.

LESLIE Fife MAP 11

Rescobie Hotel £–££

Valley Drive TEL Glenrothes (0592) 742143

A country-house hotel with impressive grounds. Vegetarians will be greeted by a full menu both at lunch – when it is cheaper – and dinner. A sample of offerings might be asparagus pancakes, a fruity summer salad and melon pearls on red fruit coulis as starters; cashew-nut roast, vegetable feuilleté or oriental stir-fry as main courses.

Open all week noon to 2, 7 to 9 Booking advisable. Table service. Licensed. Meat dishes. Fish dishes. Other diets catered for on request. Wheelchair access. Accommodation. Acccess, Amex, Diners, Visa

MELROSE Borders MAP 9

Marmion's Brasserie ££

Buccleuch Street TEL Melrose (089 682) 2245

What is simply stated as a 'vegetarian dish of the day' could turn out to be Stilton pie, black-eyed beans and mushrooms, or leek croustade; it changes daily. Simpler dishes take in potato skins and brie and gherkin kebabs.

Open Mon to Sat noon to 2, 6.30 to 10 Booking advisable. Table service. Licensed, also bring your own: corkage £2. Meat dishes. Fish dishes. Vegan dishes. Other diets catered for on request. Wheelchair access

NAIRN Highland MAP 11

Clifton Hotel ££

Viewfield Street TEL Nairn (0667) 53119

Standing head and shoulders above its companion hotels by the sea, the Clifton offers more than just dinner – 'more a theatrical experience'. Prices are not outrageous. On arrival, diners are ushered into a sitting-room for a drink and then all guests are invited in to dine together (as though staying in a large country house together). All the rooms repay attention and are busy with prints. Perhaps the fact that at least six of the staff and family are vegetarians accounts for a healthy provision of non-meat and fish dishes (more variety is available if they know you are coming). Local Scottish dishes co-exist with French ones; samphire is a welcome locally foraged starter; a cheese and tabouleh concoction turned out to be a well presented combination of garlic, lemon and cheese flavours. Home-made chewy wholegrain bread is served. Vegetables provençale is one of various main course possibilities – aubergine charlotte, lentil bake, butterbean bake or vegetable pie are alternatives. What many would regard as a prosaic item, crème caramel, comes as a large pudding from which to help yourself.

Open all week 12.30 to 1, 7 to 9.30 **Closed** Nov to Feb Booking advisable. Table service. Licensed. Meat dishes. Fish dishes. Vegan and other diets catered for on request. No-smoking area. Wheelchair access. Access, Amex, Diners, Visa

PEEBLES Borders MAP 9

Sunflower £–££

4 Bridgegate TEL Peebles (0721) 22420

The coffee-shop is predominantly vegetarian though the odd prawn, tuna fish or ham component may appear in a dish. Lunch could be soup made with vegetarian stock, home-made bread, hot dishes such as cheese and lentil loaf, leek and tomato pancake, vegetarian shepherd's pie, creamy leek croustade or, the most popular item, a salad pancake with cheese sauce. Coffee and walnut gateau is highly rated.

Open Mon to Sat noon to 2.30 Booking advisable. Table service. Licensed. Snacks. No-smoking area. Wheelchair access

PERTH Tayside MAP 11

Littlejohns £

65 Methven Street TEL Perth (0738) 39888

It's a fun place decorated with ephemera, the American-style tabloid menu bearing humorous newspaper extracts and antique advertisements for 'security hose supporters' and 'shoe dressings'. The food has a Mexican bias. A vegetarian section on the menu offers baked Brie and potato skins, deep-fried mushrooms, nachos and guacamole, to be followed by a vegetable pie, a veggieburger, pizza, lasagne and a good quesada, which is a tortilla filled with spicy vegetables, topped with sour cream and cheese, served with salad and refried beans. The bread-and-butter and the sticky-toffee puddings rate very high, though portions could be bigger. Part of a chain.

Open all week, exc Sun L, noon to 11 Table service. Licensed. Meat dishes. Fish dishes. Wheelchair access. Access, Amex, Diners, Visa

ST ANDREWS Fife **MAP 11**

Brambles £

College Street TEL St Andrews (0334) 75380

Centrally situated in an atmospheric old building, this self-service café is predominantly vegetarian with some meat and fish dishes. The main problem is overcrowding in university term time. Hot dishes, such as vegetable and potato bake, red bean curry, red bean lasagne, nut roast and vegetable terrine, are highly recommended. So are the cakes – Brambles own fudge cake, raspberry cheesecake, banoffi pie and sticky-toffee caramel dumpling. Although vegans are catered for, they will get a better choice if they ring in advance.

Open Tue to Sat 7.30am to 4.30, bank hol Mons Counter service. Licensed, also bring your own: corkage £2.50. Meat dishes. Fish dishes. Vegan dishes. Other diets catered for on request. Snacks. Take-aways. No smoking

Littlejohns £

73 Market Street TEL St Andrews (0334) 75444

One of a small chain of American-style diners serving Mexican food, pizzas and burgers. The jolly menu is decorated with old-fashioned advertisements and has a special vegetarian section: lasagne, burger, pastie, pizza and stir-fry pie.

Open all week noon to 11 (exc Sun L, 5) **Closed** 1 and 2 Jan Booking advisable. Table service. Licensed. Meat dishes. Fish dishes. Snacks. Wheelchair access. Access, Amex, Diners, Visa

New Balaka £££

3 Alexandra Place, Market Street TEL St Andrews (0334) 74825

This smart Indian restaurant near the town centre makes itself welcoming with tables laid with cloths, candles and fresh flowers, and looks after vegetarians with a special set meal (for two). The food is generally highly regarded, the herbs are either home grown or come from India. The korma is particularly recommended.

Open all week, exc Sun L, noon to 2, 5.30 to 12.30 **Closed** few days Jan Booking advisable. Table service. Licensed. Meat dishes. Seafood dishes. Take-aways. Children under 16 must be with parents. Wheelchair access. Access, Amex, Visa

SELKIRK Borders MAP 9

Philipburn House Hotel ££

TEL Selkirk (0750) 20747

Many have enjoyed meals at this hotel that treats vegetarians to a separate menu. Dishes can be taken either as starters or main courses: crispy Gruyère fritters with tarragon mayonnaise; Swiss raclette served in traditional manner with little potatoes, gherkins and tiny onions; broccoli and nut bake, and a spicy fondue.

Open all week 12.15 to 2, 7.30 to 9.30 Booking advisable. Table service. Tables outside. Licensed. Meat dishes. Fish dishes. Other diets catered for on request. Snacks at other times. No children under 14 at D. Wheelchair access. Accommodation. Access, Amex, Diners, Visa

STEWARTON Strathclyde MAP 11

Chapeltoun House £££

TEL Stewarton (0560) 82696

The turn-of-the-century house with delightful gardens can prove chilly – open fires are lit even in May. The four-course menu has a vegetarian main dish. Starters might be melon and pineapple sorbet with lychee, fruit coulis or a citrus dish, all very fruity; the main dish might be home-made tortellini filled with spinach served on a fresh herb sauce or the predictable filo pastry, but this time filled with fresh noodles, mushrooms, wild rice and a soft-poached quail's egg. Desserts tend towards creaminess. As we went to press, a new chef took over the kitchen, so the approach may change.

Open all week noon to 2, 7 to 9 **Closed** first week in Jan Booking advisable. Table service. Licensed, also bring your own: corkage varies. Meat dishes. Vegan dishes. Other diets catered for on request. Snacks at other times. No children. Accommodation. Access, Amex, Visa

STIRLING Central MAP 11

Littlejohns £

52 Port Street TEL Stirling (0786) 63222

One of a small chain of American-style diners serving Mexican food, pizzas and burgers. The jolly menu is decorated with old-fashioned advertisements and has a vegetarian section: vegetable lasagne, burger, pastie, pizza and stir-fry pie.

Open all week noon to 11 (5 Sun) **Closed** 1 and 2 Jan Booking advisable. Table service. Licensed. Meat dishes. Fish dishes. Snacks. Wheelchair access. Access, Amex, Diners, Visa

STRUAN (Isle of Skye) Highland MAP 11

Green House ££

TEL Struan (047 072) 293

The emphasis is on wholefoods and fresh local produce; the cooking uses traditional recipes and a wide selection of different kinds of bread are baked. Lunches may consist of a variety of soups, perhaps lentil and carrot or a cream of celery, potato and apple followed by hot dishes of pizza, walnut and orange roast, bulgur bake with piquant tomato sauce or chanterelles with butter and black pepper. In the evening a vegetarian might again find interesting soups – perhaps lovage and courgette – and main dishes of lentil and cheese layer bake, chickpea and tomato wedge and a special of savoury aubergine crumble. Puddings range from chocolate truffle cake to raspberry cranachan. The proprietors stock

Highland wines from Moniack Castle near Inverness: silver birch, meadowsweet or blaeberry.

Open Sun to Fri noon to 5.30, 6 to 9 **Closed** Easter to mid-Oct Table service. Licensed. Meat dishes. Fish dishes. Vegan dishes. Other diets catered for on request. Snacks. No-smoking area

SWINTON Borders MAP 10

Four Seasons £–££

Wheatsheaf Hotel TEL Swinton (089 086) 257

The long building, its frontage lined with stone setts, overlooks the village green. A popular bar serves meals such as vegetarian tortellini or spinach pancake. The cosy restaurant, with strong maroon décor set off by lace curtains and Danish white and maroon tableware, serves fish and game among which the lone vegetarian pancake seems dull. There is no great excitement in the starters, either: deep-fried Brie, Ogen melon with wild strawberries and passion-fruit sorbet; but all are tasty and made as far as possible from local produce. Cheeses are particularly good.

Open Tue to Sun 11.30am to 2.15, 6 to 10 **Closed** middle 2 weeks Feb Booking advisable. Table service. Tables outside. Licensed. Meat dishes. Fish dishes. Vegan dishes. Other diets catered for on request. No pipes or cigars in dining-room. Wheelchair access. Accommodation. Access, Visa

ULLAPOOL Highland MAP 11

Ceilidh Place ££

14 West Argyle Street TEL Ullapool (0854) 2103

'Living on its sixties past' is one wry comment, which might be an attraction for some. There's a strong emphasis on vegetarian food, manifested in dishes such as asparagus mousse, spinach roulade or apple and peanut soup followed by spiced aubergine pancake or gourmet vegetable pie and haggis. The lemon cheesecake is a must. The laid-back atmosphere may be dated, but the hotel, housed in linked whitewashed old cottages, is popular with its café, bookshop, craft shop and club-house complex. Worth a visit.

Open all week 12.15 to 3, 7 to 9 **Closed** 2 weeks Jan Booking advisable D. Table service D. Counter service L. Tables outside L. Meat dishes. Fish dishes. Other diets catered for on request. Snacks at other times. No smoking in dining-room. Wheelchair access. Accommodation. Access, Amex, Diners, Visa

Frigate £

Shore Street TEL Ullapool (0854) 2488

A no-nonsense café in décor and atmosphere, but the wholefood bias makes it out of the ordinary. There's a vegetarian dish to be gleaned among the starters and main courses, which tend towards snacks or pasta. Everything looks and tastes fresh, including home-made shortbread. With the mix of locals speaking Gaelic, lorry drivers from the ferries and smart French yacht cruisers, it's a fun place to people-watch while eating.

Open all week 7.30am to 9pm, L from noon (7.30am to 5pm in winter, also closed Sun) Table service. Licensed. Meat dishes. Fish dishes. Vegan and other diets catered for on request. Snacks. Take-aways. Access, Visa

WALLS Shetland MAP 11

Burrastow House £–££

Burrastow, Walls TEL Walls (059 571) 307

A tiny outpost of good cooking and accommodation for six people in a remote spot ideal for observing otters, seals and other wildlife. The library enables guests to bone up on local and natural history. A sheep tethered in the garden provides milk. The proprietors take turns cooking. Bo Simmons, being a vegetarian, provides good vegetarian choices with an inclination towards Mediterranean and Middle-Eastern dishes. Anne Prior is more likely to vary traditional British cookery. Local ingredients are used when possible and everything that can be is made at the hotel. Lunches are cheaper and more basic with soup, bean and almond pâté or polenta pie, for example. Sometimes the vegetarian dishes have to be asked for. Dinners are more ambitious, with starters such as nettle and oatmeal fritters or layered vegetable terrine, and main dishes such as chestnut and mushroom casserole, carrot and cumin soufflé pancakes or mushrooms and madeira in pastry. Summer pudding has been described as 'one of the best'. Home-made chocolates arrive with the coffee.

Open all week, exc Tue, 12.30 to 2.30, 7.30 to 9.30 **Closed** Jan and Feb, L Oct to Mar Booking advisable. Table service. Licensed, also bring your own: corkage 50p. Meat dishes. Other diets catered for on request. No smoking in the dining-room. Accommodation

Wales

ABERAERON Dyfed **MAP 6**

Hive on the Quay £

Cadwgan Place TEL Aberaeron (0545) 570445

The harbourside café with conservatory restaurant has an apiary attached and the Holgate family, who own and run it, make and sell honey as well as honey-related products. The honey ice-cream is famous. The café is open from the spring bank holiday to end of September but the restaurant does not open until early July. Organic produce is evident and bread, pies and cakes are home made; there are good teas, including a cream one. Apart from the crisp buckwheat pancakes, of which vegetarian versions are mushrooms in wine sauce or tomatoes, sweet peppers and herbs, there are vegetarian daily specials such as pasta with pesto, cauliflower and broccoli cheese bake with sweetcorn and potato fritters, and that old favourite, lasagne. Laverbread with cream cheese in a roulade may be served as a starter. Children are well catered for with a special menu and particularly flamboyant sundaes. Plainer puddings include a gooseberry pie bulging with gooseberries and served with whipped cream.

Open all week noon to 2, 6 to 9; café: noon to 2 **Closed** restaurant: first week Sept to first week July; café: end Sept to spring bank hol Booking advisable in high season. Table service D. Counter service 10am to 6. Tables outside. Licensed. Meat dishes. Fish dishes. Snacks at other times. Take-aways. Wheelchair access

The availability of vegan dishes is indicated in the details underneath the text of an entry.

ABERDOVEY Gwynedd MAP 6

Maybank Hotel ££

4 Penhelig Road TEL Aberdovey (065 472) 500

The converted terraced house at the edge of the village provides stunning views over the sea: the cooking, which has been commended, is modern British in the sense of emphasis on presentation, yet comes in larger portions than might be expected. Fresh local produce is a priority. The vegetarian dish might be lasagne, nut roast, fritters in sweet-and-sour sauce or stuffed peppers. Try the light chocolate mousse.

Open all week D 6.30 to 10, May to Oct; Fri and Sat D Dec to Apr, Mon to Thur for parties of 8 by arrangement **Closed** 9 Jan to 10 Feb, Nov Booking advisable. Table service. Tables outside. Licensed. Meat dishes. Fish dishes. Other diets catered for on request. Accommodation. Access, Visa

ABERYSTWYTH Dyfed MAP 6

Gannets £–££

7 St James Square TEL Aberystwyth (0970) 617164

A rather basic, large restaurant between the market hall and the castle, filled with potted plants. It is near the University and students and academics form a large proportion of the customers. Though it doesn't immediately conjure up a vegetarian image, about 10 per cent of its clientele is reported to be vegetarian, and there is a vegetarian platter at both lunch and dinner. This rather filling dish might take in a selection of vegetable pie, good garlicky ratatouille, moist nut and mushroom roast, spiced samosas, stuffed peppers, calabrese niçoise, cauliflower Mornay and cauliflower portugaise. Vegetables, which come from an organic farm nearby, are all cooked al dente. Of the good salads, the earthy beetroot version with chopped shallots and parsley is noteworthy. In season there is a good summer fruit tart full of black cherries, blackcurrants and apples. A soft, gooey hazelnut meringue might be on offer at other times.

Open Mon to Sat noon to 2, 6 to 9.30 **Closed** 1 week in autumn, 1 week in spring Booking advisable. Table service. Licensed. Meat dishes. Fish dishes. Vegan dishes. Other diets catered for on request. Take-aways. No-smoking area. Wheelchair access. Access, Visa

Pavilion

££

The Royal Pier TEL Aberystwyth (0970) 624888

In an area not spoiled for choice, the restaurant on the pier goes some way to make up for the shortage. Vegetarians are not overlooked, though by no means pampered. Typical starters include home-made French onion soup, reported as 'strong tasting with plenty of onions', or deep-fried mushrooms with mayonnaise, which were fresh and succulent. Main dishes have included lentil and tikka loaf and a strudel of mushrooms in flaky pastry with mustard sauce. Dessert fans might choose the fruit vacherin royale of three home-made meringues in a pyramid, filled with Chantilly cream and served with strawberry and blackcurrant coulis. Service is speedy and willing, though not always informed. The spacious dining-room provides large round tables for families. Diners are serenaded non-stop with live piano music – a plus or minus according to point of view.

Open Fri, Sat 7 to 9.30, Sun noon to 2.30 Booking advisable. Table service. Licensed. Meat dishes. Fish dishes. Vegan and other diets catered for on request. Access, Amex, Visa

BANGOR Gwynedd MAP 6

Herbs

£

30 Mount Street TEL Bangor (0248) 351249

Once purely a take-away, there is now a dining-room open for lunch and by arrangement for dinners for large parties. The menu is mainly vegetarian and vegan, but the occasional ham quiche or pizza is prepared. Take-away facilities still provide some good snacks such as garlic and cheese vegetable pie; vegetable plait; a hot pasta dish; red dragon pie or mushrooms in cream sauce; and nut burgers. Lunch could be ploughman's with vegetarian cheese, risotto, casserole or pancake. Dinner is rather more sophisticated: three starters and a couple of main courses might be coriander cream eggs with black olives; herb and nut salad balls; or fried vegetarian cheese with olives; followed by spinach roulade with lemon cream sauce and cheese crusted nut roll with tomato sauce. Vegetable fricassee or nut roast with fried onions and vegetable gravy have also featured. Puddings include walnut pie, greengage pie or apple pancakes.

Open Mon to Sun 10 to 3, D by arrangement for groups of 10 or more **Closed** Christmas, bank hols and 1 week Table service. Meat dishes. Vegan dishes. Snacks. Take-aways

BARMOUTH Gwynedd MAP 6

Lawrenny Lodge £

Aberamffra Road TEL Barmouth (0341) 280466

This hotel caters for vegetarians with a daily dish – a sample week's menu included cheese and lentil loaf with red wine and tomato sauce, spiced chickpeas with braised rice, aubergines Parmesan, filled vegetable rolls au gratin, lasagne, lentil croquettes with parsley sauce, and chilli bean casserole with pasta. It's also heartening to know that future seasons will include even more alternatives.

Open Mon to Sun 7 to 9 **Closed** Jan, Feb Booking advisable. Table service. Licensed, also bring your own: corkage. Meat dishes. Other diets catered for on request. Wheelchair access, exc WC. Accommodation Mar to Dec. Access, Visa

BETWS-Y-COED Gwynedd MAP 6

Bubbling Kettle ★ £

Holyhead Road TEL Betws-y-Coed (069 02 667)

'Home-cooked lunches' it says modestly outside this spick-and-span semi over the road from the cascading falls, and home-cooked they are, to perfection in simple style. The entrance to the restaurant, which is the front parlour, is through the garden. Pride of place is given to a painting of a champion Welsh terrier once owned by one of the cooks. Both cooks take an obvious pride in cooking, justifiably. Snacks and cream teas are served as well as lunches and a vegetarian dish of the day is always available. A thick vegetable soup, the only starter, proved tasty; a vegetarian moussaka made with fresh tomatoes, mushrooms and lentils and topped with a smoky cheesey custard could not have been better; the pastry of the apple pie and almond tart was short, flaky and did all it should, the almond flavour of the tart thankfully not that of almond essence. Unbelievably good value.

Open all week, exc Fri, noon to 5.30 **Closed** Oct to Mar exc for bookings Bookings advisable in high season. Table service. Tables outside. Meat dishes. Fish dishes. Snacks. No-smoking area

BORTH-Y-GEST Gwynedd MAP 6

Blossoms ££

Ivy Terrace TEL Porthmadog (0766) 513500

In the centre of the village on the harbour front is this bistro-style restaurant that serves some of the best food for miles around. Vegetarian options might be bean bake, pasta with broccoli, walnuts and cream or asparagus and mushroom crêpe. Children are welcome but parents are asked to bring them early in the evening.

Open Mon to Sat noon to 2, 7 to 10 **Closed** Mon and Tue Oct to Mar Booking advisable. Table service. Tables outside. Licensed. Meat dishes. Fish dishes. Vegan dishes. Other diets catered for on request. No-smoking area. Access, Visa

BRECON Powys MAP 6

Brown Sugar £

12 The Bulwark TEL Brecon (0874) 5501

Though not purely vegetarian, Brown Sugar will provide good-value basic dishes such as macaroni cheese, ratatouille, risotto or mushrooms in cheese sauce with rice. Starters are asparagus pancake and corn on the cob; salads, jacket potatoes and other snacks complete a short menu.

Open all week, exc Sun D, 10 to 9.30 (5.30 Oct to Apr) Table service. Tables outside. Licensed. Meat dishes. Fish dishes. Vegan dishes and other diets catered for on request. Snacks. Take-aways. Wheelchair access

Duke's, Wellington Hotel ££

The Bulwark TEL Brecon (0874) 5225

The coffee-shop serves four vegetarian main courses: stroganoff, pancake, nut roast and baked aubergine are samples. Try, perhaps, Glamorgan mushrooms as a starter – devilled peppers would be an alternative. Bar snacks are served, which include pizzas, baked potatoes and lasagne.

Open all week 11.45 to 5, 6.15 to 10 Table service. Tables outside. Licensed. Meat dishes. Fish dishes. Vegan dishes. Snacks. Wheelchair access. Accommodation. Access, Amex, Visa

BROAD HAVEN Dyfed MAP 6

Druidstone Hotel £

TEL Broad Haven (0437) 781221

Described by some as pleasantly idiosyncratic, by others as muddled, this hotel perched above the sea offers good-value food. Both bar and restaurant menus provide for vegetarians: starters of black-bean, mushroom and barley soup, falafel, a highly recommended tomato and orange soup or stuffed mushrooms could be followed by pinto bean enchilada, green lentil and spinach lasagne or spinach and Brie flan as main dishes. Ice-creams are alcoholic and home made and the lemon soufflé authentically tastes of lemon zest.

Open all week, exc Sun D, 12.30 to 2.30, 7.30 to 9.30 **Closed** Only party bookings Nov, late Jan, early Feb Booking advisable. Table service. Tables outside. Licensed. Meat dishes. Vegan and other diets catered for with prior notice. Wheelchair access. Accommodation. Access, Amex, Visa

CARDIFF South Glamorgan MAP 6

Armless Dragon ££

97 Wyvern Road, Cathays TEL Cardiff (0222) 382357

Many reporters enjoy the eclectic cuisine that ranges from Wales to the West Indies. The two vegetarian main dishes could be Mexican-inspired pancakes, stir-fried tofu with vegetables or a dish that beggars the usual description of 'vegetable platter' with its laverburger, pakora, stuffed pepper, spiced beans and more. Samphire and another Welsh speciality, laverballs, have featured as starters.

Open Mon to Sat, exc Sat L, 12.15 to 2.15, 7.30 to 10.30 **Closed** 25 Dec to 1 Jan Booking advisable. Table service. Licensed, also bring your own: corkage varies. Meat dishes. Fish dishes. Vegan dishes. Other diets catered for on request. Wheelchair access (exc wc). Access, Amex, Diners, Visa

Bo Zan £££

78 Albany Road, Roath TEL Cardiff (0222) 493617

Reckoned one of the better Chinese restaurants in Cardiff, the Bo Zan is unassuming and understated and attracts a loyal following for the quality of its food. A vegetarian section includes the usual monk's vegetables, but other dishes include fried vegetarian Singapore rice noodles, straw mushrooms, bean curd and cashew-nuts in sea spice sauce and variations on stir-fried vegetables. The toffee apple is good – crispy on the outside and soft and tender inside. Service can be cool.

Open all week, exc Sun L and Mon L, noon to 2, 6 to 11.30 Booking advisable. Table service. Licensed. Meat dishes. Vegan dishes. Other diets catered for on request. Snacks at other times. Take-aways. Wheelchair access. Access, Amex, Diners, Visa

Crumbs Salad Bar Ⓥ £

33 Morgan Arcade TEL Cardiff (0222) 395007

The main item in this vegetarian café is a salad bowl of six combinations; alternatively pick just one and add extras such as nuts, raisins, sweet-corn, cottage cheese or egg mayonnaise. There's fruit salad or yoghurt to follow and a selection of fruit juices.

Open Mon to Sat 9.30 to 3 Counter service. Vegan dishes. Other diets catered for on request. Take-aways. No-smoking area. Wheelchair access

De Courcey's £££

Tyla Morris House, Church Road, Pentyrch TEL Cardiff (0222) 892232

The menu has some interesting ideas, though they don't extend far into the vegetarian offering – possibly a collection of aubergines, courgettes and spaghetti tossed at your table in Neapolitan sauce. Starters are more tempting with Stilton and walnut tartlets or salad of vegetables with peanut dressing. Sorbets are home made, alternatively try the angel hair cake with carrot marmalade or smooth chocolate mousse with crisp almond biscuit. Allow plenty of time for a meal in this fascinating house. Made of wood, it was imported from Scandinavia as a kit in 1892; the inside is slightly over-lavish.

Open all week, exc Sat L and Sun D, noon to 2, 7.30 to 10 Booking advisable. Table service. Licensed. Meat dishes. Fish dishes. Other diets catered for on request. Snacks. Wheelchair access. Access, Amex, Diners, Visa

Gibsons ★ £ £–£££

8 Romilly Crescent, Canton TEL Cardiff (0222) 341264

An enthusiastic reader reports 'an exceptional choice of excellent veggie dishes. The set lunches and dinners remain value for money.' A menu of five or six dishes in each course varies according to availability: tomato and Gruyère salad, courgettes niçoise and burgundian mushrooms might be among the starters; leek and flageolet bean Véronique, Caerphilly and walnut stuffed aubergine and vegetables, and cottage cheese in filo among main dishes. Puddings include meringue in peach sauce or Hungarian chocolate pudding. A popular place for celebrations.

Open Wed to Mon, exc Mon D and Sat D, 12.30 to 2, 7.30 to 9.30 Booking advisable. Table service. Licensed, also bring your own: corkage £2. Meat dishes. Fish dishes. Vegan dishes. Other diets catered for on request. Access, Amex, Diners, Visa

New Harvesters ££

5 Pontcanna Street TEL Cardiff (0222) 232616

'A good example of its kind in the area,' is the verdict on this restaurant which always has a choice of vegetarian main dishes. An atmosphere of warmth and cosiness is enhanced by the deep red décor, with burgundy patterned carpet and dark stained pine furniture. Pot plants trail from a high shelf and baskets hang outside. There is nothing outstandingly original about the vegetarian food, but as a place to eat out with a meat-eater, it's useful. Starters such as garlic mushrooms, or a good cheesy omelette are followed by wholewheat pancake, savoury beans with cream and parsley, omelette or black-eyed peas and rice. The pancake is reckoned to be good, the vegetable filling crisp, served with completely plain accompanying vegetables. The unsampled desserts did not look quite as appetising.

Open Tue to Sat noon to 2.30, 7 to 10.30 (exc Sun D) Booking advisable. Table service. Licensed. Meat dishes. Fish dishes. Wheelchair access. Access, Visa

Noble House ££

9–10 St David's House, Wood Street TEL Cardiff (0222) 388430

Commendably there's a short vegetarian section to the menu at this Peking and Szechuan restaurant that vies with Bo Zan (see entry) as the best Chinese in the city. A hot and spicy dish of shredded carrot with lime juice, wrapped in lettuce leaves, and Top Hat, a mixture of vegetables in pastry, sit alongside spring rolls, fried bean curd and crispy seaweed. 'The enchantment of the cucumber' sounds intriguing. Décor is smart, service helpful. Sunday lunch is a buffet.

Open all week 12.30 to 2.30, 6 to 11.30 (1 to 3, 6.30 to 11 Sun) **Closed** 25 and 26 Dec Booking advisable. Table service. Licensed. Meat dishes. Vegan dishes. Access, Amex, Diners, Visa

Pepper Mill Diner ££

173 King Road, Canton TEL Cardiff (0222) 382476

This Mexican/American restaurant succeeds in being a cut above a café. It's a comfortable and pleasant place where vegetarians are not made to feel second-class citizens. The kitchen is on view and clearly shows that food is freshly prepared. Six choices are Mexican vegetarian, of which a crisp deep-fried pancake envelope stuffed with vegetables is good, and spinach and cheese enchilada generous. Both come with nachos and salad. Service is brisk. Home-made puddings are unusual: try hot American baked cheesecake, which is a custardy and mild filling in a wholemeal pastry case, or a 'rich, dark and powerful' concoction of layered mousse, meringue and chocolate base.

Open Mon to Sat, exc Sat L, noon to 2, 6 to 9.30 (10.30 Fri and Sat) Booking advisable. Table service. Licensed, also bring your own: corkage £1. Meat dishes. Fish dishes. Vegan dishes. Take-aways. No-smoking area. Wheelchair access. Access

Sage Wholefood ⓥ £

Wellfield Court, Wellfield Road, Roath TEL Cardiff (0222) 481223

This purely vegetarian and vegan restaurant serves lunches that change daily – leek croustade, lentil moussaka or spinach and mushroom lasagne, for instance, might appear on the blackboard. There is often some kind of bean or vegetable bake, casserole, nut loaf, flan or pizza. Colourful salads include brown rice with soy dressing, home-grown beansprout and raw beetroot and apple. The Carob Surprise pudding is a perhaps unexpected combination of Greek yoghurt, carob, banana and cashews. Other sweets include sugarless fruitcake and various fruit crumbles.

Open Tue to Sun 11.45 to 3 **Closed** 1 week Christmas Counter service. Tables outside. Licensed. Vegan dishes. Snacks at other times. Take-aways. Wheelchair access

Swallows Coffee House £

8 Royal Arcade TEL Cardiff (0222) 373816

This small, friendly coffee-house is popular at lunchtime, so be prepared for queues. Ham or tuna toasted sandwiches are the only concessions to flesh-eaters here. Possibilities include macaroni cheese, ratatouille, lentil stew and red beans with brown rice. Home-made cakes might be carrot, real cheesecake, apple and walnut, banana, a chocolate version made with ground almonds.

Open Mon to Sat 8.30 to 5 **Closed** bank hols, 25 and 26 Dec Counter service. Vegan dishes. Snacks. Take-aways. Wheelchair access

Topoli ££

218 City Road TEL Cardiff (0222) 494922

Vegetarian lovers of Greek cuisine do reasonably well with casserole topped with cheese and served with a dark powder that's a mild lemony spice, or the vegetarian meze, either as a starter or main course. All the components are of excellent quality. There is a special vegetarian Sunday lunch, too. Access to the dining-room is past the kitchen and the chef welcomes visitors individually. Particularly popular with theatre people.

Open all week exc Mon and Sat L noon to 2, 6 to 11.30 (12.30 Sat) **Closed** 25 and 26 Dec Booking advisable. Table service. Licensed. Meat dishes. Fish dishes. Other diets catered for on request. Take-aways. Wheelchair access. Access, Amex, Diners, Visa

CARDIGAN Dyfed MAP 6

Granary £

Teifi Wharf TEL Cardigan (0239) 614932

About a third of the menu caters for vegetarians and there is a strong emphasis on wholefoods and organic vegetables. Starters might include mushrooms in garlic, melon and ginger or hummus, while savoury stuffed pancakes with vegetarian cheese and parsley sauce, stuffed marrows, cauliflower cheese, ratatouille and kabli channa are some of the main dishes on offer. There's a selection of organic wines.

Open all week 11 to 10.30 (Thur to Sun only, Oct) **Closed** Nov to Easter Booking advisable. Table service. Counter service L. Tables outside. Licensed. Meat dishes. Vegan dishes. Other diets catered for on request. Snacks. Take-aways. Wheelchair access

Larders £

Rhos y Gilwen Mansion, Rhos Hill TEL Boncath (023 974) 378

The Gothic mansion was built 130 years ago on the site of a previous house; in 1985 there was a disastrous fire and restoration work still continues. The restaurant has been created from former larders and the sensibly brief menu of home-cooked food changes weekly. Home-made bread and rolls, cakes, scones and pies are cooked in an Aga. The one vegetarian meal might include a starter such as cheese pâté or vegetable soup (all soups are made with vegetarian stock). Possible main dishes are: peanut oat burgers, broccoli mushroom bake, lentil and tomato loaf, crêpe, or ratatouille flan.

Open Thur to Sun noon to 2.15 **Closed** Jan and Feb Table service. Counter service. Tables outside. Meat dishes. Snacks. Take-aways. No-smoking area. Wheelchair access

CARMARTHEN Dyfed **MAP 6**

Waverley ⓥ £

23 Lammas Street TEL Carmarthen (0267) 236521

The café is at the back of the wholefood store. The menu changes daily; lunches follow a fairly standard pattern of baked potato, quiche, lasagne, salads, with extra dishes such as vegetable Wellington, mushroom pancake provençale or lentil burgers.

Open Mon to Sat 11.30 to 2 Counter service. Licensed. Vegan dishes. Other diets catered for on request. Snacks. Take-aways. Wheelchair access

CHEPSTOW Gwent **MAP 6**

Castle View Hotel ££

16 Bridge Street TEL Chepstow (029 12) 70349

Vegetarians get short shrift in Chepstow but this hotel makes a real effort and offers a vegetarian menu. The creeper-clad traditional Welsh pub overlooks the ruins of the castle; the dining-room has an exposed stone wall and stripped-pine furniture. Although the menu has four dishes as starters and four as main course, they could not be described as exciting (chestnut and celery loaf, Gloucester and chive lasagne, quiche and omelette). A sample meal showed a reliance on a small repertoire of ingredients (in this case celery and cheese predominated). There may be a wait for puddings, but its worth it – moist chocolate roulade was made with good-quality chocolate and hot apricots in spiced syrup was much enjoyed.

Open all week noon to 2, 6.30 to 9 Booking advisable. Table service. Tables outside. Licensed. Meat dishes. Fish dishes. No smoking in dining-room. Accommodation. Access, Amex, Diners, Visa

CILGERRAN Dyfed MAP 6

Castle Kitchen £–££

TEL Cardigan (0239) 615055

Patrick and Mary Browne run this small cottagey restaurant with a friendly informal style and, on a short fixed-price menu, provide one dish for vegetarians: perhaps a fine spinach quiche or pancakes stuffed with spinach, nuts and garlic. Pancakes flamed in Cointreau and nectarines in brandy have been liked; pears in red wine have disappointed.

Open Tue to Sun, L noon to 3; Fri and Sat D 7.30 to 9; Tue to Thur D by arrangement Booking advisable. Table service. Licensed, also bring your own: corkage £2.50. Meat dishes. Fish dishes. Other diets catered for on request. Snacks at other times. No-smoking area. Access, Visa

COLWYN BAY Clwyd MAP 6

Good Taste Bistro £

18 Seaview Road TEL Colwyn Bay (0492) 534786

At the pedestrian entrance to the Colwyn Centre. Meat and vegetarian dishes are available. Lasagne, pizza and daily specials such as leeks in a pie crust, aubergines Parmesan, mushroom crumble, curry, spinach and almonds, cannelloni and stuffed courgettes are vegetarian choices. Menus will be devised for special occasions, for example they did one for Comic Relief.

Open Mon to Sat noon to 4.30 (2 Wed) Table service. Tables outside. Licensed. Meat dishes. Other diets catered for on request. Snacks. Mainly no smoking. Wheelchair access

CONWY Gwynedd MAP 6

Lodge ££

Tal y Bont, Nr Conwy TEL Dolgarrog (049 269) 766

The enormous menu of this commended hotel restaurant has melon and a vegetarian pâté, suitable for vegans, beginning the meal. Then there are three main dishes on the lines of lasagne, chasseur – fresh vegetables in wine and onion sauce – and mixed bean Indienne in a chilli, cumin and coriander sauce.

Open all week, exc Mon L, 12.15 to 1.45 (noon to 2 Sun), 7 to 9 Booking advisable. Table service. Tables outside. Licensed. Meat dishes. Fish dishes. Other diets catered for on request. Wheelchair access. Access, Visa

CRICKHOWELL Powys MAP 6

Bridge End Inn ££

TEL Crickhowell (0873) 810338

Although vegetarian choices are limited in this pub restaurant, it is one of the best places in which to eat in town; chilli, lasagne and mushroom and nut fettucine could be main dishes.

Open all week noon to 2.30, 6.30 to 10 Booking advisable. Table service. Licensed. Meat dishes. Vegan dishes and other diets catered for with prior notice. No-smoking area. Wheelchair access. Access, Visa

Cheese Press £

18 High Street TEL Crickhowell (0873) 811122

Above a gift shop, the café serves good wholefood lunches and snacks. You might find soup, followed by curry and lentil pasties, cauliflower cheese, quiche or vegetable bake. It's a fine place to bring the family.

Open Mon to Sat 9.30am to 4.45 (also Sun in summer) Counter service. Licensed. Meat dishes. Snacks. Take-aways. No-smoking area

DINAS MAWDDWY Gwynedd MAP 6

Old Station Coffee Shop ★ £

TEL Dinas Mawddwy (065 04) 338

On the A470 a mile north of Mallywd near Minllyn is this excellent café where lunches are generous. Everything is spotlessly clean and almost all the food (ice-cream is an exception) is home made. Choices include soup, lasagne, pizza, savoury flan and some six salads. Good honest puddings might be apple pie, Bakewell tart or chocolate cake. Before and after lunch there are scones, cakes and snacks on offer, the speciality being carrot and banana cake. Good value and one of the best places of its genre in Wales.

Open all week 9.30 to 5 **Closed** Nov to Mar, exc 1 week beginning 27 Dec Counter service. Tables outside. Licensed. Meat dishes. Other diets catered for. Take-aways. No-smoking area. No children in pushchairs. Wheelchair access

DOLGELLAU Gwynedd MAP 6

Abergwynant Hall ££

TEL Dolgellau (0341) 422238

Sweep down the tree-lined drive and arrive at a Victorian granite house surrounded by delightful grounds that slope down to a lake. A conservatory has been added to give dining space, filled with greenery. The lounge is more traditional, green and crimson, full of magazines and papers. Food is good value and well cooked, and vegetarians are provided with one main dish. Starters might consist of mille-feuille of avocado, or risotto, followed by asparagus pancakes. The short dessert menu has good gingersnaps with fresh fruit, excellent chocolate cups filled with hazelnut mousse served on minted cream and wonderful strawberry delight. Good Welsh cheeses.

Open Tue to Sat 7 to 9.30, Sun L 12.30 to 2.30 **Closed** 26 Dec to 1 Mar Booking advisable. Table service. Tables outside. Licensed, also bring your own: corkage £2.50. Meat dishes. Snacks. Wheelchair access. Access

Dylanwad Da ★ ££

2 Smithfield Street TEL Dolgellau (0341) 422870

Dylan Rowlands, the eponymous owner, describes this restaurant as being 'for *Guardian* readers' which, depending on your taste, could be a recommendation or a deterrent. Reports are full of praise for the informal and friendly atmosphere, boosted by an open fire in winter and fresh wild flowers on the tables. The cooking tends to be rich, with plenty of cream, and draws inspiration from an eclectic range of world cuisines. Vegetarian starters might include soup, perhaps tomato, orange and ginger, mushroom pâté or mushroom and leek mousse. Main dishes might include vegetable casserole in filo pastry, vegetable and almond turnover with parsley or Chinese vegetable and cashew pancake. A refreshing adaptability is displayed – for example, you can choose not to have a sauce with a dish, or to have two puddings and no starter. Puddings are worth saving space for: chilled Cointreau and orange custard is described as 'mouthwatering just to look at and even better to taste'; chocolate pudding with dark chocolate sauce has excellent texture and flavour and apple and mincemeat pancake is praised. Fresh ingredients are used whenever possible and everything is cooked on the premises, from the ice-cream to the complimentary chocolates which arrive with coffee.

Open all week July to Sept, D 7 to 9.30; Thur to Sat Oct to June, D 7 to 9.30 **Closed** Feb Booking advisable. Table service. Licensed. Meat dishes

ERBISTOCK Clwyd MAP 6

Boat Inn

££

TEL Bangor-on-Dee (0978) 780143

So named because the ferry used to cross here – the old winching equipment still stands by the wharf. An 'absolutely idyllic' setting is enhanced by a garden terrace with rock walls hung with aubretia. Being a couple of miles outside the town, the inn has few neighbours, except the church. The old red sandstone building has many good features, beams, flagstones and stone walls, thankfully unimproved. A vegetarian menu of three starters – terrine, fruitslaw and an unusual gnocchi in a tomato and cream cheese sauce – and three main courses – roulade, mushrooms provençale and vegetable and wild rice pancake, for instance – can be enjoyed at less cost than the meaty versions. The modern British style produces puddings such as golden syrup sponge pudding, as well as iced strawberry soufflé and home-made ice-creams, of which vanilla is praised. Bar snacks are also available, eaten in view of the ancient range.

Open all week, noon to 2pm, 7pm to 9.30pm Booking advisable. Table service. Tables outside. Licensed, also bring your own: corkage £3.50. Meat dishes. Fish dishes. Vegan dishes. Other diets catered for on request. Wheelchair access. Access, Amex, Visa

HAY-ON-WYE Powys MAP 6

Cygnet and Mallard Room, Swan Hotel ££

Church Street TEL Hay-on-Wye (0497) 821188

The imposing hotel has been modernised to provide a muted and luxurious restaurant, the Cygnet, and a slightly cheaper-priced bar, the Mallard Room. Both offer a vegetarian menu which changes about every six weeks. Service is pleasant and swift. Examples of dishes include a good vegetable terrine and a stunning courgette and mushroom timbale in two sauces: walnut and tomato. Main dishes might be pierogi, an ambitious attempt that was a little dry, but with a good crisp cream cheese pastry and a nut stuffing heightened by fresh coriander; or a pasta dish tossed in olive oil, rather too oily. Sauces are particularly good. Puddings, rotating in a glass display cabinet, tend towards the excessively sweet or very creamy.

Open all week noon to 2, 7 to 9.30 Table service. Tables outside. Licensed. Meat dishes. Fish dishes. Other diets catered for on request. No-smoking area. Wheelchair access. Accommodation. Access, Visa

Granary ££

Broad Street TEL Hay-on-Wye (0497) 820790

Granary is a good place for a snack or an informal and reasonably priced vegetarian meal. The friendly, characterful old barn with huge doors and high ceiling, beams abounding, is popular for lunches and teas; Tibetan roast, nut roast and curries give an idea of the repertoire. Cakes and teabreads are home made, with carrot cake and millionaire's shortbread the specialities. Expect to queue for lunch at the weekend.

Open all week, daytime only, noon to 5 **Closed** 25 and 26 Dec Counter service. Tables outside. Licensed. Meat dishes. Vegan dishes. Other diets catered for on request. Snacks at other times. Wheelchair access. Access, Visa

A restaurant doesn't have to be able to serve all items on the menu, although it should have most. If you think the restaurant is deliberately trying to mislead people, tell the local Trading Standards Officer.

LALESTON Mid-Glamorgan MAP 6

Great House ££

High Street TEL Bridgend (0656) 657644

The pleasantly unostentatious restoration of this historic house, combined with beautiful setting and good food, make this a place for a lavish meal with meat-eating companions. The menu seems light on vegetarian starters – filo cheese parcels or melon with Champagne sorbet – but things improve with a large collection of main dishes: feuilleté of vegetables with a mint-scented paloise sauce; stir-fried; curried vegetables; or almond and vegetable filo parcels. Home-made puddings and Welsh cheeses.

Open Mon to Sat exc Sat L noon to 2, 7 to 9.30 Booking advisable. Table service. Tables outside. Licensed. Meat dishes. Fish dishes. Other diets catered for on request. Take-aways. No pipes or cigars. Wheelchair access. Access, Diners, Visa

LLANDDERFEL Gwynedd MAP 6

Palé Hall ££

TEL Llandderfel (067 83) 285

Built in 1870 for a Scottish building engineer, the grey stone house with marvellous grounds occupies a magnificent position on the banks of the Dee. One of its claims to fame is still having the bath used on a visit by Queen Victoria. Country-house grandeur is accompanied by a friendly and welcoming atmosphere. The modern British menu may give a choice of starters: cream cheese pâté with chives and lemon on Cumberland sauce; fruit and vegetable kebab with saffron rice; fan of melon and poached pear with minted yoghurt. But there's only one main dish: nut and vegetable cutlet with provençale sauce, or baked courgettes filled with walnuts, hazelnuts and peppers on a honey sauce, for instance. Follow with sticky-toffee pudding, home-made ice-creams or strawberry Pavlova. Hand-made chocolates with coffee come at no extra charge.

Open all week noon to 2, 7 to 9.30 Booking advisable. Table service. Licensed, also bring your own: corkage £2. Meat dishes. Fish dishes. Vegan dishes. Other diets catered for on request. Snacks. No smoking in dining-room. No children under 12. Accommodation. Access, Amex, Diners, Visa

LLANDDOWROR Dyfed MAP 6

Old Mill £££

TEL St Clears (0994) 230836

Along the A477 between St Clears and Pembroke Dock is this extraordinary double act. One half is a transport café, which does vegetarian meals, too; the other is the restaurant proper. The family who run the duo are vegan and there is a full vegetarian and vegan menu. Start, perhaps, with deep-fried Stilton, pears filled with soft cheese, walnuts and port, or fresh carrot juice; go on to pasta with green garlic sauce, savoury pie topped with puff pastry, lentil and herb loaf with tomatoes, and mushrooms, or meatless shepherd's pie.

Open all week 7pm to 9, Sat, Sun L 11.30 to 1.30 Booking advisable. Table service. Tables outside. Licensed. Meat dishes. Vegan dishes. Other diets on request. Snacks. Take-aways. Wheelchair access. Access, Amex, Diners, Visa

LLANDRILLO Clwyd MAP 6

Tyddyn Llan £££

TEL Llandrillo (049 084) 264

Reports are unanimously positive for this comfortable, easy and friendly hotel where imagination is at work in the kitchen and prices are not extortionate. The restaurant is in an extension – previously the games room – to this Georgian stone house with pleasant gardens near the Dee. Log fires are plentifully fed and lit even on summer evenings if it's chilly. Daily fixed-price menus might include a good French onion soup, Anglesey egg baked with leeks and cream cheese, and main dishes of Italian courgette bake, sauté oyster mushrooms on a bed of oriental noodles, or vegetable filo purse. Treacle tart with Drambuie cream and apple and almond sponge cake are typical of the generally old-fashioned puddings. Breakfast is an experience: eggs are from the owners' own hens and preserves are home made.

Open all week, exc Mon L and Tue L, 12.30 to 2, 7.30 to 9.30 **Closed** Feb Booking advisable. Table service. Licensed, also bring your own: corkage £3. Meat dishes. Fish dishes. Other diets catered for on request. Wheelchair access. Accommodation. Access, Visa

LLANDRINDOD WELLS Powys MAP 6

Good Food Café ⓥ ★ £

High Street

The faded elegance of the Victorian shopfront and bare wood-panelled walls provides a homely and unsophisticated background for some good home cooking by a group of women. The noticeboard gives room to worthy ecological and alternative groups. A typical day's lunch provided lentil roll with excellent pastry and tasty filling, a bready mushroom pâté and a very deep pan pizza. Granary-style rolls are home made. A hot pudding of apple, rhubarb and banana pie, with an indefinable alcoholic flavour, was much enjoyed and the home-made vanilla ice-cream proved creamy and smooth. They don't stint on portions and the food is varied, fresh, and good value. No telephone, so no bookings.

Open Mon to Fri. 10.30 to 2.30 Counter service. Vegan dishes. Take-aways

LLANDUDNO Gwynedd MAP 6

Bodysgallen Hall £££

TEL Deganwy (0492) 84466

The glories of Bodysgallen include its fine seventeenth-century stone exterior, beautiful recently restored interior and antique furnishings. Outside are formal parterres and a walled garden. What is reckoned to be one of the best kitchens in Wales, supported by excellent service, produces vegetarian dishes that get more prosaic as they become main courses. For example, asparagus and walnut tart with thyme butter or artichoke bottoms filled with wild mushrooms are starters, whereas asparagus, vegetables and herbs in puff pastry or a vegetable tart are typical of main courses. Efforts are made for vegetarians and this would certainly be a memorable place for a visit if a financial splurge is in mind.

Open all week 12.30 to 2, 7.30 to 9.45 Booking advisable. Table service. Licensed, also bring your own: corkage £2.50 to £5. Meat dishes. Fish dishes. Vegan dishes. Other diets catered for on request. Snacks at other times. No smoking in dining-room. No children under 8. Wheelchair access. Accommodation. Access, Amex, Diners, Visa

Craigside Manor

Colwyn Road, Little Orme

As the Guide went to press, Craigside Manor was sold to Whitbread, the brewery, and chef David Harding moved to the St Tudno Hotel (see below).

Grafton Hotel £

Craig-y-Dom Parade TEL Llandudno (0492) 76814

The Grafton Hotel has a welcome wholefood bias and also serves organic wines. A standard menu yields three perpetual dishes for vegetarians – pancake, nut roast, or sunflower and sesame seed slice. Further daily specials extend the choice, perhaps Mexican pizza, Valencia slice, nut croquettes or Mexican corn roast. Prices are reasonable.

Open Mon to Sat 6 to 8.30 (Sun 1 to 1.30) **Closed** mid-Dec to mid-Jan Booking advisable. Table service. Licensed, also bring your own: corkage £2.50. Meat dishes. Fish dishes. Vegan dishes. Other diets catered for on request. Snacks. No smoking in restaurant. Wheelchair access to restaurant, wc and accommodation. Accommodation. Access, Visa

St Tudno Hotel ££–£££

North Parade TEL Llandudno (0492) 74411

All the advantages of a situation on the Promenade, good facilities (including swimming-pool) and a five-course menu with a vegetarian daily main dish make this a good place to stay. Starters tend to be fruity – grapefruit baked with natural Welsh honey and vinaigrette, assiette of melon and exotic fruits served on raspberry coulis; main courses of risotto – avocado, mixed nuts and diced fruits and rice – and pancake with fruits in mild curry sauce show the same inclination. There is a good selection of Welsh cheeses in addition to, for instance, lemon meringue cheesecake browned under the grill, plum cheesecake crumble or Bakewell tart. Very competent cooking.

Open all week 12.30 to 2, 6.45 to 9.30 **Closed** 2½ weeks Dec to Jan Booking advisable. Table service. Licensed. Meat dishes. Fish dishes. Other diets catered for on request. Snacks at other times. Wheelchair access. Accommodation. Access, Amex, Diners, Visa

LLANDYBIE Dyfed MAP 6

Cobblers ££

3 Church Street TEL Llandybie (0269) 850540

There's a strong Welsh slant to the food at this little restaurant opposite the village church. Glamorgan sausages, Welsh cheese soufflé and laverbread roulade with a garlic stuffing might figure as starters; main courses tread the more predictable path of moussaka, lentil bake and stuffed squash, though sauces are enterprising. Local organic ingredients and home-grown herbs are used whenever possible. A five-course vegetarian meal was on offer for £10 as we went to press.

Open Tue to Sat, exc Thur L, noon to 1.30, 7 to 9.30 Booking advisable. Table service. Licensed. Meat dishes. Vegan dishes. Other diets catered for on request. Take-aways. Wheelchair access. Access, Visa

LLANGEFNI Gwynedd MAP 6

The Whole Thing £

5 Field Street TEL Llangefni (0248) 724832

The café, over a wholefood shop, draws praise for its cooking of lentil lasagne, pizza, hot apricot slice with ice-cream and chocolate flapjack among other dishes. Though the range may not be great, do not be deterred; what is there is good. Particularly crowded on Thursday (market day).

Open Mon to Fri 11.30am to 2 **Closed** bank hols Counter service. Unlicensed, but bring your own: corkage 50p per bottle. Meat dishes. Fish dishes. Other diets catered for on request. Snacks. Take-aways. No smoking

LLANGOLLEN Clwyd **MAP 6**

Gales £

18 Bridge Street TEL Llangollen (0978) 860089 and 861427

One reasonably priced vegetarian dish graces the menu of the wine bar, part of a bed-and-breakfast enterprise with recently refurbished bedrooms. Typical dishes include harlequin bake, vegetable crumble, pilaff and tagliatelle. Starters might be mushroom pâté, quiche, soup or Stilton cream. Everything is home made.

Open Mon to Sat noon to 2, 6 to 10.15 **Closed** 25 Dec to 2 Jan Table service. Tables outside. Licensed. Meat dishes. Fish dishes. Accommodation

Good Taste Ⓥ £

Market Street TEL Llangollen (0978) 861425

This strictly vegetarian tea-room is a real find – a place where all food is home-cooked to order. Tables are covered with pretty cloths and diners can eat out on the patio in summer. The menu has starters of mushroom pâté, home-made soup or egg mayonnaise; main dishes include cobbler, mushroom vol-au-vent, cauliflower cheese, sweet-and-sour savouries, savoury pancake, quiche, mushroom pasty, and cheese croissants as well as salads and jacket potatoes. Of course there are also cream teas, teacakes, bara brith, and so on.

Open Mon to Sun 11.30 to 2.30, 3.30 to 5.30 **Closed** mid-Jan to 1 Mar, Wed Sept to 1 Mar Table service. Tables outside. Vegan dishes. Other diets catered for on request. Snacks. Take-aways. No smoking. Wheelchair access

LLANIDLOES Powys **MAP 6**

Great Oak Café Ⓥ £

12 Great Oak Street TEL Llanidloes (055 12) 3211

A purely vegetarian café run by a co-operative. Wholefood lunches will start with soup and go on to pizza, vegeburger or curry with daily dishes of such things as nut roast, crumble or quiche. Vegans will always find suitable cakes and there is a vanilla soya dessert instead of cream. Organic ingredients are used whenever possible and in addition to red and white wine, a choice of spiced elderberry, country fruit wines and elderflower.

Open Mon to Sat noon to 4.30 Counter service. Tables outside. Licensed. Vegan dishes. Other diets catered for on request. Snacks. Take-aways. No-smoking area. Wheelchair access

LLANTHONY Gwent MAP 6

Abbey Hotel ££

TEL Crucorney (0873) 890487

What a setting, and what a building, it's worth a visit for these alone. The restaurant is part of the ruined priory set in a circle of hills that are part of the Black Mountains. The bar is in the undercroft with its vaulted ceiling, and the south tower contains a few bedrooms, filled with huge pieces of furniture that give the impression of having been there since Walter Savage Landor brought his bride home. The dining-room, blessedly silent, has dark gloss paint, Gothic windows, a huge range and another vaulted ceiling. There are only five tables. The food is good and several vegetarian options are available – tomato and sage soup, stuffed pancake and herb terrine as starters; a mushroom pancake, nut roast and vegetable biriani as main dishes. Puddings are limited and the ice-cream comes from a shop. If you can't stay to enjoy the vegetarian cooked breakfast, at least wander out into the priory ruins and watch the bats before you leave.

Open all week noon to 2.30, 7 to 9 **Closed** mid-week Dec, one week before Easter Counter service. Licensed, also bring your own: corkage varies. Meat dishes. Other diets catered for on request. Snacks at other times. Take-aways

LLANWDDYN Powys MAP 6

Lake Vyrnwy Hotel £–££

TEL Llanwddyn (069 173) 692

This Edwardian sporting hotel is in an imposing position, overlooking the spectacular Lake Vyrnwy reservoir; a recent facelift has created an elegant and comfortable atmosphere, the sitting-room warmed by a log fire, and the dining-room outstanding. The food, with Welsh touches, is good and the single vegetarian main dish is not a Cinderella, but shows some thought and care. Try the savoury profiteroles filled with cream cheese or perhaps Stilton, port and celery pâté served with oatcakes as starters, and go on to Cantonese style vegetarian fritters with excellent sweet-and-sour sauce or a roulade on white wine and grape sauce. Fudge ice-cream is home made and hot lemon pancakes filled with raspberries and apple and flamed in brandy are praised. Worth a visit for a special occasion with non-vegetarian companions.

Open Mon to Sun 12.30 to 1.45, 7.30 to 9.15 Table service. Licensed, also bring your own: corkage £3. Meat dishes. Other diets catered for on request. Wheelchair access. Accommodation. Access, Amex, Diners, Visa

LLYSWEN Powys MAP 6

Griffin Inn ££

TEL Brecon (0874) 754241

This charming old fishing inn in the Upper Wye Valley provides a first-class meal with generous portions. The restaurant serves a selection of starters; deep-fried Stilton and garlic mushrooms, mushroom soup, and main courses of ratatouille pasta, or mushroom, asparagus and avocado pancakes (mushrooms have a rather overwhelming presence on the menu). Try the hazelnut and coffee yoghurt pudding for dessert. Bedrooms are cottagey, charming and spotless.

Open all week, exc Sun D, noon to 2 (2.30 in summer), 7 to 9 (9.30 in summer) Booking advisable. Table service. Tables outside. Licensed. Meat dishes. Fish dishes. Vegan dishes and other diets catered for on request. Wheelchair access. Accommodation. Access, Amex, Diners, Visa

MACHYNLLETH Powys MAP 6

Felin Crewi £

Penegoes TEL Machynlleth (0654) 3113

Two miles out of Machynlleth on the A489 is this café-cum-gift shop attached to a working water-driven flour mill. It's a place for good-value home-made cakes, teas and lunches. The flour for cakes and bread is freshly milled on site and eggs are free-range. Savoury dishes include jacket potatoes, nutburgers, tomato and courgette gratin and a good choice of Welsh cheeses. Welsh cakes give a local flavour, or try the chocolate fudge cake. A children's menu is offered.

Open all week, 11am to 5.30 **Closed** Oct to Easter Table service. Counter service. Tables outside. Licensed. Meat dishes. Vegan dishes. Other diets catered on request. Snacks. Take-aways. No-smoking inside. Wheelchair access (also wc)

Quarry Ⓥ £

Centre for Alternative Technology TEL Machynlleth (0654) 702400

After boning up on how to run your house without using the National Grid, by using wind power, water springs and watery sun, eat organically at the restaurant – though not all the products were grown in the tiny garden. In the high season and at bank holidays queues develop. The co-operative, which also runs the Quarry Shop in town (see entry below), makes all food freshly and comes up with pizzas, quiches, baked potatoes and a rather sorry-looking organic ploughman's. Salads are better. Such cakes as a chocolate and malt and an apple parkin are pleasantly light and trifle is a high spot. Tables outside offer a good view of the solar panels at work.

Open all week, L 12.30 to 2.30 **Closed** 1½ weeks Christmas Counter service. Tables outside. Vegan dishes. Other diets catered for on request. Snacks. Take-aways. Wheelchair access

Quarry Shop Ⓥ ★ £

13 Maengwyn Street TEL Machynlleth (0654) 702624

Run by the co-operative that also manages the café at the Centre for Alternative Technology, this wholefood counter is at the back of a shop. It serves simple, wholesome vegan and vegetarian lunches of thick, hearty soups, smoked tofu pâté, hummus, pizza, aubergine fritters, mushroom stroganoff, a rich-tasting butterbean and mushroom fricassee and various salads, among other dishes, plus home-made cakes. Opening is extended to Sundays during the summer and on bank holiday weekends.

Open Mon to Sat 11.30 to 3 (2 Thur) Counter service. Tables outside. Unlicensed. Vegan dishes. Snacks at other times. Take-aways. No smoking

MAENCLOCHOG Dyfed MAP 6

Post Office ££

Rosebush TEL Maenclochog (099 13) 205

The dining-room cum tea-room, which seats about 20, is in a working post office that is also a shop. The food is always piping hot and starters that have been singled out for praise include melon and cucumber in a dressing with a hint of raspberry vinegar; mushrooms stuffed with sunflower seeds and garlic; and guacamole with crudités. There are some five main courses, including Mexican bulgur with avocado, mushroom goulash and a corn and tomato lasagne that has a vegan version with soya white sauce. Fruit crumble and cheesecake have been well reported; cheeses on the board are local. The typical stone-and-slate building is pleasantly decorated inside and the welcome is warm.

Open all week 9 to 6, D Mon to Sat 7.30 to 9.30 Booking essential. Table service. Tables outside. Licensed. Meat dishes. Fish dishes. Vegan dishes. Other diets catered for on request. Snacks. Wheelchair access. Accommodation

MAENTWROG Gwynedd MAP 6

Old Rectory Hotel £

TEL Maentwrog (076 685) 305

Susan Herbert prefers to take advance orders for the good-value set vegetarian meal at her hotel near Ffestiniog, especially in the low season, so that ingredients are bought fresh, but there is always a meal of the day available. Dishes have a Middle-Eastern leaning and range from the simple, as in hummus, or tabouleh, to home-made soup, perhaps haricot bean, tomato and tarragon, and such main courses as Somerset pie with apple, onion, cabbage and cheese sauce. An Arabic special takes in Basmati rice, brown lentils and onions; chickpeas in tomato sauce with cumin; and cauliflower, onions and potato sauté in coriander and oregano.

Open all week 6.30 to 9.30, plus L noon to 2 May to Sept Booking advisable. Table service. Licensed. Meat dishes. Vegan dishes. Other diets catered for on request. Snacks. Take-aways. Accommodation. Access

MENAI BRIDGE Gwynedd MAP 6

Jodies Wine Bar and Bistro ££

Telford Road TEL Menai Bridge (0248) 714864

At the Anglesey end of the Menai Bridge, Jodies serves both meat and vegetarian dishes made to their own recipes. There's usually a pasta choice, perhaps with a sauce of onions, wheat, mung beans, red peppers and cream, followed by broccoli and cheese bake, stir-fried vegetables in sweet-and-sour sauce or vegetables in cream and tomato sauce.

Open all week noon to 2, 7 to 9.50 Table service. Tables outside. Licensed, also bring your own: corkage £1.50. Meat dishes. No-smoking area. No children under 5. Wheelchair access

NANTGAREDIG Dyfed MAP 6

Four Seasons, Cwmtwrch Farmhouse Hotel ££

TEL Nantgaredig (026 788) 238

One of the original stone farm buildings houses the family-run restaurant; another contains accommodation. The dining-room has bare stone walls, exposed beams and a welcome wood-burning stove. A conservatory extends the space. On the three-course menu a vegetarian might find good sliced avocado salad or melon and grapes, to be followed by a main course of perhaps cheese and spinach pie, tagliatelle with pesto, or lasagne. Excellent Italian strawberry trifle; grape and almond tart is a speciality. Crusty wholemeal bread is baked on the premises. Service is good but inclined to be slow.

Open Mon to Sat, D 7.30 to 9.45 **Closed** 1 week early Mar, 1 week late Sept Booking advisable. Table service. Tables outside. Licensed. Vegan dishes. Other diets catered for on request. Wheelchair access. Accommodation

The main criterion for inclusion in the guide is that an eating place offers a vegetarian main course on its standard menu, at all times, that is more than just an omelette, quiche or salad. If you find that a listed restaurant no longers caters for vegetarians, please inform the guide; the address to write to is on page 9.

NEWPORT Dyfed **MAP 6**

Cnapan ★ £–££

East Street TEL Newport (0239) 820575

The owner of this 'country house for guests' with restaurant is herself vegetarian, which may explain the originality of the vegetarian dishes. The lunch menu is limited – Welsh onion tart or various hot oat-based flans, of which the broccoli, orange and medley of cheeses is meatless. At dinner the menu may come up with Pencarreg cheese and pear flan with garlic mayonnaise, egg noodles with spicy mushroom sauce, or winter fruits marinated in port as starters, to be followed by summer-into-autumn pie with lemon and rum sauce, surprise layered loaf with parsley and chunky apricot sauce or dishes created from the bounty of seashore or hedgerow – samphire, laverbread, and sea spinach are regular ingredients. Accompanying vegetables are well cooked, overall the food is attractively presented and reliably excellent. There is always an old-fashioned pudding, and there might be coffee-flavoured crème brûlée or apricot and walnut ice-cream with a drizzle of liqueur.

Open Wed to Sun exc Tue D and Sun D 12.15 to 2.30, 7 to 9 **Closed** Feb, Mon to Thur D, Nov to Jan Booking advisable D. Table service. Tables outside. Licensed. Meat dishes. Fish dishes. Other diets catered for on request. No smoking in dining-room. No children under 4 at D. Wheelchair access. Accommodation. Access, Visa

NEWTOWN Powys **MAP 6**

Jays £

Ladywell Shopping Precinct TEL Newtown (0686) 625395

Mostly vegetarian, with a small selection for meat-eaters. Wholefood dishes are cooked every morning: potato and onion cheese bake, lasagne, stuffed marrow, lentil and vegetable crumble and various flans as well as pizzas and soups can be eaten at a reasonable price for lunch. Vegan dishes are sometimes available.

Open all week 9.30 to 4.30 Counter service. Licensed. Meat dishes. Take-aways. Wheelchair access

PONTFAEN Dyfed MAP 6

Gelli Fawr Country House ★ ££

near Fishguard TEL Newport (0239) 820343

Turn right past the Golden Lion pub in Newport and then follow signs. There is nothing pretentious about this old stone farmhouse where, in addition to bed and breakfast, self-catering accommodation and a swimming-pool, there is a welcome vegetarian menu. A love of cooking shines through in light lunches and three-course meals. Salads are described as 'works of art'; an apple strudel 'simply couldn't be bettered'. The simple and pretty dining-room is filled with flowers and a few antiques; service is friendly. The vegetarian menu sensibly allows dishes to be ordered either as starters or main dishes – deep-fried crispy vegetables, toasted Brie, lentil rissoles, vegetables en croûte, among others. Try good lemon mousse or tipsy bread-and-butter pudding. Organic wines are available.

Open all week noon to 2.30, 7.30 to 9.30 Apr to Oct, Wed to Sat Nov to May Booking advisable. Table service. Licensed, also bring your own: corkage £1 per bottle. Meat dishes. Other diets catered for on request. Snacks at other times. Take-aways. Wheelchair access. Accommodation. Access, Visa

Tregynon Farmhouse ££

Pontfaen, near Fishguard TEL Newport (0239) 820531

This would be a good choice for an overnight stay; the cooking has 'a leaning towards wholefood and vegetarian dishes.' The Heards have their own smallholding from which come many of the basic ingredients, such as eggs, milk, cheese and vegetables, all organically produced. All ice-creams are made on the premises without the use of eggs. The atmosphere is calm and civilised. Non-residents are recommended to book in advance. Daily menus are short and a vegetarian main dish features, such as stuffed aubergine in red wine sauce; pancake stuffed with cottage cheese, mushrooms, celery, onions, walnuts and apple; kofta; nutty cottage pie or lasagne. It might be said that the starters – banana appetiser; pink rose soup, apple and sweetcorn with a touch of beetroot; hot Pencarreg salad – show more inventiveness. Choose from one or two hot desserts, one a fruity one and a home-made ice-cream to round off the meal.

Open all week, D 7.30 to 9.30, L by arrangement Booking advisable. Table service. Licensed, but bring your own: corkage £3. Meat dishes. Other diets catered for on request. Snacks at other times. No-smoking in dining-room. Wheelchair access. Accommodation

PORTHMADOG Gwynedd MAP 6

Ship Inn ££

Lombart Street TEL Porthmadog (0766) 512990

This attractive old pub with huge open fireplace, comfortable seating and a friendly atmosphere offers traditional British cooking with a wholefood bias and at least three vegetarian meals on the menu, in both the bar and the restaurant upstairs. There is a mixed vegetable casserole or rice, peppers and almond omelette among other items.

Open Mon to Sat noon to 2.15, 6 to 9 **Closed** Feb Booking advisable. Table service. Licensed, also bring your own: corkage £1. Meat dishes. Fish dishes. Vegan dishes and other diets catered for on request. Snacks. No-smoking area. No children under 8 in bar. Wheelchair access. Access, Visa

PRESTATYN Clwyd MAP 6

Bells of St Mary's £

Mostyn Road, Cronant TEL Prestatyn (074 56) 3770

This vegetarian and meat restaurant provides home-cooked meals along the lines of a cheese and lentil loaf or perhaps a roasted cashew-nut and mushroom roast.

Open all week noon to 12.15, 7 to 10 **Closed** 25 Dec Table service. Tables outside. Licensed. Meat dishes. Vegan dishes. Other diets catered for with prior notice. Take-aways. No children after 8pm. Wheelchair access

If you book a table at a restaurant, you must turn up in reasonable time. If you don't keep your booking, or are very late, you're in breach of contract and the restaurant could sue you for compensation. Let the restaurant know as soon as possible if you can't make it, so the restaurant can reduce its loss by rebooking the table.

RHOSNEIGR Gwynedd MAP 6

Honey Pot ££

The Square TEL Rhosneigr (0407) 810302

Dinner at the Honey Pot is excellent and plentiful; vegetarians will have no need to feel uncomfortable, as, along with fish and game, there are stuffed courgettes, vegetable nest or good panzarotti – a type of lasagne. The proprietors seem genuinely interested in vegetarian cooking and with 24 hours' notice will cook a speciality of your choice.

Open Mon to Sat D 7 to 10.30 (all week July and Aug) Booking advisable. Table service. Licensed. Meat dishes. Fish dishes. Vegan dishes and other diets catered for on request. Wheelchair access. Access, Visa

ST DAVID'S Dyfed MAP 6

Warpool Court Hotel ££–£££

TEL St Davids (0437) 720300

Set on St David's Head with views of the sea, the hotel is approached up an avenue and provides above-average family holiday accommodation. The house bears the idiosyncratic marks of Ada Williams who lived there at the end of the nineteenth century and decorated it with her own sometimes erotic hand-painted tiles, and dotted the garden with fanciful grottoes. Vegetarians will find a scant choice of starters – a hot mustard-sauced salad or oyster mushroom soup with tarragon – and a solitary main course, perhaps mushroom mille-feuille in a rich cream sauce. Someone had the original idea of filling profiteroles with apples and using a lemon confit, with great success.

Open all week noon to 2, 7 to 9.15 Booking advisable. Table service. Tables outside. Licensed, also bring your own: corkage varies. Meat dishes. Fish dishes. Vegan dishes. Other diets catered for on request. Snacks at other times. Take-aways. Wheelchair access. Access, Amex, Diners, Visa

★ after a restaurant name indicates that the vegetarian cooking is especially good. A list of starred restaurants appears at the end of the book.

SOUTHERNDOWN Mid-Glamorgan **MAP 6**

Frolics **££**

Beach Road TEL Southerndown (0656) 880127

There is a paucity of vegetarian eateries in the area, so the restaurant is a small haven. Dinners might open with leek parcels, vegetable soup or garlic mushrooms, to be followed by mushroom tagliatelle, miniature mushroom pancakes or curry.

Open Tue to Sat D 7 to 10 Booking advisable. Table service. Licensed. Meat dishes. Fish dishes. Other diets on request. Wheelchair access. Access, Visa

SWANSEA West Glamorgan **MAP 6**

Chris's Kitchen ⓥ **£**

Stall 16D, The Market TEL Swansea (0792) 643455

A purely vegan market stall is a rarity, hence its inclusion in this guide. Chris cooks the Welsh cakes on the stall while you wait. Organically grown produce is used (subject to availability) in the pies and cakes and a local baker specialising in wholefood makes all the pasties, bread and cakes to Chris's recipes. There is laverbread pâté, nut/bean burger, tasty pizzas with extra toppings, curried rice and vegetables. Frozen oven-ready meals to take home include shepherdess pie, nut roast, chilli sin carne, curried chickpeas and lentil and vegetable hot-pot.

Open Mon to Sat 8.30 to 5.30 **Closed** Christmas to 2nd week Jan Take-away only. Telephone orders welcome, deliveries can be arranged. Vegan dishes. Other diets catered for on request. Snacks. Wheelchair access. No smoking

Green Dragon Bistro **££**

Green Dragon Lane TEL Swansea (0792) 641437

The restaurant is off Wind Street and, though not prepossessing from the outside and fairly basic inside, delivers good modern British cooking. Prices are particularly reasonable. Most dishes are meat or fish but a suitable meal might include mushrooms in ginger, or home-made soup to start, followed by Brazil nut roast with peppers, butterbean and tomato pie with cheesecrust, or spinach and ricotta crêpes.

Open Mon to Sat noon to 3 **Closed** Christmas to New Year Booking advisable. Table service. Licensed, also bring your own: corkage varies. Meat dishes. Vegan and other diets catered for on request. Wheelchair access. Access, Amex, Diners, Visa

Roots ⓥ ★ ££

2 Woodville Road, Mumbles TEL Swansea (0792) 366006

On the corner of the junction of Woodville and Queens Roads, parallel to the main street through Mumbles, is this vegetarian café-cum-restaurant, previously a delicatessen. A 1960s charm is lent by oriental hangings and pictures; pine tables are lit by candles and objects such as drift-wood and stones lie about. The co-operative uses mostly organic produce and will on occasion take advantage of local wild foods such as mushrooms, laverbread and samphire. They bake their own organic rolls – on Tuesdays these emerge hot from the oven. After 6.30 on four nights there is a menu of six each of starters, main dishes and puddings, all showing a creative cook. First courses of Stilton and celery pâté or hummus have been recommended; others include parasol mushroom fritters with garlic cream and basil sauce, Glamorgan sausages with laverbread sauce and a thick watercress soup. Main courses which have been enjoyed include, stir-fry of vegetables chestnut, wine casserole with cheese dumplings, spicy Middle-Eastern spinach, aubergine and chickpea couscous, tempura vegetables with gado-gado or an almond roast sadly overwhelmed by thyme, with red wine sauce; all come with huge salads. Try the light chocolate and chestnut roulade, plum and cinnamon tart, date, apple and hazelnut crumble served with soya milk vanilla custard, or an excellent gooseberry and ginger cream flan. Dessert crêpes are a speciality of the house. Lunches offer a similar wealth of choice.

Open Tue to Sat noon to 6.30, Wed to Sat 6.30 to 9; also Mon Apr to Sept Booking advisable. Table service. Tables outside. Unlicensed, but bring your own: corkage 50p per bottle. Vegan dishes. Other diets catered for on request. Snacks at other times. Take-aways. No-smoking area. Wheelchair access

TREARDDUR BAY Gwynedd MAP 6

Bay Leaf £££

TEL Trearddur Bay (0407) 860415

A restaurant that delights some, disappoints others. On the evidence of three dinners, many dishes on the extensive vegetarian menu are virtually identical, whether starter or main dish. All are huge, defeating some diners; many come loaded with virtually the contents of a fruit stall. This may be fine in a fruit salad, but do you want bananas in a savoury pancake? Sauces seem to be a motley collection of almonds, cashews, walnuts and dates, and sliced pineapple, apple, kiwi-fruit, starfruit, bananas and other fruit may be layered on top of every dish. Best to choose simple items, such as good soup.

Open Tue to Sat D 7 to 10.30, plus Sun and Mon in Aug Booking advisable Sat. Table service. Licensed. Meat dishes. Vegan dishes. Other diets catered for on request. Wheelchair access. Access, Diners, Visa

TREFRIW Gwynedd MAP 6

Chandler's ££

TEL Llanrwst (0492) 640991

The former chandler's shop has a cosy, cottagey atmosphere, an eccentric touch being given by the old school tables. In such an out of the way spot, the restaurant – 200 yards north of the bridge – needs support and deserves it. Starters might be inventions such as avocado with Stilton on toast, a good avocado with strawberries and lemon dressing or hot goats' cheese salad with sage dressing; the vegetarian main dish might turn out to be parsnip and cashew loaf with mushroom and sherry sauce, fruit and vegetable kebab, or spiced almond risotto with gado-gado or spanakopitta. Bread is home baked and rum and raisin cheesecake is good.

Open Tue to Sat D 7 to 10 Booking advisable. Table service, also bring your own: corkage £5. Meat dishes. Fish dishes. No smoking. Access, Visa

See the back of the guide for a list of restaurants awarded stars for especially good vegetarian cooking.

USK Gwent **MAP 6**

Bush House of Usk **££**

20 Bridge Street TEL Usk (029 13) 2929

Attached to a healthfood shop, the Bush House almost unbelievably transforms its daytime tea-shop appearance into a bistro at night. Chairs are assorted, tablecloths are gingham, and they sell paintings, dried flowers and pottery. The one vegetarian main dish at lunchtime is joined by another in the evening – dishes such as black-bean moussaka, nut and herb rissoles, tagliatelle niçoise, nut roast or Glamorgan sausages. A sample lunch (with a meat eater) yielded a better vegetarian lasagne (obviously home made) than the steak pie for the meat-eater. A starter of laverbread on toast, possibly an acquired taste, was salty and slightly slimy. Cherry sorbet and flapjack disappointed. Evenings, particularly Friday, may prove a better bet for vegetarians.

Open all week noon to 5.30, 7 to 10 Table service. Licensed. Meat dishes. Other diets catered for on request. Snacks. Take-aways

WELSHPOOL Powys **MAP 6**

Granary **£**

42 High Street TEL Welshpool (0938) 3198

It may not look much from the outside but the Granary, where meat and vegetable dishes co-exist, is pleasant and spacious inside, in the pine tradition. The food is turned out in generous portions and reasonably priced. There are such dishes as vegetable bake, pizza, ratatouille cheese pie, cheesy garlic pasties, quiches and jacket potatoes. Salads include brown rice, winter vegetables, coleslaw and mixed bean. All food is freshly made on the premises.

Open Mon to Sat 10am to 3 Nov to Easter, 10am to 4.30 Easter to Nov Counter service. Licensed. Meat dishes. Snacks. Take-aways. No-smoking area

Isle of Man

DOUGLAS Isle of Man MAP 9

Rafters ££

Peter Luis Department Store, 9 Duke Street TEL Douglas (0624) 72344

On the third floor of a department store, under the roof, is this attractively beamed room with sloping ceilings and big skylights, which make it airy and light. Meat and vegetarian snacks are available during the day and the lunch menu, served from noon, has a vegetarian dish that might be curry, pasta or lasagne. The emphasis is on fresh ingredients and the cooking is varied and interesting. The all-day menu has omelettes, garlic mushrooms, salads and Italian tomatoes with basil, oregano, Cheddar and Parmesan. Desserts are reported to be 'gorgeous' – for example, a 'big, puffy, creamy concoction' of an almond meringue. Excellent value.

Open Mon to Sat 10 to 5 Booking advisable. Table service. Licensed. Meat dishes. Seafood dishes. Other diets catered for on request. Snacks. Wheelchair access

ST JOHN'S Isle of Man MAP 9

Olde Tynwald House £–££

Main Road TEL St John's (0624) 801285

There have been good reports for this well-lit, dark-wood furnished restaurant opposite Tynwald Hill, which offers a separate and extensive vegetarian menu. Particular pains are taken to give a personal service: bookings are spaced so that time can be given to discussion of customers' wishes in a way that non-islanders might find almost too leisurely. Though both vegetarian and non-vegetarian menus are usually offered, it is best to mention a vegetarian preference when booking. There's also a good choice of vegan dishes, and all food is freshly cooked and well presented. Of the starters, probably the most interesting is quesadilla – a square, crisp pancake stuffed with cheese and onion. Main courses include stuffed peppers, pasta, lentil and cheese bake, dhal, mushroom stroganoff and cutlets. Chips are reckoned to be 'some of the best' and the sweets trolley is good. Excellent value for money.

Open Tue to Sat noon to 2, 7.30 to 9.30 Booking advisable. Table service. Licensed. Meat dishes. Fish dishes. Vegan dishes. Wheelchair access. Access, Visa

Alphabetical list of restaurants

Aagrah, Pudsey, West Yorkshire
Aagrah, Shipley, West Yorkshire
Abbey Green, Chester, Cheshire
Abbey Hotel, Llanthony, Gwent
Abergwynant Hall, Dolgellau, Gwynedd
Acorn, Church Stretton, Shropshire
Adil, Birmingham, West Midlands
Ajimura, WC2, London
Alfresco, Folkestone, Kent
Almeida Theatre Wine Bar, N1, London
Almshouses, Durham, Co Durham
Al-Omaraa, W2, London
Ana's Bistro, Kenilworth, Warwickshire
Andrew Edmunds, W1, London
Angel, Ilfracombe, Devon
Angel Food, Tiverton, Devon
Angel Hotel, Bury St Edmunds, Suffolk
Angel Inn, Stoke-By-Nayland, Suffolk
Annie's, Brighton, East Sussex
Apple Charlotte, Ledbury, Hereford & Worcester
Argyll Hotel, Isle of Iona, Strathclyde
Ark, Erpingham, Norfolk
Armadillo, Liverpool, Merseyside
Armless Dragon, Cardiff, South Glamorgan
Artistes Gourmands/ Café Des Artistes, Nottingham, Nottinghamshire
As You Like It, Henley On Thames, Oxfordshire
Au Provencal, SE24, London
Auberge De Provence, SW1, London
Baalbek, SW5, London
Baba Bhel Poori House, W2, London
Babbity Bowster, Glasgow, Strathclyde
Baedekers, Oxford, Oxfordshire
Bahn Thai, W1, London
Bakers, Bristol, Avon
Bakers Arms, Chipping Campden, Gloucestershire
Balbir's Vegetarian Ashoka, Glasgow, Strathclyde
Baldry's Wholefood, Grasmere, Cumbria
Bambayo, N8, London
Bamboo Garden, Edinburgh, Lothian
Bandung, Oxford, Oxfordshire
Banks, Bideford, Devon
Barn Owls, Pulborough, West Sussex
Barnaby's Bistro, Southsea, Hampshire
Basil's, Glasgow, Strathclyde
Bay Leaf, Trearddur Bay, Gwynedd
Bay Tree, Sheffield, South Yorkshire
Beaumonts Health Stores, Bury St Edmunds, Suffolk
Bedlington Café, W4, London
Beech, NW5, London
Bell, Aston Clinton, Buckinghamshire
Bell's Diner, Bristol, Avon
Bellamy's Brasserie, N16, London
Bells of St Mary's, Prestatyn, Clwyd
Bengal Dynasty, Knaresborough, North Yorkshire
Bengal Lancer, NW5, London
Bennett & Luck, N1, London
Berties Bistro, Elland, West Yorkshire
Bettys, Harrogate, North Yorkshire
Bettys, Ilkley, West Yorkshire
Bettys, Northallerton, North Yorkshire
Bettys, York, North Yorkshire
Bharat, Bradford, West Yorkshire
Bhel Poori House, N1, London
Bishops Mill, Salisbury, Wiltshire
Bistro, Forres, Grampian
Black Tiles, Martlesham, Suffolk
Blake Head, York, North Yorkshire
Blossoms, Leicester, Leicestershire
Blossoms, Borth-Y-Gest, Gwynedd
Blue Bell, Chester, Cheshire
Blue Elephant, SW6, London
Bluecoat Chambers Bistro, Liverpool, Merseyside
Boat Inn, Erbistock, Clwyd
Bobby's, Leicester, Leicestershire
Bobsleigh, Bovingdon, Hertfordshire
Bodysgallen Hall, Llandudno, Gwynedd
Bombay Brasserie, SW7, London
Bottle and Glass, Aylesbury, Buckinghamshire
Bowlish House, Shepton Mallet, Somerset
Bozan, Cardiff, South Glamorgan
Brambles, St Andrews, Fife
Brann's, Winchester, Hampshire
La Brasserie, Morpeth, Northumberland
Brasserie, Truro, Cornwall

Clock House, Barnet, Hertfordshire
Clouds, Plymouth, Devon
Cnapan, Newport, Dyfed
Cobblers, Llandybie, Dyfed
Cocina, Leeds, West Yorkshire
Cocked Hat, Coventry, West Midlands
Coconut Grove, Edinburgh, Lothian
Coconut Willy's, Stockport, Greater Manchester
Coffee House, Cirencester, Gloucestershire
Collin House, Broadway, Hereford & Worcester
Connolly's, SW15, London
Continental Flavour, Tunbridge Wells, Kent
Cook's Delight, Berkhamsted, Hertfordshire
Coolings, Exeter, Devon
Copper Inn, Pangbourne, Berkshire
Cordon Vert, SW19, London
Coriander, Bournemouth, Dorset
Corianders, Bexhill On Sea, East Sussex
Cork & Bottle, WC2, London
Cornerhouse, Manchester, Greater Manchester
Cornerstone, Ashford, Kent
Cornerstone Coffee House, Birmingham, West Midlands
Corse Lawn House Hotel, Corse Lawn, Gloucestershire
Cotehele Barn, Saltash, Cornwall
Cottage In The Wood, Malvern Wells, Hereford & Worcester
Country Kitchen, Southsea, Hampshire
Country Kitchen, Windsor, Berkshire
Country Life, W1, London
Craigside Manor, Llandudno, Gwynedd
Cranes, Cranbrook, Kent
Cranks, London (× 6)
Cranks, Dartington, Devon
Cretingham Bell, Debenham, Suffolk
Crispin's, Dulverton, Somerset
Crofters, Witham, Essex
Cromwellian, Kirkham, Lancashire
Crown, Southwold, Suffolk
Crown & Sandys, Ombersley, Hereford & Worcester
Crowns, Haslemere, Surrey
Crowthers, SW14, London
Crumbs, Carnoustie, Tayside
Crumbs Salad Restaurant, Cardiff, South Glamorgan
Cuilfail Hotel, Kilmelford, Strathclyde
Culloden, Inverness, Highland
Culloden House, Inverness, Highland
Curlew Café, Otley, West Yorkshire
Curry Kuteer, Stafford, Staffordshire
Cygnet and Mallard Room, Swan Hotel, Hay-On-Wye, Powys
Darlington Arts Centre Bistro, Darlington, Co Durham
Days Of The Raj, Birmingham, West Midlands
De Blank's, SW7, London
De Courcey's Cardiff, South Glamorgan
Deals, SW10, London
Demuth's Coffee House, Bath, Avon
Denbigh Arms, Lutterworth, Leicestershire
Dent Craft Centre, Dent, Cumbria
Diana's Diner, WC2, London
Dinham Hall, Ludlow, Shropshire
Dinham Weir, Ludlow, Shropshire
Dining Room, SE1, London
Diwana Bhel Poori, NW1, London
Dizzi Heights, Loughborough, Leicestershire
Dobson Restaurant, Linden Hall, Morpeth, Northumberland
Dolphin Brasserie, SW1, London
Doric Wine Bar, Edinburgh, Lothian
Down to Earth, Gloucester, Gloucestershire
Dr B's Kitchen, Harrogate, North Yorkshire
Dragon House, Newcastle Upon Tyne, Tyne & Wear
Dragon Pearl, Edinburgh, Lothian
Druid Inn, Birchover, Derbyshire
Druidstone Hotel, Broad Haven, Dyfed
Druimard Country House, Dervaig, Isle of Mull
Drunken Duck Inn, Ambleside, Cumbria
Duke's, Lancaster, Lancashire
Duke's, Wellington Hotel, Brecon, Powys
Dukes Hotel, SW1, London
Dumb Waiter, Todmorden, West Yorkshire
Dylans, Hanley, Staffordshire

Salad House, Chichester, West Sussex
Sally Ann Café, Worcester, Hereford & Worcester
La Santé, Birmingham, West Midlands
Sara's Kitchen, Tideswell, Derbyshire
Sarang, Derby, Derbyshire
Scoffs, Bath, Avon
Scott's, Much Wenlock, Shropshire
Seasons, W1, London
Seaview Hotel, Seaview, Isle Of Wight
Seeds, Edinburgh, Lothian
Seend Bridge Farm, Seend, Wiltshire
Shahanshah, Southall, Greater London
Shahee Bhelpoori, SW16, London
Shama Tandoori, Nottingham, Nottinghamshire
Shampers, W1, London
Shehbaaz, Aberdeen, Grampian
Shepherd's Purse, Whitby, North Yorkshire
Ship, Gateshead, Tyne & Wear
Ship Inn, Porthmadog, Gwynedd
Shiraz, Bradford, West Yorkshire
Singing Chef, Ipswich, Suffolk
Sir Toby's, Stratford Upon Avon, Warwickshire
Slims, Brighton, East Sussex
Sloops, Bideford, Devon
Soho Soho, W1, London
Le Soleil, E17, London
Something Else, N1, London
Sonny's, SW13, London
Sous Le Nez, Ilkley, West Yorkshire
South Of The Border, SE1, London
Spices, N16, London
Spinning Wheel, Hadleigh, Suffolk
Spread Eagle, SE10, London
Square Cat, Scarborough, North Yorkshire
Sree Krishna, SW17, London
Sri Siam, W1, London
Stables At Abbeydore Court Gardens, Abbey Dore, Hereford & Worcester
Stane Street Hollow, Pulborough, West Sussex
Stannary, Tavistock, Devon
Stanneylands Hotel, Wilmslow, Cheshire
Stanton's, Fowey, Cornwall
Stile, Willington, Co Durham
Ston Easton Park, Ston Easton, Somerset
Stone Close, Dent, Cumbria
Stones, Avebury, Wiltshire
Strawberryfields Bistro, Leeds, West Yorkshire
Sundial, Herstmonceux, East Sussex
Sunflower, Peebles, Borders
Sunflower Country Kitchen, Edinburgh, Lothian
Suruchi, N1, London
Surya, NW6, London
Sutherlands, W1, London
Swallows, Cardiff, South Glamorgan
Swan Hotel, Leighton Buzzard, Bedfordshire
Swinsty Tea Garden, Fewston, North Yorkshire
Szechuan House, Edinburgh, Lothian
Tandoori Nights, Newcastle Upon Tyne, Tyne & Wear
Tarantula, NW1, London
Tarts, Bath, Avon
Tate Gallery Coffee Shop, Liverpool, Merseyside
Taylors, York, North Yorkshire
Tea Rooms, Des Artistes, SW8, London
Tea Shoppe, Dunster, Somerset
Teignworthy Hotel, Chagford, Devon
Ten, Nottingham, Nottinghamshire
That Café, Manchester, Greater Manchester
Theatre Museum Café, WC2, London
Theatre Royal, Plymouth, Devon
Thin End, St Austell, Cornwall
Third Eye Centre, Glasgow, Strathclyde
Thornbury Castle, Thornbury, Avon
Three Chimneys, Dunvegan, Isle of Skye
Three Horseshoes, Powerstock, Dorset
Three Rowans, Kildonan, Highland
Thymes, Bideford, Devon
Tiffin, Croydon, Surrey
Tiffins On The Stray, Harrogate, North Yorkshire
Tiltyard Restaurant, East Molesey, Surrey
Tithe Barn Restaurant, Guildford, Surrey
Top Table, Burnley, Lancashire
Topkapi, W1, London
Topoli, Cardiff, South Glamorgan
Toppers, Topsham, Devon
Town House, Southampton, Hampshire
Treehouse, Norwich, Norfolk
Tregynon Farmhouse, Pontfaen, Dyfed
Trelissick Garden, Feock, Cornwall
Truffles, Easingwold, North Yorkshire

Restaurants awarded a star

A star has been awarded to restaurants that the guide feels have achieved an especially good standard of vegetarian cooking.

London

Baba Bhel Poori House, W2
Bhel Poori House, N1
Burts, W1
Cherry Orchard, E2
Chutneys, NW1
Country Life, W1
Diwana Bhel Poori, NW1
Food For Thought, WC2
Greenhouse, W1
Leith's, W1
Mary Tandoori, E1
Mildred's, W1
Neal's Yard Bakery & Tea Room, WC2
Rani, N3
Ravi Shankar, NW1
Sabras, NW10
Spices, N16
Sree Krishna, SW17
Sri Siam, W1
Tarantula, NW1
The Place Below, EC2
Veganomics, SE13

England

CHESHIRE
Chester, *Abbey Green*

CORNWALL
St Agnes, *Frins*, *Porthvean Hotel*

CO DURHAM
Shotley Bridge, *Manor House Inn*

CUMBRIA
Ambleside, *Harvest Vegetarian*
Cockermouth, *Quince & Medlar*
Dent, *Dent Crafts Centre*
Grasmere, *Lancrigg Vegetarian Country House Hotel*
Kendal, *Moon*
Kirkby Lonsdale, *Lupton Tower*

DERBYSHIRE
Birchover, *Druid Inn*
Chisworth, *Woodheys Farm*
Hope, *Poachers Arms*

DEVON
Barnstaple, *Heavens Above*
Ilfracombe, *Angel*
Newton Poppleford, *Jolly's*
Tavistock, *Stannary*

EAST SUSSEX
Brighton, *Food for Friends*

GLOUCESTERSHIRE
Corse Lawn, *Corse Lawn House Hotel*

GREATER MANCHESTER
Manchester, *That Café*

HAMPSHIRE
Southampton, *Town House*

HEREFORD & WORCESTER
Hereford, *Gaffers*

LANCASHIRE
Cleveleys, *Cleveleys Wholefood & Vegetarian Restaurant*

MERSEYSIDE
Liverpool, *Everyman Bistro*

NORFOLK
Erpingham, *Ark*
Holt, *Yetman's*
King's Lynn, *Garbo's*
Wells-next-the-Sea, *Moorings*

NORTHUMBERLAND
Otterburn, *Redesdale Arms Hotel*

NORTH YORKSHIRE
Fewston, *Swinsty Tea Garden*
Harrogate, *Tiffins on the Stray*
Whitby, *Magpie Café*
York, *Blake Head*
Kites

NOTTINGHAMSHIRE
Nottingham, *Jack Sprats*

OXFORDSHIRE
Watlington, *Well House*

SOMERSET
Glastonbury, *Ploughshares Café*
Montacute, *Milk House*
Shepton Mallet, *Bowlish House*

SOUTH YORKSHIRE
Sheffield, *Just Cooking*

SURREY
Croydon, *Hockneys*
Richmond, *Richmond Harvest*

TYNE & WEAR
Newcastle upon Tyne, *Dragon House*

WARWICKSHIRE
Leamington Spa, *Wishing Well*

WEST MIDLANDS
Birmingham *Nutters*
Wild Oats
Ryton-on-Dunsmore, *Ryton Gardens Café*

WEST SUSSEX
Plaistow, *Clements*

WEST YORKSHIRE
Todmorden, *Dumb Waiter*

WILTSHIRE
Avebury, *Stones*

Scotland

GRAMPIAN
Aberdeen, *Jaws Café*

LOTHIAN
Edinburgh, *Helios Fountain*
Hendersons
Kalpna

STRATHCLYDE
Glasgow, *Buttery*
Third Eye Centre

Wales

DYFED
Pontfaen, *Gelli Fawr Country House*
Newport, *Cnapan*

GWYNEDD
Betws-y-Coed, *Bubbling Kettle*
Dolgellau, *Dylanwad Da*
Dinas Mawddy, *Old Station Coffee Shop*

POWYS
Llandrindod Wells, *Good Food Café*
Machynlleth, *Quarry Shop*

SOUTH GLAMORGAN
Cardiff, *Gibsons*

WEST GLAMORGAN
Swansea, *Roots*

Restaurants serving only vegetarian food

* indicates a vegan restaurant.

London

Baba Bhel Poori House, W2
Bennett & Luck, N1
Bhel Poori House, N1
Cherry Orchard, E2
Chutneys, NW1
Cordon Vert, SW19
Cranks
**Country Life*, W1
Dining Room, SE1
Diwana Bhel Poori, NW1
**East West*, EC1
Food for Thought, WC2
Gate, W6
Govinda's, W1
Greenhouse, W1
Kastoori, SW17
Mandeer, W1
Manna, NW3
Millwards, N16
Neal's Yard Bakery & Tea Room, WC2
Nuthouse, W1
Raj Bhel Poori House, NW1
Rani, N3
Ravi Shankar, NW1
Raw Deal, W1
Sabras, NW10
Seasons, W1
Shahee Bhelpoori, SW16
Le Soleil, E17
Something Else, N1
Spices, N16
Suruchi, N1
Tarantula, NW1
The Place Below, EC2
**Veganomics*, SE13
Wilkins, SW1
Windmill, SW6
Woodlands, W1
Yours Naturally, WC2
ZZZZZZ's Café, WC1

England

AVON
Bath, *Broad Street Café*
Demuth's
Hat and Feather
Huckleberry's
Scoffs
Bristol, *Cherries Vegetarian Bistro*
McCreadies
Millwards

BERKSHIRE
Windsor, *Chaos Café*

CAMBRIDGESHIRE
Cambridge, *Nettles*
King's Pantry

CHESHIRE
Chester, *Abbey Green*

CORNWALL
Launceston, *Greenhouse*
Penzance, *Olive Branch*
St Ives, *Woodcote Hotel*

CO DURHAM
Barnard Castle, *Priors*

CUMBRIA
Ambleside, *Harvest Vegetarian*
Zeffirelli's
Cockermouth, *Quince & Medlar*
Grasmere, *Lancrigg Vegetarian Country House Hotel*
Kendal, *Waterside Wholefoods*
Kirkby Lonsdale, *Lupton Tower*

DERBYSHIRE
Derby, *Sarang*
Rowsley, *Caudwell's Country Parlour*

DEVON
Barnstaple, *Heavens Above*
Bideford, *Thymes*
Dartington, *Cranks*
Exeter, *Herbies Wholefood*
Exmouth, *Round the Bend*
Newton Poppleford, *Jolly's*
Plymouth, *Plymouth College of Further Education*
Tavistock, *Stannary*
Tiverton, *Reapers*
Totnes, *Willow*

DORSET
Bournemouth, *Henry's Wholefood*

EAST SUSSEX
Bexhill-on-Sea, *Corianders*
Brighton, *Food for Friends*
Slims
Hastings, *Pure Treats*

GLOUCESTERSHIRE
Gloucester, *Down to Earth*
Stroud, *Mother Nature*

GREATER LONDON
Southall, *Shahanshah*

GREATER MANCHESTER
Altrincham, *Nutcracker*
Manchester, *Greenhouse*
Greens
On The Eighth Day
Oldham, *Woody's*
Stockport, *Coconut Willy's*

HAMPSHIRE
Havant, *Nutmeg*
Southampton, *Flying Teapot*
Town House

HEREFORD & WORCESTER
Great Malvern, *Only Natural*
St Anne's Well
Hereford, *Gaffers*
Nutters
Worcester, *Sally Ann Café*

HERTFORDSHIRE
Berkhamsted, *Cook's Delight*

KENT
Chatham, *Food for Living Eats*
Folkestone, *Holland & Barrett*

LANCASHIRE
Cleveleys, *Cleveleys Wholefood & Vegetarian Restaurant*
Lancaster, *Libra*
Warehouse Café
Preston, *Roobarb*

LEICESTERSHIRE
Leicester, *Bread and Roses*
Chaat House
Good Earth
Loughborough, *Dizzi Heights*

LINCOLNSHIRE
Grantham, *Ferns*
*Lincoln, *Love & Barley*

MERSEYSIDE
Liverpool, *Greenbank*

NORFOLK
Norwich, *Treehouse*

NORTH YORKSHIRE
Fewston, *Swinsty Tea Garden*
Harrogate, *Tiffins on the Stray*
Scarborough, *Gemini*
Skipton, *Herbs*
Whitby, *Shepherd's Purse*
York, *Blake Head*
Millers Yard Café

NOTTINGHAMSHIRE
Nottingham, *Maxine's Salad Table*
**Rita's Café*
Ten

SHROPSHIRE
Ironbridge, *Olivers*
Shrewsbury, *Good Life*

SOMERSET
Castle Cary, *Old Bakehouse*
*Glastonbury, *Ploughshares Café*
Rainbow's End Café
Wells, *Good Earth*

STAFFORDSHIRE
Hanley, *Dylans*

SUFFOLK
Bury St Edmunds, *Beaumont's Health Stores*

SURREY
Croydon, *Hockneys*
Richmond, *Richmond Harvest*
Surbiton, *Pavement*

WARWICKSHIRE
Leamington Spa, *Wishing Well*
Stratford-upon-Avon *Café Natural*

WEST MIDLANDS
Birmingham, *Gingers*
Wild Oats
Ryton-on-Dunsmore, *Ryton Gardens Café*

WEST SUSSEX
Plaistow, *Clements*
Worthing, *Poppies*

WEST YORKSHIRE
Leeds, *Hansa*
Otley, *Curlew Café*

WILTSHIRE
Avebury, *Stones*

Scotland

GRAMPIAN
Aberdeen, *Jaws Café*

HIGHLAND
Invergarry, *Glendale Guest House*

LOTHIAN
Edinburgh, *Helios Fountain*
Hendersons
Kalpna
Lachana
Seeds

STRATHCLYDE
Glasgow, *Balbir's Vegetarian Ashoka*
Basil's
Third Eye Centre

Wales

CLWYD
Llangollen, *Good Taste*

DYFED
Carmarthen, *Waverley*

POWYS
Llanidloes, *Great Oak Café*
Llandrindod Wells, Good Food Café
Machynlleth, *Quarry*
Quarry Shop

SOUTH GLAMORGAN
Cardiff, *Crumbs Salad Bar*
Sage Wholefood

WEST GLAMORGAN
*Swansea, *Chris's Kitchen*
Roots

Maps

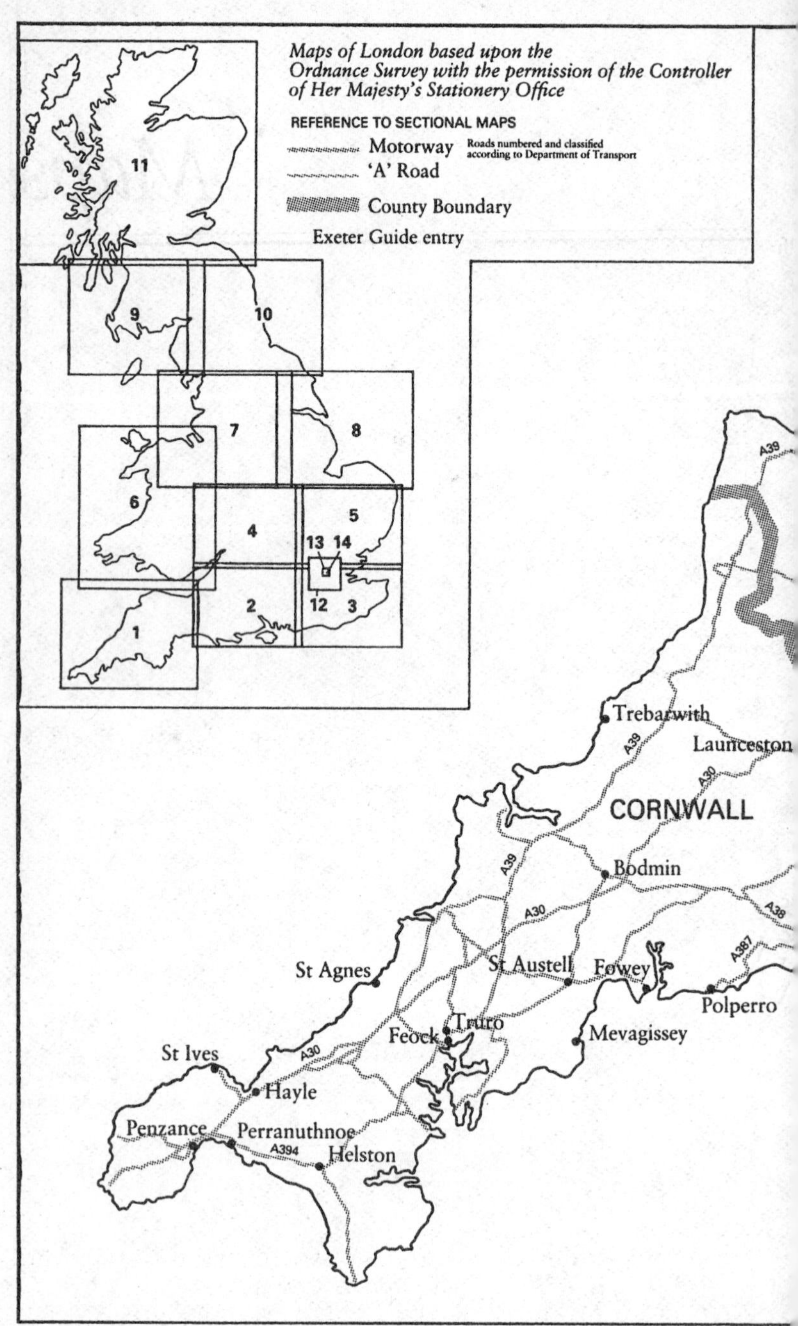
Maps of London based upon the Ordnance Survey with the permission of the Controller of Her Majesty's Stationery Office
REFERENCE TO SECTIONAL MAPS
Motorway
Roads numbered and classified according to Department of Transport
'A' Road
County Boundary
Exeter Guide entry
11
9
10
7
8
6
4
5
13
14
2
12
3
1
CORNWALL
Trebarwith
Launceston
Bodmin
St Agnes
St Austell
Fowey
Polperro
Truro
Feock
Mevagissey
St Ives
Hayle
Penzance
Perranuthnoe
Helston
A39
A30
A38
A387
A394

MAP 1

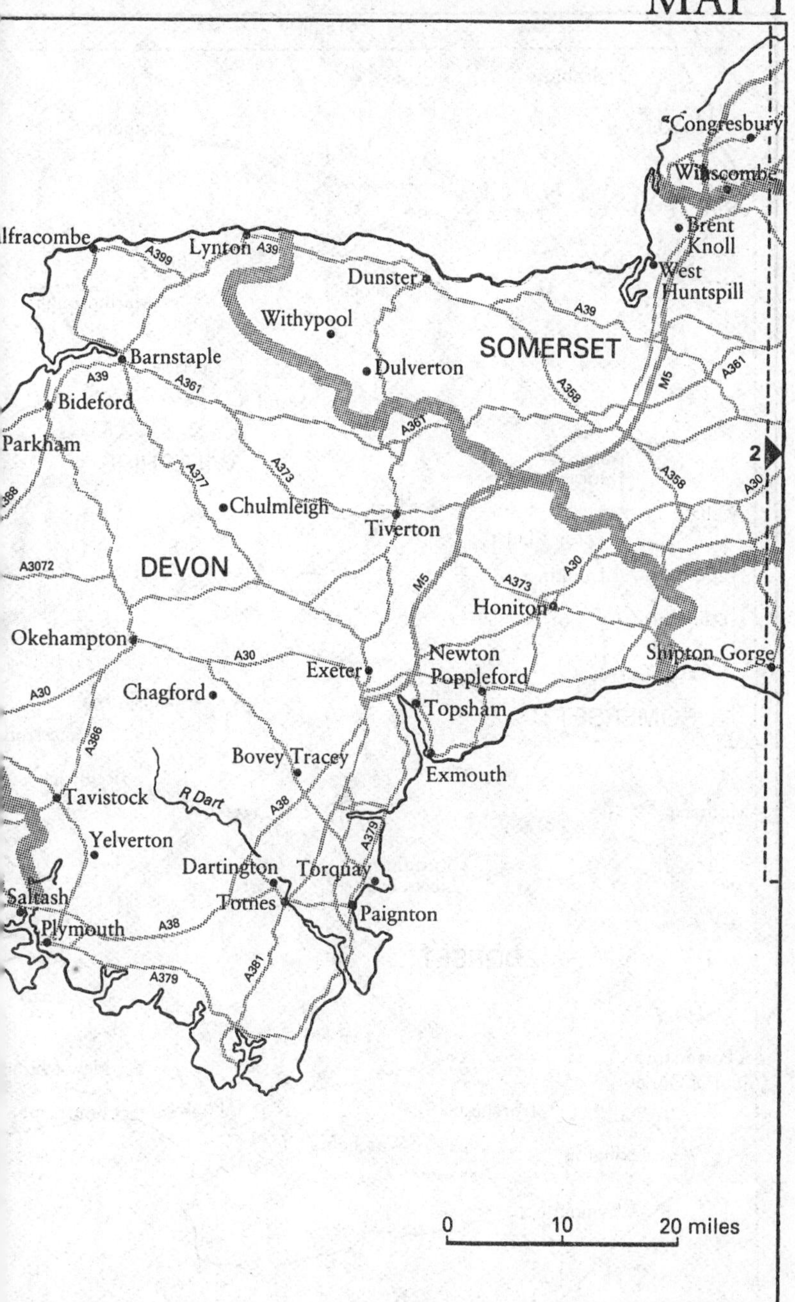

Congresbury
Winscombe
Brent Knoll
West Huntspill
Ilfracombe
Lynton
A39
A399
Dunster
Withypool
SOMERSET
Barnstaple
Dulverton
A39
A361
A358
M5
A361
Bideford
Parkham
A361
A377
A373
2
A358
A30
Chulmleigh
Tiverton
A3072
DEVON
M5
A373
A30
Honiton
Okehampton
A30
Newton Poppleford
Shipton Gorge
Exeter
A30
Chagford
Topsham
A386
Bovey Tracey
Exmouth
Tavistock
R Dart
A38
A379
Yelverton
Dartington
Torquay
Saltash
Totnes
Paignton
Plymouth
A38
A381
A379
0
10
20 miles

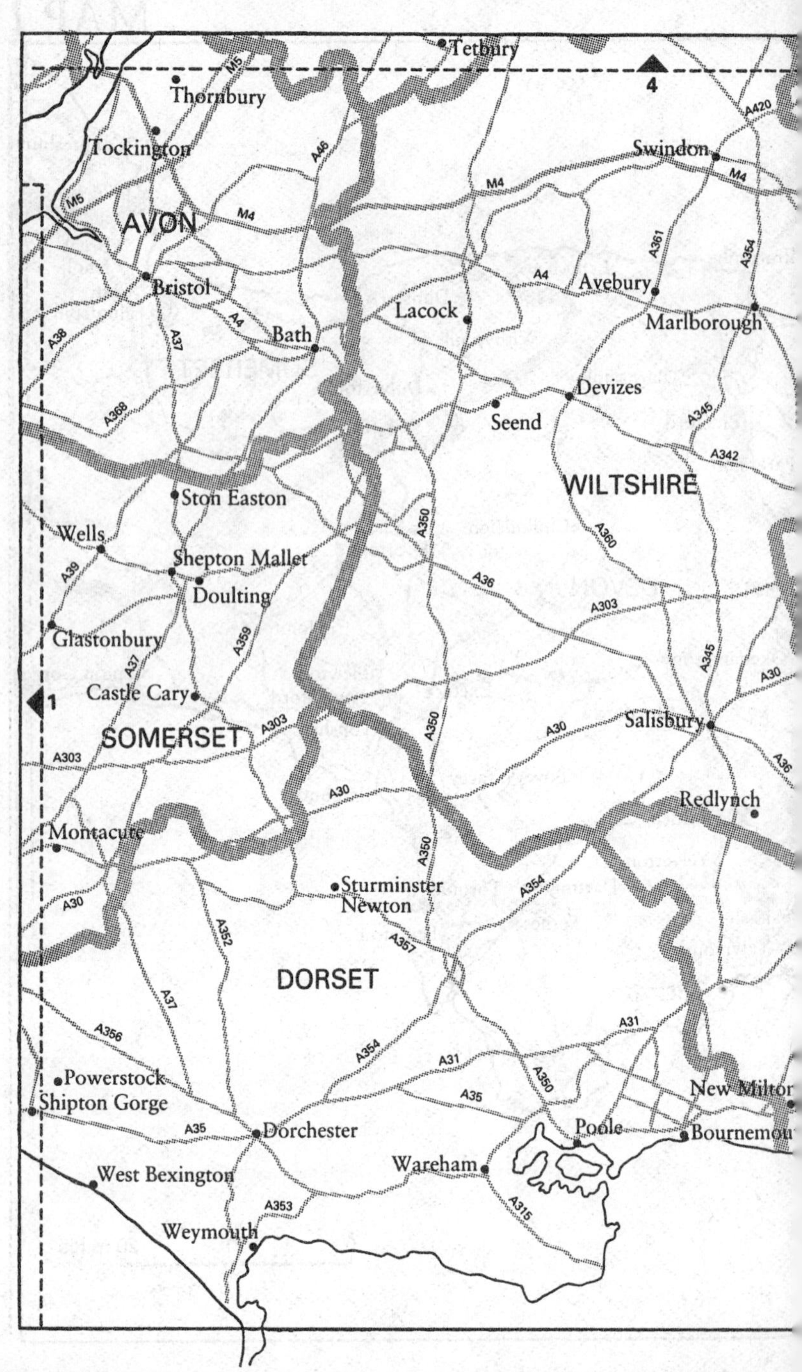

Tetbury
4
Thornbury
M5
Tockington
A46
Swindon
A420
M4
M5
AVON
M4
A361
A354
A4
Avebury
Bristol
Lacock
Marlborough
A4
Bath
A38
A37
Devizes
A368
Seend
A345
A342
WILTSHIRE
Ston Easton
A350
Wells
A360
Shepton Mallet
A39
Doulting
A36
A303
Glastonbury
A359
A37
A345
A30
1
Castle Cary
SOMERSET
A303
A350
A30
Salisbury
A303
A36
A30
Redlynch
Montacute
A350
A30
Sturminster
Newton
A354
A352
A357
DORSET
A37
A31
A356
A354
A31
A350
Powerstock
A35
New Milton
Shipton Gorge
A35
Dorchester
Poole
Bournemou
Wareham
West Bexington
A353
A315
Weymouth

MAP 2

Sutton Courtenay
Beaconsfield
Colnbrook
Henley-on-Thames
Taplow
Eton
Windsor
Pangbourne
M4
Reading
Hungerford
BERKSHIRE
A4
A338
A34
Wokingham
Camberley
A30
M3
A343
Guildford
Farnham
M3
A30
A303
A31
Godalming
HAMPSHIRE
Chawton
A343
A30
A34
Ovington
A31
Haslemere
Plaistow
Winchester
A272
3
A32
A272
A3
A36
M27
A286
Chilgrove
Southampton
Havant
A27
Lyndhurst
Chichester
Beaulieu
Portsmouth
Southsea
Seaview
A3054
A3054
ISLE OF
WIGHT
A3055
A3020
0
5
10 miles

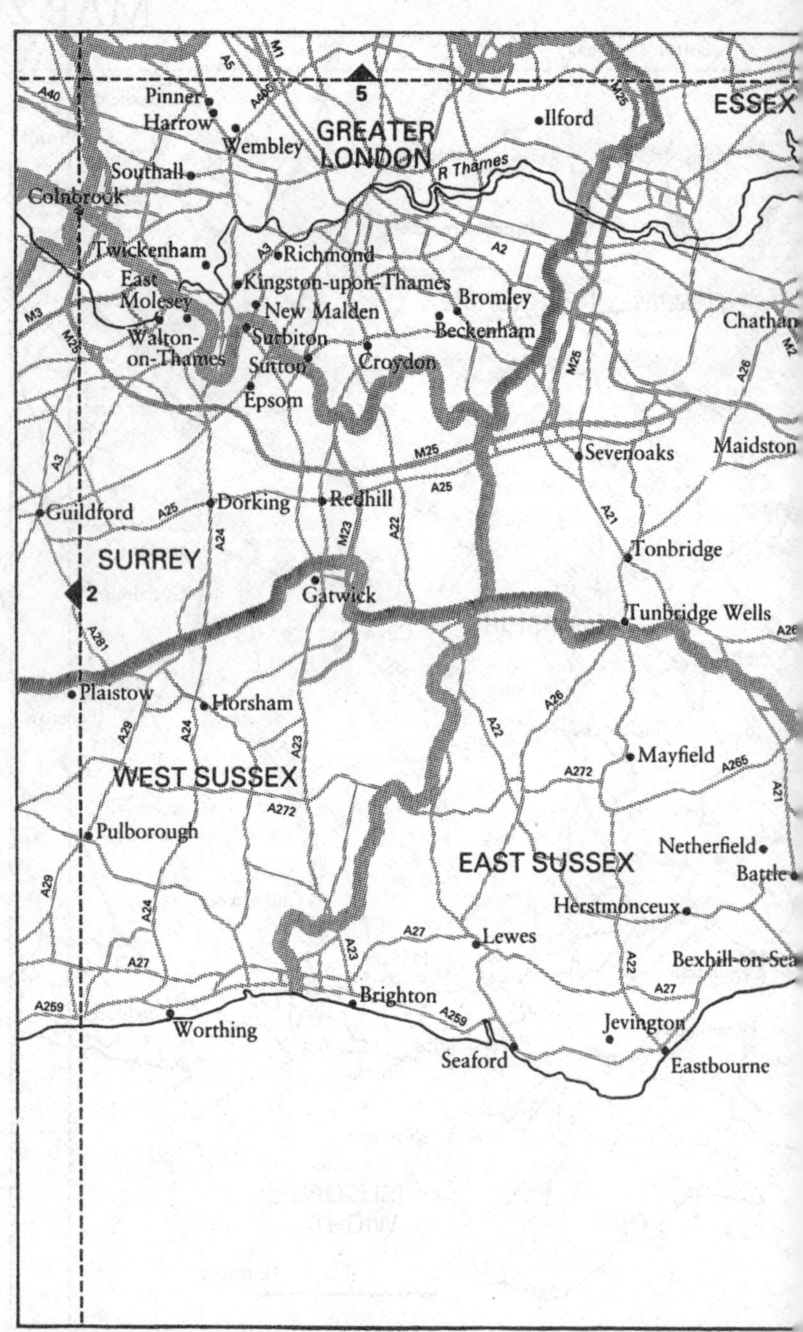
5
ESSEX
Pinner
Harrow
Wembley
GREATER
LONDON
Ilford
R Thames
Southall
Colnbrook
Twickenham
Richmond
Kingston-upon-Thames
East
Molesey
New Malden
Bromley
Beckenham
Walton-
on-Thames
Surbiton
Sutton
Croydon
Epsom
Chatham
Sevenoaks
Maidstone
Guildford
Dorking
Redhill
SURREY
Tonbridge
2
Gatwick
Tunbridge Wells
Plaistow
Horsham
Mayfield
WEST SUSSEX
Pulborough
Netherfield
EAST SUSSEX
Battle
Herstmonceux
Lewes
Bexhill-on-Sea
Brighton
Worthing
Jevington
Seaford
Eastbourne
A40
A5
M1
A406
M25
A2
A3
M3
M2
A26
A25
A24
M23
A22
A21
A281
A29
A23
A272
A265
A27
A259

MAP 3

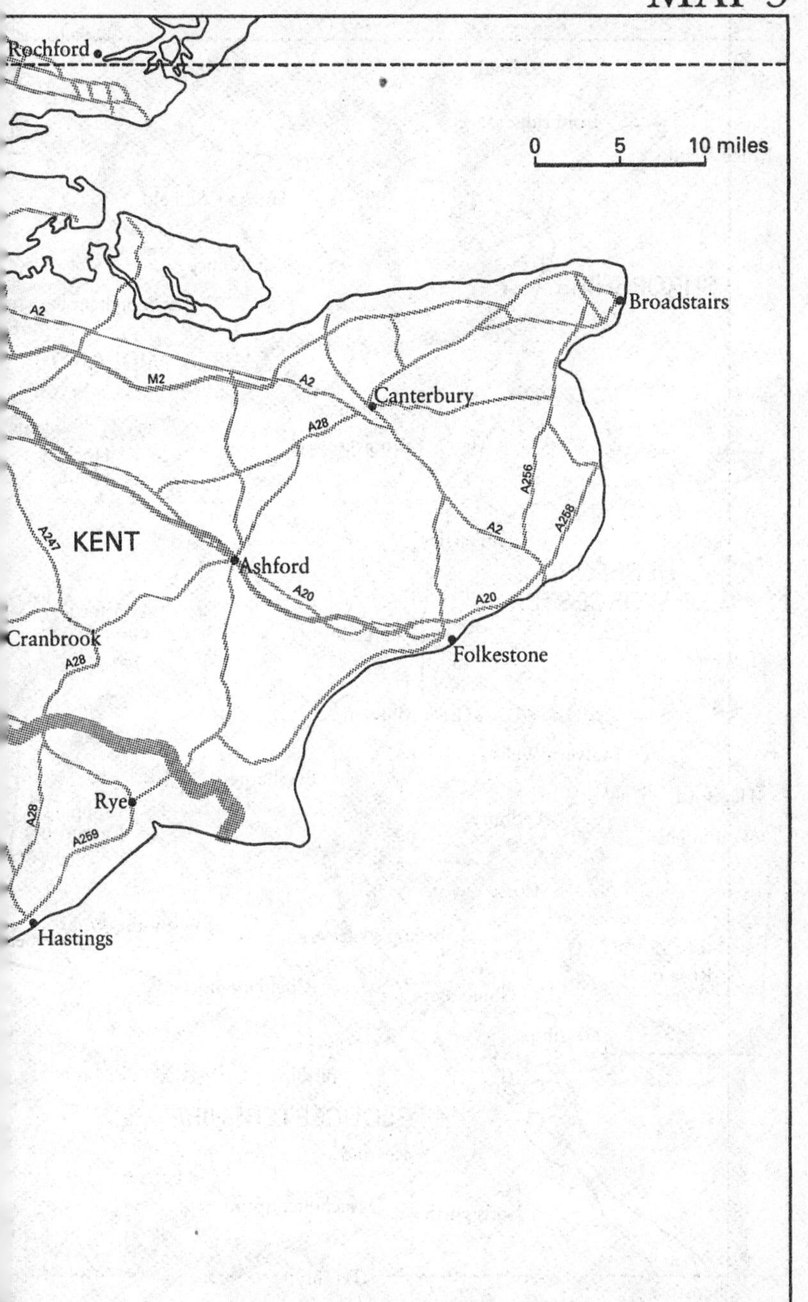

Rochford
0 5 10 miles
Broadstairs
A2
M2
A2
Canterbury
A28
A256
A258
A2
KENT
A247
Ashford
A20
A20
Cranbrook
Folkestone
A28
Rye
A28
A259
Hastings

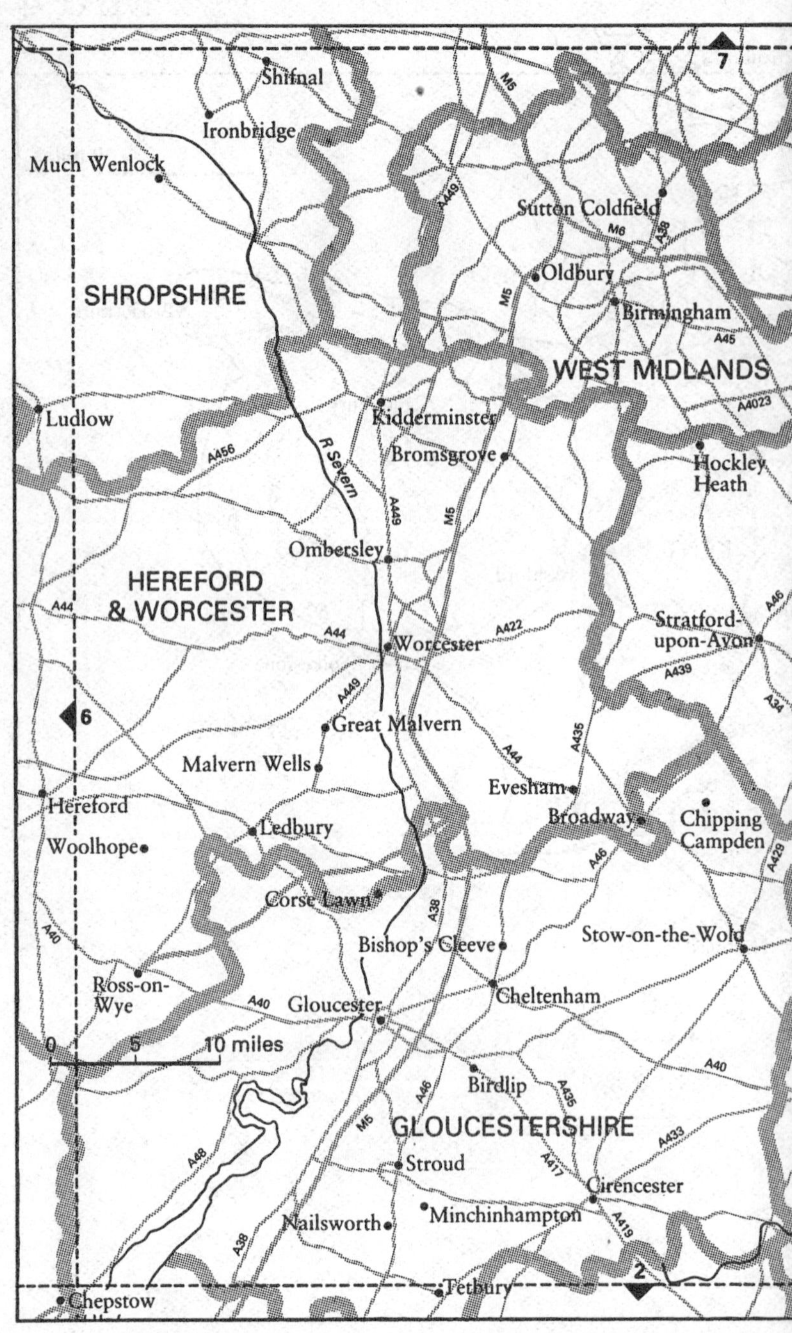
7
Shifnal
Ironbridge
Much Wenlock
M5
A449
Sutton Coldfield
M6
A38
Oldbury
SHROPSHIRE
M5
Birmingham
A45
WEST MIDLANDS
A4023
Ludlow
Kidderminster
R Severn
A456
Bromsgrove
Hockley Heath
A449
M5
Ombersley
HEREFORD & WORCESTER
A44
A46
Stratford-upon-Avon
A44
A422
Worcester
A439
A449
A34
6
Great Malvern
A435
Malvern Wells
A44
Evesham
Hereford
Broadway
Chipping Campden
Ledbury
Woolhope
A46
A429
Corse Lawn
A38
A40
Stow-on-the-Wold
Bishop's Cleeve
Ross-on-Wye
Cheltenham
A40
Gloucester
0 5 10 miles
A40
Birdlip
A435
A46
M5
GLOUCESTERSHIRE
A48
A433
A417
Stroud
Cirencester
Minchinhampton
A419
Nailsworth
A38
2
Tetbury
Chepstow

MAP 4

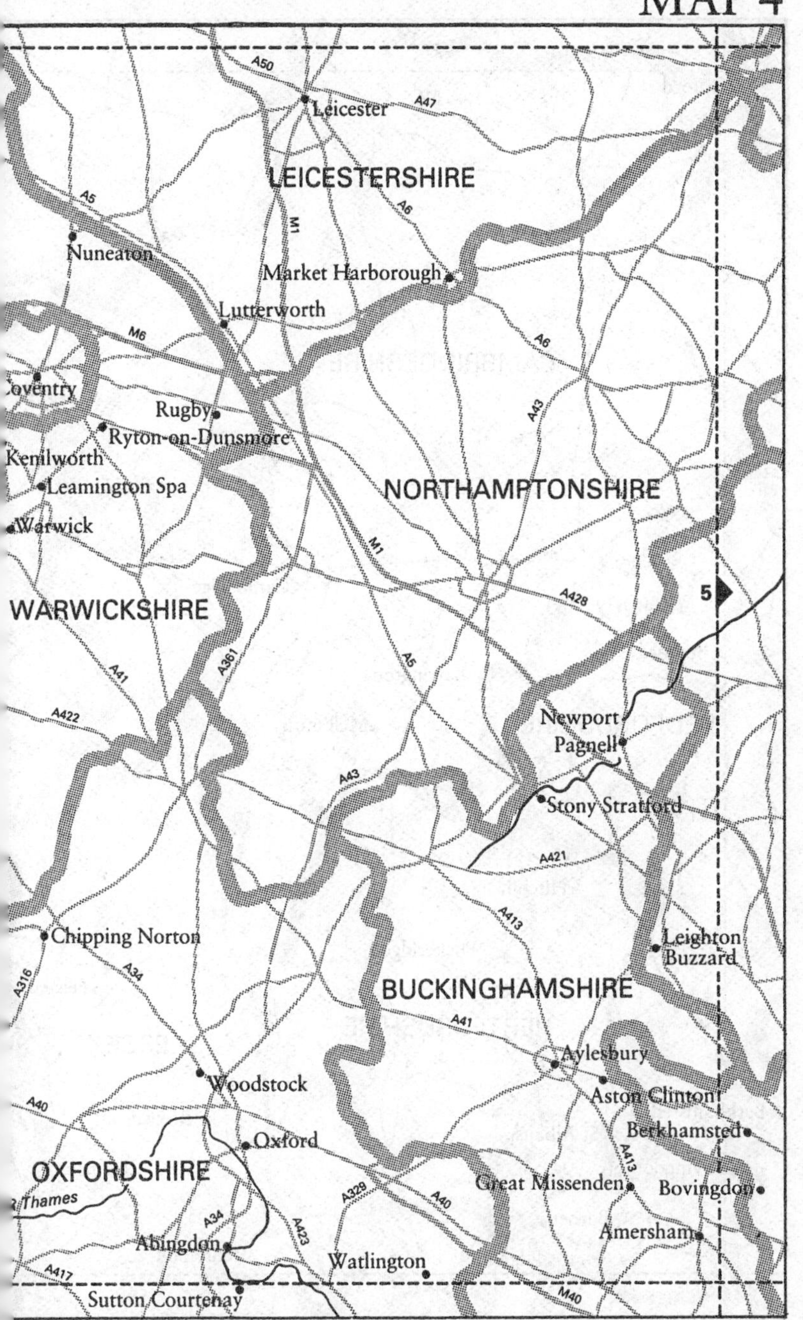

LEICESTERSHIRE
Leicester
A50
A47
A5
A6
M1
Nuneaton
Market Harborough
Lutterworth
M6
Coventry
Rugby
Ryton-on-Dunsmore
Kenilworth
Leamington Spa
Warwick
NORTHAMPTONSHIRE
A6
A43
M1
A428
5
WARWICKSHIRE
A361
A41
A5
A422
Newport
Pagnell
A43
Stony Stratford
A421
A413
Chipping Norton
Leighton
Buzzard
A316
A34
BUCKINGHAMSHIRE
A41
Aylesbury
Woodstock
Aston Clinton
A40
Berkhamsted
Oxford
OXFORDSHIRE
A413
Great Missenden
Bovingdon
R Thames
A329
A40
A34
A423
Amersham
Abingdon
Watlington
A417
Sutton Courtenay
M40

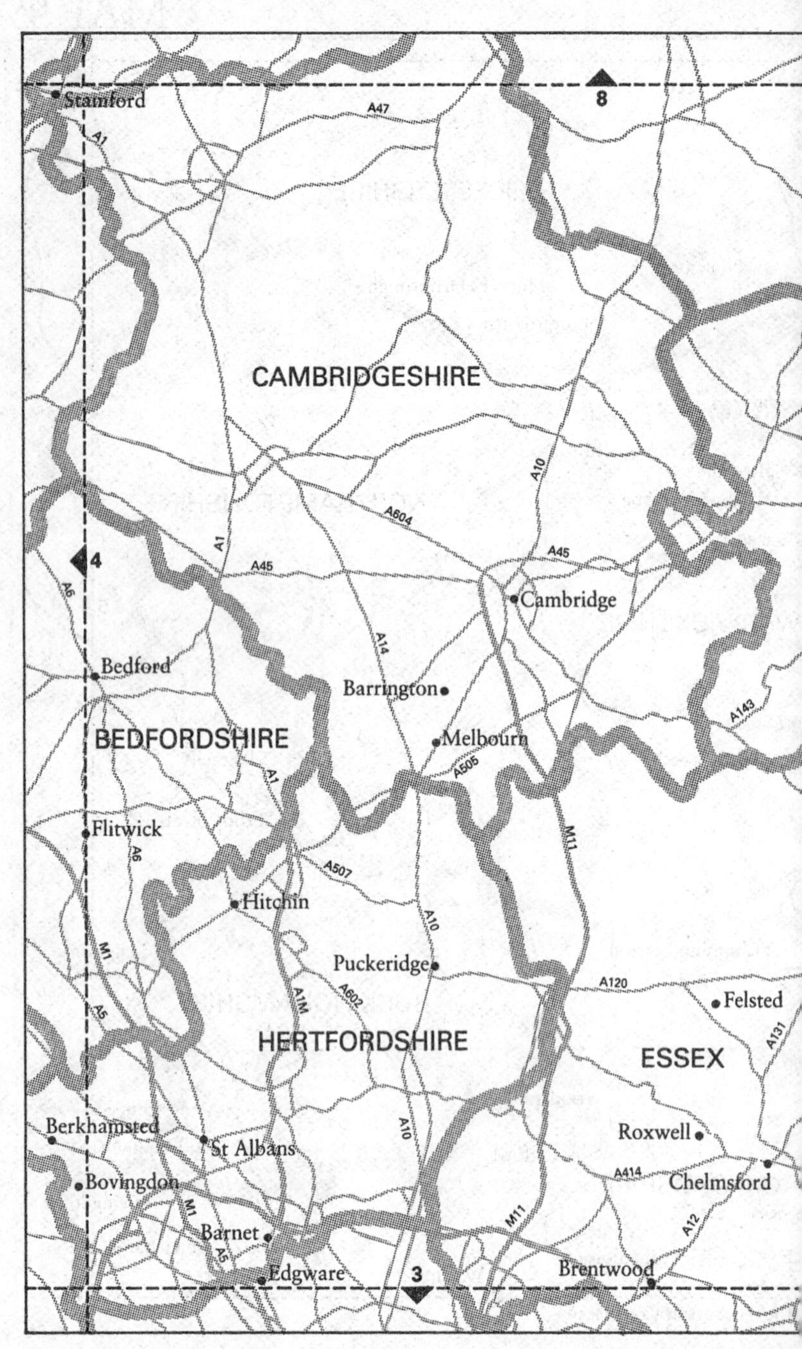

Stamford
A47
8
A1
CAMBRIDGESHIRE
A10
A604
A1
A45
A45
4
A6
Cambridge
A14
Bedford
Barrington
BEDFORDSHIRE
Melbourn
A505
A143
A1
Flitwick
A6
M11
A507
Hitchin
A10
M1
Puckeridge
A120
Felsted
A1M
A602
A5
HERTFORDSHIRE
A131
ESSEX
A10
Berkhamsted
St Albans
Roxwell
Bovingdon
A414
Chelmsford
M1
M11
A12
Barnet
A5
Edgware
3
Brentwood

MAP 5

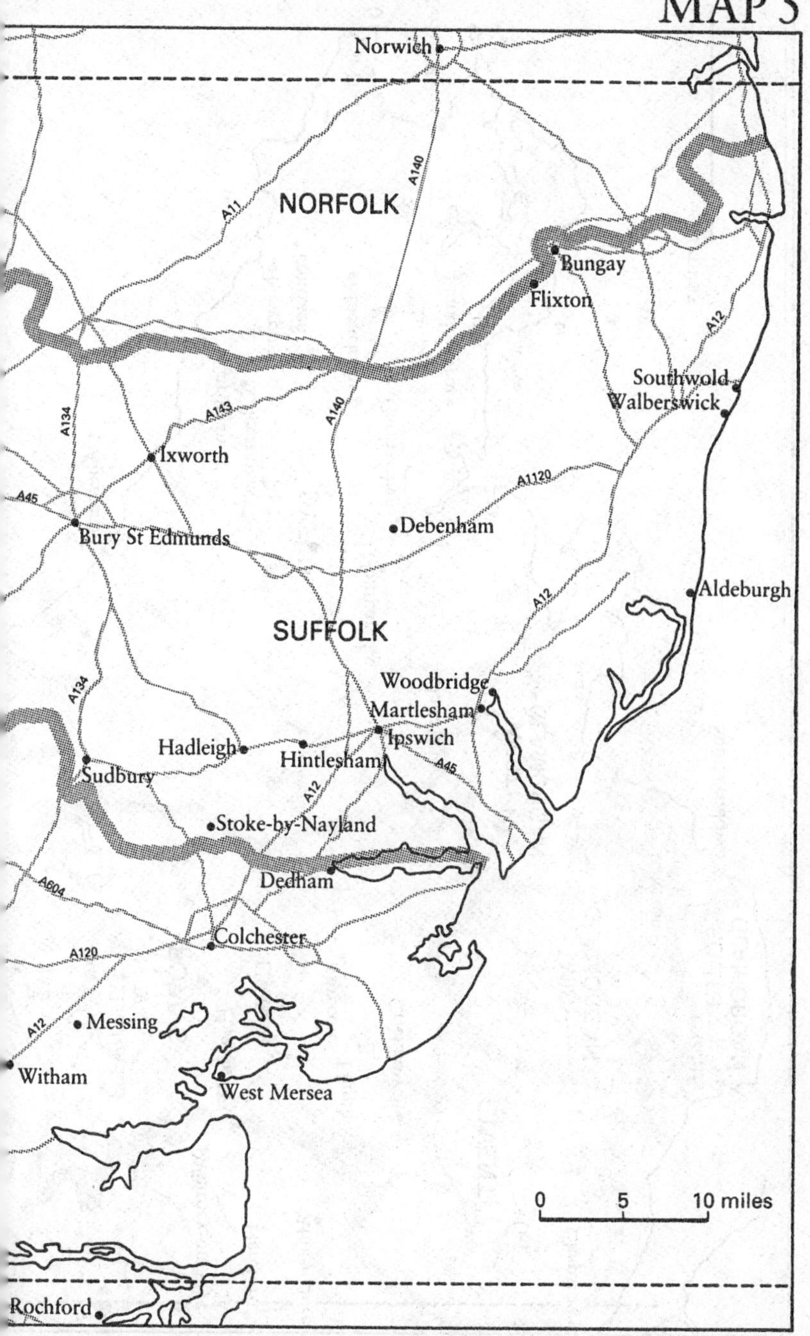

Norwich
NORFOLK
A11
A140
Bungay
Flixton
A12
Southwold
Walberswick
A134
A143
A140
Ixworth
A1120
A45
Bury St Edmunds
Debenham
Aldeburgh
A12
SUFFOLK
Woodbridge
A134
Martlesham
Ipswich
Hadleigh
Hintlesham
A45
Sudbury
A12
Stoke-by-Nayland
Dedham
A604
Colchester
A120
Messing
A12
Witham
West Mersea
0
5
10 miles
Rochford

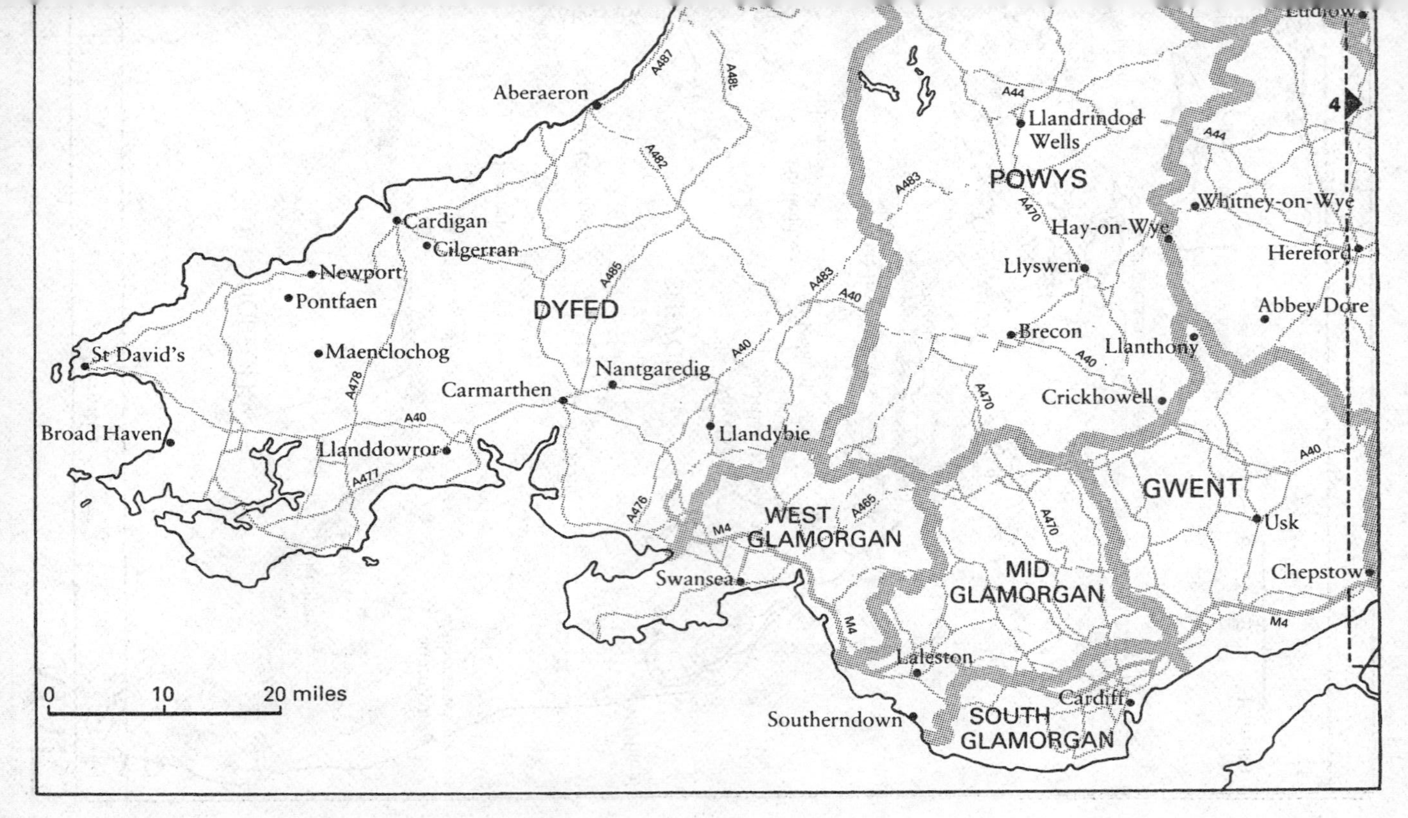

Aberaeron
A487
Llandrindod
Wells
A44
4
POWYS
A482
A483
A470
Whitney-on-Wye
Cardigan
Hay-on-Wye
Cilgerran
Hereford
Newport
Llyswen
Pontfaen
A485
DYFED
A483
A40
Abbey Dore
Brecon
St David's
Maenclochog
A40
Llanthony
Nantgaredig
A40
Carmarthen
A478
A470
Crickhowell
A40
Broad Haven
Llandybie
Llanddowror
A477
A40
GWENT
A476
A465
WEST
GLAMORGAN
M4
Usk
A470
MID
GLAMORGAN
Swansea
Chepstow
M4
M4
Laleston
Cardiff
0
10
20 miles
Southerndown
SOUTH
GLAMORGAN

MAP 6

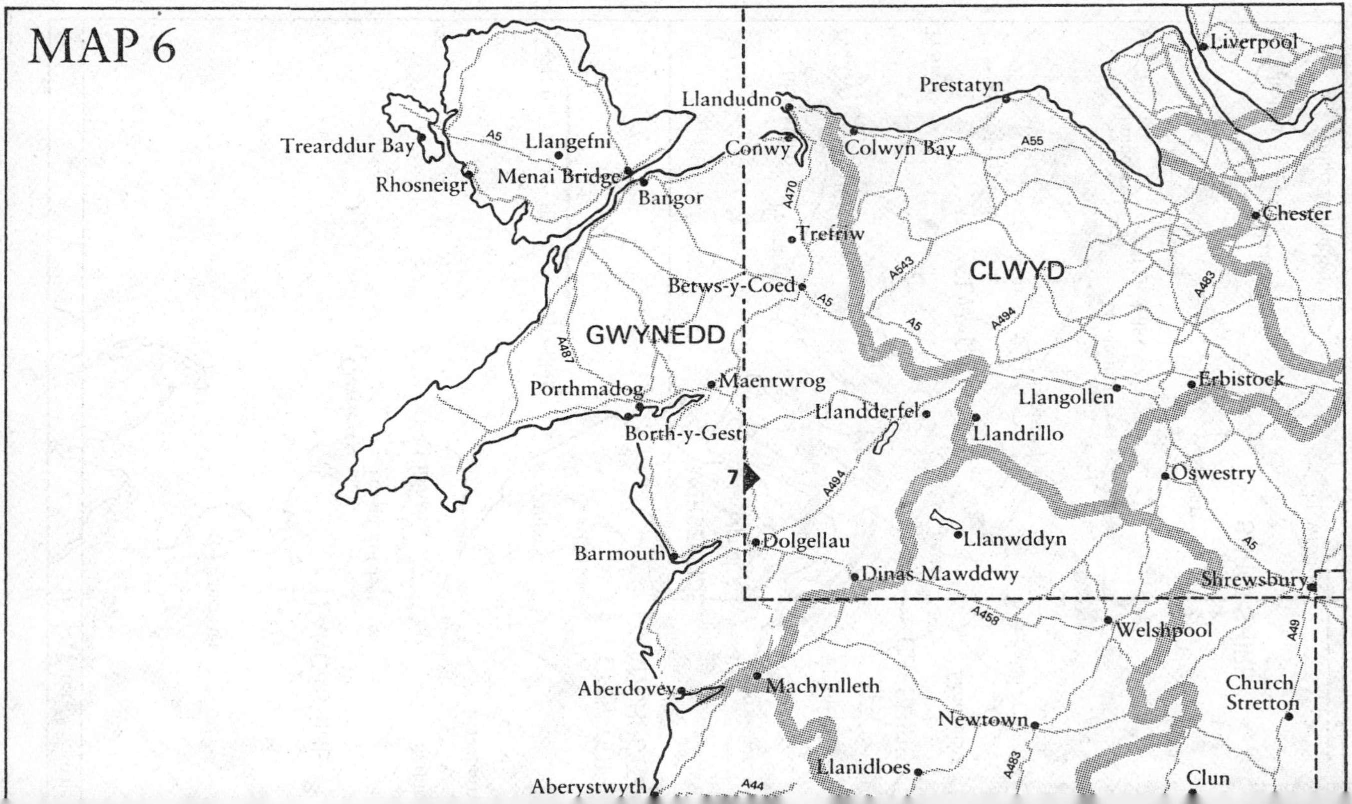

Liverpool
Prestatyn
Llandudno
Trearddur Bay
A5
Llangefni
Conwy
Colwyn Bay
A55
Rhosneigr
Menai Bridge
Bangor
Chester
A470
Trefriw
A543
CLWYD
Betws-y-Coed
A5
A483
A5
A494
GWYNEDD
A487
Maentwrog
Porthmadog
Erbistock
Llangollen
Llandderfel
Llandrillo
Borth-y-Gest
7
Oswestry
A494
Llanwddyn
Dolgellau
A5
Barmouth
Dinas Mawddwy
Shrewsbury
A458
Welshpool
A49
Church Stretton
Aberdovey
Machynlleth
Newtown
A483
Llanidloes
Clun
Aberystwyth
A44

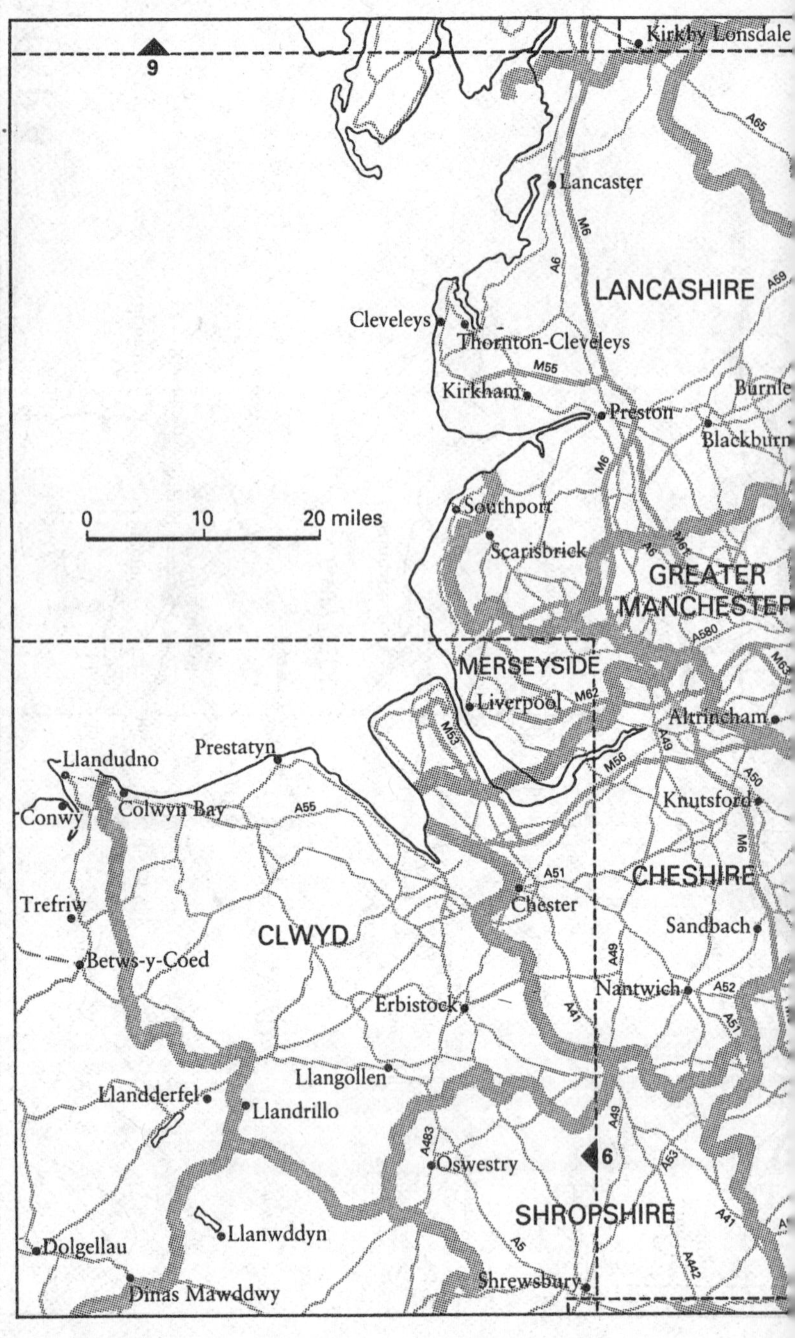

9
Kirkby Lonsdale
A65
Lancaster
M6
A6
LANCASHIRE
A59
Cleveleys
Thornton-Cleveleys
M55
Kirkham
Preston
Burnle
Blackburn
M6
Southport
0
10
20 miles
Scarisbrick
A6
M61
GREATER
MANCHESTER
A580
MERSEYSIDE
M63
Liverpool
M62
M53
Altrincham
Llandudno
Prestatyn
A49
M56
A50
Conwy
Colwyn Bay
A55
Knutsford
M6
A51
CHESHIRE
Chester
Trefriw
CLWYD
Sandbach
A49
Betws-y-Coed
Nantwich
A52
Erbistock
A41
A51
Llangollen
Llandderfel
Llandrillo
A49
A483
6
Oswestry
A53
SHROPSHIRE
A41
Llanwddyn
Dolgellau
A5
A442
Shrewsbury
Dinas Mawddwy

MAP 7

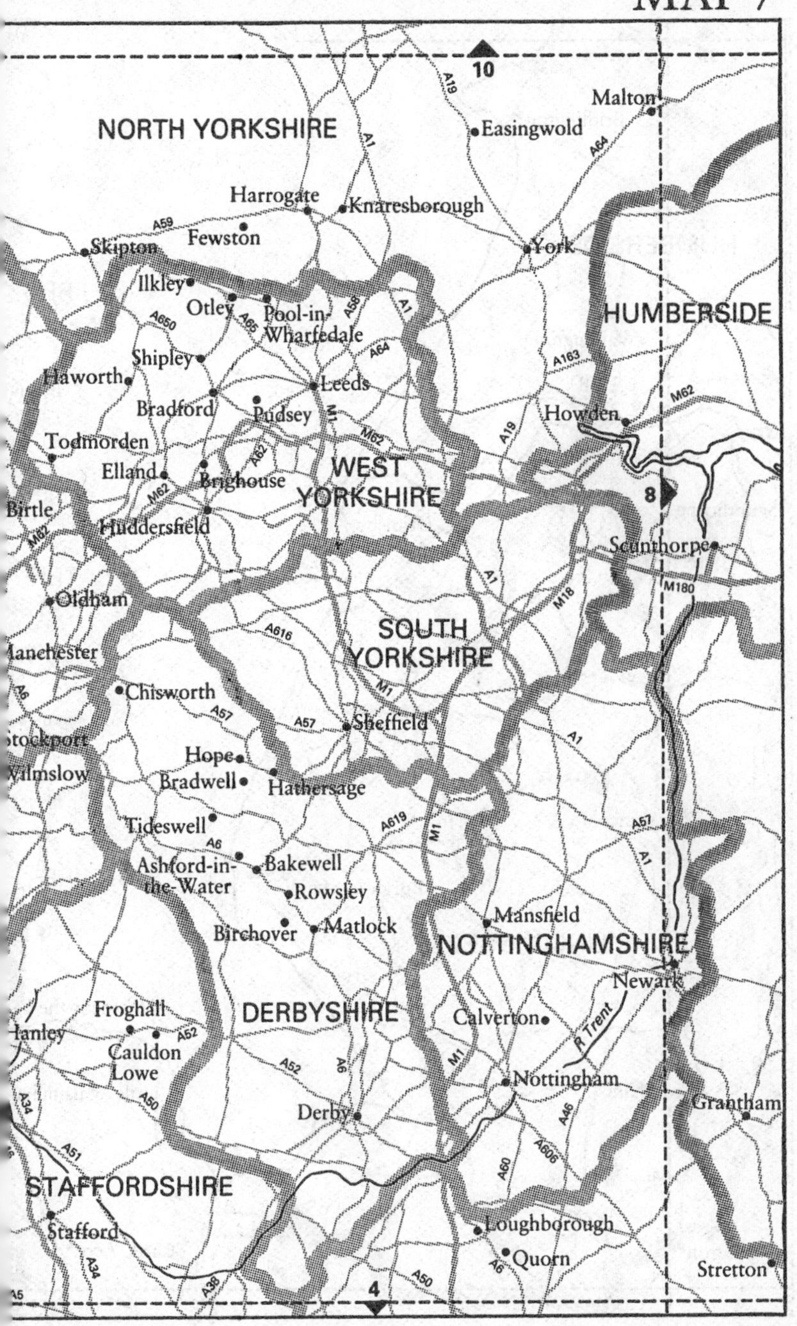

10
NORTH YORKSHIRE
Malton
Easingwold
A19
A1
A64
Harrogate
Knaresborough
A59
Fewston
Skipton
York
Ilkley
Otley
Pool-in-Wharfedale
A65
A650
A58
HUMBERSIDE
Shipley
Haworth
Leeds
A163
Bradford
Pudsey
M1
M62
Howden
Todmorden
WEST YORKSHIRE
Elland
Brighouse
A62
8
Birtle
Huddersfield
Scunthorpe
M180
Oldham
A616
M18
SOUTH YORKSHIRE
Manchester
A6
Chisworth
A57
Sheffield
Stockport
Hope
Wilmslow
Bradwell
Hathersage
Tideswell
A619
Ashford-in-the-Water
Bakewell
Rowsley
Birchover
Matlock
Mansfield
NOTTINGHAMSHIRE
Newark
Froghall
DERBYSHIRE
Calverton
R Trent
Hanley
Cauldon Lowe
A52
A34
A50
Nottingham
A46
Derby
Grantham
A51
A606
A60
STAFFORDSHIRE
Stafford
Loughborough
Quorn
A38
Stretton
A5
4

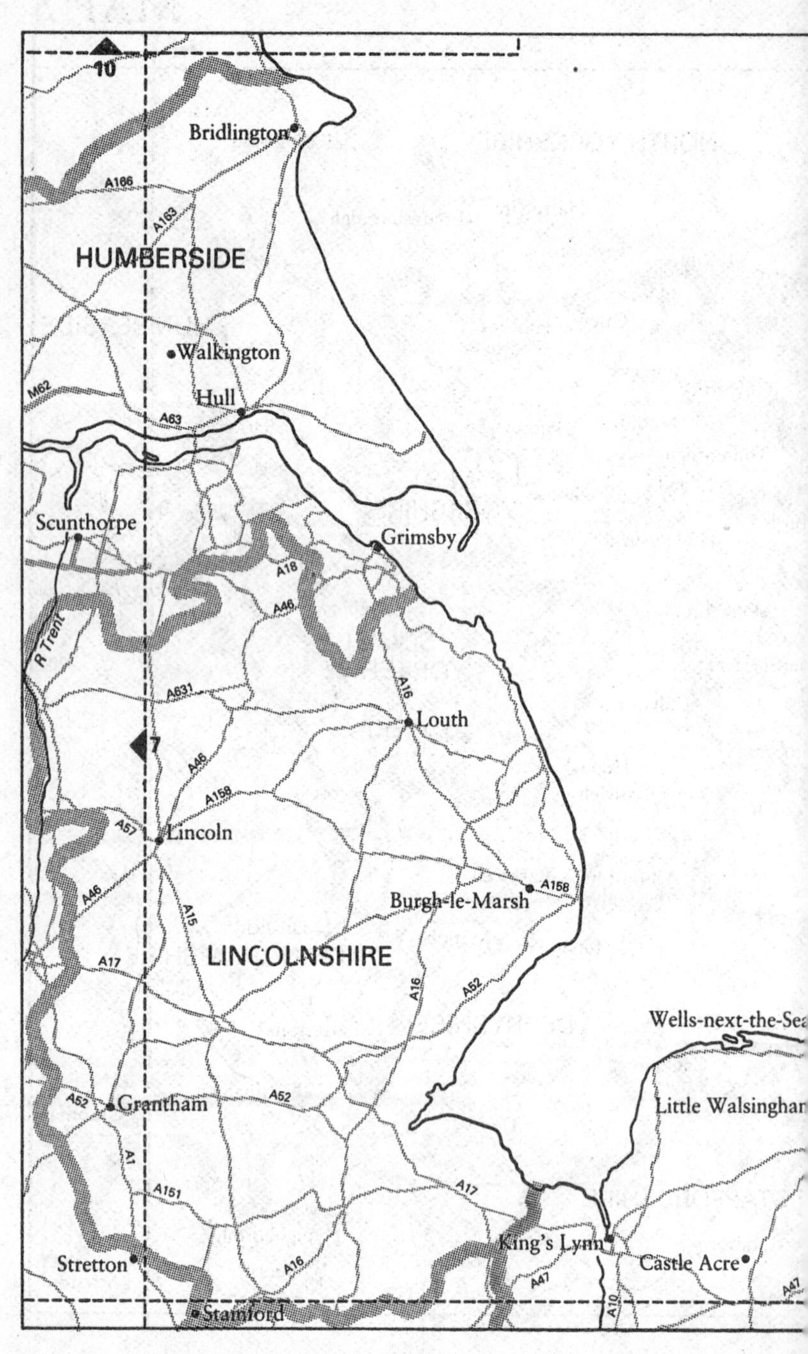
10
Bridlington
A166
A163
HUMBERSIDE
Walkington
M62
Hull
A63
Scunthorpe
Grimsby
A18
A46
R Trent
A631
A16
Louth
7
A46
A158
A57
Lincoln
A158
Burgh-le-Marsh
A46
A15
LINCOLNSHIRE
A17
A16
A52
Wells-next-the-Sea
A52
Grantham
A52
Little Walsingham
A1
A151
A17
King's Lynn
Stretton
A16
Castle Acre
A47
A47
A10
Stamford

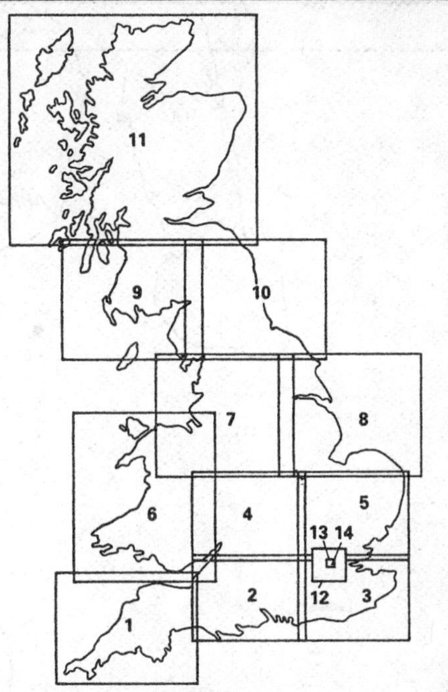

REFERENCE TO SECTIONAL MAPS

Motorway — Roads numbered and classified according to Department of Transport

'A' Road

County Boundary

Exeter Guide entry

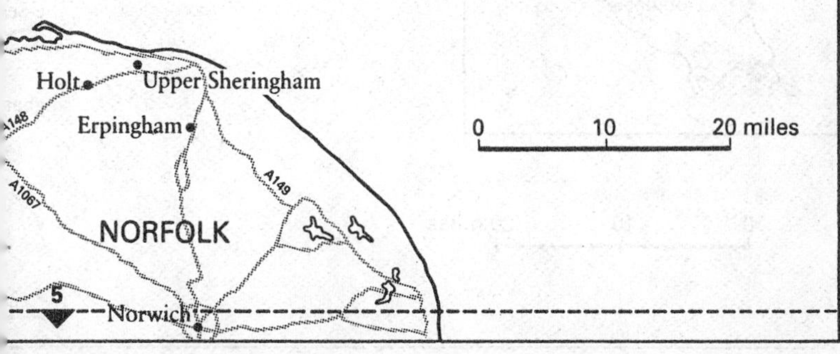

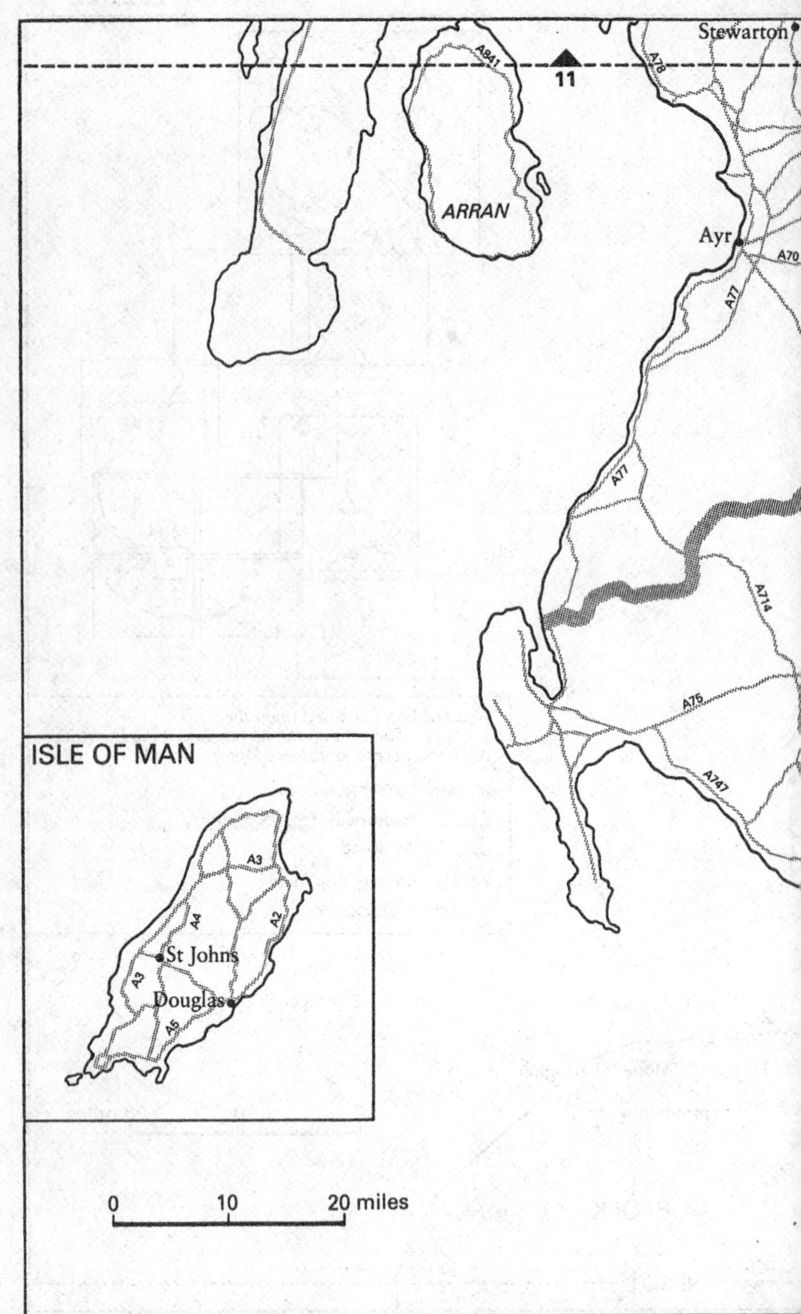
Stewarton
A841
11
A78
ARRAN
Ayr
A70
A77
A77
A714
A75
A747
ISLE OF MAN
A3
A4
A2
St Johns
A3
Douglas
A5
0
10
20 miles

MAP 9

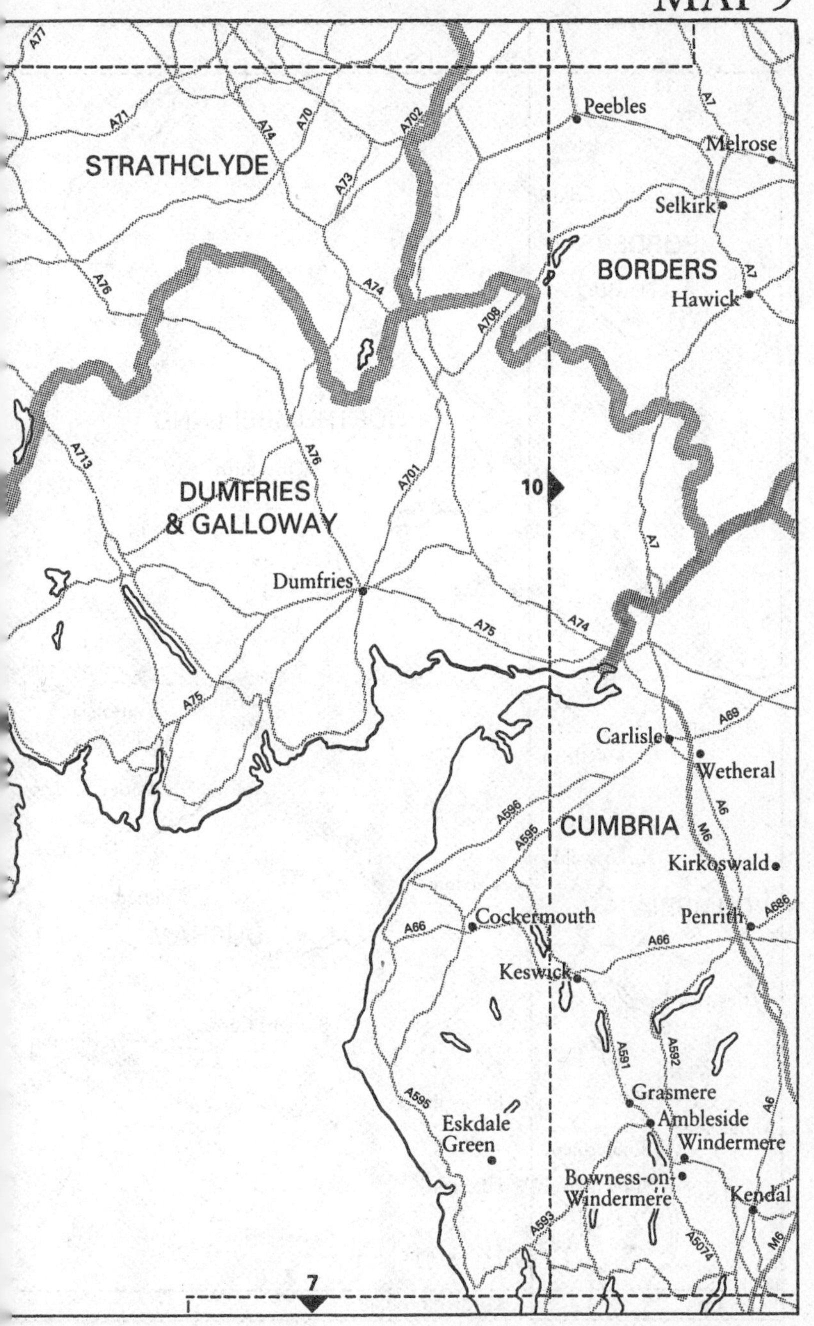

STRATHCLYDE
DUMFRIES & GALLOWAY
BORDERS
CUMBRIA
Peebles
Melrose
Selkirk
Hawick
Dumfries
Carlisle
Wetheral
Kirkoswald
Penrith
Cockermouth
Keswick
Grasmere
Ambleside
Windermere
Bowness-on-Windermere
Kendal
Eskdale Green
10
7
A77
A71
A74
A70
A702
A73
A76
A708
A713
A701
A75
A7
A69
A6
M6
A596
A595
A66
A686
A591
A592
A593
A5074

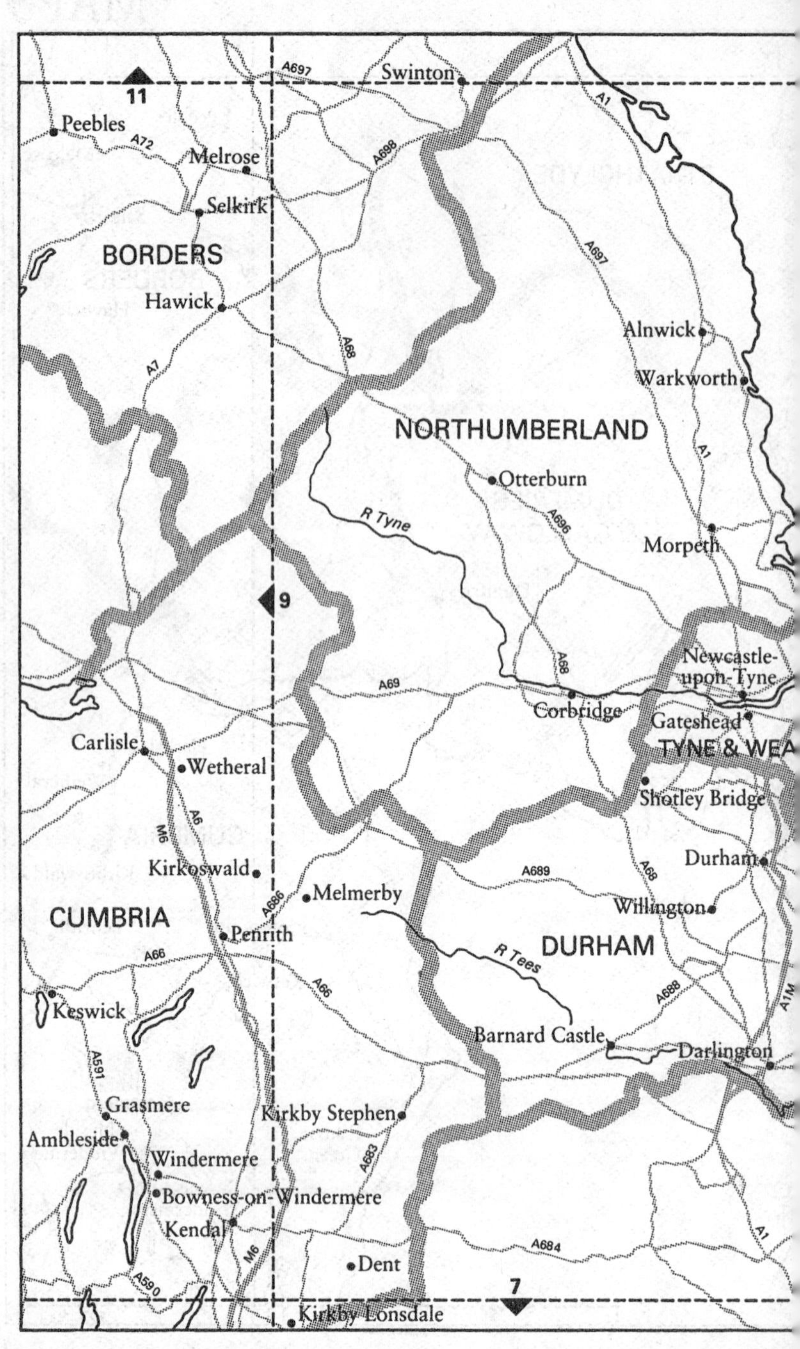
11
Swinton
A697
Peebles
A72
Melrose
A698
A1
Selkirk
BORDERS
A697
Hawick
A68
Alnwick
A7
Warkworth
NORTHUMBERLAND
A1
Otterburn
R Tyne
A696
Morpeth
9
A68
Newcastle-upon-Tyne
A69
Corbridge
Gateshead
TYNE & WEA
Carlisle
Wetheral
Shotley Bridge
A6
M6
Durham
Kirkoswald
A689
A68
Melmerby
A686
Willington
CUMBRIA
Penrith
DURHAM
R Tees
A66
A66
A688
Keswick
A1M
Barnard Castle
Darlington
A591
Grasmere
Kirkby Stephen
Ambleside
Windermere
A683
Bowness-on-Windermere
Kendal
A684
A1
M6
Dent
A590
7
Kirkby Lonsdale

MAP 10

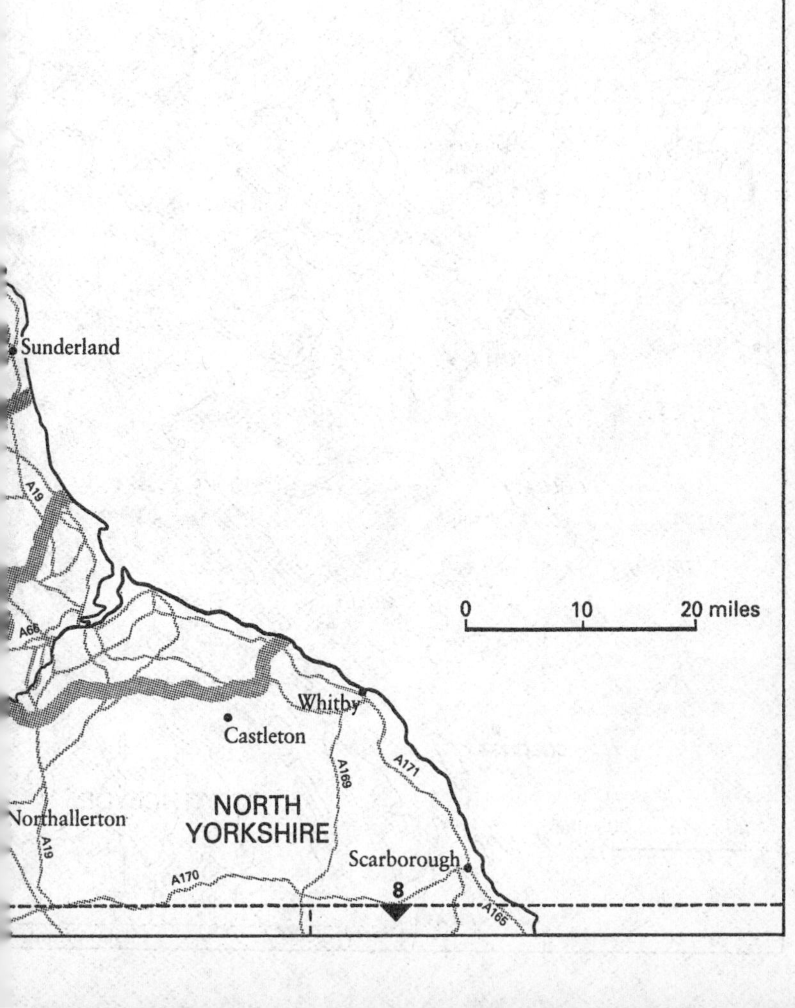

Sunderland
A19
A66
Whitby
Castleton
A171
A169
Northallerton
NORTH
YORKSHIRE
A19
Scarborough
A170
8
A165
0
10
20 miles

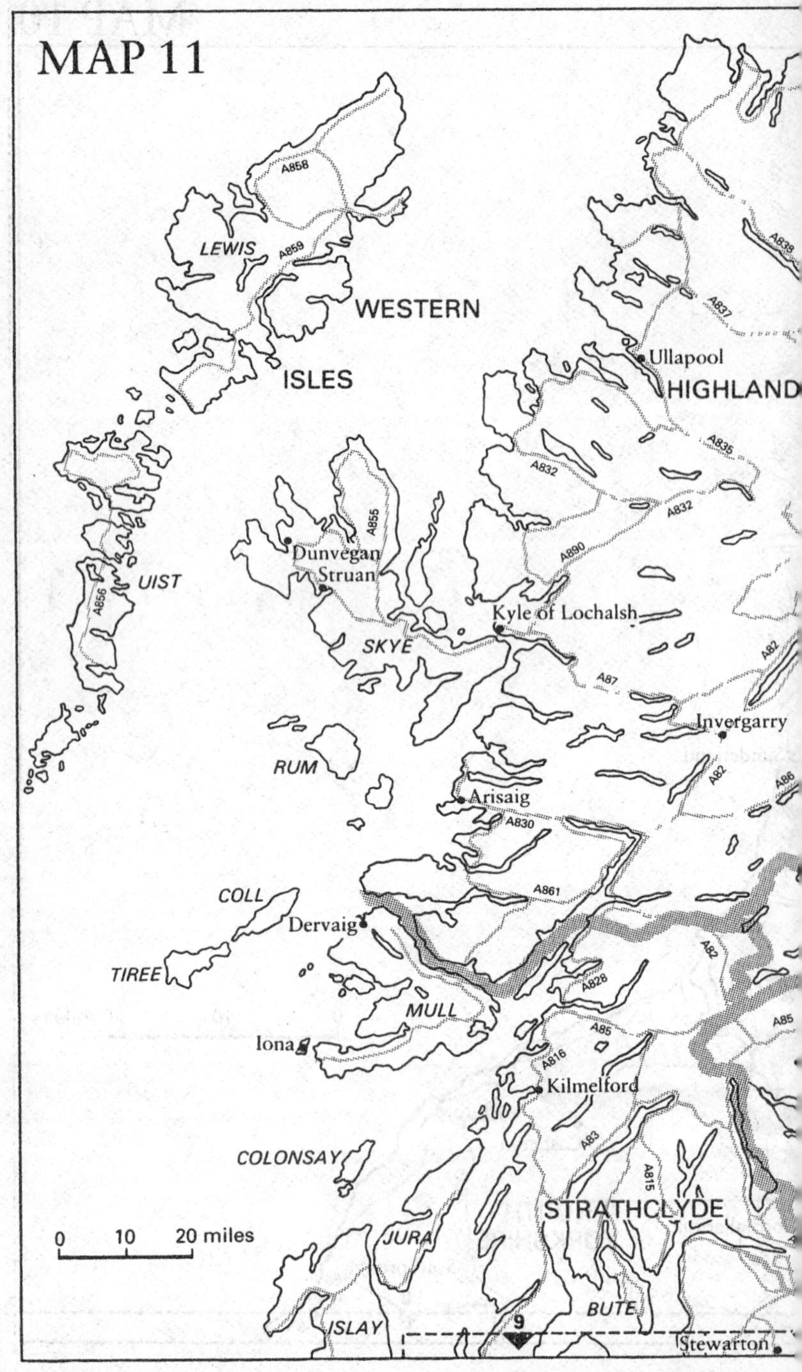
MAP 11
A858
LEWIS
A859
WESTERN
ISLES
UIST
A856
A855
Dunvegan
Struan
SKYE
RUM
Ullapool
HIGHLAND
A838
A837
A835
A832
A832
A890
Kyle of Lochalsh
A87
A82
Invergarry
A82
A86
Arisaig
A830
A861
COLL
Dervaig
TIREE
A82
A828
MULL
A85
A85
Iona
A816
Kilmelford
A83
A815
COLONSAY
STRATHCLYDE
0 10 20 miles
JURA
BUTE
ISLAY
9
Stewarton

UNST
0 10 20 miles
YELL
Walls
MAINLAND
MAINLAND
HOY
ORKNEY
SHETLAND
A836
A9
Kildonan
A836
A9
Forres
Nairn
Inverness
A96
A98
A97
A95
A9
A92
A96
A92
A97
Aberdeen
GRAMPIAN
A93
A93
A94
A9
A92
A827
A923
Auchmithie
A9
TAYSIDE
Dundee
Carnoustie
A85
A94
A85
Perth
M90
St Andrews
A9
FIFE
Blair
Drummond
Leslie
Forth
Stirling
M80
Falkirk
Edinburgh
Glasgow
LOTHIAN
A1
M8
A70
10

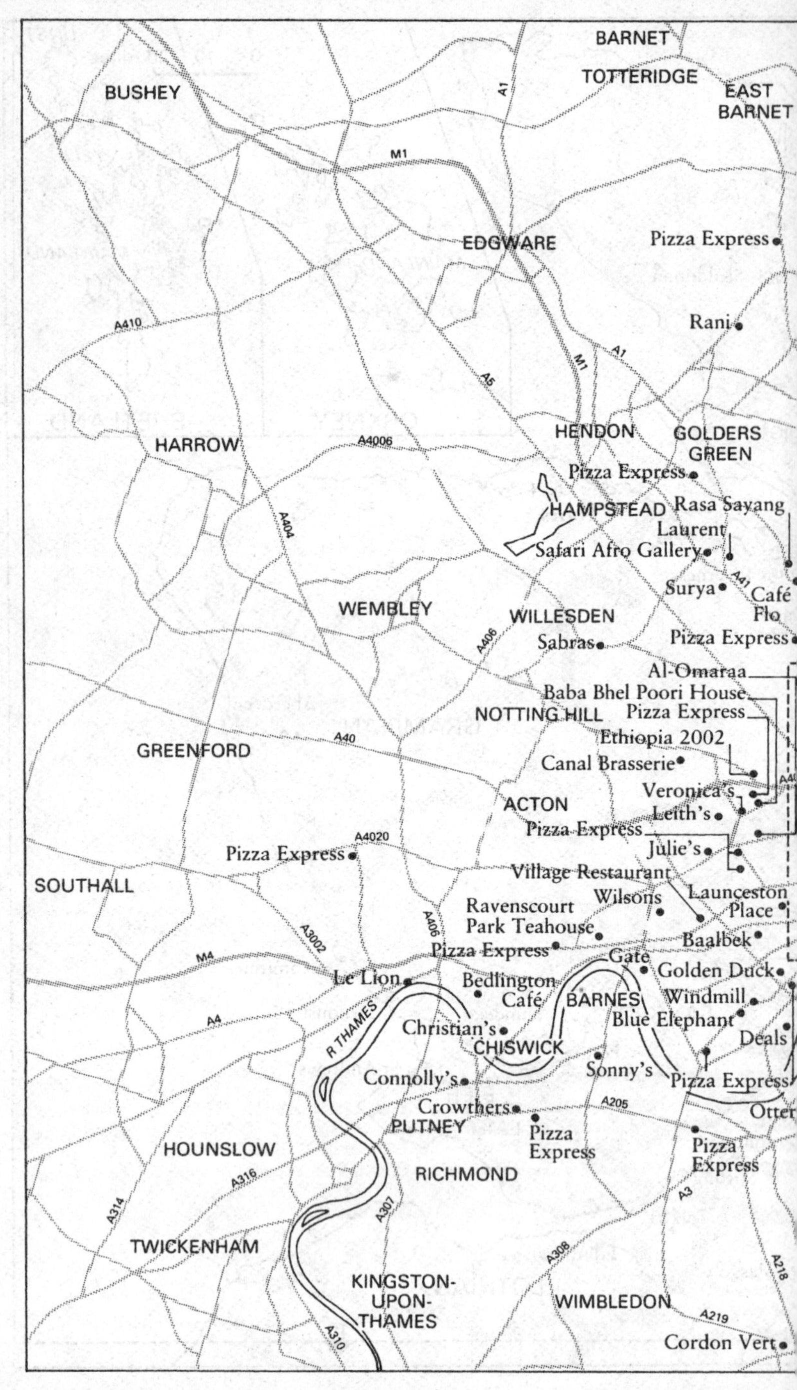
BARNET
TOTTERIDGE
EAST BARNET
BUSHEY
A1
M1
EDGWARE
Pizza Express
A410
Rani
M1
A1
A5
HENDON
GOLDERS GREEN
HARROW
A4006
Pizza Express
HAMPSTEAD
Rasa Sayang
A404
Laurent
Safari Afro Gallery
A41
Surya
Café Flo
WEMBLEY
WILLESDEN
A406
Sabras
Pizza Express
Al-Omaraa
Baba Bhel Poori House
NOTTING HILL
Pizza Express
GREENFORD
A40
Ethiopia 2002
Canal Brasserie
Veronica's
ACTON
Leith's
Pizza Express
A4020
Pizza Express
Julie's
SOUTHALL
Village Restaurant
Wilsons
Launceston Place
Ravenscourt Park Teahouse
A406
A3002
Baalbek
Pizza Express
M4
Gate
Golden Duck
Le Lion
Bedlington Café
BARNES
Windmill
A4
R THAMES
Blue Elephant
Christian's
Deals
CHISWICK
Sonny's
Connolly's
Pizza Express
Crowthers
A205
Otter
PUTNEY
Pizza Express
Pizza Express
HOUNSLOW
A316
RICHMOND
A3
A314
A307
TWICKENHAM
A308
A218
KINGSTON-UPON-THAMES
WIMBLEDON
A219
A310
Cordon Vert

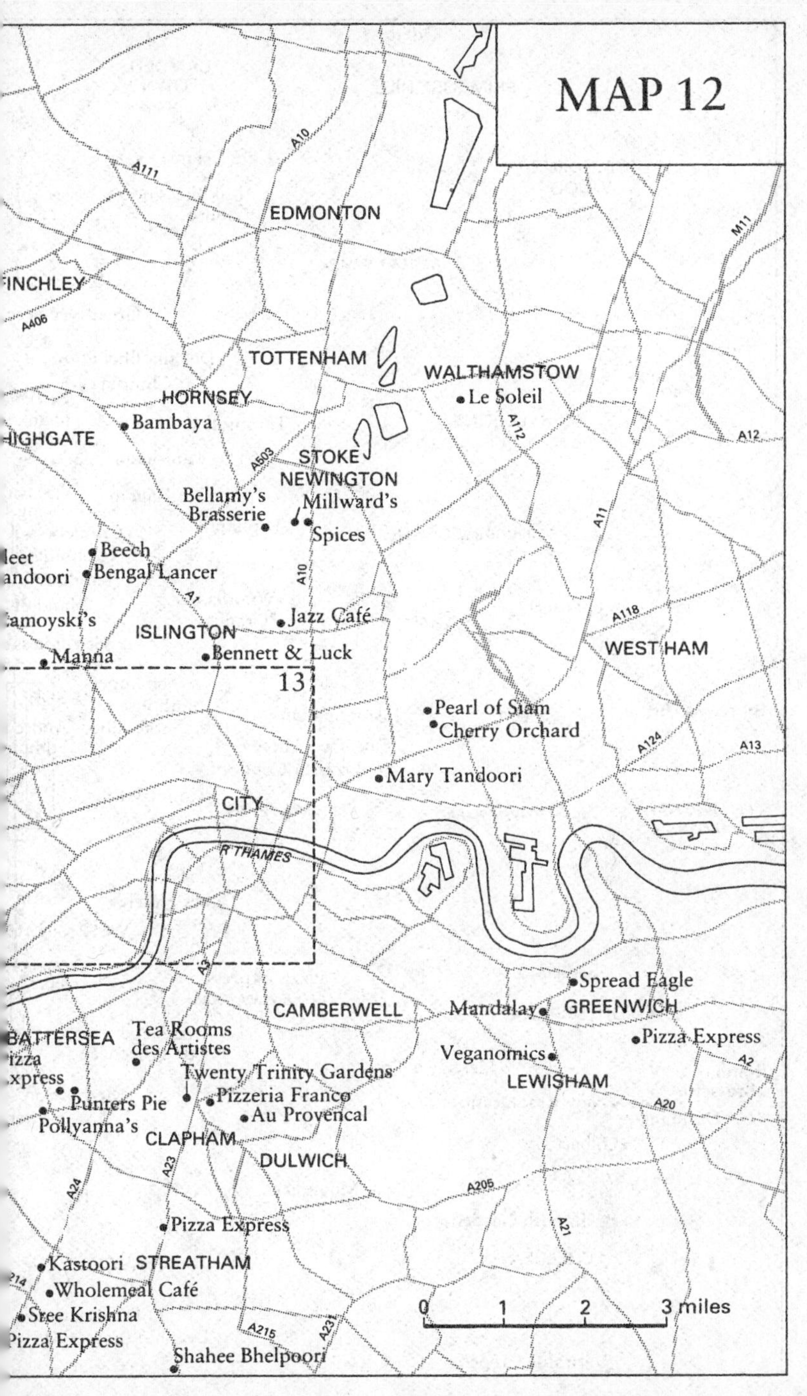

MAP 12
A10
A111
EDMONTON
M11
FINCHLEY
A406
TOTTENHAM
WALTHAMSTOW
Le Soleil
HORNSEY
Bambaya
HIGHGATE
A112
A12
A503
STOKE
NEWINGTON
Bellamy's Brasserie
Millward's
Spices
A11
Beech
Bengal Lancer
A10
A1
A118
Jazz Café
ISLINGTON
WEST HAM
Manna
Bennett & Luck
13
Pearl of Siam
Cherry Orchard
A124
A13
Mary Tandoori
CITY
R THAMES
A3
Spread Eagle
CAMBERWELL
Mandalay
GREENWICH
BATTERSEA
Tea Rooms des Artistes
Pizza Express
Veganomics
A2
Twenty Trinity Gardens
LEWISHAM
Punters Pie
Pizzeria Franco
A20
Pollyanna's
Au Provencal
CLAPHAM
DULWICH
A23
A24
A205
Pizza Express
A21
Kastoori
STREATHAM
Wholemeal Café
0 1 2 3 miles
Sree Krishna
A215
A23
Shahee Bhelpoori

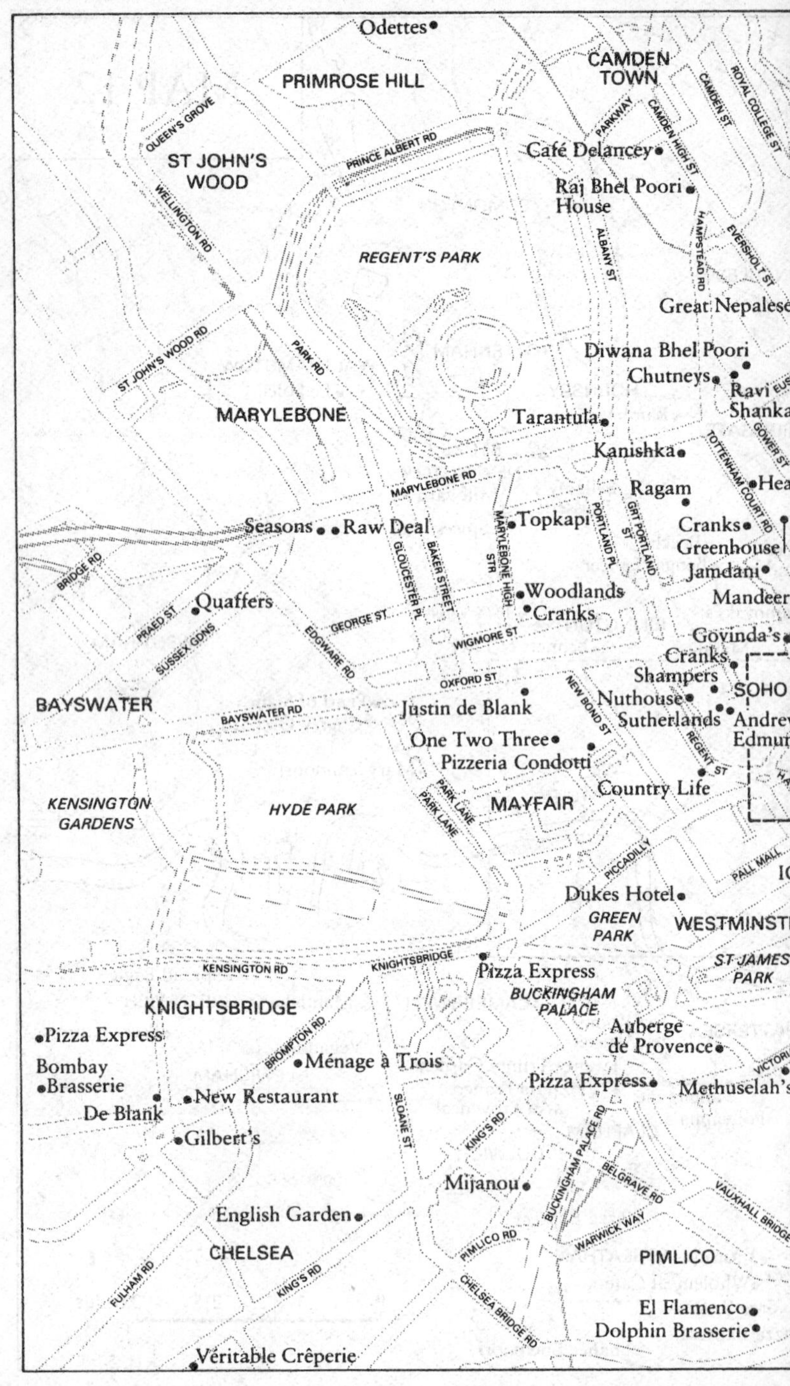
Odettes
PRIMROSE HILL
CAMDEN TOWN
ST JOHN'S WOOD
QUEEN'S GROVE
PRINCE ALBERT RD
PARKWAY
CAMDEN HIGH ST
CAMDEN ST
ROYAL COLLEGE ST
Café Delancey
Raj Bhel Poori House
WELLINGTON RD
REGENT'S PARK
ALBANY ST
HAMPSTEAD RD
EVERSHOLT ST
Great Nepalese
ST JOHN'S WOOD RD
PARK RD
Diwana Bhel Poori
Chutneys
Ravi Shanka
MARYLEBONE
Tarantula
Kanishka
GOWER ST
TOTTENHAM COURT RD
MARYLEBONE RD
Ragam
Hea
Seasons
Raw Deal
Topkapi
Cranks
Greenhouse
GLOUCESTER PL
BAKER STREET
MARYLEBONE HIGH STR
PORTLAND PL
GRT PORTLAND ST
Jamdani
BRIDGE RD
Woodlands
Cranks
Mandeer
Quaffers
PRAED ST
SUSSEX GDNS
GEORGE ST
EDGWARE RD
WIGMORE ST
Govinda's
Cranks
Shampers
OXFORD ST
SOHO
BAYSWATER
Justin de Blank
NEW BOND ST
Nuthouse
Sutherlands
Andrev
Edmun
BAYSWATER RD
One Two Three
Pizzeria Condotti
REGENT ST
Country Life
KENSINGTON GARDENS
HYDE PARK
PARK LANE
PARK LANE
MAYFAIR
PICCADILLY
PALL MALL
Dukes Hotel
GREEN PARK
WESTMINSTE
KENSINGTON RD
KNIGHTSBRIDGE
Pizza Express
BUCKINGHAM PALACE
ST JAMES' PARK
KNIGHTSBRIDGE
Pizza Express
BROMPTON RD
Auberge de Provence
Bombay Brasserie
Ménage à Trois
VICTORIA
De Blank
New Restaurant
Pizza Express
Methuselah's
SLOANE ST
Gilbert's
KING'S RD
BUCKINGHAM PALACE RD
BELGRAVE RD
Mijanou
VAUXHALL BRIDGE
English Garden
WARWICK WAY
PIMLICO RD
CHELSEA
PIMLICO
FULHAM RD
KING'S RD
CHELSEA BRIDGE RD
El Flamenco
Dolphin Brasserie
Véritable Crêperie

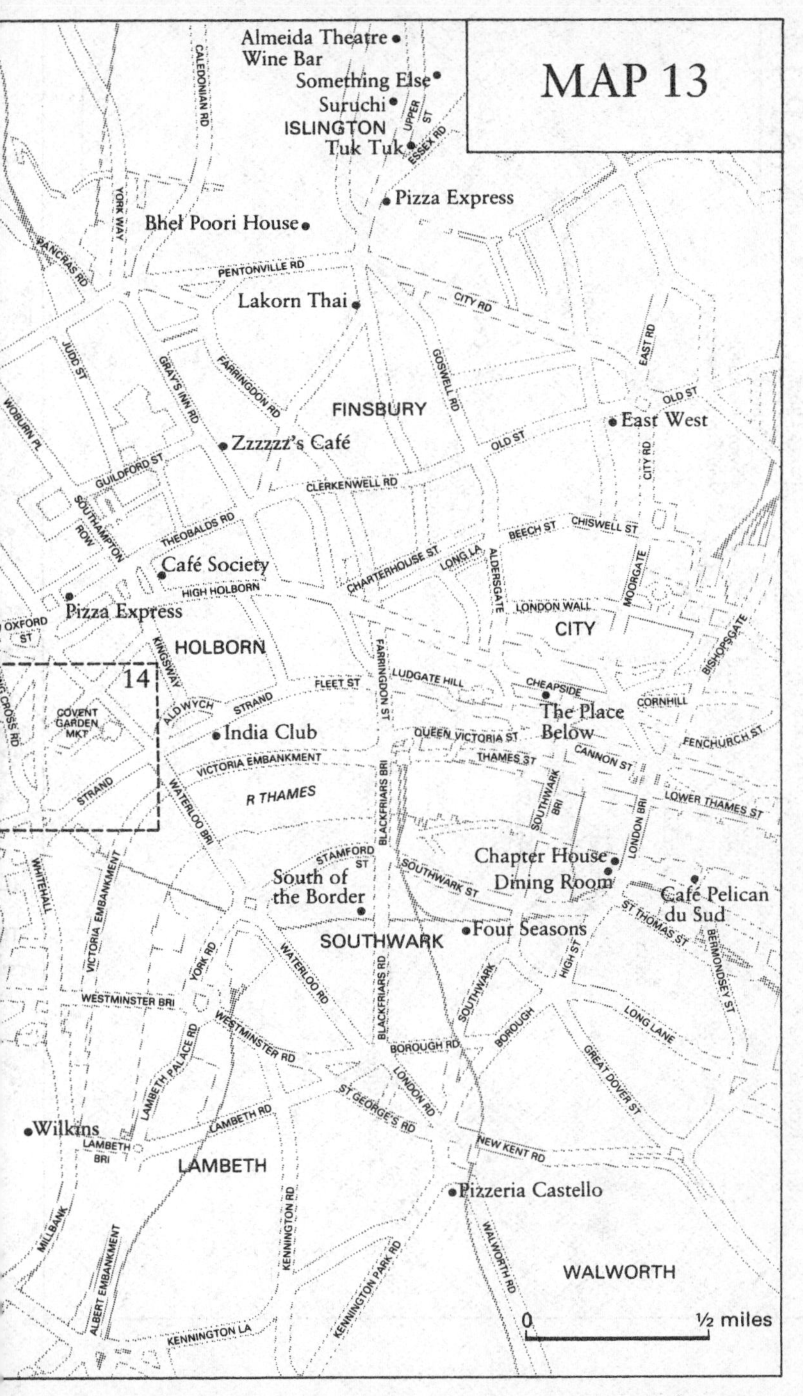
MAP 13
Almeida Theatre Wine Bar
Something Else
Suruchi
ISLINGTON
Tuk Tuk
Pizza Express
Bhel Poori House
Lakorn Thai
FINSBURY
Zzzzzz's Café
East West
Café Society
Pizza Express
HOLBORN
CITY
14
COVENT GARDEN MKT
India Club
The Place Below
R THAMES
Chapter House Dining Room
Café Pelican du Sud
South of the Border
SOUTHWARK
Four Seasons
Wilkins
LAMBETH
Pizzeria Castello
WALWORTH
0 ½ miles
CALEDONIAN RD
UPPER ST
ESSEX RD
YORK WAY
PANCRAS RD
PENTONVILLE RD
CITY RD
JUDD ST
GRAY'S INN RD
FARRINGDON RD
GOSWELL RD
EAST RD
OLD ST
WOBURN PL
GUILDFORD ST
CLERKENWELL RD
SOUTHAMPTON ROW
THEOBALDS RD
BEECH ST
CHISWELL ST
CHARTERHOUSE ST
LONG LA
ALDERSGATE
MOORGATE
HIGH HOLBORN
LONDON WALL
OXFORD ST
KINGSWAY
BISHOPSGATE
FARRINGDON ST
LUDGATE HILL
FLEET ST
CHEAPSIDE
ALDWYCH
STRAND
CORNHILL
QUEEN VICTORIA ST
FENCHURCH ST
CANNON ST
THAMES ST
VICTORIA EMBANKMENT
SOUTHWARK BRI
LOWER THAMES ST
LONDON BRI
WATERLOO BRI
BLACKFRIARS BRI
STAMFORD ST
SOUTHWARK ST
WHITEHALL
ST THOMAS ST
BERMONDSEY ST
WATERLOO RD
YORK RD
HIGH ST
WESTMINSTER BRI
BLACKFRIARS RD
SOUTHWARK
BOROUGH
LONG LANE
WESTMINSTER RD
LAMBETH PALACE RD
BOROUGH RD
LONDON RD
GREAT DOVER ST
ST GEORGE'S RD
LAMBETH RD
NEW KENT RD
LAMBETH BRI
KENNINGTON RD
MILLBANK
ALBERT EMBANKMENT
KENNINGTON PARK RD
WALWORTH RD
KENNINGTON LA

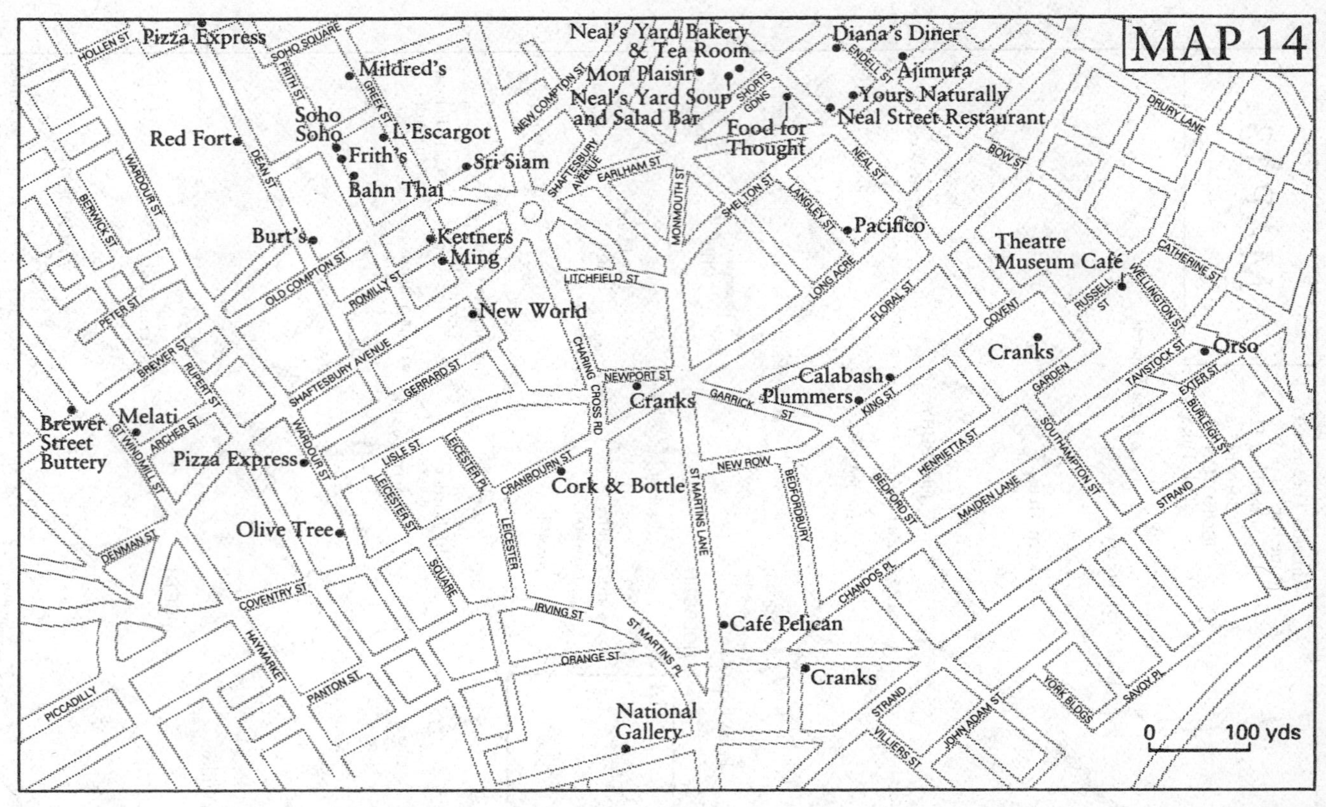
MAP 14
Pizza Express
Neal's Yard Bakery & Tea Room
Diana's Diner
Ajimura
Mildred's
Mon Plaisir
Neal's Yard Soup and Salad Bar
Yours Naturally
Neal Street Restaurant
Food for Thought
Soho Soho
Red Fort
L'Escargot
Frith's
Sri Siam
Bahn Thai
Pacifico
Theatre Museum Café
Burt's
Kettners
Ming
New World
Cranks
Orso
Calabash
Plummers
Cranks
Brewer Street Buttery
Melati
Pizza Express
Cork & Bottle
Olive Tree
Café Pelican
Cranks
National Gallery
0
100 yds
HOLLEN ST
SOHO SQUARE
FRITH ST
GREEK ST
NEW COMPTON ST
SHORTS GDNS
ENDELL ST
DRURY LANE
BOW ST
NEAL ST
DEAN ST
WARDOUR ST
BERWICK ST
SHAFTESBURY AVENUE
EARLHAM ST
MONMOUTH ST
SHELTON ST
LANGLEY ST
CATHERINE ST
WELLINGTON ST
RUSSELL ST
OLD COMPTON ST
ROMILLY ST
LITCHFIELD ST
LONG ACRE
FLORAL ST
COVENT GARDEN
PETER ST
BREWER ST
RUPERT ST
SHAFTESBURY AVENUE
GERRARD ST
CHARING CROSS RD
NEWPORT ST
GARRICK ST
KING ST
TAVISTOCK ST
EXETER ST
BURLEIGH ST
ARCHER ST
GT WINDMILL ST
WARDOUR ST
LISLE ST
LEICESTER PL
CRANBOURN ST
ST MARTINS LANE
NEW ROW
BEDFORDBURY
HENRIETTA ST
BEDFORD ST
SOUTHAMPTON ST
MAIDEN LANE
STRAND
LEICESTER ST
LEICESTER SQUARE
DENMAN ST
COVENTRY ST
IRVING ST
CHANDOS PL
ST MARTINS PL
HAYMARKET
ORANGE ST
PICCADILLY
PANTON ST
STRAND
VILLIERS ST
JOHN ADAM ST
YORK BLDGS
SAVOY PL

Report Form

V90

To *The Vegetarian Good Food Guide*
FREEPOST, 2 Marylebone Road, London NW1 1YN

I visited the following establishment on ______________________ 19 ___

and ate lunch/dinner/snack.

My meal for _____ people cost £ __________
(attach bill where possible)

Establishment name ____

Address ____

____

___________________________ Telephone __________________________

In the space below please describe what you ate and drank, and give any other details, eg of service, location and atmosphere, that you wish to add.

please continue overleaf

Does this restaurant have on its standard menu

Vegan dishes ☐ Meat ☐ Fish ☐

Any other diets catered for? (please specify) ______________________

____

From my personal experience I recommend this establishment for inclusion in/exclusion from the next edition of *The Vegetarian Good Food Guide*.

I am not connected in any way with management or proprietors.
Name and address (BLOCK CAPITALS)

____

____

____

Signed ______________________________________

____

Report Form

V90

To *The Vegetarian Good Food Guide*
FREEPOST, 2 Marylebone Road, London NW1 1YN

I visited the following establishment on ________________ 19 ____

and ate lunch/dinner/snack.

My meal for _____ people cost £ __________
(attach bill where possible)

Establishment name ______________________________

Address ______________________________

____

______________________ Telephone ______________________

In the space below please describe what you ate and drank, and give any other details, eg of service, location and atmosphere, that you wish to add.

please continue overleaf

Does this restaurant have on its standard menu

Vegan dishes ☐ Meat ☐ Fish ☐

Any other diets catered for? (please specify) ______________________

____

From my personal experience I recommend this establishment for inclusion in/exclusion from the next edition of *The Vegetarian Good Food Guide*.

I am not connected in any way with management or proprietors.
Name and address (BLOCK CAPITALS)

____

____

____

Signed ______________________________________

____

Report Form

V90

To *The Vegetarian Good Food Guide*
FREEPOST, 2 Marylebone Road, London NW1 1YN

I visited the following establishment on ____________________ 19 ____

and ate lunch/dinner/snack.

My meal for _____ people cost £ __________
(attach bill where possible)

Establishment name ______________________________

Address ______________________________

____

______________________________ Telephone ______________________________

In the space below please describe what you ate and drank, and give any other details, eg of service, location and atmosphere, that you wish to add.

please continue overleaf

Does this restaurant have on its standard menu

Vegan dishes ☐ Meat ☐ Fish ☐

Any other diets catered for? (please specify) ______________________

From my personal experience I recommend this establishment for inclusion in/exclusion from the next edition of *The Vegetarian Good Food Guide*.

I am not connected in any way with management or proprietors.
Name and address (BLOCK CAPITALS)

Signed ______________________

Report Form

V90

To *The Vegetarian Good Food Guide*
FREEPOST, 2 Marylebone Road, London NW1 1YN

I visited the following establishment on ______________________ 19 ____

and ate lunch/dinner/snack.

My meal for ______ people cost £ ______________
(attach bill where possible)

Establishment name ____

Address ____

____

____________________________ **Telephone** ___________________________

In the space below please describe what you ate and drank, and give any other details, eg of service, location and atmosphere, that you wish to add.

please continue overleaf

Does this restaurant have on its standard menu

Vegan dishes ☐ Meat ☐ Fish ☐

Any other diets catered for? (please specify) ______________________

____

From my personal experience I recommend this establishment for inclusion in/exclusion from the next edition of *The Vegetarian Good Food Guide*.

I am not connected in any way with management or proprietors.
Name and address (BLOCK CAPITALS)

____

____

____

Signed ____

____

Report Form

V90

To *The Vegetarian Good Food Guide*
FREEPOST, 2 Marylebone Road, London NW1 1YN

I visited the following establishment on ____________________ 19 ____

and ate lunch/dinner/snack.

My meal for _____ people cost £ __________
(attach bill where possible)

Establishment name ____

Address ____

____

__________________________ Telephone ____________________________

In the space below please describe what you ate and drank, and give any other details, eg of service, location and atmosphere, that you wish to add.

please continue overleaf

Does this restaurant have on its standard menu

Vegan dishes ☐ Meat ☐ Fish ☐

Any other diets catered for? (please specify) ______

From my personal experience I recommend this establishment for inclusion in/exclusion from the next edition of *The Vegetarian Good Food Guide*.

I am not connected in any way with management or proprietors.
Name and address (BLOCK CAPITALS)

Signed ______